EMC Chinese 1

真棒
Zhēn Bàng!

Senior Advisor

王昭華 Margaret M. Wong

Director of International Education / Chinese Instructor

Breck School, Minneapolis, MN

Lead Author

方虹婷 Tiffany Fang

Master of Arts in Teaching Chinese as a Second Language

Contributing Writers

陈淑华 Chen Shu-hwa 钱玲岑 Chien Ling-tsen

EMC Publishing

Editorial Director
Alejandro Vargas

Editor
Diana Moen

Associate Editors
Hannah da Veiga
Shen Yingjia

Assistant Editor
Lei Han

Copy Editor
Weihong Du

Text Designer
Jaana Bykonich

Cover Designer
Leslie Anderson

Production Specialists
Matthias Frasch
Ryan Hamner

Proofreader
International Contact, Inc.

Photo and Realia Credits: See the back of the textbook.

ISBN 978-0-82194-647-3

875 Montreal Way
St. Paul, MN 55102
Email: educate@emcp.com
Website: www.emcschool.com

Printed in the United States of America

19 18 17 16 15 6 7 8 9 10

审阅人员 Reviewers

廖勇红
Shirley Bornstein, MPA
Catholic Central High School
Burlington, Wisconsin

趙喆玄
Sara Bosa
New Trier Township High School
Winnetka, Illinois

高山
Aaron Bray
Sheboygan Falls Middle School /
Sheboygan Falls High School
Sheboygan Falls, Wisconsin

陈琰
Areana Chen, M.S.
San Diego North County Chinese School / San Diego HuaXia Chinese School
San Diego, California

陈强
Qiang (John) Chen, M.Ed.
Enloe Magnet High School
Raleigh, North Carolina

竹麗蓮
Lilien Drew, M.A.T.
Franklin High School
Somerset, New Jersey

高微
Wei Gao, M.A.
Manilus Pebble Hill School
DeWitt, New York

何静萍
Jing Ping He
Marvin Ridge High School
Waxhaw, North Carolina

黄霞
Xia Huang
Mingzhou Huaxia Chinese School
Eden Prairie, Minnesota

金晓南
Shannon Jin
Chanhassen High School /
Chaska High School
Chanhassen, Minnesota

谢洪伟
Julia Hongwei Kessel, M.A.
New Trier Township High School
Winnetka, Illinois

李堅惠
Grace Lee, M.A.
Wilson Senior High School
West Lawn, Pennsylvania

周懿
Chloe Lu
Oltman Middle School
Saint Paul Park, Minnesota

吕丽娜
Lina Lu, Ed. D.
Portland State University
Portland, Oregon

吕治萍
ZhiPing Lu
Great Wall Chinese Academy
Denver, Colorado

秦桂敏
Gwen Qin
Denver Language School
Denver, Colorado

鄭金秀
Kiki Scoggins, M.Ed. (candidate)
Clements High School
Sugarland, Texas

徐佳音
Joanne Shang
Durham Academy
Durham, North Carolina

苏纯谊
Chun-Yi Su (Coral)
Nebraska Wesleyan University /
University of Nebraska - Lincoln
Lincoln, Nebraska

田国明
Guo Ming Tian, Ph. D.
Rochester City School District
Rochester, New York

王钧
Jun (John) Wang, M.Ed., M.A.
Lyme Old Lyme High School
Old Lyme, Connecticut

王丽榕
Lirong Wang
Cannon School
Concord, North Carolina

王宇
Yu Wang, Ph.D.
Confucius Institute
Minneapolis, Minnesota

蔡麗莉
Lili Tsai-Wong, M.A.
Clovis West High School /
Buchanan High School
Fresno, California

于军
(Olivia) Jun Yu, M.A. (abd.)
Global Village Academy
Aurora, Colorado

学前寄语 To the Student

真棒！*Zhen Bàng!* When you speak Chinese to native speakers, this is an expression that you will commonly hear as a compliment. It means *Bravo!* or *Awesome!*. Since Chinese is regarded as one of the world's most difficult languages, you will definitely impress people when you pronounce it correctly and say it beautifully.

Success in studying any new language requires commitment on the part of the student. Westerners often take more time to study Chinese than they do other foreign languages, because the pronunciation and characters can be intimidating. But once you get the hang of it, you will be amazed how easily you can connect new vocabulary and concepts with your previously acquired Chinese knowledge to express yourself!

This book also introduces you to Chinese culture. You cannot truly learn a language without a sense of the underlying culture and history. You want to learn Chinese in order to communicate with Chinese people, but you cannot communicate beyond the most basic level unless you understand their innate assumptions about life, family, their identity as a people, the world around them, and so forth. Chinese is the first language of more than a quarter of the people in the world – far more than any other language. There are many people who speak the language well beyond the borders of China itself. Communities of Chinese can be found in cities all over the world. Studying the Chinese language and its cultural setting will broaden your horizons and provide you with a truly global perspective in ways you can barely imagine now.

China is emerging as a vast economic power. No one can predict exactly how its role in the world will evolve in the coming decades, but its influence will be immense, and having the tools to interface with this historical shift can only make your life more exciting. Just as people in the past fifty years have worked hard studying English, people nowadays realize that they can get a leg up on their peers in international business by taking part in the fast-growing economy of China. Knowing Chinese can expand your career options in many ways as companies now expand either their business or the manufacturing of parts to China. As an English speaker, you currently speak the most widely spoken language around the globe; but by taking this class you are adding another one that has the most native speakers on earth! Congratulations, you have made a very wise choice. Just imagine the possibilities, and set off on your journey toward learning Chinese today!

The **Pinyin System** used in

真棒！*Zhēn Bàng!* Level 1

Chinese has both a spoken form and a written form. Standard Spoken Chinese, based on the sounds of Beijing or Northern dialect is called "Putonghua" in Mainland China and "Guoyu" in Taiwan. In English, the term "Mandarin" is used.

Chinese written language is in the form of characters, which convey the meaning, rather than the sound of the language. Since there is no clear relationship between the Chinese sounds and characters, it is more efficient for beginners to learn spoken Chinese via a phonetic transcription system. Although there are many transcription systems, this book has chosen to use Pinyin, the official Romanization of Mainland China.

The sound system of Chinese is remarkably different from Western languages. For this reason, this book strives to emphasize pronunciation and the importance of spending ample time at the inception of learning on this foundation phase of Chinese. This book uses four special ways to write Pinyin*, for the express purpose of highlighting pronunciation rules and the cultivation of good habits. These are:

1. Third-tone sandhi

When two or more third tones are in sequence, we will mark the syllables before the last third-tone syllable in italics.

Example: Wǒ hěn hǎo. (I am very well.)
Wǒ hěn hǎo.

2. Marking neutral tones

The neutral tone will be indicated by a dot preceding it, while its original tone is also marked.

Example: xué.shēng = student

This way when the ".shēng" word is used in a different compound, one will know its tone.

Example: shēnghuó = life

This knowledge makes it much easier for the student, in later study, to associate the word correctly with other words or word compounds.

3. Identifying repeated syllables

When syllables are repeated, we use ".x" and when two syllables are repeated, we use ".vx",

Example: mā.x and yùndòng .vx

4. Hyphen

A hyphen is used:

a. between a number and a measure word.	Example:	yì-běn shū
b. between the verb-object.	Example:	kàn-shū
c. between verb-complements.	Example:	kàn.de-jiàn

All of these markings will be eliminated in *Zhēn Bàng!* levels 2 and 3, after the establishment of good pronunciation habits.

* This special technique was originally developed by Princeton University and is also known as The Princeton Method of Pinyin.

目录 Table of Contents

Foundation

Communication

Unit 2 我的家人 Wǒ.de Jiārén 208

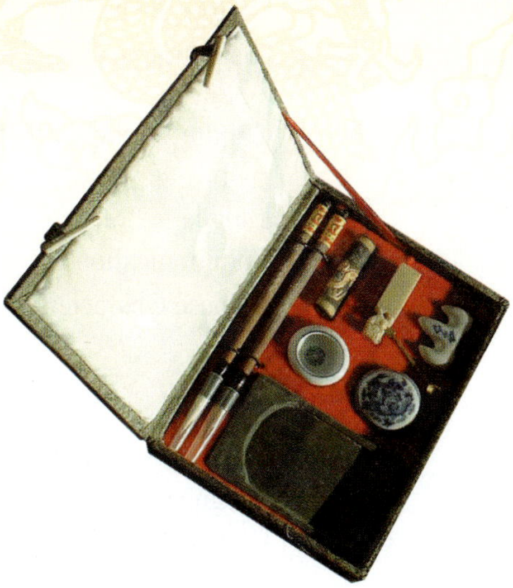

Unit 4 我要点菜! *Wǒ Yào Diǎn-cài!* 330

Unit 5 好天气 Hǎo Tiān.qì 388

Unit 6 逛街去 *Guàng-jiē .qù* 450

附录 References

The following reference pages are available in the 真棒！*Zhen Bàng!* Internet Resource Center at www.emcschool.net/zhenbang.

Abbreviations for Parts of Speech
Measure Words
Numbers 1 – 100
English Versions of the Dialogues
Chinese to English and Pinyin Vocabulary

Foundation

Foundation A

When you have completed this lesson you will be able to...

Geography / History
- find China on a map
- describe what China used to look like
- describe what China looks like today
- identify places where Chinese is spoken

Pronunciation
- pronounce four tones and the neutral tone
- pronounce initials and finals

Classroom Expressions
- use the correct Chinese expressions in certain classroom situations

Chinese Characters
- explain how Chinese characters evolved
- identify the most common Traditional radicals

Chinese Names
- define the meanings of several common Chinese first names
- introduce yourself

地理/历史 Dìlǐ / Lìshǐ

Geography / History

China on the World Map

Culture Note

China's "superlatives"

- World's biggest plaza—Tiananmen Square
- World's biggest palace—National Palace Museum
- World's biggest man-made structure—The Great Wall
- Most populated country—around 1.3 billion people
- 4th largest country in total area—around 3,673,800 miles²

China Up Close

1 按图索骥 Àntú-suǒjì / *Reading Maps*

Refer to the maps, and find answers to the questions below.

1. How many neighboring countries does China have? What are they?
2. What is the capital of China?
3. What are the two longest rivers in China? Which seas do they flow into?
4. What is the name of the mountain range on the China-Nepal border that includes the world's highest peak?

发音 Fāyīn

Pronunciation

Pinyin Initials and Finals

Chinese has both a spoken form and a written form. Standard Spoken Chinese, based on the sounds of Beijing or Northern dialect is called "Putonghua" in Mainland China and "Guoyu" in Taiwan. In English, the term "Mandarin" is used.

Chinese written language is in the form of characters, which convey the meaning, rather than the sound of the language. Since there is no clear relationship between the Chinese sounds and characters, it is more efficient for beginners to learn spoken Chinese via a phonetic transcription system. Although there are many transcription systems, this book has chosen to use Pinyin, the official Romanization of Mainland China.

A pinyin syllable can be made up of three parts: an initial, a final, and a tone. Although not every syllable in Chinese has an initial, it must have a final. Initials resemble certain English consonant sounds. There are 21 initials. Finals resemble English vowel sounds. There are 37 finals. There are four tones in Chinese, plus a neutral tone.

2 发音练习 Fāyīn Liànxí / *Pronunciation Practice*

Listen to the initials and repeat. Look at the chart for reference.

1. **b**	5. **d**	9. **g**	12. **j**	15. **zh**	19. **z**
2. **p**	6. **t**	10. **k**	13. **q**	16. **ch**	20. **c**
3. **m**	7. **n**	11. **h**	14. **x**	17. **sh**	21. **s**
4. **f**	8. **l**			18. **r**	

3 发音练习 Fāyīn Liànxí / *Pronunciation Practice*

Listen to the finals and repeat. Look at the chart for reference.

1. **a**	4. **i**	7. **ai**	11. **an**	16. **er**	17. **ia**	21. **ian**	26. **ua**	30. **uan**	34. **üe**
2. **o**	5. **u**	8. **ei**	12. **en**		18. **ie**	22. **in**	27. **uo**	31. **un***	35. **üan**
3. **e**	6. **ü**	9. **ao**	13. **ang**		19. **iao**	23. **iang**	28. **uai**	32. **uang**	36. **ün**
		10. **ou**	14. **eng**		20. **iu***	24. **ing**	29. **ui***	33. **ueng**	
			15. **ong**			25. **iong**			

Language Note

For the sake of convenience, some vowels are omitted in pinyin orthography. These include:

iou → **iu** **uei** → **ui** **uen** → **un**

However, this omission does not mean that they are left out in vocalization. Thus, when pronouncing such sounds, the speaker should stick to the original vowels.

4 发音练习 Fāyīn Liànxí *Pronunciation Practice*

Listen to the combinations of initials and finals and repeat.

1. **miù** (*ridiculous*)	7. **duì** (*correct*)	13. **gùn** (*stick*)
2. **diū** (*to throw*)	8. **tuì** (*to recede*)	14. **kǔn** (*to bind*)
3. **niú** (*cow*)	9. **guǐ** (*ghost*)	15. **hún** (*turbid*)
4. **liú** (*to stay*)	10. **huì** (*to know how to*)	16. **sūn** (*grandson*)
5. **jiù** (*old*)	11. **chuí** (*to beat*)	17. **chūn** (*spring*)
6. **qiǔ** (*embarrassing*)	12. **shuì** (*to sleep*)	18. **shùn** (*smooth*)

When i, u and ü exist alone—that is, without initials—their spelling rules are as follows:

i	**i** is written as **y**, or **y** is added before the syllable.	**i** → **yi** **ia** → **ya** **ie** → **ye**	**in** → **yin** **iu** → **you** **iao** → **yao** **ian** → **yan**	**ing** → **ying** **iang** → **yang** **iong** → **yong**
u	**u** is written as **w**, or **w** is added before the syllable.	**u** → **wu** **ua** → **wa** **uo** → **wo**	**ui** → **wei** **un** → **wen** **uai** → **wai** **uan** → **wan**	**uang** → **wang** **ueng** → **weng**
ü	**y** is added before the syllable (the two dots are dropped).	**ü** → **yu**	**üe** → **yue** **ün** → **yun**	**üan** → **yuan**

5 发音练习 Fāyīn Liànxí / Pronunciation Practice

Listen to the combinations of initials and finals and repeat.

1. **yá** (*tooth*)	6. **wú** (*no*)	11. **yǔ** (*rain*)
2. **yè** (*leaf*)	7. **wǒ** (*me*)	12. **yuē** (*appointment*)
3. **yǒu** (*to have*)	8. **wāi** (*crooked*)	13. **yún** (*cloud*)
4. **yào** (*to want*)	9. **wān** (*bay*)	14. **yuàn** (*to wish*)
5. **yìng** (*hard*)	10. **wàng** (*to forget*)	15. **yǒng** (*forever*)

The Structure of Chinese Syllables

A typical Chinese syllable is composed of three parts: an initial, a final, and a tone.

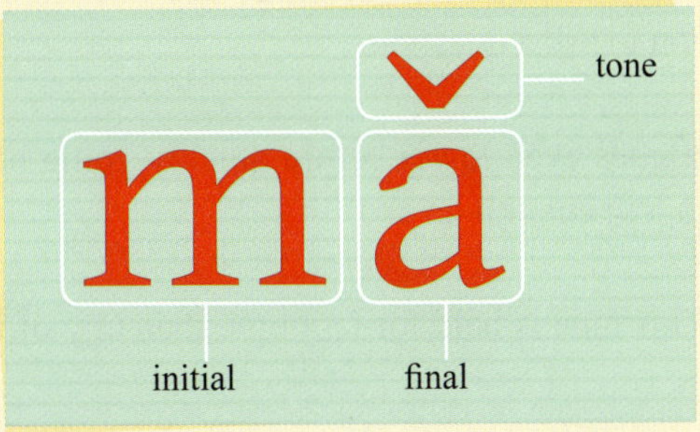

Not all syllables have an initial, but every syllable must have a final.

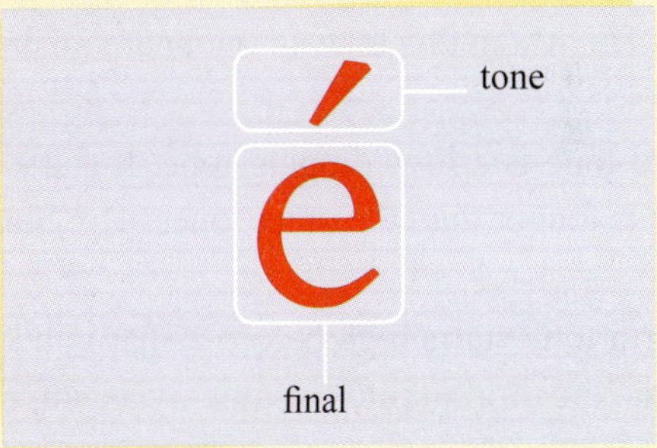

The Four Basic Tones

Tones, the pitch of syllables, are an important element of spoken Chinese. The function of tones is to distinguish meaning. Take *shuǐjiǎo* (dumplings) and *shuìjiào* (to sleep), for example. They have the same initials and finals but different tones that result in different meanings. Chinese has four basic tones and one neutral tone. Take a look at the chart below, which shows the four basic tones with examples.

Basic Tones			
1st (ˉ)	2nd (ˊ)	3rd (ˇ)	4th (ˋ)
 mā *n. mother*	 má *n. hemp*	 mǎ *n. horse*	 mà *v. to scold*

The comparative pitch of each tone is illustrated below.

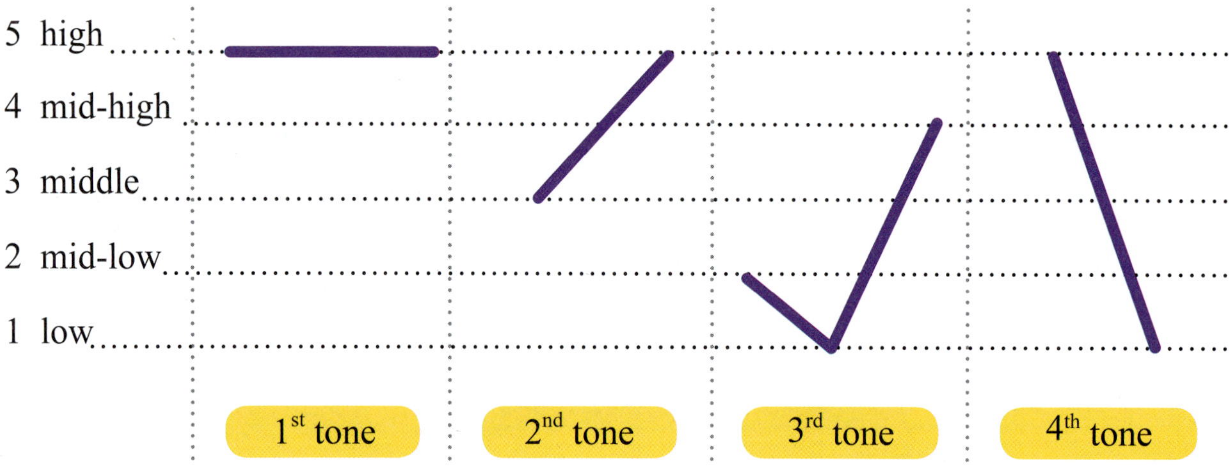

- The first tone is a high and level tone. It is steady, and is the highest of the four tones. Tip: It is important to maintain the pitch level from the beginning to the end of the syllable.

- The second tone is a high, rising tone. It begins around the middle of one's voice range and rises rapidly all the way up. Tip: Make this tone as if you are raising your intonation to ask a question.

- The third tone is a low, dipping tone. It starts quite low, then goes even lower before quickly going back up. Its duration is longer than the other tones. Tip: Start your tone at a low enough level.

- The fourth tone starts high before a sharp and sudden drop. This tone is held for less time than any of the others. Tip: Make the drop in pitch as quickly as you can.

6 发音练习 Fāyīn Liànxí *Pronunciation Practice*

Listen to the basic tones shown in the chart above and repeat in the pause provided.

The Neutral Tone

The neutral tone is toneless. It is pronounced softly, and is short, like a staccato. In transcription, the neutral tone does not carry a tone mark. For example:

gē.x	hái.zǐ	nǎi.x	bà.x
n. elder brother	*n. child*	*n. grandmother*	*n. father*

The Placement of Tonemarks

Tone marks are written above the main vowel of a syllable. The main vowel is determined by this order of importance: **a – o – e – i – u –ü.**

鸭 yā (*duck*)	猪 zhū (*pig*)	猫 māo (*cat*)

狗 gǒu (*dog*)	蝶 dié (*butterfly*)	象 xiàng (*elephant*)

Language Note

Remove the dot on the letter "i" when a tonemark is placed over it.

水 shuǐ (*water*)

There is an exception with "i" and "u." When "i" and "u" exist in the same syllable, the tone mark is always placed on the second vowel.

牛 niú (*cattle*), 腿 tuǐ (*leg*)

7 听力练习 Tīnglì Liànxí / *Listening Practice*

You will hear five Chinese words. Say if each word is first, second, third, or fourth tone.

Lì.zi: (model) first tone

8 听力练习 Tīnglì Liànxí / *Listening Practice*

Mark the initials, finals, and tones you hear on a separate sheet of paper.

Initials		Finals		Tones	
1. ☐ ǎo	3. ☐ ǒng	5. zh ☐̄	7. l ☐̀	9. te ☐	10. gai ☐
2. ☐ én	4. ☐ ín	6. k ☐̄ ng	8. sh ☐̌		

9 四声练习 Sìshēng Liànxí / Four basic tones practice

You will hear the same syllables repeated, each time with a different tone. Read along as you listen to the recording. Repeat each syllable separately, then all of them together.

1. dī dí dǐ dì
2. pū pú pǔ pù
3. fū fú fǔ fù
4. fāng fáng fǎng fàng
5. bā bá bǎ bà
6. mō mó mǒ mò
7. bāo báo bǎo bào
8. qiān qián qiǎn qiàn

10 发音练习 Fāyīn Liànxí / Pronunciation Practice

Listen to the recordings of each group of words that uses the same tone, repeat what you hear.

1. zhuō.zi sān.ge bīng.de
2. yí.ge fáng.zi pó.x
3. yǐ.zi wǒ.de yǒu.de
4. kuài.zi zhèi.ge nèi.ge

Let's Sing!

小狗在哪里 *Xiǎo*.gǒu zài *nǎ*.lǐ

Yī, èr, sān, sì, wǔ, liù, qī. Wǒ.de *xiǎo*.gǒu zài *nǎ*.lǐ?

Zài *nǎ*.lǐ? Zài *nǎ*.lǐ? Wǒ.de *xiǎo*.gǒu zài *nǎ*.lǐ?

Qī, liù, wǔ, sì, sān, èr, yī. Wǒ.de *xiǎo*.gǒu zài zhèlǐ.

Zài zhèlǐ. Zài zhèlǐ. Wǒ.de *xiǎo*.gǒu zài zhèlǐ.

Where Is My Doggy?

One, two, three, four, five, six, seven. Where is my doggy?
Where? Where? Where is my doggy?
Seven, six, five, four, three, two, one. Here is my doggy.
Here. Here. Here is my doggy.

课堂用语 Kètáng Yòngyǔ

Classroom Expressions

Situation 1

Student A: 这是第几声？
Zhè shì dì-jǐ shēng?
Which tone is this?

Student B: 这是第一声。
Zhè shì dì-yī shēng.
This is the 1st tone.

Teacher: 对，请你再说一次。
Duì, qǐng nǐ zài shuō yí-cì.
Yes, please say it again.

Situation 2

Student A: 这是第几声？
Zhè shì dì-jǐ shēng?
Which tone is this?

Student B: 这是第二声
Zhè shì dì-èr shēng.
This is the 2nd tone.

Student C: 不对，这是第三声。
Bú duì, zhè shì dì-sān shēng.
No, this is the 3rd tone.

Teacher: 不对，这是第四声。
请你们再说一次。
Bú duì, zhè shì dì-sì shēng.
Qǐng nǐ.mén zài shuō yí-cì.
No, this is the 4th tone.
Please say it again.

11 听声辨调 Tīngshēng Biàndiào *Differentiate the Tones*

With a partner, take turns pronouncing the syllables that follow. In Chinese tell your partner if he or she is correct or incorrect.

1. bǎ
2. zū
3. cè
4. hú
5. ròu
6. niǎo
7. tīng
8. jūn
9. xiǎng
10. qióng

汉字 Hànzì

Chinese Characters

The Evolution of Chinese Characters

Learning the Chinese language is easy as long as you understand its rules and how it has evolved over the years. Chinese characters came from pictures of objects in daily life that gradually evolved into text. A simple explanation of this process is as follows:

Pictographs 图像 (Túxiàng)	Oracle Bone Script 甲骨文(*Jiă*.gŭwén)	Bronze Vessel Script 金文 (Jīnwén)	Small Seal Script 小篆 (Xiăozhuàn)	Clerical Script 楷书 (Kăishū)

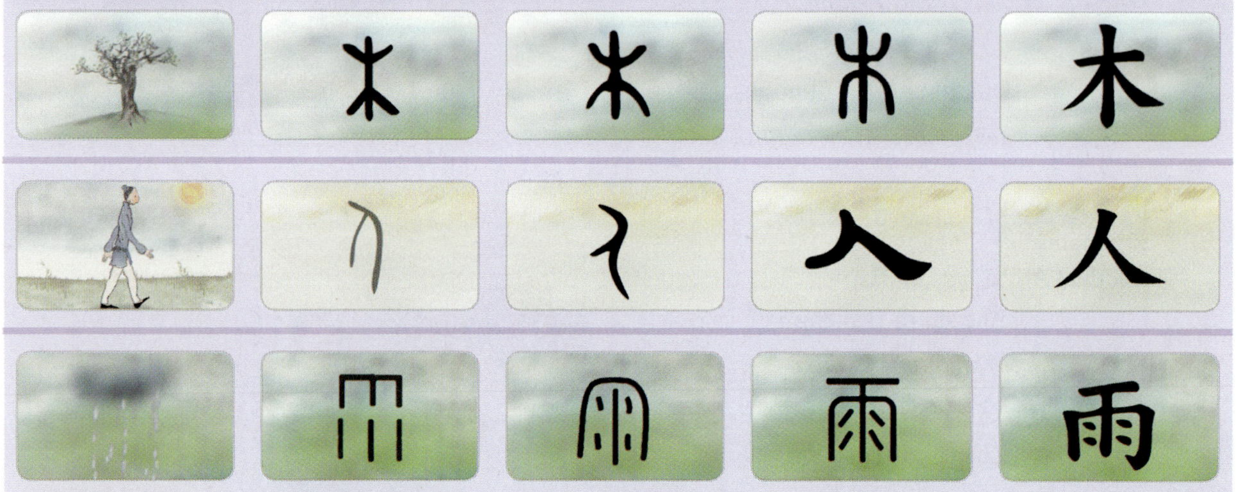

Pictographs	Before the invention of text, humans drew pictures to represent objects or record things that happened. The discovery of pictographs showed the beginning of the evolution of human language from oral to written. Chinese is the only written language to still use pictographs today.
Oracle Bone Script	In the Shang Dynasty (1600-1046 B.C.), characters were carved onto tortoise shells for divination. These characters were later seen to be the beginnings of written Chinese.
Bronze Vessel Script	In the Zhou Dynasty (146-256 B.C.), the development of bronze ware, rituals, and social hierarchy led to characters being inscribed on bronze containers and musical instruments. Bronze Vessel Script (metal text) is similar to Oracle Bone Script, but places more emphasis on stroke order. Bronze Vessel Script also set the foundation for the later Small Seal Script.
Small Seal Script	The Small Seal Script was developed after Qin Shi Huang united China in 207 B.C. It became the standard text for official documents. Because of its elegant font, the Small Seal Script is still often used in calligraphy and on carvings.
Clerical Script	Clerical Script evolved from the Small Seal Script, changing the rounder strokes to form rectilinear characters that allowed for faster character formation, making it suitable to be written on various objects. Clerical Script became the standard text of the Tang Dynasty (618-907 A.D.) and continues to be used as the 'normal' written text of today.

12 仓颉造字 Cāngjié Zàozì / *From Pictures to Characters*

Match each pictograph on the left with the character that derived from it on the right.

1. 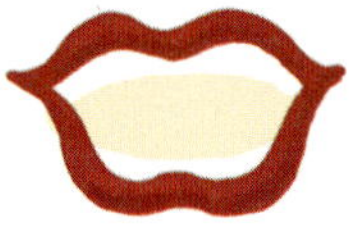	A. 山
2. 	B. 口
3. 	C. 火
4. 	D. 月
5. 	E. 鸟

50 Most Common Traditional Radicals

The radical system of Chinese writing is used for looking up meanings of words in a Chinese dictionary. Radicals are root words from which all Chinese words originate. They can be independent words or part of a character as the ideographic indicator. There are 214 radicals in total in written Chinese. Each character contains a radical, and most of the characters belonging to each radical group will carry the meaning of the radical itself. So, once you know this list of 50 common radicals, you will be able to recognize quite a few Chinese words. The radicals below are listed in the order of the number of strokes to write them. The strokes in parentheses note the ways some radicals are written when acting as side components.

Radical	Examples
1. 人(亻) rén *n. person; people*	他 tā *pron. he; him* 例 lì *n. example*
2. 刀(刂) dāo *n. knife* 	剪 jiǎn *v. to cut* 劍 jiàn *n. sword* 
3. 力 lì *n. strength*	勞 láo *n. work; labor* 勇 yǒng *adj. brave*
4. 口 kǒu *n.* mouth 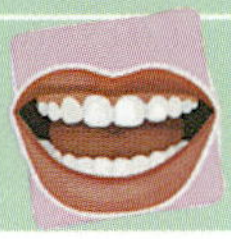	吃 chī *v. to eat* 吞 tūn *v. to swallow* 

Radical	Examples
5. 口 wéi *n. enclosure*	囚 qiú *v. to imprison* 圖 tú *n. drawing*
6. 土 tǔ *n. dirt* 	地 dì *n. land* 坐 zuò *v. to sit*
7. 大 dà *adj. large; great*	天 tiān *n. sky* 夫 fū *n. husband* 
8. 女 nǚ *n. woman*	姐 jiě *n. older sister* 妹 mèi *n. younger sister*
9. 宀 mián *n. roof*	家 jiā *n. family; house* 宮 gōng *n. palace*
10. 山 shān *n. mountain* 	岩 yán *n. rock* 峽 xiá *n. gorge*
11. 巾 jīn *n. napkin*	帕 pà *n. handkerchief* 常 cháng *adv. often*
12. 广 guǎng *n. shelter*	店 diàn *n. store* 床 chuáng *n. bed* 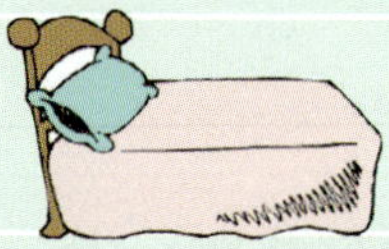
13. 彳 chì *v. to pace*	很 hěn *adv. very; quite* 待 dāi *v. to stay*
14. 心(忄)xīn *n. heart* 	思 sī *v. to think* 怕 pà *v. to fear*
15. 手(扌)shǒu *n. hand*	拉 lā *v. to slash* 拍 pāi *v. to pat*
16. 攴(攵)pū *v. to tap*	收 shōu *v. to receive* 放 fàng *v. to put*
17. 日 rì *n. sun* 	早 zǎo *n. morning* 明 míng *adj. bright*
18. 木 mù *n. wood*	樹 shù *n. tree* 森 sēn *n. forest* 
19. 水(氵)shuǐ *n. water*	海 hǎi *n. sea* 洋 yáng *n. ocean*
20. 火(灬)huǒ *n. fire* 	烤 kǎo *v. to roast* 炭 tàn *n. charcoal*

Radical	Examples
21. 牛 niú *n. ox*	牧 mù *v. to herd, to tend* 牲 shēng *n. domestic animal* 
22. 犬(犭)quǎn *n. dog*	狗 gǒu *n. dog* 狼 láng *n. wolf*
23. 玉(王)yù *n. jade*	珠 zhū *n. bead; pearl* 玩 wán *v. to play*
24. 田 tián *n. field*	男 nán *n. man; male* 界 jiè *n. boundary*
25. 疒 bìng *adj. sick*	疾 jí *n. disease* 病 bìng *n. disease; ailment*
26. 目 mù *n. eye* 	看 kàn *v. to look; to see* 省 shěng *v. to economize*
27. 石 shí *n. stone*	砂 shā *n. sand; grit* 破 pò *adj. broken*
28. 禾 hé *n. grain*	私 sī *adj. personal* 秒 miǎo *n. a second*
29. 竹(⺮)zhú *n. bamboo*	竿 gān *n. bamboo pole* 笑 xiào *v. to laugh; to smile* 
30. 米 mǐ *n. rice*	粉 fěn *n. powder* 粗 cū *adj. thick*
31. 糸(糹)sī *n. silk*	絲 sī *n. silk* 綿 mián *adj. soft*
32. 肉(月)ròu *n. flesh*	肚 dù *n. stomach* 肝 gān *n. liver*
33. 艸(艹)cǎo *n. grass*	草 cǎo *n. grass* 藻 zǎo *n. algae*
34. 虫 huǐ *n. insect* 	蟲 chóng *n. insect; worm* 蚊 wén *n. mosquito* 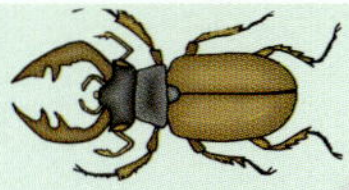
35. 衣(衤)yī *n. clothes*	初 chū *adj. first* 衫 shān *n. unlined upper garment* 
36. 言 yán *n. words*	說 shuō *v. to speak* 話 huà *n. words*

Radical	Examples
37. 貝 bèi *n. shell*	財 cái *n. wealth* 貨 huò *n. goods*
38. 足(⻊)zú *n. foot*	跑 pǎo *v. to run* 跳 tiào *v. to jump* 
39. 車 chē *n. cart*	軍 jūn *n. army* 輪 lún *n. wheel*
40. 走(辶)chuò *v. to go*	追 zhuī *v. to pursue* 逃 táo *v. to escape*
41. 邑(阝)yì *n. city*	都 dū *n. capital* 郊 jiāo *n. outskirts*
42. 金 jīn *n. metal*	錢 qián *n. money* 銀 yín *n. silver*
43. 門 mén *n. door* 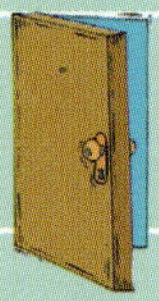	開 kāi *v. to open* 問 wèn *v. to ask*
44. 阜(阝)fù *n. plenty*	陪 péi *v. to accompany* 限 xiàn *n. limit; restriction*
45. 雨 yǔ *n. rain* 	雪 xuě *n. snow* 雲 yún *n. cloud* 
46. 頁 yè *n. heading*	頂 dǐng *n. top; peak* 類 lèi *n. kind; type*
47. 食(饣)shí *v. to eat*	飯 fàn *n. rice* 飲 yǐn *v. to drink* 
48. 馬 mǎ *n. horse*	馴 xùn *v. to tame* 騎 qí *v. to ride*
49. 鳥 niǎo *n. bird*	鶯 yīng *n. oriole* 鴨 yā *n. duck*
50. 魚 yú *n. fish* 	鯊 shā *n. shark* 鯨 jīng *n. whale*

13 按图索骥 Àntú-suǒjì / *Words with Radicals*

Match the words on the left with the corresponding radicals on the right.

1. 媽 (mā, *mother*)
2. 蝴 (hú, *butterfly*)
3. 狐 (hú, *fox*)
4. 炮 (pào, *cannon*)
5. 妻 (qī, *wife*)
6. 硬 (yìng, *hard*)
7. 炒 (chǎo, *to stir-fry*)
8. 刻 (kè, *to carve*)
9. 裳 (shāng, *clothing*)
10. 衫 (shān, *shirts*)
11. 看 (kàn, *to see*)
12. 芒 (máng, *awn*)
13. 鴨 (yā, *duck*)
14. 眠 (mián, *to sleep*)
15. 切 (qiē, *to cut*)
16. 炎 (yán, *hot*)
17. 眉 (méi, *eyebrow*)
18. 茉 (mò, *jasmine*)
19. 刃 (rèn, *blade*)
20. 磨 (mó, *grind*)

(nǚ, *female*)

(niǎo, *bird*)

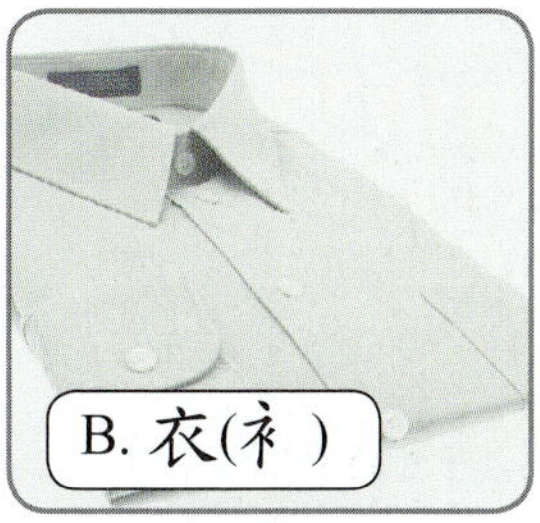

(yī, *clothes*)

(huǒ, *fire*)

(quǎn, *dog*)

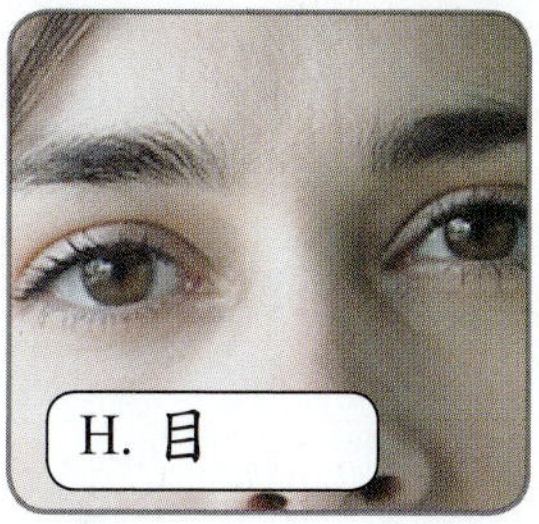

(mù, *eye*)

(dāo, *knife*)

(cǎo, *grass*)

(huǐ, *insect*)

(shí, *stone*)

14 按图索骥 Àntú-suǒjì / *Add the Radical*

Select the appropriate radical to complete each word on the left. Use the English to help you figure out what is missing.

1. □乃
nǎi, *grandmother*

2. 丘 / □
yuè, *high mountain*

3. □ / 豕
jiā, *house*

4. □戔
qián, *money*

5. □可
hé, *river*

A. 宀 (mián, *roof*)

B. 女 (nǚ, *female*)

C. 金 (jīn, *metal*)

D. 水（氵）(shuǐ, *water*)

E. 山 (shān, *mountain*)

15 按图索骥 Àntú-suǒjì / *Similar Words*

Figure out which words have the same radical. Write the words with the same radical together, along with their radical on a separate sheet of paper.

1. 切 (qiē, *to cut*)	3. 癡 (chī, *silly*)	5. 肝 (gān, *liver*)	7. 詩 (shī, *poem*)	9. 論 (lùn, *to argue*)
2. 國 (guó, *country*)	4. 困 (kùn, *to besiege*)	6. 痛 (tòng, *to hurt*)	8. 腦 (nǎo, *brain*)	10. 刻 (kè, *to carve*)

16 按图索骥 Àntú-suǒjì / *Find the Radical*

With a partner, take turns asking what the radical of each word is. Refer to the Radical Bank to identify the radicals. Follow the model.

Lì.zi: **A:** "妹" 是什么部首? "Mèi" shì shén.me bùshǒu? *What's the radical of* "妹 (*younger sister*)"?

B: "妹" 是 '女' 部。"Mèi" shì 'nǚ' bù. *The radical of* "妹 (*younger sister*)" *is* '女 (*female*)'.

Radical Bank				
人 (rén, *people*)	力 (lì, *strength*)	口 (kǒu, *mouth*)	土 (tǔ, *earth*)	女 (nǚ, *woman*)
宀 (mián, *roof*)	山 (shān, *mountain*)	心 (xīn, *heart*)	手 (shǒu, *hand*)	日 (rì, *sun*)
木 (mù, *wood*)	水 (shuǐ, *water*)	火 (huǒ, *fire*)	目 (mù, *eye*)	艸(艹) (cǎo, *grass*)
衣(衤) (yī, *clothes*)	辵(辶) (chuò, *to go*)	門 (mén, *door*)	雨 (yǔ, *rain*)	足(⻊) (zú, *foot*)

1. 看 (kàn, *to see*)	8. 怒 (nù, *angry*)	15. 松 (sōng, *pine*)
2. 時 (shí, *time*)	9. 嶽 (yuè, *high mountain*)	16. 裙 (qún, *skirt*)
3. 喝 (hē, *to drink*)	10. 烤 (kǎo, *to roast*)	17. 草 (cǎo, *grass*)
4. 坡 (pō, *slope*)	11. 婦 (fù, *woman*)	18. 跳 (tiào, *to jump*)
5. 湖 (hú, *lake*)	12. 信 (xìn, *letter*)	19. 雪 (xuě, *snow*)
6. 守 (shǒu, *to defend*)	13. 開 (kāi, *to open*)	20. 送 (sòng, *to send*)
7. 助 (zhù, *to help*)	14. 推 (tuī, *to push*)	

▲ Jade Dragon Snow Mountain (玉龙雪山) in LiJiang, Yunnan, China.

中文名字 Zhōngwén Míng.zì

Chinese Names

In China, surnames, which normally come from the father, are placed in front of given names. When picking given names for their children, Chinese parents take into consideration that certain characters are associated with one gender or the other, and that tend to choose names that contain characters related to the gender of the child. For example, 怡 (*yí*) means to be happy and comfortable, and is often used in names for girls. On the other hand, 豪 (*háo*) means unconstrained and talented, and is often used in names for boys. Here are some common characters used in names for girls and boys:

boys

俊	jùn:	to be handsome; outstanding
杰	jié:	to be exceptional
建	jiàn:	to stand; establish
强	qiáng:	to be strong
勇	yǒng:	to be brave; responsible

girls

婷	tíng:	to be fine
惠	huì:	to be mild; graceful
淑	shū:	to be kind; gentle
美	měi:	to be beautiful; pretty
雅	yǎ:	of high class; to be elegant

男孩 **Nánhái** ***Boy***		女孩 **Nǚhái** ***Girl***	
1. 明 Míng	*bright*	26. 英 Yīng	*outstanding*
2. 国 Guó	*nation*	27. 秀 Xiù	*elegant*
3. 文 Wén	*culture*	28. 玉 Yù	*jade*
4. 建 Jiàn	*build*	29. 华 Huá	*brilliant*
5. 永 Yǒng	*forever*	30. 珍 Zhēn	*treasure*
6. 华 Huá	*brilliant*	31. 兰 Lán	*orchid*
7. 德 Dé	*virtue*	32. 芳 Fāng	*fragrant*
8. 军 Jūn	*army*	33. 春 Chūn	*spring*
9. 平 Píng	*peace*	34. 云 Yún	*cloud*
10. 福 Fú	*fortune*	35. 桂 Guì	*laurel*
11. 志 Zhì	*ambition*	36. 凤 Fèng	*phoenix*
12. 忠 Zhōng	*loyalty*	37. 琴 Qín	*musical instrument*
13. 成 Chéng	*success*	38. 梅 Méi	*plum*
14. 荣 Róng	*glory*	39. 美 Měi	*beauty*
15. 伟 Wěi	*great*	40. 红 Hóng	*red*
16. 志伟 Zhìwěi	*great ambition*	41. 怡君 Yíjūn	*happy lady*
17. 建志 Jiànzhì	*to build ambition*	42. 淑芬 Shūfēn	*graceful and nice*
18. 建宏 Jiànhóng	*to establish greatness*	43. 丽君 Lìjūn	*beautiful lady*
19. 俊杰 Jùnjié	*outstanding talent*	44. 淑惠 Shūhuì	*nice and kind*
20. 俊宏 Jùnhóng	*outstanding greatness*	45. 雅惠 Yǎhuì	*elegant and nice*
21. 志强 Zhìqiáng	*strong will*	46. 雅玲 Yǎlíng	*elegant*
22. 建良 Jiànliáng	*to grow up well*	47. 美玲 Měilíng	*beautiful*
23. 志宏 Zhìhóng	*great ambition*	48. 美惠 Měihuì	*beautiful and kind*
24. 建国 Jiànguó	*to build the country*	49. 欣怡 Xīnyí	*happiness*
25. 俊男 Jùnnán	*handsome man*	50. 佩君 Pèijūn	*admirable lady*

17 男的还是女的? Nán.de Hái.shì Nǚ.de? / Boy or Girl?

With a partner, take turns asking and answering if the name is a girl's or boy's name. Follow the model.

Lì.zi:

A: 荣(glory)是男的还是女的?
Róng shì nán.de háishì nǚ.de?
Is Rong a girl or a boy?

B: 荣是男的。
Róng shì nán.de.
Rong is a boy.

A: 桂(laurel)是男的还是女的?
Guì shì nán.de háishì nǚ.de?
Is Gui a girl or a boy?

B: 桂是女的。
Guì shì nǚ.de.
Gui is a girl.

1. 郭晓玉 Guō Xiǎoyù *(jade)* 郑平成 Zhèng Píngchéng *(success)*	8. 林伟 Lín Wěi *(great)* 丁静怡 Dīng Jìngyí *(happy)*
2. 罗美玲 Luó Měilíng *(beauty)* 谢军 Xiè Jūn *(army)*	9. 李鹏 Lǐ Péng *(roc, giant mythical bird)* 陈红 Chén Hóng *(red)*
3. 林杰昌 Lín Jiéchāng *(prosperous)* 蔡琴 Cài Qín *(musical instrument)*	10. 刘刚 Liú Gāng *(strong)* 郭晶晶 Guō Jīngjīng *(crystal)*
4. 白先勇 Bái Xiānyǒng *(bravery)* 林兰 Lín Lán *(orchid)*	11. 黄蓉 Huáng Róng *(hibiscus)* 李远 Lǐ Yuǎn *(far)*
5. 吴忠德 Wú Zhōngdé *(virtue)* 张雅琪 Zhāng Yǎqí *(white gem)*	12. 康海 Kāng Hǎi *(sea)* 王淑萱 Wáng Shūxuān *(day lily)*
6. 黄杰 Huáng Jié *(outstanding)* 关颖珊 Guān Yǐngshān *(coral)*	13. 江惠珍 Jiāng Huìzhēn *(treasure)* 杨禄 Yáng Lù *(salary)*
7. 李小龙 Lǐ Xiǎolóng *(dragon)* 张美 Zhāng Měi *(beauty)*	14. 潘瑞妹 Pān Ruìmèi *(sister)* 徐福 Xú Fú *(good fortune)*

18 英文名字 Yīngwén Míng.zì / *English Names*

Below is a list of English names that have been transliterated into Chinese versions. Listen to the recording, and repeat the names.

Boys' Names		Girls' Names	
Allen	亚伦 Yàlún	Amy	艾咪 Àimī
Danny	丹尼 Dānní	Helen	海伦 Hǎilún
David	大卫 Dàwèi	Kelly	凯莉 Kǎilì
Jason	杰森 Jiésēn	Lisa	莉莎 Lìshā
Jim	吉姆 Jímǔ	Megan	梅根 Méigēn
Leo	李欧 Lǐ'ōu	Mary	玛丽 Mǎlì
Nick	尼克 Níkè	Penny	佩妮 Pèiní
Terry	泰瑞 Tàiruì	Phoebe	菲比 Fēibǐ
Tom	汤姆 Tāngmǔ	Tina	缇娜 Tínà
Sean	尚恩 Shàng'ēn	Wendy	温蒂 Wēndì

19 自我介绍 Zìwǒ Jièshào / *Self-Introduction*

Now that you have a Chinese name, try introducing yourself in Chinese and ask others their names. Follow the model.

Lì.zi: A: Nǐ jiào shén.me míng.zi?
你叫什么名字?
What's your name?

B: Wǒ jiào....
我叫…。
My name is....

20 介绍他人 Jièshào Tārén / *Introduce Others*

After the self-introduction above, you should know the Chinese names of the people sitting next to you. Use the following pattern to introduce two of them.

Lì.zi: Tā jiào....
他/她叫…。
His/Her name is....

Foundation B

When you have completed this lesson you will be able to...

Geography / History
- find the 22 Chinese provinces and capitals on a map
- explain cultural, geographical, and economic information about selected provinces

Pronunciation
- pronounce more finals and initials
- recite a tongue twister and sing a song

Classroom Expressions
- use the correct Chinese expressions in certain classroom situations

Chinese Characters
- explain how Chinese characters transformed from Traditional to Simplified
- identify the 50 most common Simplified radicals
- make the basic strokes of Chinese characters

地理/历史 Dìlǐ / Lìshǐ

Geography / History

The 22 Mainland Provinces

Province (Provincial Capital)			
1. 黑龙江(哈尔滨)	Hēilóngjiāng (Hā'ěrbīn)	12. 江西(南昌)	Jiāngxī (Nánchāng)
2. 吉林(长春)	Jílín (Chángchūn)	13. 福建(福州)	Fújiàn (Fúzhōu)
3. 辽宁(沈阳)	Liáoníng (Shěnyáng)	14. 浙江(杭州)	Zhèjiāng (Hángzhōu)
4. 河北(石家庄)	Héběi (Shíjiāzhuāng)	15. 广东(广州)	Guǎngdōng (Guǎngzhōu)
5. 河南(郑州)	Hénán (Zhèngzhōu)	16. 贵州(贵阳)	Guìzhōu (Guìyáng)
6. 山东(济南)	Shāndōng (Jǐnán)	17. 云南(昆明)	Yúnnán (Kūnmíng)
7. 山西(太原)	Shānxī (Tàiyuán)	18. 四川(成都)	Sìchuān (Chéngdū)
8. 江苏(南京)	Jiāngsū (Nánjīng)	19. 陕西(西安)	Shǎnxī (Xī'ān)
9. 安徽(合肥)	Ānhuī (Héféi)	20. 甘肃(兰州)	Gānsù (Lánzhōu)
10. 湖北(武汉)	Húběi (Wǔhàn)	21. 青海(西宁)	Qīnghǎi (Xīníng)
11. 湖南(长沙)	Húnán (Chángshā)	22. 海南(海口)	Hǎinán (*Hǎi*kǒu)

The Provinces

黑龙江 Hēilóngjiāng

Named after the biggest river within its borders, Heilongjiang is both China's most northern and eastern province. Due to its vast, fertile lands and sparse population, it has always been an agricultural province of importance in the north. **Hā'ěrbīn**, the provincial capital, known as the "city of ice," has ice sculpture festivals each year from the first of January until the Chinese New Year, which usually falls at the end of January to the early February depending on the Lunar Calendar.

▲ Ha'erbin ice sculptures.

河北 Héběi

Hé means "river," and *běi* means "north." Hebei's name comes from its location: "north of the Yellow River." It has two municipal cities within its border, Beijing and Tianjin, with **Shíjiāzhuāng** as its capital. Hebei shares the number one spot with Shaanxi as the province with the most historical artifacts. Chengde Mountain Resort, the Great Wall, and the famous Shanhai Pass are all located in Hebei.

▲ Shanhai Pass.

山东 Shāndōng

Shān means "mountain" and *dōng* means "east." Therefore the name of Shandong, east of the Taihang Mountains, comes from its location, too. **Jǐnán** is its capital city. Because of its many natural springs, it is also called the "city of springs." Shandong is rich in both history and culture, and has had a great influence on the development of Chinese civilization—the most well-known being Confucius and his teachings. It is also rich in natural resources, and home to Mount Tai—the first natural and cultural World Heritage Site named in China.

Confucius

Confucius was an important philosopher and teacher of the Spring and Autumn Period (6th century, B.C.). At the time, China's feudalism was starting to crumble, and education, which used to be a privilege of the rich, started to enter society, leading to a thirst for more knowledge. Confucius taught the philosophy of 仁 *rén* —how to be honest and kind; and 礼 *lǐ*, a social structure that emphasized moderation and respect. His school of thought, Confucianism, has since not only been adapted as the standard of empirical rule, but has also become the core of Chinese culture. Moreover, Confucianism has affected nearby countries such as Japan, Korea and Vietnam to form an East-Asian cultural circle and beyond—inadvertently becoming the catalyst for the European Renaissance.

浙江 Zhèjiāng

▲ Qiantang River wave.

Zhejiang's capital is **Hángzhōu**, a city of scenic beauty listed as one of China's seven major ancient cities. Even though Zhejiang province is one of China's smallest in terms of its area, it has a strong economy based on local investments. Zhejiang has the longest coastline in the country, and boasts the largest fishing industry in China.

云南 Yúnnán

Yunnan province is located next to China's southwestern border. Its capital, **Kūnmíng**, is one of China's most famous historical cultural cities. It is also known as "spring city" for its mild climate throughout the year. Yunnan's economy is below the national average, but it is full of natural resources, including many types of animal and plant life, metals, and herbs.

四川 Sìchuān

▲ Giant pandas.

Chéngdū is Sichuan's capital city. Sichuan is a historical province with many resources, hence its historical name, the "province of abundance." Situated in a basin surrounded by mountains, it lacks sufficient transportation. It does, however, have a booming tourism industry partly due to the giant pandas that reside within its borders. Another Sichuan sightseeing must, the Jiuzhaigou Valley Scenic and Historic Interest Area, is listed as a World Heritage Site.

▲ Jiuzhaigou Valley.

陕西 Shǎnxī

Shanxi, with its capital **Xī'ān**, is located within China's geological center, making it a place of importance throughout history. Also called the "museum of ancient history," it is home to the Terracotta Army in Xi'an.

Terracotta Army

The Terracotta Army (兵马俑 Bīng*mǎ*yǒng) was found in the burial grounds of Qin Shi Huang, emperor of the Qin Dynasty (3rd century B.C.). The army is composed of life-size clay soldiers in the model of the Qin army and placed around the circumference of the tomb to protect the emperor in his slumber.

青海 **Qīnghǎi**

▲ Qinghai prairie.

Qinghai, the only province in China named after a lake, takes its name from Lake Qinghai, the largest inland saltwater lake in the country. In Mongolian, Lake Qinghai means "green lake." Its capital city is **Xīníng**. Qinghai has vast meadows used for pasturing, which are a sight-seeing destination.

海南 **Hǎinán**

▲ Hainan Island.

Hainan, with its capital **Hǎikǒu**, is located at China's southernmost point. Weather in Hainan is warm throughout the year, with clear seasonal differences, earning it the name of "Hawaii of the East." Famous for its seafood and pearls, Hainan is a tourism hotspot that combines sightseeing, vacationing, and culture.

1 温故知新 Wēngù Zhīxīn *Remembering the Facts*

Match each province on the left with a description of the province on the right. Some provinces will be matched with more than one description.

1. Hainan	A. province of abundance
2. Heilongjiang	B. where Confucius lived
3. Ha'erbin	C. Hawaii of the East
4. Sichuan	D. the museum of ancient history
5. Shandong	E. the most northern and eastern province in China
6. Xi'an	F. where the Terracotta Army is located
7. Yunnan	G. city of ice
	H. city of springs
	I. spring city

2 角色扮演 Juésè Bànyǎn *Role Play*

With a partner, play the role of a Chinese-American businessperson at an international conference in Beijing asking a Chinese colleague where certain people are from.

Lì.zi: **A:** 他/她从哪儿来? Tā cóng nǎr lái? *Where is he/she from?*
B: 他/她从…来。Tā cóng… lái. *He/She is from (name of provincial capital).*

发音 Fāyīn

Pronunciation

3 发音练习 Fāyīn Liànxí / *Pronunciation Practice*

Listen to the finals from the chart and repeat in the pause provided.

Pronunciation Tips for Finals		
1.	**a**	Open your mouth wide and keep your tongue in a flat, relaxed position.
2.	**o**	Make your mouth round and hold your tongue in the middle of the open space.
3.	**e**	Open your mouth halfway. At the same time, spread your lips apart, as if you were smiling.
4.	**i**	Keep your mouth flat as if you were pronouncing the English letter "e."
5.	**ai**	To pronounce the combination **ai**, open your mouth and say **a** first. Then close it a bit to pronounce **i**.
6.	**ei**	To pronounce the combination **ei**, say **e** first. Then make your mouth flat to say **i**.
7.	**ao**	To pronounce the combination **ao**, open your mouth and say **a** first. Then round your mouth to say **o**.
8.	**ou**	To pronounce the combination **ou**, round your mouth and say **o** first. Then make your mouth even to say **u**.
9.	**an**	Open your mouth and say **a** first. Then close it a bit to let the air out through the nasal cavity, ending with **n**.
10.	**en**	Keep your mouth relaxed to say **e** first. Then close it a bit to let the air out through the nasal cavity, ending with **n**.
11.	**ang**	Open your mouth and say **a** first. Then let the air out through the back part of the nasal cavity, ending with **ng**.
12.	**eng**	Keep your mouth relaxed to say **e** first. Then close it a bit to let the air out through the back part of the nasal cavity, ending with **ng**.
13.	**ong**	Pronounce **o** first and then **ng**.

NOTE: Finals are like vowels in English, whereas initials, or labials, resemble consonants.

4 发音练习 Fāyīn Liànxí *Pronunciation Practice*

Listen to the initials from the chart and repeat in the pause provided.

Pronunciation Tips for Initials		
1.	**b**	Shut the lips tightly to obstruct breathing. Then open them to let out the air. This sound is not aspirated.
2.	**p**	Like with **b**, the lips are shut tightly to obstruct breathing. Open them quickly and force the air out. This sound is aspirated.
3.	**m**	Shut your lips tightly. Then let air out through the nasal cavity.
4.	**f**	Press the upper teeth against the lower lip. Let out a breath. This sound relies on friction between the teeth and the lip.

5 发音练习 Fāyīn Liànxí *Pronunciation Practice*

Read from left to right across the rows and repeat the combination of initials and finals.

	Finals \ Initials	b	p	m	f
1.	**a**	ba	pa	ma	fa
2.	**o**	bo	po	mo	fo
3.	**e**			me	
4.	**i**	bi	pi	mi	
5.	**ai**	bai	pai	mai	
6.	**ei**	bei	pei	mei	fei
7.	**ao**	bao	pao	mao	
8.	**ou**		pou	mou	fou
9.	**an**	ban	pan	man	fan
10.	**en**	ben	pen	men	fen
11.	**ang**	bang	pang	mang	fang
12.	**eng**	beng	peng	meng	feng
13.	**ong**				

NOTE: Even though certain combinations of initials and finals can be made, some do not occur in Mandarin Chinese.

6 发音练习 Fāyīn Liànxí / *Pronunciation Practice*

Now that you know the individual sounds, let's combine them together with the tones. Listen to the recording and repeat in the pause provided.

1.	**b + a**	bā bá bǎ bà	bà.x	*n. father*
2.	**b + o**	bō bó bǒ bò	bó.x	*n. uncle*
3.	**b +i**	bī bí bǐ bì	bí.zi	*n. nose*
4.	**b + ai**	bāi bái bǎi bài	báisè	*n. white*
5.	**b + ei**	bēi běi bèi	běifāng	*n. north*
6.	**b + ao**	bāo báo bǎo bào	bēibāo	*n. backpack*
7.	**b + an**	bān bǎn bàn	hēibǎn	*n. blackboard*
8.	**b + en**	bēn běn bèn	Rìběn	*n. Japan*
9.	**b + ang**	bāng bǎng bàng	bāngmáng	*v. to help*
10.	**b + eng**	bēng béng běng bèng	bēngdài	*n. bandage*

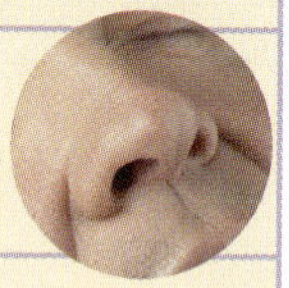

7 听力练习 Tīnglì Liànxí / *Listening Practice*

You will hear six sounds that are combined with the initial "b." Choose the correct final you hear and write the word on a separate piece of paper.

ai	ao	an	en	ang	eng

8 听力练习 Tīnglì Liànxí *Listening Practice*

Combine the initial "p" with some finals. Repeat what you hear in the pause provided.

1.	**p + a**	pā pá pà	hàipà	*adj. afraid* 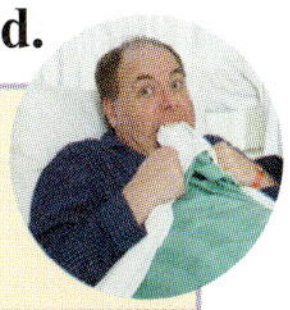
2.	**p + o**	pō pó pǒ pò	wàipó	*n. grandmother*
3.	**p + i**	pī pí pǐ pì	píxié 	*n. leather shoes*
4.	**p + ai**	pāi pái pài	páiduì	*v. to line up* 
5.	**p + ei**	pēi péi pèi	péibàn	*v. to accompany*
6.	**p + ao**	pāo páo pǎo pào	pǎobù	*v. to run*
7.	**p + an**	pān pán pàn	pán.zi	*n. plate* 
8.	**p + en**	pēn pén pèn	huāpén 	*n. flowerpot*
9.	**p + ang**	pāng páng pǎng pàng	pángxiè	*n. crab* 
10.	**p + eng**	pēng péng pěng pèng	péng.yǒu	*n. friend*

9 听力练习 Tīnglì Liànxí *Listening Practice*

Listen to the recording, and write the eight finals that begin with the initial "p" on a separate sheet of paper.

1. p____	3. p____xié	5. p____duì	7. p____.yǒu
2. p____	4. mànp____	6. wàip____	8. huāp____

10 发音练习 Fāyīn Liànxí / Pronunciation Practice

Combine the initial "m" with some finals. Repeat what you hear.

1.	**m + a**	mā má mǎ mà	mā.x	*n. mother*
2.	**m + o**	mō mó mǒ mò	móshù	*n. magic*
3.	**m + e**	me	shén.me	*qw. what*
4.	**m +i**	mī mí mǐ mì	mì.x	*n. secret*
5.	**m + ai**	mái mǎi mài	màipiàn	*n. oatmeal*
6.	**m + ei**	méi měi mèi	mèi.x	*n. younger sister*
7.	**m + ao**	māo máo mǎo mào	máoyī	*n. sweater*
8.	**m + ou**	móu mǒu	jìmóu	*n. strategy*
9.	**m + an**	mán mǎn màn	mànhuà	*n. cartoon*
10.	**m + en**	mēn mén měn mèn men	dàmén	*n. gate*
11.	**m + ang**	máng mǎng	mángguǒ	*n. mango*
12.	**m + eng**	mēng méng měng mèng	níngméng	*n. lemon*

11 听力练习 Tīnglì Liànxí / Listening Practice

You will hear six sounds that are combined with the initial "m." Choose the correct final you hear and write the word on a separate piece of paper.

a	o	ei	en	ou	ai

12 发音练习 Fāyīn Liànxí / *Pronunciation Practice*

Combine the initial "f" with some finals. Repeat what you hear.

1.	**f + a**	fā fá fǎ fà	tóu.fà	*n. hair* 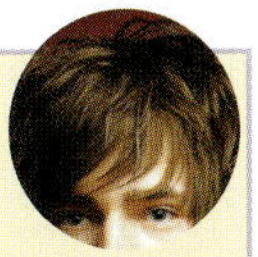
2.	**f + o**	fó	Fójiào	*n. Buddhism*
3.	**f + ei**	fēi féi fěi fèi	fēijī	*n. airplane* 
4.	**f + ou**	fǒu	fǒuzé	*adv. otherwise*
5.	**f + an**	fān fán fǎn fàn	fànguǎn	*n. restaurant* 
6.	**f + en**	fēn fén fěn fèn	fēnshù	*n. grade*
7.	**f + ang**	fāng fáng fǎng fàng	fáng.zi	*n. house* 
8.	**f + eng**	fēng féng fěng fèng	mìfēng	*n. bee*

13 听力练习 Tīnglì Liànxí / *Listening Practice*

Listen to the recording, and write the six finals that begin with the initial "f" on a separate sheet of paper.

1. mìf ____	4. f ____ .zi
2. f ____ guǎn	5. f ____ jī
3. f ____ shù	6. tóu.f ____

14 发音练习 Fāyīn Liànxí / *Pronunciation Practice*

You will hear a recording of pairs of Chinese words that may sound similar, but actually have different pronunciations. Listen carefully and repeat each word in the pause provided.

1.	**bó** (*uncle*) / **bá** (*to pull out*)	10.	**bā** (*eight*) / **fā** (*to issue*)
2.	**pāi** (*to pat*) / **pēi** (*an embryo*)	11.	**péi** (*to accompany*) / **méi** (*eyebrow*)
3.	**máo** (*feather*) / **móu** (*pupil*)	12.	**bì** (*to close*) / **pì** (*examples*)
4.	**fǎn** (*to return*) / **fěn** (*powder*)	13.	**mà** (*to scold*) / **fà** (*hair*)
5.	**bāng** (*to help*) / **bēng** (*to collapse*)	14.	**bàng** (*stick*) / **pàng** (*fat*)
6.	**mǎn** (*full*) / **mǎng** (*boa*)	15.	**péng** (*friend*) / **méng** (*to cover*)
7.	**fén** (*to burn*) / **féng** (*to sew*)	16.	**bàn** (*half*) / **màn** (*slow*)
8.	**bà** (father) / **mà** (*to scold*)	17.	**bēn** (*to run quickly*) / **mēn** (*stuffy*)
9.	**pó** (*old woman*) / **fó** (*Buddha*)	18.	**pàng** (*fat*) / **fàng** (*to put*)

15 听力练习 Tīnglì Liànxí / *Listening Practice*

Listen to the recording, and select the sound you hear by writing A or B on a separate sheet of paper.

1.	A. mā	B. mō	6.	A. mēn	B. mēng
2.	A. bǎi	B. biě	7.	A. pài	B. mài
3.	A. póu	B. pá	8.	A. bāo	B. māo
4.	A. fǎn	B. fǎng	9.	A. fán	B. pán
5.	A. pèng	B. pàng	10.	A. bǎng	B. mǎng

16 听力练习 Tīnglì Liànxí / *Listening Practice*

You will hear each word twice. The first time you listen, write the missing finals you hear. The second time, mark the tones. Write your answers on a separate sheet of paper.

Lì.zi:

bān

1. b____

2. f____zào

3. m____

4. ____ēng.zhēng

5. ____í____āo

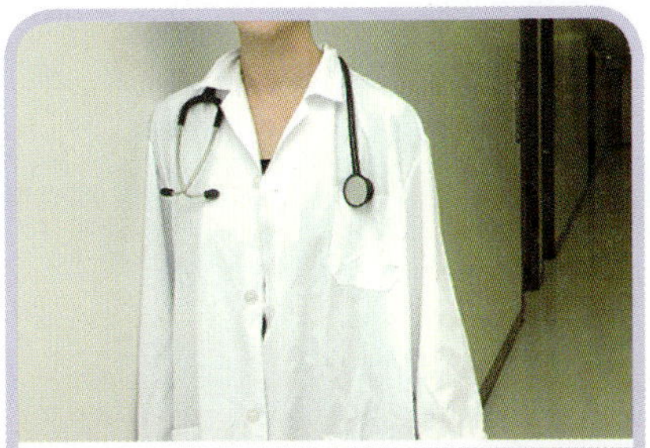

6. ____ái____áo

7. dàom____

8. p____shǒu

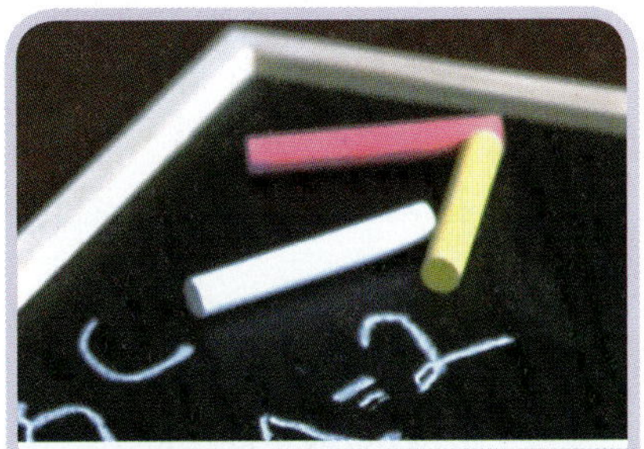

9. *f*____b____

10. m____m____

11. f____p____

12. p____sh____

Tongue Twister

花马白马 Huāmǎ Báimǎ

老马有两匹马，	*Lǎo*.mǎ *yǒu liǎng-pǐ* mǎ,
一匹花马，一匹白马。	yì-pǐ huāmǎ, yì-pǐ báimǎ.
花马花，白马白，	Huāmǎ huā, báimǎ bái,
花马白马，都是老马的小马。	huāmǎ báimǎ, dōu shì *lǎo*.mǎ .de *xiǎo* mǎ.

Old Horse has two horses
— a horse with patches and a white horse.
The patched horse has patches, and the white horse is white.
Both the horse with patches and the white horse are Old Horse's horses.

Let's Sing!

三轮车 Sānlúnchē

三轮车，跑得快，	Sānlúnchē, pǎo .de-kuài,
上面坐个老太太。	shàng.miàn zuò .ge lǎo tài.x.
要五毛，给一块，	Yào wǔ-máo, gěi yí-kuài,
你说奇怪不奇怪？	nǐ shuō qíguài bù qíguài?

Tricycle
Tricycle, it goes fast,
an old lady is sitting on it.
Ask for 50 cents and get a dollar;
do you think this is strange?

课堂用语 Kètáng Yòngyǔ

Classroom Expressions

Teacher: 这是你的讲义。
Zhè shì nǐ.de jiǎngyì.
This is your handout.

Student: 谢谢老师。
Xiè.x lǎoshī.
Thank you.

Teacher: 请坐。
Qǐng zuò.
Please sit down.

Teacher: 请站起来。
Qǐng zhàn qǐlái.
Please stand up.

Teacher: 请打开书。/请把书打开。
Qǐng dǎkāi shū. / *Qǐng* bǎ shū dǎkāi.
Please open the book.

Teacher: 请翻页。
Qǐng fān yè.
Please turn the page.

Teacher: 请看黑板。
Qǐng kàn hēibǎn.
Please look at the board.

17 老师说什么? Lǎoshī shuō shén.me? *What does the teacher say?*

Listen to the recording, and match each classroom expression to the corresponding picture. Number 1-5 on a separate sheet of paper.

汉字 Hànzì
Chinese Characters

Traditional vs. Simplified Characters

There are two types of written Chinese characters in use today: Traditional characters and Simplified characters. Traditional characters, stemming from the Qin Dynasty (221-207 B.C.), have a history of roughly 2,000 years. Simplified characters evolved later from the People's Republic of China (PRC) government's wish to reduce illiteracy; they simplified the strokes used in Traditional Chinese to achieve this goal. Thus, Simplified characters are derived from the Traditional characters. Here is an outline of the methods for simplification:

Ⓐ Adaptation of ancient characters. In olden times, text was simpler. Text grew complex over time as needs arose.

從 → 从 (cóng), 禮 → 礼 (lǐ)

Ⓑ Simplification from the people. To save time, some civilians simplified words they wrote. Thus, some Simplified characters came from these commonly used words during the Song (960-1279 A.D.) and Yuan (1271-1368 A.D.) dynasties.

聖 → 圣 (shèng), 歡 → 欢 (huān)

Ⓒ Omission of (usually more complex) strokes. Sometimes a simplified component is used in place of the complex.

Stroke omission: 尋 → 寻 (xún), 飛 → 飞 (fēi)
Stroke substitution: 勸 → 劝 (quàn), 漢 → 汉 (hàn)

Ⓓ Unification from calligraphy. In Ancient China, calligraphy had fewer strokes to form a more flowing font. Some Simplified characters evolved from the unification of these strokes used in calligraphy.

東 → 东 (dōng), 車 → 车 (chē).

The examples below show how some characters were simplified.

Calligraphy				
Simplified Characters	东 (dōng, *east*)	车 (chē, *car*)	办 (bàn, *to do*)	贝 (bèi, *shell*)

❺ Replacement of complicated phonetic components with simpler ones. Some characters are made up of form and phonetic components, where the form component gives the character meaning, while the phonetic component gives the character its pronunciation. For words like these, if the phonetic component has too many strokes, the character is simplified by replacing the complicated phonetic component with another that bears a similar sound.

襯 → 衬 (chèn), 遠 → 远 (yuǎn)

❻ Simplification of character forms and substitution of less-used characters with others of the same or similar pronunciation. Various different characters with complicated strokes that share the same pronunciation were replaced by the same simplified character in an attempt to reduce the overall number of characters in use.

復；複 → 复 (fù), 鐘；鍾 → 钟 (zhōng)

Here are some examples of how the Traditional characters were simplified. They are shown side by side for you to compare their differences.

Traditional	Simplified	Examples: from Traditional to Simplified			
糸	纟	結→结,	紙→纸,	線→线,	約→约
見	见	現→现,	規→规,	視→视,	覺→觉
言	言 *	說→说,	談→谈,	訂→订,	記→记
貝	贝	財→财,	貨→货,	責→责,	貪→贪
車	车	軍→军,	揮→挥,	較→较,	軟→软
侖	仑	論→论,	倫→伦,	輪→轮,	淪→沦
金	金 *	釘→钉,	針→针,	鈕→钮,	釵→钗
門	门	問→问,	聞→闻,	間→间,	閃→闪
頁	页	須→须,	頂→顶,	順→顺,	頑→顽
食	食 *	飢→饥,	飯→饭,	飽→饱,	飲→饮
魚	鱼	漁→渔,	鯉→鲤,	鮮→鲜,	鮭→鲑
鳥	鸟	鳴→鸣,	鴛→鸳,	鴨→鸭,	鵝→鹅

* "言," "金" and "食" are the same as their Traditional versions when written as independent characters. However, when they are used as radicals, they are written as " 讠", " 钅" and " 饣".

The 50 Most Common Simplified Radicals

Radicals are root words from which all Chinese words originate. They are used for looking up meanings of words in a Chinese dictionary. They can be independent words or part of a character as the ideographic indicator. In the first lesson you learned the 50 most commonly used Traditional radicals. Since you have also learned the transformation principles, here are the 50 most commonly used Simplified radicals.

Radical		Examples
1.	人(亻)rén *n. person; people*	从 cóng *prep. from* 仁 rén *n. kindness*
2.	彳 chì *v. to pace*	很 hěn *adv. very* 往 wǎng *prep. toward*
3.	手（扌）shǒu *n. hand*	拿 ná *v. to take* 扫 sǎo *v. to sweep*
4.	足（⻊）zú *n. foot*	跑 pǎo *v. to run* 跳 tiào *v. to jump*
5.	口 kǒu *n. mouth*	吃 chī *v. to eat* 喝 hē *v. to drink*
6.	目 mù *n. eye*	眼 yǎn *n. eye* 盲 máng *adj. blind*
7.	饣 shí *n. food*	饥 jī *adj. hungry* 饭 fàn *n. rice*
8.	礻 shì *v. to notify*	祖 zǔ *n. ancestor* 祀 sì *v. to sacrifice*
9.	父 fù *n. father*	爹 diē *n. father* 爷 yé *n. grandfather*
10.	女 nǚ *n. woman*	妈 mā *n. mother* 妻 qī *n. wife*
11.	子 zǐ *n. child*	孩 hái *n. child* 孤 gū *n. orphan*
12.	日 rì *n. sun*	明 míng *adj. bright* 早 zǎo *n. morning*
13.	月 yuè *n. moon*	脑 nǎo *n. brain* 肚 dù *n. stomach*
14.	雨 yǔ *n. rain*	雾 wù *n. fog* 雪 xuě *n. snow*

15.	水（氵） shuǐ *n. water*	海 hǎi *n. sea* 江 jiāng *n. river*
16.	冫 bīng *n. ice*	冰 bīng *n. ice* 冷 lěng *adj. cold*
17.	山 shān *n. mountain*	峰 fēng *n. peak* 峡 xiá *n. gorge*
18.	木 mù *n. wood*	村 cūn *n. village* 林 lín *n. grove*
19.	艹 cǎo *n. grass*	草 cǎo *n. grass* 花 huā *n. flower*
20.	石 shí *n. stone*	岩 yán *n. rock* 砂 shā *n. sand*
21.	虫 huǐ *n. insect(s)*	蚊 wén *n. mosquito* 蛇 shé *n. snake*
22.	疒 bìng *adj. sick*	疾 jí *n. disease* 病 bìng *n. disease; ailment*
23.	火（灬） huǒ *n. fire*	炸 zhá *v. to fry* 炮 pào *n. cannon*
24.	力 lì *n. strength*	努 nǔ *v. to exert* 动 dòng *v. to move*
25.	土（士） tǔ *n. earth*	地 dì *n. ground; earth* 坑 kēng *n. entrapment*
26.	大 dà *adj. big*	天 tiān *n. sky* 太 tài *adv. too; enough*
27.	小（⺌） xiǎo *adj. small*	少 shǎo *adj. less* 尖 jiān *adj. pointed*
28.	立 lì *v. to set up; to establish*	站 zhàn *v. to stand up* 竖 shù *adj. vertical*
29.	走 zǒu *v. to walk*	起 qǐ *v. to star* 越 yuè *v. to across*
30.	辶 chuò *v. to go*	进 jìn *v. to enter* 远 yuǎn *adj. far*

31.	页 yè *n. heading*	顶 dǐng *n. top* 顺 shùn *adj. smooth*
32.	户 hù *n. household*	扇 shàn *n. fan* 启 qǐ *v. to open*
33.	门 mén *n. door*	闭 bì *v. to close* 间 jiān *adv. between*
34.	广 guǎng *n. shelter*	店 diàn *n. store* 床 chuáng *n. bed*
35.	阜（阝）fù *n. plenty*	阳 yáng *n. sun* 际 jì *n. boundary*
36.	邑（阝）yì *n. city*	都 dū *n. capital* 邦 bāng *n. nation*
37.	皿 mǐn *n. shallow container*	盆 pén *n. basin* 盅 zhōng *n. cup without a handle*
38.	心（忄）xīn *n. heart*	忙 máng *adj. busy* 怀 huái *v. to keep (in mind)*
39.	宀 mián *n. roof*	安 ān *adj. safe* 完 wán *adj. over*
40.	又 yòu *adv. again*	难 nán *adj. difficult* 对 duì *adj. correct*
41.	刀（刂）dāo *n. knife*	切 qiē *v. to cut* 利 lì *adj. sharp*
42.	钅 jīn *n. gold*	钱 qián *n. money* 银 yín *n. silver*
43.	车 chē *n. vehicle*	辆 liàng *m. quantifier for land vehicles* 输 shū *v. to transport*
44.	衣（衤）yī *n. clothes*	衫 shān *n. shirt* 裤 kù *n. pants*
45.	纟 sī *n. silk*	红 hóng *adj. red* 级 jí *n. grade*
46.	讠 yán *n. word*	说 shuō *v. to speak* 订 dìng *v. to order*
47.	牛 niú *n. ox*	牧 mù *v. to herd domestic animals* 物 wù *n. thing*

48.	穴 xuè *n. cave*	空 kōng *adj. empty* 穿 chuān *v. to pass through*
49.	犬（犭）quǎn *n. dog*	狗 gǒu *n. dog* 狼 láng *n. wolf*
50.	囗 wéi *v. to surround*	国 guó *n. country* 困 kùn *v. to besiege*

18 找出部首 Zhǎochū Bùshǒu / *Finding the Radicals*

Knowing the radical of a character can help you look up the character in a dictionary. Match the Chinese characters that follow with the corresponding radicals.

1. 盟	3. 饭	5. 有	7. 匠	9. 莓	11. 式	13. 江	15. 冰	17. 阳	19. 受
2. 画	4. 扔	6. 老	8. 邦	10. 到	12. 国	14. 狼	16. 吃	18. 历	20. 建

A. 犭 B. 饣 C. 氵 D. 耂 E. 皿 F. 戈 G. 扌 H. 廴 I. 凵 J. 冫

K. 口 L. 厂 M. 冂 N. 刂 O. 匚 P. 阝 Q. 艹 R. 囗 S. 爫 T. 阝

19 繁体还是简体？ Fántǐ háishì Jiǎntǐ? / *Traditional or Simplified?*

Now that you have learned the difference between Traditional and Simplified characters, identify which character is Simplified from the following pairs.

1.	A. 饿	B. 頓	5.	A. 輩	B. 钗	9.	A. 頭	B. 図
2.	A. 紗	B. 赏	6.	A. 辅	B. 轉	10.	A. 鲔	B. 闊
3.	A. 红	B. 魯	7.	A. 閱	B. 讨	11.	A. 賠	B. 铜
4.	A. 托	B. 鴛	8.	A. 鸦	B. 銀	12.	A. 辉	B. 開

The Basic Strokes

As you learn to write Chinese characters, the first thing to know is how to make the strokes. Strokes are important because they show how the characters are composed and enable you to write the characters more easily. There are eight basic strokes that are commonly used. They are illustrated as follows:

1.	横 héng (Horizontal stroke)	The horizontal stroke can be either short or long. The stroke is written from left to right, not the other way around.		
	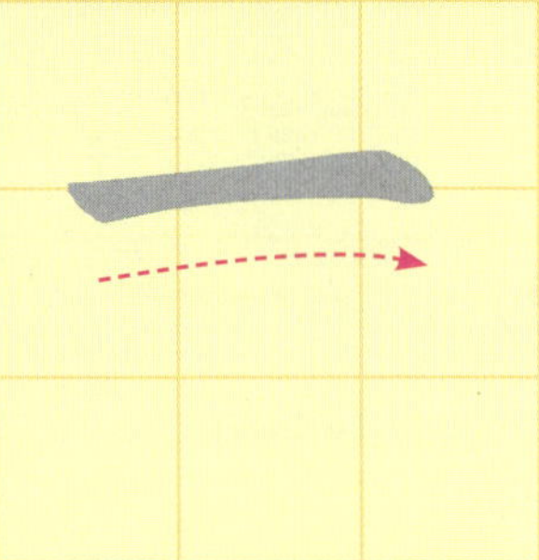	一 yī *one*	二 èr *two*	王 wáng *a Chinese family surname*
2.	竖 shù (Vertical stroke)	Always write the vertical stroke from the top downward.		
	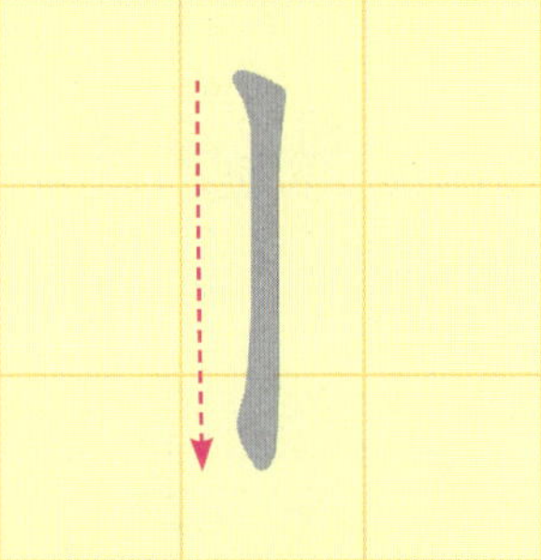	十 shí *ten*	工 gōng *work*	中 zhōng *medium*
3.	撇 piě (Left-slanted stroke)	This stroke is used in different lengths and angles, but all are only variations on the basic way of writing the stroke. Write the stroke from the top right to the bottom left.		
	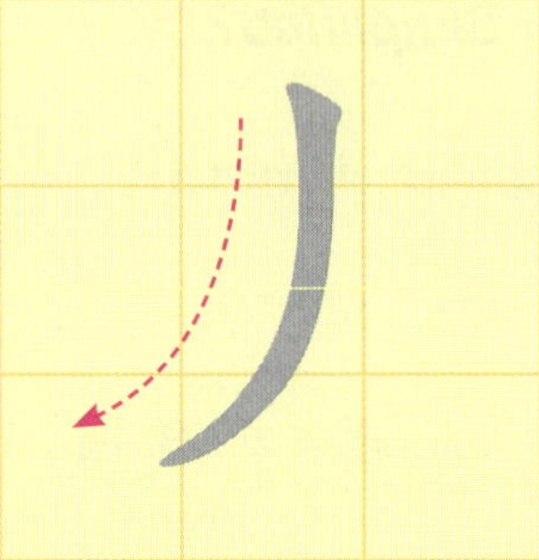	大 dà *big*	千 qiān *thousand*	手 shǒu *hand*
4.	捺 nà (Right-slanted stroke)	There are two forms of this stroke: slanted and flat. Write the stroke from the top left to the bottom right.		
	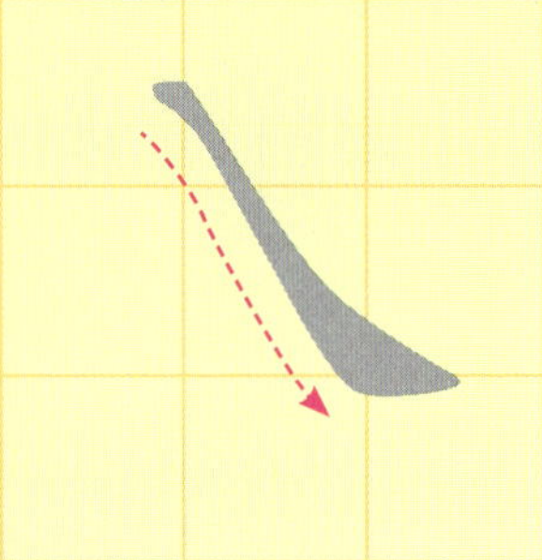	人 rén *people*	八 bā *eight*	这 zhè *this*

5.	点 diǎn (Dots)	The dot takes on many forms, as illustrated.

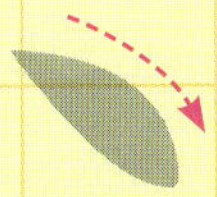

心	六	京
xīn *heart*	liù *six*	jīng *the capital of a country*

6.	提 tí (Rising stroke)	Make the rising stroke from the bottom left to the top right.

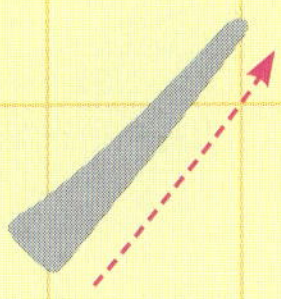

江	北	冰
jiāng *river*	běi *north*	bīng *ice*

7.	钩 gōu (Hook)	Make a small tick at the end of a stroke.

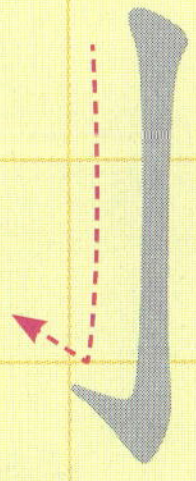

小	心	代
xiǎo *small*	xīn *heart*	dài *a generation*

8.	折 zhé (Bent stroke)	Make a turn at a certain section of a stroke.

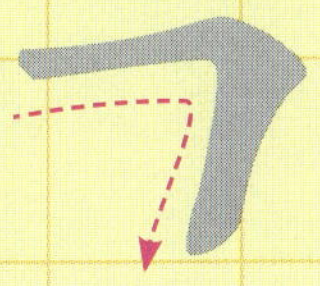

日	山	女
rì *sun*	shān *mountain*	nǚ *woman*

Foundation C

When you have completed this lesson you will be able to...

Geography / History
- locate China's municipalities and special districts on a map
- explain cultural, geographical, and economic information about the municipalities and special districts

Pronunciation
- pronounce more finals and the alveolar and velar sounds
- recite three rhymes and sing a new song

Classroom Expressions
- use the correct Chinese expressions in certain classroom situations

Chinese Characters
- define and explain Chinese pictographs
- understand and apply the stroke order rules for writing Chinese characters

地理/历史 Dìlǐ / Lìshǐ

Geography / History

A city of great political, economic and military importance or a city that has a large population is considered a provincial-level division called a municipality, similar to Washington, D.C. Municipalities are directly controlled by the government. Special Administrative Regions (SARs) are highly autonomous regions that were once foreign colonies. The existence of SARs allows the Chinese government to peacefully resolve issues stemming from their past foreign status. Although SARs are at the same level as provinces, they are governed in a different way and with a different system.

Municipalities	
1. 北京	Běijīng
2. 天津	Tiānjīn
3. 上海	Shànghǎi
4. 重庆	Chóngqìng
Special Districts	
5. 香港	Xiānggǎng
6. 澳门	Àomén

The Four Municipalities

北京 Běijīng

Beijing, home of the famous Peking Man (*homo erectus*), is estimated to have over 3,000 years of history. It is a Chinese city of cultural importance, having been the capital of five dynasties that left behind a wealth of art, relics, and other artifacts. These dynasties also bequeathed architectural wonders, such as the Palace Museum (Gùgōng), the Great Wall (Chángchéng), the Peking Man's excavation site (Zhōukǒudiàn), the Temple of Heaven (Tiāntán), the Summer Palace (Yíhéyuán), and Tiananmen Square (Tiān'ānmén *Guǎng*chǎng). After the People's Republic of China (PRC) was established in 1949, Beijing was named the capital of the PRC and became the political, economic, and cultural center of the nation. In 2008 Beijing hosted the Summer Olympics, and you can still visit the Olympic Village (Àoyùncūn). Beijing is also the largest ground and air transportation center in China, and was the first city in China to build a subway system. Nowadays, Beijing is the network hub for the railroad system. It is in Beijing where many local customs and activities originated, such as cross talk, Peking Opera, and traditional snacks like sugarcoated haws on a stick. In recent years, Beijing has experienced an economic boom, which has led to a better standard of living for many of its residents.

Culture Note

Cross talk (相声 xiàngshēng): A performing style in the form of dialogues or monologues filled with puns, cross talk is found only in Chinese-speaking countries. Society and celebrities are often the targeted themes.

Peking Opera (京剧 jīngjù): This traditional style of Peking Opera combines songs from the palace and the people. It developed in Beijing during the Qing dynasty (1636 A.D. - 1912 A.D.).

Tanghulu (糖葫芦 tánghúlú): A snack commonly found on the streets throughout China, it is made up of sugarcoated fruits on a (bamboo) stick. In the north, Chinese haws and pears are often used, while in the south, tanghulu is often made using tomatoes, strawberries, or grapes.

▲ The Temple of Heaven, where emperors offered sacrifices to the gods.

Temple of Heaven

The Temple of Heaven in Beijing is the world's largest ancient structure built to pay homage to the gods and the heavens. Built in 1420 and listed as a World Heritage Site in 1998, it was designed to emblazon the vastness of the sky and show that the heavens are above and beyond everything else. The structure was influenced by Chinese philosophy, as evidenced by its cylindrical shape and rectangular outer walls, that represents the belief that "the heavens are round; the land is square." The decorations of the Temple of Heaven are elaborate and incorporate concepts of kinetics, acoustics, and geometry. The building has great historical, scientific, and cultural value, and holds a place of importance in China's architectural history.

▲ The lotus pond in the summer.

▲ The Jade Bridge in the Summer Palace.

Summer Palace

The Summer Palace is special because of its combination of manmade structures and natural scenery. It is an example of China's era of landscape art at its peak. In 1998, the Summer Palace was listed as a World Heritage Site. The Palace site covers over 723 acres, taken up mostly by Wanshou Mountain and Kunming Lake, which covers three quarters of the surface area. At the center of the site, there is a Buddhist temple. The Summer Palace is currently China's largest and most well-preserved imperial garden. It is also one of China's four most famous gardens; sometimes it is also referred to as the Imperial Garden Museum.

▲ The largest city plaza in the world—Tiananmen Square.

Tiananmen Square

Built in 1417, Tiananmen Square is a city plaza located in the center of Beijing. Covering over 108 acres, it is the largest city plaza in the world and can accommodate a gathering of one million people. At the north of the square, China's national flag is raised and lowered with the rising and setting of the sun each day. The Chinese government has prohibited the placement of outdoor ads in the square and within 328 feet of the square's eastern and western borders.

Olympic Village

The Olympic Village was built for the Beijing Olympics in 2008. It was used to house the 16,000 athletes and staff from 205 countries. The Opening Ceremony for the Beijing Games began at eight in the evening on August 8, 2008, because the Chinese pronunciation of 8 is similar to that of 发 fā *prosperity*. The Chinese government hoped to bring good fortune to the Games beginning with the lucky number eight. It was designed with environmental, cultural, and technological precepts in mind, which is why it is sometimes referred to as "Green Olympic Village," "Cultural Olympic Village," or "Technological Olympic Village." Divided into the Residence Sector and the International Sector, the Olympic Village covers over 163 acres of land. It is situated within the Olympic Park, and is south of a forested park and north of the main stadium. The village is scenic and has convenient transportation. The Residential Sector takes up most of the village and contains a clinic for athletes, restaurants, a library, an entertainment center, a leisure center and information centers as well as apartment buildings. Welcoming ceremonies and other receptions were held in the International Sector to make it convenient for the athletes from other nations to get to know each other. After the Games, the Olympic Village was converted to residential property for civilians.

天津 Tiānjīn

Tianjin, one of China's coastal cities, has long been a city of military importance as is evidenced by its name, "the Heavenly Ford." Situated in northeast China, it became an important port with the opening of the Grand Canal in 609 A.D. and is today the nearest port to the Chinese capital, Beijing. The Bohai Sea lies to its east, and it is surrounded by Hebei province and mountains to the north. With its strong industrial accomplishments in biochemistry, automobiles and airplane production, clothing, pharmaceuticals, and food products, Tianjin is also called "the pearl of Bohai Sea." Tianjin is also full of historic sites, such as the Dagukou Ford. Its traditional and modern architecture led it to also be called the "multinational museum of architecture." In its history, Tianjin has seen eight foreign territorial concessions come and go and this past foreign influence is reflected in its buildings. Tianjin is also famous for its snacks, which include fried dough twists, steamed stuffed buns, and candied chestnuts.

▲ The Century Clock (Tianjin Shijizhong), with bronze relief carvings of the 12 symbols of the Chinese zodiac.

上海 Shànghǎi

Shanghai is located in the middle of China's coastline and is an important transportation hub. Besides being a well-situated port city, it is also an industrial base and center for trade. Shanghai formed its own unique culture by adapting some of the Euro-American culture that came with the opening of the port in 1842 as a result of the British victory in the First Opium War. Huangpu River divides the city of Shanghai into Puxi (west of Huangpu River) and Pudong (east of Huangpu River). In 1842, China lost the First Opium War and was forced to allow the British to build ports and erect stores to form the Bund, after which developments in Puxi progressed rapidly. In contrast, Pudong remained more rural until the 1990s. In 1992, the Chinese government "modernized" Pudong, filling its cityscape with skyscrapers.

▲ The city of Shanghai juxtaposes traditional and modern buildings.

Shanghai is a blend of the old and the new, the traditional and the contemporary. European-style buildings, such as banks and hotels, have become landmarks. Many immigrants resided in Shanghai before 1949, when it was named the "ten-mile foreign area." Under Chinese reform initiatives, Shanghai has hosted many cultural events and built important cultural venues, such as the Shanghai Grand Theatre and the Shanghai Museum, and is rapidly eclipsing Hong Kong as the financial and trade center of China. It is also known as a shopping paradise, and is set to host the World Expo in 2010.

▲ Once a rice field, Pudong now has tall buildings, like the one above, that have sprung up everywhere.

Culture Note

The Opium Wars:
The first Opium War broke out after China refused to allow the smuggling of opium by the British. Thus, the British started the war in 1839. The Chinese lost in 1842, and signed their first unequal treaty.

重庆 Chóngqìng

Chongqing is located in Yangtze River's upriver regions, and is one of western China's most important cities. A big industrial area, it is also a transportation hub for China's southwest. It is a hilly region that is frequently covered with fog, which is why it is also called the "city of mountains" or the "fog capital." As for food, people there have a preference for spicy dishes. One of the most famous is the Chongqing hotpot, also known as "spicy" hotpot. In 2007, Chongqing was awarded the name of the "hotpot capital of China." Chongqing is also a historical city, and home to the Dazu Rock Carvings. The famous Three Gorges Dam is located near Chongqing, drawing many tourists every year.

▶ Customers can choose two or three flavors for one hot pot. One of the most popular choices includes original and spicy soup in the same pot.

Culture Note

Hot pot (火锅 *huǒguō*): A style of cooking that uses pots (锅 *guō*) over a heat source filled with water or soup in which various ingredients (such as meat, seafood, and vegetables) are put in and cooked together. The ingredients, once cooked, can be consumed with the addition of one or a variety of sauces.

The Two Special Districts

香港 Xiānggǎng

Hong Kong, an important center of finance and marine transportation, is China's first Special Administrative Region (SAR). The central island of Hong Kong was conceded to the British at the end of the First Opium War and became a British Crown Colony in 1842. Due to its occupation by the British for a century and a half, English became a common language and British culture and institutions were woven into the fabric of the colony. In 1997, at the expiration of a 99-year lease on portions of Hong Kong, the entire colony was returned to China in a formal ceremony that was both poignant and joyful. Due to its lack of flat land to build on and large population, downtown apartments are often more than ten stories high. Hong Kong's economy is strongly based on exports, resulting in busy ports for both sea and air, giving Hong Kong its reputation as one of Asia's traditional four small "dragons" (the others being Singapore, South Korea, and Taiwan) and an international center of finance. Hong Kong is also well-known for its entertainment industry, which has led to it being called the "Hollywood in the East"; and cuisine, including its famous Dim Sum, which tourists and locals alike enjoy sampling.

▲ Large shop signs are a feature of Hong Kong's city streets.

澳门 Àomén

Macau, China's other SAR, is located off the southeastern coast of China. Throughout history, it has played an important role in international relations. The Historic Centre of Macau is listed as a UNESCO World Heritage Site. Macau was the first and the last foreign colony in China. It was leased to Portugal in 1557, and was not returned to China until 1999. Due to this long period of Portuguese influence, many Portuguese historical properties such as the *Ruínas da Antiga Catedral de São Paulo* can be found in Macau. Tourism is Macau's main industry, with many visitors coming to gamble in its fine casinos, stay in its attractive hotels, and frequent its many restaurants.

▶ Cathedral of St. Paul.

1 温故知新 Wēngù Zhīxīn *Remembering the Facts*

Select the letter that describes each municipality or special district. Some municipalities or special districts will be matched with more than one description.

1. Běijīng	A.	special district of China
2. Tiānjīn	B.	municipality of China
3. Shànghǎi	C.	the Hollywood in the East
4. Chóngqìng	D.	hotpot capital of China
5. Xiānggǎng	E.	ten-mile foreign area
6. Àomén	F.	the capital of the PRC

2 温故知新 Wēngù Zhīxīn *Remembering the Facts*

Decide if each statement is true or false. Correct any false statements.

1. The Temple of Heaven, the Summer Palace, and Tiananmen Square are all listed as World Heritage Sites.
2. The design concept of the Temple of Heaven is "the heavens are square; the land is round."
3. The land to water ratio of the Summer Palace is three to one.
4. Tiananmen Square is a place for the public to gather and voice their opinions, so there are plenty of ads and slogans to be seen.
5. The opening ceremony of the 2008 Olympics was held on August 8th, 2008, because eight is a lucky number in China.

▲ A fan at the 2008 Olymics.

3 角色扮演 Juésè Bànyǎn / Role Play

With a partner, play the roles of a Chinese-American teacher who's in a hospital in Beijing and one of the Chinese-American parents who's a chaperone for the student trip. The teacher wants to know what her students are visiting on their free day today.

Lì.zi: **A:** Justin今天参观什么地方？
Justin jīn.tiān cānguān shén.me dì.fāng?
What will Justin visit today?

B: 他今天参观奥运村。
Tā jīn.tiān cānguān Àoyùncūn.
He will visit the Olympic Village.

Yíhéyuán *(the Summer Palace)*	Gùgōng *(the Palace Museum)*
Tiāntán *(the Temple of Heaven)*	Àoyùncūn *(the Olympic Village)*
Tiān'ānmén Guǎngchǎng *(Tiananmen Square)*	Zhōukǒudiàn *(the Peking Man's excavation site)*

1. Heather / Tiananmen Square
2. Brian / the Temple of Heaven
3. Tiffany / the Peking Man's excavation site
4. Amber / the Palace Museum
5. Andrew / the Summer Palace
6. Lance / the Olympic Village

▶ Willows are prevalent plants in Jiangsu province.

发音 Fāyīn

Pronunciation

4 发音练习 Fāyīn Liànxí / *Pronunciation Practice*

Listen to the finals from the chart and repeat in the pause provided.

Pronunciation Tips for Finals		
1.	**i**	Keep your mouth flat as if you were pronouncing the English letter **e**.
2.	**ia**	Pronounce **i** first and then **a**.
3.	**iao**	Pronounce **i** first and then **ao**.
4.	**ie**	Pronounce **i** first and then **ê**.
5.	**iu***	Pronounce **i** first and then **ou**.
6.	**ian**	Pronounce **i** first and then **an**.
7.	**in**	Pronounce **i** first and then **n**.
8.	**iang**	Pronounce **i** first and then **ang**.
9.	**ing**	Pronounce **i** first and then **ng**.
10.	**iong**	Pronounce **i** first and then **ong**.

***NOTE:** There is a hidden "o" sound between "iu."

Alveolar Sounds

Alveolar sounds are made by the tongue coming into contact with the alveolar ridge. There are two alveolar ridges in the mouth—one just above the top teeth (and before the hard palate) and the other just below the bottom teeth. Some alveolar consonants in English are **[t]**, **[d]**, **[s]**, **[z]**, **[n]** and **[l]**; similarly, Chinese alveolar consonants are **d**, **t**, **n**, and **l**.

5 发音练习 Fāyīn Liànxí *Pronunciation Practice*

Listen to the initials from the chart and repeat in the pause provided.

Pronunciation Tips for Alveolar Sounds		
1.	**d**	Move the tip of the tongue so that it touches the upper ridge of your teeth. Drop the tongue to let out the air. The sound is not aspirated.
2.	**t**	Like with **d**, touch the tip of your tongue to the upper ridge of your teeth. Drop your tongue quickly to force the air out. This sound is aspirated.
3.	**n**	Let the tip of your tongue touch the upper ridge of your teeth. Let the air out through the nasal cavity.
4.	**l**	Allow the tip of your tongue to touch the back of the upper ridge of your teeth. Let the air out from both sides of the tongue.

Velar Sounds

Velar sounds are made with the back part of the tongue touching the soft palate, located toward the back of the top of the mouth. Some examples in English are the **[k]** in "skip" and the **[g]** in "get." In Chinese, velar consonants are **g**, **k**, and **h**.

6 发音练习 Fāyīn Liànxí *Pronunciation Practice*

Listen to the initials from the chart and repeat in the pause provided.

Pronunciation Tips for Velar Sounds		
1.	**g**	Raise the back of your tongue against the soft palate. Then let out the air. This sound is not aspirated.
2.	**k**	Like with **g**, put the back of your tongue against the soft palate. Then let the air out, only this time with a bit more force. This sound is aspirated.
3.	**h**	Raise the back of your tongue toward the soft palate. Then let the air flow out of the channel between your tongue and your soft palate.

7 发音练习 Fāyīn Liànxí / Pronunciation Practice

Listen to the recording and repeat the combination of initials and finals.

	Initials / Finals	d	t	n	l
1.	**i**	di	ti	ni	li
2.	**ia**				lia
3.	**iao**	diao	tiao	niao	liao
4.	**ie**	die	tie	nie	lie
5.	**iu**	diu		niu	liu
6.	**ian**	dian	tian	nian	lian
7.	**in**			nin	lin
8.	**iang**			niang	liang
9.	**ing**	ding	ting	ning	ling

8 发音练习 Fāyīn Liànxí / Pronunciation Practice

Combine the initial "d" with some finals. Listen to the recording and repeat what you hear.

1.	**d + i**	dī dí dǐ dì	dìdi	*n. younger brother*
2.	**d + iao**	diāo diǎo diào	diàoyú	*v. to fish*
3.	**d + ie**	diē dié	húdié	*n. butterfly*
4.	**d + iu**	diū	diūdiào	*v. to throw away*
5.	**d + ian**	diān diǎn diàn	zìdiǎn	*n. dictionary*
6.	**d + ing**	dīng dǐng dìng	juédìng	*v. to decide*

9 大声念 Dàshēng Niàn / *Read it Aloud*

With a partner, take turns reading the rhyme aloud.

丁丁去钓鱼。	Dīngdīng qù diàoyú.	*Dingding went fishing.*
丁丁去抓蝴蝶。	Dīngdīng qù zhuā húdié.	*Dingding went to catch butterflies.*
去钓鱼的丁丁也去抓蝴蝶。	Qù diàoyú de Dīngdīng yě qù zhuā húdié.	*The Dingding that went fishing also went to catch butterflies.*
钓到鱼的丁丁踮起脚底。	Diàodào yú de Dīngdīng diǎnqǐ jiǎodǐ.	*Dingding, after catching some fish, stood on his tiptoes.*
抓到了蝴蝶，弄丢了鱼。	Zhuādào le húdié, nòngdiū le yú.	*However, after he caught some butterflies, he lost the fish.*

10 听力练习 Tīnglì Liànxí / *Listening Practice*

You will hear four sounds that are combined with the initial "d." Choose the correct final you hear and write the word on a separate sheet of paper.

iu	ian	ing	ie

11 发音练习 Fāyīn Liànxí / *Pronunciation Practice*

Combine the initial "t" with some finals. Repeat what you hear.

1.	**t + i**	tī tí tǐ tì	diàntī	*n. elevator*
2.	**t + iao**	tiāo tiáo tiǎo tiào	tiào-wǔ	*v. to dance*
3.	**t + ie**	tiē tiě tiè	dìtiě	*n. subway*
4.	**t + ian**	tiān tián tiǎn	tiānkōng	*n. sky*
5.	**t + ing**	tīng tíng tǐng	dàtīng	*n. hall*

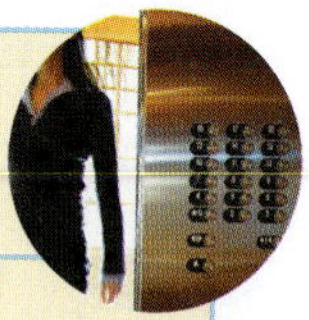

12 大声念 Dàshēng Niàn *Read it Aloud*

With a partner, take turns reading the rhyme aloud.

我搭电梯，你搭地铁。	Wǒ dā diàntī, nǐ dā dìtiě.	*I ride the elevator, you take the subway.*
我天天搭电梯，你天天搭地铁。	Wǒ tiāntiān dā diàntī, nǐ tiāntiān dā dìtiě.	*I ride the elevator every day; you take the subway every day.*
我听音乐，你爱跳舞。	Wǒ tīng yīnyuè, nǐ ài tiàowǔ.	*I listen to music, you love to dance.*
我天天听音乐，你天天爱跳舞。	Wǒ tiāntiān tīng yīnyuè, nǐ tiāntiān ài tiàowǔ.	*I listen to music every day; you love to dance every day.*

13 听力练习 Tīnglì Liànxí *Listening Practice*

You will hear five sounds that are combined with the initial "t." Choose the correct final you hear and write the word on a separate sheet of paper.

i	iao	ie	ian	ing

14 发音练习 Fāyīn Liànxí *Pronunciation Practice*

Now that you know the individual sounds, let's combine them together with the tones. Listen to the recording and repeat.

1.	**n + i**	nī ní nǐ nì	nítǔ	*n. soil*
2.	**n + iao**	niǎo niào	*xiǎo* niǎo	*n. bird* 
3.	**n + ie**	niē nié niè	niè.zi	*v. tweezers*
4.	**n + iu**	niū niú niǔ niù	niúnǎi	*n. milk* 
5.	**n + ian**	niān nián niǎn niàn	niánjì	*n. age*
6.	**n + in**	nín	nín	*pron. you (polite)*

7.	**n + iang**	niáng niàng	xīnniáng	*n.* *bride* 
8.	**n + ing**	níng nǐng nìng	níngjìng	*adj.* *quiet*

15 大声念 Dàshēng Niàn / *Read it Aloud*

With a partner, take turns reading the rhyme aloud.

宁静的早晨鸟儿叫， 向您说声早。	Níngjìng de zǎochén niǎo'r jiào, xiàng nín shuō.shēng zǎo.	*Birds chirp in the quiet morning to say hello.*
捏只泥牛给小宝宝， 祝他身体好。	Niē zhī níniú *gěi xiǎo*bǎobao, zhù tā shēn*tǐ* hǎo.	*I made a cow out of clay and gave it to the baby to wish him health.*
希望五年十年后， 换他娶新娘。	Xīwàng wǔ-nián shí-nián hòu, huàn tā qǔ xīnniáng.	*He hopes that after five or ten years, it'll be his turn to marry his bride.*

16 听力练习 Tīnglì Liànxí / *Listening Practice*

Listen to the recording and write the five finals that begin with the inital "n" on a separate sheet of paper.

1. niún__	2. xiǎo.n__	3. n__ tǔ	4. xīnn__	5. n__.zi

17 发音练习 Fāyīn Liànxí / *Pronunciation Practice*

Combine the initial "l" with some finals. Repeat what you hear.

1.	**l + i**	lī lí lǐ lì	lǐwù	*n.* *gift* 
2.	**l + iao**	liāo liáo liǎo liào	liáotiān	*v.* *to chat*
3.	**l + ie**	liē liě liè	lièrén	*n.* *hunter*
4.	**l + iu**	liū liú liǔ liù	liúxíng	*adj.* *fashionable*

5.	**l + ian**	lián liǎn liàn	xiàngliàn	*n. necklace*
6.	**l + in**	līn lín lǐn lìn	línjū	*n. neighbor*
7.	**l + iang**	liáng liǎng liàng	shànliáng	*adj. kindhearted*
8.	**l + ing**	līng líng lǐng lìng	lǐngdài	*n. necktie*

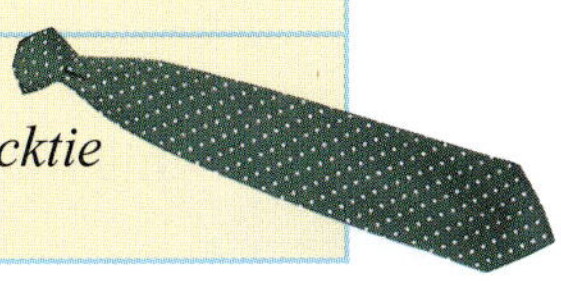

18 大声念 Dàshēng Niàn / *Read it Aloud*

With a partner, take turns reading the sentences aloud.

1. Línjū Lǐ xiān.shēng hěn shànliáng, tā cóng bù dǎliè.
   (*My neighbor, Mr. Lee, is very kind; he never goes hunting.*)
2. *Wǒ hěn* xǐ.huān liáotiān, tèbié shì liúxíng de dōng.xī.
   (*I love to chat, especially about fashion.*)
3. Nǐ sòng wǒ zhè-tiáo xiàngliàn, wǒ sòng nǐ zhè-tiáo lǐngdài.
   (*You gave me this necklace, I give you this tie.*)

19 听力练习 Tīnglì Liànxí / *Listening Practice*

Listen to the recording and complete the words below choosing the correct final to place after the inital "l."

Lì.zi: sēnl<u>ín</u>

i	ie	in	iu	iao	ian	iang	ing

1. xiàngl__	3. l__wù	5. shànl__	7. l__jū
2. l__dài	4. l__xíng	6. l__rén	8. l__tiān

20 发音练习 Fāyīn Liànxí / Pronunciation Practice

Listen to the recording of some initials combined with the final "iu." Repeat what you hear.

1.	**miù** (*ridiculous*)	6.	**jiù** (*old*)
2.	**diū** (*to throw*)	7.	**qiū** (*autumn*)
3.	**niū** (*little girl*)	8.	**qiú** (*to beg*)
4.	**niǔ** (*to twist*)	9.	**xiū** (*to rest*)
5.	**jiǔ** (*long*)	10.	**xiù** (*show*)

21 发音练习 Fāyīn Liànxí / Pronunciation Practice

You will hear a recording of pairs of Chinese words that may sound similar, but actually have different pronunciations. Listen carefully and repeat each word in the pause provided.

1.	**tiǎo** (*to stir up*) / **tiě** (*iron*)	8.	**lín** (*neighbor*) / **liáng** (*cool*)
2.	**diāo** (*to carve*) / **diū** (*to throw*)	9.	**niàn** (*to read aloud*) / **niàng** (*to ferment*)
3.	**tián** (*sweet*) / **tiáo** (*to adjust*)	10.	**nín** (*you*) / **níng** (*quiet*)
4.	**liǎng** (*a couple*) / **liǎo** (*to understand*)	11	**lǐn** (*cold*) / **lǐng** (*neck*)
5.	**liè** (*to hunt*) / **liù** (*six*)	12.	**dī** (*low*) / **tī** (*to kick*)
6.	**niè** (*tweezers*) / **niàn** (*to read aloud*)	13.	**niè** (*tweezers*) / **liè** (*to hunt*)
7.	**liú** (*to stay*) / **lián** (*to link*)	14.	**níng** (*quiet*) / **lín** (*neighbor*)

22 听力练习 Tīnglì Liànxí / *Listening Practice*

Listen to the recording, and select the word you hear by writing A or B on a separate sheet of paper.

Lì.zi: (A.) bài B. pài

1.	A. liáo	B. liú	5.	A. lín	B. líng	9.	A. diū	B. liū
2.	A. tiē	B. tiān	6.	A. tiǎo	B. tiǎn	10.	A. dǐng	B. tǐng
3.	A. niú	B. níng	7.	A. diū	B. diē	11.	A. ní	B. lí
4.	A. niàn	B. niàng	8.	A. niào	B. tiào	12.	A. lín	B. níng

23 听力练习 Tīnglì Liànxí / *Listening Practice*

You will hear each word twice. The first time you listen, write the missing finals you hear. The second time, mark the tones. Write your answers on a separate sheet of paper.

Lì.zi:

lièfèng

1. l__

3. n____

2. t__

4. d____

Let's Sing!

太阳出来了！ Tàiyáng chūlái liǎo!

公鸡啼，小鸟叫，	Gōngjī tí, *xiǎo* niǎo jiào,
太阳出来了！	tàiyáng chūlái liǎo!
太阳当空照，	Tàiyáng dāng kōng zhào,
对我微微笑。	duì wǒ wēiwēi xiào.
他笑我，年纪小，	Tā xiào wǒ, niánjì xiǎo,
又笑我，志气高。	yòu xiào wǒ, zhìqì gāo.
年纪小，志气高，	Niánjì xiǎo, zhìqì gāo,
将来作个大英豪！	jiānglái zuò .ge dà yīngháo!

The sun is out!

The rooster crows, the bird calls;
the sun is out!
The sun shines up high,
smiling at me.
He smiles because I'm young,
and he smiles because I'm ambitious.
Young and ambitious,
I'll grow to be a hero!

课堂用语 Kètáng Yòngyǔ

Classroom Expressions

Teacher: 有问题吗？
Yǒu wèntí ma?
Any questions?

Student A: 有。
Yǒu.
Yes.

Student B: 没有。
Méiyǒu.
No.

Teacher: 听懂了吗？
Tīng dǒng.le .ma?
Can you understand what you hear?

Student E: 听得懂。/ 听懂了。
Tīng.de-dǒng. / Tīng dǒng .le.
Yes (I can understand what I hear).

Student F: 听不懂。/ 没听懂。
Tīng bù-dǒng. / Méi tīngdǒng.
No (I can't understand what I hear).

Teacher: 懂了吗？
Dǒng.le .ma?
Do you understand?

Student C: 懂了。
Dǒng .le.
Yes (I understand).

Student D: 不懂。
Bù dǒng.
No (I don't understand).

24 你说什么？ Nǐ shuō shén.me? *What do you say?*

In Pinyin, write if you understand or don't understand each sentence.

1. *Wǒ* hěn gāoxìng.
2. Zhè shì dì-sì shēng.
3. *Qǐng* nǐ zài shuō yí-cì.
4. Tā shì cóng Shànghǎi lái de.
5. Jīn.tiān tiānqì *hěn* hǎo.
6. Wǒ.de *xiǎo* gǒu zài *nǎ*.lǐ?
7. Míng.tiān méi.yǒu Zhōngwén kè.
8. Wǒ.de lǎoshī shì Zhōng.guórén.

汉字 Hànzì

Chinese Characters

Pictographs

Pictographs are characters that were originally drawings of objects. For example, the pictograph for  is shaped like a crescent moon. The pictograph  looks like the profile of a tortoise with four legs and a shell. Chinese characters have changed their shape considerably over the course of the centuries, becoming much squarer in form. Look at the transformation of the pictograph  (月 yuè) into the modern form:

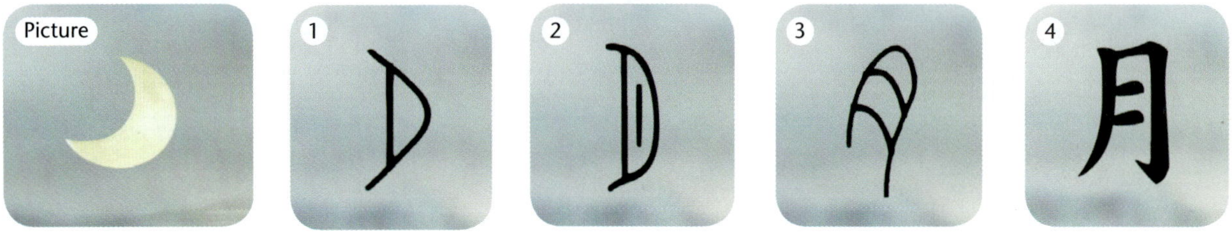

Generally speaking, pictographs can be divided into four kinds: the anatomical (body parts and people), the geographical (things in the natural world), the living (animals and plants), and the inanimate (objects). The following are examples of each category.

1. The anatomical:

Ancient form	Modern form	Pronunciation	English
	子	zǐ	*child*
	口	kǒu	*mouth*

2. The geographical:

Ancient form	Modern form	Pronunciation	English
	日	rì	*sun*
	山	shān	*mountain*

3 The living:

Ancient form	Modern form	Pronunciation	English
	牛	niú	*cow*
	木	mù	*tree*

4 The inanimate:

Ancient form	Modern form	Pronunciation	English
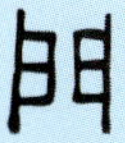	门	mén	*door*
	册	cè	*book*

25 从古到今 Cóng Gǔ Dào Jīn / *From Ancient Times to the Present*

Match each pictograph with the modern character (Traditional) of the same meaning.

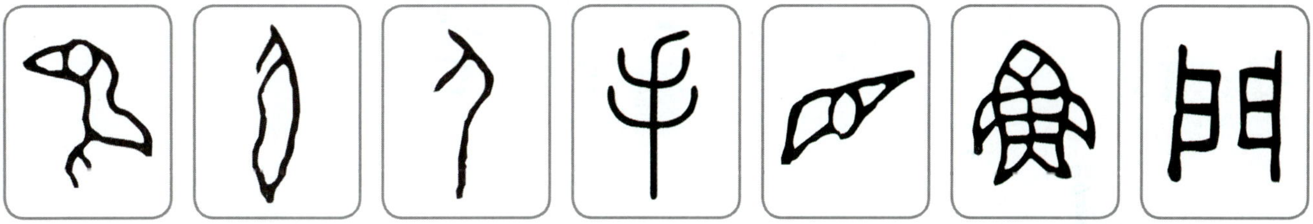

1. **2** **3.** **4.** **5.** **6.** **7.**

A. 人 *human*

B. 手 *hand*

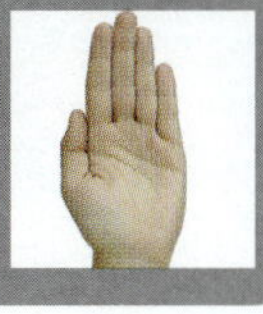

C. 鳥 *bird*

D. 目 *eye*

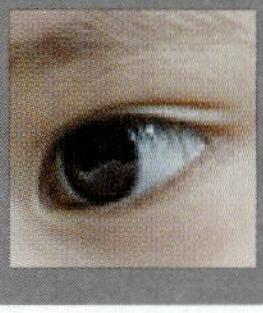

E. 弓 *bow*

F. 門 *door*

G. 魚 *fish*

Stroke Order

When writing Chinese characters, it is important to use the correct stroke order. The following rules for stroke order should be observed.

1.	Horizontal first, then vertical.	
	十 shí	一 十
	干 gān	一 二 干

2.	Top first, then bottom.	
	二 èr	一 二
	古 gǔ	

3.	Left-slanted first, then right-slanted.	
	八 bā	丿 八
	人 rén	丿 人

4. Left first, then right.

Character	Stroke order
川 chuān	
仁 rén	

5. Center first, then both sides.

Character	Stroke order
小 xiǎo	
木 mù	

6. When making a dot 丶, write it first if it is positioned on the top or upper-left. When it appears on the upper right or in the middle, write it last.

Character	Stroke order
文 wén	
斗 dǒu	
犬 quǎn	
叉	

7. With "closed" characters, make the outside strokes (left, top, right), then the strokes in the middle, then the bottom stroke that "closes" the character.

回 huí

因 yīn

8. With semi-closed characters, there are three different stroke orders:

Ⓐ Strokes in the middle before surrounding stroke(s)

凶 xiōng

言 yán

Ⓑ Surrounding strokes before strokes in the middle

同 tóng

司 sī

C Top before middle before lower-left

匹 pī	一 丌 兀 匹
匠 jiàng	一 ⺈ 了 斤 斤 匠

26 选出第一笔！ Xuǎnchū dì-yī bǐ! *Let's find the first stroke!*

Look at the characters below, and determine which stroke should be made first. Write the first stroke on a separate sheet of paper.

1. 月	6. 劣	11. 儿
2. 九	7. 四	12. 不
3. 立	8. 去	13. 说
4. 可	9. 风	14. 井
5. 河	10. 土	15. 时

▲ She practices writing characters.

Foundation D

When you have completed this lesson you will be able to...

Geography / History

- describe the different groups of people who live in China
- explain the causes and effects of the One-Child Policy
- find the five Chinese autonomous regions and capitals on a map
- explain cultural, geographical, and economic information about the autonomous regions

Pronunciation

- pronounce more finals and dental sibilants
- recite a new rhyme and sing a new song

Classroom Expressions

- use the correct Chinese expressions in certain classroom situations

Chinese Characters

- define and explain ideographs
- describe the evolution of Chinese characters
- identify some computer fonts

China's Population Density

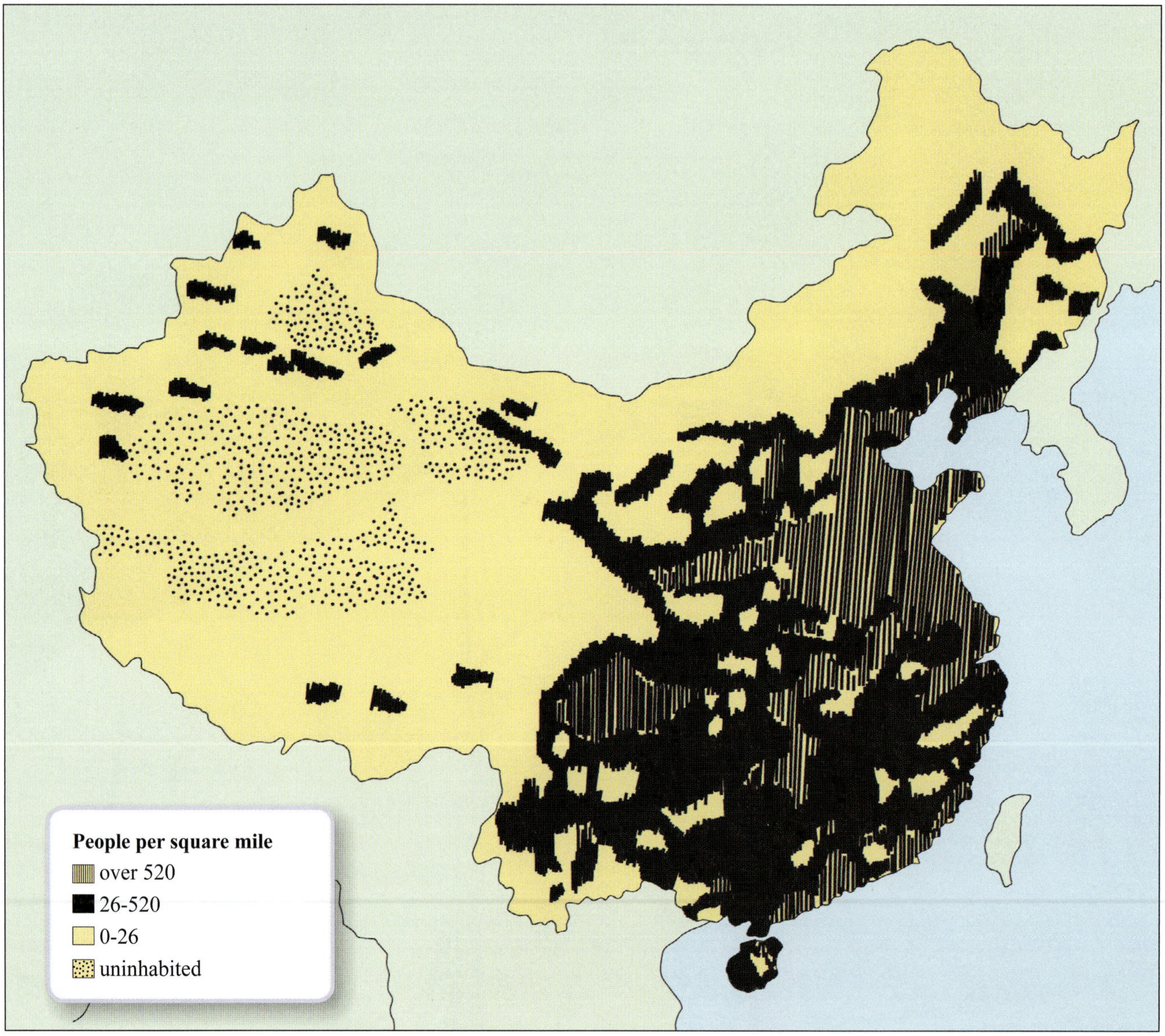

China has a population of 1.3 billion that is made up of 56 national minorities, including the Han, Mongol, Hui, Tibetan, and Uyghur. The Han people make up the majority (93%) of the overall population; the other national minorities are known as "minority tribes." Generally, the defining elements of a minority are language, homeland, and social values. In a deliberate effort to help minority people assimilate into the Han language and culture, the Central Government has set up special training centers, like the National Minorities Institute in Beijing, to train loyal minority cadres to govern in these regions. The Chinese government states that "ethnic equality and cooperation" are guiding principles, and therefore endeavors to include all national minorities in national affairs. (Even national minorities with a small population have at least one representative in the government.)

▲ The Miao people sing folk songs at a dragon boat festival.

▲ In Tibet, Khampa minority women traditionally dressed at festivals.

One-Child Policy

Due to a big population explosion in the late 1970s, the Chinese government implemented the One-Child Policy to alleviate some of the nation's problems due to lack of resources. Today, even though the population is successfully under control, a number of problems have surfaced as a result. Some issues include a larger number of boys born each year compared to girls, hidden girls in rural areas (known as a ghost population), and parents spoiling their only child.

1 温故知新 Wēngù Zhīxīn / *Remembering the Facts*

Decide if each statement is true or false. Correct any false statements.

1. The largest of the national minorities in China is the Mongols.
2. According to the Chinese government, the defining elements of a minority are language, homeland, and social values.
3. The Central Government has set up special training centers in every minority region to train loyal minority cadres.
4. The population density of coastline areas is around 520 people per square mile.
5. The One-Child Policy has been in effect for over 30 years.
6. The One-Child Policy has successfully decreased China's population without creating any social problems.

Five Autonomous Regions

Autonomous Region (Capital City)	
1. 内蒙古自治区（呼和浩特）	Nèiménggǔ Zìzhìqū (Hūhéhàotè)
2. 宁夏回族自治区（银川）	Níngxià Huízú Zìzhìqū (Yínchuān)
3. 新疆维吾尔自治区（乌鲁木齐）	Xīnjiāng Wéiwú'ěr Zìzhìqū (Wūlǔmùqí)
4. 西藏自治区（拉萨）	Xīzàng Zìzhìqū (Lāsà)
5. 广西壮族自治区（南宁）	Guǎngxī Zhuàngzú Zìzhìqū (Nánníng)

The Chinese government has established "autonomous regions" for areas where minority ethnic groups reside to allow these groups to follow their own customs and preserve their cultural heritage. However, in order to make governance easier for the state, the central government sends an administrative leader to the regions.

▲ Genghis Khan.

▲ Inner Mongolia grassland.

内蒙古自治区 Nèiménggǔ Zìzhìqū

Inner Mongolia Autonomous Region is the oldest autonomous region for minority ethnic groups in China. It is located in the north and covers a wide area. Its capital, Hohhot (呼和浩特 *Hūhéhàotè*), means "green city"—a tribute to the meadows, forests, and other natural resources that abound in the region. Inner Mongolia is important to China, due largely to its vast grasslands that allow for pasturing of cattle and other animals. It is also a popular tourist destination due to Mongolian culture, grassland scenery, the view of the Yellow River, and cultural sites left behind by Genghis Khan, who built the Mongolian Empire in the 13th century. In his day, the empire reached as far as Uzbekistan in the Middle East. In recent years, following the Chinese reformation, urban planning in the region has developed by leaps and bounds to make Mongolian cities centers of not only politics, economy, and culture, but also technological development.

宁夏回族自治区 Níngxià Huízú Zìzhìqū

The capital of Ningxia Hui Autonomous Region, home of the Hui tribe (totaling one third of the region's population), is Yinchuan (银川 *Yínchuān*). Throughout history, the Yellow River has played a great part in the region's irrigation. With abundant sunlight and rainfall, Ningxia's plains have been blessed with the production of various crops, including apples and watermelons, all famous for their unrivaled sweetness. Ningxia Hui Autonomous Region also has pastures for grazing, and produces a lot of sheepskin. The area is also rich in coal and limestone deposits.

◀ Ningxia is famous for sheepskin, melons and apples.

新疆维吾尔自治区 Xīnjiāng Wéiwú'ěr Zìzhìqū

Xinjiang Uyghur Autonomous Region is located near China's northwestern border. Its capital, Ürümqi (乌鲁木齐 *Wūlǔmùqí*), was an important stop on the Silk Road, a historic trade route between China and Europe. Xinjiang is the largest of all provincial-level administrative areas and is home to a variety of tribes, with the Uyghur in the majority. Because of this diversity, cultural influences can be seen in many of its cities. Xinjiang, which means "new frontier," is the home of the hottest, coldest, driest, and windiest areas in China. Due to its long hours of sun, the agricultural industry has flourished, with quality cotton, grapes, walnuts, and cantaloupe as some of the most important products. The area is also famous for its superb silks and carpets. Famous sites in the region include the Tian Shan mountainous range and Mogao Cave (also known as the "Cave of a Thousand Buddhas").

▲ Heaven's Lake.

▲ Potala Palace.

西藏自治区 Xīzàng Zìzhìqū

Tibet Autonomous Region is located in China's southwest, in the most elevated region of the world—the Tibetan Plateau where the Himalayas lie. Covered in snow for around six months each year, Tibet has very long days, which has resulted in it becoming a center for solar power. (Its capital, Llasa—拉萨 *Lāsà*, is called the "City of Sunlight.") Besides solar power, Tibet also produces large amounts of hydropower, geothermal energy, and wind power. The majority Tibetans have a long history and are famous for their religious culture. There are also many religious buildings in the region, one of which is Llasa's Potala Palace, a World Heritage Site.

广西壮族自治区 Guǎngxī Zhuàngzú Zìzhìqū

Guangxi Zhuang Autonomous Region is located near China's southern border, and is home to the Zhuang people. Guangxi is famous for its limestone landscape, which, coupled with the West River's clear waters, forms magnificent scenery. Pearls found along the region's northern border are of excellent quality, and it is one of the leaders in rice production. Sugarcane has also been produced here for a long time. In recent years, cities in Guangxi have seen developments in architecture and gardening. South Asian tropical plants can be found in the botanical gardens and parks of its capital city, Nanning (南宁 *Nánníng*).

▲ Limestone landscape in Guangxi.

2 温故知新 Wēngù Zhīxīn / *Remembering the Facts*

Match each description on the left with the correct region on the right. Each region may be used more than once.

1. home of the hottest and coldest place in China
2. where the Potala Palace is
3. home of the Hui national minority
4. limestone landscape
5. its capital is named the "City of Sunlight"
6. the first and oldest autonomous region
7. home of the Zhuang national minority
8. an important stop on the Silk Road
9. grasslands scenery
10. irrigation from the Yellow River

A.	Inner Mongolia Autonomous Region
B.	Ningxia Hui Autonomous Region
C.	Xinjiang Uyghur Autonomous Region
D.	Tibet Autonomous Region
E.	Guangxi Zhuang Autonomous Region

3 角色扮演 Juésè Bànyǎn / *Role Play*

With a partner, play the roles of a reporter and Mr. Zhang, an American teacher of Chinese. The reporter asks Mr. Zhang to which autonomous regions his students are going for their family stays.

Ningxia Hui Autonomous Region	Níngxià Huízú Zìzhìqū
Inner Mongolia Autonomous Region	Nèiménggǔ Zìzhìqū
Tibet Autonomous Region	Xīzàng Zìzhìqū
Guangxi Zhuang Autonomous Region	Guǎngxī Zhuàngzú Zìzhìqū
Xinjiang Uyghur Autonomous Region	Xīnjiāng Wéiwú'ěr Zìzhìqū

Lì.zi: Brian / Tibet Autonomous Region

A: Brian 去哪儿? Brian qù nǎr? *Where is Brian going?*

B: 他去西藏自治区。Tā qù Xīzàng Zìzhìqū. *He is going to Tibet Autonomous Region.*

1. Lance / Inner Mongolia Autonomous Region
2. Amy / Guangxi Zhuang Autonomous Region
3. Garrett / Xinjiang Uyghur Autonomous Region
4. Kara / Ningxia Hui Autonomous Region

发音 Fāyīn

Pronunciation

4 发音练习 Fāyīn Liànxí / *Pronunciation Practice*

Listen to the finals from the chart and repeat in the pause provided.

Pronunciation Tips for Finals		
1.	**u**	Round your lips as if you were pronouncing **oo** in English.
2.	**ua**	Pronounce **u** first and then **a**.
3.	**uo**	Pronounce **u** first and then **o**.
4.	**un**	Pronounce **ü** first and then **en**. Change the shape of your mouth from round to narrow.
5.	**uai**	Pronounce **u** first and then **ai**.
6.	**ui**	Pronounce **u** first and then **ei**.
7.	**uan**	Pronounce **u** first and then **an**.
8.	**uang**	Pronounce **u** first and then **ang**.
9.	**ueng**	Pronounce **u** first and then **eng**.
10.	**ong**	Pronounce **o** first and then **ng**.

Dental Sibilants

Sibilants are sounds formed by creating friction with the positioning of your tongue or lips while directing a jet of air toward the front of the teeth. When making dental sibilants, place your tongue at the back of the upper and lower teeth to let the air pass.

5 发音练习 Fāyīn Liànxí / *Pronunciation Practice*

Listen to the finals from the chart and repeat in the pause provided.

Pronunciation Tips for Dental Sibilants		
1.	**z**	Place the tip of your tongue against the back of your teeth. Then let the air squeeze out between your tongue and teeth. This sound is not aspirated.
2.	**c**	Place the tip of your tongue against the back of your teeth. Then let a strong breath out through the channel between your tongue and teeth. This sound is aspirated.
3.	**s**	Place the tip of your tongue against the back of your teeth. Then let the air out between your tongue and teeth, as if you were pronouncing 's' in English.
4.	**zh**	Turn up the tip of your tongue against the hard palate. Then loosen it a bit to let out the air. This sound is not aspirated.
5.	**ch**	Turn up the tip of your tongue against the hard palate. Then loosen it a bit to let out the air, only with a stronger breath. This sound is aspirated.
6.	**sh**	Turn up the tip of your tongue toward the hard palate. Then let the air squeeze out.
7.	**r**	Turn up the tip of your tongue toward the hard palate to obstruct your breath. Then let the air squeeze out.

6 发音练习 Fāyīn Liànxí / *Pronunciation Practice*

Listen to the recording and repeat the combinations of initials and finals.

	Initials / Finals	**z**	**c**	**s**	**zh**	**ch**	**sh**	**r**
1.	**u**	zu	cu	su	zhu	chu	shu	ru
2.	**ua**				zhua		shua	
3.	**uo**	zuo	cuo	suo	zhuo	chuo	shuo	ruo
4.	**un**	zun	cun	sun	zhun	chun	shun	run
5.	**uai**				zhuai	chuai	shuai	
6.	**ui**	zui	cui	sui	zhui	chui	shui	rui
7.	**uan**	zuan	cuan	suan	zhuan	chuan	shuan	ruan
8.	**uang**				zhuang	chuang	shuang	
9.	**ueng***							
10.	**ong**	zong	cong	song	zhong	chong		rong

*_Ueng_ can only stand by itself, and it is spelled *weng*.

7 发音练习 Fāyīn Liànxí / Pronunciation Practice

Combine the initial "z" with some finals. Repeat what you hear.

1.	**z + u**	zū zú zǔ	chūzūchē	*n. taxi*
2.	**z + uo**	zuó zuǒ zuò	zuótiān	*n. yesterday*
3.	**z + un**	zūn zǔn	zūnjìng	*v. to respect*
4.	**z + ui**	zuī zuǐ zuì	zuǐ.bā	*n. mouth*
5.	**z + uan**	zuān zuǎn zuàn	zuànshí	*n. diamond*
6.	**z + ong**	zōng zǒng zòng	zǒng.tǒng	*n. president*

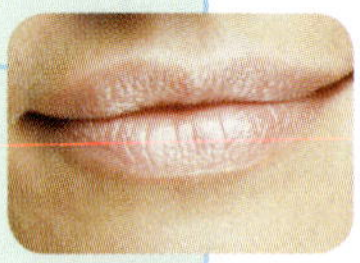

8 听力练习 Tīnglì Liànxí / Listening Practice

You will hear six sounds that are combined with the initial "z." Choose the correct final you hear and write the word on a separate piece of paper.

ui	u	uo	un	uan	ong

9 发音练习 Fāyīn Liànxí / Pronunciation Practice

Combine the initial "c" with some finals. Repeat what you hear.

1.	**c + u**	cū cú cù	cūxīn	*adj. careless*
2.	**c + uo**	cuō cuó cuǒ cuò	cuòwù	*n. mistake*
3.	**c + un**	cūn cún cǔn cùn	cūn.zi	*n. village*

4.	**c + ui**	cuī cuǐ cuì	cuìruò	*adj. fragile*
5.	**c + uan**	cuān cuán cuàn	cuàngǎi	*v. to tamper with*
6.	**c + ong**	cōng cóng	cōngmíng	*adj. smart*

10 听力练习 Tīnglì Liànxí / *Listening Practice*

Listen to the recording. Complete the words you hear by writing the correct finals after "c" on a separate sheet of paper.

1. c__xīn	2. c__míng	3. c__gǎi	4. c__.zi	5. c__ruò	6. c__wù

11 发音练习 Fāyīn Liànxí / *Pronunciation Practice*

Combine the initial "s" with some finals. Repeat what you hear.

1.	**s + u**	sū sú sù	sùdù	*n. speed*
2.	**s + uo**	suō suǒ suò	suōxiě	*n. abbreviation*
3.	**s + un**	sūn sǔn 	sūn.zi	*n. grandson*
4.	**s + ui**	suī suí suǐ suì	suīrán	*conj. although*
5.	**s + uan**	suān suàn	dàsuàn	*n. garlic* 
6.	**s + ong**	sōng sǒng sòng	qīngsōng	*adj. relaxed*

12 听力练习 Tīnglì Liànxí / Listening Practice

Listen to the recording. Complete the words you hear by writing the correct finals after "s" on a separate sheet of paper.

1. s__xiě	2. s__.zi	3. s__rán	4. s__dù	5. dàs__	6. qīngs__

13 发音练习 Fāyīn Liànxí / Pronunciation Practice

Combine the initial "zh" with some finals. Repeat what you hear.

1.	**zh + u**	zhū zhú zhǔ zhù	làzhú	*n. candle*
2.	**zh + ua**	zhuā zhuǎ	zhuāyǎng	*v. to scratch an itch*
3.	**zh + uo**	zhuō zhuó	zhuō.zi	*n. table*
4.	**zh + un**	zhūn zhǔn zhùn	zhǔnbèi	*v. to prepare*
5.	**zh + uai**	zhuāi zhuǎi zhuài	zhuài	*v. to drag*
6.	**zh + ui**	zhuī zhuì	zhuīqiú	*v. to pursue*
7.	**zh + uan**	zhuān zhuǎn zhuàn	zhuānjiā	*n. expert*
8.	**zh + uang**	zhuāng zhuàng	qiángzhuàng	*adj. strong*
9.	**zh + ong**	zhōng zhǒng zhòng	zhòngyào	*adj. important*

14 听力练习 Tīnglì Liànxí / Listening Practice

Listen to the recording, and write the number of the tone for each pair of words. Follow the model.

Lì.zi: zhu →1 zhu →3

1. zhuang→__ zhuang→__	4. zhua→ __ zhua→__	7. zhui→ __ zhui→__
2. zhun→__ zhun→__	5. zhuai→__ zhuai→__	8. zhong→ __ zhong→__
3. zhuo→__ zhuo→__	6. zhuan→ __ zhuan→__	

15 发音练习 Fāyīn Liànxí / Pronunciation Practice

Combine the initial "ch" with some finals. Repeat what you hear.

1.	**ch + u**	chū chú chǔ chù	chūkǒu	*n. exit*
2.	**ch + uo**	chuō chuò	chuòhào	*n. nickname*
3.	**ch + un**	chūn chún chǔn	chūntiān	*n. spring*
4.	**ch + uai**	chuāi chuǎi chuài	chuāicè	*v. to estimate*
5.	**ch + ui**	chuī chuí	chuīniú	*v. to boast*
6.	**ch + uan**	chuān chuán chuǎn chuàn	chuánzhēn	*n. fax*
7.	**ch + uang**	chuāng chuáng chuǎng chuàng	chuānglián	*n. curtain*
8.	**ch + ong**	chōng chóng chǒng chòng	chōnglàng	*v./n. to surf; surfing*

16 听力练习 Tīnglì Liànxí / Listening Practice

Listen to the recording, and select the sound you hear by writing A or B on a separate sheet of paper.

1. A. un B. ui	3. A. uan B. uang	5. A. uai B. uan
2. A. u B. uo	4. A. uo B. ong	6. A. uan B. un

17 发音练习 Fāyīn Liànxí / Pronunciation Practice

Combine the initial "sh" with some finals. Repeat what you hear.

1.	**sh + u**	shū shú shǔ shù	*lǎo*.shǔ	*n. mouse*
2.	**sh + ua**	shuā shuǎ shuà	shuāyá	*v. to brush teeth*
3.	**sh + uo**	shuō shuò	shuōhuà	*v. to talk*
4.	**sh + un**	shǔn shùn	shùnlì	*adj. smooth*
5.	**sh + uai**	shuāi shuǎi shuài	shuāidǎo	*v. to fall over*
6.	**sh + ui**	shuǐ shuì	shuìjiào	*v. to sleep*
7.	**sh + uan**	shuān shuàn	xiāofángshuān	*n. fire hydrant*
8.	**sh + uang**	shuāng shuǎng	shuāngfāng	*n. both sides*

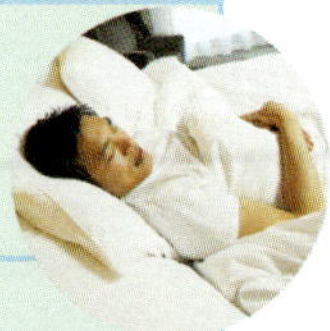

18 听力练习 Tīnglì Liànxí / Listening Practice

Listen to the recording, and select the sound you hear by writing A or B on a separate sheet of paper.

1. A. shùn B. shuì	3. A. shū B. shuō	5. A. shuǐ B. shǔn
2. A. shuāi B. shuān	4. A. shǔ B. shuǎ	6. A. shùn B. shuài

19 发音练习 Fāyīn Liànxí / Pronunciation Practice

Combine the initial "zh" with some finals. Repeat what you hear.

1.	**r + u**	rú rǔ rù	rùkǒu	*n. entrance*
2.	**r + uo**	ruò	ruòdiǎn	*n. weakness*
3.	**r + un**	rùn	lìrùn	*n. profit*
4.	**r + uan**	ruǎn	róuruǎn	*adj. soft*
5.	**r + ong**	róng rǒng	róngyì	*adj. easy*

20 听力练习 Tīnglì Liànxí / Listening Practice

Listen to the recording and write the number of the words for which you hear the 4th tone.

21 发音练习 Fāyīn Liànxí / Pronunciation Practice

Listen to the recording and pronounce the following words that have a "ui" final.

1.	**duī** *(a pile)*	6.	**cuī** *(to hurry)*
2.	**tuǐ** *(leg)*	7.	**suì** *(a year of age)*
3.	**guì** *(expensive)*	8.	**chuī** *(to blow)*
4.	**huí** *(to return)*	9.	**shuǐ** *(water)*
5.	**zuì** *(the most)*	10.	**ruì** *(sharp)*

22 发音练习 Fāyīn Liànxí / Pronunciation Practice

Listen to the recording and pronounce the following words that have a "un" final.

1.	**dūn** *(to squat)*	6.	**hūn** *(to faint)*
2.	**tūn** *(to swallow)*	7.	**zūn** *(to respect)*
3.	**lún** *(wheel)*	8.	**cún** *(to save)*
4.	**gǔn** *(to roll)*	9.	**sǔn** *(to decrease)*
5.	**kùn** *(hard-pressed)*	10.	**zhǔn** *(standard)*

23 发音练习 Fāyīn Liànxí / Pronunciation Practice

Some of the sounds may sound similar and cause confusion, so we need to know how to differentiate them. Listen to the recording and repeat each pair of words.

1.	**zhuā** *(to grab)* / **zhuō** *(table)*	8.	**cùn** *(inch)* / **cuàn** *(to flee)*
2.	**ruò** *(weak)* / **rùn** *(moist)*	9.	**zū** *(to rent)* / **cū** *(thick)*
3.	**shuǐ** *(water)* / **shuǎi** *(to fling)*	10.	**zú** *(enough)* / **sú** *(custom)*
4.	**zhuài** *(to drag)* / **zhuì** *(to fall)*	11.	**suān** *(sour)* / **shuān** *(door bolt)*
5.	**zuǐ** *(mouth)* / **zuǎn** *(to compile)*	12.	**zuó** *(yesterday)* / **zhuó** *(turbid)*
6.	**chuán** *(ship)* / **chuáng** *(bed)*	13.	**zhuǎi** *(waddling)* / **shuāi** *(to fling)*
7.	**sōng** *(loose)* / **sūn** *(grandson)*	14.	**chuí** *(to hang downward)* / **shuí** *(who)*

24 听力练习 Tīnglì Liànxí / *Listening Practice*

Listen to the recording, and select the sound you hear by writing A or B on a separate sheet of paper.

Lì.zi: (A.) zhuā B. shuā

1.	A. zuò	B. zuì	7.	A. suō	B. zhuō
2.	A. shuā	B. shuō	8.	A. zhuàng	B. chuàng
3.	A. zǔn	B. zuǐ	9.	A. suǒ	B. zuǒ
4.	A. shuài	B. shuàn	10.	A. rùn	B. shùn
5.	A. chuán	B. chuàn	11.	A. sū	B. shū
6.	A. chǔn	B. chǒng	12.	A. chún	B. cún

25 听力练习 Tīnglì Liànxí / *Listening Practice*

You will hear each word twice. The first time you listen, write the missing finals you hear. The second time, mark the tones. Write your answers on a separate sheet of paper.

Lì.zi:

z uò

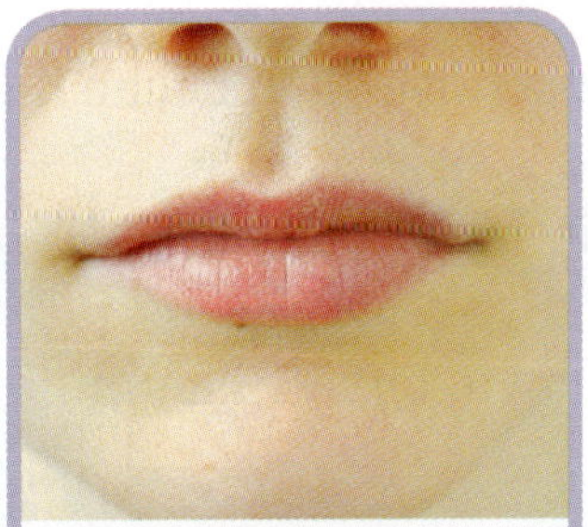

1. z____

3. g____sù

5. ch____

2. y____cōng

4. c____zhuāng

6. sh____

26 大声念 Dàshēng Niàn / *Read it Aloud*

With a partner, take turns reading the rhyme aloud.

黑夜空，月弯弯，	Hēiyèkōng, yuè wānwān,	*Dark night sky / crescent moon /*
满天星，亮晶晶，	mǎntiān xīng, liàng jīngjīng.	*full of stars / shining*
好像那，一盏盏，	Hǎoxiàng nà, yì *zhǎn*zhǎn,	*Almost like / lots of /*
小银灯，放光明。	xiǎo yíndēng, fàng guāngmíng.	*small lamps / giving off light*
大大小小，密密麻麻，	Dàdà*xiǎo*xiǎo, mìmìmámá,	*Big and small / everywhere /*
闪闪烁烁，	*shǎn*shǎnshuòshuò,	*twinkling*
数也数不清。	*shǔ yě* shǔ bù qīng.	*(and) uncountable*

Let's Sing!

蝴蝶 Húdié

蝴蝶，蝴蝶生的真美丽，	Húdié, húdié shēng.de zhēn měilì,
头戴着金丝，身穿花花衣，	tóu dài.zhe jīnsī, shēn chuān huāhuāyī,
你爱花儿，花儿也爱你，	nǐ ài huār, huār yě ài nǐ,
你会跳舞，花也甜蜜。	nǐ huì tiàowǔ, huā yě tiánmì.

Butterfly

Butterfly, butterfly, born so pretty,
With golden threads on heads, and wearing fancy clothes,
You love flowers, and they love you too,
You can dance, and the flowers are sweet.

课堂用语 Kètáng Yòngyǔ

Classroom Expressions

Teacher: 请到这儿/这里来。
Qǐng dào zhèr/ zhè.lǐ lái.
Please come here.

Teacher: 请在黑板写……。
Qǐng zài hēi*bǎn* xiě….
Please write… on the blackboard.

字 zì *word*	句子 jù.zi *sentence*
你的名字 nǐ.de míng.zì *your name*	

Teacher: 请跟我说。
Qǐng gēn wǒ shuō.
Please repeat after me.

Teacher: 我们现在听……。
Wǒ.mén xiànzài tīng….
Let's listen to… now.

绕口令 ràokǒulìng *tongue twister*	歌 gē *song*

Teacher: 请你们做做看。
Qǐng nǐ.mén zuò.x kàn.
Please try it yourselves.

27 他在做什么? Tā zài zuò shén.me? *What is he doing?*

Listen to the recording, and match each classroom expression to the corresponding picture.

A

C

E

B

D
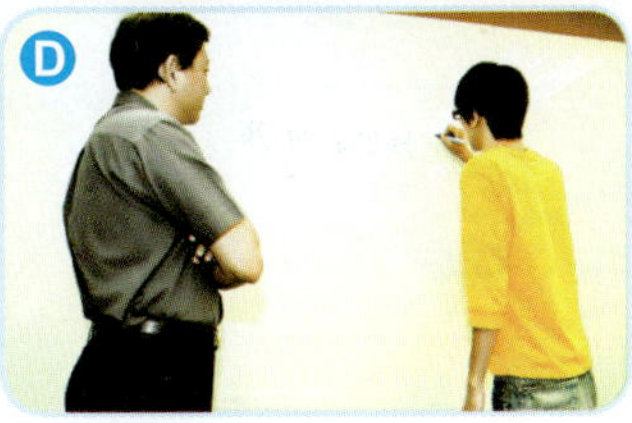

汉字 **Hànzì**

Chinese Characters

Ideographs

In the last lesson you learned that pictographs are characters that were originally drawings of concrete objects. This lesson is about ideographs, which came after pictographs. Ideographs are graphical representations of abstract ideas, such as 一 *yī* (one) and 二 *èr* (two).

Ideographs can be made in two ways. The first way is to portray abstract concepts through symbols only, such as drawing a line to show position, then making a shorter stroke above the longer line to show "up": 上 *shàng*; or one below to show "down": 下 *xià*. The character 三 *sān* is composed of three horizontal lines to represent the number three. The ancient Chinese used the base ten numeral system too, so the number ten would bring the cycle back to the beginning. Thus, to differentiate ten from one (一, *yī*), they added a vertical line to form 十 *shí*; the number ten. The character 大 *dà* shows a man with his arms and legs spread open wide to mean "big." A man with his arms down and his legs together becomes 小 *xiǎo*, meaning "small."

The other way ideographs are formed is to add an abstract symbol to a pictograph; for example, the word 刃 *rèn* (blade) was formed by adding an abstract dot to the pictograph 刀 *dāo* (knife) to show the sharpest point of a knife. Adding a dot to the pictograph 口 *kǒu* (mouth) to show the tongue tasting something makes the word 甘 *gān* (sweet). The ancient Chinese added an abstract sign to the pictograph of a man with his arms and legs spread open wide to form 天 *tiān* to refer to the sky above our heads. The character 寸 *cùn* was formed by adding an abstract sign to the bottom left of the pictograph 手 *shǒu* (hand) to refer to an inch below the palm, the place where traditional Chinese doctors felt to take the pulse of their patients. Use of this character has since evolved to refer to a unit of measurement, the inch.

28 辨认会意字 Biànrèn Huìyìzì / *Identifying Ideographs*

Make an educated guess about what each ideograph stands for.

1.	旦 dàn	Hint: This word came from the pictograph 日, meaning "sun"; the bottom line represents the horizon.
2.	本 běn	Hint: This word came from the pictograph 木, meaning "wood"; the line added to the bottom represents a location.
3.	末 mò	Hint: This word also came from the pictograph 木; the line added to the top represents a location.
4.	凸 tū	Hint: This refers to something on top of something else.
5.	凹 āo	Hint: This refers to something missing from something else.
6.	凶 xiōng	Hint: 凵 represents a hole, and the 㐅 refers to a mark where the trap is.

The Evolution of Chinese Characters

Chinese characters evolved over a period of more than five thousand years, and Chinese calligraphy has been around for just as long. From pictures and symbols to the creation and formation of text, from oracle bones through each successive dynasty to the present day, multiple writing styles have been established that show the history and culture of each Chinese character. Calligraphy, an art form for writing Chinese characters, has five basic styles that we will examine.

There are two kinds of Seal Style: large (or great) Seal Style and small Seal Style. Today, Seal Style often refers to small Seal Style, which was the first script type to be used throughout China. Seal Style is a square in shape, and is still often used by artists as the style for their seals. The characteristics of the Official Style are that the horizontal strokes are long, and the vertical strokes short. This style seems especially solemn. Compared to this style, the Standard Style is squarer in form. With each character in the Standard Style a square, written Chinese has been referred to as "square words." However, both the Official and Standard Styles take more time to write, so they were traditionally used in old official documents. Normally, when people write Chinese characters quickly, the characters may seem messy, not printed. This sort of script is called the Running Style, which, in the Han Dynasty in the 3rd century B.C., became the Cursive Style. The main function of the Cursive Style is not to convey meaning, but to present a visually pleasing effect through the connection of the characters. Let's see what these different styles look like.

篆书 zhuànshū *(Seal Style)*	隶书 lìshū *(Official Style)*	楷书 kǎishu *(Standard Style)*	行书 xíngshū *(Running Style)*	草书 cǎoshū *(Cursive Style)*
人	人	人	人	人
本	本	本	本	本
性	性	性	性	性
初	初	初	初	初
近	近	近	近	近
相	相	相	相	相

29 辨认书法字体 Biànrèn Shūfǎ Zìtǐ / *Identify Calligraphy Styles*

For the Chinese, calligraphy has been incorporated into the art of everyday life. Look at the pictures that follow and determine which calligraphy style is being used.

Computer Fonts

Nowadays, word processors provide all sorts of Chinese fonts to make Chinese text more interesting. The following are some examples:

	Name of Font		*three*	*big*	*king*	*mouth*	*heart*
1.	标楷体	biāo*kǎi*tǐ	三	大	王	口	心
2.	新细明体	xīnxìmíngtǐ	三	大	王	口	心
3.	圆体	yuántǐ	三	大	王	口	心
4.	娃娃体	wá.xtǐ	三	大	王	口	心

30 辨认电脑字体 Biànrèn Diànnǎo Zìtǐ *Identify Computer Fonts*

The sentences below all say "Chinese is interesting." Identify each computer font.

A.	中文真有意思
B.	中文真有意思
C.	中文真有意思
D.	中文真有意思

Foundation E

When you have completed this lesson you will be able to...

Geography / History

- discuss the important food crops in China and where they grow
- name and describe the ingredients of several famous Chinese dishes
- explain the history and culture of Taiwan
- identify the dialects spoken in different regions of China

Pronunciation

- pronounce more finals and palatal sounds
- recite a new rhyme and sing a new song

Classroom Expressions

- use the correct Chinese expressions in certain classroom situations

Chinese Characters

- define common combinations of pictographs and ideographs
- define common combinations of radicals and phonetic Chinese components
- understand the importance of proportion in writing characters
- understand the placement of radicals in writing characters

地理/历史 Dìlǐ / Lìshǐ

Geography / History

Important Food Crops in China

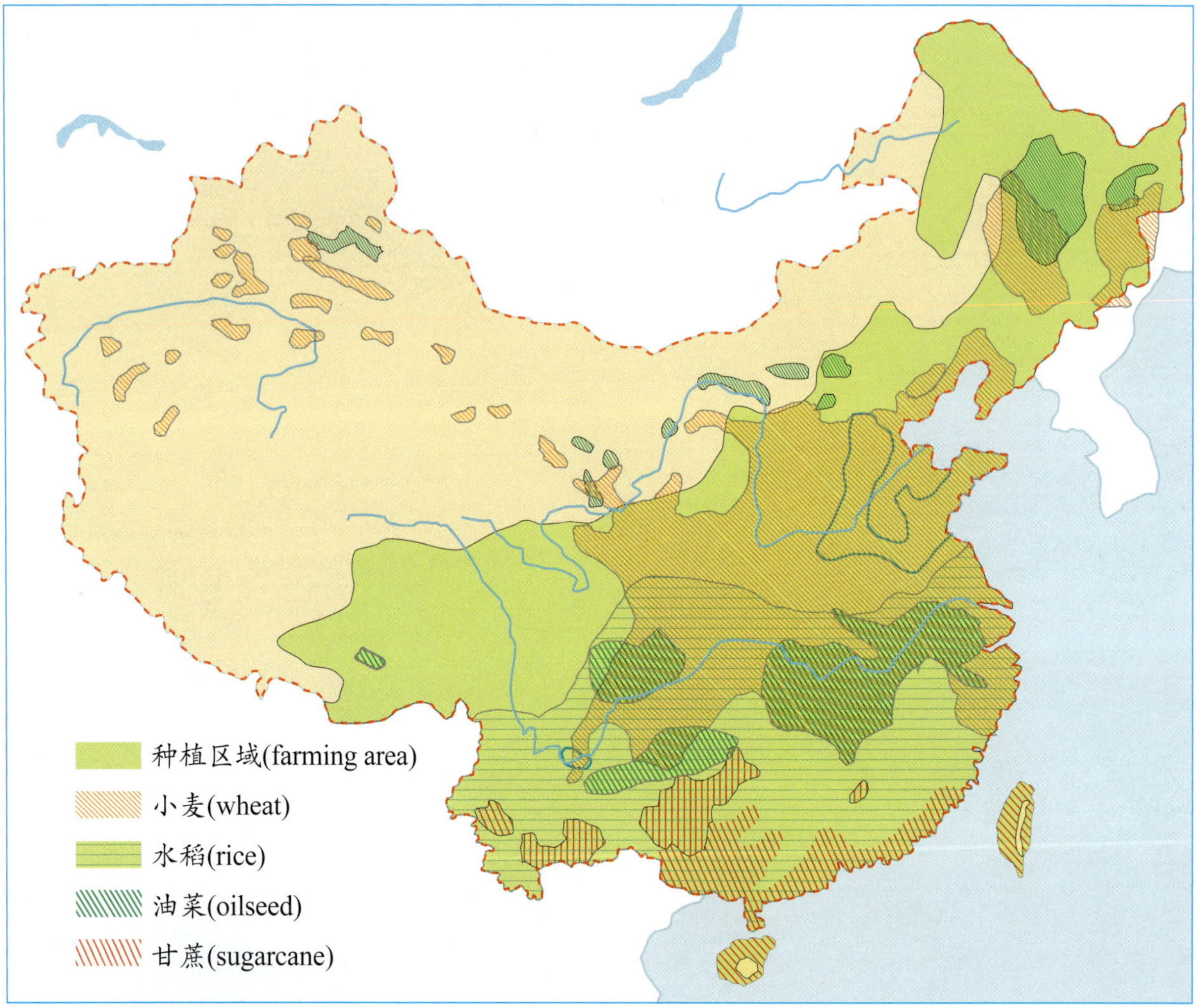

Food Crops			Used in...
小麦	xiǎomài	*wheat*	the breading for Peking Duck
水稻	shuǐdào	*rice*	a staple for every meal in southern China
玉米	yùmǐ	*corn*	fried rice
花生	huāshēng	*peanuts*	Kung Pao Chicken
油菜	yóucài	*oilseed*	Kung Pao Chicken, fried rice, and any stir-fry dishes
甜菜	tiáncài	*sugar beets*	Dongpo's Pork
甘蔗	gān.zhè	*sugarcane*	desserts and sweet products
辣椒	làjiāo	*red chilies*	Kung Pao Chicken, General Tso's Chicken, Mapo Tofu

Due to its geography and climate, China has a booming agricultural industry. The climate is influenced by seasonal winds from Siberia in the winter and the Pacific in the summer. The hot and humid summers are suitable for growing rice, wheat, and corn, for example. China also has some very fertile lands, such as the stretch of black earth in the northeast and purple soil in Sichuan that contain a high volume of nutrients. China's main food crops are: grains (wheat, rice, maize), oil-bearing crops (oilseed, peanuts), and sugar crops (sugar beets, sugarcane).

Wheat (小麦 *xiǎomài*)

▲ A vast wheat farm in northern China.

Wheat is the staple food of the Chinese people in the north. With 4,500 years of history in wheat cultivation, China was one of the first countries to domesticate the crop. There are two kinds of wheat—one that grows in winter, and one that grows in spring. Spring wheat is cultivated in China's Heilongjiang Province, Inner Mongolia and the northwest, while winter wheat is cultivated in northern China, Shanxi, south of Xinjiang, and along the Yangtze River. Up until 2005, China was ranked as the number one country for wheat production.

Rice (水稻 *shuǐdào*)

▲ Farmers transplant rice seedlings.

Rice needs warm, humid weather and short periods of sunshine. The number of rice harvests differs from region to region. In southern China and Taiwan, there can be as many as three harvests each year; crops along the Yangtze can be harvested twice per year; and as for areas in higher latitudes, rice can only be harvested once each year. The northernmost area where rice is grown is Heilongjiang Province. Rice is served with most dishes in the south.

Corn (玉米 *yùmǐ*)

Corn is grown in northern China and in the mountains in the southwest. It prefers warm weather and short periods of sun. Because it grows between the winter wheat harvests, it is grown intermittently with wheat along the Yellow River and in areas in the north where frost only appears for short periods during the year. China's largest production site for corn is in Shandong, and China ranks second in the world in corn production.

▲ Fruitful corn farms.

Peanuts (花生 *huāshēng*)

Oil-bearing peanuts are used in the production of cooking oil. It is an annual herbaceous plant that is mainly found in Shandong, the eastern portion of Liaoning, Guangdong, along the Yellow River and Huai River, and the southeastern coast. One popular dish served with peanuts is Kung Pao Chicken.

▲ Peanuts are plants with various uses.

Oilseed (油菜 *yóucài*)

▲ A scenic landscape of oilseed flowers.

Along with India, China is ranked as having the longest history of oilseed cultivation. Used in cooking, oilseed is crispy and slightly bitter to the taste. It is cultivated mainly along the Yangtze River. A biannual crop, its seeds are planted in Xinjiang, Gansu, Qinghai, and Inner Mongolia in the fall and harvested the following May. Shandong is the main production site for oilseed. The oil from the oilseed is used in the Chinese stir-fried dishes.

Sugar beets (甜菜 *tiáncài*)

In China, sugar beets are used to make sugar. They are grown mainly in the northern areas of China.

▶ Sugar beets are grown commercially for sugar production.

Sugarcane (甘蔗 *gānzhè*)

▲ Harvest of sugarcane.

▲ Bunches of sugarcane are ready to sell.

Sugarcane grows in fertile soil and in places where there is a large variance in temperature between winter and summer. It also prefers a lot of sun, so it is cultivated throughout the tropics and sub-tropics. Sugarcane is grown in China's southern provinces, such as Guangdong, Guangxi, Fujian, Sichuan, Yunnan, Jiangxi, Guizhou, Hunan, Zhejiang, and Hubei. It is also grown in Taiwan.

Chilies (辣椒 *làjiāo*)

Chilies were imported into China during the Ming Dynasty (1368-1644 A.D.). Before that, China's main spices were ginger, pepper, and Chinese red pepper. Chilies are not only hot; they are also sweet with a unique fragrance. Therefore, they are not only used as seasoning, but main dishes as well. People living in China's southwest eat the most chilies. Chilies grow in Sichuan, Hunan, Jiangxi, Guizhou, and Yunnan, so most dishes there use chilies as seasoning. There is a saying: "Sichuan people aren't afraid of spicy dishes; spicy dishes, Hunan people aren't afraid of; Guizhou people are afraid that dishes aren't spicy enough." At present, dried chilies and chili powder are two of China's important exports.

▲ Chilies are used widely in dishes from southwest China.

1 温故知新 Wēngù Zhīxīn / *Remembering the Facts*

Decide if each statement is true or false. Correct any false statements.

1. Sichuan has fertile lands for growing crops.
2. Wheat is the staple for northern China.
3. China ranks number two in the world for overall corn production.
4. Chinese people have used chilies as cooking ingredients for 2,000 years.
5. Sugarcane doesn't like sun, so it is cultivated in the tropics and sub-tropics.
6. Rice grows in a dry climate.
7. Sugar beets are used to make sugar.
8. People living in China's southwest love to eat chilies and their dishes are famous for being spicy.
9. Sugarcane is grown in northern China.
10. Chilies are a relatively new crop in China, at least compared with ginger, pepper, and Chinese red pepper.

Famous Chinese Dishes

Peking Duck (北京烤鸭 *Běijīng kǎoyā*)

Peking Duck is a Beijing delicacy that is popular with tourists. It is red on the outside and has juicy meat on the inside that has a layer of non-greasy fat. A famous dish, it is well-known throughout the world. After the duck is roasted, chefs slice it; the slices are called 片鸭 *piànyā.* There are many ways to prepare Peking Duck. Most commonly it is served with scallions, cucumber slices and sweet sauce, which are rolled up in a thin layer of breading.

Fried Rice (炒饭 *chǎofàn*)

Fried rice is made by stir-frying cooked rice with other ingredients such as eggs, vegetables, meat, or seafood. Fried rice is an international rice dish that is sold in almost all Chinese restaurants across the world. The most famous fried rice dish in China is Yangzhou Fried Rice (扬州炒饭 *Yángzhōu chǎofàn*) which is made with rice, eggs, char siu, ham strips, vegetables, and shrimp.

Kung Pao Chicken (宫保鸡丁 *gōngbǎo jīdīng*)

Kung Pao Chicken is a traditional Sichuan dish. It is made by stir-frying diced chicken and peanuts with dried red chili, resulting in a spicy dish that is widely popular.

Dongpo's Pork (东坡肉 *Dōngpō ròu*)

Dongpo's Pork is a famous Hangzhou dish. It was rumored to have been invented by the poet 苏东坡 *Sū Dōngpō*, whom the dish is named after.

Dongpo's Pork is made by cutting a piece of half fatty pork into a two-by-two inch square, then stewing it together with scallions, ginger, sugar, and soy sauce.

General Tso's Chicken (左宗棠鸡 *Zuǒ Zōngtáng jī*)

General Tso's Chicken is a famous Hu'nan dish named after General Tso (左宗棠 *Zuǒ Zōngtáng*), who was rumored to love eating it. Its ingredients need to be prepared according to certain specifications. For example, the chicken used must have not laid eggs before, and all the bones must be removed. To make this dish, remove the chicken bones then dice the meat. Then, remove the chili seeds and cut the chili into pieces. After that, fry the chicken, then add the chilies, soy sauce, vinegar, ground garlic and ground ginger and stir fry. Lastly, add some starch to thicken the sauce, and sprinkle with sesame oil. When the dish is served, the chicken is golden in color and tastes crispy on the outside, but tender on the inside.

Mapo Tofu (麻婆豆腐 *mápó dòufǔ*)

Mapo Tofu is Sichuan's representative dish. Its main ingredients are tofu, minced beef (or pork), chili, and Sichuan pepper. This dish is an example of 麻辣 *málà*, with Sichuan pepper contributing to the numbness (麻 *má*) and the chilies to the spiciness (辣 *là*).

2 角色扮演 Juésè Bànyǎn / *Role Play*

With a partner, play the roles of a server and a customer in a Chinese restaurant.

Li.zi: **A:** 你要点什么？
Nǐ yào diǎn shén.me?
What would you like to order?

B: 我要点…。
Wǒ yào diǎn….
I'd like to order….

1. 北京烤鸭
Běijīng kǎoyā
Peking Duck

2. 麻婆豆腐
mápó dòufǔ
Mapo Tofu

3. 左宗棠鸡
Zuǒ Zōngtáng jī
General Tso's Chicken

4. 宫保鸡丁
gōngbǎo jīdīng
Kung Pao Chicken

5. 牛肉面
niúròumiàn
Beef Noodles

6. 饺子
jiǎo.zi
Dumpling

7. 炒饭
chǎofàn
Fried Rice

8. 酸辣汤
suānlàtāng
Sweet & Sour Soup

The Cities and Counties in Taiwan

①基隆市	Jīlóng Shì	*Keelung City*
②台北县	Táiběi Xiàn	*Taipei County*
③台北市	Táiběi Shì	*Taipei City*
④桃园县	Táoyuán Xiàn	*Taoyuan County*
⑤新竹县	Xīnzhú Xiàn	*Hsinchu County*
⑥新竹市	Xīnzhú Shì	*Hsinchu City*
⑦苗栗县	Miáolì Xiàn	*Miaoli County*
⑧台中县	Táizhōng Xiàn	*Taichung County*
⑨台中市	Táizhōng Shì	*Taichung City*
⑩南投县	Nántóu Xiàn	*Nantou County*
⑪彰化县	Zhānghuà Xiàn	*Changhua County*
⑫云林县	Yúnlín Xiàn	*Yunlin County*
⑬嘉义县	Jiāyì Xiàn	*Chiayi County*
⑭嘉义市	Jiāyì Shì	*Chiayi City*
⑮台南县	Táinán Xiàn	*Tainan County*
⑯台南市	Táinán Shì	*Tainan City*
⑰高雄县	Gāoxióng Xiàn	*Kaohsiung County*
⑱高雄市	Gāoxióng Shì	*Kaohsiung City*
⑲屏东县	Píngdōng Xiàn	*Pingtung County*
⑳宜兰县	Yílán Xiàn	*Yilan County*
㉑花莲县	Huālián Xiàn	*Hualien County*
㉒台东县	Táidōng Xiàn	*Taitung County*
㉓澎湖县	Pénghú Xiàn	*Penghu County*
㉔连江县	Liánjiāng Xiàn	*Lienchiang County*
㉕金门县	Jīnmén Xiàn	*Kinmen County*

3 按图索骥 Àntú-suǒjì / *Reading Maps*

Look at the map and answer the questions below.

1. Where is Taiwan in relation to mainland China?
2. What is the one county in Taiwan that does not have a coastline?
3. Where is the capital of Taiwan, Taipei City, located?
4. Which is the largest county in Taiwan?
5. How many island counties are there in Taiwan?

About Taiwan

Taiwan is an island situated off mainland China's southeastern shore. It covers 14,040 miles^2, and has 18 counties, two municipalities, and five cities. Though small in area, its population density is ranked ninth in the world, with 248 people per square mile. Before 1949, the government of the Republic of China (ROC) controlled all of China, but this ended when they lost the civil war against the Chinese Communist Party. After losing the war, the government of the ROC relocated to Taiwan and made Taipei its capital city. Since then, Taiwan and mainland China have been separated politically. Both governments seek to resolve the remaining problems peacefully.

While mainland China and Taiwan share the same official language, Mandarin, the former has adopted Simplified Chinese, while the latter still uses Traditional characters.

Taiwan, formed from the clashing of two tectonic plates, has a diverse topography with mountains, basins, and hills. Most of the land is mountainous. Taiwan's Central Mountain Range, which offers magnificent scenery, runs vertically through Taiwan. Mt. Jade, Taiwan's highest peak at 12,962.56 feet is an important landmark. Alishan, another mountain range, is a great spot to watch dawn break, and is also famous for the railway that runs through its forest. Most of Taiwan's plains are in the west; Chianan Plain in the southwest is the largest and the center of agricultural production in Taiwan.

▲ There are 100 mountains more than 3,000 feet above sea level in Taiwan.

Due to the inclines of the mountain ranges, rivers in Taiwan are short and flow from west to east or vice versa, eroding the mountains to form narrow valleys, of which the Taroko Gorge in Hualien is a prime example.

◀ Taipei 101 was the tallest building in the world, until January 2010.

Taiwan has mild winters but hot summers and typhoons in autumn, which result in plenty of precipitation. With the mountainous terrain and rainfall come strong currents and numerous waterfalls, resources that led to the development of hydroelectricity. High-tech electronics are the key industry. Most of Taiwan's electronic industry is in the north, while the south focuses more on heavy industry and exportation. Eastern Taiwan focuses on tourism.

▲ Endemic species in Taiwan—Formosa salmon.

Taiwan has a diverse array of animal and plant life. Among the fauna are the Taiwanese Black Bear—the largest land animal in Taiwan with the famous white "V" on its chest, —and other species that originated during the Ice Age, such as the Formosa salmon, hundred-pace snake, cloud leopard, Chelonia mydas, and Phalaenopsis.

▲ Nowadays, Phalaenopsis are regarded as a work of art.

Rice is Taiwan's main crop, followed by sugarcane and tea. The geography and climate of Taiwan, coupled with advancing agricultural technology, allow the island, called—the "kingdom of fruit,"—to grow many fruits, including the banana, tangerine, and apple.

Two advantages of living in Taiwan are its quality of life and diversity. Convenience stores are open 24 hours and are easy to find; they pop up on an average of every 327 yards. There are plenty of malls that make shopping very convenient, as well as night markets for snacks and entertainment. Taiwan is also rich in art and culture, home to performing groups such as the contemporary Cloud Gate Dance Company; Yi Wan Ran Hand Puppet Group, which performs with hand puppets in the Taiwanese Hand Puppet Theater; and Ming Hwa Yuan Culture and Arts Group, experts at folk opera.

▲ Night markets are a must-see place for visitors to Taiwan.

▲ Hand Puppet Theater is traditional Taiwanese performance.

Decide if each statement is true or false. Correct any false statements.

1. Taiwan is located southwest of China.
2. Mainland China uses Simplified Chinese, and Taiwan uses Traditional Chinese.
3. Taiwan is full of plains and lacks plateaus, so agriculture is well-developed.
4. Taiwan's southwest is where most of Taiwan's crops are produced.
5. Eastern Taiwan's main industry is tourism.
6. Taiwan's highest peak is Alishan.
7. Taiwan's high-tech developments have given it the name "kingdom of fruit."
8. Life is convenient in Taiwan, with theaters open 24 hours a day.

▲ Taiwan is the kingdom of fruit. The fruits from left to right are: mango, starfruit, bell apple, longan, and litchi nut.

Language Map of China

The Chinese language is extremely complex and diverse, due in part to its number of speakers; however, the main reason lies in the vast area of land that these speakers inhabit. China is a multi-cultural and multi-lingual country, made up of 56 national minorities and languages and dialects from five major language families: the Han-Tibetan, the Altaic, the Austronesia, the South-Asian, and the Indo-European. Thus, Chinese is in actuality a language family made up of several dialects and languages separated by region or ethnicity. A speaker in one region cannot necessarily comprehend a speaker from another region. This situation is further complicated by the fact that most Chinese dialects have no written expression.

An attempt to unify Chinese into one language was made through the promotion of Mandarin Chinese, which is why most people immediately think of Mandarin when discussing Chinese language. However, Mandarin is far from being the only form of Chinese spoken in China. Nowadays, the Chinese language family is composed of China's lingua franca, Mandarin—both spoken and written—and other languages and dialects. Dialects of the Han people, who make up 91.59 percent of the Chinese population, are often divided by region into seven strands: the Northern dialect, the Wu dialect, the Xiang dialect, the Gan dialect, Hakka, Cantonese, and the Min dialect. China's other ethnic groups also speak their own languages, such as Mongolian and Tibetan.

The map on the next page shows the major dialects and the languages of China's minority groups spoken in different regions of China today.

① Shanghainese

Shanghainese, spoken in and around Shanghai, saw its golden era in the 1930s, when it was heard on most radio and television broadcasts. Since the late 1980s, schools in Shanghai began to teach in Mandarin, which led to a decrease in the use of Shanghainese. Today there are young people who cannot speak Shanghainese fluently.

② Hakka

Hakka is widely used among the Hakka people in southern China, in areas such as Guangdong, Fujian, Jiangxi, and Guangxi. It is also spoken in Taiwan. Hakka is also used by many overseas Chinese.

③ Hokkien

Hokkien is used in Fujian, Guangdong, Hainan, Guangxi, Zhejiang, and Taiwan, plus other countries in Southeast Asia. Despite a steady population of users in Taiwan and in an ongoing theatrical culture (such as puppet shows and folk opera), the promotion of Mandarin in Taiwan in recent years has led to a younger generation that does not speak Taiwanese (a dialect of Hokkien in Taiwan); some people in Taiwan do not understand Taiwanese at all.

④ Cantonese

Cantonese is mainly spoken in the midwest of Guangdong, south of Guangxi, and in Hong Kong and Macau. It is also widely spoken by overseas Chinese, and is regarded as one of the most influential Chinese dialects after Mandarin.

⑤ Mongolian

Mongolian is used in the northern areas of China, namely Inner Mongolia, Liaoning, Jilin, and Heilongjiang, where Mongolian is the mother tongue of about 4.9 million people.

⑥ Tibetan

Modern Tibetan looks completely different from other Chinese languages. It is spoken within and around the Tibet Autonomous Region of China.

5 温故知新 Wēngù Zhīxīn / *Remembering the Facts*

Complete the following statements.

1. Cantonese is mainly spoken in the midwest of Guangdong, south of Guangxi, and in ___ and Macau.
2. Hokkien is used in Fujian, Guangdong, Hainan, Guangxi, Zhejiang, and ___.
3. ___, spoken in and around Shanghai, saw its golden era in the 1930s, when it was heard on most radio and television broadcasts.
4. Modern Tibetan looks ___ from other Chinese languages. It is spoken within and around the Tibet Autonomous Region of China.
5. ___ is used in northern China, namely Inner Mongolia, Liaoning, Jilin, and Heilongjiang.
6. ___ is widely used among the people in southern China and by overseas Chinese.

6 角色扮演 Juésè Bànyǎn / *Role Play*

With a partner, take turns asking and telling what language each foreign exchange student speaks.

Lì.zi: Juan (Mexico) **A:** Juan说什么语言? Juan shuō shén.me yǔyán?
What language does Juan speak?
B: 他说西班牙语 Tā shuō Xībānyáyǔ.
He speaks Spanish.

语言 Yǔyán *Languages*					
中文	Zhōngwén	*Chinese*	法语	Fǎyǔ	*French*
日语	Rìyǔ	*Japanese*	德语	Déyǔ	*German*
韩语	Hányǔ	*Korean*	英语	Yīngyǔ	*English*
泰语	Tàiyǔ	*Thai*	意大利语	Yìdàlìyǔ	*Italian*
广东话	Guǎngdōnghuà	*Cantonese*	西班牙语	Xībānyáyǔ	*Spanish*

1. Felicity (England)
2. David (Colombia)
3. Jean-Pierre (France)
4. Mingming (Macau)
5. Klaus (Germany)
6. Taro (Japan)
7. Maria (Italy)
8. Na-Yok (Thailand)
9. Eunah (Korea)

发音 Fāyīn

Pronunciation

7 发音练习 Fāyīn Liànxí / *Pronunciation Practice*

Listen to the finals from the chart and repeat after the speaker.

Pronunciation Tips for Finals		
1.	**ü**	First, pronounce **i**. Then, change the shape of your mouth from unrounded to rounded.
2.	**üe**	Pronounce **ü** first and then **ê**. Change the shape of your mouth from rounded to narrow.
3.	**üan**	Pronounce **ü** first and then **an**. Change the shape of your mouth from rounded to narrow.
4.	**ün**	Pronounce **ü** first and then **en**. Change the shape of your mouth from rounded to narrow.

8 发音练习 Fāyīn Liànxí / *Pronunciation Practice*

Listen to the finals from the chart and repeat after the speaker.

Pronunciation Tips for Palatal Sounds		
1.	**j**	Raise the front of your tongue to the hard palate and press the tip against the back of the lower teeth. Then squeeze air out through this channel. This sound is not aspirated.
2.	**q**	As with **j**, raise the front of your tongue to the hard palate and press the tip against the back of the lower teeth. Then let the air out, only with a stronger breath. This sound is aspirated.
3.	**x**	Raise the front of your tongue toward the hard palate. Then let the air flow out through the channel formed between your tongue and hard palate.

NOTE: Palatals are sounds articulated with the back of the tongue raised against the hard palate to form a narrow channel through which air passes.

Language Note

1. Finals with **-ü** can all stand by themselves. The finals **ü** and **üe** are spelled **yu** and **yue** when they stand alone.
2. The initials "j," "q," and "x" can only be combined with **i** and **ü** families.
3. When "j," "q," or "x" is spelled together with the **ü** family, the two dots on top of **ü** should be removed: for example, *jǔ* (to lift). However, when combining **ü** with **n** and **l**, the two dots should be kept: for example, *nǚ* (female).

9 发音练习 Fāyīn Liànxí *Pronunciation Practice*

Repeat the combination of initials and finals after the speaker.

	Initials / Finals	**j**	**q**	**x**
1.	**i**	ji	qi	xi
2.	**ü**	ju	qu	xu
3.	**üe**	jue	que	xue
4.	**üan**	juan	quan	xuan
5.	**ün**	jun	qun	xun

10 发音练习 Fāyīn Liànxí *Pronunciation Practice*

Combine the initial "j" with some finals. Repeat what you hear.

1.	**j + i**	jī jí jǐ jì	jīdàn	*n. egg* 
2.	**j + ü**	jū jú jǔ jù	jú.zi	*n. tangerine* 
3.	**j + ue**	juē jué juě juè	juédìng	*v. to decide*
4.	**j + uan**	juān juǎn juàn	juānxuě	*v. to donate blood*
5.	**j + un**	jūn jùn	jūnrén	*n. soldier*

11 听力练习 Tīnglì Liànxí / Listening Practice

Listen carefully to each pair of words. Select the word you hear by saying A or B.

1.	A. juēzuǐ	B. juézuǐ	3.	A. jīlì	B. jílì
2.	A. jù.zi	B. jú.zi	4.	A. yānjuǎn	B. yànjuàn

12 发音练习 Fāyīn Liànxí / Pronunciation Practice

You will hear the combination of the initial "q" with other finals. Repeat what you hear.

1.	**q + i**	qī qí qǐ qì	jīqì	*n. machine*
2.	**q + ü**	qū qú qǔ qù	xìngqù	*n. interest*
3.	**q + üe**	quē qué què	máquè	*n. sparrow*
4.	**q + üan**	quān quán quǎn quàn	quán.tóu	*n. fist* 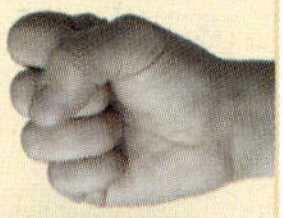
5.	**q + ün**	qūn qún	qún.zi	*n. skirt* 

13 听力练习 Tīnglì Liànxí / Listening Practice

You will hear some words that start with the initial "q" and are combined with one of the finals below. Select the final that you hear.

1. üan *or* üe	2. üan *or* ün	3. i *or* ü	4. ün *or* üan

14 发音练习 Fāyīn Liànxí / Pronunciation Practice

Listen to the combination of the initial 'x' with some finals. Repeat what you hear.

1.	**x + i**	xī xí xǐ xì	xìjù	*n. drama*

2.	**x + ü**	xū xú xǔ xù	xùjí	*n. sequel*
3.	**x + üe**	xuē xué xuě xuè	xuéxiào	*n. school*
4.	**x + üan**	xuān xuán xuǎn xuàn	xuǎnzé	*n. choice*
5.	**x + ün**	xūn xún xùn	xùnliàn	*v. to train*

15 听力练习 Tīnglì Liànxí *Listening Practice*

The sounds you will hear can be combined with the initial "x." Complete the words below on a separate sheet of paper.

1. x__zhǐ	2. x__huān	3. x__wèn	4. x__ruò	5. dòngx__

16 发音练习 Fāyīn Liànxí *Pronunciation Practice*

Listen to the recording and repeat each pair of words.

1.	**jú** *(orange)* / **jué** *(to feel)*	4.	**jǔ** *(to raise)* / **qǔ** *(to marry)*
2.	**què** *(but)* / **quàn** *(to advise)*	5.	**qué** *(lame)* / **xué** *(to learn)*
3.	**xuán** *(to revolve)* / **xún** *(to look for)*		

17 发音练习 Fāyīn Liànxí *Pronunciation Practice*

With a partner, take turns pronouncing the words below. Tell your partner if he or she is correct (*duì*) or incorrect (*bú duì*).

1.	**jìxìn** (*to send a letter*)	5.	**xìjù** (*drama*)
2.	**jīxù** (*savings*)	6.	**juānzèng** (*to donate*)
3.	**qìjù** (*utensil*)	7.	**quānxuǎn** (*to choose and circle*)
4.	**xīqǔ** (*to absorb*)		

18 听力练习 Tīnglì Liànxí / *Listening Practice*

Listen to the recording, and select the word you hear.

1.	A. qún	B. qú	3.	A. jūn	B. jū	5.	A. xún	B. qún
2.	A. xuè	B. xuàn	4.	A. juǎn	B. quǎn	6.	A. juè	B. juàn

19 听力练习 Tīnglì Liànxí / *Listening Practice*

Listen carefully to the following words. You will hear each word twice. The first time you hear the word, write it on a separate sheet of paper. The second time you hear the word, mark the tones.

júhuā

ü	ing	i	üan	ün	üe

1. dùj__

4. l__xíng

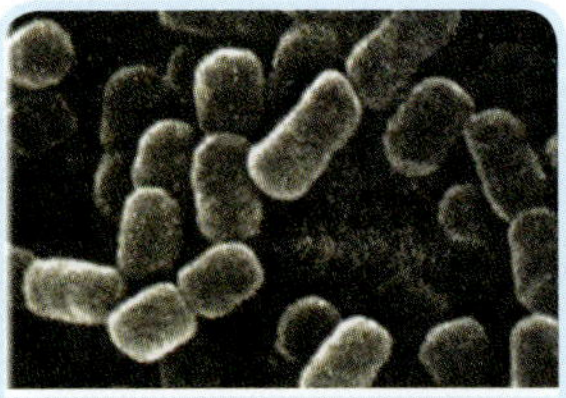

7. xìj__

2. yóuq__

5. x__.zi

8. l__

3. n__rén

6. l__sè

9. q__tíng

20 大声念 Dàshēng Niàn / Read it Aloud

With a partner, take turns reading the rhyme aloud.

圆圈圆，圈圆圈，	Yuánquān yuán, quān yuánquān,	*Round circles, circling circles,*
萱萱娟娟学画圈，	Xuānxuān Juānjuān xué huà quān.	*Xuanxuan and Juanjuan learn to draw circles.*
娟娟画的圈像月，	Juānjuān huà.de quān xiàng yuè,	*Juanjuan's circles look like moons,*
萱萱画的圈像拳，	Xuānxuān huà.de quān xiàng quán.	*Xuanxuan's circles look like fists.*
娟娟萱萱比圆圈，	Juānjuān Xuānxuān bǐ yuánquān,	*Juanjuan and Xuanxuan compare their circles,*
看看谁的圆圈圆。	kànkàn shéi.de yuánquān yuán.	*to see whose are rounder.*

Let's Sing!

小毛驴 Xiǎo Máolǘ

我有一只小毛驴，
我从来也不骑。
有一天我心血来潮，
骑着去赶集。
我手里拿着小皮鞭，
我心里正得意。
不知怎么哗啦啦啦啦，
我摔了一身泥。

Wǒ yǒu yì-zhī xiǎo máolǘ,
wǒ cónglái yě bù qí.
Yǒu yì-tiān wǒ xīnxuè láicháo,
qí.zhe qù gǎnjí.
Wǒ shǒulǐ ná.zhe xiǎo píbiān,
wǒ xīn.lǐ zhèng déyì.
Bù zhī zěn.me huā lā lā lā lā,
wǒ shuāi.le yì-shēn ní.

Little Donkey

I have a little donkey that I never ride.
One day I got motivated and rode him to market.
I held a whip in my hands and was pleased with myself
When all of a sudden, not knowing what happened, I fell
and got covered in mud.

课堂用语 Kètáng Yòngyǔ
Classroom Expressions

Common High School Subjects					
英文	中文	数学	历史	音乐	体育
Yīngwén	Zhōngwén	Shùxué	Lìshǐ	Yīnyuè	Tǐyù
English	*Chinese*	*math*	*history*	*music*	*P. E.*

Situation 1

Student A: 你上什么课?
Nǐ shàng shén.me kè?
What class do you have now?

Student B: 我上中文课。
Wǒ shàng Zhōngwén kè.
I have Chinese class.

Situation 2

Student A: 这个学期你修什么课?
Zhèi.ge xuéqī nǐ xiū shén.me kè?
What classes are you taking this semester?

Student B: 这个学期我修中文和数学课。
Zhèi.ge xuéqī wǒ xiū Zhōngwén hé shùxué kè.
This semester, I am taking Chinese and math.

21 我的课 Wǒ.de Kè *My Classes*

With a partner, take turns asking and telling what class you have at certain times of the day.

Lì.zi: A: 你上什么课?
Nǐ shàng shén.me kè?
What class do you have now?

B: 我上历史课。
Wǒ shàng lìshǐ kè.
I have history class.

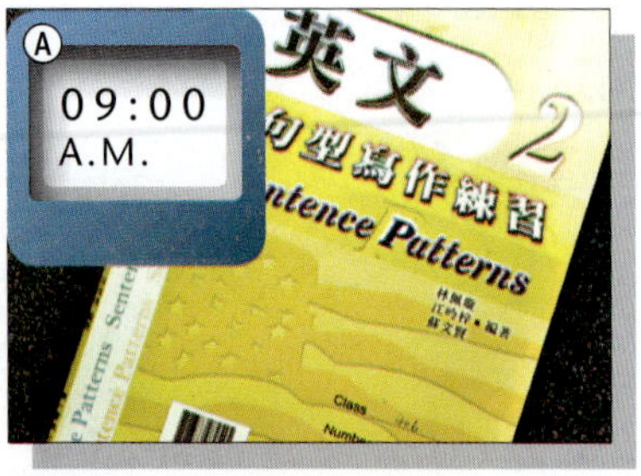

汉字 **Hànzì**

Chinese Characters

Combinations of Pictographs and Ideographs

With the development of Chinese civilization, thoughts and ideas that needed to be conveyed became more complex. Thus, when the time came that pictographs and ideographs were not enough, a new type of character appeared that combined the meaning of two or more elements to form a new meaning. For example, the character 日 (*rì*, sun) and the character 月 (*yuè*, moon) were put together to form the character 明 (*míng*), which means "bright." Below you will see some examples of these combinations.

人 *(people)*	+	木 *(tree)*	=	休 (xiū, *to rest*)
宀 *(roof)*	+	女 *(woman)*	=	安 (ān, *peace*)
女 *(woman)*	+	子 *(child)*	=	好 (hǎo, *good*)
亡 *(die)*	+	目 *(eyes)*	=	盲(máng, *blind*)
少 *(few)*	+	力 *(strength)*	=	劣 (liè, *inferior*)
手 *(hand)*	+	目 *(eyes)*	=	看 (kàn, *to see*)
心 *(heart)*	+	中 *(middle)*	=	忠 (zhōng, *loyalty*)
日 *(sun)*	+	一 *(one)*	=	旦 (dàn, *dawn*)

22 造字游戏 Zàozì Yóuxì / *Creating New Characters*

Look at the meanings of the pictographs and ideographs to determine what the new combinations mean.

1. 木 (mù, *tree*) + 木 (mù, *tree*) = 林 (lín)
2. 人 (rén, *people*) + 言 (yán, *speech*) = 信 (xìn)
3. 人 (rén, *people*) + 口 (wéi, *enclosure*) = 囚 (qiú)
4. 田 (tián, *field*) + 心 (xīn, *heart*) = 思 (sī)
5. 日 (rì, *sun*) + 日 (rì, *sun*) + 日 (rì, *sun*) = 晶 (jīng)

Combinations of Radicals and Phonetics

Characters can also consist of a radical indicator and a phonetic indicator. Radicals represent a word's meaning or type; for example, words with the radical 女 *nǚ* often have to do with females. The phonetic element gives a word its sound; for example, words containing 马 *mǎ* often sound similar to it—such as *mā*, *má*, *mǎ* or *mà*. Ninety percent of Chinese characters are derived in this way.

Radical		Phonetic		Combinations
女 (*woman*)	+	马 (mǎ)	=	妈 (mā, *mother*)
木 (*wood*)	+	才 (cái)	=	材 (cái, *building materials*)
水 (*water*)	+	羊 (yáng)	=	洋 (yáng, *ocean*)
言 (*speech*)	+	己 (jǐ)	=	记 (jì, *to remember*)
心 (*heart*)	+	相 (xiāng)	=	想 (xiǎng, *to think*)
人 (*people*)	+	主 (zhǔ)	=	住 (zhù, *to live*)

23 造字游戏 Zàozì Yóuxì *More Combinations*

Combine each radical with the phonetic of 曼 *màn*. Then select the letter of the correct meaning of the new word.

1. 心 (*heart*)	+	曼 (màn)	=	慢		A.	eel
2. 水 (*water*)	+	曼 (màn)	=	漫		B.	overflow
3. 鱼 (*fish*)	+	曼 (màn)	=	鳗		C.	slow
4. 草 (*grass*)	+	曼 (màn)	=	蔓		D.	trailing plant
5. 土 (*earth*)	+	曼 (màn)	=	墁		E.	put rock on ground
6. 金 (*metal*)	+	曼 (màn)	=	镘		F.	trowel

▶ Cangjie claimed to be the inventor of Chinese characters five thousand years ago. Legend has it that he had four eyes and eight pupils.

The Importance of Proportion When Writing Characters

Chinese words may look complicated, but in fact, their structures are logical and easy to analyze. Chinese characters are called "square" characters, meaning no matter how simple or complex, each character fits inside a square. They can be divided into five main structures, which are listed below. Once these five structures are mastered, the makeup of Chinese characters will be much more familiar and less intimidating to you. These structures will not only help you memorize characters, but also reduce problems with missing dots or strokes when writing. Understanding these structures will make even complex characters easy to remember.

Characters should be written with a sense of symmetry and proportion. A character can be formed as a one-picture character, a two-picture character, a three-picture character, or a four-picture character. One-picture characters fit inside a square. There are two possibilities for dividing a square for two-picture characters. Three-picture characters come in five different patterns. The square for four-picture characters can be subdivided in three ways. Understanding how to mentally plot out a character within a square will give you one of the fundamentals needed for effective written communication in Chinese.

	Structure		**Examples**
1.	One-Picture Character		刀 dāo *n. knife*
			女 nǚ *n. female*
2.	Two-Picture Character	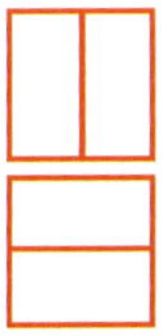	叫 jiào v. *to shout*
			早 zǎo *adj. early*
3.	Three-Picture Character		例 lì *n. example*
			意 yì *n. meaning; idea*
			部 bù *n. part*
			然 rán *adv. really*
			增 zēng *v. to add*
4.	Four-Picture Character		能 néng *v. to be able to*
			慢 màn *adj. slow*
			湖 hú *n. lake*

24 拆解文字 Chāijiě Wénzì / Let's Find the Structure!

Look at the following Chinese characters. For each one determine if it is a one, two, three, or four picture character.

1. 心	4. 为	7. 胖	10. 思
2. 杏	5. 求	8. 洗	11. 大
3. 侧	6. 页	9. 战	12. 流

25 物以类聚 Wù Yǐ Lèi Jù / Characters with the Same Written Structure

Match each character in the first row with a character in the second row that has the same written structure.

1. 树　2. 人　3. 射　4. 忘　5. 剖　6. 培　7. 单

A. 香　B. 华　C. 湖　D. 火　E. 语　F. 敬　G. 烙

The Placement of Radicals

Previously, we learned about radicals and components of characters and where they are placed. There are rules for where to place radicals, too. Let's look at the table below to learn the rules for placing radicals.

	Placement of Radicals	Radicals	Examples
1.	left of the character	亻 *person*	你 nǐ *n. you*
		犭 *animal*	狗 gǒu *n. dog*
		日 *sun*	明 míng *adj. bright*
2.	right of the character	攵 *tap*	故 gù *n. reason*
		阝 *city*	都 dū *n. city*
		刂 *knife*	到 dào *v. to arrive*

3.	top of the character	宀 *roof*	家 jiā *n. home*
		冖 *cover*	写 xiě *v. to write*
		艹 *grass*	草 cǎo *n. grass*
4.	bottom of the character	灬 *fire*	热 rè *adj. hot*
		心 *heart*	想 xiǎng *v. to think*
5.	whole-word frames	口 *enclose*	国 guó *n. country*
		匚 basket	区 qū *n. area*
		冂 *border*	网 wǎng *n. net*
		凵 *receptacle*	画 huà *n. painting*
		疒 *disease*	病 bìng *n. disease*
		辶 *to go*	追 zhuī *v. to pursue*

26 拆解文字 Chāijiě Wénzì / *Let's Find the Structure!*

First, identify the radical for each word and give its meaning. Then, say the structure of it according to the chart "Placement of Radicals."

1. 洗 xǐ *v. to wash*
2. 笔 bǐ *n. pen*
3. 医 yī *n. doctor*
4. 季 jì *n. season*
5. 胖 pàng *adj. fat*
6. 攻 gōng *v. to attack*
7. 盆 pén *n. basin*
8. 芽 yá *n. sprout*
9. 团 tuán *n. group*
10. 对 duì *adj. correct*
11. 阴 yīn *adj. cloudy*
12. 助 zhù *v. to help*
13. 亨 hēng *adj. prosperous*
14. 务 wù *n. affair*

Foundation F

When you have completed this lesson you will be able to...

Geography / History

- describe features of China's natural landscape and locate them on a map
- locate the Great Wall and the Grand Canal on a map
- to explain the history of the Great Wall and the Great Canal

Pronunciation

- pronounce a variety of tonal changes
- understand Pinyin spelling rules
- understand other Chinese spelling systems
- sing two new songs

Classroom Expressions

- use the correct Chinese expressions in certain classroom situations

Chinese Characters

- define examples of borrowed characters
- examine how Chinese vocabulary is created

The Natural Environment of China

China is a large country and has a very diverse landscape. The topography comprises mountains, hills, basins, plains, and plateaus. Among them, mountains and plateaus occupy 59% of the total land. The terrain of China slopes from west to east, forming a flight of three tiers. The first tier is made up of mountains and plateaus in the west; the second tier is of plateaus and basins; the third tier is of flat plains in the east.

Important Landforms in China		
1. 黑龙江	Hēilóng Jiāng	*Heilongjiang*
2. 东北平原	Dōngběi Píngyuán	*Northeast China Plain*
3. 大兴安岭	Dàxīng'ānlǐng	*Greater Khingan Range*
4. 内蒙古高原	Nèiménggǔ Gāoyuán	*Inner Mongolia Plateau*
5. 黄土高原	Huángtǔ Gāoyuán	*Loess Plateau*
6. 太行山	Tàiháng Shān	*Taihang Mountains*

7. 黄河	Huáng Hé	*Yellow River*
8. 华北平原	Huáběi Píngyuán	*North China Plain*
9. 长江	Cháng Jiāng	*Yangtze River*
10. 南岭	Nán Lǐng	*Nanling Mountains*
11. 珠江	Zhū Jiāng	*Pearl River*
12. 秦岭	Qín Lǐng	*Qinling Mountains*
13. 四川盆地	Sìchuān Péndì	*Sichuan Basin*
14. 昆仑山	Kūnlún Shān	*Kunlun Mountains*
15. 青藏高原	Qīngzàng Gāoyuán	*Tibetan Plateau*
16. 喜马拉雅山	*Xǐ*mǎlāyǎ Shān	*Himalaya Range*
17. 阿尔泰山	Ā'ěrtài Shān	*Altai Mountains*
18. 准噶尔盆地	Zhǔngá'ěr Péndì	*Junggar Basin*
19. 天山	Tiān Shān	*Tian Shan*
20. 塔里木盆地	*Tǎ*lǐmù Péndì	*Tarim Basin*
21. 塔克拉玛干沙漠	Tǎkèlāmǎgān Shāmò	*Taklamakan Desert*

太行山 Tàiháng Shān

The Taihang Mountains provide an important topographical border, with Loess Plateau to their west and the North China Plain to their east. The mountain range is famous for its magnificent scenery that includes rivers and valleys, rock formations, and an abundance of trees, as well as various historical artifacts. Two key features are the Taihang Grand Canyon, which is also known as "Colorado in the East," and Wuzhi Mountain with its five peaks that look like fingers. Every year, a lot of people visit the Taihang Mountains to camp, relax, hang glide or rock climb.

▶ The magnificent scenery of Taihang Mountains.

黄河 Huáng Hé

The Yellow River is China's second-longest river. Known as "Mother River," it is traditionally considered to be the home of the Chinese. The river's midstream flows through Loess Plateau, whose sediments turn the water yellow. The Yellow River carries the most sand of any river in the world. In addition to this, the volume of the river is inconsistent. The Chinese government is now trying to reduce the Yellow River's sedimentation and erosion problem.

长江 Cháng Jiāng

The Yangtze River is China's longest and the world's third-longest river. Along its banks, crop production amounts to almost half of China's total, with rice crops taking up 70 percent. China's most densely populated and prosperous cities can be found along its banks, such as Shanghai, Nanjing, Wuhan, Chongqing, and Chengdu. The Yangtze and Qiantang Rivers flow out to sea to form the Yangtze River Delta, an area of great economic development. The famous Three Gorges—consisting of the Qutang Gorge, Xiling Gorge, and Wu Gorge—make up a scenic area along the Yangtze.

▲ A tranquil section of the Yangtze River.

南岭 Nán Lǐng

The Nanling Mountains are the largest group of mountains south of the Yangtze River; they run through the Guangdong, Hunan, and Jiangxi provinces, as well as the Guangxi Zhuang Autonomous Region. The basins in the west of the Nanling Mountains are made up primarily of limestone, while the basins in the east, made up of red rocks, are equally spectacular due to the weathering and erosion that has occurred. Places south of the Nanling Mountains have a warm climate throughout the year, while places north of the mountains have colder winters with a higher chance of snowfall, making the Nanling Mountains an important geographical border. The mountains are also rich in colored metals, especially tungsten and antimony.

秦岭 Qín Lǐng

The Qinling Mountains are located right in the middle of China, and are the country's only east-west mountain range. The mountains are an important geographical border that separates China's north from its south, and the water systems of the Yangtze and Yellow Rivers. The mountains are also a border that separates the bio-organisms into the Palearctic and Indo-Malaya ecozones. In addition, the mountains divide the tropical and temperate climate zones.

四川盆地 Sìchuān Péndì

The Sichuan Basin has fertile ground suitable for agriculture. Because it has always produced plentiful crops, it earned the name "Land of Abundance." It is also called the "Red Basin" due to the Dawn Redwood that dots the surface. Coal, liquid petroleum, natural gas, salt, phosphorus, and sulfates can also be found here, making the area an important place for industry in China's southwest.

青藏高原 Qīngzàng Gāoyuán

The Tibetan Plateau is China's largest. The most elevated plateau in the world, it is also known as the "Roof of the World." Two mountain ranges—the

Himalayas and the Kunlun Mountains—intersect the plateau to form many basins, valleys, and lakes. The lakes, a large feature of the Tibetan Plateau, are a great source of hydropower and the origin of many big rivers in Asia.

▲ Roof of the World.

喜马拉雅山 *Xǐmǎlāyǎ Shān*

The Himalaya Range is Asia's greatest and most majestic mountain range and home to many of the world's tallest peaks, including the world's tallest peak, Mount Everest. These peaks are covered in ice and snow all year round, prompting the name "Himalaya," which means "abode of snow" in Sanskrit. For adventurous mountain climbers, the Himalaya Range is the most attractive destination in the world.

1 按图索骥 Àntú-suǒjì / *True or False*

Decide if each statement is true or false. Correct any false statements.

1. The Yellow River is higher than the Yangtze River in latitude.
2. The highest mountain in China is Tian Shan.
3. Inner Mongolia is a basin.
4. Like the Nanling Mountains, the Qinling Mountain range is north to south.
5. The north-east part of China is a mountainous area.

2 温故知新 Wēngù Zhīxīn / *Remembering the Facts*

Identify each geographical feature on a separate sheet of paper.

1. This place is called the "Land of Abundance," in a basin in China's southwest, because of its agricultural production, natural gases, and mineral deposits.
2. The second longest river in China, also known as the "Mother River" of the Chinese, it got its name from the yellow sand that is carried along by its currents.
3. Some features in this place led to it being called the "Colorado in the East."
4. This mountain range is covered in snow all year round, and is home to the world's highest peak, Mount Everest.
5. China's only east-west mountain range separates the Yellow and the Yangtze Rivers. Geographically, it is an important border that divides the north and south into different climate zones.
6. Places north of these mountains have a colder climate and places south of them have a warmer climate.
7. The most elevated plateau in the world, it is known as the "Roof of the World."
8. The river is the longest one in China, and the third-longest in the world.

Place Names

In China, place names are usually made up of directions, geographical nouns, and adjectives. The following is a table of common words that are used to make up place names. It will help you better understand the names of important places in China.

Direction	东 (dōng, *east*)	南 (nán, *south*)	西 (xī, *west*)	北 (běi, *north*)
Nouns	海 (hǎi, *sea*)	江 (jiāng, *river*)	河 (hé, *river*)	湖 (hú, *lake*)
	津 (jīn, *ferry*)	港 (gǎng, *harbor*)	城 (chéng, *city*)	京 (jīng, *capital*)
	山 (shān, *mountain*)	林 (lín, *forest*)	天 (tiān, *sky*)	疆 (jiāng, *border*)
Adjective	黄 (huáng, *yellow*)	长 (cháng, *long*)	香 (xiāng, *fragrant*)	吉 (jí, *lucky*)

3 地理名称 Dìlǐ Míngchēng *Geographical Names*

Decode the Chinese place names below, using the chart above. Follow the model.

Lì.zi: 北京 Běijīng

Capital of the north

1.	黄河 Huánghé
2.	吉林 Jílín
3.	山东 Shāndōng
4.	香港 Xiānggǎng
5.	长城 Chángchéng
6.	天津 Tiānjīn
7.	南京 Nánjīng
8.	山西 Shānxī
9.	河北 Héběi
10.	天山 Tiānshān

▼ Xiānggǎng

4 角色扮演 Juésè Bànyǎn / *Role Play*

Almost three million American tourists visit China each year. With a partner take turns asking and answering which locations the tourists are visiting.

Lì.zi: Mrs. Johnson / 青藏高原 / Qīngzàng Gāoyuán

A: Mrs. Johnson参观什么地方？ Mrs. Johnson cānguān shén.me dì.fāng?

What is Mrs. Johnson seeing?

B: 她参观青藏高原。 Tā cānguān Qīngzàng Gāoyuán.

She is seeing the Tibetan Plateau.

1.	Mr. Jones	Tàiháng Shān	*Taihang Mountains*
2.	Miss Stephanie	Xǐmălāyǎ Shān	*Himalaya Range*
3.	Mr. Bulaya	Cháng Jiāng	*Yangtze River*
4.	Mrs. Wallace	Huáng Hé	*Yellow River*
5.	Miss Choi	Sìchuān Péndì	*Sichuan Basin*

▲ The Yellow River is named after its color.

The Great Wall and the Grand Canal

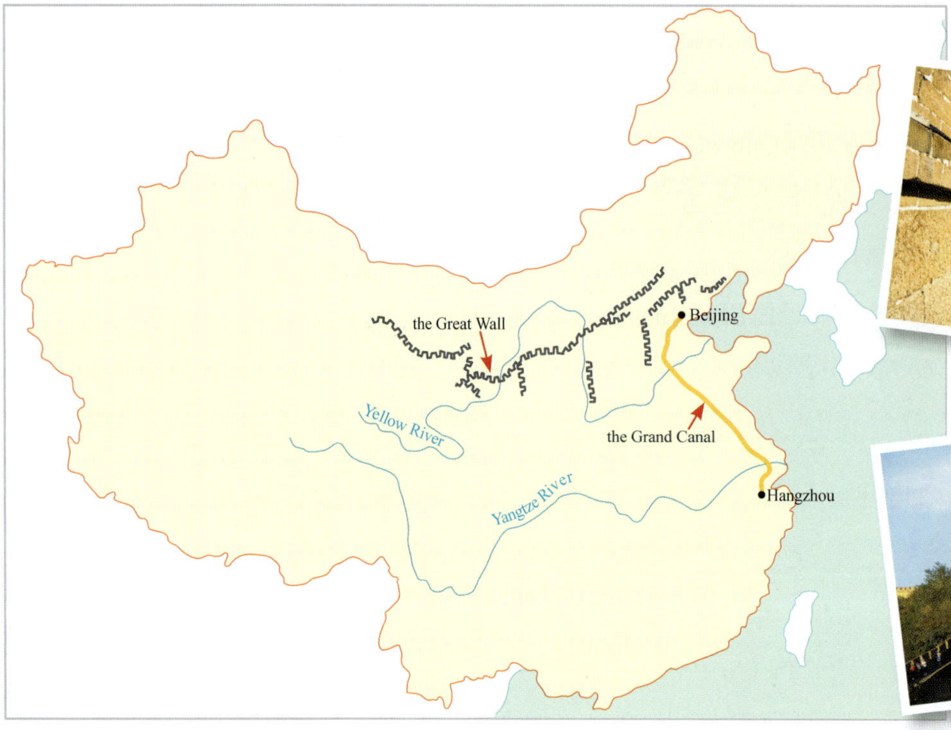

长城 Chángchéng The Great Wall

The Great Wall currently stretches from Shanhaiguan (in Hebei Province) in the east to Lop Nur (in Xinjiang Uyghur Autonomous Region) in the west. Built to prevent invasion from tribes of nomads in the north, its construction was a huge military affair that started in the Spring and Autumn Period (770-221 B.C.) and ended after the unification of China in the Qin Dynasty (221-207 B.C.). Successive dynasties following the Qin era made repairs to the Wall: The Han (202 B.C.-220 A.D.) and Ming (1368-1644 A.D.) dynasties made the most ambitious extensions and repairs. Emperors Wen and Xuan of the Han Dynasty extended the Great Wall and made it almost 10,000 kilometers in length. Repairs and construction of the Great Wall were made for military purposes. However, nowadays, most repairs are for preservation of the site and to encourage tourists to visit. The Great Wall was listed as a World Heritage Site in 1987, and is considered one of the Seven Wonders of the Medieval World.

大运河 Dàyùnhé The Grand Canal

The Great Wall and the Grand Canal are considered the two greatest constructions of ancient China and are known around the world. The Grand Canal is the world's longest canal; it also took the longest time to build. The construction of the Grand Canal began during the Spring and Autumn Period (770-476 B.C.) and was completed in the Yuan Dynasty (1271-1368 A.D.). The Canal starts in Beijing, and then passes through Tianjin, Hebei, Shandong, Jiangsu, and Zhejiang to end in Hangzhou. It links the waterways of the Hai, Yellow, Huai, Yangtze, and Qiantang Rivers in its 1,113-mile course. The Grand Canal made it possible for economic and cultural exchanges through the flow of goods between China's north and south. The Grand Canal is a boon for the industry, agriculture, and urban development of the areas along its course. Throughout history, the Grand Canal has contributed a lot to China's economy, unification, social progress, and cultural prosperity—a pattern that continues in modern-day China.

5 按图索骥 Àntú-suǒjì / *Reading Maps*

Look carefully at the map on the opposite page, then answer the following questions.

1. Which river does the Great Wall intersect?
2. Which city is close to the northern end of the Grand Canal?
3. Which city is close to the southern end of the Grand Canal?

6 温故知新 Wēngù Zhīxīn / *Remembering the Facts*

Match each description to its corresponding site.

(A) The Great Wall (B) The Grand Canal

1. World Heritage Site
2. the symbol of China
3. links several waterways
4. its construction has been a military affair
5. one of the Seven Wonders of the Medieval World
6. a boon for industry, agriculture, and urban development along its trajectory
7. built to prevent invasion from tribes of nomads in the north
8. allows for economic and cultural exchanges between China's north and south

发音 Fāyīn

Pronunciation

Tonal Changes

Every Chinese character is pronounced as a single syllable. However, the tonal value of a syllable changes when pronounced in sequence.

Half-Third Tone

The half-third tone is a variant of the regular third tone. It begins as the full-third does, but, having reached its low point, remains at that level without rising again. As with the first tone, you may check yourself on the half-third tone by seeing whether you can prolong it at a constant pitch.

A third-tone syllable is pronounced in the half-third tone when a syllable in the first, second, or fourth tone immediately follows. A full-third tone is pronounced only when no syllable immediately follows, i.e., only at the end of a phrase, or by itself. When spelling in Pinyin, no distinction is made between a full-third and a half-third tone. Look for examples of half-third tones in the following chart.

简单	女人	跑步	好书	打折	五块
jiǎndān	nǚrén	pǎobù	hǎo shū	dǎzhé	wǔ kuài
simple	*woman*	*to run*	*good book*	*discount*	*five dollars*

Transformation of the Third Tone

When a syllable with the third tone is at the end of a sentence or phrase, it remains in the third tone. The third tone transforms, however, when there are more than two third-tone words in sequence.

1. When a third tone syllable is followed by another third tone syllable, the first syllable transforms into the second tone, as in these examples:

	很好	老鼠	表演	语法
	hěn hǎo	*lǎo*shǔ	*biǎo*yǎn	*yǔ*fǎ
pronounced as →	ˊ ˇ	ˊ ˇ	ˊ ˇ	ˊ ˇ
	very good	*mouse*	*performance*	*grammar*

2. When three syllables with the third tone come in sequence, the pronunciation transforms according to context. This usually becomes [third-second-third] or [second-second-third]. Can you find these patterns in the examples below?

	小老板	炒米粉	展览馆	总统府
	xiǎo *lǎo*bǎn	chǎo *mǐ*fěn	*zhǎnlǎn* guǎn	*zǒngtǒng* fǔ
pronounced as →	ˇ ˊ ˇ	ˇ ˊ ˇ	ˊ ˊ ˇ	ˊ ˊ ˇ
	"junior" boss	*stir-fried rice noodles*	*exhibition center*	*presidential palace*

Tone Transformation of 一 *yī*

一 *yī* is pronounced using the first tone, but its tone changes in the following situations:

1. When 一 *yī* is a one-word phrase or at the end of the sentence, it remains in the first tone, as can be seen in these examples:

	十一	第一	万一	星期一
	shíyī	dì-yī	wànyī	Xīngqīyī
tones →	ˊ —	ˋ —	ˋ —	— — —
	eleven	*first*	*just in case*	*Monday*

2. When 一 *yī* is followed by another syllable, it is transformed into the second or fourth tone.

	yī + 1st tone	yī + 2nd tone	yī + 3rd tone	yī + 4th tone	yī + neutral tone
	一杯	一年	一口	一岁	一个
	yì-bēi	yì-nián	yì-kǒu	yí-suì	yí .gè
tones →	ˋ —	ˋ ˊ	ˋ ˇ	ˊ ˋ	ˊ
	one cup	*one year*	*one bite*	*one year-old*	*one item*

Tone Transformation of 不 *bù*

不 *bù* is a fourth-tone character. When 不 *bù* is pronounced as a single syllable or at the end of a phrase or clause, it is pronounced in the fourth tone. If it is followed by a first, second, or third-tone syllable, its tone remains as the fourth. If it is followed by another fourth-tone syllable, it then transforms into the second tone. Look at the chart to find examples of the tone transformation of 不 *bù*.

	bù + 1st tone	bù + 2nd tone	bù + 3rd tone	bù + 4th tone
	不高	不行	不想	不要
	bù gāo	bù xíng	bù xiǎng	bú yào
tones →	ˋ —	ˋ ˊ	ˋ ˇ	ˊ ˋ
	not tall	*no way*	*do not want*	*wouldn't like*

Fourth-Tone Sandhi

The modified fourth tone begins where the full fourth tone begins, but in the same amount of time, falls only about half as far as the full fourth.

Some experts believe that this modified fourth tone is in fact better represented as a matter of stress rather than a matter of tone alteration. Since the second syllable of any two-syllable compound—not just fourth-tone compounds—tends to receive slightly more stress than the first, the fourth-plus-fourth phenomenon does not need to be considered a theoretical exception. However, it is still a good idea for beginning language learners to focus on the fourth-plus-fourth combination as a special case. In the chart you will see some examples of the fourth-tone sandhi.

看报	度假	卖画	大骂	气候	误会
kàn-bào	dù jià	mài-huà	dà mà	qìhòu	wùhuì
to read a newspaper	*to spend one's holidays*	*to sell paintings*	*to scold*	*climate*	*misunderstanding*

7 发音练习 Fāyīn Liànxí *Pronunciation Practice*

Listen and then repeat each word, expression, or sentence after the speaker.

1. 本人 běnrén (*oneself*)
2. 保守 *bǎo*shǒu (*conservative*)
3. 潜水艇 qián*shuǐ*tǐng (*submarine*)
4. 米老鼠 mǐ*lǎo*shǔ (*Mickey Mouse*)
5. 打草稿 dǎ *cǎo*gǎo (*to make a draft*)
6. 吃喜酒 chī *xǐ*jiǔ (*to go to a wedding banquet*)
7. 洗脸水 *xǐliǎn* shuǐ (*water used for face washing*)
8. 老古董 lǎo *gǔ*dǒng (*old antique*)
9. 老李买水饺。 *Lǎo* Lǐ mǎi *shuǐ*jiǎo. (*Old Li buys dumplings.*)
10. 他很想去洗手间。 Tā *hěn* xiǎng qù *xǐ*shǒujiān. (*He really wants to go to the bathroom.*)
11. 我有好几把雨伞。 *Wǒ* yǒu *hǎo jǐ* bǎ *yǔ*sǎn. (*I have several umbrellas.*)
12. 你请柳小姐买手表。 *Nǐ* qǐng Liǔ *xiǎo*jiě mǎi *shǒu*biǎo. (*You ask Miss Liu to buy you a watch.*)

8 标出声调 Biāochū Shēngdiào *Mark the Tones*

Copy each expression on a separate sheet of paper. Then mark the tones you hear.

Lì.zi: měilì

1. yiqi	2. bu xiao	3. tongyi	4. bu keyi	5. yi ge ren

9 听力练习 Tīnglì Liànxí *Listening Practice*

You will hear five sets of words pronounced differently. Choose the letter of the pronunciation that matches the word you see.

Lì.zi: **A.** búshì

1. yí-jiàn	2. bùnéng	3. yì-tiān	4. bùhǎo	5. chūyī

10 标出声调 Biāochū Shēngdiào / *Mark the Tones*

Copy the sentences that follow on a separate sheet of paper. Then listen to the recording, and mark the tones.

Lì.zi: Xiǎo Chén jīntiān bú zài-jiā.

1. Wo you yi-ge jie.x.
2. Wo bu renshi zhe yi-wei xiao pengyou.
3. Lin xiansheng sanshiyi-sui, bu gao, bu ai, bu pang, bu shou.

11 发音练习 Fāyīn Liànxí / *Pronunciation Practice*

Listen to each pair of words below and repeat.

1.	**nǚrén** *(woman)*	**lǚrén** *(traveler)*
2.	**huìhuà** *(conversation)*	**fèihuà** *(useless or nonsensical word or statement)*
3.	**Xiānggǎng** *(Hong Kong)*	**shānggǎng** *(business harbor)*
4.	**rùkǒu** *(entrance)*	**lùkǒu** *(intersection)*
5.	**zhǎodào** *(to find)*	**zǎodào** *(to arrive early)*
6.	**shàngsī** *(boss)*	**sàngshī** *(to lose)*
7.	**yuàn.zi** *(yard)*	**yàn.zi** *(swallow)*
8.	**qùwèi** *(interest)*	**cùwèi** *(vinegar flavor)*
9.	**dàlóu** *(multi-story building)*	**dàluó** *(big gong)*
10.	**rénshēn** *(ginseng)*	**rénshēng** *(life)*

12 发音练习 Fāyīn Liànxí / *Pronunciation Practice*

Listen to the recording, and select the word you hear.

Lì.zi: Ⓐ mínshēng (*livelihood*) B. míngshēng (*reputation*)

1.	A. jiānyù *(jail)*	B. jiāngyù *(territory)*
2.	A. gǒushí *(dog food)*	B. guǒshí *(fruit)*
3.	A. jù.zi *(sentence)*	B. zhù.zi *(pillar)*
4.	A. jīnrén *(modern people)*	B. jūnrén *(soldier)*
5.	A. zǎo.zi *(dates)*	B. jiǎo.zi *(dumpling)*

13 听力练习 Tīnglì Liànxí / *Listening Practice*

Listen to the recording and select the word you hear by writing A or B on a spearate sheet of paper.

Lì.zi: A. fāfēng B. huāfēng

1.	A. nuǎnshēn	B. luǎnshēng	4.	A. nèixiàn	B. nèixiàng
2.	A. huāngtáng	B. fāngtáng	5.	A. *gǎn*rǎn	B. *gǎn*lǎn
3.	A. qídào	B. chídào	6.	A. chénfēng	B. shénfēng

Pinyin Spelling Rules

Placement of tone marks

Tone marks are written above the main vowel of a syllable. The main vowel is determined by this order of precedence: **a** – **o** – **e** – **i** – **u** –**ü**. What is the main vowel in the following words?

鸭 yā (*duck*) 猪 zhū (*pig*)

猫 māo (*cat*) 狗 gǒu (*dog*)

蝶 dié (*butterfly*) 象 xiàng (*elephant*)

However, there is an exception with **i** and **u**. That is, when **i** and **u** exist in the same syllable, the tone mark is always placed on the second vowel. For example: 牛 niú (*cattle*), 腿 tuǐ (*leg*)

The dot in the letter **i** is removed when a tone mark is placed over it. For example: 水 shuǐ (*water*).

Finals for ü change in the following situations

-ü, -üē, -üān, -ün		
Remove the two dots when...		Keep the two dots when...
there are no initials.	combined with **j**, **q** and **x**.	combined with **n** and **l**.
月 yuè (*moon*) 圆 yuán (*round*)	橘 jú (*orange*) 裙 qún (*skirt*)	女 nǚ (*girl*) 绿 lǜ (*green*)

Capital Letters

1. Capitalize the first letter of all proper nouns.

孔子 *Kǒngzǐ* (*Confucius*)

香港 Xiānggǎng (*Hong Kong*)

李先生 Lǐ xiān.shēng (*Mr. Li*)

2. Capitalize the first letter of the first word in a sentence.

苹果很好吃。 Píngguǒ *hěn* hǎochī. (*Apples are very delicious.*)

我们去公园吧！ Wǒ.mén qù gōngyuán .ba! (*Let's go to the park!*)

In order to avoid confusion, an apostrophe (') is used to divide two syllables when the combination may cause uncertainty or ambiguity.

饥饿 jī'è (*hunger*)

平安 píng'ān (*safety*)

▶ Confucius is a great teacher and philosopher in China.

Write the correct combinations of initials, finals, and tones from those provided. Note that (X) means there is no initial.

	initial	final	tone	combination		initial	final	tone	combination
Lì.zi:	b	a	ˇ	bǎ					
1.	p	o	ˊ		7.	(X)	iao	ˋ	
2.	t	ao	ˊ		8.	q	üe	ˋ	
3.	sh	ou	ˉ		9.	l	ü	ˇ	
4.	(X)	uan	ˇ		10.	(X)	iao	ˊ	
5.	m	iu	ˋ		11.	(X)	un	ˇ	
6.	(X)	i	ˇ						

Pinyin vs. Other Spelling Systems

Wade-Giles

Thomas Wade was the British ambassador to China and later the first professor of Chinese at Cambridge. He published the first Chinese textbook in English in 1867, using his own method of phonetic Romanization. His successor at Cambridge, Herbert Giles, assisted by his son Lionel Giles, refined the system in his 1912 edition.

Mandarin Phonetic System (MPS)

In 1918, the Republic of China (ROC) developed the Mandarin Phonetic System I (or Bopomofo). This became a part of the compulsory teaching of written Chinese in elementary schools, and is still the primary spelling system used in Taiwan today. The People's Republic of China (PRC) stopped using this system after implementing the Pinyin System in 1958.

Gwoyeu Romatzyh (G.R.)

In 1928, the ROC adopted "Gwoyeu Romatzyh" (also known as MPS II) developed by Zhao Yuanren, which spells the tones into the syllable. However, because of its complexity, it was only used for a while before being replaced by the more popular Bopomofo.

Yale

In 1943, George Kennedy from the Far-Eastern Languages Center at Yale University created Yale Romanization—a spelling system that followed English spellings for the military to use in the Far East. Although this system uses similar spelling practices to what English speakers are used to, it doesn't fully represent Chinese phonetics and so is not widely used.

▲ Yale University.

Pinyin

The Pinyin System uses the 26 letters of the Roman alphabet and a few symbols to mark tones. Developed by Zhou Youguang, an economic professor and Chinese émigré who returned to China in the 1950s, Pinyin was approved as the official Romanization for the PRC by the Fifth Session of the First National People's Congress in 1958. It was later adopted by the International Organization for Standardization in 1982 and by the United Nations in 1986. Because the Pinyin System's principles are simple and fit Chinese pronunciation well, it has become the standard spelling system used both in and outside of China.

The following charts are for your reference. Take a look at how the different spelling systems represent initials and finals.

Initials				
Wade-Giles	MPS	G.R.	Yale	Pinyin
p-	ㄅ	b-	b-	b-
p'	ㄆ	p-	p-	p-
m-	ㄇ	m-	m-	m-
f-	ㄈ	f-	f-	f-
t-	ㄉ	d-	d-	d-
t' -	ㄊ	t-	t-	t-
n-	ㄋ	n-	n-	n-
l-	ㄌ	l-	l-	l-
k-	ㄍ	g-	g-	g-
k'-	ㄎ	k-	k-	k-
h-	ㄏ	h-	h-	h-
ch(i)-	ㄐ	j(i)-	j(y)-	j-
ch'(i)-	ㄑ	ch(i)-	ch(y)-	q-
hs(i)-	ㄒ	sh(i)-	sh(y)-	x-
ch-	ㄓ	j-	j-	zh-
ch'-	ㄔ	ch-	ch-	ch-
sh-	ㄕ	sh-	sh-	sh-

j-	ㄖ	r-	r-	r-
ts-	ㄗ	tz-	dz-	z-
ts'-	ㄘ	ts-	ts-	c-
s-	ㄙ	s-	s-	s-

Finals				
Wade-Giles	MPS	G.R.	Yale	Pinyin
-a	ㄚ	-a	-a	-a
-o	ㄛ	-o	-o	-o
-e	ㄜ	-e	-e	-e
-(i)e	ㄝ	-(i)e	-(i)e	-(i)e
-ai	ㄞ	-ai	-ai	-ai
-ei	ㄟ	-ei	-ei	-ei
-au	ㄠ	-au	-au	-au
-ou	ㄡ	-ou	-ou	-ou
-an	ㄢ	-an	-an	-an
-en	ㄣ	-en	-en	-en
-ang	ㄤ	-ang	-ang	-ang
-eng	ㄥ	-eng	-eng	-eng
-er	ㄦ	-er	-er	-er
-i	ㄧ	-i	-i	-i
-u	ㄨ	-u	-u	-u
-u	ㄩ	-iu	-yu	-ü

Some examples of words in the different spelling systems:

Spelling systems / Words	Wade-Giles	MPS	G.R.	Yale	Pinyin
人 *human*	jen	ㄖㄣ	ren	rén	rén
猪 *pig*	chu	ㄓㄨ	ju	jū	zhū
狗 *dog*	kou	ㄍㄡ	gou	gǒu	gǒu
唱歌 *to sing*	ch'angke	ㄔㄤ ㄍㄜ	changge	chànggē	chànggē
说话 *to talk*	shuohua	ㄕㄨㄛ ㄏㄨㄚ	shuohua	shuōhuà	shuōhuà

15 回答问题 Huídá Wèntí / *Answering Questions*

Answer the following questions about the different spelling systems. Write the answers on a separate sheet of paper.

1. What is the standard spelling system in China?
2. What nationalities were the people who invented Wade-Giles?
3. In what year was the first Chinese textbook published?
4. Where is the Mandarin Phonetic System used today?
5. Why was Gwoyeu Romatzyh replaced by MPS?
6. Why was Yale Romanization first created?
7. Why is Yale Romanization not widely used?
8. In what year did the People's Republic of China implement the Pinyin System?

Culture Note

毛泽东 Máo Zédōng

Mao Zedong was an important political and military leader of 20th-century China. He became the first leader of the People's Republic of China. His most famous book on Chinese socialism, *The Quotations from Chairman Mao Zedong* (aka *The Little Red Book*) has been translated into over 65 languages.

16 大声念 Dàshēng Niàn *Read it Aloud*

With a partner, take turns reading the rhyme aloud.

城门城门几丈高?	Chéngmén chéngmén jǐ-zhàng gāo?	*Town gate, town gate, how tall is it?*
三十六把刀，	sānshíliù-bǎ dāo,	*Thirty-six blades (tall),*
骑大马，带把刀，	qí dà mǎ, dài bǎ dāo,	*Riding a big horse holding a blade,*
走进城门滑一跤。	zǒu jìn chéngmén huá yì-jiāo.	*slip when walking through the town gate.*

Let's Sing!

西风的话 Xīfēng .de huà

去年我回去，
你们刚穿新棉袍。
今年我来看你们，
你们变胖又变高。
你们可记得，池里荷花变莲蓬。
花少不愁没颜色，
我把树叶都染红。

Qùnián wǒ huíqù,
nǐ.mén gāng chuān xīn miánpáo.
Jīnnián wǒ lái kàn nǐ.mén,
nǐ.mén biàn pàng yòu biàn gāo.
Nǐ.mén kě jì.de, chí.lǐ héhuā biàn liánpéng,
Huā shǎo bù chóu méi yánsè,
wǒ bǎ shùyè dōu rǎn hóng.

The West Wind's Words

Last year when I returned,
you had just donned your quilted coats.
This year I visit you,
you've all gotten chubbier and taller.
Do you still remember the lotus flowers in the pond turning into pods,
Do not fret over a lack of color because the flowers are few,
I've dyed all the leaves red.

课堂用语 Kètáng Yòngyǔ
Classroom Expressions

Teacher: 请看……。
Qǐng kàn….
Please look at….

地图	白板	黑板
dìtú	báibǎn	hēibǎn
map	*whiteboard*	*blackboard*

Teacher: 请把……拿出来。
Qǐng bǎ… ná chūlái.
Please take out….

笔	铅笔	书	纸	作业/功课
bǐ	qiānbǐ	shū	zhǐ	zuòyè/gōngkè
pen	*pencil*	*book*	*paper*	*homework*

Teacher: 请把……收起来。
Qǐng bǎ… shōu qǐlái.
Please put... away.

手机	背包	书包	MP3 播放器
shǒujī	bēibāo	shūbāo	MP sān bōfàngqì
cell phone	*backpack*	*bookbag*	*mp3 player*

17 我说你做 Wǒ shuō nǐ zuò / *Do as I say*

Put a pen, pencil, a piece of paper, your homework and textbook on your desk. When your teacher tells you which item to take, hold it up.

Borrowed Characters

Back in the days when there were more words to speak than characters to express them, people would borrow an established character to write a word with a similar sound. For example, once there were two versions of the character for scorpion. One of them (), showing the head, tail, and claws, was pronounced *chài*; another (), showing the head, tail, claws, and legs, was pronounced *wàn*. But *wàn* also meant "ten thousand" but had no written equivalent. The character for *wàn* (scorpion) was borrowed—claws, head, legs and all—to express "ten thousand" and has now metamorphosed into the modern character for "ten thousand," (万 *wàn*). Below are more examples:

Oracle bones	Modern character	Original meaning	Borrowed meaning
	求 qiú	*fur*	*to request*
	自 zì	*nose*	*self*
	亦 yì	*armpit(s)*	*also*
	豆 dòu	*a dish used for meat or other foods*	*soybeans*
	其 qí	*sieve*	*that one's*

字 zì and 词 cí

The noun 字 *zì* (character) is comprised of one character and sometimes has an independent meaning. Each 字 *zì* is one syllable. A 词 *cí* (word) may be comprised of one or more 字 *zì*; therefore, 词 *cí* may be one or more syllables. Most 词 *cí* in Chinese are composed of two 字 *zì*.

Here are some examples of 词 *cí* as one character, two characters, and three characters.

One character	人 (rén, *human*)	狗 (gǒu, *dog*)	书 (shū, *book*)
Two character	学生 (xué.shēng, *student*)	冷气 (lěngqì, *air conditioner*)	早上 (zǎo.shàng, *morning*)
Three character	图书馆 (túshūguǎn, *library*)	篮球场 (lánqiúchǎng, *basketball court*)	幼儿园 (yòu'éryuán, *kindergarten*)

Many of the 25,000 or so individual 字 *zì* are combined to create compounds perceived as single words; and a 字 *zì* may or may not retain its original meaning when used in a compound. For example:

中 zhōng (*middle*)	+	国 guó (*kingdom*)	→	中国 Zhōngguó (*China*)
高 gāo (*high*)	+	兴 xìng (*pleasure*)	→	高兴 gāoxìng (*cheerful*)
说 shuō (*to speak*)	+	话 huà (*word*)	→	说话 shuōhuà (*to speak*)
吃 chī (*to eat*)	+	饭 fàn (*rice*)	→	吃饭 chīfàn (*to eat*)
毛 máo (*fur*)	+	笔 bǐ (*pen*)	→	毛笔 máobǐ (*writing brush made of fur*)
天 tiān (*sky*)	+	气 qì (*air*)	→	天气 tiānqì (*weather*)
明 míng (*clear; bright*)	+	天 tiān (*sky*)	→	明天 míngtiān (*tomorrow*)
运 yùn (*fortune*)	+	气 qì (*air*)	→	运气 yùnqì (*luck*)

When new words come from abroad, the Chinese have three responses. One is to translate these foreign words into Chinese. The other option is to transliterate them by representing the sounds of a foreign word in Chinese characters. Sometimes translation and transliteration are creatively combined. Therefore, although thousands of new and foreign words are added to the language, very few 字 *zì* are being created.

Here are some examples of translations and transliterations:

Translations	
toothpaste	牙膏 yágāo (*tooth ointment*)
refrigerator	冰箱 bīngxiāng (*icebox*)
car	汽车 qìchē (*gas vehicle*)
rocket	火箭 huǒjiàn (*fire arrow*)
airplane	飞机 fēijī (*fly machine*)
helicopter	直升机 zhíshēngjī (*straight-rising-machine*)
calculator	计算机 jìsuànjī (*figure-count-machine*)
wireless	无线电 wúxiàndiàn (*no-wire electric*)
astronaut	航天员 hángtiānyuán (*avigator-sky-man*)
atom bomb	原子弹 yuánzǐdàn (*atom-bullet*)

	Transliteration
coffee	咖啡 kāfēi
bus	巴士 bāshì
scone	司康 sīkāng
pudding	布丁 bùdīng
vitamin	维他命 wéitāmìng
the Beatles	披头士 Pītóushì (*hair around the shoulders men*)
club	俱乐部 jùlèbù (*a place full of complete happiness*)
chocolate	巧克力 qiǎokèlì

18 按图索骥 Àntú-suǒjì *Analyzing Compound Words*

The following compound words all use the character 电 *diàn*, meaning "electricity," to construct new words. Select the letter of the correct meaning of each Chinese word.

1. 电+视 shì (*watch*)	A. television
2. 电+梯 tī (*ladder*)	B. battery
3. 电+流 liú (*flow*)	C. radio station
4. 电+影 yǐng (*shadow*)	D. trolley car
5. 电+车 chē (*vehicle*)	E. electric current
6. 电+台 tái (*platform*)	F. telephone
7. 电+池 chí (*pool*)	G. movie
7. 电+话 huà (*speech*)	H. elevator

19 外来语 Wàiláiyǔ / *Loan Words with Foreign Origins*

The following words are transliterated from languages other than Chinese. With a partner, take turns pronouncing them and matching them with the correct meaning.

1. 酷 kù	A.	toast
2. 幽浮 yōufú	B.	jacket
3. 马达 mǎdá	C.	gene
4. 香槟 xiāngbīn	D.	guitar
5. 基因 jīyīn	E.	burger
6. 柠檬 níngméng	F.	UFO
7. 吉他 jítā	G.	champagne
8. 土司 tǔsī	H.	lemon
9. 汉堡 hànbǎo	I.	motor
10. 夹克 jiákè	J.	cool

20 他是谁？ Tā shì shéi? / *Who is he/she?*

The following are Chinese translations of American figures. With a partner, take turns pronouncing them and figure out who each person is.

1. 奥巴马 Àobāmǎ	4. 罗斯福 Luósīfú	7. 汤姆克鲁斯 Tāngmǔ Kèlǔsī
2. 林肯 Línkěn	5. 麦当娜 Màidāngnà	8. 乔治克鲁尼 Qiáozhì Kèlǔní
3. 布什 Bùshí	6. 布拉德皮特 Bùlādé Pítè	

21 这是什么地方? Zhè shì shén.me dì.fāng? / *Where is it?*

The following words are Chinese translations of place names in the United States. With a partner, take turns pronouncing them and figure out what they are.

1. 华盛顿 Huáshèngdùn	4. 洛杉矶 Luòshānjī	7. 加利福尼亚 Jiālìfúníyà
2. 纽约 Niǔyuē	5. 芝加哥 Zhījiāgē	8. 拉斯维加斯 Lāsīwéijiāsī
3. 波士顿 Bōshìdùn	6. 密西西比 Mìxīxībǐ	

Communication

Unit 1

你好！ *Nǐ hǎo!*

When you have completed this unit, you will be able to...

- greet someone politely and say goodbye
- introduce yourself and others
- tell what time of day it is
- ask how someone is and tell how you are
- tell someone your nationality, age, and grade in school
- ask someone else's name, nationality, age, and grade in school
- talk about school subjects
- count from one to twenty

Lesson A

发音 Fāyīn
Pronunciation

m n f l + a i o

词汇 Cíhuì
Vocabulary

招呼语 Zhāohūyǔ *Greetings*

老师 (老師)
lǎoshī
n. teacher

校长 (校長)
xiàozhǎng
n. principal

我 (我)
wǒ
pron. I

你 (你)
nǐ
pron. you

您 (您)
nín
pron. you (polite)

先生 (先生)
xiān.shēng
n. Mr.

小姐 (小姐)
xiǎo.jiě
n. Miss

你们 (你們)
nǐ.men
pron. you (plural)

太太 (太太)
tài.tài
n. Mrs.

Nouns

名字（名字）	míng.zì	*name*
们（們）	men	*(a plural suffix for pronouns; sometimes a suffix for nouns)*
中文（中文）	Zhōngwén	*Chinese language*

Demonstratives

这（這）	zhè; zhèi	*this*

Verbs

姓（姓）	xìng	*to be surnamed*
叫（叫）	jiào	*to be called*
是（是）	shì	*to be*

Adjectives

好（好）	hǎo	*good*
贵（貴）	guì	*noble; honored*

Question Words

什么（甚麼）	shén.me	*what*

Particles

呢（呢）	ne	*(a final particle used in follow-up questions)*

Interjections

嘿（嘿）	hei	*Hey*

NOTE: Vocabulary charts in this book will show the simplified Chinese characters, followed by the traditional Chinese characters in parentheses, the Pinyin, and the English translation or explanation.

1 他们说什么? Tā.mén shuō shén.me? *What do they say?*

With a partner, play the roles of two students who say hello to each other at the two different times indicated below.

A.

B.

2 中文怎么说? Zhōngwén zěn.me shuō? *How would you say it in Chinese?*

Write in Pinyin what you say in the following situations.

1. You meet your teacher in the morning.
2. You meet your friends in the cafeteria.
3. You want to ask what another student's name is.
4. You want to greet Miss Song on the street.
5. You greet Mr. and Mrs. Wu at their apartment.

句型介绍 Jùxíng Jièshào
Language Patterns

Greeting Others

To greet others, first we address the person, and then add the greeting.

name/title + **greeting** !

A: 老师，早安！ Lǎoshī, zǎo'ān!

B: 姚祥，早安！ Yáo Xiáng, zǎo'ān!

The Question Word 什么 *shén.me*

The question word 什么 *shén.me* asks "What"? Inserting a noun after 什么 *shén.me* asks for further details about the noun.

什么 *shén.me* + **noun**

A: 你叫什么名字？ Nǐ jiào shén.me míng.zì?

B: 我叫林朋。 Wǒ jiào Lín Péng.

Language Note

To ask someone's last name, we usually say 你/您贵姓 *Nǐ / Nín guì xìng*?. It is more polite and considerate. Young people use the more informal 你姓什么 *Nǐ xìng shén.me*? To reply to both of the questions, just say 我姓.... *Wǒ xìng*.... plus your last name.

中文

The Interrogative Particle 呢 *.ne*

When 呢 *.ne* is used at the end of a sentence, it is an interrogative. If the previous sentence has already provided some context, we can use a new subject or topic followed by 呢 *.ne* to form a question. In Chinese, 呢 *.ne* is used the same way as "how about...?" in English.

declarative sentence + **pronoun** + 呢 *.ne*?

A: 你好！我姓鲁，你呢？ *Nǐ* hǎo! Wǒ xìng Lǔ, nǐ .ne?

B: 我姓钱。 Wǒ xìng Qián.

会话 Huìhuà
Dialogue

你叫什么名字? Nǐ jiào shén.me míng.zì? *What's your name?*

Bai Ping and Zhang Guohua are talking outside the classroom.

白苹:	你好。	Bái Píng:	*Nǐ* hǎo.
张国华:	你好。	Zhāng Guóhuá:	*Nǐ* hǎo.
白苹:	你叫什么名字?	Bái Píng:	Nǐ jiào shén.me míng.zì?
张国华:	我叫张国华，你呢?	Zhāng Guóhuá:	Wǒ jiào Zhāng Guóhuá, nǐ .ne?
白苹:	我姓白，叫白苹。	Bái Píng:	Wǒ xìng Bái, jiào Bái Píng.
张国华:	早安。	Zhāng Guóhuá:	Zǎo'ān.

Lin Shufang approaches them.

林书芳:	你们早。	Lín Shūfāng:	Nǐ.mén zǎo.
张国华:	这是林书芳。	Zhāng Guóhuá:	Zhè shì Lín Shūfāng.
林书芳:	你好。你叫什么名字?	Lín Shūfāng:	*Nǐ* hǎo, nǐ jiào shén.me míng.zì?
白苹:	你好。我叫白苹。	Bái Píng:	*Nǐ* hǎo, wǒ jiào Bái Píng.

3 他们叫什么名字? Tā.mén jiào shén.me míng.zì? *What are their names?*

Complete each sentence with the name of the person.

1. 她叫 Tā jiào ____。
(*She is...*)

2. 他叫 Tā jiào ____。
(*He is...*)

3. 她叫 Tā jiào ____。
(*She is...*)

4 懂了吗? Dǒng .le .ma? *Do you understand?*

Answer the following questions.

1. What are the names of the two people who meet at the beginning of the dialogue?
2. How do they greet each other?
3. Do they know each other's names? How can you tell?
4. What is the name of the third person?
5. What is the time of day?
6. Who knows Lin Shufang? How do you know?

文化橱窗 Wénhuà Chúchuāng

Culture Window

Chinese Names

Chinese names are divided into two parts, last names and first names. Unlike Western names, the last name always precedes the first name. Children usually take their father's last name. Traditionally, wives place their husband's last names before their own, but this custom is hardly practiced anymore.

Chinese family names also stand for a family's origin. In former times, families with the same last name were not allowed to intermarry, but this is no longer enforced.

Most Chinese family names are monosyllabic, such as 陈 *Chén*, 王 *Wáng*, or 林 *Lín*. Two-syllable family names, such as 司马 *Sīmǎ* or 欧阳 *Ōuyáng* are less common. Parents usually give their children a beautiful and meaningful name. For example, if a boy is named 强 *Qiáng*, his parents probably hope for him to be "strong." Let's look at the names of three famous Chinese people.

Ang Lee, a famous director from Taiwan, won an Academy Award for Best Director for the movie Brokeback Mountain in 2006.

姓 (xìng, ***last name***)	名 (míng, ***first name***)	
姚 (Yáo)	明 (Míng, *bright*)	*Ming Yao*
李 (Lǐ)	安 (Ān, *peace*)	*Ang Lee*
马 (Mǎ)	友友 (Yǒu.yǒu, *friend*)	*Yo Yo Ma*

Courtesy in Making Introductions

Usually, Chinese people introduce themselves by giving their full names. On formal occasions, they shake hands and give their names, titles, or positions. When people give out business cards, they deliver them with both hands to show respect. Traditionally, to show respect to older people, superiors, or women, these people are introduced first.

Chinese people give business cards with both hands.

5 文化动动脑 Wénhuà Dòng.dòngnǎo / *Culture Check-up*

On a separate sheet of paper, write a short answer in English for each question.

1. In what order do the Chinese give their first and last names?
2. Today do Chinese women always change their last name when they marry?
3. What do you think was the concern behind the old law that said people with the same last names couldn't marry?
4. Are Chinese last names always monosyllabic and first names always two syllables long?
5. On formal occasions, how do Chinese people greet each other when they meet for the first time?
6. How should a businessperson give his or her business card to others?
7. When introducing your friends to your parents, who should you introduce first? How about introducing your parents to your 24-year-old teacher?

Language Practice

6 找出问题 Zhǎochū Wèntí / *Identify the Questions*

Listen to the following eight sentences, and say "yes" if what you hear is a question or "no" if it is not.

7 谁在说话? Shéi zài shuōhuà? / *Identify the Speaker*

You will hear three dialogues. Choose the photo that corresponds to each one.

A

B

C

开口说 Kāikǒu Shuō
Communication

8 问候同学 Wènhòu Tóngxué / *Greeting a Classmate*

With a partner, play the roles of two students who greet each other at school.

- Say good morning or hi.
- Ask each other's name.
- Tell your name.
- Ask each other's Chinese name.
- Give your Chinese name.

9 介绍他人 Jièshào Tārén / *Introducing Someone*

In the morning, you greet a friend from Chinese class. Then the Chinese exchange student approaches you. Introduce him or her to your friend.

10 名片 Míngpiàn / *Business Card*

Look at the following business cards and then answer the questions that follow. Note: the top one is in simplified characters, and the bottom one is in traditional characters.

1. What are the last names of these two people?
2. How would you address both of these people if you were to meet them for the first time?

汉字天地 Hànzì Tiāndì

Chinese Characters

早 ■ zǎo ■ morning

The character 早 is composed of two individual characters. The 日 on top is the sun in the sky, and the 十 on the bottom stands for the shadow of all things. The two combined represent morning, a time when light and the shadows of all things under the sun can be seen.

Stroke Order

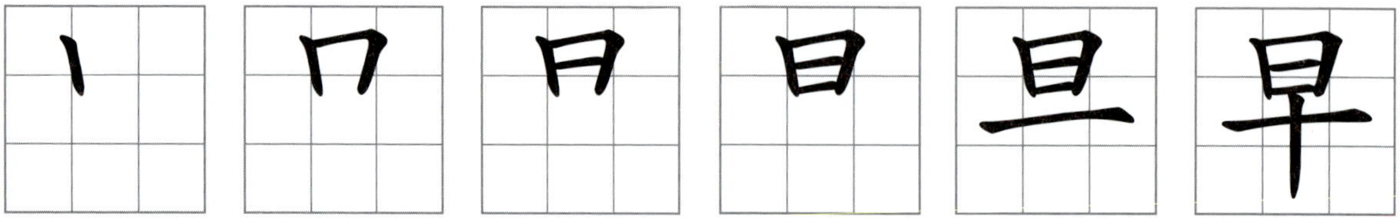

11 词汇延伸 Cíhuì Yánshēn / *Vocabulary Builder*

Below are some characters that can be combined with 早 *zǎo* to create new words. Match the Chinese words on the left with the appropriate English meaning on the right.

餐 cān *n. meal*	安 ān *n. peace*	上 shàng *adj. up*	操 cāo *n. exercise*	晚 wǎn *n. evening*

1. 早餐 zǎocān — A. *morning exercise*
2. 早安 zǎo'ān — B. *sooner or later*
3. 早上 zǎo.shàng — C. *morning*
4. 早操 zǎocāo — D. *breakfast*
5. 早晚 *zǎo*.wǎn — E. *good morning*

12 汉字侦探 Hànzì Zhēntàn / *Visual Detective*

Can you find 早 in the following pictures?

Lesson B

发音 Fāyīn
Pronunciation

m n f l + ai ao

词汇 Cíhuì
Vocabulary

时间词 Shíjiān Cí *Time Words*

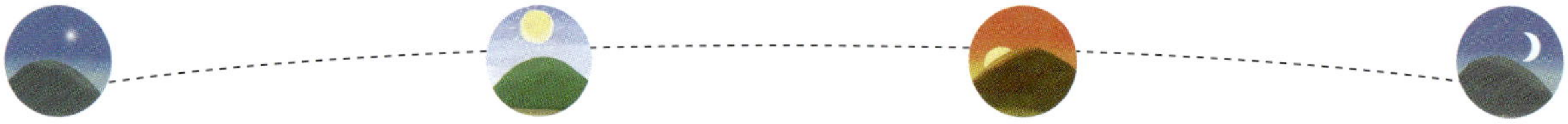

06:00 ~ 12:00	12:00 ~ 13:00	13:00 ~ 18:00	18:00 ~ 24:00
早上 (早上)	中午 (中午)	下午 (下午)	晚上 (晚上)
zǎo.shàng	zhōng.wǔ	xià.wǔ	wǎn.shàng
morning	*the noon hour*	*afternoon*	*evening*

同学 (同學)
tóngxué
n. classmate

好久不见 (好久不見)!
Hǎo jiǔ bú jiàn!
Long time no see!

你好吗 (你好嗎)? *Nǐ* hǎo .ma? *How are you?*

很好 (很好) *hěn* hǎo *great*	不错 (不錯) búcuò *fine*	还行 (還行) hái xíng *not bad*	不太好 (不太好) bú tài hǎo *not so good*

A: 王校长，再见 (王校長，再見)。

Wáng xiàozhǎng, zàijiàn. *Good-bye, Principal Wang.*

B: 罗老师，再见 (羅老師，再見)。

Luó lǎoshī, zàijiàn. *Good-bye, Mr. Luo.*

明天见 (明天見)。

Míng.tiān jiàn. *See you tomorrow.*

一会儿见(一會兒見)。

Yí huìr jiàn. *See you in a little bit.*

最近好吗
(最近好嗎)?
Zuìjìn hǎo .ma?
How have you been lately?

很好，你呢
(很好，你呢)?
Hěn hǎo, nǐ .ne?
Great. How about you?

Adverbs

不（不）	bù / bú	*no; not*
很（很）	hěn	*very*

Auxiliary Verbs

得（得）	děi	*to need; to have to*

Question Words

吗（嗎）	.ma	*(a particle used at the end of a declarative sentence to form a yes/no question)*

Verbs

见（見）	jiàn	*to see*
走（走）	zǒu	*to go; to walk*
去（去）	qù	*to go*

Verb-objects

上课（上課）	shàng-kè	*to go to class*
回家（回家）	huí-jiā	*to go home*
睡觉（睡覺）	shuì-jiào	*to sleep*

1 哈啰 Hā.lou *Hello*

You will listen to a dialogue twice. Say if each of the following statements are true or false based on the dialogue.

1. It is morning.
2. Wang Jing hasn't been well recently.
3. Cai Meili hasn't seen Wang Jing in a long time.
4. Teacher Xiao has been well recently.

2 打招呼 Dǎ zhāohū *Greetings*

With your classmates, greet each other based on the pictures.

3 中文怎么说? Zhōngwén zěn.me shuō? / *How would you say it in Chinese?*

What do you say when you…

1. see the principal as you walk through the school gate in the morning?
2. say good-bye to your teacher after class?
3. meet a friend you haven't seen in a long time?
4. say good-bye to your classmates on the school bus on the way home?
5. are walking to class with your classmates but need to leave?
6. meet a friend you haven't seen for a long time and wish to find out how he's been?
7. say good night to your parents before bed?

4 回应问候 Huíyìng Wènhòu / *Responses to a Greeting*

Select the response to 你好吗? *Nǐ hǎo .ma?* that corresponds to each facial expression.

1. 

2. 

3. 

4. 

A. 还行 Hái xíng

B. 很好 *Hěn* hǎo

C. 不太好 Bú tài hǎo

D. 不错 Búcuò

句型介绍 Jùxíng Jièshào
Language Patterns

The Question Word 吗 *.ma*

A question can be formed by adding 吗 *.ma* to the end of a declarative statement. Responses include 是 *shì* (yes) or 不是 *bú shì* / 不 *bù* (no). The negative answer 不 *bù* is the short answer of 不是 *bú shì*.

Language Note

The original pronunciation of 不 is *bù*. However, when followed by a fourth-tone, it is pronounced as *bú*.

他叫吴柏熊。 Tā jiào Wú Bóxióng.

他叫吴柏熊吗? Tā jiào Wú Bóxióng .ma?

A: 你是苏先生吗? Nǐ shì Sū xiān.shēng .ma?

B: 是，我是。 Shì, wǒ shì.

A: 她是李小姐吗？ Tā shì Lǐ *xiǎo*jiě .ma?

B: 不是，她是林小姐。 Bú shì, tā shì Lín *xiǎo*jiě.

"How are you?" + Response

To ask about someone's condition, give the name of the person or the last name with the title, then add 你好吗 *Nǐ hǎo .ma*?

Name / Last name and title + **你好吗 *Nǐ* hǎo .ma?**

A: Mary，你好吗？ Mary, *nǐ* hǎo .ma?

B: 我很好。 *Wǒ hěn* hǎo.

A: 李校长，你好吗？ Lǐ xiàozhǎng, *nǐ* hǎo .ma?

B: 我很好，谢谢。 *Wǒ hěn* hǎo, xiè.x.

The Auxiliary Verb 得 *děi*

The auxiliary verb 得 *děi* means "to have to" or "must." The pattern below indicates that an action needs to be done shortly.

得 *děi* + **Verb Phrase** + 了 *.le*

A: 我得睡觉了，晚安。 *Wǒ* děi shuì-jiào .le, wǎn'ān.

B: 晚安。 Wǎn'ān.

A: 我得上课了，一会儿见。 *Wǒ* děi shàngkè .le, yí-huìr jiàn.

B: 一会儿见。 Yí-huìr jiàn.

会话 Huìhuà
Dialogue

你好吗？ *Nǐ* hǎo .ma? *How are you?*

Lin Shufang and Zhang Guohua meet each other at the entrance of the school.

张国华：	林书芳，下午好。	Zhāng Guóhuá:	Lín Shūfāng, xià.*wǔ* hǎo.
林书芳：	张国华，下午好。	Lín Shūfāng:	Zhāng Guóhuá, xià.*wǔ* hǎo.
张国华：	你好吗？	Zhāng Guóhuá:	*Nǐ* hǎo .ma?
林书芳：	很好，谢谢。你呢？	Lín Shūfāng:	*Hěn* hǎo, xiè.x. Nǐ .ne?
张国华：	不错。	Zhāng Guóhuá:	Búcuò.

Bai Ping comes and joins them.

白苹：	你们好。	Bái Píng:	Nǐ.mén hǎo.
林书芳：	你好吗？	Lín Shūfāng:	*Nǐ* hǎo .ma?
白苹：	很好，谢谢你。	Bái Píng:	*Hěn* hǎo, xiè.x nǐ.
张国华：	我得走了。再见。	Zhāng Guóhuá:	*Wǒ děi* zǒu .le. Zàijiàn.
白苹：	再见。	Bái Píng:	Zàijiàn.

5 懂了吗？ Dǒng .le .ma? / *Do you understand?*

Answer the following questions.

1. What are the names of the two people who meet at the beginning of the dialogue?
2. What do they say to greet each other?
3. How is Zhang Guohua?
4. Which character is doing better today?
5. Who comes to join Zhang Guohua and Lin Shufang?
6. Who has to leave first in the second part of the dialogue?

6 他们好吗？ Tā.men hǎo .ma? / *How are they?*

With a partner, take turns asking and telling how you are. One of you asks the question. The other answers for the characters based on the dialogue.

❶ 

❷ 

❸ 

Lì.zi: A: 林书芳，你好吗？
Lín Shūfāng, *nǐ* hǎo .ma?

B: 很好。
Hěn hǎo.

文化橱窗 Wénhuà Chúchuāng

Culture Window

Bow with hands clasped (拱手作揖, gǒngshǒu zuòyī)

In ancient China, behavior was restricted by rigid social hierarchies. People of a different social status could not speak to each other without good reason, and even those from the same social circle followed complex rules in greeting each other. Smiling at another person, or having any kind of physical contact, such as hand-holding or hugging, was considered impolite or even offensive. In this cultural environment, 拱手作揖 *gǒngshǒu zuòyī* developed. The expression 拱手 *gǒngshǒu means* "to make fists with both hands and raise them to the chest" and 作揖 *zuòyī means* "to bow." The concept of 拱手作揖 *gǒngshǒu zuòyī* allowed people to express courtesy and respect in a restrained and formal manner.

Nowadays, most Chinese use gestures (a nod of the head, a smile, or a wave) to greet others. A traditional greeting is 吃了吗? *Chī .le .ma*? ("Have you eaten?"). This expression developed because China's population used to be comprised mainly of farmers, who needed a good meal to have the strength to work in the fields. In modern times, there are fewer people working in agriculture, which makes this greeting irrelevant. As a result, is it now mostly used by the older generation, and most young people just greet each other with 你好 *Nǐ hǎo*.

Comparisons

1. How do young people in the United States greet each other?
2. Generally, are the Chinese or Americans more demonstrative in their greetings and leave-takings?

Taboos when saying good-bye

In Western society, bidding someone good-bye is very common. However, the Chinese do not use the phrase 再见 *zàijiàn* ("good-bye") on some occasions. The word 再 *zài* means "again," while 见 *jiàn* means "to see." Hence, 再见 *zàijiàn* literally means "to see someone again," After ceremonies such as funerals and wakes, some Chinese people will leave quietly without saying goodbye to one another, believing that saying 再见 *zàijiàn* is a bad omen that could cause another sad gathering.

7 文化动动脑 Wénhuà Dòng.dòngnăo / *Culture Check-up*

Write a short answer in English for each question, or do what is asked.

1. In the past, why couldn't the Chinese talk to anyone they wanted?
2. Greet your classmate in Chinese using the 拱手作揖 *gǒngshǒu zuòyī* pose and gesture.
3. What insight do you get into ancient Chinese culture by learning about the greeting 拱手作揖 *gǒngshǒu zuòyī*?
4. How do younger Chinese people greet each other today? Are there any special gestures?
5. What is the cultural significance behind the greeting 吃了没？ *Chī .le méi?*
6. In which situations is saying "good-bye" a taboo for the Chinese? Why?

Language Practice

8 角色扮演 Juésè Bànyǎn / *Role Play*

Complete the dialogue between two friends. Then, with a partner, say the dialogue aloud.

1. **A:** ___！
2. **B:** 早！Zǎo!
3. **A:** ___？
4. **B:** 很好。___？ *Hěn* hǎo. ___?
5. **A:** 还行，谢谢。Hái xíng, xiè.x.
6. **B:** 林华最近好吗？Lín Huá zuìjìn hǎo .ma?
7. **A:** 她最近___。她生病了。Tā zuìjìn___. Tā shēngbìng .le
8. **B:** 我得___了。*Wǒ* děi ___ .le.
9. **A:** 我得回家了。*Wǒ* děi huí-jiā .le.
10. **B:** ____。
11. **A:** 再见。Zàijiàn.

9 换句话说 Huàn jù huà shuō *Forming Questions*

Change the following declarative statements into questions by adding 吗 *.ma.*

1. 这是白华。 Zhè shì Bái Huá.
2. 大卫姓张。 Dàwèi xìng Zhāng.
3. 她叫林安安。 Tā jiào Lín Ān'ān.
4. 芳芳生病了。 Fāngfāng shēngbìng .le.
5. 谢老师很好。 Xiè lǎoshī *hěn* hǎo.
6. 你得上课了。 *Nǐ* děi shàng-kè .le.
7. 他们得回家了。 Tā.mén děi huí-jiā .le.

10 他们得做什么? Tā.men děi zuò shén.me? *What do they have to do?*

Say what each person has to do.

❶

林安安 Lín Ān'ān

❷

董国 Dǒng Guó 董书 Dǒng Shū

❸
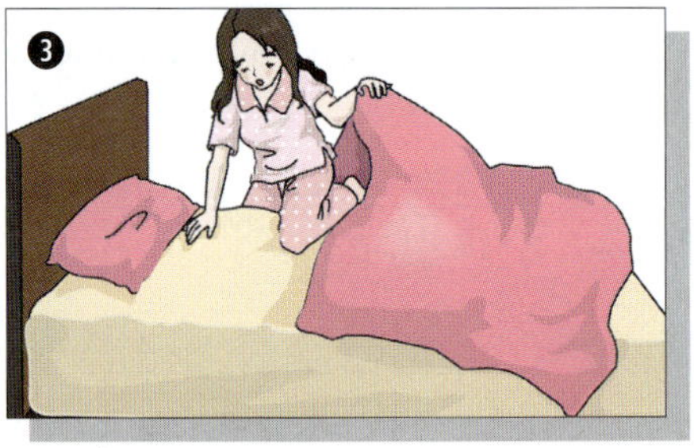
张芳 Zhāng Fāng

❹

李文 Lǐ Wén

开口说 Kāikǒu Shuō *Communication*

11 问候同学 Wènhòu Tóngxué *Greeting a Classmate*

With a partner, play the roles of two students who greet each other at school.

A: Say your classmate's name, and wish him/her "good morning" or "good afternoon." Then ask how he or she is.

B: Greet your classmate and say how you are.

A: Say you must leave.

B: Say good-bye.

12 问候朋友 Wènhòu Peng.you / *Greeting a Friend*

With a partner, take turns asking and telling how you are, based on the visual cues. Begin by greeting each other.

13 聊天室 Liáotiānshì / *Chat Room*

Sharon has an online friend in China whom she communicates with in the evening. Fill in the blanks in the conversation using an appropriate expression from the box. Then answer the questions that follow.

A. 好久不见 *hǎo* jiǔ bú jiàn
B. 再见 zàijiàn
C. 晚上好 wǎn.shàng hǎo
D. 陈先生好吗 Chén xiān.shēng hǎo .ma

陈芳Chén Fāng: 晚上好！ Wǎn.shàng hǎo!
Sharon: (1.)___
陈芳Chén Fāng: 好久不见！ *Hǎo* jiǔ bú jiàn!
Sharon: (2.)___
陈芳Chén Fāng: 你最近好吗？ Nǐ zuìjìn hǎo .ma?
Sharon: ☺我很好！ *Wǒ hěn* hǎo! (3.)___？
陈芳Chén Fāng: 他不太好。他最近生病了。 Tā bú tài hǎo. Tā zuìjìn shēngbìng .le.
Sharon: 😳
陈芳Chén Fāng: 我得做晚饭了。明天见！ *Wǒ* děi zuò wǎnfàn .le. Míng.tiān jiàn!
Sharon: 好，(4.)___。

5. What's the name of Sharon's online friend?
6. Based on this conversation, when will Sharon next chat with her?

14 传简讯 Chuán Jiǎnxùn / *Sending a Text Message*

Jin Ming asked his classmate Wang Mu if he had time to play basketball, and got the text message that follows in reply. Read the message. Then answer the questions that follow.

金铭 Jīn Míng:

早上我得上课，下午好吗？

Zǎo.shàng *wǒ* děi shàng-kè, xià.*wǔ* hǎo .ma?

王沐 Wáng Mù

1. When does Wang Mu want to play basketball?
2. Can Wang Mu make it at the time Jin Ming proposed? If not, why?
3. If Jin Ming had time, how would he have replied to Wang Mu's message?

汉字天地 Hànzì Tiāndì

Chinese Characters

见 (見) ■ jiàn ■ *to see*

From the Oracle Bones Script (罒) of the character 见, we can see that it is in the form of a person with his eyes wide open and looking forward. As time passed, the pictograph became more linear and evolved to 見, which has been simplified as 见.

Stroke Order

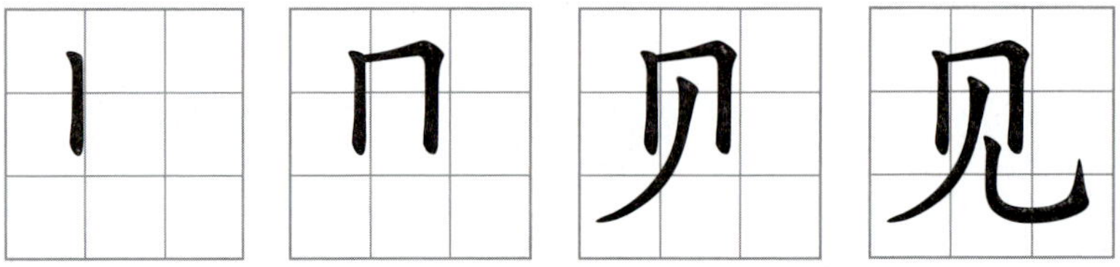

15 词汇延伸 Cíhuì Yánshēn / *Vocabulary Builder*

Below are some characters that can be combined with 见 *jiàn* to create new words. Match the Chinese words on the left with the appropriate English meaning on the right.

面 miàn *n. face*	闻 wén *n. to hear*	再 zài *adv. again*	习 xí *v. to practice*	主 zhǔ *n. master*

1. 见面 jiànmiàn — *A. one's own judgment*
2. 见闻 jiànwén — *B. to meet*
3. 再见 zàijiàn — *C. good-bye*
4. 见习 jiànxí — *D. knowledge*
5. 主见 zhǔjiàn — *E. internship*

16 汉字侦探 Hànzì Zhēntàn / *Visual Detective*

Can you find 见 (見) in the following pictures?

Lesson C

发音 Fāyīn
Pronunciation

m n f l + an ang

词汇 Cíhuì
Vocabulary

Pronouns			
我（我）wǒ	*I*	我们（我們）wǒ.mén	*we*
你（你）nǐ	*you*	你们（你們）nǐ.mén	*you (plural)*
他（他）tā	*he*	他们（他們）tā.mén	*they (m.)*
她（她）tā	*she*	她们（她們）tā.mén	*they (f.)*
它（它）tā	*it*	它们（它們）tā.mén	*they (neuter)*

国家 Guójiā *Countries*

美国(美國)
Měi.guó
United States

中国(中國)
Zhōng.guó
China

英国(英國)
Yīng.guó
England

德国(德國)
Dé.guó
Germany

法国(法國)
Fǎ.guó
France

西班牙(西班牙)
Xībānyá
Spain

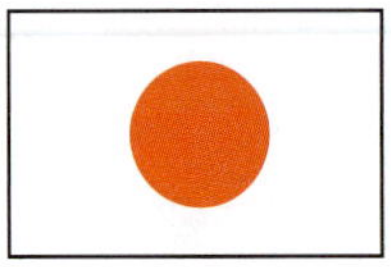
日本(日本)
Rìběn
Japan

韩国(韓國)
Hán.guó
Korea

意大利(義大利)
Yìdàlì
Italy

加拿大(加拿大)
Jiā'nádà
Canada

新加坡(新加坡)
Xīnjiāpō
Singapore

印度(印度)
Yìndù
India

泰国(泰國)
Tài.guó
Thailand

马来西亚(馬來西亞)
Mǎláixīyà
Malaysia

越南(越南)
Yuènán
Vietnam

Language Note

Saying nationalities in Chinese is simple. Just combine the name of the country with 人 *rén*.

Name of Country + 人 *rén* = **Nationality**

For example,
"墨西哥 *Mòxīgē* Mexico" + "人 *rén*" = "墨西哥人 *Mòxīgērén* Mexican"

我是意大利人，你呢
(我是義大利人，你呢)?
Wǒ shì Yìdàlìrén, nǐ .ne?
I'm Italian. How about you?

我是加拿大人
(我是加拿大人)。
Wǒ shì Jiā'nádàrén.
I'm Canadian.

A: 你是德国人吗 (你是德國人嗎)?
Nǐ shì Dé.guórén .ma? *Are you German?*

B: 不，我是西班牙人 (不，我是西班牙人)。
Bù, wǒ shì Xībānyárén. *No, I'm Spanish.*

你是哪国人
(你是哪國人)?
Nǐ shì nǎi-guó rén?
What's your nationality?

他是韩国人，我们是中国人 (他是韓國人，我們是中國人)。
Tā shì Hán.guórén, wǒ.mén shì Zhōng.guórén.
He's Korean, and we are Chinese.

A: 很高兴认识你 (很高興認識你)。
Hěn gāoxìng rèn shí nǐ. *Nice to meet you.*

B: 我也很高兴认识你 (我也很高興認識你)。
Wǒ yě hěn gāoxìng rèn shí nǐ. *Nice to meet you, too.*

我是中国人
(我是中國人)。
Wǒ shì Zhōng.guórén.
I'm Chinese.

Adjectives

高兴 (高興)	gāoxìng	*happy; glad*

Adverbs

也 (也)	yě	*also; too*

Interjections

嗨 (嗨)	hāi	*hi; hello*

Nouns

国 (國)	guó	*country*
人 (人)	rén	*person; people*
课 (課)	kè	*class; course*
朋友 (朋友)	péng.yǒu	*friend*

Pronouns

大家 (大家)	dàjiā	*all; everyone*

Question Words

哪 (哪)	nǎ	*which*

Verbs

问 (問)	wèn	*to ask*
请问 (請問)	qǐngwèn	*may I ask*
认识 (認識)	rèn shí	*to know (people)*

1 他们是哪国人? Tā.men shì něi-guó rén? *What are their nationalities?*

You will hear three dialogues. Select the letter of the flags that represent the people's nationalities that you hear.

2 他们从哪儿来? Tā.men cóng shì nǎr lái.de? / *Where are they from?*

Tell where each tourist in Beijing is from, based on his or her country's flag.

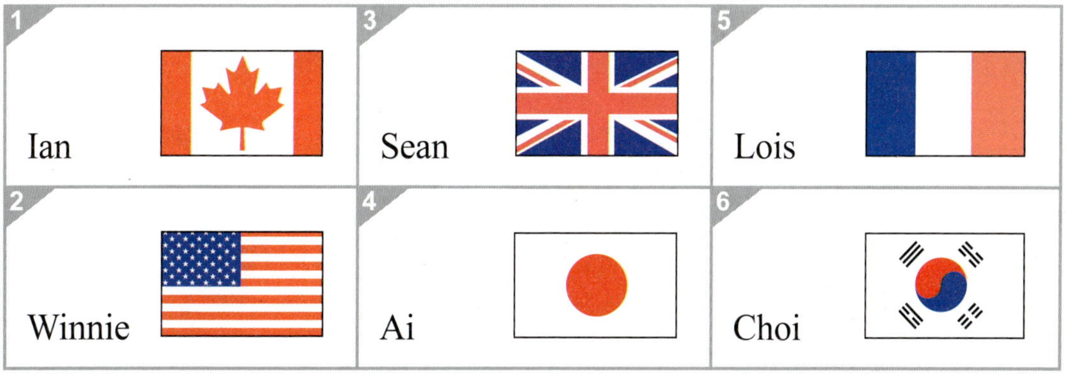

3 谁认识谁? Shéi rèn shí shéi? / *Who knows whom?*

Ask your partner if the first person from the dialogue knows the second. Your partner will respond, based on his or her knowledge of the dialogues.

Lì.zi: *(Model)* 白苹Bái Píng / 张国华 Zhāng Guóhuá

A: 白苹认识张国华吗? Bái Píng rèn shí Zhāng Guóhuá .ma?

B: 白苹认识张国华。 Bái Píng rèn shí Zhāng Guóhuá.

1. 张国华 Zhāng Guóhuá / 林书芳 Lín Shūfāng

2. 林书芳 Lín Shūfāng / 董军 Dǒng Jūn

3. 董军 Dǒng Jūn / 张国华 Zhāng Guóhuá

4. 张国华 Zhāng Guóhuá / 白苹 Bái Píng

5. 白苹 Bái Píng / 林书芳 Lín Shūfāng

4 中文怎么说? Zhōngwén zěn.me shuō? / *How would you say it in Chinese?*

Imagine you are an exchange student in China. What would you say in the following situations?

1. You want to greet the student next to you.
2. You want to tell the student your name.
3. You want to tell the student your nationality.
4. You ask if the student knows the teacher.
5. You ask if the student is Chinese.

句型介绍 Jùxíng Jièshào

Language Patterns

The Particle 的 *.de*

The particle 的 *.de* is used between a modifier and a noun. The modifier plus 的 *.de* always precede the noun.

Modifier + 的 *.de* + **noun / pronoun**

我的朋友 wǒ.de péng.yǒu

我们的老师 wǒ.mén.de lǎoshī

Modifiers can be other nouns, pronouns, adjectives, or whole clauses as in these examples:

老师的姓 lǎoshī .de xìng

我的名字 wǒ.de míng.zì

很好的朋友 *hěn* hǎo .de péng.yǒu

那个姓张的学生 nèi.-ge xìng Zhāng .de xué.shēng

Comparisons

What are "my" and "our" called in English? What are the corresponding forms for "you," "he," "she," and "they"?

The Question Word 哪 *nǎ*

The question word 哪 *nǎ (něi)* is used to make inquiries, similar to "which" in English. It is usually followed by a measure word and then a noun. The words in this type of question follow the word order of a declarative sentence. The phrase 哪国人 *něi*-guó rén* is used to ask what someone's nationality is.

哪 *nǎ* + **Measure Word** + **Noun?**

A: 你是哪国人? Nǐ shì něi-guó rén?

B: 我是美国人。 Wǒ shì Měi.guórén.

A: 请问你是哪国人? Qǐngwèn nǐ shì něi-guó rén?

B: 我是英国人。你呢? Wǒ shì Yīng.guórén. Nǐ .ne?

A: 我是法国人。 Wǒ shì Fǎ.guórén.

墨西哥 Mòxīgē *Mexico*

Language Note

The question word 哪 *nǎ* is pronounced *něi* when it is followed by a measure word.

哪个 *něi-.ge*? 哪国 *něi-guó*?

The Adverb 也 *yě*

The adverb 也 *yě* means "too" or "also." In Chinese, adverbs always precede verbs; therefore, it cannot move around in a sentence. Also, note that adverbs cannot appear without a corresponding verb. Thus, there is no equivalent in Chinese of the shortened English form "Me too."

Subject + **也 *yě*** + **(negation)** + **Verb**

A: 我是加拿大人。 Wǒ shì Jiā'nádàrén.

B: 我也是加拿大人。 *Wǒ* yě shì Jiā'nádàrén.

A: 我不是日本人。 Wǒ bú shì Rìběnrén.

B: 我也不是日本人。 *Wǒ* yě bú shì Rìběnrén.

Comparisons

Is "too" locked into one position by the verb in an English sentence? Look at the examples below:

He too is my friend.

He is my friend too.

The Negative Adverb 不 *bù / bú*

The adverb 不 *bù / bú* is used to make an affirmative sentence negative.

Noun / Pronoun + **不 *bù / bú*** + **Adjective / Verb**

我不是日本人。我是美国人。 Wǒ bú shì Rìběnrén. Wǒ shì Měi.guórén.

A: 你是黄依吗？ Nǐ shì Huáng Yī .ma?

B: 不，我不是黄依。我是黄怡。 Bù, wǒ bú shì Huáng Yī. Wǒ shì Huáng Yí.

Language Note

The original pronunciation of 不 is *bù*. However, when followed by a fourth-tone, it is pronounced as *bú*.

不高兴 *bù gāoxìng*; 不回家 *bù huí-jiā*; 不好 *bù hǎo*; 不错 *bú cuò*.

会话 Huìhuà

Dialogue

外国交换学生 Wàiguó Jiāohuàn Xué.shēng

The Foreign Exchange Student

At school, Lin Shufang is talking to Dong Jun.

林书芳：你好，我叫林书芳。

董军：你好，我的名字叫董军。很高兴认识你。

林书芳：你是哪国人？

董军：我是韩国人，你也是韩国人吗？

林书芳：不是，我是中国人。

Lín Shūfāng: *Nǐ* hǎo, wǒ jiào Lín Shūfāng.

Dǒng Jūn: *Nǐ* hǎo, wǒ.de míng.zì jiào Dǒng Jūn. Hěn gāoxìng rèn shí nǐ.

Lín Shūfāng: Nǐ shì něi-guó rén?

Dǒng Jūn: Wǒ shì Hán.guórén, *nǐ* yě shì Hán.guórén .ma?

Lín Shūfāng: Bú shì, wǒ shì Zhōng.guórén.

Teacher Li approaches them.

李老师：林书芳、董军，你们好。

董、林：李老师好。

李老师：你们是日本人吗？

林书芳：不是，他是韩国人，我是中国人。

Lǐ lǎoshī: Lín Shūfāng, Dǒng Jūn, nǐ.mén hǎo.

Dǒng, Lín: *Lǐ* lǎoshī hǎo.

Lǐ lǎoshī: Nǐ.mén shì Rìběnrén .ma?

Lín Shūfāng: Bú shì, tā shì Hán.guórén, wǒ shì Zhōng.guórén.

5 懂了吗？ Dǒng .le .ma? *Do you understand?*

Answer the following questions.

1. How many people are there in the dialogue?
2. What are their names?
3. Where do the boy and the girl come from?
4. Later, who approaches and talks to them?
5. Where does the teacher think these two students are probably from?

6 他们是哪国人？ Tā.mén shì něi-guó rén? *What are their nationalities?*

Tell the nationality of the following two people in the dialogue.

文化橱窗 Wénhuà Chúchuāng

Culture Window

The Importance of Titles

The Chinese place a lot of importance on titles, which may reflect a person's age, social standing, and gender. For example, to address a teacher, you should always use the title 老师 *lǎoshī* instead of 先生 *xiān.shēng* (Mr.) or 太太 *tài.tài* (Mrs.). Also, in situations where an employee is addressing his or her manager, it would be more polite to address him as 经理 *jīnglǐ* (manager) instead of just 先生 *xiān.shēng* (Mr.).

Addressing someone correctly shows good manners, while a title misspoken may result in offending the addressee. For example, we can examine how married women are addressed traditionally. The title 大姐 *dàjiě* refers to women who are married and a little bit older than you, 大嫂 *dàsǎo* is used to address women who are married and older than you, and 伯母 *bómǔ* refers to women who are married and a lot older than you. If one of these titles were used to address a young lady, that young lady might feel extremely insulted. Therefore, it is always better to address women as 小姐 *xiǎojiě* (Miss) or 女士 *nǚshì* (Ms.). Another form of address, 女士 *nǚshì*, is a more polite form for addressing ladies.

The Chinese Meaning of "China"

The literal meaning of China (中国 *Zhōng guó*) is "middle kingdom." This is because in ancient China, as in many other ancient cultures, people naturally thought that their country was the center of the known world. As Chinese culture became more advanced and compared itself with its neighbors, 中国 *Zhōng guó* came to connote more than a simple geographical concept—that China was the center of civilization, with its emperor the leader.

Neighboring Countries

China has long had interactions with its neighboring countries in trade, art, scholarship, and culture. An early example is the Silk Road in Xinjiang that connected China to the Mideast and Europe 2,000 years ago for the exportation of silk, tea, and other desirable products. During the Tang Dynasty (618-907 A.D.), China influenced Japan's political, economic, and social systems, as well as its system of writing. Of all its neighboring countries in Asia, China continues to interact the most with Japan and Korea. Every year, the import and export figures from these two neighbors are ranked right at the top. Academic exchange, too, is frequent. For example, Beijing's University of Technology has a cooperative relationship with many institutions in Japan, including Tokyo University of Technology, Hokkaido University, and Kyushu University. South China Normal University also has an exchange program with Korea's Chung-Ang, Hangyang, and Kongyang Universities.

▲ Camels are a means of transportation in Silk Road.

7 文化动动脑 Wénhuà Dòng.dòngnǎo / *Culture Check-up*

On a separate sheet of paper, write a short answer in English for each question.

1. What areas of a person's life might a title refer to?
2. Why may one person have different titles?
3. Why is it important to address someone correctly?
4. What sort of person would you address using 大姐 *dàjiě*, 大嫂 *dàsǎo*, or 伯母 *bómǔ*?
5. What is the literal meaning of 中国 *Zhōng.guó*?
6. What was the name of the transportation link China used for trade with the Mideast and Europe?
7. What did China export to other countries at that time?
8. During which dynasty did the Japanese adopt written Chinese?
9. China has the closest relations with which two of its neighboring countries?
10. What types of exchanges are frequent amongst China and Japan and Korea?

▶ Many students from neighboring countries come to China to study.

Language Practice

8 校园关系 Xiàoyuán Guānxì / *Relationships at School*

Form sentences using 的 *.de* to show people's relationships at school.

Lì.zi: *Mr. Li / Luo Ming's / teacher*
李先生是罗明的老师。Lǐ xiān.shēng shì Luó Míng .de lǎoshī.

1. Wesley / Tiffany's / classmate
2. he / Miss Jones'/ friend
3. Mrs. Wong / Lance's / principal
4. Feng / Mr. Fang's / student
5. Zhiqiang / Mrs. Wang's / student

9 他/她是哪国人？ Tā/tā shì něi-guó rén? / *Where is he/she from?*

With a partner, take turns asking and telling the nationalities of the teens on the map.

Lì.zi: **A:** Sakura是哪国人？ Sakura shì něi-guó rén?
B: Sakura是日本人。 Sakura shì Rìběnrén.

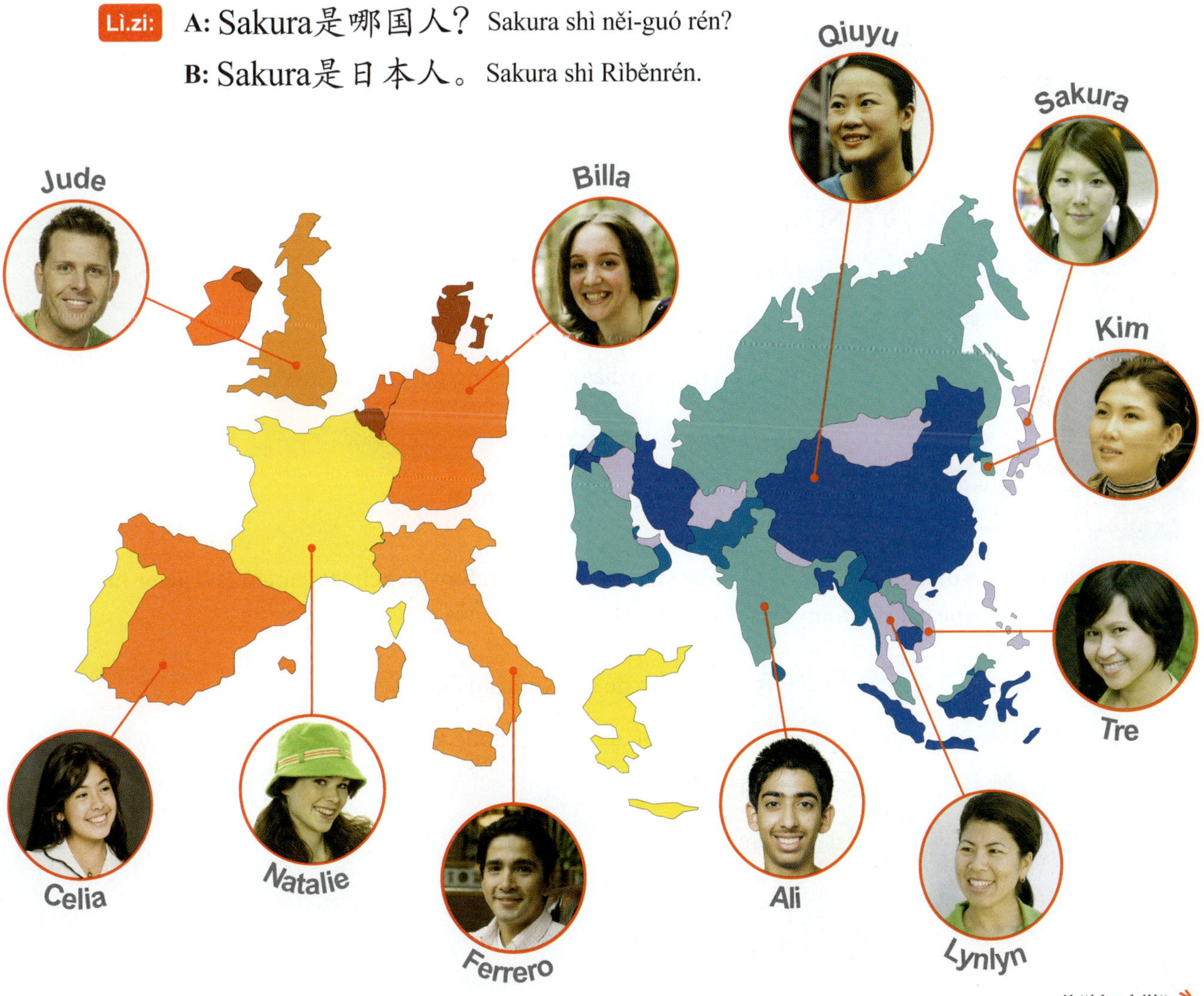

10 他/她也是… Tā/ tā yě shì… *He/She is also from....*

Write sentences saying that the second person is from the same country as the first.

Lì.zi: Peter是英国人。Peter shì Yīng.guórén. (Felicity)
Felicity也是英国人。Felicity yě shì Yīng.guórén.

1. 东是中国人。Dong shì Zhōng.guórén. (Wenrong)
2. Yu 是马来西亚人。Yu shì Mǎláixīyàrén. (Feng)
3. Treva 是加拿大人。Treva shì Jiā'nádàrén. (Sasha)
4. Claudia 是德国人。Claudia shì Dé.guórén. (Helena)
5. Paul 新加坡人。Paul shì Xīnjiāpōrén. (Patrick)

11 回答问题 Huídá Wèntí *Answer the Questions*

With a partner, take turns asking and answering the questions.

Lì.zi: **A:** 你叫Linda吗？Nǐ jiào Linda .ma?
B: 不，我不叫Linda，我叫Alice。Bú, wǒ bú jiào Linda, wǒ jiào Alice.

1. 你姓Copperfield吗？Nǐ xìng Copperfield .ma?
2. 你叫Kerwin吗？Nǐ jiào Kerwin .ma?
3. 你是法国人吗？Nǐ shì Fǎ.guórén .ma?
4. 你是老师吗？Nǐ shì lǎoshī .ma?
5. 你的校长是中国人吗？Nǐ.de xiàozhǎng shì Zhōng.guórén .ma?

12 听力练习 Tīnglì Liànxí *Listening Practice*

Listen to the dialogue followed by four statements below. Say if each statement is true or false based on the dialogue. Correct any false statements.

1. 男的(*male voice*)是新加坡人。Nán.de shì Xīnjiāpōrén.
2. 女的(*female voice*)也是中国人。Nǚ.de yě shì Zhōng.guórén.
3. 男的姓梁。Nán.de xìng Liáng.
4. 女的不姓梁。Nǚ.de bú xìng Liáng.

13 听力练习 Tīnglì Liànxí / *Listening Practice*

You will hear four mini-dialogues. Choose the photo that corresponds to each one.

开口说 Kāikǒu Shuō

Communication

14 认识新朋友 Rèn shí Xīn Péng.yǒu / *Meeting New Friends*

You are at a party for foreign exchange students in Shanghai. Working with two partners, play the parts of the students as they get to know each other.

A, B, C: Introduce yourselves.

A: Ask the nationality of the other exchange students.

B: Say you are Korean.

C: Say you are Indian.

A: Say that it is nice to meet them.

B: Say you must go.

C: Say good-bye.

15 介绍 Jièshào *Introductions*

With a partner, write a dialogue for this situation: two foreign exchange students meet and exchange information in Chinese, giving their names and telling where they're from.

16 他/她是哪国人? Tā/tā shì něi-guórén? *Where is he / she from?*

Each name tag below has the name of an exchange student and the flag of the country he or she is from. The teacher has matched up the exchange students with the American students, who are going to give the exchange students their name tags. Answer the questions that follow.

A.

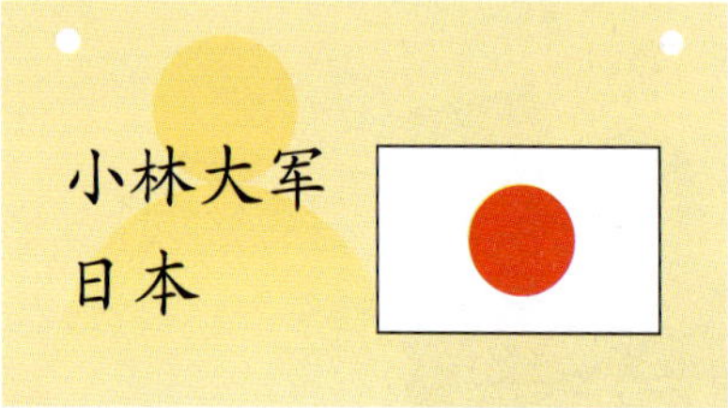

B.

C.

1. Which name tag does Brent give to Dong Fangshu?
2. Which name tag does Alicia give to Zhang Jian?
3. Which name tag does Mark give to Xiaolin Dajun?

17 他/她是… Tā/ tā shì… *He/She is from....*

This is a list of foreign exchange students attending a school in Haerbin this year. With a partner, take turns asking and telling where each exchange student is from.

Lì.zi: **A:** Trong是越南人，对不对? Trong shì Yuènánrén, duì.bú duì?
B: 对，他是越南人。 Duì, tā shì Yuènánrén.

外国交换学生 Wàiguó Jiāohuàn Xué.shēng *Foreign Exchange Students*

名字 **Míng.zì** ***Name***	国籍 **Guójí** ***Nationality***
1. Antony Chaumont	French
2. Henry Wei	Singaporean
3. Julia McNeil	Canadian
4. Marylene Kayser	German
5. Susumu Yokohama	Japanese
6. Tanya Escobar	Spanish
7. Trong Nuyn	Vietnamese
8. Yoon Kim	Korean

汉字天地 Hànzì Tiāndì

Chinese Characters

人 ■ rén ■ person; people

The pictograph 人 *rén* originally depicted a man standing sideways with his hands stretched out. Gradually it transformed into the character in use now. It is also a common radical for words related to a person or people. When 人 *rén* is used as the radical for other words, is often written as 亻.

Stroke Order

丿 人

18 词汇延伸 Cíhuì Yánshēn *Vocabulary Builder*

Below are some characters that can be combined with 人 *rén* to create new words. Match the Chinese words on the left with the appropriate English meaning on the right.

生 shēng	口 kǒu	亲 qīn	情 qíng	超 chāo
n. existence	*m. a measure word for people*	*adj. related by blood*	*n. affection*	*suf. super*

1. 人生 rénshēng
2. 人口 rénkǒu
3. 亲人 qīnrén
4. 情人 qíngrén
5. 超人 chāorén

A. *superman*
B. *kinsfolk*
C. *population*
D. *sweetheart*
E. *life*

19 汉字侦探 Hànzì Zhēntàn *Visual Detective*

Can you find 人 in the following pictures?

Lesson D

发音 Fāyīn
Pronunciation

b p + a ai ao an ang

词汇 Cíhuì
Vocabulary

在学校里 Zài xuéxiào lǐ *In the school*

Common Subjects in Chinese High Schools			
语文(語文) yǔwén *language arts*	英语(英語) Yīngyǔ *English*	外语(外語) wàiyǔ *foreign language*	数学(數學) shùxué *math*
历史(歷史) lìshǐ *history*	地理(地理) dìlǐ *geography*	物理(物理) wùlǐ *physics*	化学(化學) huàxué *chemistry*
生物(生物) shēngwù *biology*	音乐(音樂) yīnyuè *music*		美术(美術) měishù *art*
信息技术(信息技術) xìnxī jìshù *information technology*	通用技术(通用技術) tōngyòng jìshù *general technology*	政治(政治) zhèngzhì *political education*	体育(體育) tǐyù *physical education*

Other Subjects			
中文(中文) Zhōngwén *Chinese*	法语(法語) Fǎyǔ *French*	德语(德語) Déyǔ *German*	西班牙语(西班牙語) Xībānyáyǔ *Spanish*
写作(寫作) xiězuò *composition*	文学(文學) wénxué *literature*	计算机科学(計算機科學) jìsuànjī kēxué *computer science*	
乐队(樂隊) yuèduì *band*		合唱团(合唱團) héchàngtuán *choir*	戏剧(戲劇) xìjù *theater*

中学 (中學) zhōngxué *n. high school*		中学生(中學生) zhōngxué.shēng *n. high school student*	
初中(初中) chūzhōng *n. junior high school*	高中(高中) gāozhōng *n. senior high school*	初中生(初中生) chūzhōng.shēng *n. junior high school student*	高中生(高中生) gāozhōng.shēng *n. senior high school student*

Junior High and High School Grades

	7th grade	8th grade	9th grade	10th grade	11th grade	12th grade
美国	七年级 (七年級) qī-niánjí	八年级 (八年級) bā-niánjí	九年级 (九年級) jiǔ-niánjí	十年级 (十年級) shí-niánjí	十一年级 (十一年級) shíyī-niánjí	十二年级 (十二年級) shí'èr-niánjí
中国	初中一年级 (初中一年級) chūzhōng yì-niánjí	初中二年级 (初中二年級) chūzhōng èr-niánjí	初中三年级 (初中三年級) chūzhōng sān-niánjí	高中一年级 (高中一年級) gāozhōng yì-niánjí	高中二年级 (高中二年級) gāozhōng èr-niánjí	高中三年级 (高中三年級) gāozhōng sān-niánjí

我学数学 (我學數學)。

Wǒ xué shùxué. *I study math.*

林老师是我的数学老师 (林老師是我的數學老師)。

Lín lǎoshī shì wǒ.de shùxué lǎoshī. *Miss Lin is my math teacher.*

我上日语。他上德语。(我上日語。他上德語)。

Wǒ shàng Rìyǔ. Tā xiū Déyǔ. *I take Japanese. He takes German.*

A: 你上几年级?

Nǐ shàng jǐ-niánjí? *What grade are you in?*

B: 我上三年级。

Wǒ shàng sān-niánjí. *I'm in the third grade.*

Let's count!

0	1	2	3	4	5	6	7	8	9	10
零 líng	一 yī	二 èr	三 sān	四 sì	五 wǔ	六 liù	七 qī	八 bā	九 jiǔ	十 shí

Numbers in Chinese are easy to learn. For example, the number 11 is *shíyī*, a combination of *shí* (10) and *yī* (1). In the same vein, the number 20 is *èr* (2) and *shí* (10) put together. The numbers 11 to 20 are listed below.

11	12	13	14	15	16	17	18	19	20
十一 shíyī	十二 shí'èr	十三 shísān	十四 shísì	十五 shíwǔ	十六 shíliù	十七 shíqī	十八 shíbā	十九 shíjiǔ	二十 èr.shí

To say "tens," just put the cardinal numbers 2 to 9 before 10 *shí* (as shown in the table below.)

From 10 to 100:

10	20	30	40	50	60	70	80	90	100
十 shí	二十 èr.shí	三十 sān.shí	四十 sì.shí	五十 wǔ.shí	六十 liù.shí	七十 qī.shí	八十 bā.shí	九十 jiǔ.shí	一百 yìbǎi

Adjectives

对（對）	duì	*correct; right*

Interjections

嗯（嗯）	.en	*um*

Measure Words

年级（年級）	-niánjí	*grade*
岁（歲）	-suì	*year (of age)*

Nouns

教室（教室）	jiàoshì	*classroom*

Common Expressions

对不对（對不對）	duì .bú duì	*Is that right?*

Verbs

修（修）	xiū	*to take (a college class)*
学（學）	xué	*to study; to learn*
上	shàng	*to attend, to take (a class)*

1 你上什么课? Nǐ shàng shén.me kè? *What classes do you take?*

Ask if your partner is taking the following classes. Then switch roles.

Lì.zi: **A:** 你上数学课吗？ Nǐ shàng shùxué kè .ma?

B: 对，我上数学课。 Duì, wǒ shàng shùxué kè.

Comparisons

Which classes are offered in Chinese schools that are not part of your school's curriculum?

2 他们几年级? Tā.men jǐ-niánjí? *What grades are they in?*

Tell what grades the following students are in.

3 数字 Shùzì *Numbers Sequence*

Complete each sequence up to 20.

1. yī, sān, wǔ....
2. èr, sì, liù....
3. sān, liù, jiǔ....
4. sì, bā, shí'èr....

4 看课表 Kèchéng Bǎo / *Class Schedule*

Refer to the class schedule and answer the questions that follow.

学生：叶星			年级：高一年级		
Monday	星期一 Xīngqīyī	星期二 Xīngqī'èr	星期三 Xīngqīsān	星期四 Xīngqīsì	星期五 Xīngqīwǔ
8:00-8:50	外语 wàiyǔ	政治 zhèngzhì	数学 shùxué	外语 wàiyǔ	数学 shùxué
9:00-9:50	数学 shùxué	外语 wàiyǔ	物理 wùlǐ	政治 zhèngzhì	通用技术 tōngyòng jìshù
10:00-10:50	物理 wùlǐ	数学 shùxué	语文 yǔwén	语文 yǔwén	语文 yǔwén
11:00-11:50	语文 yǔwén	地理 dìlǐ	地理 dìlǐ	数学 shùxué	外语 wàiyǔ
14:00-14:50	历史 lìshǐ	化学 huàxué	外语 wàiyǔ	生物 shēngwù	美术 měishù
15:00-15:50	生物 shēngwù	语文 yǔwén	信息技术 xìnxī jìshù	体育 tǐyù	信息技术 xìnxī jìshù
16:00-16:50	班会* bānhuì	体育 tǐyù	历史 lìshǐ	化学 huàxué	自习* zìxí

*班会 bānhuì: *class meeting* *自习 zìxí: *individual study*

1. How many subjects is the student taking?
2. What grade is the student in?
3. Which classes does he have the most often?
4. It is 11:30 on Monday morning. Which class is he in now?
5. It is 2:15 on Wednesday afternoon. Which class is he in now?
6. It is 8:30 on Friday morning. Which class is he in now?

Comparisons

Do Chinese students have the same classes every day? What are the advantages and disadvantages of a Chinese schedule?

5 个人问题 Gèrén Wèntí / *Personal Questions*

Answer each question in Chinese and ask a classmate these questions.

1. 这是数学教室吗？ Zhè shì shùxué jiàoshì .ma?
2. 你上中文课吗？ Nǐ shàng Zhōngwén kè .ma?
3. 谁是你的中文老师？ Shéi shì nǐ.de Zhōngwén lǎoshī?
4. 你上历史吗？ Nǐ shàng lìshǐ .ma?
5. 你上几年级？ *Nǐ* shàng jǐ-niánjí?
6. 你几岁？ *Nǐ* jǐ-suì?

句型介绍 Jùxíng Jièshào

Language Patterns

The Question Word 几 *jǐ*

The question word 几 *jǐ* ("How many?") is needed to tell what grade you're in and what your age is. It functions grammatically like a number in the pattern:

Number + **Measure Word** + **Noun**

几年级 jǐ-niánjí　　几岁 jǐ-suì

A: 我上十年级，你上几年级？ Wǒ shàng shí-niánjí, nǐ shàng jǐ-niánjí?
B: 我也上十年级。 *Wǒ* yě shàng shí-niánjí.

A: 我十六岁，你几岁？ Wǒ shíliù-suì, *nǐ* jǐ-suì?
B: 我十五岁。 Wǒ shíwǔ-suì.

Language Note

To ask the age of people 20 years old or more, you may also use 你多大? *Nǐ duó dà*? or 你多大年纪? *Nǐ duó dà niánjì*?

Confirm something by using 对不对 *duì .bú duì*

The interrogative phrase 对不对 *duì .bú duì* ("Is that right?") is added at the end of a statement to make it into a question and asks for confirmation of the information in the statement.

Sentence + **对不对 *duì .bú duì*?**

To give a short answer to 对不对 *duì .bú duì* questions , say 对 *duì* for "correct", and 不 *bù* or 不对 *bú duì* for "no". The former is the short form of 不对 *bú duì*.

对 *duì* + **Sentence** **OR** **不对 *bú duì*** + **Sentence**

A: 李老师是中国人，对不对？ *Lǐ* lǎoshī shì Zhōng.guórén, duì .bú duì?
B: 对。 Duì.

A: 这是日语教室，对不对？ Zhè shì Rìyǔ jiàoshì, duì .bú duì?
B: 不对，这是中文教室。 Bù duì, zhè shì Zhōngwén jiàoshì.

A: Michael Schumacher 是西班牙人，对不对？ Michael Schumacher shì Xībānyárén, duì .bu duì?
B: 不对，他不是西班牙人，他是德国人。 Bú duì, tā bú shì Xībānyárén, tā shì Dé.guórén.

会话 Huìhuà
Dialogue

找教室 Zhǎo jiàoshì Looking for the Classroom

Looking for his next class at this international school, Dong Jun approaches Zhang Guohua.

董军：这是法语教室吗？
张国华：不是，这是中文教室。

董军：你修中文课吗？
张国华：对，你也修中文课吗？

董军：嗯，我也修中文课。
张国华：你上几年级？
董军：我上高一年级。你上高二年级，对不对？
张国华：对。
董军：你几岁？
张国华：我十六岁。
董军：我十五岁。

Dǒng Jūn: Zhè shì *Fǎ*yǔ jiàoshì .ma?
Zhāng Guóhuá: Bú shì, zhè shì Zhōngwén jiàoshì.

Dǒng Jūn: Nǐ xiū Zhōngwén kè .ma?
Zhāng Guóhuá: Duì, *nǐ* yě xiū Zhōngwén kè .ma?

Dǒng Jūn: .En, *wǒ* yě xiū Zhōngwén kè.
Zhāng Guóhuá: Nǐ shàng jǐ-niánjí?
Dǒng Jūn: Wǒ shàng gāo yī-niánjí. Nǐ shàng gāo èr-niánjí, duì .bú duì?
Zhāng Guóhuá: Duì.
Dǒng Jūn: *Nǐ* jǐ-suì?
Zhāng Guóhuá: Wǒ shíliù-suì.
Dǒng Jūn: Wǒ shíwǔ-suì.

6 他们多大？ Tā.mén duó dà? *Information about the Characters*

With a partner, take turns asking and telling the ages and grades of the characters in the dialogue.

❶

❷

7 懂了吗? Dǒng .le .ma? *Do you understand?*

Answer the following questions according to the dialogue.

1. 这是地理教室吗? Zhè shì dìlǐ jiàoshì .ma?
2. 谁修中文课? Shéi xiū Zhōngwén kè?
3. 董军上几年级? Dǒng Jūn shàng jǐ-niánjí?
4. 张国华上几年级? Zhāng Guóhuá shàng jǐ-niánjí?
5. 董军几岁? Dǒng Jūn jǐ-suì?
6. 张国华几岁? Zhāng Guóhuá jǐ-suì?

文化橱窗 Wénhuà Chúchuāng
Culture Window

Grade levels in Chinese schools

The most common educational system used in China is the 6-3-3 system, which describes a format of six years of elementary school, three years of junior high, and three years of senior high. Currently, 65 percent of schools in China follow the 6-3-3 system. Since 1986, the first nine years of education are mandatory. Kindergarten usually begins at age five and students usually complete high school at age 18.

Transportation to school

In densely populated cities in China, most elementary schools are within walking distance of the pupils' homes. However, most students in junior and senior high have to take public transportation, such as buses, the metro, or trains, to get to school. Some schools provide buses, but they are very rare. Students who are in a rush to get to school might also take a taxi. Biking to school is also an option for those who live closer; some students ride motorized

▲ School students are on their way to school.

bicycles. Because China is so large, there are many areas that lack public transportation. Schools in those areas usually provide room and board for students. Nowadays, many families, especially those living in cities, own their own cars. So some parents drive their children to school and pick them up after school.

Foreign language instruction in China

Foreign language classes are taught in the 80,000 middle schools and high schools in China four or five times per week. In addition, there are about 50 foreign language schools that provide six to eight classes of language instruction per week. English classes are compulsory at the middle school, high school, and university level, which makes English the most widely studied foreign language in China. Since 1994, elementary schools in China have also started teaching English, with plans to have classes available for an additional million pupils each year. Russian and Japanese are the second and third most popular foreign languages, and preferred by students from China's three northeastern provinces and Inner Mongolia. Other popular foreign languages–offered at most foreign language schools–are French, German, Spanish, and Italian.

8 文化动动脑 Wénhuà Dòng.dòngnǎo / *Culture Check-up*

On a separate sheet of paper, write a short answer in English for each question.

1. In China, the educational system is expressed numerically. Which system is currently in use by 65 percent of the schools?
2. In which year did China implement mandatory education?
3. Education is mandatory for how many years?
4. In China, where can children before the age of six go to school?
5. What forms of transportion are available for senior high students who live in cities?
6. If public transportation isn't available, what do schools usually offer?
7. Which foreign language is the most widely studied in China?
8. Why do you think interest in taking Japanese and Russian is so high?

Language Practice

9 他/她几年级? Tā/tā jǐ-niánjí? / *What grade is he/she in?*

With a partner, take turns asking and telling what grade each student is in. Follow the model.

Lì.zi: 德昌 Déchāng / 9th

A: 德昌上几年级?
Déchāng shàng jǐ-niánjí?

B: 他上九年级。
Tā shàng jiǔ-niánjí.

1. 程成 Chéng Chéng / 11th	4. 怡君 Yíjūn / 7th
2. 冯琴 Féng Qín / 8th	5. 建志 Jiànzhì / 12th
3. 王文 Wáng Wén / 9th	6. 董兰 Dǒng Lán / 10th

10 他们几岁? Tā.mén jǐ-suì? *How old are they?*

With a partner, take turns asking and telling how old these people are. Follow the model.

Lì.zi:

Chen Hua　　Liu Qiang

A: 陈华几岁? Chén Huá jǐ-suì?

B: 她十八岁。柳强几岁? Tā shíbā-suì. Liǔ Qiáng jǐ-suì?

A: 他十七岁。 Tā shíqī-suì.

1. 6	4	3. 19	12	5. 8	13
Wu Jian	Qian Ling	Gong Hui	Zhao Tong	Wu Junping	Cai Mengzhen
2. 16	14	4. 1	1	6. 5	7
Sun Bin	Pan Quan	Zhong Li	Zhong Yu	Fang Meishan	Xie Jiarong

11 对不对? Duì .bú duì? *Is that right?*

With a partner, take turns asking and answering questions. Follow the model.

Lì.zi: 叫Nelson Sue jiào Nelson Sue

A: 你叫Nelson Sue，对不对? Nǐ jiào Nelson Sue, duì .bú duì?

B: 不对，我叫Martinelli Jacob。 Bú duì, wǒ jiào Martinelli Jacob.

1. 很好 *hěn* hǎo	3. 十年级 shí-niánjí
2. 美国人 Měi.guórén	4. 十五岁 shíwǔ-suì

Language Note

The interrogative phrase 对不对 *duì .bú duì* is used to confirm information, and the final particle 呢 *.ne* is used in follow-up questions.

中文

12 回答问题 Huídá Wèntí / Answering Questions

With a partner, take turns asking and answering questions. When asking a question, complete the question that has been started by adding 对不对 *duì .bu duì*. When answering a question, give an affirmative or negative response. Follow the model.

Lì.zi: 你叫… Nǐ jiào…

A: 你叫Wally Wilson，对不对？ Nǐ jiào Wally Wilson, duì .bú duì?

B: 不对，我叫Walt Wilson。 Bú duì, wǒ jiào Walt Wilson.

1. 你姓… Nǐ xìng….	6. 老师姓…，叫… Lǎoshī xìng…, jiào….
2. 你是…人 Nǐ shì… rén	7. 老师是…人 Lǎoshī shì… rén
3. 你…岁 Nǐ… suì	8. 这是…教室 Zhè shì… jiàoshì
4. 你…年级 Nǐ… niánjí	9. 你是我的… Nǐ shì wǒ.de….
5. 你修…课 Nǐ xiū… kè	

13 认识新朋友 Rèn shí Xīn Péng.yǒu / Getting to Know New Friends

You will hear a dialogue followed by four statements below. Say if each statement is true or false based on the dialogue.

1. Gao Zhan is in the 8th grade.
2. Gao Zhan asked He Qingqing's grade.
3. He Qingqing is 13 years old.
4. He Qingqing and Gao Zhan take the same Chinese class.

14 这是我的教室吗？ Zhè shì wǒ.de jiàoshì .ma? / Is This My Classroom?

Yaeko, a 14-year-old Japanese 9th-grader, who is a foreign exchange student at an international school in Beijing, walks into a classroom. The French teacher looks at a new student form and asks the student questions: What is your nationality? How old are you? etc. With a partner, play the roles of Yaeko and the teacher as they try to determine if she is in the right classroom.

新生名单 Xīnshēng Míngdān New Student Form

- 日本人 Rìběnrén
- 十四岁 shísì-suì
- 九年级 jiǔ-niánjí
- 法语课 *Fǎyǔ* kè
- 叫Yaeko Kahoko jiào Yaeko Kahoko

Yaeko在对(duì, *right*)的教室吗？
Yaeko zài duì .de jiàoshì .ma?

开口说 Kāikǒu Shuō

Communication

15 遇见同学 Yùjiàn Tóngxué / *Meeting a Classmate*

With a partner, play the roles of two students who meet for the first time.

A: Say good-morning or good afternoon and introduce yourself to a classmate. Ask what grade he or she is in.
B: Say which grade you are in, guess your classmate's age, and ask if you are correct.
A: Confirm your age and ask what classes your classmate is taking.
B: Say which classes you are taking. Ask which classes your classmate is taking.
A: Say which classes you are taking. Then say you have to go.
B: Say good-bye.

16 小小调查 Xiǎo.xiǎo Diàochá / *A Survey*

To find out if students in your class are taking another foreign language, draw a grid like the one that follows. In the grid write the names in Chinese of four foreign languages and number 1 to 10. Then poll ten of your classmates.

Lì.zi: **A:** 你上德语课吗? Nǐ shàng Déyǔ kè .ma?
B: 对，我上德语课。 Duì, wǒ shàng Déyǔ kè.
....
A: 五个学生上西班牙语课，三个学生上法语课，两个学生上德语课。
Wǔ-.ge xué.shēng shàng Xībānyáyǔ kè, sān-.ge xué.shēng shàng *Fǎ*yǔ kè, liǎng-.ge xué.shēng shàng Déyǔ kè.

	1	2	3	4	5	6	7	8	9	10	Total
法语课 *Fǎ*yǔ kè			X		X		X				3
德语课 Déyǔ kè	X			X							2
西班牙语课 Xībānyáyǔ kè		X				X		X	X	X	5
日语课 Rìyǔ kè											10

17 这是谁的书？ Zhè shì shéi .de shū? *Whose book is it?*

Imagine that you pick up a book in the classroom that is not yours. You open the book and see the page below. Answer the questions.

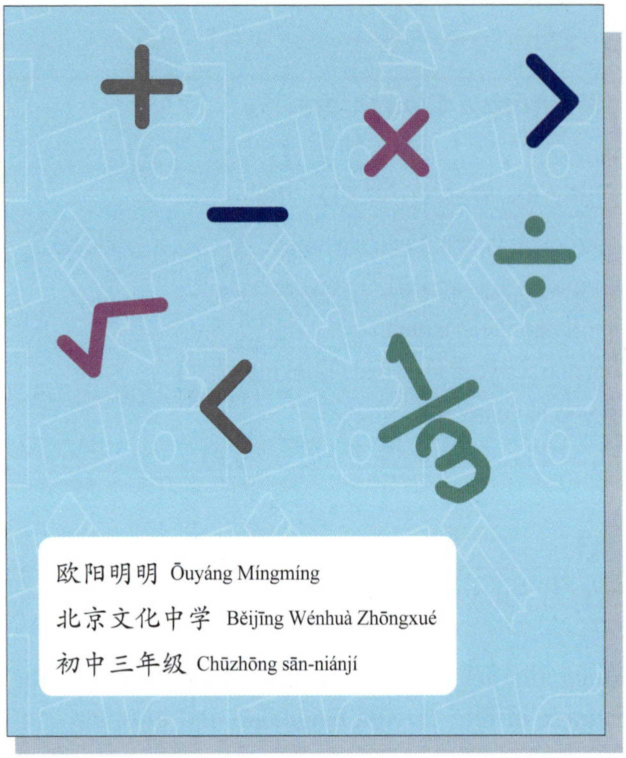

1. What is the last name of the owner of the book? What is his or her first name?
2. What grade is the owner of the book in?
3. What class is the book for?
4. If you are two years ahead of the owner of the book, what grade are you in?

汉字天地 Hànzì Tiāndì

Chinese Characters

中 ■ zhōng ■ *middle*

The ideograph 中 *zhōng*, which means "middle," resembles a flag on a pole standing in the middle of a circle.

Stroke Order

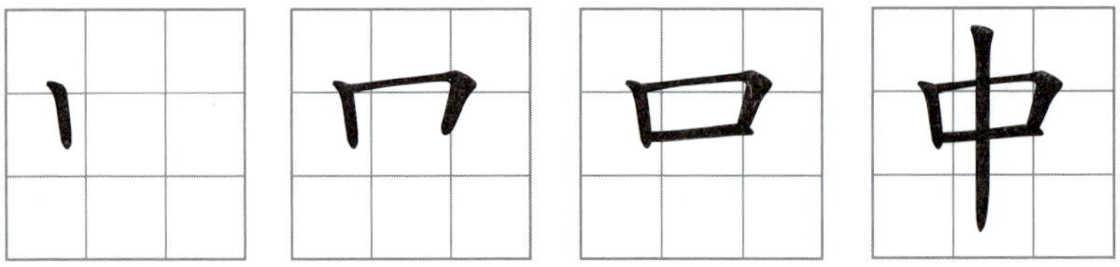

18 词汇延伸 Cíhuì Yánshēn / *Vocabulary Builder*

Below are some characters that can be combined with 中 *zhōng* to create new words. Match the Chinese words on the left with the appropriate English meaning on the right.

国 guó *n. country*	年 nián *n. age*	立 lì *v. to stand*	级 jí *n. grade*	途 tú *n. road*

1. 中国 Zhōng.guó — A. *middle-aged*
2. 中年 zhōngnián — B. *China*
3. 中立 zhōnglì — C. *neutral*
4. 中级 zhōngjí — D. *halfway*
5. 中途 zhōngtú — E. *intermediate level*

19 汉字侦探 Hànzì Zhēntàn / *Visual Detective*

Can you find 中 in the following pictures?

Unit 2

我的家人 Wǒ.de Jiārén

When you have completed this unit, you will be able to...

- identify and describe family members and pets
- use words of measurement when discussing quantities
- discuss dates and months of the year
- ask for someone's telephone number and give your own telephone number
- discuss hobbies
- express your likes and dislikes
- ask others what they like and dislike
- give and respond to invitations

Lesson A

发音 Fāyīn
Pronunciation

d t + a ai ao an ang

词汇 Cíhuì
Vocabulary

家庭成员 Jiātíng Chéngyuán *Family Members*

1. 外公（外公）
   wàigōng
   n. maternal grandfather
2. 外婆（外婆）
   wàipó
   n. maternal grandmother
3. 爷爷 (爺爺)
   yé.x
   n. paternal grandfather
4. 奶奶（奶奶）
   nǎi.x
   n. paternal grandmother
5. 妈妈 (媽媽)
   mā.x
   n. mother
6. 爸爸（爸爸）
   bà.x
   n. father
7. 姐姐（姐姐）
   jiě.x
   n. older sister

Pets and the Sounds They Make

宠物 (寵物) chǒngwù *n. pets*					
狗 (狗) gǒu *n. dog*	猫 (貓) māo *n. cat*	鸟 (鳥) niǎo *n. bird*	鱼 (魚) yú *n. fish*	天竺鼠 (天竺鼠) tiānzhúshǔ *n. guinea pig*	兔子 (兔子) tù.zǐ *n. rabbit*

A: 这是谁 (這是誰)? Zhè shì shéi? *Who is this?*

B: 这是我妈妈 (這是我媽媽)。 Zhè shì wǒ mā.x. *This is my mother.*

A: 这是你的狗吗 (這是你的狗嗎)? Zhè shì nǐ.de gǒu .ma? *Is this your dog?*

B: 不是，这是我外婆的狗 (不是，這是我外婆的狗)。

Bú shì, zhè shì wǒ wàipó .de gǒu. *No, this is my (maternal) grandmother's dog.*

A: 你的猫叫什么名字 (你的貓叫什麼名字)?

Nǐ.de māo jiào shén.me míng.zì? *What is your cat's name?*

B: 它叫胖胖 (它叫胖胖)。 Tā jiào Pàng.x. *Its name is Pangpang.*

A: 你的宠物是什么 (你的寵物是什麼)?

Nǐ.de chǒngwù shì shén.me? *What kind of pet do you have?*

B: 我的宠物是兔子，它很大也很胖 (我的寵物是兔子，它很大也很胖)。

Wǒ.de chǒngwù shì tù.zǐ, tā hěn dà *yě* hěn pàng. *I have a pet rabbit. It is big and fat.*

Adjectives

大（大）	dà	*big*
小（小）	xiǎo	*small*
可爱（可愛）	kě'ài	*cute; adorable*
胖（胖）	pàng	*fat*

Demonstratives

那（那）	nà	*that*

Nouns

家（家）	jiā	*home; family*
人（人）	rén	*people*
家人（家人）	jiārén	*family members*

1 他们家有什么人？ Tā.mén jiā yǒu shén.me rén? *Who are their family members?*

With a partner, take turns asking and answering which of Jane and Rick's family members are shown in the photos.

A.

B.

2 真真的家人 Zhēnzhēn .de Jiārén *Zhenzhen's Family Members*

Give the name of everyone in Zhenzhen's family. Follow the model.

Lì.zi: 妈妈 / 李枫 mā.x / Lǐ Fēng
真真的妈妈叫李枫。 Zhēnzhēn .de mā.x jiào Lǐ Fēng.

1. 爸爸 / 吴强 bà.x / Wú Qiáng
2. 姐姐 / 吴宁 jiě.x / Wú Níng
3. 外婆 / 金兰 wàipó / Jīn Lán
4. 奶奶 / 刘君 nǎi.x / Liú Jūn

3 他们多大年纪? Tā.mén duó dà niánjì? *How old are they?*

With a partner, take turns asking and answering how old Bai Cheng's family members are. Follow the model.

Lì.zi: 爷爷 yé.x (60)
A: 白成的爷爷多大年纪? Bái Chéng .de yé.x duó dà niánjì?
B: 他六十岁。 Tā liù.shí-suì.

1. 外婆 wàipó (70)
2. 爸爸 bà.x (50)
3. 妈妈 mā.x (40)
4. 姐姐 jiě.x (20)
5. 奶奶 nǎi.x (60)
6. 外公 wàigōng (50)

4 小华的宠物 Xiǎohuá .de Chǒngwù *Xiaohua's Pets*

Describe Xiaohua's pets. Are they big, small, adorable, or fat? Follow the model.

Lì.zi: 小华的天竺鼠很大。 Xiǎohuá .de tiānzhúshǔ hěn dà.

1. 
2. 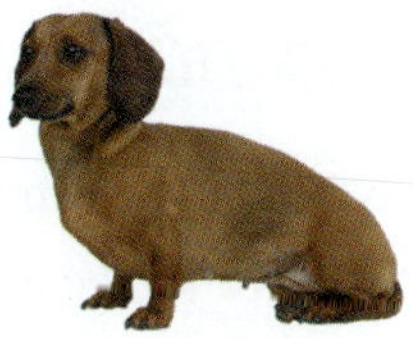
3. 
4. 

5 中文怎么说? Zhōngwén zěn.me shuō? *How would you say it in Chinese?*

What do you say in Chinese in the following situations?

1. You see your classmate's family portrait and want to find out who his or her (maternal) grandmother is.
2. You meet a classmate when you are out walking your dog and you introduce your dog to him or her.
3. A cat jumps in through your window. You pick it up and ask your neighbors if it is their cat.
4. You find out that the cat belongs to your neighbors and ask them its name.
5. You want to know if your classmate has any pets.
6. You are asked if you have any pets.

句型介绍 Jùxíng Jièshào

Language Patterns

Omitting 的 *.de*

As you know, 的 *.de* resembles the possessive "-'s" in English. When two people have a close relationship, such as family members or close friends, 的 *.de* can be omitted.

N1 + **的 *.de*** + **N2 (N1's N2)**

我的妈妈 wǒ.de mā.x → 我妈妈 wǒ mā.x

我的朋友 wǒ.de péng.yǒu → 我朋友 wǒ péng.yǒu

Language Note

When talking about their pets, the Chinese say 我的狗 *wǒ.de gǒu* or 我的猫 *wǒ.de māo*. It would be incorrect to say 我狗 *wǒ gǒu* or 我猫 *wǒ māo*.

The Demonstratives 这 *zhè* and 那 *nà*

The demonstratives 这 *zhè* and 那 *nà* are used similarly but have different meanings. The demonstrative 那 *nà* indicates an object that is far from the speaker, while the demonstrative 这 *zhè* indicates an object that is close to the speaker.

这是我爷爷，那是我奶奶。 Zhè shì wǒ yé.x, nà .shì *wǒ* nǎi.x.

When followed by a number or measure word, 这 *zhè* and 那 *nà* are pronounced 这 *zhèi* and 那 *nèi*.

这只狗叫小白，那只狗叫小黑。 Zhèi-zhī gǒu jiào Xiǎobái, nèi-zhī gǒu jiào Xiǎohēi.

The Question Word 谁 *shéi*

The question word 谁 *shéi* is used to ask "who" or "whom." The word order in questions that use a question word is the same as the word order used in the answers.

Here is the formula to use when 谁 *shéi* is in the subject position:

谁是 *Shéi shì* + **Noun / Pronoun** **?**

A: 谁是我们的老师？ Shéi shì wǒ.mén.de lǎoshī?

B: 王老师是我们的老师。 Wáng lǎoshī shì wǒ.mén.de lǎoshī.

A: 谁是你姐姐？ Shéi shì *nǐ* jiě.x?

B: 那个人是我姐姐。 Nèi-.ge rén shì *wǒ* jiě.x.

If 谁 *shéi* is in the object position, the answer will be in the same position.

Noun / Pronoun + **是谁 *shì shéi*** **?**

A: 王老师是谁？ Wáng lǎoshī shì shéi?

B: 王老师是我们的老师。 Wáng lǎoshī shì wǒ.mén.de lǎoshī.

A: 他们是谁？Tā.mén shì shéi?

B: 他们是高二年级的学生。 Tā.mén shì gāo 'èr-niánjí .de xué.shēng.

会话 Huìhuà Dialogue

那个人是谁？ Nèi-.ge rén shì shéi? *Who is that?*

In Bai Ping's home, Lin Shufang is pointing to a photo and talking to her new friend.

林书芳：	那个人是你吗？	Lín Shūfāng:	Nèi-.ge rén shì nǐ .ma?
白苹：	对，是我。	Bái Píng:	Duì, shì wǒ.
林书芳：	这是谁？	Lín Shūfāng:	Zhè shì shéi?
白苹：	这是我姐姐。	Bái Píng:	Zhè shì *wǒ* jiě.x.
林书芳：	他们是你爸爸妈妈吗？	Lín Shūfāng:	Tā.mén shì nǐ bà.x mā.x .ma?
白苹：	不是，他们是我爷爷奶奶。	Bái Píng:	Bú shì, tā.mén shì wǒ yé.x nǎi.x.
林书芳：	这是你的狗吗？它叫什么名字？	Lín Shūfāng:	Zhè shì nǐ.de gǒu .ma? Tā jiào shén. me míng.zì?
白苹：	它叫小可爱。	Bái Píng:	Tā jiào *Xiǎo*kě'ài.
林书芳：	那是你的猫吗？	Lín Shūfāng:	Nà shì nǐ.de māo .ma?
白苹：	是，它叫大胖。	Bái Píng:	Shì, tā jiào Dàpàng.

6 他们是谁? Tā.mén shì shéi? *Who are they?*

Give the names of each person, animal or character based on the descriptions in the dialogue.

1. 

2. 

3. 

7 懂了吗? Dǒng .le .ma? *Do you understand?*

Answer the following questions.

1. Whose photo are they talking about?
2. According to the dialogue, what family members are in the photo?
3. Besides family members, who else is in the photo?
4. How many pets does Bai Ping have?
5. What are their names?

文化橱窗 Wénhuà Chúchuāng

Culture Window

Pets in China

About 56 percent of Chinese people have pets, mostly dogs, but also cats, fish, birds, turtles/tortoises, and rabbits. For most Chinese people, keeping pets is a way of life, like having a friend around for fun and entertainment. Of course, there are also people who keep pets for practical purposes—cats to catch mice and dogs to guard the door, for example.

▲ Koi fish, pets of the rich in ancient China.

People in ancient China also kept pets. In those days, pets commonly included horses, cattle, birds, and koi fish, and were mainly owned by the rich. Back then, domestic animals weren't just kept as companion animals but for other purposes; horses were used for traveling, and koi fish were kept to symbolize wealth in the family.

Today, in more densely populated areas in China, such as Guangzhou, Beijing, and Tianjin, dogs must be registered with the government, and there are rules in place to reduce the number of strays. An incentive for people living in provinces where registration is mandatory is free pet vaccinations. Because the province requires a 5,000 Yuan (approximately $750) registration fee, there is an increasing number of unregistered and unvaccinated dogs, now known as 黑狗 (*hēi gǒu*, "black dogs"). The government is now making changes to the restrictions, such as lowering registration fees, in hopes that this problem can be solved.

Here is a list of some popular names for dogs and cats:

狗 *gǒu*, dog	小白 Xiǎobái 小黑 Xiǎohēi	旺财 Wàngcái 狗狗 *Gǒu*gǒu
猫 *māo*, cat	咪咪 Mīmī 喵喵 Miāomiāo	贝贝 Bèibèi 猫猫 Māomāo

Nowadays, many Chinese people give their pets English names. When this trend first started, many pets were named Lucky or Money. Now, names like Molly, Max and Charlie are also common.

Comparisons

Are there any rules that dog owners must follow in your community? If so, do you agree with them? If not, what rules do you think should be implemented?

8 文化动动脑 Wénhuà Dòng.x nǎo / *Culture Check-up*

Choose the correct answer.

1. What is the most popular pet in China today?
   A. cat B. dog C. fish
2. For the ancient Chinese, what did koi fish signify?
   A. wealth B. food C. competition

3 Are you able to keep a pet dog without any restrictions in densely populated Chinese cities such as Tianjin?
   A. Yes, this is the people's right.
   B. No, you must register your dog first.
   C. It depends on the number of dogs you have.

4. In China, what are the non-registered pet dogs called?
   A. stray dogs B. little dogs C. black dogs

Language Practice

9 这是…，那是… Zhè shì..., nà shì... *This is..., that is....*

Decide if the statements you hear about the photos are true or false.

1. 

2. 

3. 

4. 

5. 

6. 

10 家庭照片 Jiātíng Zhàopiàn *Family Photo*

Bring a picture of your parents and grandparents to school. Point out each family member to your partner. Follow the model.

Lì.zi: 这是我妈妈。 Zhè shì wǒ mā.x.

11 宠物动物园 Chǒngwù Dòngwùyuán *At a Petting Zoo*

Use 这 *zhè* and 那 *nà* to name the pets in the photo depending on their distance from the boy. Follow the model.

Lì.zi: 这是猫，那是狗。 Zhè shì māo, nà shì gǒu.

12 陈小姐的家人 Chén *Xiǎo*jiě .de Jiārén / *Miss Chen's Family*

As you hear descriptions of Miss Chen's family members, identify each relative in the photo. Follow the model.

Lì.zi: 这是陈小姐的爸爸。 Zhè shì Chén *xiǎo*jiě .de bà.x.

13 他们是哪国人? Tā.mén shì něi-guó rén? / *What is their nationality?*

The yearbook staff needs to know the nationalities of the international students at school in order to put their photos under the correct flag. Replace 谁 *shéi* in the question with the subject in parentheses.

Lì.zi: 谁是日本人? Shéi shì Rìběnrén? (Fu)
Fu是日本人。 Fu shì Rìběnrén.

1. 谁是德国人? Shéi shì Dé.guórén? (Siegfried)
2. 谁是西班牙人? Shéi shì Xībānyárén? (Belia)
3. 谁是印度人? Shéi shì Yìndùrén? (Satyajit)
4. 谁是泰国人? Shéi shì Tài.guórén? (Chailai)

14 写问题 Xiě Wèntí / *Writing Questions*

In Pinyin, write the question that would come before each statement. The underlined words will help you form a question. Follow the model.

Lì.zi: Taro是我的同学。 Taro shì wǒ.de tóngxué.
Taro是谁? Taro shì shéi?

1. 她姓白。 Tā xìng Bái.
2. 他叫张国华。 Tā jiào Zhāng Guóhuá.
3. 这是中文教室。 Zhè shì Zhōngwén jiàoshì.
4. 我们修法语课。 Wǒ.mén xiū *Fǎ*yǔ kè.
5. 这个人是我外公。 Zhèi-.ge rén shì wǒ wàigōng.
6. 那个人是我的同学。 Nèi-.ge rén shì wǒ.de tóngxué.
7. 我姐姐上高三。 *Wǒ* jiě.x shàng gāo sān.

开口说 Kāikǒu Shuō
Communication

15 介绍家人 Jièshào Jiārén / My Favorite Relative

Show a photo of a favorite relative, or a famous person you might pretend is your relative, to a group of classmates. Prepare a presentation in which you describe the person in the photo. Include the following in your presentation:

- relationship to you
- name
- age
- physical description
- nationality
- pets he/she owns

16 身份证 Shēnfènzhèng / I.D. Card

Below is the front and back of a Taiwanese ID (identity card). Answer the questions that follow.

xìngmíng: Lín Guóhuá

chūshēng nián yuè rì: Mínguó liù.shíliù nián Sìyuè wǔ rì

xìngbié: nán

tǒngyī biānhào: A125529099

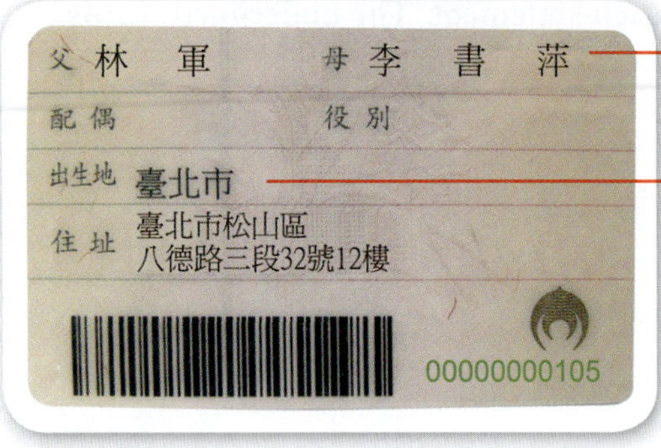

fù: Lín Jūn   mǔ: Lǐ Shūpíng

chūshēngdì: Táiběi shì

Note: The Republic of China was formed in 1911. Thus, an ROC year (民國 *Mínguó*) is the same as the western year minus 1911.

1. 他叫什么名字？ Tā jiào shén.me míng.zì?
2. 他几岁？ Tā jǐ-suì?
3. 他的爸爸、妈妈叫什么名字？ Tā.de bà.x, mā.x jiào shén.me míng.zì?
4. 这是台湾身份证(Taiwanese ID)，对不对？ Zhè shì Táiwān shēnfènzhèng, duì .bú duì?

汉字天地 Hànzì Tiāndì
Chinese Characters

妈 ■ mā ■ mother

The noun 妈 *mā*, meaning mother, is a combination character, composed of a radical and a phonetic component. On the left is the radical for "female", 女 *nǚ*; and on the right is the phonetic component 马 *mǎ*.

Stroke Order

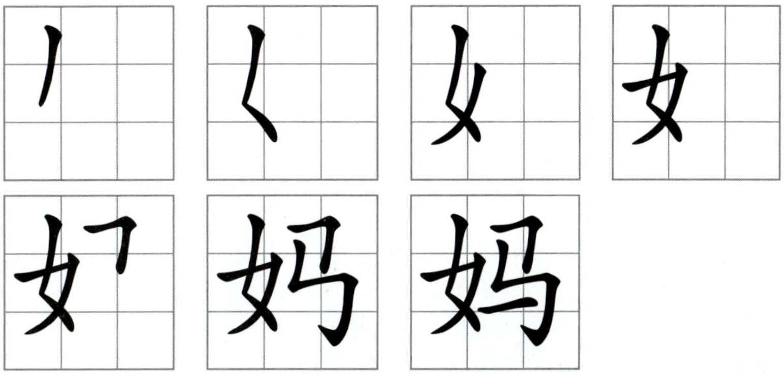

17 词汇延伸 Cíhuì Yánshēn / *Vocabulary Builder*

Below are some characters that can be combined with 妈 *mā* to create new words. Match the Chinese words on the left with the appropriate English meaning on the right.

舅 jiù *n. uncle*	奶 nǎi *n. milk*	干 gān *adj. relatives not linked by blood*	后 hòu *n. later*	星 xīng *n. star*

1. 舅妈 jiùmā
2. 奶妈 nǎimā
3. 干妈 gānmā
4. 后妈 hòumā
5. 星妈 xīngmā

A. *nursing mother*
B. *mother by affection*
C. *aunt*
D. *stepmother*
E. *a celebrity's mom*

18 汉字侦探 Hànzì Zhēntàn / *Visual Detective*

Can you find 妈 in the following pictures?

Lesson B

发音 Fāyīn Pronunciation

g k h a + ai ao an ang

词汇 Cíhuì Vocabulary

兄弟姐妹 Xiōngdì-jiěmèi *Siblings*

照片(照片)
zhàopiàn
n. photo

弟弟(弟弟)
dì.x
n. younger brother

哥哥(哥哥)
gē.x
n. elder brother

妹妹(妹妹)
mèi.x
n. younger sister

姐姐(姊姊)
jiě.x
n. elder sister

乌龟(烏龜)
wūguī
n. turtle

书(書)
shū
n. book

纸(紙)
zhǐ
n. paper

鞋子(鞋子)
xié.zi
n. shoe(s)

衣服(衣服)
yī.fú
n. clothes

笔(筆)
bǐ
n. pen

可乐(可樂)
kělè
n. cola

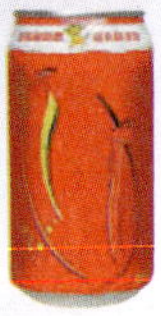

茶(茶)
chá
n. tea

背包(背包)
bēibāo
n. backpack

水(水)
shuǐ
n. water

A: 你家有什么人(你家有什麼人)?
Nǐ jiā yǒu shén.me rén? *Who are the members of your family?*

B: 我家有爸爸、妈妈和我(我家有爸爸、媽媽和我)。
Wǒ jiā yǒu bà.x、mā.x hé wǒ. *There are my father, mother, and I in my family.*

A: 你家有几口人(你家有幾口人)?
Nǐ jiā yǒu *jǐ*-kǒu rén? *How many people are there in your family?*

B: 我家有三口人(我家有三口人)。
Wǒ jiā yǒu sān-kǒu rén. *There are three people in my family.*

A: 你们有宠物吗(你們有寵物嗎)?
Nǐ.mén *yǒu* chǒngwù .ma? *Do you (pl.) have pets?*

B: 我没有宠物(我沒有寵物)。
Wǒ .méi.*yǒu* chǒngwù. *I don't have a pet.*

C: 我有乌龟(我有烏龜)。
Wǒ yǒu wūguī. *I have a turtle.*

Culture Note

Children usually call their parents 爸爸 *bà.x* and 妈妈 *mā.x*. In more formal situations, 父亲 *fù.qīn* is used for father and 母亲 *mǔ.qīn* for mother.

Conjunctions

可是 (可是)	kě.shì	*but; however*
和 (和)	hé	*and*

Measure Words

个 (個)	-.ge	*a common measure word*
口 (口)	-kǒu	*a measure word for people*

Numbers

两 (兩)	liǎng	*two*

Question Words

几 (幾)	jǐ	*how many*

Verbs

有 (有)	yǒu	*to have*
没有 (沒有)	.méi.yǒu	*to not have (the negation of 有 yǒu)*

1 词汇分类 Cíhuì Fēnlèi *Vocabulary Categorization*

Look at the words for family members below, and then group them according to gender.

1. 爷爷 yé.x
2. 奶奶 nǎi.x
3. 外公 wàigōng
4. 外婆 wàipó
5. 爸爸 bà.x
6. 妈妈 mā.x
7. 哥哥 gē.x
8. 姐姐 jiě.x
9. 妹妹 mèi.x
10. 弟弟 dì.x

2 她的家人 Tā.de Jiārén *A Girl's Family*

You will hear a short dialogue about a girl's family. Listen carefully and then answer the following questions.

1. 这个女生(nǚshēng, *girl*)叫什么名字? Zhèi-.ge nǚshēng jiào shén.me míng.zì?
2. 她有兄弟姐妹吗? Tā yǒu xiōngdì-jiěmèi .ma?
3. 她有几个兄弟姐妹? Tā *yǒu* jǐ-.ge xiōngdì-jiěmèi?
4. 她家有几口人? Tā jiā yǒu *jǐ*-kǒu rén?
5. 她家有什么人? Tā jiā yǒu shén.me rén?

3 家庭成员 Jiātíng Chéngyuán *Family Members*

You will hear three mini-dialogues, choose the photo that corresponds to each one.

4 他们有什么? Tā.mén yǒu shén.me? *What do they have?*

Match the descriptions on the left with the appropriate visual on the right.

1. 小白有书。 Xiǎobái yǒu shū.
2. 英英有可乐。 Yīngyīng *yǒu* kělè.
3. 国华有笔。 Guóhuá *yǒu* bǐ.
4. 芳芳有纸。 Fāngfāng *yǒu* zhǐ.
5. 可可有鞋。 *Kě*kě yǒu xié.
6. 小明有水。 Xiǎomíng *yǒu* shuǐ.
7. 林校长有茶。 Lín xiào*zhǎng* yǒu chá.
8. 董太太有狗。 Dǒng tài.x *yǒu* gǒu.
9. 白小姐有衣服。 Bái *xiǎo*jiě yǒu yī.fú.
10. 李先生有猫。 Lǐ xiān.shēng yǒu māo.

5 个人问题 Gèrén Wèntí *Personal Questions*

Answer the following questions in Chinese.

1. 你有弟弟吗? *Nǐ* yǒu dì.x .ma?
2. 你有妹妹吗? *Nǐ* yǒu mèi.x .ma?
3. 你有几个兄弟姐妹? *Nǐ yǒu* jǐ-.ge xiōngdì-jiěmèi?
4. 你家有几口人? Nǐ jiā yǒu *jǐ*-kǒu rén?
5. 你有宠物吗? *Nǐ yǒu* chǒngwù .ma?

句型介绍 Jùxíng Jièshào
Language Patterns

The Verb 有 *yǒu*

The verb 有 *yǒu* means "to have" or "there is," "there are." The negative of 有 *yǒu* is not 不 *bù*, as with all other verbs, but 没 *méi*: 没有 *.méi.yǒu*.

(没 *méi*) + 有 *yǒu* + **Noun**

我有哥哥，没有姐姐。*Wǒ* yǒu gē.x, .méi.yǒu jiě.x.

A: 你有笔吗？ *Nǐ yǒu* bǐ .ma?

B: 我没有笔。 Wǒ .méi.*yǒu* bǐ.

The verb 有 *yǒu* can be omitted from a sentence if it is followed by a noun.

我没有书。Wǒ .méi.yǒu shū. → 我没书。Wǒ méi shū.

However, 有 *yǒu* must be used if a noun doesn't follow.

我没有。Wǒ .méi.yǒu.

Measure Words

In Chinese, when you want to count or identify nouns, measure words are needed. They help categorize the kind of object in question.

这 *zhèi* / 那 *nèi* + **Measure Word** + **Noun**

OR

Number + **Measure Word** + **Noun**

Common Measure Words		
个(個) -.ge	the most common measure word for objects and people, like 人 *rén*, a person	一个哥哥 yí-.ge gē.x
罐(罐) -guàn	used for things that come in a can, like 可乐 *kělè*, a can of cola	两罐可乐 liǎng-guàn kělè
只(隻) -zhī	used for small animals, like 狗 *gǒu*, a dog	三只狗 sān-zhī gǒu

件(件) -jiàn	used for clothing and events, like 衣服 *yī.fú*, an article of clothing	四件衣服 sì-jiàn yī.fú
双(雙) -shuāng	used for pairs, like 鞋子 *xié.zi*, a pair of shoes	五双鞋 wǔ-shuāng xié
瓶(瓶) -píng	used for things that come in a bottle, like 水 *shuǐ*, a bottle of water	六瓶水 liù-píng shuǐ
本(本) -běn	used for books, albums, like 书 *shū*, a "volume" of a book	七本书 qī-běn shū
杯(杯) -bēi	used for liquids contained in a cup, like 茶 *chá*, a cup of tea	八杯茶 bā-bēi chá
支(枝) -zhī	used for stick-like things, like 笔 *bǐ*, a "stick" of a pen	九支笔 jiǔ-zhī bǐ
张(張) -zhāng	used for flat things like 纸 *zhǐ*, a sheet of paper	十张纸 shí-zhāng zhǐ

Language Note

中文

As you know, the number two is 二 *èr*. However, when it is followed by a measure word, it usually becomes 两 *liǎng*, as in these examples:

两只猫 liǎng-zhī māo
两个人 liǎng-.ge rén

The Question Word 几 *jǐ*

The question word 几 *jǐ* asks "how many?" It is always combined with a measure word and usually used when the amount being discussed is ten or less.

几 *jǐ* + **Measure Word** + **Noun**

A: 你有几双鞋子？ *Nǐ yǒu* jǐ-shuāng xié.zi?
B: 我有十双鞋子。 *Wǒ* yǒu shí-shuāng xié.zi.

A: 你有几本书？ *Nǐ yǒu jǐ*-běn shū?
B: 我有两本书。 *Wǒ yǒu liǎng*-běn shū.

会话 Huìhuà Dialogue

全家福 Quánjiāfú *Family Photo*

In the classroom, Lin Shufang shows a photo on her cell phone to Bai Ping.

白　苹：	这是你姐姐吗？	Bái Píng:	Zhè shì *nǐ* jiě.x .ma?
林书芳：	不是，这是我妹妹。	Lín Shūfāng:	Bú shì, zhè .shì wǒ mèi.x.
白　苹：	你有几个兄弟姐妹？	Bái Píng:	*Nǐ yǒu* jǐ-.ge xiōngdì-jiěmèi?
林书芳：	两个，一个姐姐，一个妹妹。	Lín Shūfāng:	Liǎng-.ge, yí-.ge jiě.x, yí-.ge mèi.x.
白　苹：	我有姐姐，可是我没有妹妹。	Bái Píng:	*Wǒ yǒu* jiě.x, kě.shì wǒ .méi.yǒu mèi.x.
林书芳：	你家有几口人？	Lín Shūfāng:	Nǐ jiā yǒu *jǐ*-kǒu rén?
白　苹：	我家有六口人。	Bái Píng:	Wǒ jiā yǒu liù-kǒu rén.
林书芳：	你家有什么人？	Lín Shūfāng:	Nǐ jiā yǒu shén.me rén?
白　苹：	我爸爸、妈妈、哥哥、姐姐、弟弟，和我。	Bái Píng:	Wǒ bà.x、mā.x、gē.x、jiě.x、dì.x, hé wǒ.

6 谁的家人？ Shéi .de jiārén? *Whose family is it?*

Refer to the dialogue above to determine which of the portraits shows Lin Shufang's family, and which shows Bai Ping's family.

❶

❷

7 懂了吗? Dǒng .le .ma? *Do you understand?*

Answer the following questions in Chinese.

1. 谁有照片? Shéi yǒu zhàopiàn?
2. 林书芳家有什么人? Lín Shūfāng jiā yǒu shén.me rén?
3. 白苹家有什么人? Bái Píng jiā yǒu shén.me rén?
4. 林书芳有什么兄弟姐妹? Lín Shūfāng yǒu shén.me xiōngdì-jiěmèi?
5. 白苹有几个兄弟姐妹? Bái Píng *yǒu* jǐ-.ge xiōngdì-jiěmèi?

文化橱窗 Wénhuà Chúchuāng

Culture Window

Names for Family Members in Chinese

The Chinese place great emphasis on relationships within large families. In the past, it was common for an entire extended family to live under one roof. Compared to Westerners, the way Chinese people refer to relatives is much more precise. First of all, let's take a look at siblings. An older brother is called 哥哥 *gē.x*, and an older sister 姐姐 *jiě.x*. A younger brother is referred to as 弟弟 *dì.x*, and a younger sister as 妹妹 *mèi.x*.

For family members of the same generation on the mother's side or children of one's father's sisters ("first cousins"), the word 表 *biǎo* is added to the word that describes a sibling, for example. 表哥 *biǎogē*, 表姐 *biǎojiě*, 表弟 *biǎodì*, or 表妹 *biǎomèi*. For children of one's father's brothers, the word 堂 *táng* is added to form 堂哥 *tánggē*, 堂姐 *tángjiě*, 堂弟 *tángdì*, or 堂妹 *tángmèi*.

There is also a distinction made about the children of one's siblings ("nephews" or "nieces"), depending on whether they are children of a person's sisters or brothers. Sons of a brother are known as 侄子 *zhí.zi* and nieces are known as 侄女 *zhí.nǚ*; sons of a person's sister are referred to as 外甥 *wàishēng*, and daughters of a person's sister are 外甥女 *wàishēngnǚ*.

Paternal grandparents are called 祖父母 *zǔfùmǔ*. Or individually, 祖父 *zǔfù* is used for grandfathers and 祖母 *zǔmǔ* for grandmothers. Similarly, maternal grandfathers are called 外祖父 *wàizǔfù* and maternal grandmothers 外祖母 *wàizǔmǔ*. Together, they are 外祖父母 *wàizǔfùmǔ*.

Due to recent changes in society, households are now usually made up of immediate family consisting of only two parents and their children. It is now rare for grandparents to live with other family members, though in some rural areas, this is still the norm.

8 文化动动脑 Wénhuà Dòng.x nǎo / *Culture Check-up*

Select the letter of the correct answer.

1. In China, what criteria determines the names of family members?

   A. social status　　B. number of people　　C. age and gender

2. What should you call a boy in your nuclear family who is older than you?

   A. 表哥 *biǎogē*　　B. 哥哥 *gē.x*　　C. 堂哥 *tánggē*

3. To which family members are you referring when you use 堂 *táng*?

   A. the children of your father's brothers

   B. the children of your father's sisters

   C. the children of your mother's brothers

▶ Due to the one-child policy, most families in China have only one child.

Language Practice

9 买上学的东西 Mǎi shàng-xué .de dōng.xī / *Shopping for School*

At the end of summer, you want your mother to take you shopping for school. Tell her what you don't have.

Lì.zi: 我要买一本书。

Wǒ yào mǎi yì-běn shū.

1.	2.	3.	4.	5.
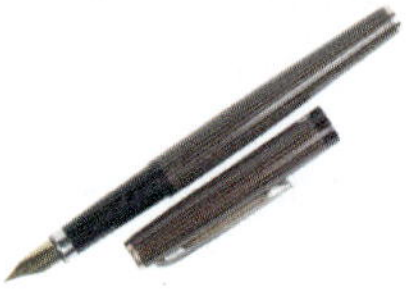			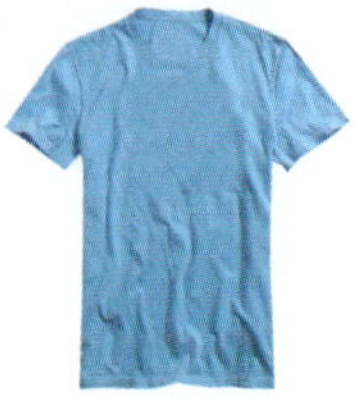	

10 有几个？ Yǒu jǐ-.ge? How many are there?

Use measure words to say how many items there are.

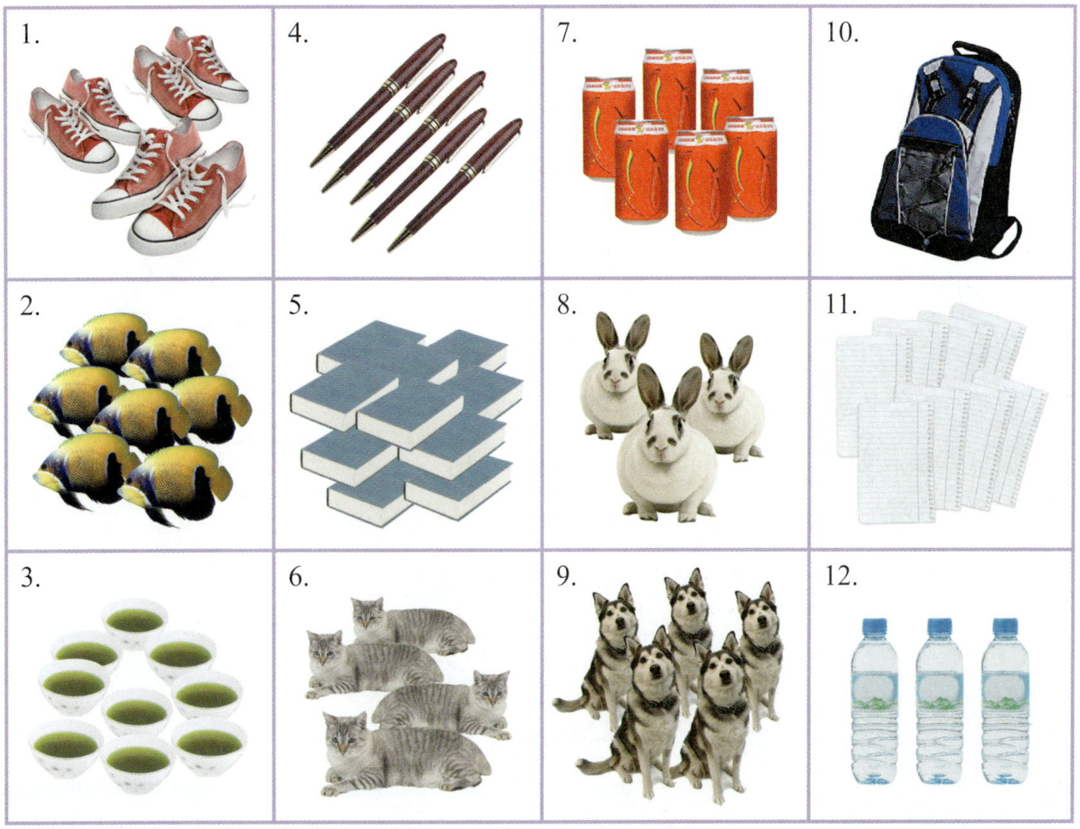

11 我有两个 Wǒ Yǒu Liǎng-.ge Two of Everything

Working in pairs, take turns asking what your partner has and answering that you have two of each object.

Lì.zi: 我有两本书。

Wǒ yǒu liǎng-běn shū.

12 找出问题 Zhǎochū Wèntí | *Questions*

Write down the number of each sentence that is a question. Note that all the question marks have been removed, so you will need to look for question words.

1. 他没有弟弟，对不对 Tā .méi.yǒu dì.x, duì .bú.duì
2. 这是谁的哥哥 Zhèi shì shéi .de gē.x
3. 你家有几口人 Nǐ jiā yǒu *jǐ*-kǒu rén
4. 我有三支笔 *Wǒ* yǒu sān-zhī bǐ
5. 你有两本书吗 *Nǐ* yǒu *liǎng*-běn shū .ma
6. 我也有哥哥 *Wǒ yě* yǒu gē.x
7. 你家有什么人 Nǐ jiā yǒu shén.me rén
8. 我没有兄弟姐妹 Wǒ .méi.yǒu xiōngdì-jiěmèi
9. 我家有爸爸、妈妈和我 Wǒ jiā yǒu bà.x, mā.x hé wǒ
10. 他姐姐叫什么名字 Tā jiě.x jiào shén.me míng.zì

开口说 Kāikǒu Shuō

Communication

13 我的家庭 Wǒ.de Jiātíng | *My Family*

Working in pairs, talk about your families, and include the following information in your conversation:

- the number of people in your family
- how many siblings you have
- the names, ages, and grade levels of your siblings
- whether or not you have nieces and nephews
- what pets you have (if any) and their names

14 我同学的兄弟姐妹 Wǒ Tóngxué .de Xiōngdì-jiěmèi / *My Classmates' Siblings*

Interview three classmates, asking them their name, the number of siblings they have, and the names of their siblings. Fill in a graphic organizer like the one below for each classmate you interview.

Lì.zi: **A:** 你叫什么名字？ Nǐ jiào shén.me míng.zì?

B: 我叫林华。 Wǒ jiào Lín Huá.

A: 你有几个兄弟姐妹？ *Nǐ yǒu* jǐ-.ge xiōngdì-jiěmèi?

B: 我有一个哥哥和一个妹妹。 *Wǒ* yǒu yí-.ge gē.x hé yí-.ge mèi.x.

A: 你的兄弟姐妹叫什么名字？ Nǐ.de xiōngdì-jiěmèi jiào shén.me míng.zì?

B: 我哥哥叫林军，我妹妹叫林苹。 Wǒ gē.x jiào Lín Jūn, wǒ mèi.x jiào Lín Píng.

A: 他们几岁？ Tā.mén jǐ-suì?

B: 我哥哥十六岁，我妹妹十二岁。 Wǒ gē.x shíliù-suì, wǒ mèi.x shí'èr-suì.

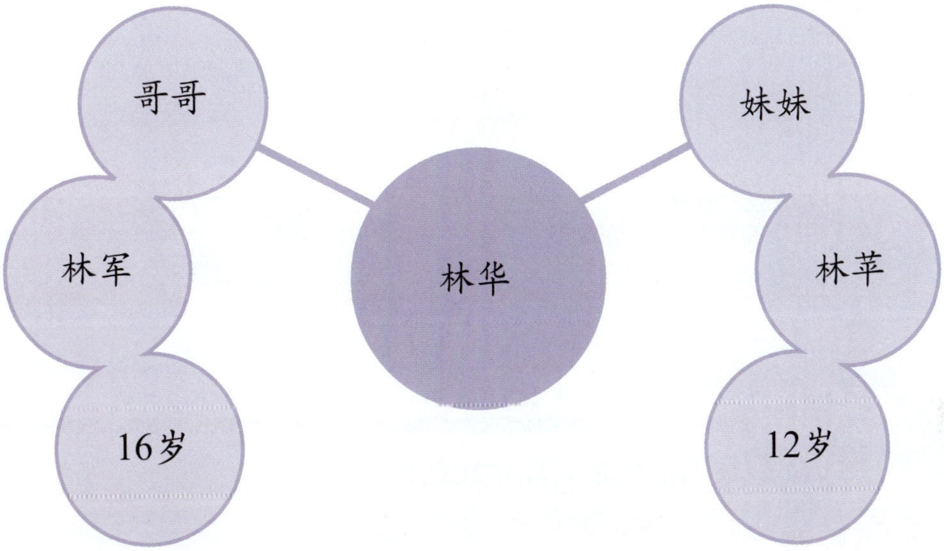

15 写一写 Xiě yì xiě / *Let's write!*

Now use your graphic organizers to write short paragraphs in Pinyin that give each classmate's name, the number of siblings he or she has and their names.

16 家庭关系图 Jiātíng Guānxì Tú / *A Family Tree*

Answer the following questions about the family tree below.

1. What should E call A and B?
2. What should H call A and B?
3. What should H call C and D?
4. What should K call A and B?
5. What should I call H and K?
6. What should I call G and J?

汉字天地 Hànzì Tiāndì

Chinese Characters

口 ■ kǒu ■ mouth

The pictograph 口 *kǒu* shows the shape of a mouth. It is also a common radical for words related to the mouth.

Stroke Order

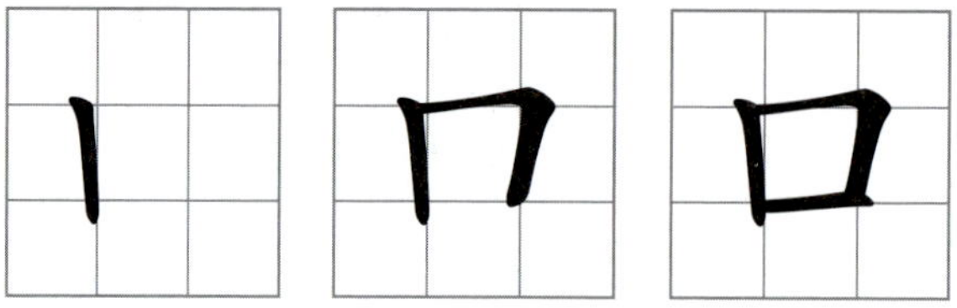

17 词汇延伸 Cíhuì Yánshēn / *Vocabulary Builder*

Below are some characters that can be combined with 口 *kǒu* to create new words. Match the Chinese words on the left with the appropriate English meaning on the right.

袋 dài *n. bag*	水 shuǐ *n. water*	红 hóng *n. red*	罩 zhào *n. cover*	门 mén *n. door*

1. 口袋 kǒudài — A. *entrance*
2. 口水 *kǒu*shuǐ — B. *saliva*
3. 口红 kǒuhóng — C. *pocket*
4. 口罩 kǒuzhào — D. *surgical mask*
5. 门口 ménkǒu — E. *lipstick*

18 汉字侦探 Hànzì Zhēntàn / *Visual Detective*

Can you find 口 in the following pictures?

Lesson C

发音 Fāyīn
Pronunciation

z zh + a ai ao an ang

词汇 Cíhuì
Vocabulary

月份 Yuèfèn *Months of the Year*

一月 Yīyuè
January

二月 Èryuè
February

三月 Sānyuè
March

四月 Sìyuè
April

五月 Wǔyuè
May

六月 Liùyuè
June

七月 Qīyuè
July

八月 Bāyuè
August

九月 Jiǔyuè
September

十月 Shíyuè
October

十一月 Shíyīyuè
November

十二月 Shí'èryuè
December

Culture Note

Chinese New Year is based on the lunar calendar, so it does not begin in January. Instead, it falls between late January and early February.

万圣节是十月三十一日(萬聖節是十月三十一日)。
Wànshèngjié shì Shíyuè sān.shíyī rì. *Halloween is October 31st.*

圣诞节是十二月二十五日(聖誕節是十二月二十五日)。
Shèngdànjié shì Shí'èryuè èr.shíwǔ rì. *Christmas Day is December 25th.*

A: 今天是几月几号(今天是幾月幾號)?
Jīn.tiān shì jǐ-yuè jǐ-hào? *What's the date today?*

B: 今天是七月二号(今天是七月二號)。
Jīn.tiān shì Qīyuè èr hào. *It's July 2nd.*

Language Note

In spoken Chinese, we say "#月 *yuè* #号 *hào*" to express the date, but on paper or in formal situations, we say "#月 *yuè* #日 *rì*."

生日(生日)
shēng.rì *n. birthday*

生日快乐(生日快樂)
shēng.rì kuàilè *ce. happy birthday*

生日蛋糕(生日蛋糕)
shēng.rì dàngāo *n. birthday cake*

生日卡片(生日卡片)
shēng.rì kǎpiàn *n. birthday card*

生日礼物(生日禮物)
shēng.rì lǐwù *n. birthday gift*

A. 生日晚会是几月几号（生日晚會是幾月幾號）？

Shēng.rì wǎnhuì shì jǐ-yuè jǐ-hào? *What date is the birthday party?*

B: 五月一号（五月一號）。

Wǔyuè yī hào. *It's on May 1st.*

A. 你的生日是几月几号（你的生日是幾月幾號）？

Nǐ.de shēng.rì shì jǐ-yuè jǐ-hào? *When is your birthday?*

B: 我的生日是九月二十号（我的生日是九月二十號）。

Wǒ.de shēng.rì shì Jiǔyuè èr.shí hào. *My birthday is September 20th.*

A. 你有他的电话号码吗（你有他的電話號碼嗎）？

Nǐ yǒu tā.de diànhuà hàomǎ .ma? *Do you have his telephone number?*

B: 我没有他的电话号码（我沒有他的電話號碼）。

Wǒ .méi.yǒu tā.de diànhuà hàomǎ. *I don't have his telephone number.*

A. 这是不是你的手机（這是不是你的手機）？

Zhè shì .bú.shì nǐ.de shǒujī? *Is this your cell phone?*

B: 是，谢谢你（是，謝謝你）！

Shì, xiè.x nǐ! *Yes, thanks!*

Let's Count!

For numbers after 20, simply add 1 to 9 after the "tens."

21	22	23	24	25
二十一 èr.shíyī	二十二 èr.shí'èr	二十三 èr.shísān	二十四 èr.shísì	二十五 èr.shíwǔ
36	47	58	69	
三十六 sān.shíliù	四十七 sì.shíqī	五十八 wǔ.shíbā	六十九 liù.shíjiǔ	

Interjections

哇（哇）	.wa	*wow*

Measure Words

月（月）	yuè	*month*
号（號）	hào	*date*

Nouns

号码（號碼）	hàomǎ	*number*

1 一年的月份 Yì nián .de Yuèfèn / *Months of the Year*

Say the month that correctly completes each sequence below.

1. 一月 Yīyuè, 二月 Èryuè....
2. 十月 Shíyuè, 十一月 Shíyīyuè....
3. 五月 Wǔyuè, 六月 Liùyuè....
4. 八月 Bāyuè, 九月 Jiǔyuè....
5. 四月 Sìyuè, 五月 Wǔyuè....
6. 七月 Qīyuè, 八月 Bāyuè....

2 数一数 Shǔ Yì Shǔ / *Numbers*

Complete each sequence of numbers.

1. 10 shí, 20 èr.shí, …, 90 jiǔ.shí
2. 2 èr, 12 shí'èr, …, 92 jiǔ.shí'èr
3. 51 wǔ.shíyī, 53 wǔ.shísān, …, 69 liù.shíjiǔ
4. 30 sān.shí, 32 sān.shí'èr, …, 50 wǔ.shí
5. 81 bā.shíyī, 82 bā.shí'èr, …, 99 jiǔ.shíjiǔ
6. 42 sì.shí'èr, 52 wǔ.shí'èr, ..., 92 jiǔ.shí'èr
7. 72 qī.shí'èr, 74 qī.shísì, ..., 100 yìbǎi
8. 30 sān.shí, 35 sān.shíwǔ, ..., 95 jiǔ.shíwǔ
9. 6 liù, 16 shíliù, …, 96 jiǔ.shíliù
10. 5 wǔ, 10 shí, …, 100 yìbǎi

中文数字很简单！
Zhōngwén shùzì *hěn* jiǎndān!
Chinese numbers are easy!

3 几月几号? Jǐ-yuè jǐ-hào? *What's the date?*

Give the date in Chinese for each illustrated holiday.

1.

3.

5.

2.

4.

6.

4 Heather的生日 Heather .de Shēng.rì *Heather's Birthday*

Heather Zhang is an American student living in China with her parents. Answer the questions about her birthday celebration.

1. 今天是几月几号? Jīn.tiān shì jǐ-yuè jǐ-hào?
2. 今天是谁的生日? Jīn.tiān shì shéi .de shēng.rì?
3. 她几岁? Tā jǐ-suì?
4. 谁给她礼物? Shéi gěi tā lǐwù?
5. 谁给她卡片? Shéi gěi tā kǎpiàn?

5 中文怎么说? Zhōngwén zěn.me shuō? *How would you say it in Chinese?*

What do you say in Chinese in the following situations?

1. You ask your mother today's date.
2. You tell your older sister that today is May 17th.
3. You tell your teacher that you don't have Susan's telephone number.
4. You ask your classmate if he/she has Susan's telephone number.
5. You ask your classmate for Teacher Lin's telephone number.
6. You pick up the book the girl in front of you leaves on the desk and ask if it's hers.
7. You tell your friend your telephone number.
8. You tell your new friend when your birthday is.

6 个人问题 Gèrén Wèntí *Personal Questions*

Answer each question in Chinese.

1. 你的生日是几月几号? Nǐ.de shēng.rì shì jǐ-yuè jǐ-hào?
2. 你有手机吗? *Nǐ yǒu* shǒujī .ma?
3. 你的电话号码是多少? Nǐ.de diànhuà hàomǎ shì duōshǎo?
4. 你爸爸多大年纪? 妈妈呢? Nǐ bà.x duó dà niánjì? Mā.x .ne?
5. 他们的生日是几月几号? Tā.mén.de shēng.rì shì jǐ-yuè jǐ-hào?
6. 你的爷爷多大年纪? 奶奶呢? Nǐ.de yé.x duó dà niánji? Nǎi.x .ne?

句型介绍 Jùxíng Jièshào

Language Patterns

Saying the Date

To express the date in Chinese, start with the year and continue in order with the month, day, hour and minute. Remember this order by starting with the largest unit of time and continuing down to the smallest.

年 ***nián*** + 月 ***yuè*** + 号 ***hào*** / 日 ***rì***

2012年8月15日（2012.8.15）èr líng yī èr nián Bāyuè shíwǔ rì

林肯的生日是一八零九年二月十二日。 Línkěn .de shēng.rì shì yī bā líng jiǔ nián Èryuè shí'èr rì.

Language Note

To say the year, pronounce each number separately.

2013年 èr líng yī sān nián

1996年 yī *jiǔ* jiǔ liù nián

1978年 yī jiǔ qī bā nián

Using the Question Word 几 *jǐ* to Ask About Dates

In the previous lesson, we learned that 几 *jǐ* means "how many." We also use 几 *jǐ* as the question word to ask about dates.

A: 今天是几月几号？ Jīn.tiān shì jǐ-yuè jǐ-hào?

B: 今天是三月十二号。 Jīn.tiān shì Sānyuè shí'èr hào.

Using the Question Word 多少 *duōshǎo* to Ask for Phone Numbers

The original meaning of the question word 多少 *duōshǎo* is "how many" or "how much." Here, it is used to ask for a phone number.

A: 你的电话号码是多少？ Nǐ.de diànhuà hàomǎ shì duōshǎo?

B: 我的电话号码是18776933。 Wǒ.de diànhuà hàomǎ shì yī bā qī qī liù jiǔ sān sān.

A: 大卫的手机号码是多少？ Dàwèi .de shǒujī hàomǎ shì duōshǎo?

B: 他的手机号码是1325-754-6089。 Tā.de shǒujī hàomǎ shì yī sān èr wǔ qī wǔ sì liù líng bā jiǔ.

会话 Huìhuà
Dialogue

你的电话号码是多少？ Nǐ.de diànhuà hàomǎ shì duōshǎo?
What is your phone number?

In the cafeteria, Dong Jun is talking to Zhang Guohua.

董军：	你的生日是几月几号？	Dǒng Jūn:	Nǐ.de shēng.rì shì jǐ-yuè jǐ-hào?
张国华：	我的生日是十一月二十二号，你呢？	Zhāng Guóhuá:	Wǒ.de shēng.rì shì Shíyīyuè èr.shíèr hào, nǐ .ne?
董军：	一月一号。	Dǒng Jūn:	Yīyuè yī hào.
张国华：	哇！一月一号！	Zhāng Guóhuá:	.Wa! Yīyuè yī hào!
董军：	你的电话号码是多少？	Dǒng Jūn:	Nǐ.de diànhuà hàomǎ shì duōshǎo?
张国华：	我的电话号码是 6513-0828。	Zhāng Guóhuá:	Wǒ.de diànhuà hàomǎ shì liù wǔ yī sān líng bā èr bā.
董军：	你有手机吗？	Dǒng Jūn:	*Nǐ* yǒu shǒujī .ma?
张国华：	有。	Zhāng Guóhuá:	Yǒu.
董军：	你的手机号码是多少？	Dǒng Jūn:	Nǐ.de shǒujī hàomǎ shì duōshǎo?
张国华：	196-2347-6902。	Zhāng Guóhuá:	Yī jiǔ liù èr sān sì qī liù jiǔ líng èr.

7 个人资料 Gèrén Zīliào / *Personal Information*

Copy the table below on a separate sheet of paper. Based on the dialogue above, fill in the table with the correct information. Some information applies to only one of the characters.

Information \ Name	Dong Jun 	Zhang Guohua 
生日 shēng.rì		
电话号码 diànhuà hàomǎ		
手机号码 shǒujī hàomǎ		

8 懂了吗? Dǒng .le .ma? / *Do you understand?*

Answer the following questions in Chinese.

1. 董军的生日是几月几日？ Dǒng Jūn .de shēng.rì shì jǐ-yuè jǐ-rì?
2. 张国华的生日是几月几日？ Zhāng Guóhuá .de shēng.rì shì jǐ-yuè jǐ-rì?
3. 张国华的电话号码是多少？ Zhāng Guóhuá .de diànhuà hàomǎ shì duōshǎo?
4. 张国华有手机吗？ Zhāng Guóhuá *yǒu* shǒujī .ma?
5. 张国华的手机号码是多少？ Zhāng Guóhuá .de shǒujī hàomǎ shì duōshǎo?

文化橱窗 Wénhuà Chúchuāng
Culture Window

How the Chinese Celebrate Birthdays

Traditionally, the Chinese only celebrate a person's first birthday, and then do not celebrate the person's birthday again until the age of 40. Each birthday is an occasion for a family gathering, so in China, birthdays are considered family occasions.

A child's first birthday is called 周岁 *zhōu suì*, and is considered the most important birthday. There are events for this occasion, such as 抓周 *zhuāzhōu*, which is a ritual of placing many objects in front of the baby for him or her to grab. It is believed that the object the infant chooses will determine his or her future; for example, grabbing an abacus represents success in the business world, picking up a drumstick means the child will never go hungry, taking a stethoscope suggests the child will become a doctor, and reaching for a book means that the child will do well in school.

When celebrating the birthdays of middle-aged and senior adults, age noodles (寿面 *shòumiàn*), pork knuckle noodles, and red eggs are often prepared to wish the recipient a long life and good health. In recent years, due to intercultural influences, many Chinese now celebrate birthdays in the western style by singing songs and eating cakes.

▲ The character 寿 *shòu* (in the background) means longevity.

Cell Phones in Mainland China

Cell phones in China are called 移动电话 (*yídòng diànhuà*, mobile phones) or 手提电话 (*shǒutí diànhuà*, handheld phones), and are simplified as 手机 *shǒujī*. Increasingly important in Chinese society, cell phones have become the most used form of communication for many young people. According to surveys, over half the people in China have a cell phone.

Mainland China's cell phone numbers begin with a number from 130 to 139, from 150-159, or from 180-189, and are composed of 11 digits. An area code follows the first three digits, such as 010 for Beijing, 020 for Guangzhou, and 021 for Shanghai. To call numbers in another city, a 0 must be added in front of the number, making a total of 12 digits. A country code is needed when calling from another country, like the United States. What is the country code for China?

Comparisons

Which birthday is especially important for teen Hispanic girls? Is turning 16 ("Sweet Sixteen") a special birthday in your family? What other birthdays are considered significant in the United States? What do they signify, for example, turning 18 and 21?

	first few digits	country code
Mainland China	130-139, 159...	86
Hong Kong	6, 9	852
Taiwan	09	886

9 文化动动脑 Wénhuà Dòng.x nǎo / *Culture Check-up*

Select the letter of the correct answer.

1. What does 周岁 *zhōu suì* refer to?
   A. first birthday B. celebration one week after birth C. 20th birthday

2. According to Chinese beliefs, which of the following statements concerning infants' *zhuazhou* and their future careers is incorrect?
   A. grabbing an abacus—future career in business
   B. grabbing a stethoscope—future career in medicine
   C. grabbing a drumstick—future career in the arts

3. At a Chinese birthday celebration, you see age noodles, pork knuckle noodles, and red eggs. This leads you to believe that this is a birthday celebration for whom?
A. a small child B. a teenager C. someone over 40

4. What is the percentage of cell phone usage in China?
A. over 50% B. over 100% C. over 150%

5. Which number must you add to the original cell phone number to make a phone call from Shanghai to Shenzhen?
A. 2 B. 1 C. 0

6. If your friend's cell phone number is 13001086551, where does he probably live?
A. Shanghai B. Beijing C. Guangzhou

7. Taiwan's cell phone numbers begin with what set of numbers?
A. 886 B. 136 C. 09

Language Practice

10 几月几号? Jǐ-yuè jǐ-hào? *What's the date?*

Listen to the recording and select the date that you hear.

1. A. 6.30 B. 12.13
2. A. 8.5 B. 5.8
3. A. 1.21 B. 1.11
4. A. 7.19 B. 1.19
5. A. 12.24 B. 2.24
6. A. 10.6 B. 10.16

11 出生年份 Chūshēng Niánfèn *The Year of Birth*

Listen to the recording and write down the year that each of Wang Mei's relatives was born.

12 美国历史 Měi.guó Lìshǐ *American History*

Write in English the dates that you hear. When you are done, look up these dates and write down what happened in American history on that day.

13 保持联络 Bǎochí Liánluò / *Keeping in Touch*

Write down the phone number mentioned in each mini-dialogue you hear. Follow the model.

Lì.zi: 1300-106-6541.

开口说 Kāikǒu Shuō
Communication

14 中国节日 Zhōng.guó Jiérì / *Chinese Holidays*

The following are some traditional Chinese holidays. With a partner, take turns asking and telling each other the dates of the holidays. Note that the dates are based on the Lunar Calendar.

Lì.zi: A: 春节是几月几号？ Chūnjié shì jǐ-yuè jǐ-hào?

B: 春节是一月一号。 Chūnjié shì Yīyuè yī hào.

January 1st	January 15th	May 5th	July 7th	July 15th	August 15th

春节 Chūnjié *Spring Festival (Chinese New Year)*	元宵节 Yuánxiāojié *Lantern Festival*	端午节 Duānwǔjié *Dragon Boat Festival*	七夕节 Qīxìjié *Chinese Valentine's Day*	鬼节 Guǐjié *Ghost Festival*	中秋节 Zhōngqiūjié *Mid-Autumn Festival*

Culture Note

The Lunar Calendar is a traditional Chinese calendar, and it has been in use since the 11th century, B.C. Traditional festivals like the above-mentioned are all based on it.

15 排排站 Pái.x Zhàn / *Form a line*

Ask your classmates when their birthdays are and place yourselves in a line, in birthday order. Students with January birthdays should start to line up on the left side of the room.

16 演唱会日期 Yǎnchànghuì Rìqī / *Concert Dates*

With a partner, take turns asking each other who is performing at Kennedy Center on certain dates. Follow the model.

Lì.zi: 5.14 / 9.20

A: 谁五月十四号在Kennedy Center有演唱会?

Shéi Wǔyuè shísì hào zài Kennedy Center *yǒu* yǎnchànghuì?

B: Justin Timberlake.

B: 谁九月二十号有演唱会?

Shéi Jiǔyuè èr.shí hào *yǒu* yǎnchànghuì?

A: Andrea Bocelli.

Date	Performer	Date	Performer
5.14	Justin Timberlake	7.28	Kylie Minogue
5.26	Alicia Keys	8.1	Lindsay Lohan
6.7	Leona Lewis	8.17	Black Eyed Peas
6.23	Gwen Stefani	9.20	Andrea Bocelli
7.19	Beyonce	9.30	Linkin Park

1. 5.26 / 8.1
2. 6.7 / 7.19
3. 6.23 / 9.30
4. 7.28 / 8.17

17 我同学的电话 Wǒ Tóngxué .de Diànhuà / *My Classmates' Phone Numbers*

You want to keep in touch with five of your classmates during vacation. With each classmate, take turns asking for phone numbers and writing them down in a chart like the one that follows.

Lì.zi: **You:** 你的电话号码是多少？

Nǐ.de diànhuà hàomǎ shì duōshǎo?

Audrey: 我的电话号码是651-555-1234。

Wǒ.de diànhuà hàomǎ shì
liù wǔ yī *wǔ wǔ* wǔ yī èr sān sì.

☺ Audrey	☎ 651-555-1234
☺	☎
☺	☎
☺	☎
☺	☎
☺	☎

18 护照 Hùzhào / *Passport*

Look at the passport below and answer the questions that follow.

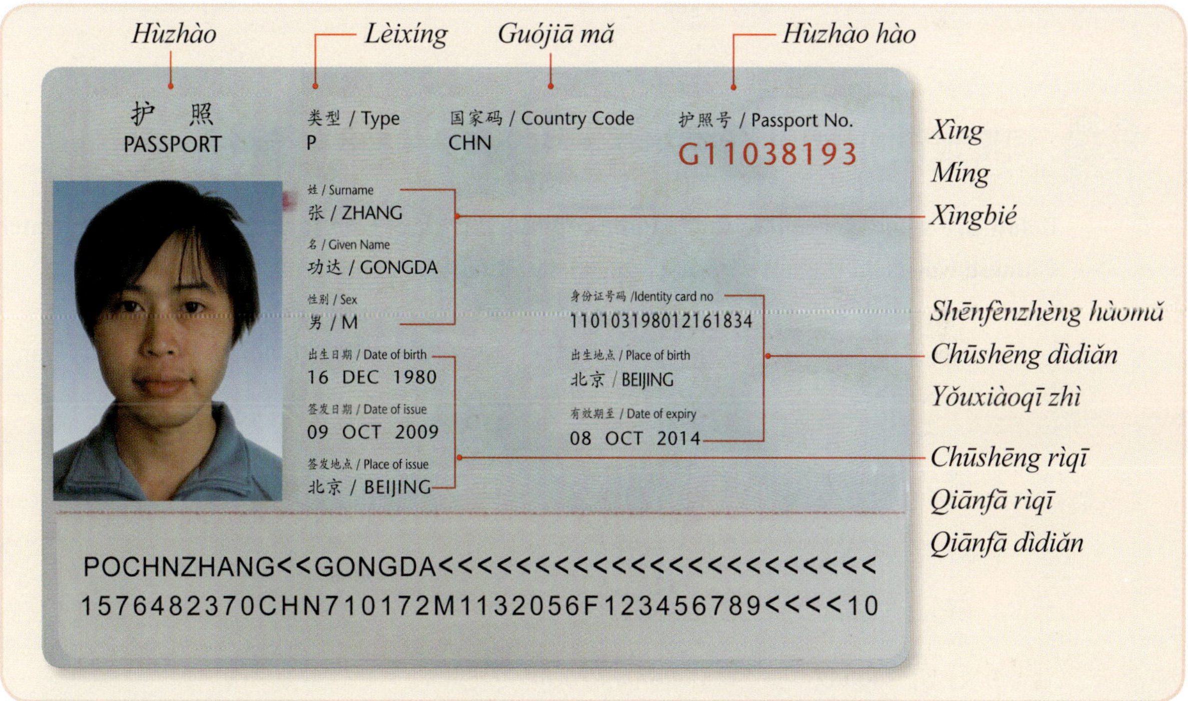

1. Whose passport is this?
2. What is the passport number?
3. What is the passport owner's identity card number?
4. When is his birthday?
5. Where was he born?
6. When was the passport issued?
7. Where was the passport issued?
8. When does this passport expire?

汉字天地 Hànzì Tiāndì
Chinese Characters

好 ■ hǎo ■ goodness

The character 好 *hǎo* is a combination of two pictographs. The pictograph 女 means "female." The second pictograph means "son." In ancient China, once a man married a woman, the first thing he and his family wanted was a son, considered to be the "greatest of goods." The two pictographs combined represent a symbol of goodness: a woman holding a new-born baby boy in her arms.

Stroke Order

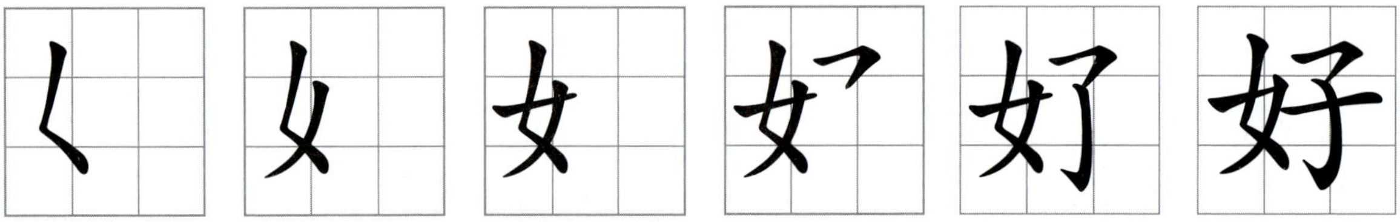

19 词汇延伸 Cíhuì Yánshēn / *Vocabulary Builder*

Below are some characters that can be combined with 好 *hǎo* to create new words. Match the Chinese words on the left with the appropriate English meaning on the right.

人 rén *n. person*	吃 chī *v. to eat*	心 xīn *n. heart*	听 tīng *v. to listen*	看 kàn *v. to see*

1. 好人 hǎorén — A. *good person*
2. 好吃 hǎochī — B. *good-looking*
3. 好心 hǎoxīn — C. *delicious*
4. 好听 hǎotīng — D. *pleasant to hear*
5. 好看 hǎokàn — E. *kindhearted*

20 汉字侦探 Hànzì Zhēntàn *Visual Detective*

Can you find 好 in the pictures below?

Lesson D

发音 Fāyīn
Pronunciation

c ch + a ai ao an ang

词汇 Cíhuì
Vocabulary

休闲活动 Xiūxián Huódòng *Leisure Activities*

篮球 (籃球)
lánqiú
n. basketball

足球 (足球)
zúqiú
n. soccer

滑板 (滑板)
huábǎn
n. skateboarding

棒球 (棒球)
bàngqiú
n. baseball

排球 (排球)
páiqiú
n. volleyball

冰球 (冰球)
bīngqiú
n. ice hockey

游泳 (游泳)
yóuyǒng
v./n. to swim; swimming

上网 (上網)
shàngwǎng
v. to surf the Internet

电子游戏 (電子遊戲)
diànzǐ yóuxì
n. video games

一起逛街吧 (一起逛街吧)!
Yìqǐ guàngjiē .ba! *Let's go shopping!*

听音乐 (聽音樂)
tīng-yīnyuè
vo. to listen to music

唱歌 (唱歌)
chàng-gē
vo. to sing

跳舞 (跳舞)
tiào-wǔ
vo. to dance

画画 (畫畫)
huà.x
vo. to paint; to draw

写字 (寫字)
xiě-zì
vo. to write

看书 (看書)
kàn-shū
vo. to read (books)

吃饭 (吃飯)
chī-fàn
vo. to eat

说话 (說話)
shuō-huà
vo. to speak

你喜欢做什么
(你喜歡做什麼)？
Nǐ xǐ.huān zuò shén.me?
What do you like to do?

我喜欢看电影
(我喜歡看電影)。
Wǒ xǐ.huān kàn-diànyǐng.
I like watching movies.

A: 你们打不打排球 (你們打不打排球)？
Nǐ.mén dǎ .bù.dǎ-páiqiú? *Do you play volleyball?*

B: 我很喜欢打排球 (我很喜歡打排球)。
Wǒ hěn xǐ.huān dǎ-páiqiú. *I like playing volleyball a lot.*

C: 我有时候打排球 (我有時候打排球)。
Wǒ yǒushí.hòu dǎ-páiqiú. *I like playing volleyball sometimes.*

A: 你的爱好是什么 (你的愛好是什麼)？
Nǐ.de àihào shì shén.me? *What are your pastimes?*

B: 我的爱好是跳舞和画画 (我的愛好是跳舞和畫畫)。
Wǒ.de àihào shì tiào-wǔ hé huà.x. *My pastimes are dancing and painting.*

Adverbs

一起 (一起)	yìqǐ	*together*

Conjunctions

那 (那)	nà	*then; in that case*

Idiomatic Expressions

对了 (對了)	duì.le	*by the way*

Nouns

球 (球)	qiú	*ball*
爱好 (愛好)	àihào	*pastime*
电影 (電影)	diànyǐng	*movie*

Particles

吧 (吧)	.ba	*(used at the end of a sentence to make a suggestion)*

Time Words

明天 (明天)	míng.tiān	*tomorrow*

Verbs

喜欢 (喜歡)	xǐ.huān	*to like*
做 (做)	zuò	*to do; to make*
打 (打)	dǎ	*to hit; to play (a ball sport)*
踢 (踢)	tī	*to kick; to play (soccer)*
玩 (玩)	wán	*to play (sports or recreational activities)*
看 (看)	kàn	*to see; to look at*

Language Note

Different verbs are used for different sports. For sports like basketball, baseball, and hockey, 打 *dǎ* is used. For soccer, the verb is 踢 *tī*, and for skateboarding and video games, 玩 *wán* is used.

1 青少年的爱好 Qīngshàonián .de Àihào *Teen Pastimes*

You will hear six activities. Select the photo that corresponds to the activity you hear by choosing A or B.

1. A. 
   B. 

2. A. 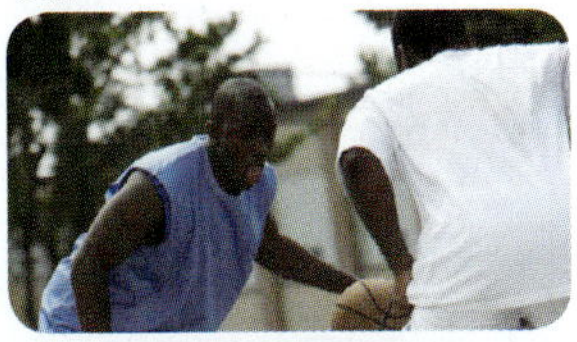
   B. 

3. A. 
   B. 

4. A. 
   B. 

5. A. 
   B. 

6. A. 
   B. 

2 什么球? Shén.me qiú? *What sport do they like?*

Say whether the following teens like playing basketball, baseball, or soccer.

Lì.zi: Pamela 

Pamela喜欢打篮球。 Pamela xǐ.huān dǎ-lánqiú.

1	2	3	4	5	6	7	8	9
马英 Mǎ Yīng 	Victor 	柳元 Liǔ Yuán 	Sandra 	白心怡 Bái Xīnyí 	王育成 Wáng Yùchéng 	林白和林华 Lín Bái hé Lín Huá 	吴文 Wú Wén 	明明 Míngmíng 

3 找找人 Zhǎo.x Rén / *Find someone who....*

To interview your classmates about what activities they like, make a grid like the one that follows. Number the questions from 1 to 8. Ask your classmates the following questions one at a time. For each affirmative answer, get that person's signature. Get a signature from a different person for each question.

Lì.zi: **Daniel:** 你喜欢踢足球吗？ *Nǐ* xǐ.huān tī-zúqiú .ma?

Bob: 我不喜欢踢足球。 Wǒ bù xǐ.huān tī-zúqiú.

Tanya: 我喜欢踢足球。 *Wǒ* xǐ.huān tī-zúqiú. (Tanya signs your paper.)

你喜欢… **Nǐ xǐ.huān…**	**Names**
1. 踢足球吗？ tī-zúqiú .ma?	Tanya
2. 打篮球吗？ dǎ-lánqiú .ma?	
3. 游泳吗？ yóuyǒng .ma?	
4. 玩滑板吗？ wán-huábǎn .ma?	
5. 玩电子游戏吗？ wán-diànzǐ yóuxì .ma?	
6. 打棒球吗？ dǎ-bàngqiú .ma?	
7. 上网吗？ shàngwǎng .ma?	
8. 唱歌吗？ chàng-gē .ma?	
9. 听音乐吗？ tīng-yīnyuè .ma?	

4 个人问题 Gèrén Wèntí / *Personal Questions*

Answer each question in Chinese.

1. 你的爱好是什么？ Nǐ.de àihào shì shén.me?
2. 你喜欢什么运动(*sport*)？ *Nǐ* xǐ.huān shén.me yùndòng?
3. 你不喜欢什么运动(*sport*)？ Nǐ bù xǐ.huān shén.me yùndòng?
4. 你很喜欢听音乐吗？ *Nǐ hěn* xǐ.huān tīng-yīnyuè .ma?
5. 你有时候喜欢画画吗？ *Nǐ* yǒushí.hòu xǐ.huān huà.x .ma?
6. 你明天想(*to want*)做什么？ Nǐ míng.tiān xiǎng zuò shén.me?

句型介绍 Jùxíng Jièshào

Language Patterns

Verb-Object Compounds

Certain verbs are commonly paired with certain nouns to form "verb-object" compounds, such as 吃饭 *chī-fàn* ("eat rice"), 说话 *shuō-huà* ("speak words"), and 写字 *xiě-zì* ("write characters") . The verb-object compound 吃饭 *chī-fàn* should be translated not as "eat rice," but simply as "eat." Similarly, other verb-object compounds are to be translated as intransitive verbs. In a sense, the objects of these compounds are "dummy" objects. For example:

写字 xiě-zì *to write* (lit. to write characters)	看书 kàn-shū *to read* (lit. to look at books)	唱歌 chàng-gē *to sing* (lit. to sing songs)
吃饭 chī-fàn *to eat* (lit. to eat rice)	跳舞 tiào-wǔ *to dance* (lit. to dance a dance)	说话 shuō-huà *to speak* (lit. to speak words)
画画 huà.x *to paint; to draw* (lit. to paint pictures)		

我们吃饭。 Wǒ.mén chī-fàn.

他喜欢说话。 Tā xǐ.huān shuō-huà.

他们写字。 Tā.mén xiě-zì.

Because V-O compounds are intransitive, they cannot take an object. In order to add an object, simply replace the "dummy" object with the object you want.

我说话。 Wǒ shuō-<u>huà</u>. (sentence with "dummy" object)

Yīngwén = Wǒ shuō Yīngwén. (sentence with desired object)

In other words, verbs like 吃 *chī*, 说 *shuō*, and 写 *xiě* are transitive when they appear without their "dummy" objects. When they appear with no objects at all, they are still transitive. Therefore, to translate them into English, you often have to supply the word "it." For example:

你吃不吃? Nǐ chī .bù.chī? *Do you eat (it)?*

请你写。 *Qǐng nǐ* xiě. *Please write (it).*

V-O compounds can be split when a specific feature or description needs to be added. For example,

我看<u>中文</u>书。

Wǒ kàn <u>Zhōngwén</u> shū.

他们说<u>很多</u>话。

Tā.mén shuō <u>hěn duō</u> huà

Comparisons

Look up the adjective "transitive" in the dictionary. Then determine if each underlined English verb below is transitive or intransitive.

I <u>called</u> Jeremy.

We <u>went</u> out.

"V 不 *bù* / *bú* V" Questions

The particle 吗 *.ma* at the end of a sentence changes a statement into a yes / no question. Although this may seem like an easy way to ask questions in Chinese, you shouldn't use it all the time because Chinese speakers use V not-V questions more often. V not-V questions offer the listener a choice between something and its negation. To answer this kind of question, you must answer either "V" or "not-V."

V + **不 *bù / bú*** + **V** + **O**

Question: 你是不是学生？ Nǐ shì .bú.shì xué.shēng?

Positive response: 我是学生。 Wǒ shì xué.shēng.
(or 我是 Wǒ shì.)
(or 是 Shì.)

Negative response: 我不是学生。 Wǒ bú .shì xué.shēng.
(or 我不是 Wǒ bú .shì.)
(or 不是 Bú.shì.)

The "not-V" form of 有 *yǒu* is 没有 *méi.yǒu*, so the V not-V questions for the verb 有 *yǒu* is 有没有 *yǒu .méi.yǒu*.

他们有没有手机？ Tā.mén yǒu .méi.yǒu shǒujī?
你有没有兄弟姐妹？ *Nǐ* yǒu .méi.yǒu xiōngdì-jiěmèi?

The Suggestive Particle 吧 *.ba*

The particle 吧 *.ba* is used at the end of a sentence to make a suggestion to others, similar to the "Let's (do something)" expression in English.

Sentence + **吧 *.ba***

A: 我们明天做什么？ Wǒ.mén míng.tiān zuò shén.me?
B: 我们看电影吧！ Wǒ.mén kàn-diànyǐng .ba!
明天一起吃饭吧！ Míng.tiān yìqǐ chī-fàn .ba!

会话 Huìhuà
Dialogue

邀请新朋友 Yāoqǐng Xīn Péng.yǒu *Inviting a New Friend*

Walking to the subway after school, Zhang Guohua and Dong Jun discuss their likes and dislikes.

张国华：	你喜欢做什么？	Zhāng Guóhuá:	*Nǐ* xǐ.huān zuò shén.me?
董军：	我喜欢打球。	Dǒng Jūn:	*Wǒ* xǐ.huān dǎ-qiú.
张国华：	你喜欢打什么球？	Zhāng Guóhuá:	*Nǐ* xǐ.huān dǎ shén.me qiú?
董军：	我喜欢打篮球，你呢？	Dǒng Jūn:	*Wǒ* xǐ.huān dǎ-lánqiú, nǐ .ne?
张国华：	我不喜欢打篮球。对了，你看不看电影？	Zhāng Guóhuá:	Wǒ bù xǐ.huān dǎ-lánqiú. Duì .le, nǐ kàn .bú.kàn-diànyǐng?
董军：	我看，我很喜欢法国电影。	Dǒng Jūn:	Wǒ kàn, *wǒ hěn* xǐ.huān Fǎ.guó diànyǐng.
张国华：	我也喜欢。	Zhāng Guóhuá:	*Wǒ yě* xǐ.huān.
董军：	那我们明天一起看电影吧！	Dǒng Jūn:	Nà wǒ.mén míng.tiān yìqǐ kàn-diànyǐng .ba!
张国华：	好啊。	Zhāng Guóhuá:	Hǎo .a.

5 谁喜欢什么？ Shéi xǐ.huān shén.me? *Who likes what?*

Give the name of the character who is being described. For some sentences you will need to give both names.

1. 他喜欢打球。 Tā xǐ.huān dǎ-qiú.
2. 他喜欢打篮球。 Tā xǐ.huān dǎ-lánqiú.
3. 他喜欢看电影。 Tā xǐ.huān kàn-diànyǐng.
4. 他很喜欢看法国电影。 Tā xǐ.huān kàn Fǎ.guó diànyǐng.
5. 他明天要去看电影。 Tā míng.tiān yào qù kàn-diànyǐng.

6 对还是错? Duì hái.shì cuò? *True or false?*

Decide if each statement about the dialogue is true or false. Correct any false statements.

1. 董军喜欢打篮球。 Dǒng Jūn xǐ.huān dǎ-lánqiú.
2. 张国华也喜欢打篮球。 Zhāng Guóhuá *yě* xǐ.huān dǎ-lánqiú.
3. 他们都喜欢看电影。 Tā.mén dōu xǐ.huān kàn-diànyǐng.
4. 董军喜欢法国电影，张国华不喜欢法国电影。
   Zhāng Guóhuá xǐ.huān Fǎ.guó diànyǐng, Zhāng Guóhuá bù xǐ.huān Fǎ.guó diànyǐng.
5. 他们明天一起打篮球。 Tā.mén míng.tiān yì*qǐ* dǎ-lánqiú.

文化橱窗 Wénhuà Chúchuāng

Culture Window

Basketball in China

▲ Yao Ming is the basketball idol of many Chinese teens.

Americans introduced basketball to the Chinese in 1894, and since then, it has become one of China's favorite sports. Activities and events are held in cities all over China. The Chinese don't just love to watch basketball—they do very well in competitions, too. Since the Summer Olympic Games of 1984, the Chinese Men's Basketball Team has placed as high as eighth place, and the Women's Team has won a silver medal.

Basketball is also a popular sport with students. Almost every school has a basketball court, and students will form teams to compete against each other. Students very much look forward to interschool competitions and they avidly follow teams and players in both the Chinese Basketball Association (CBA) and America's National Basketball Association (NBA). There are also basketball schools in China to train Chinese basketball hopefuls, such as the famous school in Chengdu.

Yao Ming joined the CBA when he was 18. At seven feet, six inches, he is able to shoot baskets with ease. This, along with his agility and personal technique, has allowed him to become one of the best centers in the world today. At the Sydney Summer Olympics in 2000, he and fellow teammates Wang Zhizhi and Mengke Bateer were called "The

Walking Great Wall." In 2003, Yao received the Laureus World Newcomer of the Year award.

Wang Zhizhi is a seven-foot-one left-hander with nimble footwork that has allowed him to fool many opponents and win multiple international games for the Chinese National Team. He was also the first Chinese player to play in the NBA, and became the MVP of the CBA finals in 2007.

Mengke Bateer, a Mongolian player, first appeared on the basketball scene in the Asian Games in 1994 when he was 19 years old. He then became a regular fixture on the national team. Mengke Bateer was the second Chinese basketball player to play in the NBA, and the first to win the championship when he played with the San Antonio Spurs.

At six-foot-11 inches, Yi Jianlian is a great shot and has lots of strength, making him one of the few Chinese players who like to slam-dunk. In 2004, he was picked for the Chinese National Team and became the youngest MVP in CBA history in 2005. He was considered to be one of China's best newcomers to professional basketball, and entered the NBA draft in 2007.

7 文化动动脑 Wénhuà Dòng.x nǎo / *Culture Check-up*

Choose the correct answer.

1. When and from where did the sport of basketball travel to China?
   A. 1894, from the United States B. 1893, from Canada C. 1895, from Mexico

2. What have been the best rankings for the Chinese Men's and Women's basketball teams?
   A. second, first B. eighth, second C. fifth, third

3. Yao Ming's height is one of his advantages on the court. How tall is he?
   A. seven feet, six inches B. eight feet, one inch C. seven feet

4. At the 2000 Olympics, Yao Ming, Wang Zhizhi and Mengke Bateer combo was called what?
   A. the Moving China B. the Walking Great Wall C. the Moving World

5. Who were the first and second Chinese players to be drafted into the NBA?
   A. Yao Ming, Wang Zhizhi B. Yi Jianlian, Yao Ming
   C. Wang Zhizhi, Mengke Bateer

6. An excerpt of an interview with one of the Chinese basketball players is as follows: "...is one of China's best centers. Although he is very tall, he is very agile. This, combined with his left-handedness, often keeps his opponents on their feet." Who is this person?
   A. Yi Jianlian B. Wang Zhizhi C. Mengke Bateer

7. Mengke Bateer belongs to which of China's ethnic groups?
   A. Xinjiang B. Zhuang C. Mongolian

8. Which of the following is NOT one of Yi Jianlian's achievements?
   A. awarded the MVP in the CBA finals
   B. once played for the Chinese men's national team
   C. was the youngest MVP in CBA history

Language Practice

8 他们喜欢做什么？ Tā.mén xǐ.huān zuò shén.me? *What do they like to do?*

Say what each teen likes to do according to the photos below.

1. James 	3. Wàn Yuè 	5. Tina 
2. Liú Fēng 	4. Melody 	6. Guān Tíng 

9 留学 Liúxué *Study Abroad*

Say what language the following foreign exchange students from China are speaking this year.

1. 林秀 Lín Xiù
2. 赵国 Zhào Guó
3. 黄梅 Huáng Méi
4. 高健 Gāo Jiàn

10 换句话说 Huàn jù huà shuō / *Will you or won't you?*

You will hear eight questions ending in 吗 .*ma.* Change them into "affirmative-negative" questions.

Lì.zi: **A:** 他喜欢打篮球吗？ Tā xǐ.huān dǎ-lánqiú .ma?
B: 他喜不喜欢打篮球？ Tā xǐ .bù xǐ.huān dǎ-lánqiú?

1. 林先生打棒球吗？ Lín xiān.shēng dǎ-bàngqiú .ma?
2. 她看电影吗？ Tā kàn-diànyǐng .ma?
3. 张小姐有妹妹吗？ Zhāng *xiǎojiě* yǒu mèi.x .ma?
4. 你认识白老师吗？ Nǐ rèn.shì Bái lǎoshī .ma?
5. 他的生日是二月二号吗？ Tā.de shēng.rì shì Èryuè èr hào .ma?
6. 你有他的电话号码吗？ *Nǐ* yǒu tā.de diànhuà hàomǎ .ma?

11 你喜欢做什么？ *Nǐ* xǐ.huān zuò shén.me? / *What do you like to do?*

Ask if your partner does the activities in the photos. Use the "V + 不 bù/bú + V + O" pattern.

Lì.zi: **A:** 你喜不喜欢看电影？ *Nǐ* xǐ bù xǐ.huān kàn-diànyǐng?
B: 我喜欢。 *Wǒ* xǐ.huān.
OR 我不喜欢。 Wǒ bù xǐ.huān.

1.	2.	3.	4.	5.

12 我们一起…吧！ Wǒ.mén yìqǐ… .ba! / *Let's…!*

Based on what your classmates tell you, suggest an activity for the two of you to do together.

Lì.zi: 董书：我踢足球。 Dǒng Shū: Wǒ tī-zúqiú.
我们一起踢足球吧！ Wǒ.mén yìqǐ tī-zúqiú .ba!

1. 林苹：我看书。 Lín Píng: Wǒ kàn-shū.
2. 白军：我打棒球。 Bái Jūn: *Wǒ* dǎ-bàngqiú.
3. 李爱：我打篮球。 Lǐ Ài: *Wǒ* dǎ-lánqiú.
4. 王可可：我玩滑板。 Wáng *Kěkě*: Wǒ wán-huábǎn.
5. 张华：我看中国电影。 Zhāng Huá: Wǒ kàn-Zhōng.guó diànyǐng.

13 谈谈爱好 Tán.x Àihào / *Talking about Pastimes*

Select the photo that corresponds to the activity in the mini-dialogue you hear.

A. 

C. 

E. 

B. 

D. 

F. 

开口说 Kāikǒu Shuō

Communication

14 你的爱好是什么? Nǐ.de àihào shì shén.me? / *What are your pastimes?*

With a partner, play the roles of two students who are discussing their pastimes.

A: Greet your classmate and ask how he or she is doing.
B: Tell your partner how you are doing.
A: Ask your classmate what his or her hobbies are.
B: Name an activity you like to do. Ask your classmate if he or she likes that activity too.
A: Say "yes, I like that activity a lot."
B: Suggest doing the activity together.

15 我的伙伴的爱好 Wǒ.de Huǒbàn .de Àihào / *My Partner's Likes and Dislikes*

With a partner, take turns asking and telling each other what you like to do for fun. Make a grid like the one that follows and put a check mark in the appropriate column.

你喜欢…吗? *Nǐ* xǐ.huān… .ma? Do you like...?

	是 shì	不 bù		是 shì	不 bù
1. 玩滑板 wán-huábǎn			5. 吃东西 chī-dōng.xi		
2. 游泳 yóuyǒng			6. 踢足球 tī-zúqiú		
3. 打篮球 dǎ-lánqiú			7. 说中文 shuō-Zhōngwén		
4. 上网 shàngwǎng			8. 写字 xiě-zì		

16 周末计划 Zhōumò Jìhuà / *Weekend Plans*

In small groups of four, tell two things you like to do in your free time. The person on the right of the speaker will ask who likes to do those activities.

Lì.zi: **A:** 我喜欢打篮球。 *Wǒ* xǐ.huān dǎ-lánqiú.
B: 谁喜欢打篮球? Shéi xǐ.huān dǎ-lánqiú?
(*All four group members raise their hands.*)

17 志伟的电子邮件 Zhìwěi .de Diànzǐ Yóujiàn / *Zhiwei's E-mail*

To organize a composition about what you and your key pal like, make intersecting circles. In the first circle list the four pastimes you like best; in the second circle list the things your key pal likes best; in the section where the circles intersect list the things that both of you like.

我喜欢玩滑板、看电影、听音乐和上网。你喜欢做什么?
Wǒ xǐ.huān wán-huábǎn, kàn-diànyǐng, tīng-yīnyuè hé shàngwǎng.
Nǐ xǐ.huān zuò shén.me?

志伟 Zhìwěi

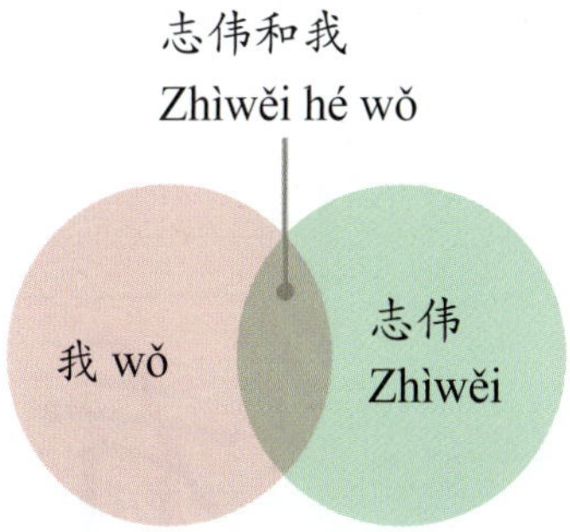

Now that you have completed your graphic organizer, write your composition. First say what you like to do. Then say what Zhiwei likes to do. Finally, state what you both like to do.

Look at the movie ticket and answer the questions.

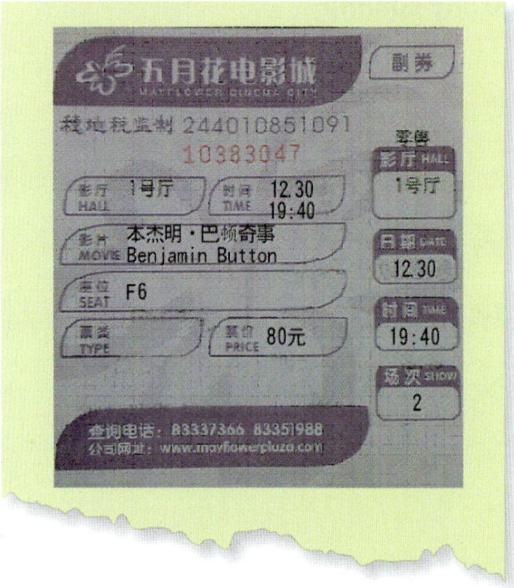

1. On what dates did she watch the movie?
2. At what time did the movie start?
3. How much was the ticket?

汉字天地 Hànzì Tiāndì

Chinese Characters

看 ■ kàn ■ to see

The character 看 *kàn* combines the two pictographs 手 *shǒu* and 目 *mù*. The 手 *shǒu* character on top means "hand," while the 目 *mù* character on the bottom means "eye." Combined, the two represent "to see" by portraying a man putting his hand above his eyes to shade them from the sun's rays.

Stroke Order

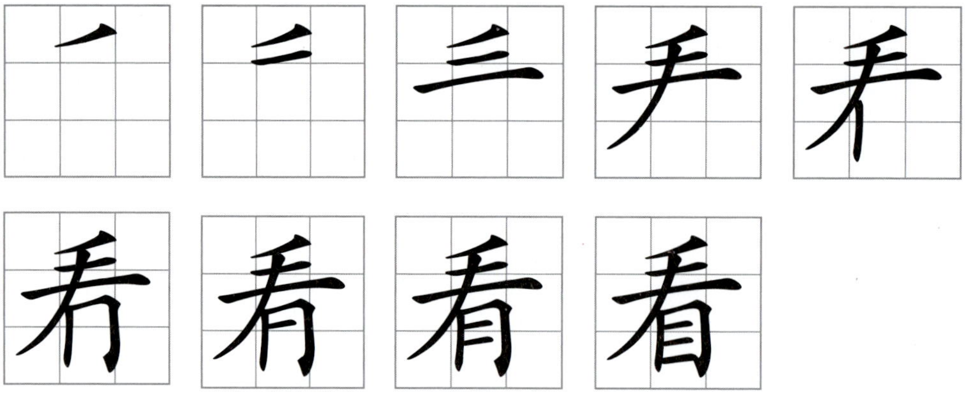

19 词汇延伸 Cíhuì Yánshēn / *Vocabulary Builder*

Below are some characters that can be combined with 看 *kàn* to create new words. Match the Chinese words on the left with the appropriate English meaning on the right.

法 fǎ *n. method*	书 shū *n. book*	轻 qīng *adj. light*	病 bìng *n. sick*	重 zhòng *adj. heavy*

1. 看法 kànfǎ — A. *opinion*
2. 看书 kànshū — B. *to underestimate*
3. 看轻 kànqīng — C. *to regard as important*
4. 看病 kànbìng — D. *to read*
5. 看重 kànzhòng — E. *to see a doctor*

20 汉字侦探 Hànzì Zhēntàn / *Visual Detective*

Can you find 看 in the following pictures?

Unit 3

在学校里 Zài Xuéxiào Lǐ

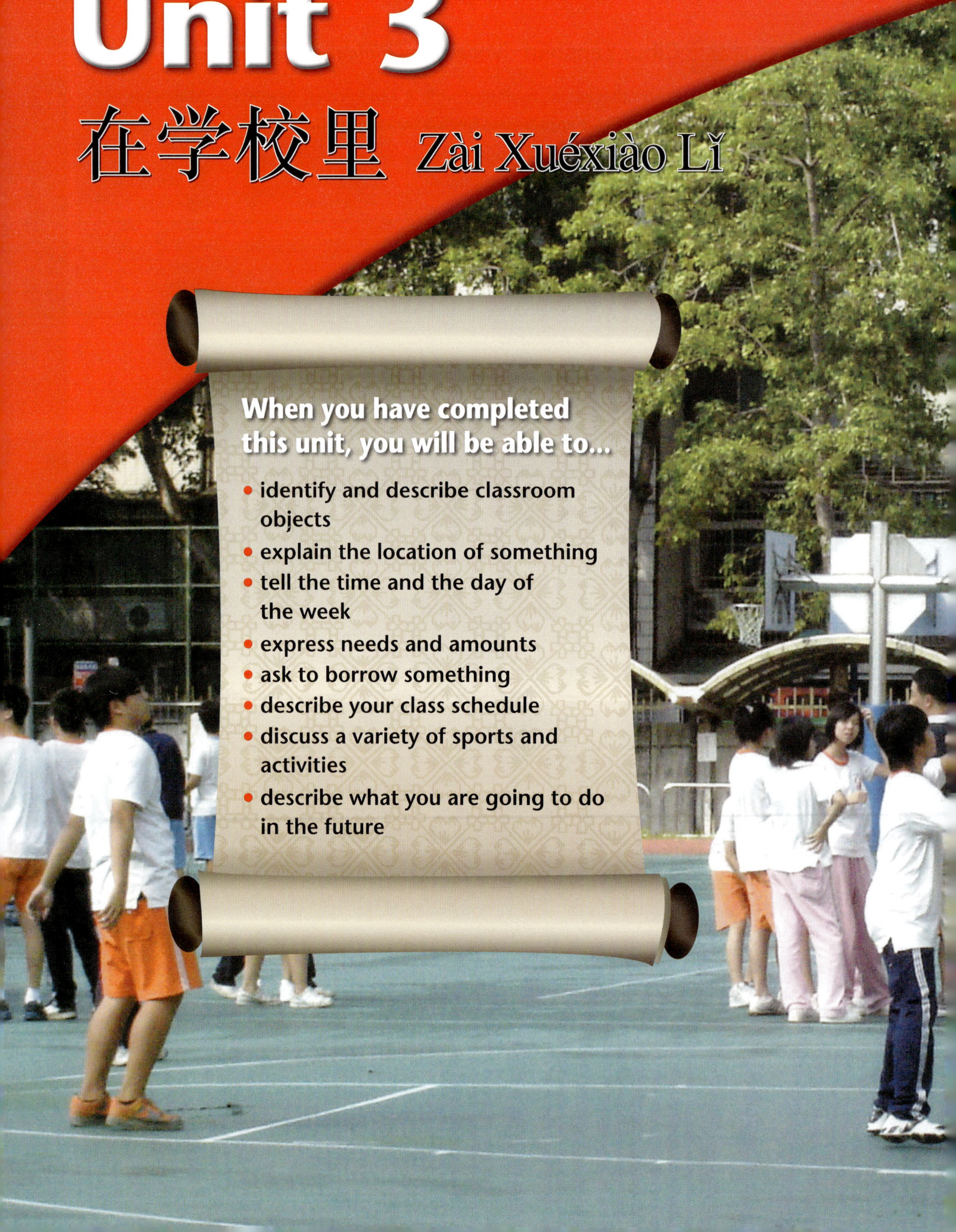

When you have completed this unit, you will be able to...

- identify and describe classroom objects
- explain the location of something
- tell the time and the day of the week
- express needs and amounts
- ask to borrow something
- describe your class schedule
- discuss a variety of sports and activities
- describe what you are going to do in the future

Lesson A

发音 Fāyīn
Pronunciation

s sh r + a ai ao an ang

词汇 Cíhuì
Vocabulary

教室 Jiàoshì *The Classroom*

1. 白板 (白板)
báibǎn
n. whiteboard

2. 板擦 (板擦)
bǎncā
n. board eraser

3. 白板笔 (白板筆)
bái*bǎn*bǐ
n. white board marker

4. 开电脑 (開電腦)
kāi diànnǎo
v.o. turn on the computer

5. 电脑 (電腦)
diànnǎo
n. computer

6. 海报 (海報)
hǎibào
n. poster

7. 地图 (地圖)
dìtú
n. map

8. 讲台 (講台)
jiǎngtái
n. podium

9. CD播放机 (CD播放機)
CD bōfàngjī
n. CD player

10. 光盘 (光盤)
guāngpán
n. compact disc (CD)

11. 投影机 (投影機)
tóuyǐngjī
n. projector

12. 桌子 (桌子)
zhuō.zi
n. table; desk

13. 背包 (背包)
bēibāo
n. backpack

14. 书包 (書包)
shūbāo
n. schoolbag

15. 课本 (課本)
kèběn
n. textbook

16. 椅子 (椅子)
yǐ.zi
n. chair

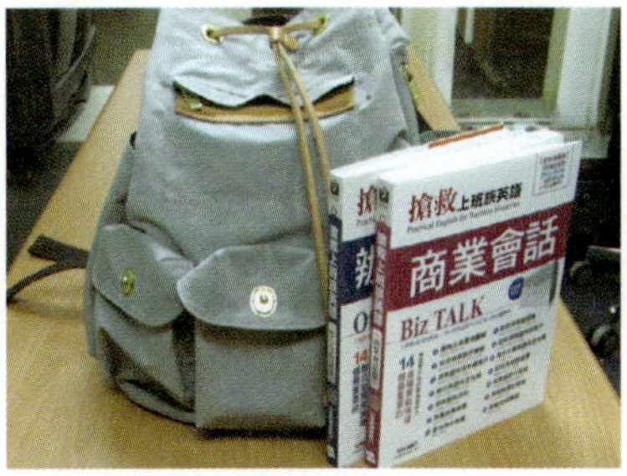

书在背包前面
(書在背包前面)。
Shū zài bēibāo qián.miàn.
The books are in front of the backpack.

书在背包后面
(書在背包後面)。
Shū zài bēibāo hòu.miàn.
The books are behind the backpack.

书在背包上面
(書在背包上面)。
Shū zài bēibāo shàng.miàn.
The books are on top of the backpack.

书在背包下面
(書在背包下面)。
Shū zài bēibāo xià.miàn.
The books are under the backpack.

书在背包旁边
(書在背包旁邊)。
Shū zài bēibāo pángbiān.
The book is next to the backpack.

书在背包外面
(書在背包外面)。
Shū zài bēibāo wài.miàn.
The book is outside the backpack.

背包在课本中间
(背包在課本中間)。
Bēibāo zài kèběn zhōngjiān.
The backpack is between the textbooks.

课本在背包右边
(課本在背包右邊)。
Kèběn zài bēibāo yòu.biān.
The textbook is to the right of the backpack.

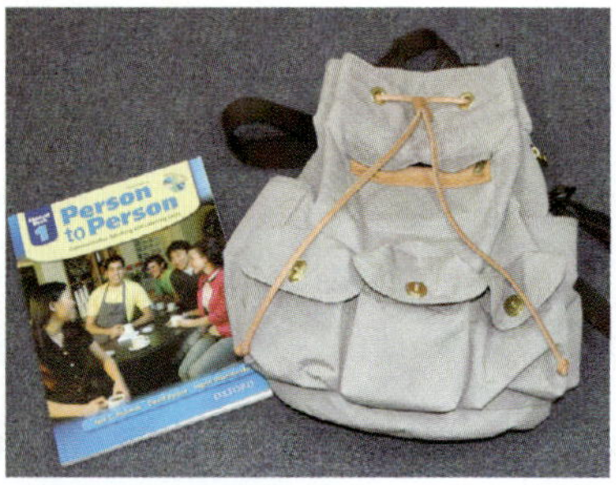

课本在背包左边
(課本在背包左邊)。
Kèběn zài gǒu zuǒ.biān.
The textbook is to the left of the backpack.

A: 奇怪 (奇怪)...
Qíguài... *That's strange...*

B: 怎么了 (怎麼了)?
Zěn.me .le? *What's wrong?*

A: 你的生物课本在哪儿 (你的生物課本在哪兒)?
Nǐ.de shēngwù kèběn zài nǎr? *Where is your biology textbook?*

B: 在教室里面 (在教室裡面)。
Zài jiàoshì lǐ.miàn. *It's in the classroom.*

Adjectives

奇怪 (奇怪)	qíguài	*strange*

Nouns

黑板 (黑板)	hēibǎn	*blackboard*
粉笔 (粉筆)	fěnbǐ	*chalk*

Question Words

哪儿 (哪兒)	nǎr	*where*
哪里 (哪裡)	nǎlǐ	*where*

Verbs

在 (在)	zài	*indicates the position of a person or thing*
找 (找)	zhǎo	*to look for; to search*

1 教室用品 Jiàoshì Yòngpǐn / *Classroom Objects*

Listen to the recording, and say the letter of the object being described.

2 老师的桌子上 Lǎoshī .de Zhuō.zi Shàng *On the Teacher's Desk*

Write a paragraph about six imaginary items on a teacher's desk. Indicate the relation of each object to another object. Then exchange your paragraph with that of your partner, who will draw what you have described. Finally, switch roles.

3 吴修在哪儿? Wú Xiū zài nǎr? *Where is Wu Xiu?*

Look at the pictures, and say where Wu Xiu is in relation to the table.

Lì.zi: 吴修在桌子上。Wú Xiū zài zhuō.zi shàng.

1.

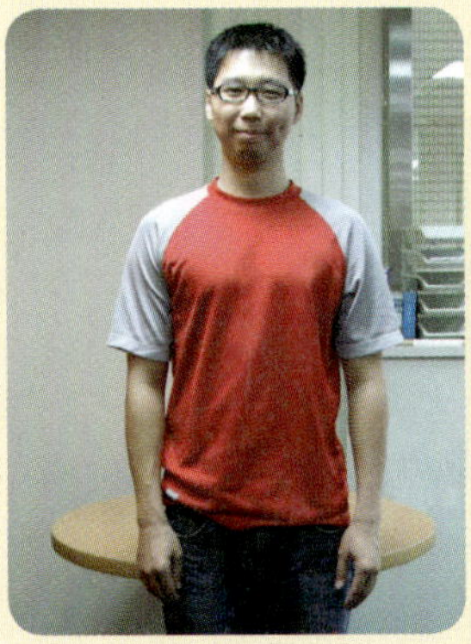

2.

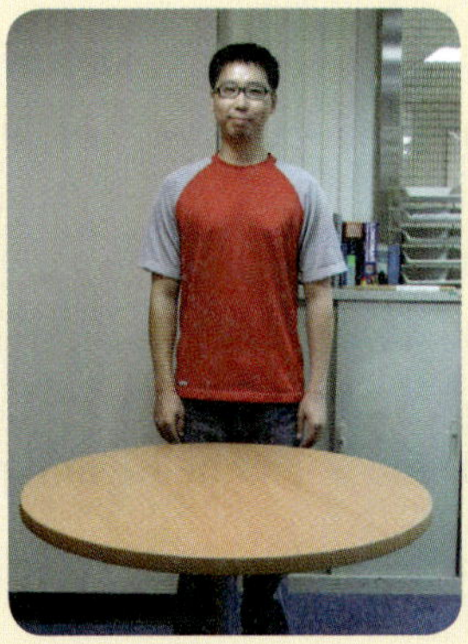

3.

4.

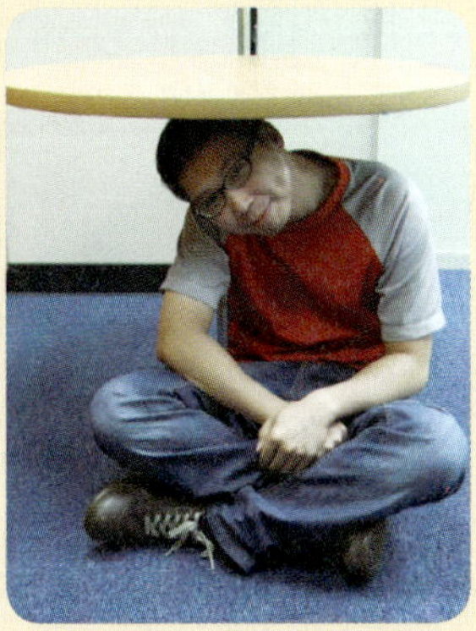

4 光盘在哪儿? Guāngpán zài nǎr? *Where is the CD?*

Look at the pictures, and say where the CD is in relation to the CD player.

Lì.zi: 光盘在CD播放机后面。Guāngpán zài CD bōfàngjī hòu.miàn.

1.

2.

3.

4.

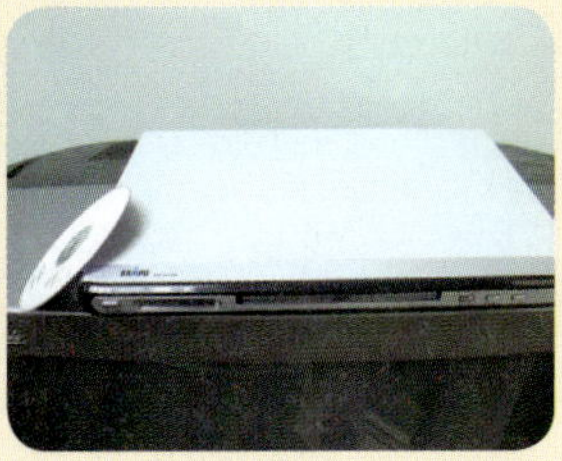

5 在哪儿? Zài nǎr? Where is it?

Write the question that would come before each answer.

Lì.zi: 狗在哥哥和妹妹中间。Gǒu zài gē.x hé mèi.x zhōngjiān.
狗在哪儿? Gǒu zài nǎr?

1. 狗在奶奶前面。Gǒu zài nǎi.x qián.miàn.
2. 妈妈在妹妹后面。Mā.x zài mèi.x hòu.miàn.
3. 爸爸在爷爷右边。Bà.x zài yé.x yòu.biān.
4. 哥哥在爷爷前面。Gē.x zài yé.x qián.miàn.
5. 奶奶在爷爷左边。Nǎi.x zài yé.x zuǒ.biān.
6. 爷爷在爸爸和奶奶中间。
   Yé.x zài bà.x hé nǎi.x zhōngjiān.

句型介绍 Jùxíng Jièshào
Language Patterns

The Question Word 哪儿 *nǎr*

The question word 哪儿 *nǎr* asks "where." The question word is placed in the position where it can be found in the answer, which makes it easy to give a response.

Subject + 在 *zài* + 哪儿 *nǎr* ?

A: 你家在哪儿? Nǐ jiā zài nǎr?
B: 我家在美国。Wǒ jiā zài Měi.guó.

A: 我的中文课本在哪儿? Wǒ.de Zhōngwén kèběn zài nǎr?
B: 我的中文课本在桌子下面。Wǒ.de Zhōngwén kèběn zài zhuō.zi xià.miàn.

Comparisons

What does the second sentence of the example mean in English? Did you use "in" or "at"? What are words such as these called in English? Some more examples are "to," "above," and "from."

Place Words and Relative Location

We use 在 *zài* and place words to express the relative location of the subject. The place words are usually formed as "noun / pronoun + localizer." With the help of noun or pronoun, it is easier to show the relative location.

Subject + 在 *zài* + **Place Word**

A: 小狗在哪儿？ *Xiǎo*gǒu zài nǎr?
B: 小狗在弟弟的后面。 *Xiǎo*gǒu zài dì.x .de hòu.miàn.

A: 你的课本在书包外面吗？ Nǐ.de kèběn zài shūbāo wài.miàn .ma?
B: 不是，我的课本在书包里面。 Bú shì, wǒ.de kèběn zài shūbāo lǐ.miàn.

A: 你爸爸在哪儿？ Nǐ bà.x zài nǎr?
B: 我爸爸在日本。 Wǒ bà.x zài Rìběn.

Language Note

Place words are a special group of nouns that are called for in certain grammatical patterns. There are three types of place words:

1. Geographical place names, e.g. 美国 *Měi.guó*, 中国 *Zhōng.guó*, 法国 *Fǎ.guó*, etc.
2. Localizers: 哪儿 *nǎr* or 哪里 *nǎ.lǐ* ("what place?" "where?")
   这儿 *zhèr* or 这里 *zhèlǐ* ("this place," "here")
   那儿 *nàr* or 那里 *nàlǐ* ("that place" "there")
   Other localizers: 里面 *lǐ.miàn*, 后面 *hòu.miàn*, 上面 *shàng.miàn*, 下面 *xià.miàn*, etc.
3. These localizers often combine with a noun or a pronoun.
   e.g. 教室外面 *jiàoshì wài.miàn*, or 我这儿 *wǒ zhèr*, 你那儿 *nǐ nàr*.
   Frequently the 面 *miàn* or 上 *shàng* part of the localizer can be dropped, e.g. 桌子上面 *zhuō.zi shàng.miàn* can be 桌子上 *zhuō.zi shàng* ("on the desk," "on top of the desk").

The English, "there is," "there are" is translated in Chinese in this pattern:

Place Word + 有 *yǒu* / 没有 *méi.yǒu* + **Noun**

桌子上有一本书。 Zhuō.zi.shàng yǒu yì-běn shū.

会话 Huìhuà Dialogue

东西不见了 Dōng.xī bú jiàn .le *Something is Missing*

In the classroom, Bai Ping is looking for something.

白 苹：	奇怪···	Bái Píng:	Qíguài...
张国华：	怎么了？	Zhāng Guóhuá:	Zěn.me .le?
白 苹：	我的英文课本在哪儿？	Bái Píng:	Wǒ.de Yīngwén kèběn zài nǎr?
张国华：	不在书包里面吗？	Zhāng Guóhuá:	Bú zài shūbāo lǐ.miàn .ma?
白 苹：	嗯，不在书包里面，也不在桌子上面。	Bái Píng:	Ēn, bú zài shūbāo lǐ.miàn, yě bú zài zhuō.zi shàng.miàn.

Zhang Guohua rummages through the pile of books on Bai Ping's desk.

张国华：	嘿，你看。	Zhāng Guóhuá:	Hēi, nǐ kàn.
白 苹：	我的英文课本！	Bái Píng:	Wǒ de Yīngwén kèběn!

6 谁在说话？ Shéi zài shuō-huà? *Who is the speaker?*

Identify who said each line from the dialogue.

1. 不在书包里面吗？ Bú zài shūbāo lǐ.miàn .ma?
2. 奇怪··· Qíguài...
3. 也不在桌子上面。 Yě bú zài zhuō.zi shàng.miàn.
4. 我的英文课本在哪儿？ Wǒ.de Yīngwén kèběn zài nǎr?

7 懂了吗? Dǒng .le .ma? Do you understand?

Decide if each statement is true or false. Correct any false statements.

1. 白苹的书包不见了(*lost*)。 Bái Píng .de shūbāo bú jiàn .le.
2. 白苹找她的课本。 Bái Píng zhǎo tā.de kèběn.
3. 张国华找他的中文课本。 Zhāng Guóhuá zhǎo tā.de Zhōngwén kèběn.
4. 白苹的课本不在书包里面。 Bái Píng .de kèběn bú zài shūbāo lǐ.miàn.
5. 张国华找到(*found*)白苹的课本。 Zhāng Guóhuá zhǎodào Bái Píng .de kèběn.
6. 白苹的课本在桌子上面。 Bái Píng .de kèběn zài zhuō.zi shàng.miàn.

文化橱窗 Wénhuà Chúchuāng
Culture Window

Cram Schools (补习班 *bǔxíbān*)

▲ Outside of a cram school.

As competition for admittance into top Chinese universities intensifies, it is more and more common for students to attend cram schools. There are two basic types of cram schools, those that develop talent and those that build academic skills. Talent schools are mostly targeted toward grade school children. Since most parents nowadays have one or two children, they can afford to spend money on their kids to improve their skills in abacus, English (or other languages), music or art, among others. The atmosphere of these classes is usually more lively compared to traditional schools, so that the students enjoy what they are doing. A lot of the talent cram schools are named after famous educators, such as Piaget or Montessori, on whom they base their teaching philosophy. Language schools are targeted toward children and adults of all ages. Most language schools also provide test preparation classes, which are intended to help their students pass tests like the GMAT (an admissions requirement for many graduate business schools) or TOEFL (a test recognized for assessing English skills), and often required for admission to overseas schools and universities.

Academic cram schools are targeted more toward students in junior and senior high, as there are national entrance exams they have to take at those levels. These cram schools have a much more tense atmosphere than day school. Discipline is strict and practice tests are frequent. Children often go to these cram schools after class on weekdays to improve skills in their weaker subjects, for example, English or math, or they may spend consecutive months (normally during summer or winter vacation) preparing for an important exam, much like a boot camp. During these pre-exam period cramming sessions, lunch and dinner are provided. Students whose exam results are less than satisfactory may choose to retake the exam the following year. In such cases, the cram school will often become students' second home, as they feverishly prepare to retake the test.

▲ Cram schools for all kinds of entrance examinations.

Comparisons

Ask some American relatives or acquaintances if they know about any courses or prep books designed to help students enter college or graduate school. You may also want to do some online research. In small groups, share your information and make a group list of these resources to hand in to your teacher.

8 文化动动脑 Wénhuà Dòng.x nǎo / *Culture Check-up*

Complete each statement with an appropriate word or expression.

1. Cram schools develop students' ___ and academic skills.
2. Talent cram schools include classes such as ___, English (or other languages), ___ or art.
3. Talent schools are mostly targeted toward ___ children.
4. Because nowadays parents have only ___ or ___ children, they can afford to spend money on their kids to go to talent cram schools.
5. Some talent cram schools are named after ___, such as Piaget or Montessori, on whom they base their teaching philosophy.
6. Both ___ and ___ of all ages go to language schools.
7. The atmosphere in cram school is ___ than day school.
8. Students who go to academic cram school are mostly ___ or ___ students because there are national entrance exams for them to pass.
9. Children often go to cram schools ___ on weekdays or they may spend their ___ in cram schools just to prepare for an important exam.
10. The cram school will often become the students' second ___ as they prepare to retake the exam the following year.

Language Practice

9 观光客在哪儿? Guānguāngkè zài nǎr? *Where are the tourists?*

Tell where each American tourist is by referring to the map.

10 在哪儿? Zài nǎr? *Where is it?*

With a partner, take turns asking and telling where the objects are.

1. 

2. 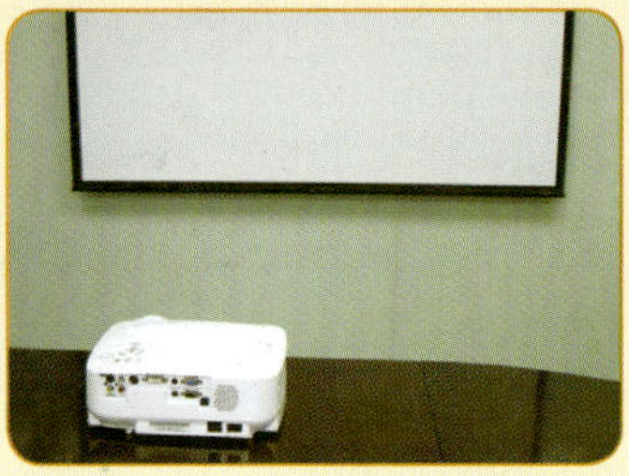

3. 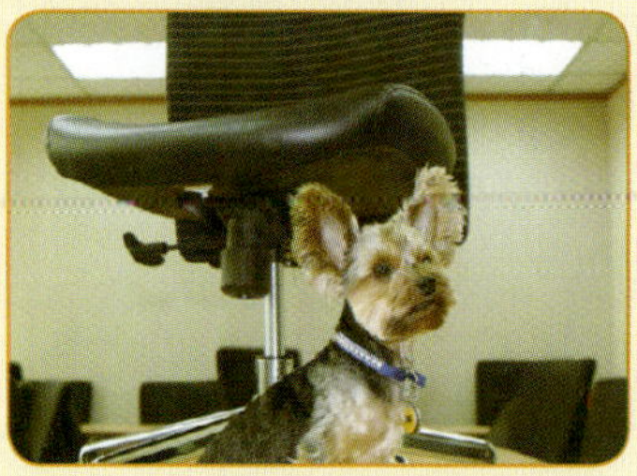

4. 

5. 

6. 

开口说 Kāikǒu Shuō
Communication

11 我的小狗在哪儿? Wǒ.de *xiǎo*gǒu zài nǎr? *Where is my dog?*

With a partner, play the roles of two siblings who are looking for their dog.

A: Ask your sibling what's wrong.
B: Ask where the dog is.
A: Ask if it's under the table.
B: Say it's not under the table.
A: Say "Hey, look!" and that it's under the chair.

12 白板笔在哪儿? Bái*bǎn*bǐ zài nǎr? *Where is the marker?*

Read the paragraph. Then write a sentence saying where the marker is.

教室里有一张桌子。桌子上有一个背包、一本文学课本 和一片光盘。白板笔不在背包前面，也不在背包后面。白板笔不在背包上面，也不在背包下面。白板笔不在背包旁边。白板笔不在文学课本前面，也不在文学课本下面。白板笔不在文学课本里面。白板笔不在光盘前面，也不在光盘后面。白板笔不在光盘上面，也不在光盘下面。白板笔不在光盘旁边。白板笔在哪儿?

Jiàoshì *lǐ* yǒu yī-zhāng zhuō.zi. Zhuō.zi.shàng yǒu yī-.ge bèibāo, yì-běn wénxué kèběn hé yí-piàn guāngpán. Bái*bǎn*bǐ bú zài bēibāo qián.miàn, yě bú zài bēibāo hòu.miàn. Bái*bǎn*bǐ bú zài bēibāo shàng.miàn, yě bú zài bēibāo xià.miàn. Bái*bǎn*bǐ bú zài bēibāo pángbiān. Bái*bǎn*bǐ bú zài wénxué kèběn qián.miàn, yě bú zài wénxué kèběn hòu.miàn. Bái*bǎn*bǐ bú zài wénxué kèběn shàng.miàn, yě bú zài wénxué kèběn xià.miàn. Bái*bǎn*bǐ bú zài wénxué kèběn lǐ.miàn. Bái*bǎn*bǐ bú zài guāngpán qián.miàn, yě bú zài guāngpán hòu.miàn. Bái*bǎn*bǐ bú zài guāngpán shàng.miàn, yě bú zài guāngpán xià.miàn. Bái*bǎn*bǐ bú zài guāngpán pángbiān. Bái*bǎn*bǐ zài nǎr?

13 教室物品在哪儿？ Jiàoshì wùpǐn zài nǎr? / *Where are the classroom objects?*

With a partner, take turns asking and answering where the objects are.

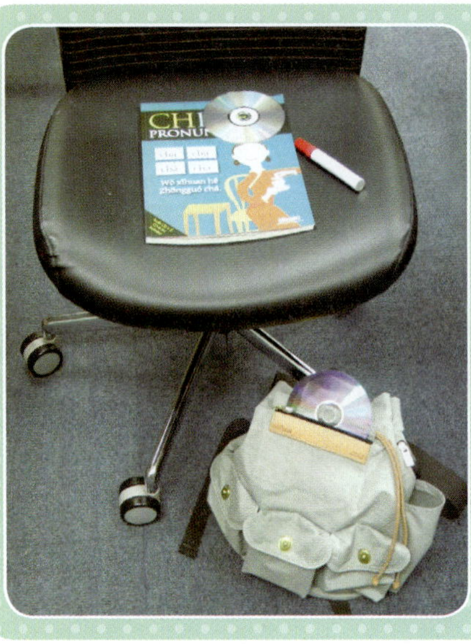

1. 背包 bēibāo
2. 白板笔 bái*bǎn*bǐ
3. 课本 kèběn
4. 光盘 guāngpán

14 便笺 Biànjiān / *Notes*

Look at the notes and answer the questions that follow.

A.

国华 Guóhuá：
你的早餐* 在桌子上面。
Nǐ.de zǎocān zài zhuō.zi shàng.miàn.
妈妈 mā.x

B.

弟弟 dì.x：
你的篮球在我的房间*里面！
Nǐ.de lánqiú zài wǒ.de fángjiān lǐ.miàn.
哥哥 gē.x

C.

惠美 Huìměi：
我的手机在哪儿?
Wǒ.de shǒujī zài nǎr?
李奇 LǐQí

* 早餐 zǎocān *n. breakfast*
* 房间 fángjiān *n. room*

1. Who wrote Note A?
2. Where is Guohua's breakfast?
3. Who is Note B for?
4. Where is the basketball?
5. For Note C, who is looking for things?
6. What is he looking for?

汉字天地 Hànzì Tiāndì
Chinese Characters

上 ■ shàng ■ up; above

The ideograph 上 *shàng* is composed of two horizontal planes. The one on the bottom that is lower and longer represents the horizon; the short line above the horizon indicates "up or above."

Stroke Order

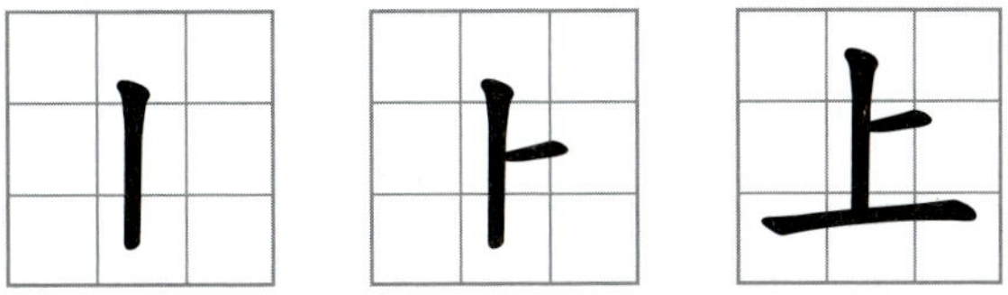

15 词汇延伸 Cíhuì Yánshēn / *Vocabulary Builder*

Below are some characters that can be combined with 上 *shàng* to create new words. Match the Chinese words on the left with the appropriate English meaning on the right.

衣 yī *n. clothes*	午 wǔ *n. noon*	等 děng *n. grade*	网 wǎng *n. net*	班 bān *n. duty*

1. 上衣 shàngyī
2. 上午 shàngwǔ
3. 上等 shàngděng
4. 上网 shàngwǎng
5. 上班 shàngbān

A. *upper garment*
B. *to go to work*
C. *morning*
D. *first-class, first-rate*
E. *to use the Internet*

16 汉字侦探 Hànzì Zhēntàn / *Visual Detective*

Can you find 上 in the following pictures?

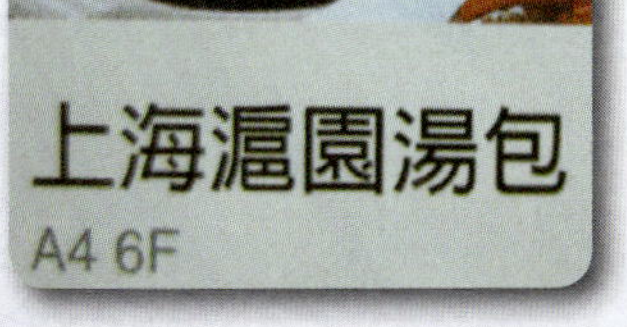

Lesson B

发音 Fāyīn
Pronunciation

b p m f d t n l g k
h z c s zh ch sh r
+ o u ou

词汇 Cíhuì
Vocabulary

文具 Wénjù *School Supplies*

铅笔盒（鉛筆盒）
qiānbǐhé
n. pencil box

修正液（修正液）
xiūzhèngyè
n. correction fluid

纸（紙）
zhǐ
n. paper

铅笔（鉛筆）
qiānbǐ
n. pencil

尺子（尺子）
chǐ.zi
n. ruler

剪刀（剪刀）
jiǎndāo
n. scissors

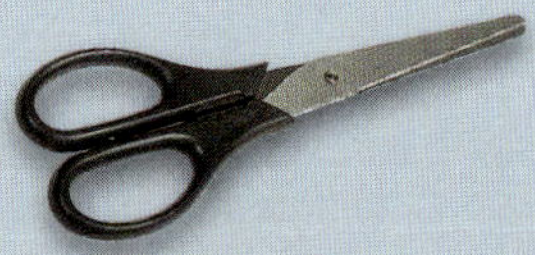

圆珠笔（圓珠筆）
yuánzhūbǐ
n. ballpoint pen

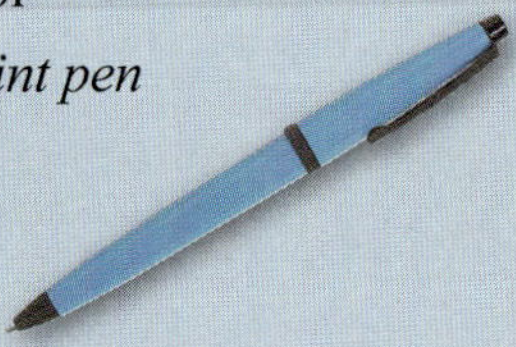

订书机（釘書機）
dìngshūjī
n. stapler

笔记本（筆記本）
bǐjìběn
n. notebook

橡皮（橡皮）
xiàngpí
n. eraser

胶水（膠水）
jiāoshuǐ
n. glue

文件夹（文件夾）
wénjiànjiā
n. folder

A: 请借给我一支笔和一张纸(請借給我一枝筆和一張紙)。

Qǐng jiè *gěi* wǒ yì-zhī bǐ hé yì-zhāng zhǐ. *Please lend me a pen and a piece of paper.*

A: 大华给芳芳一本笔记本(大華給芳芳一本筆記本)。

Dàhuá gěi Fāngfāng yì-běn bǐjìběn. *Dahua gives Fangfang a notebook.*

A: 小苹借给阿国一瓶胶水(小蘋借給阿國一瓶膠水)。

Xiǎopíng jiè gěi Āguó yì-píng jiāoshuǐ. *Xiaoping lends Aguo the glue.*

A: 你可以借给我修正液吗(你可以借給我修正液嗎)?

Nǐ kěyǐ jiè *gěi* wǒ xiūzhèngyè .ma? *Can you lend me the correction fluid?*

B: 当然(當然)!

Dāngrán! *Of course!*

A: 现在几点(現在幾點)?

Xiànzài *jǐ*-diǎn? *What time is it?*

B:

09:00

九点(九點)

jiǔ-diǎn

07:05

七点五分(七點五分)

qī-diǎn wǔ-fēn

04:28

四点二十八分(四點二十八分)

sì-diǎn èr.shíbā-fēn

01:30

一点三十分(一點三十分)

yì-diǎn sān.shí-fēn

一点半(一點半)

yì-diǎn bàn

06:15

六点十五分(六點十五分)

liù-diǎn shíwǔ-fēn

六点一刻(六點一刻)

liù-diǎn yí-kè

谢谢你（謝謝你）。
Xiè.x nǐ. *Thank you.*

不客气（不客氣）。
Bú kè.qì. *You're welcome.*

Adjectives

半（半）	bàn	*half*

Auxiliary Verbs

可以（可以）	kěyǐ	*can; may*

Idiomatic Expressions

不客气（不客氣）	bú kè.qì	*you're welcome*

Measure Words

支（支）	-zhī	*for stick-like things*
张（張）	-zhāng	*for a piece of paper*
点（點）	-diǎn	*o'clock*
分（分）	-fēn	*minute*
刻（刻）	-kè	*quarter*

Movable Adverbs

当然（當然）	dāngrán	*of course*

Particles

啊（啊）	.a	*a particle with many functions. (It expresses surprise and at the end of a sentence or indicates that a strong opinion has been expressed.)*

Time Words

现在（現在）	xiànzài	*now*

Verbs

请（請）	qǐng	*to request ("please")*
借（借）	jiè	*to borrow; to lend*
要（要）	yào	*to want; to need*
给（給）	gěi	*to give*

1 他们有什么? Tā.mén yǒu shén.me? / *What do they have?*

Say what each student has. Follow the model.

Lì.zi: 董大朋有书包和地图。

Dǒng Dàpéng yǒu shūbāo hé dìtú.

Dǒng Dàpéng

1. Lǐ Qiáng	3. Zhōng Shù	5. Gōng Sānhuì

2. Wáng Méifēn	4. Wú Zhōngxīng	6. Hé Guāng

2 开学第一天 Kāixué Dì-yī Tiān / *The First Day of School*

It's the first day of school and some students have come unprepared. The prepared students are willing to share their school supplies. Say who gives what to whom. Follow the model.

Lì.zi: Jiarong / Shuhui / paper

家荣给淑惠一张纸。 Jiāróng gěi Shúhuì yī-zhāng zhǐ.

1. Kevin / Kim / Chinese textbook
2. Wenhua / Zhichao / scissors
3. Abu / Tony / eraser
4. Ruby / Meijuan / stapler
5. Yizhen / Jean / folder
6. Richard / Abby / ruler

3 假期 Jiàqī / *Vacation*

Say what Junhong wants to do during vacation and with whom. Follow the model.

Lì.zi: play soccer / Chunmei

俊鸿和春梅一起踢足球。 Jùnhóng hé Chūnméi yìqǐ tī-zúqiú.

1. listen to music / Shufen
2. watch a movie / Ying
3. play volleyball / Fang
4. go shopping / Mei
5. play basketball / Gui
6. play video games / Fenfen

4 课表 Kèbiǎo *Class Schedule*

With a partner, take turns asking and answering when you have various classes. Follow the model.

Lì.zi: **A:** 你的生物课几点？ Nǐ.de shēngwùkè *jǐ*-diǎn?

B: 我的生物课两点。 Wǒ.de shēngwùkè *liǎng*-diǎn.

1. Chinese
2. physical education
3. history
4. literature
5. biology
6. math

5 有多少？ Yǒu duōshǎo? *How many are there?*

Say how many of each item there are. Follow the model.

Lì.zi: 十张纸

shí-zhāng zhǐ

1. 	4. 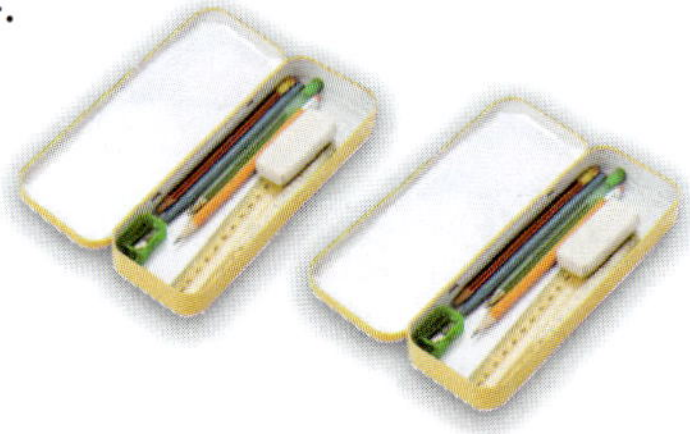	7. 
2. 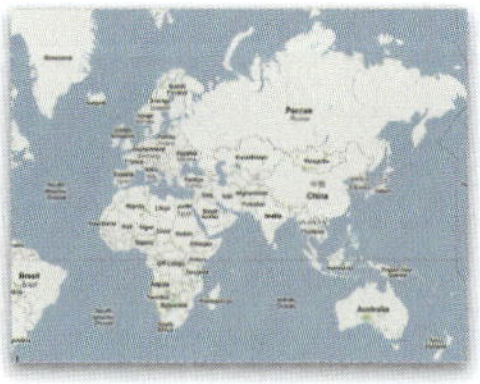	5. 	8. 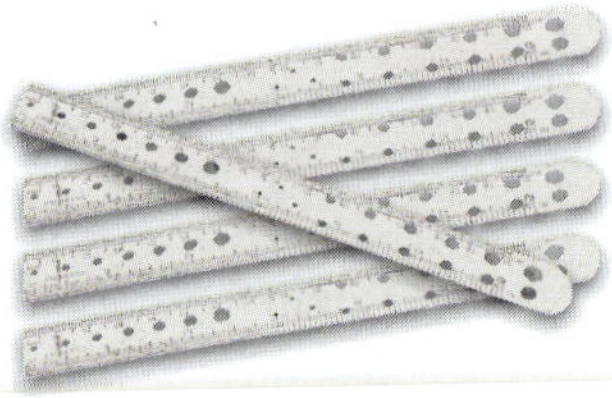
3. 	6. 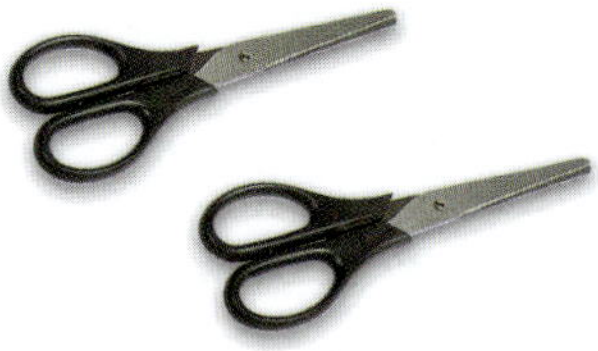	9. 

6 现在几点? Xiànzài jǐ-diǎn? *What time is it?*

With a partner, take turns asking and stating the indicated time.

Lì.zi: A: 现在几点? Xiànzài *jǐ*-diǎn?

B: 现在一点。 Xiànzài yì-diǎn.

7 李琴忙碌的一天 Lǐ Qín Mánglù.de Yì Tiān *Li Qin's Busy Day*

Look at Li Qin's agenda below and say what she does at each of the times indicated.

9:00	听音乐	tīng-yīnyuè
10:15	买东西	mǎi-dōng.xī
12:45	跟朋友见面	gēn péng.yǒu jiàn-miàn
1:30	踢足球	tī-zúqiú
6:00	跟家人吃饭	gēn jiārén chī-fàn
7:50	看电影	kàn-diànyǐng

8 个人问题 Gèrén Wèntí *Personal Questions*

Answer each question in Chinese.

1. 你有几支笔? *Nǐ yǒu* jǐ-zhī bǐ?
2. 你有没有纸? *Nǐ* yǒu méi.*yǒu* zhǐ?
3. 你有课本吗? *Nǐ* yǒu kèběn .ma?
4. 你有什么课本? *Nǐ* yǒu shén.me kèběn?
5. 现在几点? Xiànzài *jǐ*-diǎn?

句型介绍 Jùxíng Jièshào

Language Patterns

The Verb 借 *jiè*

Unlike English, the verb 借 *jiè* means both "to lend to," and "to borrow from," therefore, "给 *gěi* + person" is often used with the verb 借 *jiè*.

Person A + **借给 *jiè gěi*** + **Person B** + **Something**

王星借给我一支笔。 Wáng Xīng jiè *gěi* wǒ yì-zhī bǐ. *Wang Xing lent me a pen.*

Person A + **借 *jiè*** + **Something** + **给 *gěi*** + **Person B**

王星借一支笔给我。 Wáng Xīng jiè yì-zhī bǐ *gěi* wǒ. *Wang Xing lent a pen to me.*

The Auxiliary Verb 可以 *kěyǐ*

To ask permission to do something from someone in authority, use 可以 *kěyǐ*. The negative form of 可以 *kěyǐ* is 不可以 *bù kěyǐ* or 不能 *bù néng*.

Subject + **可以 *kěyǐ*** + **VP** + **吗 *.ma*** ?

YES → 可以 *kěyǐ*。

NO → 不可以 *bù kěyǐ*。

OR 不能 *bù néng*。

A: 我们可以一起看电影吗？ Wǒ.mén *kěyǐ* yìqǐ kàn diànyǐng .ma?

B: 当然可以。 Dāngrán *kěyǐ*.

A: 你明天可以打球吗？ Nǐ míng.tiān *kěyǐ* dǎ-qiú .ma?

B: 不可以。 Bù *kěyǐ*.

OR 不能。 Bù néng.

会话 Huìhuà
Dialogue

借东西 Jiè dōng.xī *Borrowing Stuff*

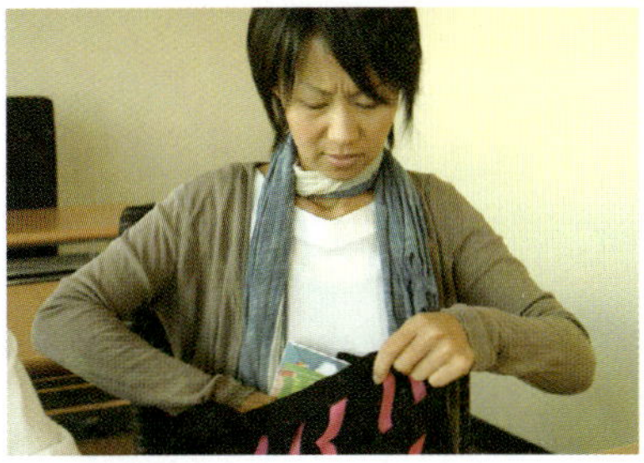

In the classroom, Lin Shufang is looking in her schoolbag for her missing pencil box.

林书芳：啊，我的铅笔盒在家里。
白苹：你要笔吗？
林书芳：谢谢，请借给我一支笔。
白苹：你要不要纸？
林书芳：要，请给我两张。
白苹：还要什么？
林书芳：我也没有书。我们可以一起看吗？
白苹：当然可以。
林书芳：谢谢你！现在几点？
白苹：现在八点五十五分。

Lín Shūfāng: .A, wǒ.de qiānbǐhé zài jiā lǐ.
Bái Píng: Nǐ yào bǐ .ma?
Lín Shūfāng: Xiè.x, qǐng jiè *gěi* wǒ yì-zhī bǐ.
Bái Píng: Nǐ yào .bú.yào zhǐ?
Lín Shūfāng: Yào, *qǐng gěi wǒ* liǎng-zhāng.
Bái Píng: Hái yào shén.me?
Lín Shūfāng: *Wǒ* yě méi.yǒu shū. Wǒ.mén *kě*yǐ yìqǐ kàn .ma?
Bái Píng: Dāngrán *kě*yǐ.
Lín Shūfāng: Xiè.x nǐ! Xiànzài *jǐ*-diǎn?
Bái Píng: Xiànzài bā diǎn wǔ.shíwǔ fēn.

9 她借什么？ Tā jiè shén.me? *What does she borrow?*

Say how many of each item Lin Shufang borrows from Bai Ping.

1. 	3. 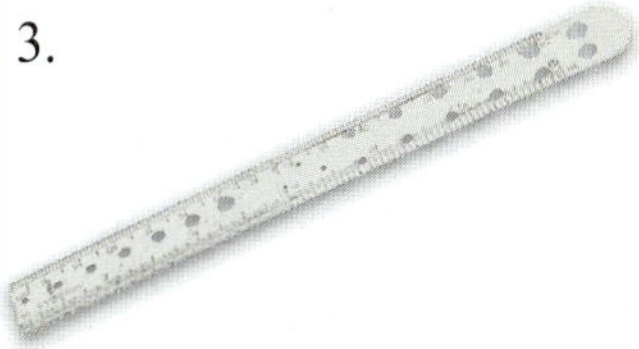	5. 
2. 	4. 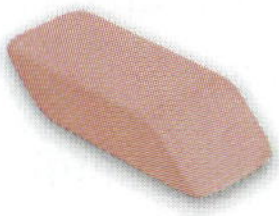	6. 

10 懂了吗? Dǒng .le .ma? Do you understand?

Answer the following questions.

1. 他们在哪儿？ Tā.mén zài nǎr?
2. 现在几点？ Xiànzài *jǐ*-diǎn?
3. 林书芳找什么？ Lín Shūfāng zhǎo shén.me?
4. 林书芳有铅笔盒吗？ Lín Shūfāng yǒu qiānbǐhé .ma?
5. 林书芳的铅笔盒在哪儿？ Lín Shūfāng .de qiānbǐhé zài nǎr?
6. 白苹借给林书芳什么？ Bái Píng jiè gěi Lín Shūfāng shén.me?
7. 白苹借给林书芳几支笔？几张纸？ Bái Píng jiè gěi Lín Shūfāng jǐ-zhī bǐ? jǐ-zhāng zhǐ?
8. 谁没有课本？ Shéi méi.yǒu kèběn?

文化橱窗 Wénhuà Chúchuāng
Culture Window

The Four Treasures of the Study (文房四宝 Wénfáng Sì Bǎo)

Historically, a scholar was a man who would spend many years in concentrated study of the works of Confucius and of other philosophical writings. Scholars often sat for competitive exams to become government officials for a district in China. Scholars were seen as men of great refinement, with a very strong sense of duty to their superiors, but also to those they governed. Wherever they went, they took 文房四宝 *Wénfáng sì bǎo* with them. In Chinese, 文房 *wénfáng* means "study room," and 四宝 *sì bǎo* means the "four treasures." The four treasures is a reference to the brush, ink, paper, and inkstone. Ink is often solidified into inksticks for easier transportation, and the inkstone is a stone mortar for the grinding of inksticks. The four treasures are tools needed for East Asian calligraphy.

▲ The four treasures of the study.

Apart from being the written language, the writing of characters is also seen as the art form of calligraphy. Therefore, it is not unusual to see the four treasures used to make Chinese landscape paintings. In Chinese history, calligraphy has played an important role in both literature and art. For a long time, the educated were expected to be proficient in calligraphy. Many famous poets and emperors wrote important and revered texts using calligraphy that have been passed down and are now national treasures. Today, writing phrases or texts in calligraphy is still used to mark special occasions.

To use the four treasures of the study, follow the steps below:

1. Pour an adequate amount of clear water onto the inkstone.

2. Grind the inkstick on the inkstone softly with steady movements.

3. Dip the brush into the ink. Try not to bend the hairs on the brush.

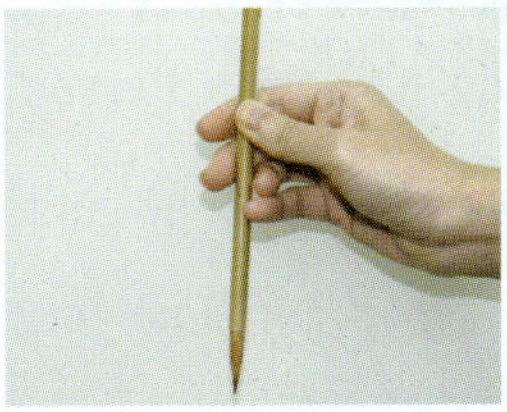

4. Hold the brush over the paper, and begin.

5. After use, clean the brush with your fingers by running water along the hairs. Try not to damage the hairs of the brush. Dry with a clean cloth. The inkstone should also be washed with water and a soft cloth.

6. Leave the brush and inkstone in a cool, dark place to dry.

11 文化动动脑 Wénhuà Dòng.x nǎo / *Culture Check-up*

Complete each statement with an appropriate word or expression.

1. A scholar was a man who would spend many years in concentrated study of the works of ___ and of other philosophical writings.
2. In Chinese, 文房 *wénfáng* means "___," and 四宝 *sì bǎo* means the "___."
3. 文房四宝 *Wénfáng sì bǎo* refers to four items: ___, ___, ___, and ___.
4. The four treasures are tools needed for East Asian ___.
5. Besides from being the written language, the ___ of characters is also seen as the art form of calligraphy.
6. It is not outside the norm to see the four treasures used to create Chinese ___ paintings.
7. In Chinese history, calligraphy has played an important role in both ___ and ___.
8. Many national treasures right now are important and revered texts using ___ written by famous poets and emperors.
9. Today, writing phrases or texts in calligraphy is still used to mark ___ occasions.
10. To make the ink, first you have to pour an adequate amount of ___ onto the inkstone, and then ___ the inkstick on the ___ softly with steady movements.

12 换句话说 Huà jù huà shuō / *Paraphrasing*

Change the following sentences to "Person A + 借给 *jiè gěi* + Person B + something" or "Person A + 借 *jiè* + something + 给 *gěi* + Person B." Follow the model.

Lì.zi: 他借给同学一个橡皮。 Tā jiè gěi tóngxué yí-.ge xiàngpí.
他借一个橡皮给同学。 Tā jiè yí-.ge xiàngpí gěi tóngxué.

1. 她借给我一支笔。 Tā jiè *gěi* wǒ yì-zhī bǐ.
2. 林小姐借一个手机给我。 Lín *xiǎo*jiě jiè yí-.ge shǒujī *gěi* wǒ.
3. 爸爸借给李先生一个光盘。 Bà.x jiè *gěi* Lǐ xiān.shēng yí-.ge guāngpán.
4. 我借一本书给弟弟。 Wǒ jiè yì-běn shū gěi dì.x.
5. 请借给我三张纸。 Qǐng jiè *gěi* wǒ sān-zhāng zhǐ.
6. 可以借给我这本书吗? *Kě*yǐ jiè *gěi* wǒ zhèi běn shū .ma?
7. 张书苹借几支笔给他? Zhāng Shūpíng jiè jǐ-zhī *bǐ* gěi tā?
8. 我借给毛欢欢一本英文课本。 Wǒ jiè gěi Máo Huānhuān yì-běn Yīngwén kèběn.

13 莉君的劳作 Lìjūn .de Láozuò / *Lijun's Art Project*

Lijun has made a list of the supplies she already has for her art project. She has a list from her art teacher of what supplies she needs. Compare the two lists and say which items Lijun needs to borrow from the teacher. Follow the model.

Lì.zi: 莉君要跟老师借胶水。 Lìjūn yào gēn lǎoshī jiè jiāoshuǐ.

What Lijun has:	Teacher's list:
• pencil	• stapler • eraser
• paper	• glue • scissors
• eraser	• paper • pencil
• stapler	• pen • ruler

14 生日礼物 Shēng.rì Lǐwù *Birthday Presents*

Say what Meihui's family members and friends are giving her for her birthday. Follow the model.

Lì.zi: 爸爸跟妈妈 / 衣服 bà.x gēn mā.x / yī.fú
爸爸跟妈妈给她衣服。 Bà.x gēn mā.x gěi tā yī.fú.

1. 姐姐 / 书 jiě.x / shū
2. 弟弟 / 笔 dì.x / bǐ
3. 哥哥 / 背包 gē.x / bēibāo
4. 外祖父跟外祖母 / 鞋 wàizǔfù gēn wàizǔmǔ / xié
5. 雅龄 / 茶 Yǎlíng / chá
6. 明修 / 铅笔盒 Míngxiū / qiānbǐhé

15 请求允许 Qǐngqiú Yǔnxǔ *Asking Permission*

With a partner, play the roles of a student who asks for permission to do certain things and a teacher who gives or doesn't give permission. Before you begin, check the Foundation lessons for any classroom expressions you don't remember.

1. 看地图 kàn-dìtú
2. 用手机 yòng-shǒujī
3. 写黑板 xiě-hēibǎn
4. 听MP3 tīng-MP3
5. 在黑板上写我的名字 zài hēibǎn shàng *xiě* wǒ.de míng.zì
6. 看书 kàn-shū

16 听力练习 Tīnglì Liànxí *Listening Practice*

Listen to the recording, and choose the photo that corresponds to each dialogue.

A.

B.

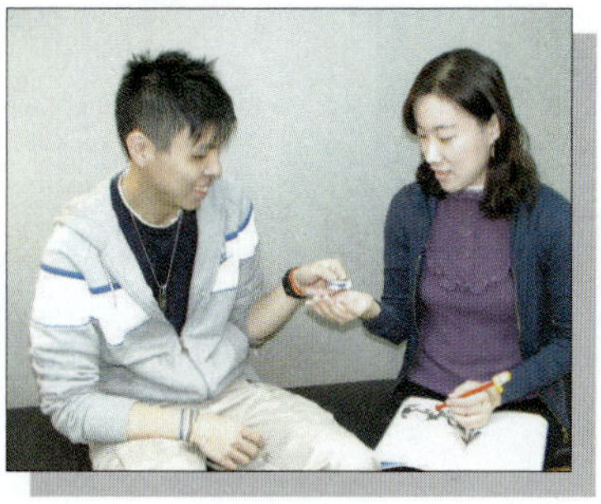

C.

开口说 Kāikǒu Shuō
Communication

17 同学帮帮忙 Tóngxué Bāng.x Máng / Give Me a Hand

With a partner, play the roles of two students who are getting ready for class.

A: Greet B.

B: Greet A and ask A for the time.

A: Say what time it is.

B: Say what you forgot to bring to class.

A: Ask if your classmate needs to borrow those items.

B: Say how many of each item you need.

A: Ask if your classmate needs anything else.

B: Say thank you.

A: Say you're welcome.

18 描述教室 Miáoshù Jiàoshì / Describe the Classroom

Write a paragraph in Pinyin that describes the people and objects in this classroom.

19 这个周末 Zhèi.ge Zhōumò / *This Weekend*

Poll your classmates about what they want to do this weekend.

- Ask 10 classmates about what they want to do this weekend.
- Note each response.
- Finally, count how many people want to do the same things and report your findings to your small group.

Lì.zi: 俊杰：这个周末你要做什么？

Jùnjié: Zhèi-.ge zhōumò nǐ yào zuò shén.me?

虹霖：我要看电影。

Hónglín: Wǒ yào kàn diànyǐng.

……

俊杰：四个学生要看电影，三个学生要…

Jùnjié: Sì-.ge xué.shēng yào kàn diànyǐng, sān-.ge xué.shēng yào…

20 你可以借给我吗？ *Nǐ kěyǐ jiè gěi wǒ .ma?* / *Can you lend it to me?*

Borrow the listed classroom objects from several classmates. Then tell your small group how many of each item you borrowed. Use the chart like the one below to record your answers.

Lì.zi: **A:** 你可以借给我铅笔吗？ *Nǐ kě*yǐ jiè *gěi* wǒ qiānbǐ .ma?

B: 可以 / 不可以。 *Kě*yǐ. / Bù *kě*yǐ.

A: 你可以借给我几支铅笔？ *Nǐ kě*yǐ jiè wǒ jǐ-zhī qiānbǐ?

B: 我可以借给你两支铅笔。 *Wǒ kě*yǐ jiè nǐ liǎng-zhī qiānbǐ.

……

A: 我借到*四支铅笔，两个橡皮和一本笔记本。

Wǒ jiè.dào sì-zhī qiānbǐ, liǎng-.ge xiàngpí hé yì-běn bǐjìběn.

*借到 *jiè.dào*: to have borrowed. Here it means that one has succeeded in borrowing things one wants.

	铅笔	原珠笔	橡皮	修正液	笔记本	文件夹	尺
Classmate A	2						
Classmate B							
Classmate C							
Total:							

21 失物招领 Shīwù Zhāolǐng / *Lost and Found*

Below is the writing on a Lost and Found notice board. Read what is written and use pinyin to answer the questions.

中文教室失物招领[1]

书包，里面有一个手机，
一个铅笔盒，两本书，三个光盘。
公告日期：九月十七日

联络[2]电话：0991-675-6521 陈老师

1. 失物招领 shīwù zhāolǐng *n.lost and found*
2. 联络 liánluò *n.contact*

1. Where was this school bag found?
2. When did this notice go up?
3. What are in the school bag?
4. Whom should you contact to claim this bag if it is yours?
5. What is the telephone number provided?

汉字天地 Hànzì Tiāndì
Chinese Characters

下 ■ xià ■ down; under

The ideograph 下 *xià* is composed of two horizontal planes. The longer plane at the top indicates the horizon and the lower plane indicates "*down or under*."

Stroke Order

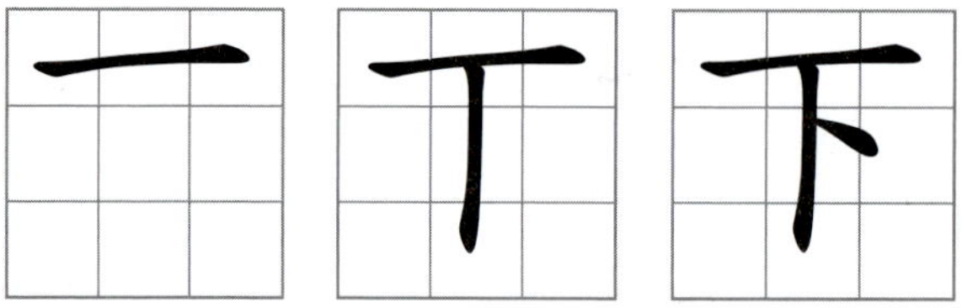

22 词汇延伸 Cíhuì Yánshēn / Vocabulary Builder

Below are some characters that can be combined with 下 xià to create new words. Match the Chinese words on the left with the appropriate English meaning on the right.

列 liè	午 wǔ	策 cè	班 bān	手 shǒu
v. to list	*n. noon*	*n. scheme*	*n. duty*	*n. hand*

1. 下列 xiàliè	A. *following*
2. 下午 xiàwǔ	B. *to get off work*
3. 下策 xiàcè	C. *afternoon*
4. 下班 xiàbān	D. *to start*
5. 下手 xiàshǒu	E. *very unwise move*

23 汉字侦探 Hànzì Zhēntàn / Visual Detective

Can you find 下 in the following pictures?

Lesson C

发音 Fāyīn
Pronunciation

b p m f d t n l g
k h z c s zh ch sh r + e ei

词汇 Cíhuì
Vocabulary

日历（日曆）Rìlì *Calendar*

Mon	Tue	Wed	Thu	Fri	Sat	Sun
星期一（星期一）Xīngqīyī *Monday*	星期二（星期二）Xīngqī'èr *Tuesday*	星期三（星期三）Xīngqīsān *Wednesday*	星期四（星期四）Xīngqīsì *Thursday*	星期五（星期五）Xīngqīwǔ *Friday*	星期六（星期六）Xīngqīliù *Saturday*	星期日（星期日）Xīngqīrì *Sunday*
4:00 P.M. 去图书馆（去圖書館）qù túshūguǎn *go to the library*	9:00 A.M. 数学考试（數學考試）shùxué kǎoshì *math test*	5:30 P.M. 读中文（讀中文）dú Zhōngwén *study Chinese*	10:40 A.M. 中文小考（中文小考）Zhōngwén xiǎokǎo *Chinese quiz*	7:55 P.M. 健身房锻练（健身房鍛練）jiànshēnfáng duànliàn *exercise at a fitness center*	11:00 A.M. 去爷爷家（去爺爺家）qù yé.x jiā *go to grandpa's house*	2:00 P.M. 看书（看書）kàn-shū *read books*

前天（前天）qián.tiān *n. the day before yesterday*

昨天（昨天）zuó.tiān *n. yesterday*

今天（今天）jīn.tiān *n. today*

明天（明天）míng.tiān *n. tomorrow*

后天（後天）hòu.tiān *n. the day after tomorrow*

A: 今天星期几 (今天星期幾)？ Jīn.tiān xīngqī jǐ? *What day is it today?*

B: 今天星期四 (今天星期四)。 Jīn.tiān Xīngqīsì. *It's Thursday.*

有意思(有意思)
yǒu yì.sī
adj. interesting

没有意思
(沒有意思)
méi.yǒu yì.sī
adj. uninteresting

容易(容易)
róngyì
adj. easy

难 (難)
nán
adj. difficult

有挑战性 (有挑戰性)
yǒu tiǎozhànxìng
adj. challenging

好玩儿(好玩兒)
hǎo.wánr
adj. fun

无聊(無聊)
wúliáo
adj. boring

A: 我觉得数学课很难 (我覺得數學課很難)。
Wǒ jué.de shùxué kè hěn nán. *I think math class is very hard.*

B: 我也觉得数学课很难， 可是很有意思 (我也覺得數學課很難，可是很有意思)。
Wǒ yě jué.de shùxué kè hěn nán, kě.shì *hěn* yǒu yì.sī.
I also think math class is very hard, but it is very interesting.

A: 我昨天上体育和地理， 你呢 (我昨天上體育和地理，你呢)？
Wǒ zuó.tiān shàng tǐyù hé dìlǐ, nǐ .ne? *I had PE class and geography class yesterday, what about you?*

B: 我上生物和物理 (我上生物和物理)。
Wǒ shàng shēngwù hé wùlǐ. *I had biology and physics.*

你明天有考试吗(你明天有考試嗎)？
Nǐ míng.tiān *yǒu* kǎoshì .ma?
Do you have tests tomorrow?

有，两个小考(有，兩個小考)。
Yǒu, liǎng-.ge *xiǎo*kǎo.
Yes, two quizzes.

A: 你星期几有历史课(你星期幾有歷史課)？
Nǐ xīngqī *jǐ* yǒu lìshǐ kè? *What day do you have history class?*

B: 星期一和星期三(星期一和星期三)。
Xīngqīyī hé Xīngqīsān. *Monday and Wednesday.*

A: 我得去图书馆了(我得去圖書館了)。
Wǒ děi qù túshūguǎn .le. *I have to go to the library now.*

Adverbs

还(還)	hái	*still, in addition, and also*

Common Expressions

好了(好了)	hǎo .le	*okay*

Conjunctions

可是(可是)	kě.shì	*but*

Measure Words

堂(堂)	-táng	*period of class*

Nouns

考试(考試)	kǎoshì	*test, exam*
大考(大考)	dàkǎo	*final exam*
小考(小考)	*xiǎo*kǎo	*quiz*

Verbs

觉得(覺得)	jué.de	*to feel; think*
来(來)	lái	*to come*

1 一星期的日子 Yì Xīngqī .de Rì.zi / *Days of the Week*

You will hear several days of the week. Say in Chinese the day that comes before the one you hear.

2 课表 Kèbiǎo / *Class Schedule*

Make a class schedule in Chinese. Place the days of the week horizontally at the top, the time each class starts vertically on the left, and the classes you have under each day of the week.

3 你的课怎么样? Nǐ.de kè zěn.meyàng? / *How are your classes?*

Exchange your class schedule with that of your partner. Ask your partner how he or she feels about certain classes on the schedule. Follow the model.

Lì.zi: A: 你喜欢美术课吗? *Nǐ* xǐ.huān měishù kè .ma?

B: 我喜欢美术课。美术课很有意思。*Wǒ* xǐ.huān měishù kè. Měishù kè *hěn* yǒu yì.sī.

4 他们去哪儿? Tā.mén qù nǎr? / *Where are they going?*

Say where the following people are going. Follow the model.

Lì.zi: 李华 Lǐ Huá / school

李华去学校。 Lǐ Huá qù xuéxiào.

1. Bái Píng / fitness center
2. Yǎhuì / grandma's house
3. Yú Lì / home
4. Wèi Qíng / library
5. Měilíng / literature class
6. Jiànguó / older sister's house
7. Zhēnzhēn / English class

5 中文怎么说? Zhōngwén zěn.me shuō? / *How would you say it in Chinese?*

Write in Pinyin what you would say in the following situations.

1. Ask what classes your friend has today.
2. Tell your friend that you had music and math class yesterday.
3. Ask your friend what day he or she has English class.
4. Ask if your friend likes Chinese class.
5. Ask if your friend has a test tomorrow.
6. Tell your friend that you have two tests the day after tomorrow.
7. Tell your friend that you have to go to French class.

6 个人问题 Gèrén Wèntí *Personal Questions*

Answer each question in Chinese.

1. 你今天有什么课？ Nǐ jīn.tiān yǒu shén.me kè?
2. 你觉得什么课很难？ Nǐ jué.de shén.me kè hěn nán?
3. 你觉得什么课很容易？ Nǐ jué.de shén.me kè hěn róngyì?
4. 你明天有大考吗？有小考吗？ Nǐ míng.tiān yǒu dàkǎo .ma? *yǒu xiǎo*kǎo .ma?
5. 你今天下课以后(*after school*)要去哪儿？ Nǐ jīn.tiān xià-kè yǐhòu yào qù nǎr?

句型介绍 Jùxíng Jièshào

Language Patterns

Word Order for Time Words

In Chinese, time words are movable adverbs. They can come either before or after the subject.

Time Word + **Subject** + **Time Word** + **Verb Phrase**

〔我们〕〔星期日〕〔看德国电影〕。 Wǒ.mén Xīngqīrì kàn Dé.guó diànyǐng.

Subject *Time* *Verb Phrase*

〔星期日〕〔我们〕〔看德国电影〕。 Xīngqīrì wǒ.mén kàn Dé.guó diànyǐng.

Time *Subject* *Verb Phrase*

Language Note

Time words are listed from the bigger unit to the smaller unit. For example, we say: 十月一日星期五早上八点二十分 *Shíyuè yīrì Xīngqīwǔ zǎo.shàng bā-diǎn èr.shí-fēn* for "8:20 A.M., Friday, the 1st of October."
This Chinese example shows the day first, followed by the date and the hour.

The Adverb 还 *hái*

The adverb 还 *hái* means "also" or "in addition" and signifies an increase beyond the original level or supplies extra information. It must be placed after the subject and before the verb. In this pattern, 还 *hái* should be put before the second verb phrase.

Subject + **VP1** + **还 *hái*** + **VP2**

我有三只猫，还有一只狗。

Wǒ yǒu sān-zhī māo, hái yǒu yì-zhī gǒu.

她星期三有一个小考，星期五还有两个大考。

Tā Xīngqīsān yǒu yí-.ge *xiǎo*kǎo, *Xīng*qīwǔ hái *yǒu* liǎng-.ge dàkǎo.

Adjectives in Chinese

Adjectives in Chinese sometimes function as verbs. In that sense, a verb is not necessary in a sentence that uses adjectives. However, adverbs are usually used to modify such adjectives, for example, 不 *bù* (not), 很 *hěn* (very, quite), 太 *tài* (too), and 非常 *fēicháng* (very).

Subject + **Adverb** + **Adjective**

考试很难。 Kǎoshì .hěn nán. *The test is quite difficult.*

音乐教室不大。 Yīnyuè jiàoshì bú dà. *The music classroom is not big.*

Language Note

Although 很 *hěn* is translated as meaning "very," it doesn't necessarily mean it unless it is stressed. In sentences with adjectives like 英文课很难 *Yīngwén kè .hěn nán*, 很 *hěn* is always regularly used. However, if one wishes to express the degree of "very," simply stressing 很 *hěn* will still retain its original meaning.

今天的考试难。 Jīn.tiān .de kǎoshì nán.

Today's test was difficult.

今天的考试很难。 Jīn.tiān .de kǎoshì .hěn nán.

Today's test was quite difficult.

The Verbs 来 *lái* and 去 *qù*

Both 来 *lái* (to come) and 去 *qù* (to go) indicate motion and direction, and are usually followed by a place word. There is a difference between the verbs 来 *lái* and 去 *qù* in much the same way that "to come" and "to go" have different meanings in English. With 来 *lái*, it means the subject is moving to the direction where the speaker is, whereas with 去 *qù*, the subject is moving away from where the speaker is

来 *lái* / 去 *qù* + **Place**

我去学校。 Wǒ qù xuéxiào.

她今天来我家。 Tā jīn.tiān lái wǒ jiā.

会话 Huìhuà
Dialogue

课表 Kèbiǎo *Class Schedules*

At the school entrance, Dong Jun is talking to Lin Shufang.

董军:	你今天上什么课?	Dǒng Jūn:	Nǐ jīn.tiān shàng shén.me kè?
林书芳:	我今天上英文和数学。	Lín Shūfāng:	Wǒ jīn.tiān shàng Yīngwén hé shùxué.
董军:	我今天上英文、数学，还上化学。	Dǒng Jūn:	Wǒ jīn.tiān shàng Yīngwén, shùxué, hái shàng huàxué.
林书芳:	化学课很有意思吗?	Lín Shūfāng:	Huàxué kè *.hěn* yǒu yì.sī .ma?
董军:	很有意思，可是很难。	Dǒng Jūn:	*.Hěn* yǒu yì.sī, kě.shì .hěn nán.
林书芳:	我也觉得很难。	Lín Shūfāng:	*Wǒ* yě jué.de .hěn nán.
董军:	好了，我得去图书馆了。	Dǒng Jūn:	Hǎo .le, *wǒ* děi qù túshūguǎn .le.
林书芳:	你星期几有考试?	Lín Shūfāng:	Nǐ xīngqī jǐ *yǒu* kǎoshì?
董军:	我星期五有两个小考。	Dǒng Jūn:	Wǒ Xīngqī*wǔ yǒu* liǎng-.ge *xiǎo*kǎo.

7 懂了吗? Dǒng le ma? *Do you understand?*

Answer the following questions.

1. 林书芳今天上什么课? Lín Shūfāng jīn.tiān shàng shén.me kè?
2. 董军今天上什么课? Dǒng Jūn jīn.tiān shàng shén.me kè?
3. 董军觉得化学课很有意思吗? Dǒng Jūn jué.de huàxué kè *.hěn* yǒu yì.sī .ma?
4. 董军觉得化学课很难吗? Dǒng Jūn jué.de huàxué kè .hěn nán .ma?
5. 林书芳也觉得化学课很难吗? Lín Shūfāng yě jué.de huàxué kè .hěn nán .ma?
6. 董军得去哪儿? Dǒng Jūn děi qù nǎr?
7. 谁有考试? Shéi *yǒu* kǎoshì?
8. 他星期几有考试? Tā xīngqī *jǐ yǒu* kǎoshì?
9. 他有几个考试? Tā *yǒu* jǐ-.ge kǎoshì?

文化橱窗 Wénhuà Chúchuāng

Culture Window

A Day in School

For high school students in China, the school day starts at around 7:30 in the morning. In some schools, homeroom before the first period is devoted to tests or school assemblies. As most senior high schools place great emphasis on English, most schools have English listening tests during homeroom to improve students' English listening abilities. If no tasks are assigned in homeroom, students may take that time to study more difficult subjects such as chemistry, mathematics, or history. The first period follows homeroom at 8:00. In most schools, a period is 45 or 50 minutes long, followed by a 10 or 15 minute break.

Most schools have assemblies—times when all students and staff members gather together on the field or in the main hall for morning exercises or to listen to reports of recent happenings by the principal or dean. Awards are also given out at this time.

▲ Morning assembly for all students and staff members.

Lunch break is often an hour or 90 minutes long. During this time, students may eat their lunch or rest. Many schools in China do not have cafeterias, so most students choose to either bring a packed lunch from home, buy something to eat from the school store, or order a school lunch. After lunch break, classes continue until around 3:30 or 5:00. In most schools, there is also a cleaning period which lasts roughly 20 minutes in the afternoon. During this time, each student has to do his delegated cleaning job around the school. "Normal" high schools, as opposed to vocational high schools, place greater emphasis on higher education after graduation. Because of this, afterschool coaching—an extra period tagged on at the end of the day for more difficult subjects—has become a trend. For seniors who face impending college entrance exams, it is not unusual to stay until 9:00 P.M. after school ends to study together.

▲ Time for PE class.

One big difference between schools in China and the United States is that high school students in China do not switch classrooms between classes except for PE, art, music, or home economics. Students may not need to leave their homerooms all day. Therefore, the classroom becomes the students' home away from home; teachers and students work together to decorate the classroom and keep it clean. There are even "classroom decoration" contests in Taiwan. Students in the East are also not as free as students in the West in choosing their own schedules; electives are provided not as singles but blocks. For example, if a student chooses to go into natural sciences, he or she would be signed up automatically for biology, chemistry, physics, and advanced math. A humanities student would likewise be assigned many classes in the social sciences.

Comparisons

Do you think assigning students cleaning jobs would work in American schools? Would you like to be involved with decorating your classrooms? What are the advantages and disadvantages in staying in the same classroom all day long?

8 文化动动脑 Wénhuà Dòng.x nǎo *Culture Check-up*

Complete each statement with an appropriate word or expression.

1. High school students in China must arrive at school at around ____ , and they might have ____ or ____ before the first period.
2. In most schools, a period is ____ long, followed by a ____ break.
3. Morning assembly is a time when all the _____ and _____ gather together on the field or in the hall for morning exercises or to listen to reports of recent happenings by the principal or dean. ____ are also given out at this time.
4. During lunch break, students may ____ or ____.
5. Many schools in China do not have cafeterias, so most students choose to either bring a ____ from home, buy something to eat from the school store, or order a school lunch.

6. After lunch break, classes continue until around ____ or ____.
7. ____ high schools, as opposed to vocational high schools, place greater emphasis on higher ____ after graduation.
8. For seniors who face impending ____ exams, it is not unusual to stay until 9:00 P.M. after school ends to study together.
9. Students in China _____ switch classrooms between classes except for PE, art, music, or home economics.
10. Students in the ____ are also not as free as students in the ____ in choosing their own schedules.

Language Practice

9 时间放哪儿？ Shíjiān fàng nǎr? *Inserting time expressions*

Insert each time expression at the right place.

1. 我在家。 Wǒ zài jiā. (四点半 sì-diǎn bàn)
2. 哥哥上课。 Gē.x shàng-kè. (九点 *jiǔ*-diǎn)
3. 他看电影。 Tā kàn-diànyǐng. (星期日 Xīngqīrì)
4. 他们去图书馆。 Tā.mén qù túshūguǎn. (下午三点二十分 xià.wǔ sān-diǎn èr.shí-fēn)
5. 你们来我家。 Nǐ.mén lái wǒ jiā. (晚上七点半 wǎn.shàng qī-diǎn bàn)
6. 我们有中文考试。 Wǒ.mén yǒu Zhōngwén kǎoshì. (星期四早上十点 Xīngqīsì zǎo.shàng shí-diǎn)
7. 我的中国朋友来美国。 Wǒ.de Zhōng.guó péng.yǒu lái Měi.guó. (后天 hòu.tiān)
8. 白苹和我打篮球。 Bái Píng hé *wǒ* dǎ lánqiú. (明天下午五点 míng.tiān xià.*wǔ wǔ*-diǎn)
9. 李老师来学校。 *Lǐ* lǎoshī lái xuéxiào. (星期五早上八点十五分 Xīngqī*wǔ* zǎo.shàng bā-diǎn shíwǔ-fēn)
10. 我和爸爸妈妈去日本。 Wǒ hé bà.x mā.x qù Rìběn. (七月十三日晚上六点四十二分 Qīyuè shísān rì wǎn.shàng liù-diǎn sì.shí'èr-fēn)

10 连接句子 Liánjiē jù.zi *Combine the sentences*

Form one sentence by combining the two sentences with 还 *hái*.

Lì.zi: 我有一只猫。我有一只狗。 *Wǒ* yǒu yì-zhī māo. *Wǒ* yǒu yì-zhī gǒu.
我有一只猫，还有一只狗。 *Wǒ* yǒu yì-zhī māo, hái yǒu yì-zhī gǒu.

1. 弟弟修数学和化学。弟弟修音乐。 Dì.x xiū shùxué hé huàxué. Dì.x xiū yīnyuè.
2. 她有三个弟弟。她有一个哥哥。 Tā yǒu sān-.ge dì.x. Tā yǒu yí-.ge gē.x.
3. 我昨天上英文课。我昨天上中文课。
   Wǒ zuó.tiān shàng Yīngwén kè. Wǒ zuó.tiān shàng Zhōngwén kè.
4. 爸爸喜欢打篮球。爸爸喜欢打棒球。
   Bà.x xǐ.huān dǎ-lánqiú. Bà.x xǐ.huān dǎ-bàngqiú.
5. 他今天看法国电影。他今天看日本电影。
   Tā jīn.tiān kàn Fǎ.guó diànyǐng. Tā jīn.tiān kàn Rìběn diànyǐng.
6. 他们星期六去图书馆。他们星期日去图书馆。
   Tā.mén Xīngqīliù qù túshūguǎn. Tā.mén Xīngqīrì qù túshūguǎn.
7. 老师有一个电话。老师有两个手机。
   Lǎoshī yǒu yí-.ge diànhuà. Lǎoshī *yǒu* liǎng-.ge shǒujī.

11 你有几个？ *Nǐ* yǒu jǐ-.ge? *How many do you have?*

Say how many of each object you have. Follow the model.

Lì.zi: 我有一个足球，还有两个篮球。
Wǒ yǒu yí-.ge zúqiú, hái *yǒu* liǎng-.ge lánqiú.

1.

3.

5.

2.

4.
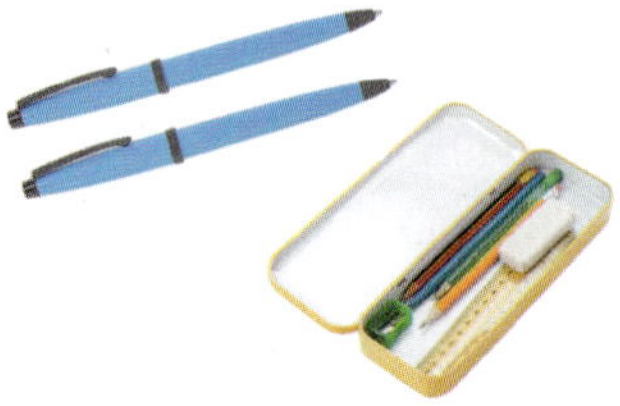

6.

12 校园调查 Xiàoyuán Diàochá / *A Survey about School*

Find out what classes your classmates think are interesting. Make a grid like the one that follows. Interview 10 students and put an X in the appropriate column. Finally, report your findings to your small group.

Lì.zi: **Zhong:** 数学课有意思吗？ Shùxué kè yǒu yì.sī .ma?

Feng: 数学课没有意思。 Shùxué kè méi.yǒu yì.sī.

	数学 shùxué	中文 Zhōngwén	文学 wénxué	化学 huàxué	历史 lìshǐ	…
有意思 yǒu yì.sī						
没有意思 méi.yǒu yì.sī	X					

13 朱琴的日历 Zhū Qín .de Rìlì / *Zhu Qin's Calendar*

Based on her calendar, say where Qin is going at the indicated time.

1. 8:50
2. 5:58
3. 7:10
4. 4:33
5. 12:55
6. 1:46
7. 8:00
8. 3:40

7:15	学校 xuéxiào
8:05	生物课 shēngwù kè
8:55	图书馆 túshūguǎn
1:00	信息技术课 xìnxī jìshù kè
1:50	数学课 shùxué kè
3:45	英文课 Yīngwén kè
4:35	体育课 tǐyù kè
6:00	哥哥家 gē.x jiā

开口说 Kāikǒu Shuō

Communication

14 聊聊学校 Liáo.x Xuéxiào / *Talking about School*

With a partner, play the roles of two students who are discussing the day they just had at school.

A: Say what classes you had today.

B: Ask what your classmate thinks about one of the classes.

A: Give your opinion. Ask if your classmate had any tests or quizzes today.

B: Say you had a quiz in Chinese.

A: Ask if it was easy.

B: Give your opinion.

15 我喜欢的课 Wǒ Xǐ.huān .de Kè / *The Classes I Like*

Give a presentation to your small group that includes the classes you have, the ones you like and how you feel about other classes. Follow the model.

Lì.zi: 我今天上…。 Wǒ jīn.tiān shàng…

我喜欢…。 *Wǒ* xǐ.huān.…

我觉得…很有意思。 Wǒ jué.de… .*hěn* yǒu yì.sī.

16 志伟的一天 Zhìwěi .de Yì Tiān *Zhiwei's Day at School*

Write a paragraph in Pinyin that describes Zhiwei's day at school yesterday. Make sure you answer the questions at the bottom in your paragraph.

1.

2.

3.

1. (*frame 1*) 志伟昨天在哪儿? Zhìwěi zuó.tiān zài nǎr?
2. 他上什么课? Tā shàng shén.me kè?
3. 他觉得生物课无聊吗? Tā jué.de shēngwù kè wúliáo .ma?
4. (*frame 2*) 他觉得数学考试很难吗? Tā jué.de shùxué kǎoshì .hěn nán .ma?
5. (*frame 3*) 他去哪儿? Tā qù nǎr?
6. 他在那儿做什么? Tā zài nàr zuò shén.me?

17 看课表 Kàn kèbiǎo / *Check out the school schedule*

Below is the school schedule of a student in 10th grade in China. Answer the questions that follow.

江苏省南通市高中课表 Jiāngsūshěng Nántōngshì Gāozhōng Kèbiǎo						
时间 shíjiān	节次 jiécì	星期一 Xīngqīyī	星期二 Xīngqī'èr	星期三 Xīngqīsān	星期四 Xīngqīsì	星期五 Xīngqīwǔ
6:25 7:05	早自习 zǎozìxí	英文 Yīngwén	中文 Zhōngwén	英文 Yīngwén	中文 Zhōngwén	英文 Yīngwén
7:15 7:55	一 yī	地理 dìlǐ	数学 shùxué	英文 Yīngwén	物理 wùlǐ	中文 Zhōngwén
8:05 8:45	二 èr	英文 Yīngwén	数学 shùxué	英文 Yīngwén	历史 lìshǐ	中文 Zhōngwén
8:55 9:35	三 sān	历史 lìshǐ	生物 shēngwù	生物 shēngwù	化学 huàxué	生物 shēngwù
10:00 10:40	四 sì	数学 shùxué	中文 Zhōngwén	中文 Zhōngwén	数学 shùxué	物理 wùlǐ
10:50 11:35	五 wǔ	生物 shēngwù	中文 Zhōngwén	体育 tǐyù	数学 shùxué	物理 wùlǐ
午休 wǔxiū						
14:00 14:40	六 liù	生物 shēngwù	政治 zhèngzhì	数学 shùxué	地理 dìlǐ	英文 Yīngwén
14:50 15:35	七 qī	信息 xìnxī	化学 huàxué	信息 xìnxī	中文 Zhōngwén	体育 tǐyù
15:45 16:25	八 bā	中文 Zhōngwén	英文 Yīngwén	物理 wùlǐ	生物 shēngwù	数学 shùxué
16:35 17:40	九 jiǔ	班会 bānhuì	生物 shēngwù	物理 wùlǐ	英文 Yīngwén	数学 shùxué

班会 bānhuì *n. class meeting*

自习 zìxí *n. self-study*

1. Based on this schedule, how many periods a day does this student have (excluding homeroom)?
2. What time does class begin for the day? At what time does the school day end?
3. How many days a week must students go to school?
4. What language classes can you see on the schedule?
5. What humanities classes can you see on the schedule?
6. What math/science classes can you see on the schedule?

汉字天地 Hànzì Tiāndì
Chinese Characters

天 ■ tiān ■ sky; day

The pictograph 天 *tiān* depicts a person stretching out his arms to the sky. This character represents both "sky" and "day."

Stroke Order

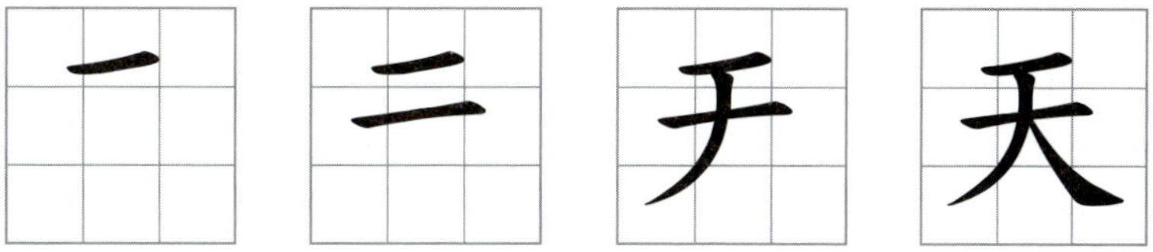

18 词汇延伸 Cíhuì Yánshēn / *Vocabulary Builder*

Below are some characters that can be combined with 天 *tiān* to create new words. Match the Chinese words on the left with the appropriate English meaning on the right.

生 shēng	气 qì	价 jià	堂 táng	桥 qiáo
v. to give birth to	*n. air*	*n. price*	*n. hall*	*n. bridge*

1. 天生 tiānshēng — A. *weather*
2. 天气 tiānqì — B. *inborn*
3. 天价 tianjià — C. *extremely high price*
4. 天堂 tiāntáng — D. *overpass*
5. 天桥 tiānqiáo — E. *heaven*

19 汉字侦探 Hànzì Zhēntàn / *Visual Detective*

Can you find 天 in the following pictures?

Lesson D

发音 Fāyīn
Pronunciation

b p m f d t n l g
k h z c s zh ch sh r + en eng

词汇 Cíhuì
Vocabulary

运动 (運動) Yùndòng *Sports*

慢跑 (慢跑)
mànpǎo *v./n. to jog; jogging*

骑自行车 (騎自行車)
qí-zìxíngchē *vo. to go biking*

冲浪 (衝浪)
chōng-làng *vo./n. to surf; surfing*

打排球 (打排球)
dǎ-páiqiú *vo. to play volleyball*

打网球 (打網球)
dǎ-wǎngqiú *vo. to play tennis*

做瑜珈 (做瑜珈)
zuò-yújiā *vo. to do yoga*

看电视 (看電視)
kàn-diànshì *vo. to watch TV*

打高尔夫 (打高爾夫)
dǎ-gāo'ěrfū *vo. to play golf*

滑雪 (滑雪)
huá-xuě *vo. to ski*

打台球（打台球）
dǎ-táiqiú *vo. to play pool*

做有氧运动（做有氧運動）
zuò yǒuyǎng yùndòng *vo. to do aerobics*

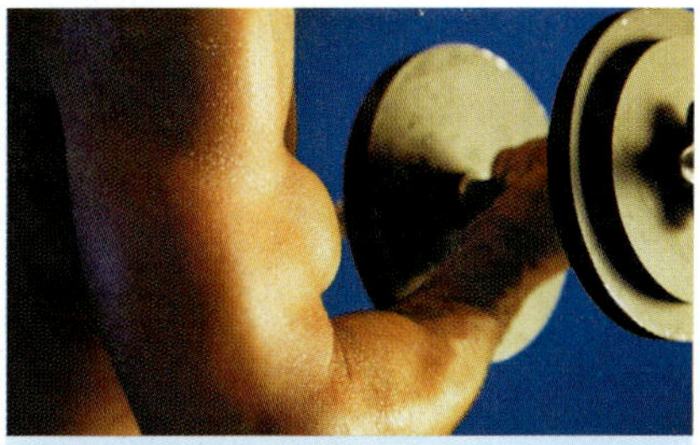

举重（舉重）
jǔzhòng *vo. to lift weights*

公园（公園）
gōngyuán *n. park*

A: 你想做什么（你想做什麼）?

Nǐ xiǎng zuò shén.me? *What would you like to do?*

B: 我想去公园（我想去公園）。

Wǒ xiǎng qù gōngyuán. *I would like to go to the park.*

篮球场（籃球場）
lánqiúchǎng *n. basketball court*

A: 你要去篮球场吗（你要去籃球場嗎）?

Nǐ yào qù lánqiúchǎng .ma? *Are you going to the basketball court?*

B: 我不去篮球场（我不去籃球場）。

Wǒ bú qù lánqiúchǎng. *No, I'm not going to the basketball court.*

购物中心（購物中心）
gòuwù zhōngxīn *n. mall*

A: 你们在哪儿（你們在哪兒）?

Nǐ.mén zài nǎr? *Where are you?*

B: 我们在购物中心（我們在購物中心）。

Wǒ.mén zài gòuwù zhōngxīn. *We are at the mall.*

A: 周末你要去哪儿（周末你要去哪兒）?

Zhōumò nǐ yào qù nǎr? *Where are you going this weekend?*

B: 我要跟我爸妈去爷爷家（我要跟我爸媽去爺爺家）。

Wǒ yào gēn wǒ bà-mā qù yé.x jiā. *I'm going to my grandparents' with my mom and dad.*

海边（海邊）
hǎibiān *n. beach*

A: 你要做什么（你要做什麼）？
Nǐ yào zuò shén.me? *What are you going to do?*

B: 我要去海边游泳，还要去打排球（我要去海邊游泳，還要去打排球）。
Wǒ yào qù hǎibiān yóuyǒng, hái yào qù dǎ-páiqiú. *I'm going swimming and playing volleyball at beach.*

美术馆（美術館）
měishùguǎn *n. art museum*

我们在美术馆看画（我們在美術館看畫）。
Wǒ. zài měishùguǎn kàn-huà.
I am looking at paintings in the art museum.

A: 周末快乐（周末快樂）！
Zhōumò kuàilè! *Have a nice weekend!*

B: 谢谢，周末快乐（謝謝，周末快樂）。
Xiè.x, zhōumò kuàilè! *Thank you. Have a nice weekend!*

Adjectives

快乐（快樂）	kuàilè	*happy; joyful*

Auxiliary Verbs

要（要）	yào	*to be going to*

Nouns

周末（週末）	zhōumò	*weekend*
场（場）	chǎng	*court*
海（海）	hǎi	*sea*
博物馆（博物館）	bówùguǎn	*museum*

Prepositions

跟（跟）	gēn	*with*

Language Note

"Preposition + noun" in Chinese often precede the verb, e.g. 我跟朋友去海边。*Wǒ gēn péng.yǒu qù hǎibiān.* Therefore, adverbs like 不 *bù* should be attached in front of it, e.g. 我不跟朋友去海边。*Wǒ bù gēn péng.yǒu qù hǎibiān.*

1 听力练习 Tīnglì Liànxí *Listen and Match*

Select the photo that corresponds to the location mentioned in the mini-dialogue.

A.

C.

E.

B.

D.

F.

2 建良的周末 Jiànliáng .de Zhōumò *Jianliang's Weekend*

Say where Jianliang is going on the weekend. Then name one thing he will most likely do there.

Lì.zi: 建良去海边。他去冲浪。

Jiànliáng qù hǎibiān. Tā qù chōng-làng.

1.
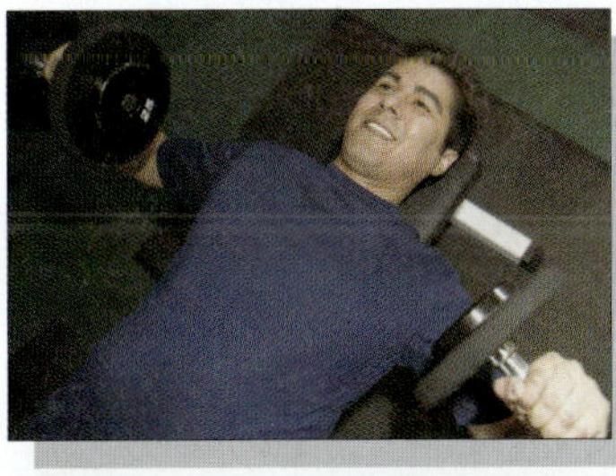

3.

5.

2.

4.

6.

3 你喜欢吗? Nǐ xǐ.huān .ma? Do you like it?

With a partner, take turns asking and telling whether or not you like to do each activity.

Lì.zi: **A:** 你喜欢骑自行车吗? Nǐ xǐ.huān qí-zìxíngchē .ma?

B: 我喜欢。 Wǒ xǐ.huān.

OR 我不喜欢。 Wǒ bù xǐ.huān.

1.

3.

5.

2.

4.

6.

4 他们在做什么? Tā.mén zài zuò shén.me? What are they doing?

With a partner, talk about what various people are doing. Student A asks questions and Student B answers them. Follow the model.

Lì.zi: 王先生 Wáng xiān.shēng (骑自行车 qí-zìxíngchē / 打台球 dǎ-táiqiú)

A: 王先生骑自行车吗? Wáng xiān.shēng qí-zìxíngchē .ma?

B: 不，他不骑自行车，他打台球。 Bù, tā bù qí-zìxíngchē, tā dǎ-táiqiú.

1. 李小姐 Lǐ xiǎo.jiě (慢跑 mànpǎo / 做瑜珈 zuò-yújiā)
2. 哥哥 gē.x (打网球 dǎ-wǎngqiú / 打篮球 dǎ-lánqiú)
3. 方老师 Fāng lǎoshī (画画 huà.x / 看书 kàn-shū)
4. 爸爸 bà.x (打高尔夫 dǎ-gāo'ěrfū / 举重 jǔzhòng)
5. 妈妈 mā.x (看电视 kàn-diànshì / 做有氧运动 zuò yǒuyǎng yùndòng)
6. 林校长 Lín xiàozhǎng (去美术馆 qù měishùguǎn / 去公园 qù gōngyuán)

句型介绍 Jùxíng Jièshào

Language Patterns

The Auxiliary Verb 要 *yào*

The auxiliary verb 要 *yào* means "to be going to." It is put before a verb to indicate the action is going to happen.

要 *yào* + **Verb**

我们明天要看电影。 Wǒ.mén míng.tiān yào kàn-diànyǐng.

他周末要去看书。 Tā zhōumò yào qù kàn-shū.

The Purpose Indicating Pattern: "去 *qù* / 来 *lái* + Verb clause"

As you know, 去 *qù* (to go) and 来 *lái* (to come) can be followed by a place word. But when 去 *qù* / 来 *lái* is followed by a verb clause, it indicates the subject is going to do something.

Note: If the action moves away from the speaker, use 去 *qù*; if the action moves toward the speaker, use 来 *lái*.

Subject + **去 *qù* / 来 *lái*** + **Verb clause**

A: 你要做什么？ Nǐ yào zuò shén.me?

B: 我去慢跑。 Wǒ qù mànpǎo.

A: 星期日林先生要来我们家。 Xīngqīrì Lín xiān.shēng yào lái wǒ.mén jiā.

B: 他来做什么？ Tā lái zuò shén.me?

A: 他来看爸爸。 Tā lái kàn bà.x.

The Preposition 跟 *gēn*

The word 跟 *gēn* is both a preposition and a conjunction. When it functions as a preposition, it means "with," and it means "and" when it functions as a conjunction. As a preposition, 跟 *gēn* must come before the main verb and after the subject.

Subject 1 + **跟 *gēn*** + **Subject 2** + **Verb Phrase**

我跟爸妈去海边。 Wǒ gēn bà-mā qù hǎibiān.

小狗跟我去公园，小狗也跟我去打篮球。

*Xiǎo*gǒu gēn wǒ qù gōngyuán, *xiǎogǒu* yě gēn wǒ qù dǎ lánqiú.

Comparisons

In English sentences, where is "with"?

Mark is going to the dance with Heather.

Mark will eat with his family first.

If these sentences were translated into Chinese, "with" would fall between what two nouns?

会话 Huìhuà
Dialogue

周末 Zhōumò *The Weekend*

At the bus stop, Bai Ping is talking to Zhang Guohua.

白苹：	你要去篮球场吗？	Bái Píng:	Nǐ yào qù lánqiúchǎng .ma?
张国华：	我不去篮球场，我要回家。	Zhāng Guóhuá:	Wǒ bú qù lánqiúchǎng, wǒ yào huí-jiā.
白苹：	周末你要去哪儿？	Bái Píng:	Zhōumò nǐ yào qù nǎr?
张国华：	我要去海边。	Zhāng Guóhuá:	Wǒ yào qù hǎibiān.
白苹：	你要去游泳吗？	Bái Píng:	Nǐ yào qù yóuyǒng .ma?
张国华：	对，我要去游泳，还要去打排球。你呢？你要做什么？	Zhāng Guóhuá:	Duì, wǒ yào qù yóuyǒng, hái yào qù dǎ-páiqiú. Nǐ .ne? Nǐ yào zuò shén.me?
白苹：	我要跟我爸妈去爷爷家。	Bái Píng:	Wǒ yào gēn wǒ bà-mā qù yé.x jiā.
张国华：	嗯，周末快乐！	Zhāng Guóhuá:	Ēn, zhōumò kuàilè!
白苹：	周末快乐！	Bái Píng:	Zhōumò kuàilè!

5 懂了吗？ Dǒng .le .ma? *Do you understand?*

Answer the following questions.

1. 白苹要去篮球场吗？ Bái Píng yào qù lánqiúchǎng .ma?
2. 张国华要去篮球场吗？ Zhāng Guóhuá yào qù lánqiúchǎng .ma?
3. 谁要回家？ Shéi yào huí-jiā?
4. 张国华周末要做什么？ Zhāng Guóhuá zhōumò yào zuò shén.me?
5. 白苹周末要做什么？ Bái Píng zhōumò yào zuò shén.me?
6. 他们最后(*at the end*)说什么？ Tā.mén zuìhòu shuō shén.me?

文化橱窗 Wénhuà Chúchuāng

Culture Window

Popular Pastimes for Teens in China

▲ Singing with subtitles on the screen.

Chinese teens engage in various indoor and outdoor pastimes. Let's look at an example of each. For indoor activities, many young people in China love to go to places called KTVs for karaoke (卡拉OK *kălā-OK*). They love to sing songs with a microphone, following the subtitles on the screen as the music video plays. Usually, larger KTVs are well-decorated with great facilities and new songs. Sometimes, they also provide food and beverages. Inviting a group of friends to party in a KTV booth is one of the most popular indoor activities of teens today.

One of the most popular outdoor activities for young people is to go to a night market. Night markets are like miniature shopping malls that have many tasty snacks and delicacies as well as an assortment of clothes, accessories, and products for daily use, made all the more appealing by the low prices and uniqueness of the venues. For example, Beijing's most famous night market, the Donghuamen Night Market (东华门夜市 *Dōnghuámén Yèshì*) is known for its rare and "special" snacks that include silkworm cocoons, millipedes, seahorses, and scorpions. However, Beijing residents consider 簋街 *Guĭ Jiē*, with its red lanterns and banners, their most representative night market. This street of markets is also known as 鬼街 *Guĭ Jiē* ("Ghost" Street) since it is open all night.

▲ Donghuamen Night Market.

▲ "Special" snacks.

▲ Starfish can also be found there.

Comparisons

Use anecdotal evidence to discuss with your small group what you like to do with a free evening. Make a list and share it with the class.

Morning in the Park

If you ever get the chance to visit a city in China, you will probably find that the parks are extraordinarily lively in the morning. With people getting in groups to do tai-chi (太极 *tàijí*), qi-gong (气功 *qìgōng*), dance, meditation, or even bird-walking, the park is never a dull place. The best part is newcomers are free to join in. It's just like a gym, but free.

▲ People do tai-chi in the park in the morning.

No matter what kind of group you choose, you are bound to get a friendly welcome. Then, while you're doing your workout, you'll be able to hear the news and catch up on all the latest gossip. You have to admit that this sounds like a lot more fun than going to the gym.

Generally speaking, Chinese city-dwellers live in apartments. As they don't have front or back yards like people in the West, they don't have much of a chance to interact with their neighbors. Thus parks in China serve as places where residents can meet up with old friends and make new ones. Along the way, people can stretch their legs and get a bit of exercise. The next time you're in China, make sure you're up early enough to take part in "park time."

6 文化动动脑 Wénhuà Dòng.x nǎo *Culture Check-up*

Complete each statement with an appropriate word or expression.

1. In a ___, you can sing songs with a microphone, and follow the subtitles on the screen as the music video plays.
2. KTVs are usually well-decorated with great ___ and new songs.
3. Sometimes, KTVs also provide ___ and ___.
4. One of the most popular indoor activities of teens today could be having a party in a ___.
5. The most popular outdoor activities for young people is to go to a ___.
6. Night markets are like miniature ___.
7. Beijing's most famous night market, the ___ night market is known for its rare and "special" snacks.
8. 簋街 *Guǐ Jiē* is also known as 鬼街 *Guǐ Jiē* ("Ghost" Street) because ___.
9. ___ could be an extraordinarily lively place to be in the morning.
10. The park is never a dull place because there are people getting in groups doing ___, ___, dance, ___, or even bird-walking.
11. The best part about the parks is that ___ are free to join in. It's just like a gym, but ___.
12. Generally speaking, Chinese city-dwellers live in ___.

Language Practice

7 暑假 Shǔjià *Summer Vacation*

Say how Yijun is going to keep busy during summer vacation. Follow the model.

Lì.zi: 怡君要打棒球。
Yíjūn yào dǎ-bàngqiú.

1. 	3. 	5. 	7. 
2. 	4. 	6. 	8. 

8 你要做什么？ Nǐ yào zuò shén.me? *What are you going to do?*

With a partner, take turns asking and answering what you are going to do every day this week. Follow the model.

Lì.zi: **A:** 你星期一要做什么？ Nǐ Xīngqīyī yào zuò shén.me?

B: 我星期一要去图书馆。 Wǒ Xīngqīyī yào qù túshūguǎn.

9 连接句子 Liánjiē jù.zi *Combine the Sentences*

Combine the following two sentences with 跟 *gēn* to form a single sentence.

Lì.zi: 董军去滑雪。张国华去滑雪。 Dǒng Jūn qù huá-xuě. Zhāng Guóhuá qù huá-xuě.
董军跟张国华去滑雪。 Dǒng Jūn gēn Zhāng Guóhuá qù huá-xuě.

1. 爸爸去看电影。妈妈去看电影。 Bà.x qù kàn-diànyǐng. Mā.x qù kàn-diànyǐng.
2. 我在家听音乐。姐姐在家听音乐。 Wǒ zài jiā tīng-yīnyuè. Jiě.x zài jiā tīng-yīnyuè.
3. 李伯伯来我家。王伯伯来我家。 Lǐ bó.x lái wǒ jiā. Wáng bó.x lái wǒ jiā.
4. 白苹去美术馆。林书芳去美术馆。 Bái Píng qù měishùguǎn. Lín Shūfāng qù měishùguǎn.
5. 他去中文教室。我去中文教室。 Tā qù Zhōngwén jiàoshì. Wǒ qù Zhōngwén jiàoshì.

10 一起做事情 Yìqǐ Zuò Shì.qíng / *Doing Things Together*

Say with whom the following people are doing the activity. Follow the model.

Lì.zi: 高兰跳舞。 Gāo Lán tiào-wǔ. (王福 Wáng Fú)

高兰跟王福跳舞。 Gāo Lán gēn Wáng Fú tiào-wǔ.

1. 丽君踢足球。 Lìjūn tī-zúqiú. (芸琳 Yúnlín)
2. 永国唱歌。 Yǒngguó chàng-gē. (淑惠 Shūhuì)
3. 佩君画画。 Pèijūn huà.x (志宏 Zhìhóng)
4. 明俊打篮球。 Míngjùn dǎ-lánqiú. (建宏 Jiànhóng)
5. 欣怡慢跑。 Xīnyí mànpǎo. (俊男 Jùnnán)
6. 邓桂买东西。 Dèng Guì mǎi dōng.xī. (蔡英 Cài Yīng)
7. 志强打高尔夫。 Zhìqiáng dǎ-gāo'ěrfū. (信鸿 Xìnhóng)
8. 文兴打网球。 Wénxīng *dǎ*-wǎngqiú. (建国 Jiànguó)

开口说 Kāikǒu Shuō

Communication

11 周末计划 Zhōumò Jìhuà / *Weekend Plan*

With a partner, play the roles of two students who are planning their weekend.

A, B: Greet each other.

A: Ask where your classmate is going for the weekend.

B: Tell where you are planning to go, with whom you are going, and what you are going to do there. Then ask where your classmate is going for the weekend.

A: Tell where you are planning to go, with whom you are going, and what you are going to do there. Then say you have to go.

B: Wish your classmate a nice weekend.

A: Say good-bye.

我要去海边。
Wǒ yào qù hǎibiān.

12 便笺 Biànjiān / *Memo*

Look at the memo, and answer the questions that follow.

朱丽叶 Zhū Lìyè:

你好，我叫罗密欧，高二年级。我是你中文课的同学。

我喜欢上中文课，还很喜欢看中国电影。

你喜不喜欢中国电影呢？

我后天（星期六）要去看电影。你要不要跟我一起去？

这是我的手机号码：0952604627。

周末快乐

六月三日　罗密欧 Luó Mì'ōu

1. Who wrote this note, and to whom?
2. On what day of the week was this note written?
3. The person who wrote this note is in which grade?
4. How does Luo Mi'ou know Zhu Liye?
5. What is the relationship between the note giver and receiver?
6. What does the author of the note like to do?
7. On what day is the author of the note planning to go to the movies?
8. What is the cell phone number of the person who wrote the note?

13 我最喜欢的周末 Wǒ Zuì Xǐ.huān .de Zhōumò / *My Favorite Weekend*

In class show a photo or drawing of a favorite weekend. Prepare a presentation in which you describe what you did in the photo. In your presentation:

- tell where you went
- tell when you went there
- tell with whom you went
- tell what you did there
- give an opinion about the activity

周末我喜欢去冲浪。
Zhōumò *wǒ* xǐ.huān qù chōng-làng.

14 中国人的周末活动 Zhōng.guórén .de Zhōumò Huódòng Chinese People's Weekend Activities

This is the outcome of a questionnaire about what Chinese people do on weekends. Look at the chart and answer the questions that follow.

在家休息 zài jiā xiū.xī *rest at home*	50%
郊游踏青 jiāoyóu tàqīng *go for an outing*	11%
运动健身 yùndòng jiànshēn *exercise*	8%
娱乐活动 yúlè huódòng *do some recreation*	8%
聚餐聊天 jùcān liáotiān *eat and chat*	7%
购物消费 gòuwù xiāofèi *go shopping*	5%
探访亲友 tànfǎng qīn-yǒu *visit relatives or friends*	3%
进修学习 jìnxiū xué.xí *study*	3%
其它 qítā *other*	5%

1. What do most people do on weekends?
2. What is the second most popular activity which Chinese people do?
3. Do many people visit relatives or friends on weekends?
4. Compared to going shopping, do more people get together and chat on weekends?
5. If there is a chart about what Americans do on weekends, what do you think are the top three activities?

15 小小调查 Xiǎo.x Diàochá A Survey

Find out what five students in your class like to do on the weekends, draw a grid like the one shown with this activity. In the grid write the names in Chinese of five weekend activities, and then poll your classmates. Each interviewee chooses his or her favorite activity. Finally, share the results of your survey with the class.

Lì.zi: A: 你周末喜欢做什么？ Nǐ zhōumò xǐ.huān zuò shén.me?

B: 我周末喜欢…。 Wǒ zhōumò xǐ.huān….

……….

A: 三个学生周末喜欢上网，两个学生周末喜欢去购物中心。
Sān-.ge xué.shēng zhōumò xǐ.huān shàngwǎng, liǎng-.ge xué.shēng zhōumò xǐ.huān qù gòuwù zhōngxīn.

Activity / Student	看电影 kàn-diànyǐng	打篮球 dǎ-lánqiú	上网 shàngwǎng	看书 kàn-shū	去购物中心 qù gòuwù zhōngxīn
建华 Jiànhuá		✓			

汉字天地 Hànzì Tiāndì
Chinese Characters

家 ■ jiā ■ home; family

The character 家 *jiā* combines the two pictographs 宀 *mián* and 豕 *shǐ*. The top pictograph 宀 *mián* stands for a roof, and the 豕 *shǐ* on the bottom represents a pig. In ancient China, most households raised pigs as domestic animals. The image of a pig under a roof, therefore, came to stand for "home" or "family."

Stroke Order

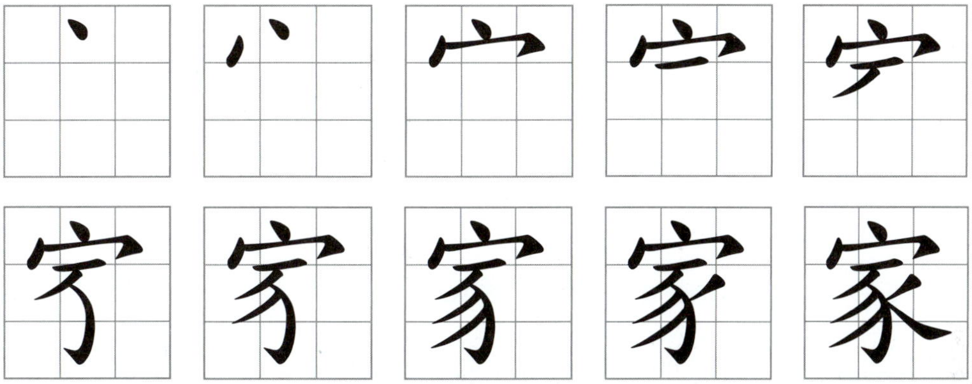

16 词汇延伸 Cíhuì Yánshēn / *Vocabulary Builder*

Below are some characters that can be combined with 家 *jiā* to create new words. Match the Chinese words on the left with the appropriate English meaning on the right.

国 guó *n. country*	人 rén *n. people*	具 jù *n. utensil*	长 zhǎng *adj. older*	务 wù *n. task*

1. 国家 guójiā — A. *parents*
2. 家人 jiārén — B. *family member*
3. 家具 jiājù — C. *household chores*
4. 家长 jiāzhǎng — D. *nation*
5. 家务 jiāwù — E. *furniture*

17 汉字侦探 Hànzì Zhēntàn / *Visual Detective*

Can you find 家 in the picture?

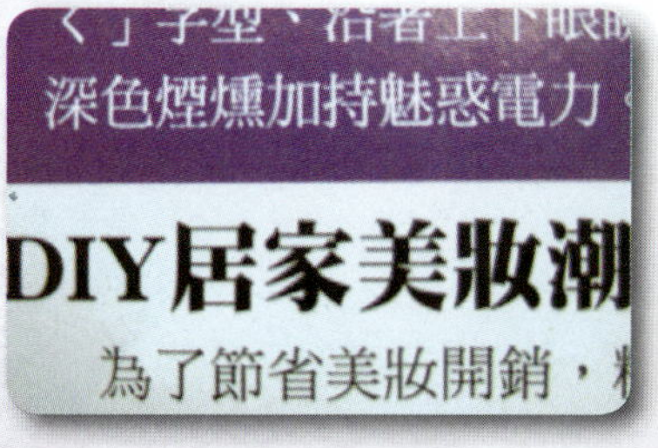

Unit 4

我要点菜！Wǒ Yào Diǎn-cài!

When you have completed this unit, you will be able to...

- order food and beverages in a restaurant
- use courtesy expressions appropriately
- discuss prices and quantities
- make a purchase and count change
- describe how different foods taste

Lesson A

发音 Fāyīn
Pronunciation

b p m f d t n l + i ia iao

词汇 Cíhuì
Vocabulary

食物 Shíwù Foods

汉堡包 (漢堡包)
hànbǎobāo
n. hamburger

吉士汉堡包 (吉士漢堡包)
jíshì hànbǎobāo
n. cheeseburger

三明治 (三明治)
sānmíngzhì
n. sandwich

热狗 (熱狗)
règǒu
n. hotdog

薯条 (薯條)
shǔtiáo
n. French fries

色拉 (色拉)
sèlā
n. salad

洋芋片 (洋芋片)
yángyùpiàn
n. chips

苹果 (蘋果)
píngguǒ
n. apple

茶 (茶)
chá
n. tea

汽水 (汽水)
qìshuǐ
n. soda

果汁 (果汁)
guǒzhī
n. juice

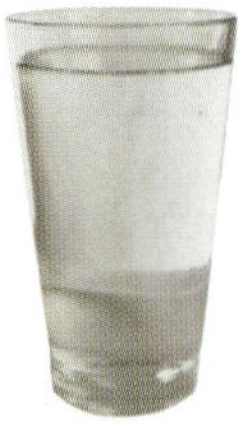

水 (水)
shuǐ
n. water

咖啡 (咖啡)
kāfēi
n. coffee

A: 你要咖啡还是茶(你要咖啡還是茶)？

Nǐ yào kāfēi hái.shì chá? *Do you want coffee or tea?*

B: 我要咖啡 (我要咖啡)。

Wǒ yào kāfēi. *I want coffee.*

A: 你要大杯还是小杯

(你要大杯還是小杯)?

Nǐ yào dà bēi hái.shì xiǎo bēi?

Do you want a large or a small?

B: 大杯，谢谢 (大杯，謝謝)。

Dà bēi, xiè.x. *Large, thanks.*

 大 (大) dà *adj. large*	 中 (中) zhōng *adj. medium*	 小 (小) xiǎo *adj. small*
 大杯 (大杯) dà bēi *adj. large (cup)*	 中杯 (中杯) zhōng bēi *adj. medium (cup)*	 小杯 (小杯) xiǎo bēi *adj. small (cup)*

Conjunctions

还是 (還是)	hái.shì	*or*

Measure Words

份 (份)	fèn	*a share of; a portion of*

Nouns

饮料 (飲料)	yǐnliào	*beverage*
是 (是)	shì	*to be*

Number + Measure Words

一下 (一下)	yí.xià	*(used after a verb to indicate short duration)*

Verbs

点 (點)	diǎn	*to order*
喝 (喝)	hē	*to drink*
等 (等)	děng	*to wait*

1 他们点什么? Tā.mén diǎn shén.me? *What do they order?*

You will hear 5 people ordering some food and drinks from the items below. Say the letter and quantity of each item ordered. You will hear each order twice.

Lì.zi: E 1, A 3

A.

C.

E.

G.

B.

D.

F.

H.

2 大的还是小的? Dà.de hái.shì xiǎo.de? *Large or Small?*

With a partner, take turns playing the roles of a customer and a server at a restaurant. Place your order according to the pictures .

Lì.zi: **A:** 你要点什么? Nǐ yào diǎn shén.me?
B: 我要点大杯咖啡。 Wǒ yào diǎn dà bēi kāfēi.

1.

2.
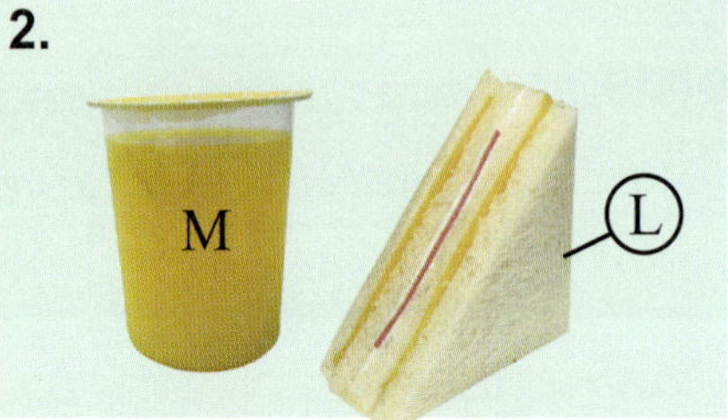

3.

句型介绍 Jùxíng Jièshào

Language Patterns

The Conjunction 还是 *hái.shì*

The conjunction 还是 *hái.shì* means "or." It is used only when asking someone to choose between two alternatives.

Choice 1 + 还是 *hái.shì* + **Choice 2**

A: 你要原珠笔还是铅笔？ Nǐ yào yuánzhūbǐ hái.shì qiānbǐ?
B: 我要铅笔，谢谢。 Wǒ yào qiānbǐ, xiè.x.

A: 这是中文教室还是法文教室？ Zhè.shì Zhōngwén jiàoshì hái.shì Fǎwén jiàoshì?
B: 这是法文教室。 Zhè.shì Fǎwén jiàoshì.

A: 你要去游泳，还是去打篮球？ Nǐ yào qù yóu-yǒng, hái.shì qù dǎ lánqiú?
B: 我要去游泳。 Wǒ yào qù yóu-yǒng.

Comparisons

Explain to a classmate how the conjunction "or" is used in English. Look at the two sentences below for examples.

Do you want bacon or sausage links?
Do you want to study or listen to music?

Language Note

The other word for "or" in Chinese is 或 *huò*. It means "or; either...or..." Look at the example:

A: 你要喝茶还是咖啡？ Nǐ yào hē-chá hái.shì kāfēi?
Do you want to drink tea or coffee?

B: 茶或咖啡都可以。 Chá huò kāfēi dōu *kě*.yǐ.
Either tea or coffee is fine.

Modifying Verbs with 一下 *yí.xià*

In Chinese, “once” or “for a while” is expressed with 一下 *yí.xià*. It can be used after a verb to indicate that an action is of short duration or to express the idea of giving something a try. It can also soften the tone of an expression so that it sounds less formal.

Verb + 一下 *yí.xià*

我看一下这本书。 Wǒ kàn yí.xià zhèi-běn shū.

请你们等一下。 *Qǐng* nǐ.mén děng yí.xià.

Language Note

In the case of a VO compound, 一下 *yí.xià* should be inserted between the verb and the object. For example, 看一下书 *kàn yí.xià shū*, 听一下音乐 *tīng yí.xià yīnyuè*.

会话 Huìhuà *Dialogue*

在快餐店 Zài Kuàicāndiàn *At the Fast-food Restaurant*

At the counter of a western restaurant, Zhang Guohua is ordering.

服务员：	你好！你要点什么？	Fúwùyuán:	*Nǐ* hǎo! Nǐ yào diǎn shén.me?
张国华：	我要一个汉堡包。	Zhāng Guóhuá:	Wǒ yào yí.ge hànbǎobāo.
服务员：	你要喝什么？果汁还是汽水？	Fúwùyuán:	Nǐ yào hē shén.me? Guǒzhī hái.shì qìshuǐ?
张国华：	我要汽水。	Zhāng Guóhuá:	Wǒ yào qìshuǐ.
服务员：	你要大杯还是小杯？	Fúwùyuán:	Nǐ yào dà bēi hái.shì xiǎo bēi?
张国华：	小杯。	Zhāng Guóhuá:	Xiǎo bēi.
服务员：	好，请等一下。	Fúwùyuán:	Hǎo, *qǐng* děng yí.xià.

3 他点什么？ Tā diǎn shén.me? *What does he order?*

Select the food Zhang Guohua orders and write each item in Pinyin.

1. 

2. 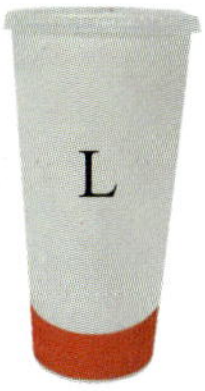

3. 

4. 

5. 

6. 

文化橱窗 Wénhuà Chúchuāng

Culture Window

International Food and Drink Franchises in China

Today there are many international coffee shops and restaurant chains in China. McDonald's, for instance, announced plans in 2009 to open 500 new stores in China over the next three years. The coffee giant Starbucks, already celebrating its ten-year anniversary in China, opened 80 new stores there in one recent year alone. Despite the popularity of Starbucks, there was a strong cultural backlash when Starbucks opened a location inside the "Forbidden City." Similarly, Kentucky Fried Chicken (KFC) was forced to move from Beihai Park, another major cultural center, after its lease expired. There is, however, still a McDonald's located near Tiananmen Square.

▲ Starbucks are popular coffee shops in China.

Despite some initial hurdles, international food and drink franchises have had a profound impact on local businesses in China. In order to compete, local restaurants and shops have had to improve their standards of cleanliness in order to attract customers. This, of course, is a positive development for local consumers.

The buying habits of Chinese people have also changed with the introduction of large convenience store chains. In Shanghai, for example, there are now thousands of 24-hour convenience stores, such as Family Mart, dotting every corner of the city and selling all types of products. These have all but replaced the *xiaomaibu*, the privately-owned convenience stores, of earlier times. In Beijing, however, the story is much different. The government, wishing to preserve the local culture, is much slower to grant licenses to chain stores, even local ones, in order to prevent the much-loved family stores from dying out.

▲ 24-hour convenience stores are dotting every corner in big cities.

Comparisons

The calorie-laden fried foods and sodas sold in fast food restaurants not only contribute to weight gain but also lead to health problems in children, such as the early onset of puberty and certain hormonal imbalances. After the first fast food restaurant opened in China in 1990, the number of overweight children increased, especially in cities. The situation mirrors what has been going on in the United States for the past 50 years. Today, 30 percent of all children in American are labeled overweight. Researchers are correlating this alarming trend to, among other things, fast food and reminding parents to take a more active role in understanding their children's dietary habits.

4 文化动动脑 Wénhuà Dòng.x nǎo / *Culture Check-up*

Decide if each statement is true or false. Correct the false statements to make them true.

1. Starbucks has already celebrated its 20th anniversary in China.
2. There is a McDonald's near Tiananmen Square.
3. McDonald's will open 500 new stores in China in 2010 alone.
4. International food and drink franchises have forced China's local restaurants to improve their standard of cleanliness.
5. International food and drink franchises have changed the buying habits of the Chinese people.
6. Family Mart is a convenience store that can be found in Shanghai.
7. There are more convenience stores in Shanghai than in Beijing.
8. The Chinese for convenience store is "xiaomaibu."
9. The first fast food restaurant opened in China in 1980.
10. Today, 30 percent of children in the United States are overweight.
11. There are more overweight children in China now than there were 20 years ago.
12. In the United States, the increase in the number of overweight children has been a problem for the past 50 years.

Language Practice

5 你的选择？ Nǐ.de Xuǎnzé? *Your Choice?*

With a partner, take turns asking and answering what you would like to eat. Use the conjunction 还是 *hái.shì* in forming your questions.

Lì.zi: **A:** 你要吉士汉堡包还是三明治？
Nǐ yào jíshì hànbǎobāo hái.shì sānmíngzhì?
B: 我要三明治。 Wǒ yào sānmíngzhì.

1.

3.
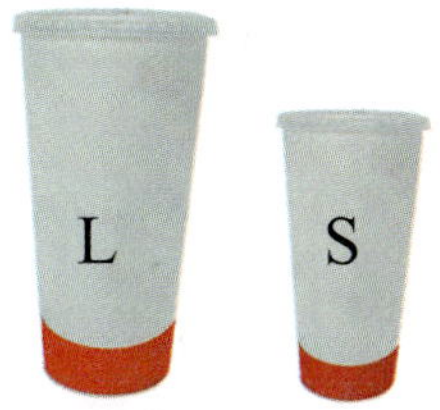

5.

7.

2.

4.

6.

8.

6 客气一点儿 Kè.qi Yì.diǎnr *Being Polite*

Add 一下 yí.xià to the following sentences to make them sound more polite.

Lì.zi: 我看电视。 Wǒ kàn-diànshì.
我看一下电视。 Wǒ kàn yí.xià diànshì.

1. 我早上慢跑。 *Wǒ* zǎo.shàng mànpǎo.
2. 你要听音乐吗？ Nǐ yào tīng-yīnyuè .ma?
3. 我要上网。 Wǒ yào shàng wǎng.
4. 请你吃这个汉堡包。 *Qǐng* nǐ chī zhèi.ge hànbǎobāo.
5. 爸爸晚上看书。 Bà.x wǎn.shàng kàn-shū.
6. 王芳得去图书馆。 Wáng Fāng děi qù túshūguǎn.
7. 你可以来我家吗？ *Nǐ kě*.yǐ lái wǒ jiā .ma?
8. 他要去海边游泳。 Tā yào qù hǎibiān yóu-yǒng.

7 个人问题 Gèrén Wèntí / *Personal Questions*

Ask your partner if he or she has the following items.

Lì.zi: soda / juice

A: 你有可乐还是果汁? *Nǐ* yǒu qìshuǐ hái.shì guǒzhī?

B: 我没有可乐，我有果汁。Wǒ méi.yǒu kělè, *wǒ* yǒu guǒzhī.

1. younger brother / older brother
2. younger sister / older sister
3. niece / nephew
4. cat / dog
5. pen / pencil
6. Chinese teacher / American teacher

8 晚饭以前 Wǎnfàn Yǐqián / *Before Dinner*

The following students have a bit of time before dinner. Tell what they are doing for a while.

Lì.zi:

王芳
Wáng Fāng

晚饭以前，她想游一下泳。
Wǎnfàn yǐqián, tā xiǎng yóu yí.xià yǒng.

1.

马明
Mǎ Míng

2.
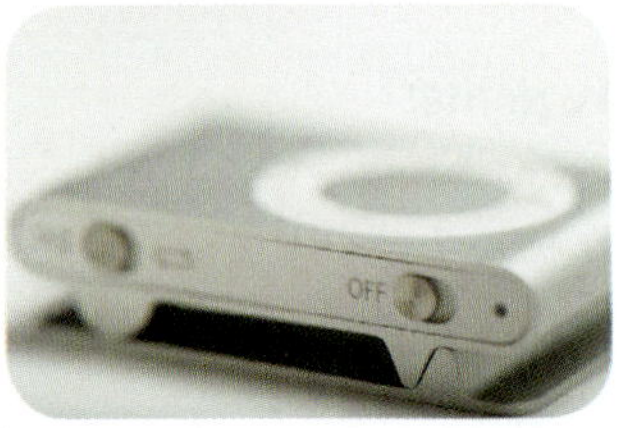

魏鸿
Wèi Hóng

3.
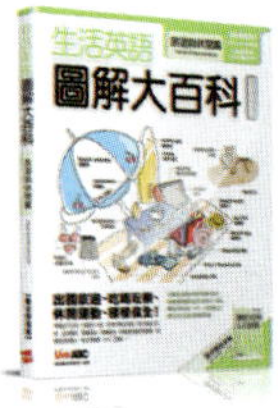

董廷
Dǒng Tíng

4.

刘怡君
Liú Yíjūn

5.

何青青
Hé Qīngqīng

6.

张蓉
Zhāng Róng

开口说 Kāikǒu Shuō

Communication

9 晚饭吃什么? Wǎnfàn chī shén.me ? / *What's for dinner?*

You want to pick up some dinner for your friend. Give him or her two choices on what to order. Follow the model.

Lì.zi: coffee / water

A: 你要咖啡还是水？ Nǐ yào kāfēi hái.shì shuǐ?

B: 我要咖啡。 Wǒ yào kāfēi.

1. hamburger / cheeseburger
2. French fries / chips
3. apple / salad
4. soda / juice

10 在快餐店里 Zài Kuàicān Diàn Dǐ / *At the Fast-food Restaurant*

With a partner, take turns saying what the following people would like to eat.

11 在餐厅里 Zài Cāntīng.lǐ / *In a Restaurant*

With two of your classmates, play the roles of two customers who order something to eat and drink in a restaurant and the server who waits on them.

- The server greets the customers and asks what they would like to eat and drink.
- Each customer orders something to eat and drink.
- The server asks what size drink they would like.
- Each customer expresses if he or she wants a small, medium, or large.
- The server repeats the two orders and politely asks the customers to wait for a while.

12 优惠券 Yōuhuìquàn / Coupon

Refer to the fast-food coupons to answer the questions below.

A.

B.

C.

1. What food items can coupon A be used for?
2. How much can you save if you order using coupon A?
3. If Bai Ping buys a salad using coupon C, what beverage will she be given?
4. If you order a hot dog, fries, and a small juice using coupon B, how much would you have to pay?
5. Zhang Guohua only has 11 Yuan on him. Which coupon can he use to order a meal?
6. Dong Jun wants a hotdog; his friend wants juice and some fires. Which coupon should they share?
7. Which coupon can be used to get a small drink?

汉字天地 Hànzì Tiāndì

Chinese Characters

果 ■ guǒ ■ fruit

The pictograph 果 *guǒ* is a combination of the 日 *rì* (sun) and 木 *mù* (tree), resulting in the bearing of fruit.

Stroke Order

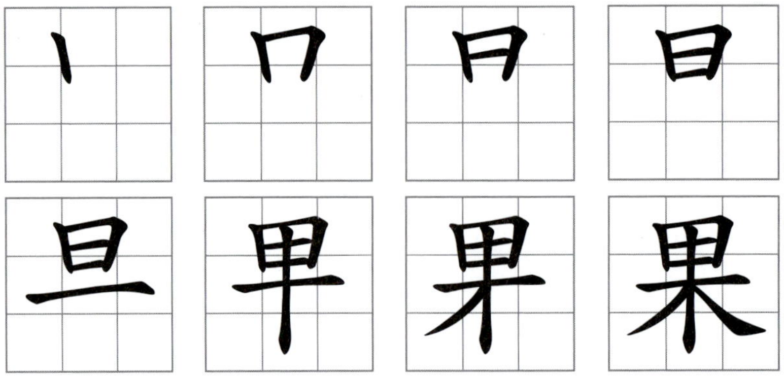

13 词汇延伸 Cíhuì Yánshēn / *Vocabulary Builder*

Below are some characters that can be combined with 果 *guǒ* to create new words. Match the Chinese words on the left with the appropriate English meaning on the right.

汁 zhī *n. juice*	酱 jiàng *n. sauce*	园 yuán *n. garden*	树 shù *n. tree*	肉 ròu *n. meat*

1. 果汁 guǒzhī — A. *orchard*
2. 果酱 guǒjiàng — B. *jam; jelly*
3. 果园 guǒyuán — C. *fruit juice*
4. 果树 guǒshù — D. *fruit flesh*
5. 果肉 guǒròu — E. *fruit tree*

14 汉字侦探 Hànzì Zhēntàn / *Visual Detective*

Can you find 果 in the following pictures?

Lesson B

发音 Fāyīn
Pronunciation

b p m f d t n l + ie iu

词汇 Cíhuì
Vocabulary

饮料 Yǐnliào *Beverages*

红茶(紅茶)
hóngchá
n. black tea

奶茶(奶茶)
nǎichá
n. milk tea

奶昔(奶昔)
nǎixī
n. milk shake

绿茶(綠茶)
lǜchá
n. green tea

热巧克力(熱巧克力)
rè qiǎo.kèlì
n. hot chocolate

橙汁(橙汁)
chéngzhī
n. orange juice

花茶(花茶)
huāchá
n. herbal tea

柠檬水(檸檬水)
níngméngshuǐ
n. lemonade

葡萄汁(葡萄汁)
pú.táozhī
n. grape juice

乌龙茶(烏龍茶)
wūlóngchá
n. oolong tea

冰沙(冰沙)
bīngshā
n. smoothie

苹果汁(蘋果汁)
píngguǒzhī
n. apple juice

数量 **Shùliàng** ***Quantities***				

一杯(一杯) yì-bēi *a cup*	一瓶(一瓶) yì-píng *a bottle*	一罐(一罐) yí-guàn *a can*	一壶(一壺) yì-hú *a pot*	一份(一份) yí-fèn *a share / portion*

A: 你们有什么茶(你們有什麼茶)?

Nǐ.mén yǒu shén.me chá? *What kind of tea do you have?*

B: 红茶、绿茶，还有乌龙茶(紅茶、綠茶，還有烏龍茶)。

Hóngchá, lǜchá, hái yǒu wūlóngchá. *Black tea, green tea, and oolong tea.*

A: 我要点吃的东西。你们有什么吃的东西(我要點吃的東西。你們有什麼吃的東西)?

Wǒ yào diǎn chī .de dōng.xī. Nǐ.mén yǒu shén.me chī .de dōng.xī?

I'd like to order something to eat. What do you have?

B: 我们有薯条、热狗和三明治(我們有薯條、熱狗和三明治)。

Wǒ.mén yǒu shǔtiáo, règǒu hé sānmíngzhì.

We have French fries, hot dogs, and sandwiches.

A: 我要点热狗和薯条(我要點熱狗和薯條)。

Wǒ yào diǎn règǒu hé shǔtiáo.

I'll have a hot dog and French fries.

Adverbs

只 (只)	zhǐ	*only*

Common Expressions

对不起 (對不起)	duì.bùqǐ	*sorry*
请问 (請問)	qǐngwèn	*May I ask…?*
不用 (不用)	búyòng	*no (need)*

Measure Words

杯 (杯)	-bēi	*measure word for cup*

Nouns

东西 (東西)	dōng.xī	*thing(s), stuff*
香草 (香草)	xiāngcǎo	*vanilla*

Verbs

问 (問)	wèn	*to ask*
吃 (吃)	chī	*to eat*

1 他们有什么？ Tā.mén yǒu shén.me? / *What are available?*

With a partner, take turns playing the roles of a customer and a server in a restaurant. The customer asks if the following items are available, and the server politely says they are not. Follow the model.

Lì.zi: **A:** 你们有没有奶昔？ Nǐ.mén yǒu .méi.yǒu nǎixī?

B: 对不起，我们没有奶昔。 Duì.bùqǐ, wǒ.mén méi.yǒu nǎixī.

1. 	2. 	3. 	4. 	5. 

2 他们点什么? Tā.mén diǎn shén.me? *What do they order?*

Look at the pictures, and say what everyone orders. Be sure to use the correct measure word for each item.

1.林员
Lín Yuán

3.白文中
Bái Wénzhōng

5.张汉
Zhāng Hàn

7.董日生
Dǒng Rìshēng

2.包美美
Bāo *Měi*.měi

4.林欢
Lín Huān

6.李书
Lǐ Shū

3 可以点什么? Kě.yǐ diǎn shén.me? *What can you order?*

Look at the menu below and decide what to order based on the amount of money you have to spend.

清净茶馆

红茶	¥ 6.00	巧克力	¥ 8.00
绿茶	¥ 6.50	橙汁	¥ 9.50
花茶	¥ 7.50	柠檬水	¥ 9.00
奶昔	¥ 10.00	葡萄汁	¥ 10.00
奶茶	¥ 8.50		

1. ¥ 6.50
2. ¥ 7.50
3. ¥ 8.50
4. ¥ 9.00
5. ¥ 9.50
6. ¥ 10.00

4 你要什么？ Nǐ yào shén.me? *What would you like?*

Based on the photos, say what each person would like to order for their table. Follow the model.

Lì.zi: 俊鸿要一杯葡萄汁。
Jùnhóng yào yì-bēi pú.táozhī.

俊鸿 Jùnhóng

1. 	3. 	5. 
国华 Guóhuá	建宏 Jiànhóng	永光 Yǒngguāng
2. 	4. 	6. 
宜秀 Yíxiù	春梅 Chūnméi	俊男 Jùnnán

5 个人问题 Gèrén Wèntí *Personal Questions*

Answer the following questions in Chinese.

1. 你喜欢咖啡还是茶？ *Nǐ* xǐ.huān kāfēi hái.shì chá?
2. 你喜欢什么茶？ *Nǐ* xǐ.huān shén.me chá?
3. 你早上喝果汁吗？ *Nǐ* zǎo.shàng hē guǒzhī .ma?
4. 你喜欢巧克力奶昔还是香草奶昔？ *Nǐ* xǐ.huān qiǎo.kèlì nǎixī hái.shì xiāngcǎo nǎixī?
5. 你的兄弟姐妹喜欢热巧克力吗？ Nǐ.de xiōngdì-jiěmèi xǐ.huān rè qiǎo.kèlì .ma?

句型介绍 Jùxíng Jièshào

Language Patterns

Asking Questions with 有没有 *yǒu méi.yǒu*

The verb 有 *yǒu* means "to have" or "there is (are)." It does not use 不 *bù* for the negative. It uses 没 *méi.*

我没有笔。 Wǒ méi.yǒu bǐ. (*I don't have a pen.*)

If a noun follows the negative form, you can shorten 没有 *méi.yǒu* to 没 *méi* e.g.

我没笔。 Wǒ méi bǐ.

However, if there is no noun following the negative, then 有 *yǒu* must be used e.g.

我没有。 Wǒ méi.yǒu.

The interrogative forms are:

Closed: 你有没有笔？ *Nǐ* yǒu méi.yǒu bǐ?

Open: 你有笔没有？ *Nǐ yǒu* bǐ méi.yǒu?

有没有 *yǒu méi.yǒu* + **Noun**

A: 你有没有中文书？ *Nǐ* yǒu méi.yǒu Zhōngwén shū?

B: 有。 Yǒu. OR 没有 Méi.yǒu.

A: 你有没有兄弟姐妹？ *Nǐ* yǒu méi.yǒu xiōngdì-jiěmèi?

B: 没有，我是独生女。 Méi.yǒu, wǒ shì dúshēngnǚ.

Comparisons

Look at the two questions below. In which language is the question more specific? In which language is the question more open-ended?

你有没有红茶？ *Nǐ* yǒu méi.yǒu hóngchá?

Do you have black tea?

The Verb + 的东西 .de dōng.xī

The noun 东西 *dōng.xī* means "thing." It is only used after a verb. For example, 喝的东西 *hē .de dōng.xī* means "something to drink," 游泳的东西 *yóu-yǒng .de dōng.xī* means "something for swimming."

Verb + 的东西 *.de dōng.xī*

A: 你要点喝的东西吗？ Nǐ yào diǎn hē .de dōng.xī .ma?

B: 我要一杯红茶。 Wǒ yào yì-bēi hóngchá.

A: 我要买吃的东西。你呢？ Wǒ yào mǎi chī .de dōng.xī. Nǐ .ne?

B: 我要买喝的东西。 Wǒ yào mǎi hē .de dōng.xī.

Answers to 要 *yào* Questions

To answer 要 *yào* questions, say 要 *yào* for "yes." However, for "no," say 不用 *búyòng* (no need), which is more polite than 不要 *bú yào*.

要不要 *yào bú.yào* + **Noun / Verb**

A: 你们要茶吗？ Nǐ.mén yào chá .ma?

B: 要，请给我们一壶茶。 Yào, *qǐng gěi* wǒ.mén yì-hú chá.

A: 你要不要喝水？ Nǐ yào .bú.yào hē-shuǐ?

B: 不用，谢谢。 Búyòng, xiè.x.

会话 Huìhuà Dialogue

在茶馆里 Zài Cháguǎn.lǐ *At the Tea Shop*

Lin Shufang and her friend are ordering drinks at a tea shop.

林书芳：	请问你们有没有果汁？	Lín Shūfāng:	Qǐngwèn nǐ.mén yǒu .méi.yǒu guǒzhī?
服务员：	对不起，我们现在只有茶和汽水。	Fúwùyuán:	Duì.bùqǐ, wǒ.mén xiànzài *zhǐ* yǒu chá hé qìshuǐ.
林书芳：	你们有什么茶？	Lín Shūfāng:	Nǐ.mén yǒu shén.me chá?
服务员：	红茶、绿茶，还有花茶。	Fúwùyuán:	Hóngchá, lǜchá, hái yǒu huāchá.
林书芳：	我要一杯红茶。	Lín Shūfāng:	Wǒ yào yì-bēi hóngchá.
白　苹：	我们要两杯绿茶。	Bái Píng:	Wǒ.mén yào liǎng-bēi lǜchá.
服务员：	你们要点吃的东西吗？	Fúwùyuán:	Nǐ.mén yào diǎn chī .de dōng.xī .ma?
林书芳：	不用，谢谢。	Lín Shūfāng:	Búyòng, xiè.x.

6 他们要什么？ Tā.mén yào shén.me? / *What are they having?*

Say if Lin Shufang and her friend are having or not having the following items.

1.	2.	3.	4.	5.	6.

7 关于茶店 Guānyú Chádiàn / *Statements About the Tea Shop*

Decide if each statement is true or false according to the dialogue. Correct any false statements.

1. 林书芳起初(*at first*)要点奶昔。 Lín Shūfāng qǐchū yào *diǎn* nǎixī.
2. 这个茶店现在只有茶和果汁。 Zhèi.ge chádiàn xiànzài *zhǐ* yǒu chá hé guǒzhī.
3. 这个茶店只卖饮料。 Zhèi.ge chádiàn zhǐ mài yǐnliào.
4. 这个茶店有三种茶。 Zhèi.ge chádiàn yǒu sān-zhǒng chá.
5. 林书芳点一杯花茶。 Lín Shūfāng diǎn yì-bēi huāchá.
6. 白苹点绿茶。 Bái Píng diǎn lǜchá.
7. 她们不要点吃的东西。 Tā.mén bú yào diǎn chī .de dōng.xī.

文化橱窗 Wénhuà Chúchuāng

Culture Window

Chinese Tea Culture

Tea-drinking habits around China differ depending on the tea that is produced locally. For example, people in the north like to drink jasmine tea, Fujian people drink oolong, and people in Guangzhou and Yunnan drink Puer tea. There is a wide range of Chinese teas. Teas are classified as black tea, green tea, white tea, yellow tea, and dark tea. When drinking tea, some people like to eat certain snacks. Some common tea snacks are peanuts (花生 *huāshēng*), sunflower seeds (瓜子 *guāzǐ*) and green soybeans (毛豆 *máodòu*). Other tea snacks include local delicacies such as Beijing's soybean flour cakes (驴打滚 *lǘdǎgǔn*) or Jiangnan's osmanthus-scented jam sweet cakes (桂花糕 *guìhuāgāo*).

Tea Houses

The people of Guangdong and Hong Kong developed the unique culture of "dim sum (点心 *diǎn.xīn*)". Dim Sum, meaning "a dot to the heart" or "a little delight," is the name for Chinese snacks, prepared in bite-size pieces or small portions. The development of a dim sum culture gave birth to a branch of tea houses, called tea restaurants (茶餐厅 *chá cāntīng*). The image of the 茶餐厅 *chá cāntīng* has become rooted in the minds of Westerners, who appreciate the efficient waiters and energetic atmosphere of these cozy Chinese tea restaurants. This was especially true after an influx of Chinese immigrants led to the opening of Cantonese tea houses in the States and Canada in the 20th century.

▲ Bite-size dim sum.

Comparisons

Are there any beverage cultures here in the United States? Where do Americans go to get these beverages? How old is this tradition?

The Varieties of Tea

	乌龙茶 Wūlóngchá *Oolong Tea* Strong flavor, between green and black tea in oxidation	
	香片 Xiāngpiàn *Silver Jasmine* Green tea base, enhanced with jasmine	
	铁观音 Tiěguānyīn *Tieguanyin Tea* Light orange tea, sustained and strong natural orchid aroma	
	普洱茶 *Pǔ'ěrchá* *Puer Tea* Mellow and uniquely aged taste, recommended as the "tea for beauty"	

How to make tea the Chinese way:

Pour boiling water into a teapot to pre-heat it. Discard the water.

Fill the teapot one third full with tea leaves.

Rinse the tea leaves by covering them with hot water and draining the tea leaves again.

Pour boiling water into the pot one more time, allowing the water to overflow. Use the teapot lid to scrape any bubbles off the surface. Wait 30 seconds for the tea to brew.

Pour the tea into the serving pitcher. Use the serving pitcher to fill each teacup. Make sure the tea in every cup has a consistent color.

NOTE: When you're drinking tea, remember that the first cup is only to be savored for its aroma. The second cup, after the teapot has been refilled, is easily the most flavorful. Usually by the third, the aroma has disappeared. But don't worry. The flavor will still be nice and full.

8 文化动动脑 Wénhuà Dòng.x nǎo / *Culture Check-up*

Decide is each statement is true or false. Correct the false statements.

1. Tea-drinking habits in China differ according to the tea that is produced locally.
2. People in northern China like to drink oolong.
3. Some people eat sesame as snacks when they drink tea.
4. Sour bean flour cakes are Beijing delicacies.
5. Dim Sum means "a little delight."
6. An influx of Chinese immigrants led to the opening of tea houses in North America in the 19th century.
7. To make Chinese tea, you should preheat the teapot before placing tea leaves inside it.
8. You should fill a teapot two-thirds full with tea leaves.
9. It takes around 30 seconds to brew a pot of tea.
10. The first cup of tea poured from a pot is only savored for its aroma and is the most flavorful.
11. By the third cup, the aroma of tea will have mostly disappeared, but the flavor will still be full.

Comparisons

A coffee-shop connoisseur from the United States might find the traditional tea shops of China different, if not interesting. First off, tea shops don't normally sell snacks. If you want to eat, you have to take care of that yourself. Secondly, while the cafes provide patrons with comfortable seating, including couches and armchairs, Chinese tea shops are more austere. There are usually no chairs or tables. People come, buy and go, and they probably won't hear cool jazz or classical music, let alone a live band. Chinese visitors to America, on the other hand, will have a hard time finding a well-made, fresh pot of tea. If you order tea in an American coffee shop, chances are they'll give you a tea bag. And it won't be cheap either. The best advice, whether in China or the United States, is "when in Rome, do as the Romans do."

Language Practice

9 我有的东西 Wǒ Yǒu .de Dōng.xī / What I Have

Use 有没有 *yǒu .méi.yǒu* to say if you have or don't have the following relatives or pets. Refer to Unit 2 if you need help remembering some of these words.

Lì.zi: **A:** 你有没有狗？ *Nǐ* yǒu méi.yǒu gǒu?

B: 我有狗。 *Wǒ yǒu* gǒu.

OR 我没有狗。 Wǒ méi.yǒu gǒu.

1. 你有没有弟弟？ *Nǐ* yǒu méi.yǒu dì.x?
2. 你有没有姐姐？ *Nǐ* yǒu méi.yǒu jiě.x?
3. 你有没有妹妹？ *Nǐ* yǒu méi.yǒu mèi.x?
4. 你有没有哥哥？ *Nǐ* yǒu méi.yǒu gē.x?
5. 你有没有兔子？ *Nǐ* yǒu méi.yǒu tù.zi?
6. 你有没有鸟？ *Nǐ* yǒu méi.yǒu niǎo?
7. 你有没有鱼？ *Nǐ* yǒu méi.yǒu yú?
8. 你有没有天竺鼠？ *Nǐ* yǒu méi.yǒu tiānzhúshǔ?

10 你有没有…？ Nǐ yǒu .méi.yǒu…? / Do you have…?

With a partner, take turns asking and answering if you have the following items. Follow the model.

Lì.zi: **A:** 你有橙汁吗？ *Nǐ* yǒu chéngzhī .ma?

B: 有，我有橙汁。 Yǒu, *wǒ* yǒu chéngzhī.

OR, 没有，我没有橙汁。 Méi.yǒu, wǒ méi.yǒu chéngzhī.

1.
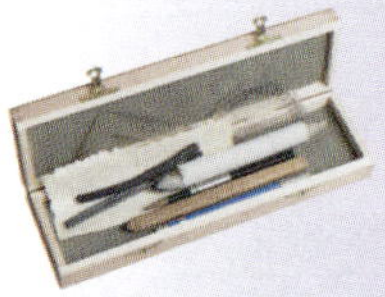

2.

3.

4.

5.
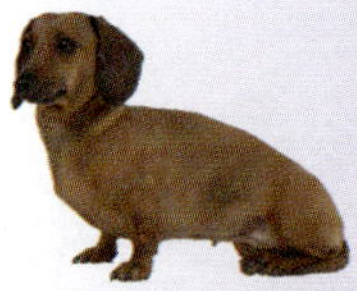

6.

7.

8.

11 中文课 Zhōngwén-Kè / *Chinese Class*

With a partner, take turns asking each other what he/she needs for the Chinese class using 要不要 *yào .bú.yào*. Refer to Unit 3 if you need help remembering some of these words. Follow the model.

Lì.zi: **A:** 你要不要中文课本？ Nǐ yào bú.yào Zhōngwén kèběn ?

B: 要。 Yào.

1. 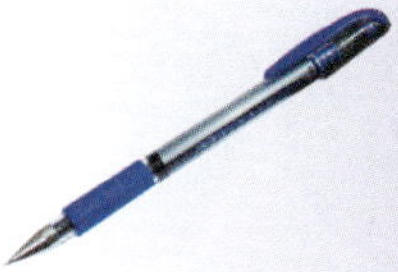
2. 
3. 
4. 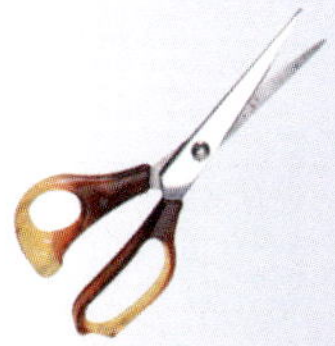
5. 
6. 
7. 
8. 

12 要吃的或喝的东西？ Yào chī .de huò hē .de dōng.xī? / *Something to eat or to drink?*

Based on the photos, which indicate what each person is hungry for, ask if he or she wants something to eat or drink.

Lì.zi:

王帅 Wáng Shuài

王帅，你要喝奶昔吗？ Wáng Shuài, nǐ yào hē nǎixī .ma?

1.  欣怡 Xīnyí
2.  俊男 Jùnnán
3.  芳仪 Fāngyí
4.  建华 Jiànhuá
5.  桂枝 Guìzhī
6.  志明 Zhìmíng
7.  雅玲 Yǎlíng
8.  志伟 Zhìwěi

13 海边一日游 Hǎibiān Yí-rì Yóu / *A Day at the Beach*

Li Ping and his friends are planning a day at the beach. Say what each person wants to bring (带 *dài*) there. Follow the model.

Lì.zi: 李屏要带吃的东西。

Lǐ Píng yào dài chī .de dōng.xī.

李屏 Lǐ Píng

1. 	3. 	5. 
洪君 Hóng Jūn	刘忠 Liú Zhōng	董凯 *Dǒng* Kǎi
2. 	4. 	6. 
陈佩 Chén Pèi	黄梅 Huáng Méi	张美 Zhāng Měi

14 你渴吗? *Nǐ kě .ma?* / *Are you thirsty?*

With a partner, take turns asking and answering is you would like the first beverage. When it's your turn to answer, either say that you would like the second beverage in the list or respond by using 不用 búyòng. Follow the model.

Lì.zi: 绿茶 lǜchá / 乌龙茶 wūlóngchá

A: 你要喝绿茶吗? Nǐ yào hē lǜchá .ma?

B: 我要喝乌龙茶。Wǒ yào hē wūlóngchá.

OR

不用，谢谢。Búyòng, xiè.x.

1.	柠檬水 níngméngshuǐ / 奶昔 nǎixī	5.	奶茶 nǎichá / 咖啡 kāfēi
2.	橙汁 chéngzhī / 乌龙茶 wūlóngchá	6.	葡萄汁 pú.táozhī / 苹果汁 píngguǒzhī
3.	红茶 hóngchá / 热巧克力 rè qiǎo.kèlì	7.	水 shuǐ / 汽水 qìshuǐ
4.	冰沙 bīngshā / 花茶 huāchá	8.	可乐 kělè / 茶 chá

开口说 Kāikǒu Shuō

Communication

15 做张茶单 Zuò .Zhāng Chádān / *Create a Menu*

With two of your classmates, create a Chinese menu of a tea shop that has at least seven beverages, and give your tea shop a Chinese name.

16 来喝茶吧！ Lái Hē-chá .Ba! / *Tea Time!*

Using the menu you created in the previous activity above, play the roles of two customers in the tea shop and the server who waits on them.

- The server greets the two customers and asks what they would like to drink.
- The first customer asks whether the drink he/she would like is available.
- The server apologizes that the drink the customer would like is unavailable.
- The server suggests other drinks.
- The second customer asks the server what kind of tea they have.
- The server lists the kinds of tea the shop has.
- The customers order different kinds of tea.
- The server repeats the complete order.
- The customers thank the server.

17 我的派对 Wǒ.de Pàiduì / *My Party*

You are having a party and need to know which beverages to buy. To find out what your guests want to drink, draw a grid like the one that follows. In the grid write the question you will ask and list four cold beverages. Then poll eight of your classmates.

Lì.zi: 雅惠：你要喝柠檬水、橙汁、苹果汁，还是汽水？

Nǐ yào hē níngméngshuǐ, chéngzhī, píngguǒzhī, hái.shì qìshuǐ?

俊宏：我要喝橙汁。 Wǒ yào hē chéngzhī.

雅惠：你要喝柠檬水、橙汁、苹果汁，还是汽水？？ Nǐ yào hē níngméngshuǐ, chéngzhī, píngguǒzhī, hái.shì qìshuǐ?								
	1	2	3	4	5	6	7	8
柠檬水 níngméngshuǐ								
橙汁 chéngzhī	✕							
苹果汁 píngguǒzhī								
汽水 qìshuǐ								

Look at the menu of Xianghe Tea House below and answer the following questions.

翔和茶馆
Xianghe Tea House

【饮料类】

红茶	￥16.00
绿茶	￥16.25
花茶	￥17.00
乌龙茶	￥26.50
普洱茶	￥27.50
奶茶	￥17.25
汽水	￥18.00
橙汁	￥18.00

【点心类】

瓜子	￥16.50
花生	￥16.50
毛豆	￥18.50
豆干	￥20.00
桂花糕	￥22.00
驴打滚	￥23.50
艾窝窝	￥30
奶酪	￥32.00

1. What kinds of tea does this tea house offer?
2. What may non-tea drinkers order to drink?
3. If you have 50 RMB, how many cups of black tea can you order?
4. Which two drinks have the same price?
5. From which two categories the menu lists items?
6. If you and your family (four people in total) have a budget of 100 RMB and wish to each order a drink at the tea house, what can you order?

汉字天地 Hànzì Tiāndì
Chinese Characters

木 ■ mù ■ wood; tree

The pictograph 木 *mù* reflects the shape of a tree. The middle part of the character "丨", reflects a tree trunk. The horizontal line "一" reflects branches and "丿" reflects roots. The pictograph 木 *mù* has gradually transformed into the character we use now. It is also a common radical for words related to wood or trees. It can help us better understand the meaning of some Chinese words.

Stroke Order

一 十 才 木

19 词汇延伸 Cíhuì Yánshēn / *Vocabulary Builder*

Below are some characters that can be combined with 木 *mù* to create new words. Match the Chinese words on the left with the appropriate English meaning on the right.

材 cái *n. material*	刻 kè *v. to carve*	片 piàn *n. slice*	工 gōng *n. worker*	器 qì *n. utensil*

1. 木材 mùcái
2. 木刻 mùkè
3. 木片 mùpiàn
4. 木工 mùgōng
5. 木器 mùqì

A. *wood chip*
B. *carpenter*
C. *woodcut*
D. *lumber*
E. *wooden furniture*

20 汉字侦探 Hànzì Zhēntàn / *Visual Detective*

Can you find 木 in the following pictures?

Lesson C

发音 Fāyīn
Pronunciation

b p m f d t n l + ian iang

词汇 Cíhuì
Vocabulary

中式早餐 Zhōngshì Zǎocān *Chinese Breakfast*

馒头 (饅頭)
mán.tóu
n. steamed bread

烧饼 (燒餅)
shāobǐng
n. sesame seed cake

馄饨 (餛飩)
hún.tún
n. wontons

鸡蛋 (雞蛋)
jīdàn
n. egg

包子 (包子)
bāo.zi
n. steamed buns with meat filling

油条 (油條)
yóutiáo
n. deep-fried twisted dough sticks

麦片 (麥片)
màipiàn
n. cereal

豆浆 (豆漿)
dòujiāng
n. soybean milk

面包 (麵包)
miànbāo
n. bread

煎饼 (煎餅)
jiānbǐng
n. pancake

炸鸡 (炸雞)
zhájī
n. fried chicken

牛奶 (牛奶)
niúnǎi
n. milk

A: 炸鸡多少钱 (炸雞多少錢)?

Zhájī duō.shǎo qián? *How much is a piece of fried chicken?*

B: 炸鸡两块钱 (炸雞兩塊錢)。

Zhájī liǎng-kuài qián. *It is two dollars.*

A: 一共多少钱 (一共多少錢)?

Yígòng duō.shǎo qián? *How much in total?*

B: 一共九块五毛钱 (一共九塊五毛錢)。

Yígòng jiǔ-kuài wǔ-máo qián. *It's nine fifty.*

人民币 (人民幣)
Rénmínbì
Chinese Renminbi

新台币 (新台幣)
Xīntáibì
New Taiwan dollar

港币 (港幣)
Gǎngbì
Hong Kong dollar

新加坡币 (新加坡幣)
Xīnjiāpōbì
Singapore dollar

日元 (日元)
Rìyuán
Japanese yen

韩元 (韓元)
Hányuán
South Korean won

欧元 (歐元)
Ōuyuán
Euro

英镑 (英鎊)
Yīngbàng
British pound

美元 (美元)
Měiyuán
US dollar

A: 你有人民币吗 (你有人民幣嗎)?

Nǐ yǒu Rénmínbì .ma? *Do you have Renminbi?*

B: 我有两百二十二块人民币，还有六十七块五毛港币 (我有兩百二十二塊人民幣，還有六十七塊五毛港幣)。

*Wǒ yǒu liǎng*bǎi èrshí'èr-kuài Rénmínbì, hái yǒu liùshíqī-kuài wǔ-máo Gǎngbì.

I have 222 RMB and 67 Hong Kong dollars.

你有没有人民币
(你有没有人民幣)?
Nǐ yǒu méi.yǒu Rénmínbì?
Do you have Renminbi?

我只有英镑和欧元
(我只有英鎊和歐元)。
Wǒ zhǐ yǒu Yīngbàng hé Ōuyuán.
I only have British pounds and Euros.

大钞 (大鈔) dàchāo *large denomination bills*	钞票 (鈔票) chāopiào *paper money*	铜板/硬币 (銅板/硬幣) tóngbǎn/yìngbì *coin*	零钱 (零錢) língqián *change*

A: 请找我铜板 (請找我銅板)。

Qǐng zhǎo wǒ tóngbǎn. *Please give me coins for change.*

B: 对不起，我只有钞票可以找你 (對不起，我只有鈔票可以找你)。

Duì.bùqǐ, *wǒ zhǐ* yǒu chāopiào *kě.yǐ zhǎo* nǐ. *Sorry, I only have paper money for you.*

A: 请问你有没有零钱 (請問你有沒有零錢)?

Qǐngwèn *nǐ* yǒu méi.yǒu língqián? *Excuse me, do you have any change?*

B: 不好意思，我只有大钞 (不好意思，我只有大鈔)。

Bùhǎoyì.sī, *wǒ zhǐ* yǒu dàchāo. *I'm sorry; I only have large bills.*

谢谢你
(謝謝你)!
Xiè.x nǐ!
Thank you!

小事，不用客气
(小事，不用客氣)。
Xiǎoshì, búyòng kè.qì.
It's nothing; don't mention it.

Possessive Pronouns			
我的（我的）wǒ.de	*mine*	我们的（我們的）wǒ.mén.de	*ours*
你的（你的）nǐ.de	*yours*	你们的（你們的）nǐ.mén.de	*yours (plural)*
他的（他的）tā.de	*his*	他们的（他們的）tā.mén.de	*theirs (m.)*
她的（她的）tā.de	*hers*	她们的（她們的）tā.mén.de	*theirs (f.)*

Adverbs

一共（一共）	yígòng	*altogether; in all*

Idiomatic Expressions

小事（小事）	xiǎoshì	*a triviality; something petty; It's nothing. (phr.)*

Measure Words

块（塊）	kuài	*dollar (in spoken Chinese, equal to 100 pennies), a chunk, or a piece of something*
分（分）	fēn	*penny*
毛（毛）	máo	*one tenth of a* 元 *yuán, a dime or 10 pennies*
件（件）	jiàn	*measure word for things and matters*

Nouns

事（事）	shì	*matter; affair; thing*
钱（錢）	qián	*money*
早餐（早餐）	zǎocān	*breakfast*

Numerals

七（七）	qī	*seven*
八（八）	bā	*eight*
九（九）	jiǔ	*nine*
零（零）	líng	*zero*
百（百）	bǎi	*hundred*

Verbs

找（找）	zhǎo	*to return change after a purchase*

Verb-Objects

找钱（找錢）	zhǎo-qián	*to give change*

Language Note

	Dollar	dime	pennies
Spoken Chinese	块（塊）kuài	毛（毛）máo	分（分）fēn
Written Chinese	元（元）yuán	角（角）jiǎo	分（分）fēn

The noun 钱 *qián*, can appear at the end of a string, but is often omitted

一块五毛(钱) *yí-kuài wǔ-máo* (*qián*) = $1.50

In spoken style, 毛 *máo* and 分 *fēn* are often omitted if it is the last item in a string

一块五(毛) *yí-kuài wǔ* (*máo*) = $1.50, or 一块五毛五(分) *yí-kuài wǔ-máo wǔ* (*fēn*) = $1.55

1 这是什么? Zhè.shì shén.me? *What is this?*

Identify each object.

Lì.zi: 这是炸鸡。

Zhè.shì zhájī

2 一共多少钱? Yígòng duō.shǎo qián? *How much in total?*

With a partner, take turns asking and telling the total price of any three items from the box. Follow the model.

Lì.zi: **A:** 色拉和果汁一共多少钱?

Sèlā hé guǒzhī yígòng duō.shǎo qián?

B: 一共十三块。

Yígòng shísān-kuài.

价目表

色拉	sèlā	¥ 6	果汁	guǒzhī	¥ 7
面包	miànbāo	¥ 4.5	可乐	kělè	¥ 3
汉堡包	hànbǎobāo	¥ 8	水	shuǐ	¥ 4
炸鸡	zhájī	¥ 10.5	牛奶	niúnǎi	¥ 9
麦片	màipiàn	¥ 7	豆浆	dòujiāng	¥ 8

3 个人问题 Gèrén Wèntí / Personal Questions

Answer the following questions in Chinese.

1. 早餐你喜欢吃什么？ Zǎocān *nǐ* xǐ.huān chī shén.me?
2. 你早上喝牛奶吗？ *Nǐ* zǎo.shàng hē niúnǎi .ma?
3. 你早上吃鸡蛋吗？ *Nǐ* zǎo.shàng chī jīdàn .ma?

句型介绍 Jùxíng Jièshào

Language Patterns

The Question Word 多少 *duō.shǎo*

The question word 多少 *duō.shǎo* means "how many" or "how much." It is used to ask for an amount.

多少 *duō.shǎo* + **Noun**

A: 你的中文课有多少人？ Nǐ.de Zhōngwén-kè yǒu duō.shǎo rén?
B: 我的中文课有二十五个人。 Wǒ.de Zhōngwén-kè yǒu èrshíwǔ.ge rén.

A: 这本书多少钱？ Zhèi-běn shū duō.shǎo qián?
B: 这本书九十九块钱。 Zhèi-běn shū jiǔshíjiǔ-kuài qián.

Language Note

Both 多少 *duō.shǎo* and 几 *jǐ* mean "how many." However, there are two differences between them.

1. 多少 *duō.shǎo* also has the meaning of "how much," and can be used with uncountable nouns. On the other hand, 几 *jǐ* can only be used with countable nouns.
   多少 *duō.shǎo* + Noun
   几 *jǐ* + Measure Word + Noun
2. 多少 *duō.shǎo* is used when the speaker expects an answer larger than ten, and 几 *jǐ* is used for questions concerning amounts that total to less than ten.

(larger than 10) 多少 *duō.shǎo* + Noun

A: 这个多少钱？ Zhèi.ge duō.shǎo qián?
B: 二十三块五毛。 Èrshísān-kuài wǔ-máo.

(under 10) 几 *jǐ* + Measure Word + Noun

A: 这个几块钱？ Zhèi.ge jǐ-kuài qián?
B: 这个五块五(毛)。 Zhèi.ge wǔ-kuài wǔ (máo).

Numbers 100-999

It is also easy to say hundreds in Chinese: just tag the word 百 bǎi (hundred) to a number.

Let's count!

100	200	300	400	500	600	700	800	900	1000
一百 yìbǎi	两百 *liǎng*bǎi	三百 sānbǎi	四百 sìbǎi	五百 *wǔ*bǎi	六百 liùbǎi	七百 qībǎi	八百 bābǎi	九百 *jiǔ*bǎi	一千 yìqiān

When numbers include a zero, remember to say 零 *líng* (zero) without having to mention the measure word that is omitted.

101	102	103	104	105
一百零一 yìbǎi líng yī	一百零二 yìbǎi líng èr	一百零三 yìbǎi líng sān	一百零四 yìbǎi líng sì	一百零五 yìbǎi líng wǔ
106	107	108	109	
一百零六 yìbǎi líng liù	一百零七 yìbǎi líng qī	一百零八 yìbǎi líng bā	一百零九 yìbǎi líng jiǔ	

For three-digit numbers with a ten, like 110, we say 一百一十 *yìbǎi yīshí*. The character 一 *yī* needs to be added in front of 十 *shí*.

111	112	113	114	115
一百一十一 yìbǎi yīshíyī	一百一十二 yìbǎi yīshí'èr	一百一十三 yìbǎi yīshísān	一百一十四 yìbǎi yīshísì	一百一十五 yìbǎi yīshíwǔ
116	117	118	119	120
一百一十六 yìbǎi yīshíliù	一百一十七 yìbǎi yīshíqī	一百一十八 yìbǎi yīshíbā	一百一十九 yìbǎi yīshíjiǔ	一百二十 yìbǎi èrshí

Language Note

The preferred way of saying "two" before a measure word is 两 *liǎng* . Exceptions: 月 *yuè* and 号 *hào* are measure words, but use 二 *èr* for 二月 *Èryuè* (February), 二号 *èr-hào* (2nd day of the month).

会话 Huìhuà Dialogue

在自助餐厅 Zài Zìzhù Cāntīng *In the Cafeteria*

In the school cafeteria, Lin Shufang brings food back for her friends.

林书芳:	这是白苹的面包和果汁。这是张国华的炸鸡和可乐。	Lín Shūfāng:	Zhè.shì Bái Píng .de miànbāo hé guǒzhī. Zhè.shì Zhāng Guóhuá .de zhájī hé kělè.
白苹:	一共多少钱?	Bái Píng:	Yígòng duō.shǎo qián?
林书芳:	面包五块，果汁七块，一共十二块。	Lín Shūfāng:	Miànbāo wǔ-kuài, guǒzhī qī-kuài, yígòng shí'èr-kuài.
张国华:	我的多少钱?	Zhāng Guóhuá:	Wǒ.de duō.shǎo qián?
林书芳:	炸鸡十七块，可乐八块五毛九，一共二十五块五毛九。	Lín Shūfāng:	Zhájī shíqī-kuài, kělè bā-kuài wǔ-máo jiǔ, yígòng èrshíwǔ-kuài wǔ-máo jiǔ.
白苹:	我只有一百块。	Bái Píng:	*Wǒ zhǐ* yǒu yìbǎi-kuài.
林书芳:	找你八十八块。	Lín Shūfāng:	*Zhǎo* nǐ bāshíbā-kuài.
张国华:	我的不用找。	Zhāng Guóhuá:	Wǒ.de búyòng zhǎo.
白苹:	书芳，谢谢你。	Bái Píng:	Shūfāng, xiè.x nǐ.
林书芳:	小事，不用客气。	Lín Shūfāng:	Xiǎoshì, búyòng kè.qì.

4 他们吃什么？ Tā.mén chī shén.me? *What are they eating?*

With a partner, ask and tell what the characters in the dialogue ordered according to the dialogue.

❶ 

❷ 

5 …多少钱？ …duō.shǎo qián? *How much is…?*

With a partner, ask and tell the price of the food items according to the dialogue.

❶ 

❷ 

❸ 

❹ 

6 懂了吗？ Dǒng .le .ma? *Do you understand?*

Answer the following questions in Chinese.

1. 谁买吃的东西？ Shéi mǎi chī .de dōng.xī?
2. 白苹的东西一共多少钱？ Bái Píng .de dōng.xī yígòng duō.shǎo qián?
3. 张国华的东西一共多少钱？ Zhāng Guóhuá .de dōng.xī yígòng duō.shǎo qián?
4. 白苹有多少钱？ Bái Píng yǒu duō.shǎo qián?
5. 林书芳找白苹多少钱？ Lín Shūfāng zhǎo Bái Píng duō.shǎo qián?
6. 林书芳要不要找张国华钱？ Lín Shūfāng yào bú.yào zhǎo Zhāng Guóhuá qián?

文化橱窗 Wénhuà Chúchuāng

Culture Window

Lunchtime for Students

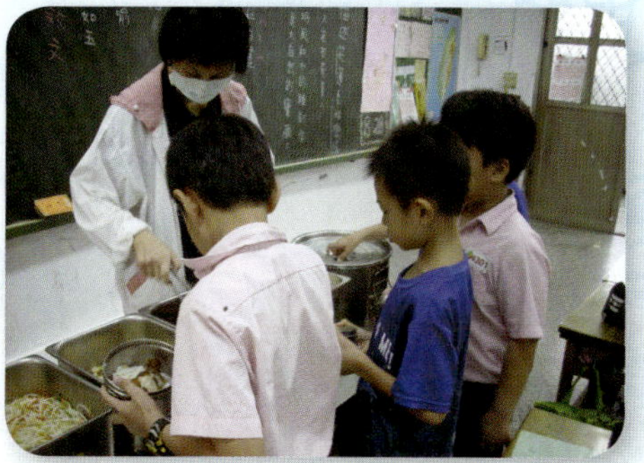

Do you know what Chinese high-school students eat for lunch? The answer is not as simple as sandwiches in a brown paper bag! The following are some of the lunches that Chinese high-school students typically eat.

The schools provide caterers to cook for all the students. At lunchtime, students line up for lunch with their own utensils. The food is diverse and prepared according to nutrition guidelines.

Lunchboxes that are often filled with rice or noodles, ribs or chicken and some vegetables are called 饭盒 *fànhé*. Lunchbox caterers (often two different suppliers) are picked by the school and deliveries are made at lunchtime.

Steamed packed lunches are more popular in Taiwan than in Mainland China. They are often made by packing last night's dinner leftovers into a metallic lunchbox until they are placed in a steam-cooker at school the next day and reheated for lunch. Before other school lunches were popular, steamed packed lunches were the norm.

Another choice for lunch is found at the school store, called 小卖部 *xiǎomàibù*. The school store sells simple lunchboxes or bread and milk, and is open all day so students can buy something to eat whenever they are hungry. Some parents have complained about school stores selling snacks and chips and even allowing students to keep a tab. This has resulted in the closing of some stores in schools.

Comparisons

If you studied in a Chinese high-school, which of the four kinds of lunches would you prefer? Why? Are lunches at your school similar to the ones mentioned above?

7 文化动动脑 Wénhuà Dòng.x nǎo / *Culture Check-up*

Answer the following questions.

1. How is the menu of school lunches decided?
2. What is a 饭盒 *fànhé*? Is there something similar in the United States?
3. If you bring a metallic lunchbox to school from home, what should you do with it once you reach school?
4. Zhang Guohua has just finished gym class and he is very hungry. Where can he go to buy something to eat in the afternoon?

Language Practice

8 数一数！ Shǔ yì.shǔ! / *Let's Count!*

Complete each sequence.

1. 100, 200, 300, …, 900
2. 100, 150, 200, …, 950
3. 520, 521, 522, …, 529
4. 601, 602, 603, …, 609
5. 810, 811, 812, …, 829
6. 110, 210, 310, …, 910
7. 230, 232, 234, …, 250
8. 441, 443, 445, …, 459

9 一共多少钱? Yígòng duō.shǎo qián? / *How much in total?*

Give the total.

1. 100 + 250=
2. 400 + 40=
3. 330 + 68=
4. 510 + 46=
5. 200 + 20=
6. 850 + 7=
7. 600 + 1=
8. 700 + 19=

10 你有多少钱? Nǐ yǒu duō.shǎo qián? / *How much do you have?*

Look at the following pictures and say how much you have. Use the correct currency.

Lì.zi: 我有一百块英镑。 *Wǒ* yǒu yìbǎi-kuài Yīngbàng.

1. 

2. 

3. 

4. 

5. 

6. 

11 多少钱? Duō.shǎo qián? *How much?*

Listen to the recording and give the correct price for each item.

1.

2.

3.

4.

5.
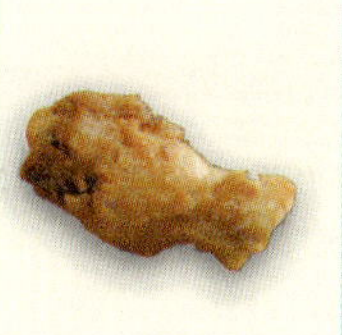

6.

12 这是谁的? Zhè.shì shéi.de? *Whose is this?*

You are placing a food order for your friends. To make sure you have the orders correct, say what each friend ordered and the total price.

1.

Taylor $ 11.50

2.

Sean $ 22.00

3.

Stephanie $ 26.00

开口说 Kāikǒu Shuō

Communication

13 聊聊天 Liáo.x tiān *Let's have a chat*

With a partner, discuss the following topics.

- Ask your partner what he/she had for breakfast.
- Ask your partner how much each breakfast item costs.
- Ask your partner what he/she had for lunch yesterday.
- Ask your partner how much each lunch item costs.

14 在早餐店 Zài Zǎocān Diàn / *At a Breakfast Restaurant*

Look at the board at a breakfast restaurant, and answer the following questions.

● 套餐 *tàocān* combo ● 单点 *dāndiǎn* a la carte ● 饮料 *yǐnliào* beverage

1. What is the currency used here?
2. If you order a sesame seed cake and a wonton, how much is that in total?
3. Which combo can you order if you wish to have milk tea?
4. Which combo can you order if you wish to have steamed buns with meat filling?
5. Which combo comes with egg?
6. If you have 50 RMB, how much will you have left after you buy combo three and four?

15 练习点餐 Liànxí Diǎn-cān / *Practice Ordering*

With a partner, practice ordering food in Chinese.

Lì.zi: **A:** 我要一个一号餐、一个炸鸡，还要一大杯红茶。

Wǒ yào yí.ge yī-hào cān, yí.ge zhájī, hái yào yì dà bēi hóngchá.

B: 好，请等一下。 Hǎo, *qǐng* děng yí.xià.

A: 一共多少钱？ Yígòng duō.shǎo qián?

B: 一共五十四块。 Yígòng wǔshísì-kuài.

A: 这是一百块。 Zhè.shì yìbǎi-kuài.

B: 找你四十六块。 *Zhǎo* nǐ sìshíliù-kuài.

A: 谢谢。 Xiè.x.

汉字天地 Hànzì Tiāndì
Chinese Characters

钱 / 錢 ■ qián ■ money

The character 钱 *qián* is a combination of a radical and a phonetic component. The left part of this character—金 *jīn*—is the radical for metal. And the right part of this character—戋 *jiān*—is the phonetic component that gives the character 钱 *qián* its sound.

Stroke Order

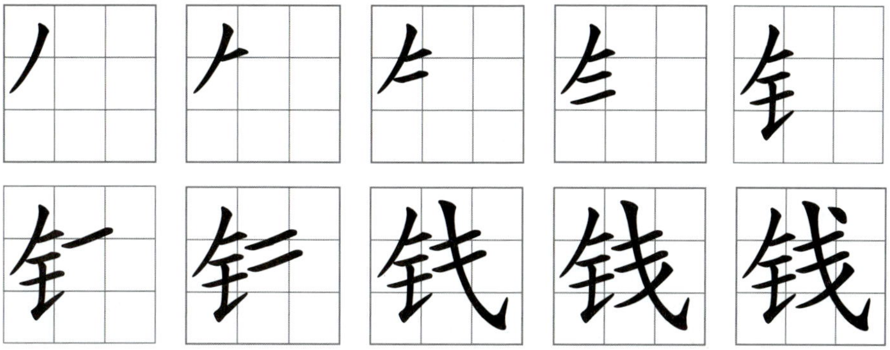

16 词汇延伸 Cíhuì Yánshēn / *Vocabulary Builder*

Below are some characters that can be combined with 钱 *qián* to create new words. Match the Chinese words on the left with the appropriate English meaning on the right.

包 bāo *n. bag; sack*	省 shěng *v. to save*	值 zhí *n. value*	存 cún *v. to store*	价 jià *n. price*

1. 钱包 qiánbāo — A. *valuable*
2. 省钱 shěng-qián — B. *wallet*
3. 值钱 zhí-qián — C. *save money*
4. 存钱 cún-qián — D. *price*
5. 价钱 jiàqián — E. *to deposit*

17 汉字侦探 Hànzì Zhēntàn / *Visual Detective*

Can you find 钱 in the following pictures?

Lesson D

发音 Fāyīn
Pronunciation

b p m f d t n l + in ing

词汇 Cíhuì
Vocabulary

在餐厅里 Zài cāntīng.lǐ *In a Restaurant*

 米饭 (米飯) mǐfàn *n. cooked rice*	 面 (麵) miàn *n. noodles*	 汤 (湯) tāng *n. soup*
菜 (菜) cài *n. dish* 	肉 (肉) ròu *n. meat* 	汤面 (湯麵) tāngmiàn *n. noodle soup* 

A: 我想吃点儿东西 (我想吃點兒東西)。
Wǒ xiǎng chī .diǎnr dōng.xī.
I want to eat something.

A: 我想吃面，您想吃什么 (我想吃麵，你想吃什麼)？
Wǒ xiǎng chī-miàn, *nǐ* xiǎng chī shén.me?
I want to eat noodles. What do you want to eat?

B: 我想吃米饭 (我想吃米飯)。
Wǒ xiǎng chī-mǐfàn. *I want to eat rice.*

A: 我们要点菜 (我們要點菜)。
Wǒ.mén yào diǎn-cài. *We'd like to order.*

B: 好，马上来 (好，馬上來)。
Hǎo, mǎshàng lái. *Okay, I'll be right there.*

Culture Note

Many Chinese meals both in homes and at restaurants are served family style, with people choosing food from different bowls and platters. Usually the number of entrees ordered will be equal to the number of people at the table, with one of the dishes being soup. Each person also will have a small bowl of rice to combine with the other food. Many restaurants have a lazy Susan that makes it easy to sample all of the dishes.

酸（酸）
suān
adj. sour

甜（甜）
tián
adj. sweet

苦（苦）
kǔ
adj. bitter

辣（辣）
là
adj. spicy

咸（鹹）
xián
adj. salty

清淡（清淡）
qīngdàn
adj. light

油（油）
yóu
adj. greasy

脆（脆）
cuì
adj. crispy

A: 鸡汤面油不油(雞湯麵油不油)？
Jītāngmiàn yóu .bù.yóu?
Is chicken noodle soup greasy?

B: 鸡汤面不油，很清淡(雞湯麵不油，很清淡)。
Jītāngmiàn bù yóu, hěn qīngdàn.
Chicken noodle soup is not greasy; it's very light.

好吃(好吃)
hǎochī
adj. delicious (good to eat)

难吃(難吃)
nánchī
adj. bad-tasting (for food)

好喝(好喝)
hǎohē
adj. delicious (good to drink)

难喝(難喝)
nánhē
adj. bad-tasting (for drinks)

A: 牛肉面好不好吃(牛肉麵好不好吃)？
Niúròumiàn hǎo .bù hǎochī?
Are the beef noodles good to eat?

B: 牛肉面很好吃(牛肉麵很好吃)。
Niúròumiàn *hěn* hǎochī.
The beef noodles are very delicious.

牛肉 (牛肉) niúròu *n. beef*	猪肉 (豬肉) zhūròu *n. pork*	鸡肉（牛肉） jīròu *n. chicken*	羊肉（羊肉） yángròu *n. lamb*	鸭肉 (鴨肉) yāròu *n. duck*

 饺子 (餃子) jiǎo.zi *n. dumplings*	 火锅 (火鍋) huǒguō *n. hot pot*	 酸辣汤 (酸辣湯) suānlàtāng *n. hot and sour soup*
 北京烤鸭 (北京烤鴨) Běijīng kǎoyā *n. Beijing roast duck*	 宫保鸡丁 (宮保雞丁) gōngbǎo jīdīng *n. Kung Pao chicken*	 麻婆豆腐 (麻婆豆腐) mápó dòu.fu *n. Mapo Tofu*

Adjectives

有名（有名）	yǒumíng	*famous*

Adverbs

都（都）	dōu	*both; all*
马上 (馬上)	mǎshàng	*at once; right away*

Measure Words

道（道）	dào	*course of a meal*

Nouns

饭（飯）	fàn	*cooked meal*
餐馆（餐館）	cānguǎn	*restaurant*
餐厅 (餐廳)	cāntīng	*cafeteria; dining room*
服务员 (服務員)	fúwùyuán	*waiter / waitress*

Particles

了（了）	.le	*(a particle placed at the end of a sentence to indicate change)*

Verbs

想（想）	xiǎng	*to want*

Verb-Objects

点菜（點菜）	diǎn-cài	*to order*

1 什么味道？ Shén.me wèidào? *What does it taste like?*

With a partner, take turns telling each other what each of the following items tastes like. Follow the model.

Lì.zi: 薯条很油。Shǔtiáo hěn yóu.

1. 	3. 	5. 	7. 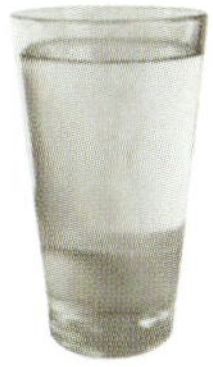
2. 	4. 	6.  Mapo Tofu	8.  hot and sour soup

2 好吃吗？ Hǎochī .ma? *Is it delicious?*

With a partner look at the photos and take turns telling each other if you think each food item is delicious or not. Follow the model.

Lì.zi: 汤面很好喝，我喜欢汤面。Tāngmiàn *hěn* hǎohē, *wǒ* xǐ.huān tāngmiàn.
汤面不好喝，我不喜欢汤面。Tāngmiàn bù hǎohē, wǒ bù xǐ.huān tāngmiàn.

1. 	3. 	5. 	7. 
2. 	4. 	6. 	8. 

3 个人问题 Gèrén Wèntí / *Personal Questions*

Answer the following questions in Chinese.

1. 你喜欢面还是米饭？ *Nǐ* xǐ.huān miàn hái.shì mǐfàn?
2. 你喜欢喝汤吗？ *Nǐ* xǐ.huān hē-tāng .ma?
3. 你喜欢吃什么肉？ *Nǐ* xǐ.huān chī shén.me ròu?
4. 美国菜油不油？ Měi.guó-cài yóu .bu.yóu?
5. 汉堡包很咸吗？ Hànbǎobāo hěn xián .ma?

句型介绍 Jùxíng Jièshào

Language Patterns

To express an upcoming action with (快)要…了 *(kuài) yào…le*

We use the following pattern to describe an action that is about to happen or will soon happen at a specific time in the near future. By adding 快 *kuài* ("soon") to this pattern, the meaning of your sentence remains the same, but carries more emphasis. Note that 快 *kuài* is optional.

(快)要 *(kuài) yào* + **Verb Phrase** + 了 *.le*

The word 了 *.le* has many meanings. Here, it is placed at the end of a sentence, and signifies a new state or status.

我们要点菜了。 Wǒ.mén yào diǎn-cài .le.

他要去篮球场了。 Tā yào qù lánqiúchǎng .le.

Choice-type questions with the Negation Adverb 不 *bù*

We learned in Unit 2, Lesson D that another way to form yes-no questions is to form choice-type questions. For example, 你是不是学生？ *Nǐ shì .bu.shì xué.shēng?* In Chinese, adjectives function as verbs, so adjectives can form choice-type questions by themselves with the help of the negation 不 *bù* (is an adverb) followed by an adjective.

Subject + **Adj.** + 不 *bù / bú* + **Adj.**

这杯咖啡苦不苦？ Zhèi-bēi kāfēi kǔ .bù.kǔ? = 这杯咖啡苦吗？ Zhèi-bēi kāfēi kǔ .ma?

酸辣汤酸不酸？ Suānlàtāng suān .bu.suān? = 酸辣汤酸吗？ Suānlàtāng suān .ma?

The Adverb 都 *dōu*

The adverb 都 *dōu* means "both; all." It must be placed after the nouns it refers to and right before the verb. Note that 都 *dōu* is not a movable adverb; its place in a sentence is fixed.

Nouns + 都 *dōu* + **Verb Phrase**

我和他都点牛肉面。 Wǒ hé tā dōu diǎn niúròumiàn.

你们都是美国人。 Nǐ.mén dōu shì Měi.guórén.

咖啡和茶我都喜欢喝。 Kāfēi hé chá wǒ dōu xǐ.huān hē.

Language Note

*都你和我是美国人。 Dōu nǐ hé wǒ shì Měi.guórén.
This is not a correct sentence. The correct one should be:
你和我都是美国人。 Nǐ hé wǒ dōu shì Měi.guórén.
You and I are both Americans.

*我喝都咖啡、茶。 Wǒ hē dōu kāfēi, chá.
This is not a correct sentence. The correct one should be:
咖啡、茶，我都喝。 Kāfēi, chá, wǒ dōu hē.
Coffee and tea, I drink both. (I drink both coffee and tea.)

会话 Huìhuà
Dialogue

在中国餐馆 Zài Zhōng.guó Cānguǎn *At a Chinese Restaurant*

In a restaurant, Dong Jun signals a waiter to come over.

服务员：	您好！您要点菜了吗？	Fúwùyuán:	Nín hǎo! Nín yào diǎn-cài .le .ma?
董军：	请问这道菜辣不辣？	Dǒng Jūn:	Qǐngwèn zhèi-dào cài là .bú.là?
服务员：	这道菜很辣。您喜欢辣的菜吗？	Fúwùyuán:	Zhèi-dào cài hěn là. Nín xǐ.huān là .de cài .ma?
董军：	不喜欢。	Dǒng Jūn:	Bù xǐ-huān.
服务员：	您想吃什么？	Fúwùyuán:	Nín xiǎng chī shén.me?
董军：	我想吃面。	Dǒng Jūn:	*Wǒ* xiǎng chī-miàn.
服务员：	我们的鸡汤面和牛肉面都很有名。	Fúwùyuán:	Wǒ.mén.de jītāngmiàn hé niúròumiàn dōu *hěn* yǒumíng.
董军：	请给我牛肉面。	Dǒng Jūn:	*Qǐng gěi* wǒ niúròumiàn.
服务员：	好，马上来。	Fúwùyuán:	Hǎo, mǎshàng lái.

4 懂了吗？ Dǒng .le .ma? *Do you understand?*

Answer the following questions in Chinese.

1. 董军要点菜了吗？ Dǒng Jūn yào diǎn-cài .le .ma?
2. 董军喜欢辣的菜吗？ Dǒng Jūn xǐ.huān là .de cài .ma?
3. 董军想吃什么？ Dǒng Jūn xiǎng chī shén.me?
4. 这家餐厅什么有名？ Zhèi-jiā cāntīng shén.me yǒumíng?
5. 董军要吃什么？ Dǒng Jūn yào chī shén.me?

文化橱窗 Wénhuà Chúchuāng

Culture Window

The Differences Between Chinese and Western Food

Due to geological and cultural differences and different customs, Chinese people eat very differently than Westerners.

Staple foods in the West consist mostly of various breads or root vegetables (such as potatoes). However, this is not the case in China. Traditionally using the Yellow River as a divider, southern China has rice as their staple food, while the staple food in the north is noodles or other flour-based products. This is because the climate of northern China is dry, while the south is hot and humid. There are also more plains suitable for cultivation in the south.

Comparisons

People in Northern China eat a lot of noodles, while people in Southern China eat a lot of rice. What are some differences in traditional diet between people in the northern and southern United States?

Chicken and pork became the main meats consumed because, in the past, China was made up of agricultural societies in which every household kept their own animals and poultry. People who lived along the coast ate mostly fish for protein. Before the days of agricultural machinery, cattle were needed by farmers to pull carts and plow fields—so Chinese rarely ate beef. However, due to Western dietary influence, and the fact that cattle are seldom used for farm work nowadays, eating beef has become more popular in Chinese societies.

For Chinese people, all ingredients must be fully cooked before they can be consumed, so most Chinese would stay away from rare or medium steaks. The same rule applies to vegetables. Salads made of raw vegetables are not part of traditional Chinese cuisine. Most vegetables are stir-fried in a short amount of time to preserve their taste and nutritional values that might otherwise have been lost if they were boiled.

The meat and vegetable portions on a Chinese dinner table also differ to that of Westerners. For the Chinese, there are always more vegetables than meat. The Chinese eat approximately 600 kinds of vegetables; that's 500 more than what Westerners usually eat. Thus, the Chinese are known as a people who choose vegetables for entrees. Chinese dishes place a lot of emphasis on taste, and can make almost any kind of ingredient into a tasty dish. For example, bamboo shoots and bean products rarely appear in Western cuisine, but both are consumed by the Chinese on a regular basis. This creative cooking is perhaps why Chinese food seems to have more variety than Western food.

▲ Cattle used to be a great help for farmers.

5 文化动动脑 Wénhuà Dòng.x nǎo / Culture Check-up

Answer the following questions.

1. What kind of meat did Chinese people eat in the past?
2. Why didn't the Chinese eat beef in the past?
3. Why has consumption of beef become more popular for the Chinese?
4. Are the Chinese used to eating raw / uncooked food?
5. How do the Chinese cook vegetables? Why?
6. Are there more meat or vegetable dishes on a Chinese dinner table?
7. Why do Chinese dishes have more variety than Western dishes?
8. When eating in Chinese restaurants in the past, what differences did you find between Chinese and American food?

Language Practice

6 换句话说 Huàn Jù Huà Shuō / Forming Questions

Change the following 吗 *.ma* questions into "Adj. 不 *.bù* Adj." choice-type questions.

Lì.zi: 炸鸡油吗？ Zhájī yóu .ma?
炸鸡油不油？ Zhájī yóu .bù.yóu?

1. 绿茶苦吗？ Lǜchá kǔ .ma?
2. 炸鸡油吗？ Zhájī yóu .ma?
3. 苹果汁甜吗？ Píngguǒzhī tián .ma?
4. 葡萄汁酸吗？ Pú.táozhī suān .ma?
5. 你爸爸好吗？ Nǐ bà.x hǎo .ma?
6. 这道菜咸吗？ Zhèi-dào cài xián .ma?
7. 他快乐吗？ Tā kuàilè .ma?
8. 那只狗可爱吗？ Nèi-zhī *gǒu* kě'ài .ma?
9. 中国汤面清淡吗？ Zhōng.guó tāngmiàn qīngdàn .ma?
10. 这家餐厅的菜好吃吗？ Zhèi-jiā cāntīng .de cài hǎochī .ma?

7 回答问题 Huídá Wèntí / Answer Questions

After changing the 吗 *.ma* questions in the previous activity into the choice-type questions, now with a partner, take turns asking and answering the questions.

Lì.zi: **A:** 炸鸡油不油？ Zhájī yóu .bù.yóu?

B: 炸鸡很油。 Zhájī hěn yóu. (Note that the modifier 很 *hěn* is unstressed.)

OR

炸鸡不油。 Zhájī bù yóu.

8 换句话说 Huàn jù huà shuō / Paraphrasing

Use 都 *dōu* to change the following 也 *yě* sentences.

Lì.zi: 你是英国人，他也是英国人。 Nǐ shì Yīng.guórén, tā yě shì Yīng.guórén.

你和他都是英国人。 Nǐ hé tā dōu shì Yīng.guórén.

1. 芳芳姓林，苹苹也姓林。 Fāng.x xìng Lín, Píng.x yě xìng Lín.
2. Jun是韩国人，Hyung也是韩国人。 Jun shì Hán.guórén, Hyung yě shì Hán.guórén.
3. 王先生五十岁，董先生也五十岁。 Wáng xiān.shēng wǔshí-suì, Dǒng xiān.sheng *yě* wǔshí-suì.
4. 张国华上高一年级，白苹也上高一年级。
   Zhāng Guóhuá shàng gāo-yī niánjí, Bái Píng yě shàng gāo-yī niánjí.
5. 我的生日是五月十三号，他的生日也是五月十三号。
   Wǒ.de shēng.rì shì Wǔyuè shísān-hào, tā.de shēng.rì yě shì Wǔyuè shísān-hào.
6. 中文课很有意思，英文课也很有意思。 Zhōngwén-kè *hěn* yǒu yì.sī, Yīngwén-kè *yě hěn* yǒu yì.sī.
7. 爸爸点大杯的汽水，妈妈也点大杯的汽水。
   Bà.x diǎn dà bēi .de qìshuǐ, mā.x *yě* diǎn dà bēi .de qìshuǐ.
8. Sam不吃猪肉，Sam也不吃羊肉。 Sam bù chī zhūròu, Sam yě bù chī yángròu.

9 怎么了? Zěn.me .le? What's up?

Use (快)要…了 *(kuài) yào*…le to say what is going to happen.

Lì.zi: 我上课。Wǒ shàng-kè.
我要上课了。Wǒ yào shàng-kè .le.

1. 弟弟九岁。 Dì.x jiǔ-suì.
2. 你们明天考试。 Nǐ.mén míng.tiān kǎoshì.
3. 爷爷来我们家。 Yé.x lái wǒ.mén jiā.
4. 他们去海边。 Tā.mén qù hǎibiān.
5. 我们去慢跑。 Wǒ.mén qù mànpǎo.
6. 董军上高二年级。Dǒng Jūn shàng gāo-èr niánjí.
7. 李小姐点菜。 *Lǐ xiǎo*.jiě diǎn-cài.
8. 我吃牛肉面。 Wǒ chī niúròumiàn.

10 请给我… Qǐng gěi wǒ… Please give me…

With a partner, take turns asking and answering each other the following questions.

Lì.zi: **A:** 你要牛肉面还是鸡汤面? Nǐ yào niúròumiàn hái.shì jītāngmiàn?
B: 请给我鸡汤面。 *Qǐng gěi* wǒ jītāngmiàn.

▲ 你要点什么? Nǐ yào diǎn shén.me?

1. 你要大杯还是小杯? Nǐ yào dà bēi hái.shì xiǎo bēi?
2. 你要咖啡还是牛奶? Nǐ yào kāfēi hái.shì niúnǎi?
3. 你要红茶还是绿茶? Nǐ yào hóngchá hái.shì lǜchá?
4. 你要果汁还是汽水? Nǐ yào guǒzhī hái.shì qìshuǐ?
5. 你要鸡块还是炸鸡? Nǐ yào jīkuài hái.shì zhájī?
6. 你要色拉还是三明治? Nǐ yào sèlā hái.shì sānmíngzhì?
7. 你要包子还是馒头? Nǐ yào bāo.zi hái.shì mán.tou?
8. 你要煎饼还是面包? Nǐ yào jiānbǐng hái.shì miànbāo?
9. 你要柠檬水还是苹果汁? Nǐ yào níngméngshuǐ hái.shì píngguǒzhī?
10. 你要牛肉汉堡包还是猪肉汉堡包? Nǐ yào niúròu hànbǎobāo hái.shì zhūròu hànbǎobāo?

11 你喜欢…吗? *Nǐ* xǐ.huān… .ma? / *Do you like…?*

With a partner, take turns asking if he or she likes the indicated foods.

Lì.zi: 牛奶 / 豆浆 niúnǎi / dòujiāng

A: 你喜欢牛奶吗? *Nǐ* xǐ.huān niúnǎi .ma?

B: 我喜欢牛奶。你喜欢豆浆吗? *Wǒ* xǐ.huān niúnǎi. *Nǐ* xǐ.huān dòujiāng .ma?

A: 我不喜欢豆浆。Wǒ bù xǐ.huān dòujiāng.

1. 花茶 / 红茶 huāchá / hóngchá
2. 热巧克力 / 咖啡 rè qiǎo.kèlì / kāfēi
3. 辣的菜 / 酸的菜 là .de cài / suān .de cài
4. 油条 / 烧饼 yóutiáo / shāobǐng
5. 热狗 / 三明治 règǒu / sānmíngzhì
6. 奶昔 / 冰沙 nǎixī / bīngshā

开口说 Kāikǒu Shuō

Communication

12 我们(快)要点菜了。 Wǒ.mén (kuài) yào diǎn-cài .le. / *We are ready to order.*

With two of your classmates, play the roles of two customers at a restaurant and the server who waits on them.

- The server greets the two customers and asks what they would like.
- Each customer asks a question about the food on the menu (the taste, etc.).
- The server answers the customers' questions and asks what the customers prefer.
- The customers say what they prefer.
- The server gives some recommendations, like, the house specialties.
- The customers order.
- The server tells the customers the price of the foods they ordered.
- The customers pay the bill and thank the server.
- The server says you're welcome.

Look at the website below and answer the questions.

鍋王 网上购物

麻辣锅...more
60 块/一份

酸菜白肉锅....more
65 块/一份

牛肉 25 块/一份

猪肉 20 块/一份

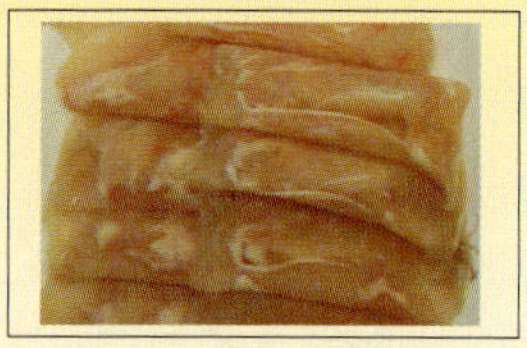

鸡肉 20 块/一份

今天点菜，明天马上到！ 运费 20块

我要点菜

Q1：酸菜白肉锅辣不辣？（07/04 09：10 by 李小姐）

A1：酸菜白肉锅不辣，很酸。（07/04 09：36 by 锅王）

Q2：哪个锅好吃？（07/07 12：10 by 陈先生）

A2：两个锅都很好吃，一个是酸的，一个是辣的，您喜欢哪个？
（07/07 13：10 by 锅王）

Q3：我要买两个酸菜白肉锅和一个麻辣锅，一共多少钱？
（07/11 15：33 by 方小姐）

运费 *yùnfèi n. delivery charge*

1. What is the name of this restaurant?
2. How many different types of hot pots does this restaurant provide?
3. Which hot pot should people who want to eat spicy foods order? And sour foods?
4. Which hot pot is the most expensive? How much is it?
5. How many types of meat are provided? What are they? Which is the most expensive?
6. How much should Miss Fang pay including postage?

汉字天地 Hànzì Tiāndì
Chinese Characters

菜 ■ cài ■ vegetable; dish

The character 菜 *cài* is a combination of radicals and phonetic components and means "vegetable; dish (in a Chinese meal)." The upper part of it—艹 *cǎo*—is the radical meaning "grass", and the lower part of this character—采 *cǎi*—is the phonetic component that gives 菜 *cài* its sound.

Stroke Order

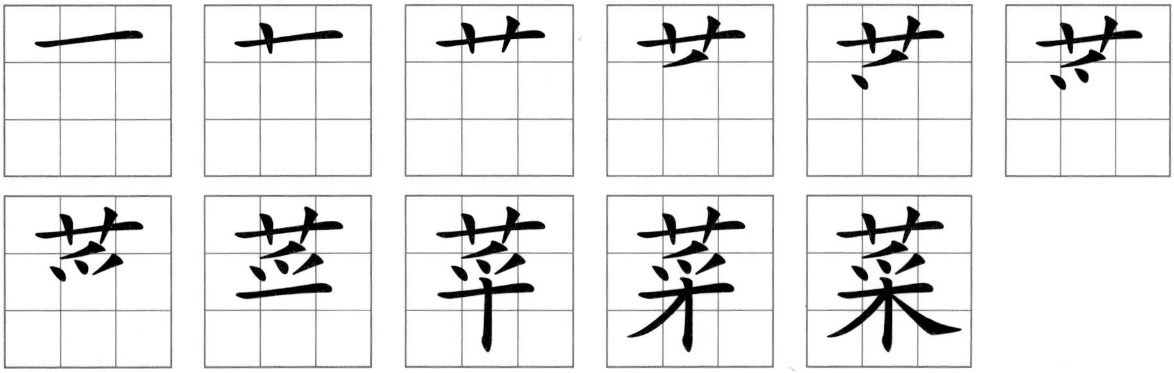

14 词汇延伸 Cíhuì Yánshēn *Vocabulary Builder*

Below are some characters that can be combined with 菜 *cài* to create new words. Match the Chinese words on the left with the appropriate English meaning on the right.

小 xiǎo	刀 dāo	园 yuán	农 nóng	油 yóu
adj. little	*n. knife*	*n. garden*	*n. agriculture*	*n. oil*

1. 小菜 xiǎocài — A. *vegetable grower*
2. 菜刀 càidāo — B. *vegetable garden*
3. 菜园 càiyuán — C. *vegetable oil*
4. 菜农 càinóng — D. *Chinese chopper*
5. 菜油 càiyóu — E. *pickles*

15 汉字侦探 Hànzì Zhēntàn *Visual Detective*

Can you find 菜 in the following pictures?

Unit 5

好天气 Hǎo Tiān.qì

When you have completed this unit, you will be able to...

- describe and discuss temperatures and the weather
- describe and discuss the seasons of the year
- talk about future events
- make comparisons between objects
- describe and discuss Chinese festivals and customs

Lesson A

发音 Fāyīn
Pronunciation

j q x + i ia iao ie iu ian in iang ing iong

词汇 Cíhuì
Vocabulary

天气 Tiān.qì *Weather*

晴天 (晴天)
qíng.tiān *n. sunny day*

阴天 (陰天)
yīn.tiān *n. cloudy day*

云(雲)
yún *n. cloud*

多云(多雲)
duōyún *adj. cloudy*

雪(雪)
xuě *n. snow*

下雪(下雪)
xià-xuě *vo. to snow*

雷(雷)
léi *n. thunder*

打雷(打雷)
dǎ-léi *vo. to thunder*

雨(雨)
yǔ *n. rain*

雨天(雨天)
yǔ.tiān *n. rainy day*

下雨(下雨)
xià-yǔ *vo. to rain*

风(風)
fēng *n. wind*

有风(有風)
yǒufēng *adj. windy*

刮风(刮風)
guā-fēng *vo. the wind is blowing very hard*

上上个星期
(上上個星期)
shàng shàng.ge xīngqī
the week before last

上个星期
(上個星期)
shàng.ge xīngqī
last week

这个星期 (這個星期)
zhèi.ge xīngqī
this week

下个星期 (下個星期)
xià.ge xīngqī
next week

下下个星期 (下下個星期)
xià xià.ge xīngqī
the week after next

今天天气真好
(今天天氣真好)。
Jīn.tiān tiān.qì zhēn hǎo.
Today's weather is great!

是啊，我喜欢晴天
(是啊，我喜歡晴天)。
Shì .a, wǒ xǐ.huan qíng.tiān.
Yeah, I like sunny days.

A: 这个星期都下雨(這個星期都下雨)。
Zhèi.ge xīngqī dōu xià-yǔ. *It has rained every day this week.*

B: 真讨厌(真討厭)！
Zhēn tǎoyàn! *It's really annoying!*

A: 明天天气怎么样(明天天氣怎麼樣)?
Míng.tiān tiān.qì zěn.meyàng? *What will the weather be like tomorrow?*

B: 明天会下雪(明天會下雪)。
Míng.tiān huì xià-xuě. *It will snow tomorrow.*

A: 下个星期六一起看电影吧(下個星期六一起看電影吧)！
Xià.ge Xīngqīliù yìqǐ kàn diànyǐng .ba! *Let's watch a movie together next Saturday!*

B: 好啊，下个星期六见(好啊，下個星期六見)！
Hǎo .a, xià.ge Xīngqīliù jiàn! *Okay, see you next Saturday!*

Adjectives

上 (上)	shàng	*last*
下 (下)	xià	*next*
讨厌 (討厭)	tǎoyàn	*annoying*

Adverbs

真 (真)	zhēn	*really*

Auxiliary Verbs

会 (會)	huì	*will*

Interjections

唉呀 (唉呀)	āiyā	*oh (to express surprise or unhappiness)*

Nouns

天气 (天氣)	tiān.qì	*weather*
网球 (網球)	wǎngqiú	*tennis*

Particles

啊 (啊)	.a	*(used at the end of a sentence to convey a feeling of admiration or as a warning)*

Question Words

怎么样 (怎麼樣)	zěn.meyàng	*how; what about...*

Verbs

见 (見)	jiàn	*to see*

Verb + Objects

打网球 (打網球)	*dǎ*-wǎngqiú	*to play tennis*

1 天气怎么样? Tiān.qì zěn.meyàng? *How is the weather?*

With a partner, take turns asking and answering how the weather is in each of the pictures below.

Lì.zi: **A:** 今天天气怎么样? Jīn.tiān tiān.qì zěn.meyàng?

B: 今天下雪。 Jīn.tiān xià-xuě.

2 中国城市天气 Zhōng.guó Chéngshì Tiān.qì *Weather of Cities in China*

With a partner, take turns asking and answering about the current weather of the Chinese cities indicated. Follow the model using a city in Mongolia.

Lì.zi: **A:** 蒙古天气怎么样? Ménggǔ tiān.qì zěn.meyàng?

B: 蒙古刮风。 Ménggǔ guā-fēng.

3 个人问题 Gèrén Wèntí / Personal Questions

Answer the following questions in Chinese.

1. 你不喜欢雨天，对不对？ Nǐ bù xǐ.huān yǔ.tiān, duì .bú.duì?
2. 晴天和阴天，你都喜欢吗？ Qíng.tiān hé yīn.tiān, nǐ dōu xǐ.huān .ma?
3. 今天天气怎么样？ Jīn.tiān tiān.qì zěn.meyàng?
4. 这个星期都是晴天吗？ Zhèi.ge xīngqī dōu shì qíng.tiān .ma?
5. 上个星期下雪了吗？ Shàng.ge xīngqī xià-xuě .le .ma?
6. 下个星期会下雨吗？ Xià.ge xīngqī huì xià-yǔ .ma?
7. 现在有没有风？ Xiànzài yǒu méi.yǒu fēng?
8. 要刮风了吗？ Yào guā-fēng .le .ma?
9. 现在天空(*sky*)有很多云吗？ Xiànzài tiānkōng *yǒu* hěn duō yún .ma?

句型介绍 Jùxíng Jièshào

Language Patterns

上 *shàng* / 下 *xià* + Time Word

As localizers, 上 *shàng* means "up; above," and 下 *xià* means "down; below." For example, 桌子上 *zhuō.zi .shàng*, 椅子下 *yǐ.zi .xià*. These two words are also used to refer to time. In such instances, 上 *shàng* means "last," and 下 *xià* means "next." However, 上 *shàng* and 下 *xià* cannot be used with "day" and "year."

上 *shàng* / 下 *xià* + 个 *.ge* + 星期 *xīngqī* / 月 *yuè*

上个星期六我去看电影了。 Shàng.ge Xīngqīliù wǒ qù kàn diànyǐng .le.

下个月五号是我的生日。 Xià.ge yuè wǔ-hào shì wǒ.de shēng.rì.

Language Note

We can even use 上 *shàng* and 下 *xià* to refer to two weeks/months ago or two weeks/months from now. So, 上上 *shàng shàng* means "before last," and 下下 *xià xià* means "after next."

上个周末 shàng.ge zhōumò	下个星期一 xià.ge Xīngqīyī
上上个周末 shàng shàng.ge zhōumò	下下个星期一 xià xià.ge Xīngqīyī

Note that we don't use 上 *shàng* and 下 *xià* for measure words such as 天 *tiān* and 年 *nián*. Their expressions are as follows:

前天 qián.tiān	昨天 zuó.tiān	今天 jīn.tiān	明天 míng.tiān	后天 hòu.tiān
前年 qián.nián	去年 qù.nián	今年 jīn.nián	明年 míng.nián	后年 hòu.nián

The Question Word 怎么样 *zěn.meyàng*

The Question Word 怎么样 *zěn.meyàng* means "how." It is a useful expression that is used in many ways.

Subject + 怎么样 *zěn.meyàng*?

- To ask how something or someone is doing?
  A: 西班牙七月的天气怎么样？ Xībānyá Qīyuè .de tiān.qì zěn.meyàng?
  B: 西班牙七月的天气很好。 Xībānyá Qīyuè .de tiān.qì *hěn* hǎo.
- To ask how someone thinks about something (used to solicit someone's opinion).
  A: 你觉得这个汤怎么样？ Nǐ jué.de zhèi.ge tāng zěn.meyàng?
  B: 我觉得这个汤很好喝。 Wǒ jué.de zhèi.ge tāng *hěn* hǎohē.
- To be used among friends, as a greeting roughly equivalent to "How's it going?" in English.
  A: 嘿，怎么样？ Hēi, zěn.meyàng?
  B: 不错，你呢？ Búcuò, nǐ .ne?

The Auxiliary Verb 会 *huì*

As you know, there are no verb tenses in Chinese. However, an auxiliary verb can add to the meaning of the verb, like 会 *huì* to mean "will most likely" to indicate an anticipated event or action.

Subject + 会 *huì* + **Verb Phrase**

明天会下雨。 Míng.tiān huì xià-yǔ.

这个星期五我会去打网球。 Zhèi.ge Xīngqīwǔ wǒ huì qù *dǎ*-wǎngqiú.

Time Word + 见 *jiàn*

To talk about seeing someone at a certain time in the future, we can use this pattern.

Time Word + 见 *jiàn*

明天见！ Míng.tiān jiàn!

下个月见！ Xià.ge yuè jiàn!

Language Note

If the place of the meeting is also known, then, according to the sentence sequence in Chinese, we can put the Place Word after the time. Note that 在 *zài* in front of the Place Word is frequently omitted in speech. Here is the pattern:

Time Word + (在 *zài*) **Place Word** + 见 *jiàn*

五点(在)篮球场见！ *Wǔ*-diǎn (zài) lánqiúchǎng jiàn!
星期六(在)海边见！ Xīngqīliù (zài) hǎibiān jiàn!

会话 Huìhuà
Dialogue

好天气 Hǎo Tiān.qì *A Sunny Day*

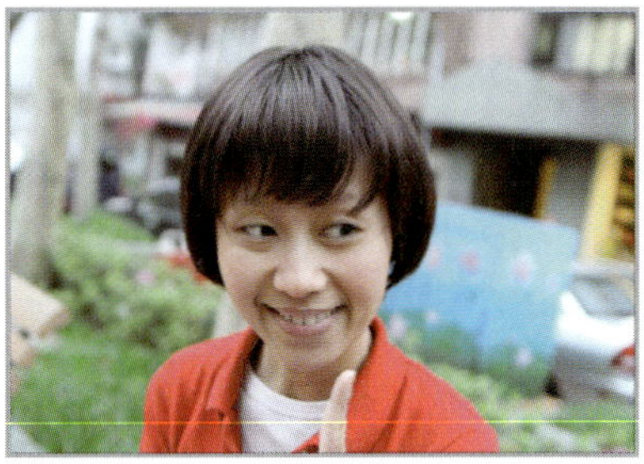

At Beihai Park, Bai Ping and Lin Shufang are sitting on a bench.

白　苹：	今天天气真好。	Bái Píng:	Jīn.tiān tiān.qì zhēn hǎo.
林书芳：	是啊，我喜欢晴天。	Lín Shūfāng:	Shì .a, *wǒ* xǐ.huān qíng.tiān.
白　苹：	这个星期都是好天气。	Bái Píng:	Zhèi.ge xīngqī dōu shì hǎo tiān.qì.
林书芳：	下个星期天气怎么样？	Lín Shūfāng:	Xià.ge xīngqī tiān.qì zěn.meyàng?
白　苹：	下个星期会下雨。	Bái Píng:	Xià.ge xīngqī huì xià-yǔ.
林书芳：	唉呀，真讨厌。	Lín Shūfāng:	Āiyā, zhēn tǎoyàn.
白　苹：	你明天要打网球吗？	Bái Píng:	Nǐ míng.tiān yào *dǎ*-wǎngqiú .ma?
林书芳：	好啊，一点？	Lín Shūfāng:	Hǎo .a, yì-diǎn?
白　苹：	好，明天见。	Bái Píng:	Hǎo, míng.tiān jiàn.

4 天气变化 Tiān.qì Biànhuà / *The Changing Weather*

Describe how the weather has been this week or will be next week based on the dialogue.

5 懂了吗? Dǒng .le .ma? / *Do you understand?*

Answer the following questions in Chinese.

1. 今天天气怎么样? Jīn.tiān tiān.qì zěn.meyàng?
2. 林书芳喜欢什么天气? Lín Shūfāng xǐ.huān shén.me tiān.qì?
3. 这个星期的天气怎么样? Zhèi.ge xīngqī .de tiān.qì zěn.meyàng?
4. 下个星期的天气怎么样? Xià.ge xīngqī .de tiān.qì zěn.meyàng?
5. 林书芳喜欢雨天吗? Lín Shūfāng xǐ.huān yǔ.tiān .ma?
6. 林书芳觉得雨天怎么样? Lín Shūfāng jué.de yǔ.tiān zěn.meyàng?
7. 他们明天要做什么? Tā.mén míng.tiān yào zuò shén.me?
8. 他们明天几点见面(*to meet*)? Tā.mén míng.tiān *jǐ*-diǎn jiàn-miàn?

文化橱窗 Wénhuà Chúchuāng

Culture Window

Beihai Park (北海公园 *Běihǎi Gōngyuán*)

Beihai Park is located in Beijing's city center. Beihai Lake is in the middle of the park and takes up over half of the entire area (175 acres). The park was built in the Liao Dynasty (907-1125 A.D.), and is the oldest, most complete and has the most diverse landscape of all of China's imperial parks. It is also the oldest surviving imperial garden to be built in the world. In 1925, it was reconstructed from a garden to a park, but was not open to the public. In 1961, the People's Republic of China named Beihai one of the first national treasures protected by the government. In 1969, the government closed the park to the public, and reopened it to the public in 1979. In 1996, Beihai Park was added to the World Heritage standby list by the United Nations.

Beihai Park is known for its "one lake, three mountains (一池三仙台 *yì-chí sān-xiāntái*)," namely Beihai Lake, Qionghua Island, Tuancheng and Xishantai. There is a legend pertaining to these places: It was said that there was a mythical place called "Penglai Fairyland (蓬莱仙境 *Pénglái Xiānjìng*)," within which were three magic mountains called Penglai, Yingzhou, and Fangzhang. Gods lived on those mountains, and magic elixirs could be found there. The design of Beihai Park was based on the legend of Penglai Fairyland.

▲Yong'an Temple.

The park is divided into Qionghua Island, the East Coast and the North Coast sectors. It is filled with religious imagery and beautiful scenery. The "Qionghua" of Qionghua Island means "beautiful jade," signifying that the island is made up of jade. It is one of the eight famous sights of ancient Beijing. At the top of Qionghua Island, there is a white tower called Yong'an Temple, which is one of Beihai's representative buildings. The tower stands at 117.75 feet, and is cylindrical at the top but cube-shaped at the bottom. It is decorated with suns, moons and flames to represent the brightness of the light of Buddhism. The buildings in the East and North Coast sectors were mostly built in the Qing Qianlong period (1711-1799 A.D.) and are Buddhist or Taoist buildings. Because of this, one can say that in Beihai Park, one can find the styles of the imperial palace and gardens as well as temples all in one place.

6 文化动动脑 Wénhuà Dòng.x nǎo / *Culture Check-up*

On a separate sheet of paper, write a short answer in English for each question.

1. Where in China is Beihai Park located? How big is it?
2. When was Beihai Park originally built? How old is it now?
3. In 1996, Beihai Park made it onto which United Nations list?
4. What is Beihai Park famous for?
5. What kind of place is Penglai Fairyland and what does it have to do with Beihai Park's design?
6. What is "Qionghua Island" and what does that name mean?
7. Which building is most representative of Beihai Park?
8. Which religion is represented in the Yong'an Temple?
9. What patterns can be seen on Yong'an Temple? What do these designs represent?
10. Which religious buildings can be found in Beihai Park? Are there places with religious undertones like Beihai Park in the United States?

Comparisons

In ancient China, Beihai Park was an imperial garden. Are there famous gardens in the United States? Can you name some of them? How do they compare to Beihai Park?

Language Practice

7 天气怎么样? Tiān.qì zěn.meyàng? / How's the weather?

With a partner, take turns asking and answering how the weather is at the times indicated. Follow the model.

Lì.zi: the day before yesterday / rainy day

A: 前天天气怎么样? Qián.tiān tiān.qì zěn.meyàng?

B: 前天下雨，是雨天。 Qián.tiān xià-yǔ, shì yǔ.tiān.

1. last week / sunny
2. this Thursday / cloudy
3. next month / sunny
4. last Wednesday / snow
5. this Monday / thunder
6. the week after next week / very windy
7. the week before last week / rain
8. next Tuesday / cloudy

8 未来 Wèilái / The Future

Use 会 *huì* to restate the following sentences.

Lì.zi: 我明天去图书馆。 Wǒ míng.tiān qù túshūguǎn.

我明天会去图书馆。 Wǒ míng.tiān huì qù túshūguǎn.

1. 后天下雨。 Hòu.tiān xià-yǔ.
2. 明天天气不好。 Míng.tiān tiān.qì bù hǎo.
3. 下个星期都是晴天吗? Xià.ge xīngqī dōu shì qíng.tiān .ma?
4. 我今天晚上去打球。 Wǒ jīn.tiān wǎn.shàng qù dǎ-qiú.
5. 我们下个周末去海边吗? Wǒ.mén xià.ge zhōumò qù hǎibiān .ma?
6. 妹妹明天下午上中文课。 Mèi.x míng.tiān xià.wǔ shàng Zhōngwénkè.
7. 哥哥下个月有很多考试。 Gē.x xià.ge yuè *yǒu* hěn duō kǎoshì.
8. 她们下个星期三一起游泳。 Tā.mén xià.ge Xīngqīsān yìqǐ yóuyǒng.
9. 他们下个星期五去看电影吗? Tā.mén xià.ge Xīngqīwǔ qù kàn-diànyǐng .ma?
10. 爸爸妈妈下下个星期日去爷爷家。 Bà.x mā.x xià xià.ge Xīngqīrì qù yé.x jiā.

9 什么时候见? Shén.me shí.hòu jiàn? / *When to meet?*

Based on the time and place provided, use the pattern "Time Word + (在 *zài*) Place Word + 见 *jiàn*" to say when and where to meet others. First say when; secondly say when and where. Follow the model.

Lì.zi: tomorrow / school

明天见。 Míng.tiān jiàn.

明天学校见。 Míng.tiān xuéxiào jiàn.

1. afternoon / basketball court
2. evening / movie theater
3. tomorrow morning / park
4. the day after tomorrow / restaurant
5. next Monday / Chinese classroom
6. next weekend / grandma's house
7. the weekend after next weekend / beach
8. next week / library
9. the week after next week / my house
10. next month / Japan
11. the month after next month / Lili's birthday party
12. next year / the United States

10 时间表 Shíjiānbiǎo / *Schedule*

Look at Josh's schedule for December on the following page. Today is the 16th. Say what Josh did or will do on the days listed, and the weather of those days.

1. 今天天气怎么样? Jīn.tiān tiān.qì zěn.meyàng?
2. 他昨天下午做什么? Tā zuó.tiān xià.wǔ zuò shén.me?
3. 他前天有考试吗? 几个? Tā qián.tiān *yǒu* kǎoshì .ma? Jǐ.ge?
4. 他明天晚上要做什么? Tā míng.tiān wǎn.shàng yào zuò shén.me?
5. 他后天几点跟白苹看电影? Tā hòu.tiān *jǐ*-diǎn gēn Bái Píng kàn-diànyǐng?
6. 他上个星期一有什么考试? Tā shàng.ge Xīngqīyī yǒu shén.me kǎoshì?
7. 他上上个星期六去谁家? Tā shàng shàng.ge Xīngqīliù qù shéi jiā?
8. 他这个星期一做什么? Tā zhèi.ge Xīngqīyī zuò shén.me?
9. 下个星期日他要去哪儿? Xià.ge Xīngqīrì tā yào qù nǎer?
10. 他什么时候有化学考试? Tā shén.me shí.hòu yǒu huàxué kǎoshì?
11. 他什么时候上画画课? Tā shén.me shí.hòu shàng huà.x kè?
12. 小美的生日是什么时候? *Xiǎo*měi .de shēng.rì shì shén.me shí.hòu?

十二月

一	二	三	四	五	六	日
		1. 在家念书 zài jiā niàn-shū	2.	3. 跟哥哥玩电子游戏 gēn gē.x wán diàn.zǐ yóuxì	4. 去爷爷家 qù yé.x jiā	5. 我的生日晚会 wǒ.de shēng.rì wǎnhuì
6. 中文小考 Zhōngwén *xiǎo*kǎo	7. 数学大考 shùxué dàkǎo	8. 下午去图书馆 xià.wǔ qù túshūguǎn	9. 晚上跟爸爸打网球 wǎn.shàng gēn bà.x *dǎ* wǎngqiú	10. 在家看电影 zài jiā kàn diànyǐng	11. 下午跟朋友打篮球 xià.wǔ gēn péng.you dǎ lánqiú	12. 下午跟同学去海边 xià.wǔ gēn tóngxué qù hǎibiān
13. 合唱团 héchàngtuán	14. 9:10两个小考 liǎng.ge *xiǎo*kǎo	15. 下午去图书馆 xià.wǔ qù túshūguǎn	今天 16. 晚上跟爸爸打网球 wǎn.shàng gēn bà.x *dǎ* wǎngqiú	17. 去健身房 qù jiànshēnfáng	18. 14:30跟白苹看电影 gēn Bái Píng kàn diànyǐng	19.
20. 合唱团 héchàngtuán	21. 上游泳课 shàng yóuyǒng-kè	22.	23. 下雨 xià-yǔ	24. 小美生日 *Xiǎo*měi shēng.rì	25. 圣诞节 Shèngdànjié	26. 去购物中心 qù gòuwù zhōngxīn
27. 合唱团 héchàngtuán	28.	29. 上画画课 shàng-huà.x kè	30. 化学考试 huàxué kǎoshì	31. 19:30新年party! Xīnnián party!		

开口说 Kāikǒu Shuō
Communication

11 讨论天气 Tǎolùn Tiān.qì / *Talking About the Weather*

With a partner, look at the weather forecast online or in a newspaper. Talk about how the weather has been recently or will be soon.

- Talk about today's weather.
- Talk about last week's weather.
- Talk about this week's weather.
- Ask your partner if this week had/will have a sunny day.
- Ask your partner if it will rain next week.
- Ask your partner about next Sunday's forecast.
- Tell your partner your favorite kind of weather.

12 世界天气 Shìjiè Tiān.qì / *The World Weather*

With a partner, check the Internet for information on the weather of countries around the world. Use the countries you learned in Unit 1. Take turns asking each other how the weather will be tomorrow in those places.

Lì.zi: **A:** 中国明天天气怎么样？ Zhōng.guó míng.tiān tiān.qì zěn.meyàng?

B: 中国明天天气很好。 Zhōng.guó míng.tiān tiān.qì *hěn* hǎo.

汉字天地 Hànzì Tiāndì
Chinese Characters

雨 ■ yǔ ■ rain

The original character for the pictograph 雨 *yǔ* shows a mountain, which represents the sky, with four dots below representing raindrops. This character has the appearance of rain falling from the sky.

Stroke Order

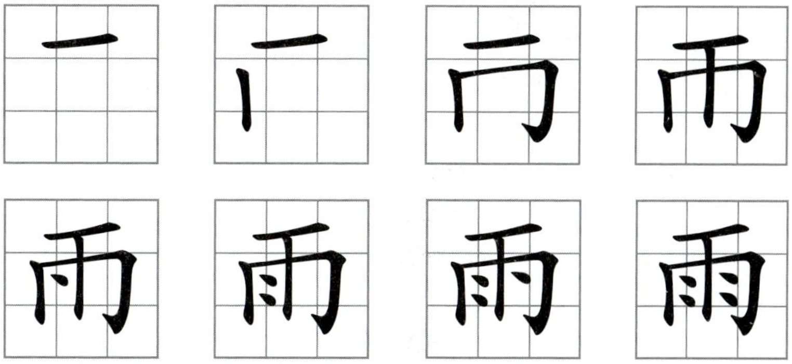

13 词汇延伸 Cíhuì Yánshēn / *Vocabulary Builder*

Below are some characters that can be combined with 雨 *yǔ* to create new words. Match the Chinese words on the left with the appropriate English meaning on the right.

衣 yī *n. clothes*	鞋 xié *n. shoes*	季 jì *n. season*	天 tiān *n. day*	量 liàng *n. quantity*

1. 雨衣 yǔyī — A. *rainfall*
2. 雨鞋 yǔxié — B. *rainy day*
3. 雨季 yǔjì — C. *raincoat*
4. 雨天 yǔtiān — D. *rainy season*
5. 雨量 yǔliàng — E. *rain boots*

14 汉字侦探 Hànzì Zhēntàn / *Visual Detective*

Can you find 雨 in the following pictures?

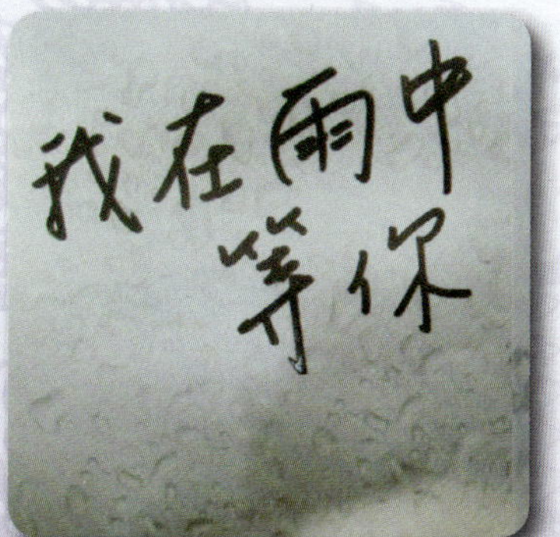

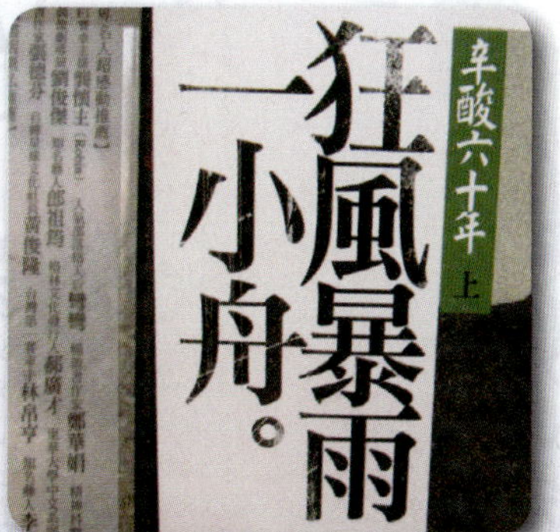

Lesson B

发音 Fāyīn

Pronunciation

b p m f d t n l g
k h z c s zh ch sh r + u ua uo

词汇 Cíhuì

Vocabulary

四季 Sì-Jì *The Four Seasons*

春天（春天）
chūn.tiān
n. spring

夏天（夏天）
xià.tiān
n. summer

秋天（秋天）
qiū.tiān
n. autumn

冬天（冬天）
dōng.tiān
n. winter

冷（冷）
lěng
adj. cold

凉（涼）
liáng
adj. cool

温暖（溫暖）
wēnnuǎn
adj. warm

热（熱）
rè
adj. hot

空调（空調）
kōngtiáo
n. air conditioner

暖气（暖氣）
nuǎnqì
n. heater; heating system

摄氏（攝氏）
Shèshì
n. Celsius

华氏（華氏）
Huáshì
n. Fahrenheit

渴（渴）
kě
adj. thirsty

饿（餓）
è
adj. hungry

冰淇淋（冰淇淋）
bīng.qílín
n. ice cream

口味（口味）kǒuwèi *n. flavor*		
香草（香草） xiāngcǎo *n. vanilla*	巧克力（巧克力） qiǎo.kèlì *n. chocolate*	草莓（草莓） cǎoméi *n. strawberry*
抹茶（抹茶） mǒchá *n. matcha*	红豆（紅豆） hóngdòu *n. red bean*	芝麻（芝麻） zhī.má *n. sesame*

Culture Note

Mainland China and Taiwan offer many ice cream flavors that might seem strange to Westerners, who might not be used to eating things like red beans and sesame in ice cream form. Other unusual flavors include bitter melon, carrot, curry and the stinky fruit durian. If that's not strange enough, one can try flavors such as soybean curd or pig's feet.

What ice cream flavors are common in the United States that might seem strange to someone from China?

A: 我又饿又渴（我又餓又渴）。

Wǒ yòu è yòu kě. *I'm hungry and thirsty.*

B: 来，吃点儿东西，喝一点儿水（來，吃點兒東西，喝一點兒水）。

Lái, chī .diǎnr dōng.xī, hē yì.diǎnr shuǐ. *Here, eat something, and drink a little water.*

A: 天气太热了（天氣太熱了）。

Tiān.qì tài rè .le. *The weather is too hot.*

B: 夏天的时候，天气总是这么热（夏天的時候，天氣總是這麼熱）。

Xià.tiān .de shí.hòu, tiān.qì zǒng.shì zhè.me rè. *In summer, it's always this hot.*

我们去吃冰淇淋吧
(我們去吃冰淇淋吧)。
Wǒ.mén qù chī bīng.qílín .ba.
Let's go eat ice-cream.

好啊 (好啊)。
Hǎo .a. *Okay.*

A: 请你打开空调 (請你打開空調)。
Qǐng nǐ dǎkāi kōngtiáo. *Please turn on the air conditioner.*

B: 没问题 (沒問題)。
Méi wèntí. *No problem.*

A: 唉，空调坏了 (唉，空調壞了)。
Āi, kōngtiáo huài .le. *Oh, the air conditioner's broken.*

B: 真糟糕 (真糟糕)。
Zhēn zāogāo. *That's awful.*

A: 现在几度 (現在幾度)?
Xiànzài jǐ-dù? *What's the temperature now?*

B: 现在二十五度 (現在二十五度)。
Xiànzài èrshíwǔ-dù. *It's 25 degrees Celsius now.*

A: 摄氏零度是华氏三十二度 (攝氏零度是華氏三十二度)。
Shèshì líng-dù shì Huáshì sānshí'èr-dù. *Zero degrees Celsius is 32 degrees Fahrenheit.*

Comparisons

One can convert temperature from Fahrenheit to Celsius with this formula:
$F = C \times 9/5 + 32$

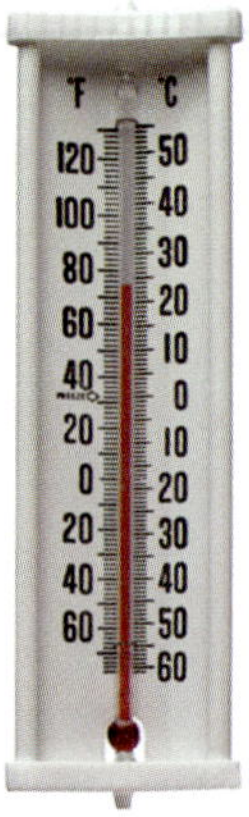

Fahrenheit (° F)	Celsius (° C)
32° F	0° C
50° F	10° C
68° F	20° C
86° F	30° C
104° F	40° C
212° F	100° C

Adjectives

坏（壞）	huài	*broken*
糟糕（糟糕）	zāogāo	*awful*

Adverbs

又（又）	yòu	*both… and…*
比较（比較）	bǐjiào	*fairly; comparatively*
太（太）	tài	*too*
总/总是（總/總是）	zǒng/zǒng.shì	*always*
这么（這麼）	zhè.me	*such; so; like this*

Common Expressions

没问题（沒問題）	méi wèntí	*no problem*

Idiomatic Expressions

一点儿（一點兒）	yì.diǎnr	*a little*

Interjections

唉（唉）	āi	*oh (a sound of sadness or regret)*

Measure Words

度（度）	dù	*a unit or measurement for temperature*

Nouns

饮料（飲料）	yǐnliào	*beverages; drink*
时候（時候）	shí.hòu	*time; moment*
空调（空調）	kōngtiáo	*air conditioner*

Verbs

打开（打開）	dǎkāi	*to turn on; to open*

Language Note

When combined with a measure word or a number, the word 这 *zhè* is pronounced 这 *zhèi*.

这杯 *zhèi-bēi*, 这两个 *zhèi liǎng.ge*.

However, when combined with 么 *.me*, the combination should be *zèm* (这 *zhè* + 么 *.me*).

1 天气怎么样? Tiān.qì zěn.meyàng? *How is the weather?*

With a partner, identify the season in each picture, then talk about the weather in each particular season. Use the model to practice the first one with your partner.

Lì.zi: **A:** 这是春天吗? Zhè.shì chūn.tiān .ma?

B: 对，这是春天。 Duì, zhè.shì chūn.tiān.

A: 春天天气怎么样? Chūn.tiān tiān.qì zěn.meyàng?

B: 春天天气很温暖。 Chūn.tiān tiān.qì hěn wēnnuǎn.

1. 

2. 

3. 

4. 

2 气象专家 Qìxiàng Zhuānjiā *Weather Expert*

Look at the weather forecast and answer the following questions.

今天

07/23 星期五	07/24 星期六	07/25 星期日	07/26 星期一	07/27 星期二	07/28 星期三	07/29 星期四

29℃	27℃	31℃	33℃	32℃	35℃	29℃

1. 今天几度? Jīn.tiān jǐ-dù?
2. 今天天气不好，对不对? Jīn.tiān tiān.qì bù hǎo, duì .bù.duì?
3. 上个星期五几度? Shàng.gè Xīngqīwǔ jǐ-dù?
4. 明天会不会下雨? Míng.tiān huì .bu.huì xià-yǔ?
5. 后天几度? Hòu.tiān jǐ-dù?
6. 后天天气比较热吗? Hòu.tiān tiān-qì bǐjiào rè .ma?
7. 昨天天气好不好? Zuó.tiān tiān.qì hǎo .bu.hǎo?
8. 前天天气怎么样? Qián.tiān tiān.qì zěn.meyàng?

3 饿还是渴? È hái.shì Kě? *Hungry or Thirsty?*

Say if you are hungry or thirsty according to the pictures.

Lì.zi:  我很渴。 *Wǒ hěn* kě.

句型介绍 Jùxíng Jièshào

Language Patterns

The Pattern 又 *yòu*...又 *yòu*...

The pattern 又…又… *yòu...yòu...* means "both… and…." But unlike "both" and "and" in English, 又 *yòu* is an adverb and therefore must always precede a verb or adjective, never a noun. There can even be three or more 又 *yòu* in a series.

我们又有可乐，又有果汁，又有茶。

Wǒ.mén yòu yǒu kělè, yòu yǒu guǒzhī, yòu yǒu chá.

(*We have cola, and juice and tea.* → It emphasizes that we have all three.)

Although this is a parallel construction, the adjectives that follow 又 *yòu* do not necessarily have to be both positive or both negative in meaning.

Subject + **又 *yòu*** + **Adjective 1 / Verb 1** + **又 *yòu*** + **Adjective 2 / Verb 2**

这道菜又香又辣。 Zhèi-dào cài yòu xiāng yòu là.

他又吃汉堡包又喝可乐。 Tā yòu chī hànbǎobāo yòu hē kělè.

The Comparative Word 比较 *bǐjiào*

The adverb 比较 *bǐjiào* means "fairly, comparatively." It is placed before an adjective to compare the subject to something else. It expresses a smaller degree than if it were not preceded by 比较 *bǐjiào*.

Subject + **比较 *bǐjiào*** + **Adjective**

昨天比较冷。 Zuó.tiān bǐjiào lěng.

巧克力冰淇淋比较好吃。 Qiǎo.kèlì bīng.qílín bǐjiào hǎochī.

The Pattern 太...了 *tài....le*

The adverb 太 *tài* means "too." It is placed in front of an adjective to show that something has reached a certain degree or has gone beyond the speaker's expectation. The pattern 太...了 *tài....le* is used to show surprise and an emotional reaction.

太 *tài* + **Adjective** + **了 *.le***

这道菜太咸了。 Zhèi-dào cài tài xián .le.

我觉得数学太难了。 Wǒ jué.de shùxué tài nán .le.

Indicating Specific Time with 的时候 *.de shí.hòu*

The time expression 的时候 *.de .shí.hòu* means "when." It functions as an indicator of a specific time, one that the speaker wants to point out. The phrase before 的时候 *.de .shí.hòu* can either be a time word, a verb phrase, or a clause. As a time adverb phrase, it is usually in front of a main sentence.

Time Word / Verb Phrase / Clause + **的时候 *.de .shí.hòu*** , **Sentence**

早上的时候，妈妈喜欢去游泳。 Zǎo.shàng .de .shí.hòu, mā.x xǐ.huān qù yóuyǒng.

睡觉的时候，我会打开空调。 Shuì jiào .de .shí.hòu, wǒ huì dǎkāi kōngtiáo.

朋友来我家的时候，我请他们喝饮料。 Péng.yǒu lái wǒ jiā .de .shí.hòu, *wǒ* qǐng tā.men hē yǐnliào.

会话 Huìhuà Dialogue

打羽毛球以后 Dǎ Yǔmáoqiú Yǐhòu *After Badminton*

After playing badminton, Bai Ping and Lin Shufang go back home and rest.

白苹：	我又热又渴。	Bái Píng:	Wǒ yòu rè yòu kě.
林书芳：	来，喝一点儿冰的饮料。	Lín Shūfāng:	Lái, hē yì.diǎnr bīng .de yǐnliào.
白苹：	谢谢。	Bái Píng:	Xiè.x.
林书芳：	现在几度？	Lín Shūfāng:	Xiànzài jǐ-dù?
白苹：	今天比较热，三十四度。	Bái Píng:	Jīn.tiān bǐjiào rè, sānshísì-dù.
林书芳：	我觉得太热了。	Lín Shūfāng:	Wǒ jué.de tài rè .le.
白苹：	夏天的时候，天气总是这么热。	Bái Píng:	Xià.tiān .de .shí.hòu, tiān.qì zǒng.shì zhè.me rè.
林书芳：	请你打开空调。	Lín Shūfāng:	*Qǐng nǐ* dǎkāi kōngtiáo.
白苹：	没问题。唉，空调坏了。	Bái Píng:	Méi wèntí. Āi, kōngtiáo huài .le.
林书芳：	真糟糕，我们去吃冰淇淋吧。	Lín Shūfāng:	Zhēn zāogāo, wǒ.mén qù chī bīng.qílín .ba.

4 对还是错？ Duì hái.shì Cuò? *True or False?*

Decide if each statement is true or false. Correct any false statements.

1. 林书芳给白苹一杯热咖啡。 Lín Shūfāng gěi Bái Píng yì-bēi rè kāfēi.
2. 今天的天气比较热。 Jīn.tiān .de tiān.qì bǐjiào rè.
3. 今天三十度。 Jīn.tiān sānshí-dù.
4. 她们觉得今天真是太热了。 Tā.mén jué.de jīn.tiān zhēn shì tài rè .le.
5. 空调坏了，她们不可以吹空调。 Kōngtiáo huài .le, tā.mén bù *kě*.yǐ chuī kōngtiáo.
6. 她们会去喝冰的饮料。 Tā.mén huì qù hē bīng .de yǐnliào.

5 懂了吗? Dǒng .le .ma? Do you understand?

Answer the following questions in Chinese.

1. 白苹觉得怎么样? Bái Píng jué.de zěn.meyàng?
2. 林书芳给白苹什么东西? Lín Shūfāng gěi Bái Píng shén.me dōng.xī?
3. 现在温度几度? Xiànzài wēndù jǐ-dù?
4. 林书芳请白苹打开什么? Lín Shūfāng qǐng Bái Píng dǎkāi shén.me?
5. 空调怎么了? Kōngtiáo zěn.me .le?
6. 她们要去吃什么? Tá.mén yào qù chī shén.me?

文化橱窗 Wénhuà Chúchuāng

Culture Window

The Metric System in China

Emperor Qin Shi Huang (秦始皇 *Qínshǐhuáng*) first standardized units of measure in China in the Qin Dynasty (221-207 B.C.). Only some traditional Chinese units of measure are still in use today; most of Chinese society now uses the metric system.

Here are some examples of the traditional Chinese units of measure:

1亩 *mǔ* = 797.326 square yards	1里 *lǐ* = 500 meters
1尺 *chǐ* = 1.09 feet (33.3 cm)	1寸 *cùn* = 1.31 inches
1市斤 *shìjīn* = 1.1 pounds	1两 *liǎng* = 1.76 ounces

In 1959, China converted to the metric system and limited use of the imperial system so that China could communicate better with the international world. In 1984, the Chinese government issued the "PRC Law of Measurements" stating that the metric system must be used for lengths, weights, electricity, time, and speed. This further standardized the units of measure in China. Also in 1959, the government announced the "City Standard (市制 *shìzhì*)" that had been in use since 1920 and would not be used after 1990. The City Standard was a transitional system announced by the Chinese government that converted traditional Chinese measurements to metric. Nowadays, most people have stopped using the City Standard, but its use and the use of traditional Chinese measurements can still be found.

Six Important Sports in China

The saying "Six Important Sports" refers to the six most popular sports played in China: basketball, volleyball, soccer, badminton, table tennis and tennis. Generally speaking, China performs better in the three latter categories than in the three former categories.

China's women's volleyball team has achieved remarkable results in recent decades. In the 1980s, they won five consecutive championships and the gold medal in the 2004 Summer Olympic Games. China's women's basketball team is fast and accurate, and has also performed well. The Chinese men's basketball team has many famous players such as Yao Ming and Wang Zhizhi, and is much loved by the Chinese public. Although the men's basketball team has managed to win gold in all but three occasions in the Asian Basketball Championships, they have yet to squeeze into the top eight in world rankings. China's men's volleyball team came fifth in the 1981 World Cup—their best result to date. China's women's soccer team was once ranked as high as number four, and the men's soccer team was the first Chinese team to play in international championships.

Badminton and table tennis have always been China's strengths. Table tennis is China's national sport, and the Chinese team recently won the 50th International Table Tennis Championships. There aren't many countries in the world that can compete with China in badminton and table tennis. China's performances in tennis, however, usually leave much to be desired.

▲ The Chinese like table tennis a lot.

6 文化动动脑 Wénhuà Dòng.x nǎo / *Culture Check-up*

Answer the following questions.

1. Who first standardized China's traditional units of measure?
2. Which measurement system is used in China now? Which measurement system is used in the United States?
3. When was the "City Standard" announced, and why?
4. Is the "City Standard" still in use in China?
5. What are the six most popular sports played in China?
6. How has the Chinese men's basketball team performed in Asia and in the world?
7. What is China's national sport?
8. Out of the six important sports, in which three sports has China had better performances worldwide?

Comparisons

What are the most popular sports in the United States? How has the United States performed in these sports internationally?

Language Practice

7 照样造句。 Zhào-yàng zào-jù. *Make sentences with this pattern.*

Make sentences with the pattern 又…又…。 *yòu…yòu….*

Lì.zi: 他 / 热 / 渴 tā / rè / kě

他又热又渴。 Tā yòu rè yòu kě.

1. 王先生 / 饿 / 渴 Wáng xiān.shēng / è / kě
2. 这道菜 / 辣 / 咸 zhèi-dào cài / là / xián
3. 我的猫 / 胖 / 可爱 wǒ.de māo / pàng / kě'ài
4. 这个面包 / 大 / 好吃 zhèi.ge miànbāo / dà / hǎochī
5. 今天的功课 / 多 / 难 jīn.tiān .de gōngkè / duō / nán
6. 果汁 / 甜 / 好喝 guǒzhī / tián / hǎohē

8 换句话说 Huàn jù huà shuō *Paraphrasing*

Change the following 很 *hěn* sentences into 太…了 *tài… .le* sentences.

Lì.zi: 这本书很奇怪。 Zhèi-běn shū hěn qíguài.

这本书太奇怪了。 Zhèi-běn shū tài qíguài .le.

1. 你的狗很胖。 Nǐ.de *gǒu* hěn pàng.
2. 他们很高兴。 Tā.mén hěn gāoxìng.
3. 她妹妹很可爱。 Tā mèi.x *hěn* kě'ài.
4. 这杯果汁很小。 Zhèi-bēi guǒzhī *hěn* xiǎo.
5. 李先生很客气。 Lǐ xiān.shēng hěn kè.qì.
6. 他觉得中文很难。 Tā jué.de Zhōngwén hěn nán.
7. 那个汉堡包很大。 Nèi.ge hànbǎobāo hěn dà.
8. 法国电影很有意思。 Fǎ.guó diànyǐng *hěn* yǒu yì.sī.
9. 这个星期的天气很热。 Zhèi.ge xīngqī .de tiān.qì hěn rè.
10. 他们的牛肉面很有名。 Tā.mén.de niúròumiàn *hěn* yǒumíng.

9 比一比 Bǐ .yì .bǐ *Let's compare!*

With a partner, take turns describing the pictures below.

Lì.zi: A: 这只狗比较大。 Zhèi-zhī gǒu bǐjiào dà.

B: 这只狗比较小。 Zhèi-zhī gǒu bǐjiào xiǎo.

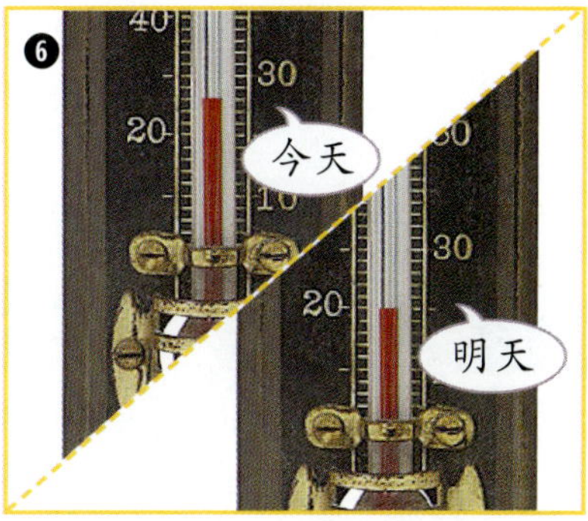

10 …的时候 .de .shí.hòu *When….*

With a partner, take turns asking and answering the following questions.

Lì.zi: A: 上历史课的时候，你很高兴吗？ Shàng lìshǐ-kè .de .shí.hòu, *nǐ* hěn gāoxìng .ma?

B: 上历史课的时候，我很高兴。 Shàng lìshǐ-kè .de .shí.hòu, *wǒ* hěn gāoxìng.

1. 看电影的时候，你吃东西吗？
   Kàn-diànyǐng .de .shí.hòu, nǐ chī dōng.xī .ma?
2. 中午的时候，你吃什么？喝什么？
   Zhōng.wǔ .de .shí.hòu, nǐ chī shén.me? Hē shén.me?
3. 今天晚上八点的时候，你要上网吗？
   Jīn.tiān wǎn.shàng bā-diǎn .de .shí.hòu, nǐ yào shàngwǎng .ma?
4. 上中文课的时候，你觉得很有意思吗？
   Shàng Zhōngwénkè .de .shí.hòu, nǐ jué.de *hěn* yǒu yì.sī .ma?

开口说 Kāikǒu Shuō Communication

11 天气怎么样? Tiān.qì zěn.meyàng? *How is the weather?*

With a partner, talk about the recent weather.

- Talk about today's weather and how you feel about it.
- Ask for the current temperature.
- Compare today's weather to yesterday's weather.
- Compare last week's weather to this week's weather.
- Ask your partner if he/she has air conditioning or a heater/central heating at home.
- Discuss if you think the weather you've been having is typical of the current season.
- Suggest an activity that is suitable in this weather.

12 小小调查 *Xiǎo* Diàochá *A Survey*

On a separate sheet of paper, draw a table like the one below. Conduct a survey in Chinese to find the most popular ice cream flavor in your class. In the table, write the names of five flavors in Chinese, then ask ten of your classmates for their favorite ice cream flavors.

Lì.zi:
A: 你喜欢什么口味? *Nǐ* xǐ.huān shén.me kǒuwèi?
B: 我喜欢巧克力。 *Wǒ* xǐ.huān qiǎo.kèlì.
A: 四个人喜欢巧克力，三个人喜欢香草，三个人喜欢抹茶。
Sì.ge rén xǐ.huān qiǎo.kèlì, sān.ge rén xǐ.huān xiāngcǎo, sān.ge rén xǐ.huān mǒchá.

巧克力	香草	草莓	咖啡	抹茶
×				

13 现在几度? Xiànzài jǐ-dù? *What temperature is it?*

With a partner, take turns asking for and giving the temperature according to the chart.

Lì.zi: A: 星期一几度? Xīngqīyī jǐ-dù?

B: 星期一十八度。 Xīngqīyī shíbā-dù.

星期一	星期二	星期三	星期四 (today)	星期五	星期六	星期日
6/15	6/16	6/17	6/18	6/19	6/20	6/21
18℃	19℃	17℃	15℃	20℃	22℃	21℃
6/22	6/23	6/24	6/25	6/26	6/27	6/28
22℃	21℃	23℃	24℃	24℃	23℃	25℃

14 四季活动 Sì-jì Huódòng *Four-Season Activity*

Working in small groups, talk about the activities you enjoy during different times of the year according to the season. Include details such as when and with whom you do an activity, what the weather is like at that time of year, and why you like the activity.

汉字天地 Hànzì Tiāndì

Chinese Characters

冰 ■ bīng ■ ice

The Chinese character for "ice" is 冰 bīng, which is a combination of the ideograph (on the left) resembling two ice blocks and the pictograph (on the right) 水 *shuǐ*, meaning water, indicating that ice comes from water.

Stroke Order

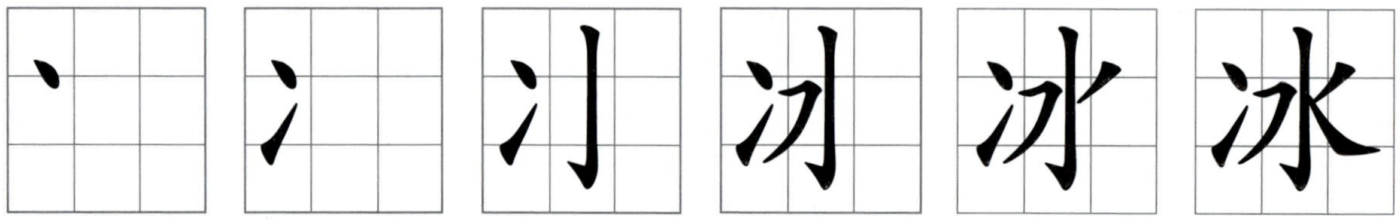

15 词汇延伸 Cíhuì Yánshēn *Vocabulary Builder*

Below are some characters that can be combined with 冰 *bīng* to create new words. Match the Chinese words on the left with the appropriate English meaning on the right.

箱 xiāng *n. box*	山 shān *n. mountain*	棒 bàng *n. stick*	鞋 xié *n. shoes*	冻 dòng *v. to freeze*

1. 冰箱 bīngxiāng — A. *ice skates*
2. 冰山 bīngshān — B. *iceberg*
3. 冰棒 bīngbàng — C. *refrigerator*
4. 冰鞋 bīngxié — D. *popsicle*
5. 冰冻 bīngdòng — E. *frozen*

16 汉字侦探 Hànzì Zhēntàn *Visual Detective*

Can you find 冰 in the following pictures?

Lesson C

发音 Fāyīn
Pronunciation

d t g k h z c s zh ch sh r + uai ui

词汇 Cíhuì
Vocabulary

中国节日 Zhōng.guó Jié.rì *Chinese Holidays and Festivals*

新年 (新年)
Xīnnián
n. the New Year

除夕 (除夕)
Chúxī
n. Chinese New Year's Eve

新年快乐
(新年快樂)
Xīnnián kuàilè
ie. Happy New Year

恭喜 (恭喜)
gōngxǐ
ie. congratulations

春节 (春節)
Chūnjié
n. Chinese New Year

春联 (春聯)
chūnlián
n. Spring Festival couplets

鞭炮 (鞭炮)
biānpào
n. firecrackers

红包 (紅包)
hóngbāo
n. red envelopes

元宵节 (元宵節)
Yuánxiāojié
n. Lantern Festival

清明节 (清明節)
Qīngmíngjié
n. Tomb-sweeping Festival

端午节 (端午節)
Duānwǔjié
n. Dragon Boat Festival

重阳节 (重陽節)
Chóngyángjié
n. Double Ninth Festival

中秋节 (中秋節)
Zhōngqiūjié
n. Mid-Autumn Festival

教师节 (教師節)
Jiàoshījié
n. Teacher's Day

Culture Note

Chinese Holiday / Festival	Chinese Lunar Date
New Year's Eve	December 31st
Chinese New Year (beginning of the Spring Festival)	January 1st
Lantern Festival	January 15th
Tomb-sweeping Festival	March 3rd
Dragon Boat Festival	May 5th
Mid-Autumn Festival	August 15th
Double Ninth Festival	September 9th
Chinese Holiday / Festival	**Date**
Teacher's Day	September 10th *

* Teacher's Day is celebrated on September 28th in Taiwan.

A: 暑假快要结束了 (暑假快要結束了)。
Shǔjià kuài yào jiéshù .le.
Summer vacation is almost over.

B: 新学期要到了 (新學期要到了)。
Xīn xuéqī yào dào .le.
The new semester is almost here.

我六月底会去中国，八月初会回美国
(我六月底會去中國，八月初會回美國)。
Wǒ Liùyuè dǐ huì qù Zhōng.guó, Bāyuè chū huì huí Měi.guó.
I will go to China at the end of June and return to the United States at the beginning of August.

A: 中国新年是哪天(中國新年是哪天)?

Zhōng.guó Xīnnián shì něi-tiān? *On what day is the Chinese New Year?*

B: 得看农历(得看農曆)。

Děi kàn nónglì. *It depends on the Lunar Calendar.*

A: 为什么你今年夏天要去中国(為什麼你今年夏天要去中國)?

Wèishén.me nǐ jīn.nián xià.tiān yào qù Zhōng.guó? *Why are you going to China this summer?*

B: 因为我想学中文, 所以我要去中国
(因為我想學中文, 所以我要去中國)。

Yīn.wèi *wǒ* xiǎng xué Zhōngwén, suǒ.yǐ wǒ yào qù Zhōng.guó.

I'm going to China because I want to study Chinese.

A: 我觉得元宵节很好玩儿(我覺得元宵節很好玩兒)。

Wǒ jué.de Yuánxiāojié *hěn* hǎowánr. *I think Lantern Festival is fun.*

B: 我觉得新年更好玩儿(我覺得新年更好玩兒)。

Wǒ jué.de Xīnnián gèng hǎowánr. *I think Chinese New Year is even more fun.*

A: 学期已经结束了(學期已經結束了)。

Xuéqī yǐ.jīng jiéshù .le. *This semester is finished.*

Adverbs

快 (快)	kuài	*soon; before long*
已经 (已經)	yǐ.jīng	*already*
更 (更)	gèng	*more*

Auxiliary Verbs

应该 (應該)	yīnggāi	*should*

Conjunctions

因为 (因為)	yīn.wèi	*because; since (reason)*
所以 (所以)	*suǒ*.yǐ	*so; therefore*

Nouns

学期 (學期)	xuéqī	*semester*
农历 (農曆)	nónglì	*the lunar calendar*
节日 (節日)	jié.rì	*festival*

Prepositions

到 (到)	dào	*to*

Question Words

为什么 (為什麼)	wèishén.me	*why*

Time Words

通常 (通常)	tōngcháng	*usually*
以前 (以前)	yǐqián	*before*

Verbs

结束 (結束)	jiéshù	*to end*
到 (到)	dào	*to arrive; to reach*
懂 (懂)	dǒng	*to understand*
过 (過)	guò	*to celebrate; to pass through time*

Verb-Objects

过年 (過年)	guò-nián	*to celebrate / spend the New Year*

1 什么节日? Shén.me jié.rì? *What festival Is It?*

Listen to the recording and say 是 *shì* if what you hear matches the picture or 不是 *bú shì* if it doesn't.

1.

3.

2.

4.

2 初?中?底? Chū? Zhōng? Dǐ? Beginning? Middle? End?

Look at the following dates and say whether they are at the 初 *chū*, 中 *zhōng*, or 底 *dǐ* of each month. Follow the model.

Lì.zi: 一月十五号 Yīyuè shíwǔ-hào
一月中 Yīyuè zhōng

一月

星期日	星期一	星期二	星期三	星期四	星期五	星期六
	1	2	3	4	5	6
7	8	9	10	11	12	13
14	15	16	17	18	19	20
21	22	23	24	25	26	27
28	29	30	31			

1. 三月二十二号 Sānyuè èrshí'èr-hào
2. 九月八号 Jiǔyuè bā-hào
3. 六月一号 Liùyuè yī-hào
4. 十二月三十一号 Shí'èryuè sānshíyī-hào
5. 七月十三号 Qīyuè shísān-hào
6. 二月二十五号 Èryuè èrshíwǔ-hào
7. 四月十九号 Sìyuè shíjiǔ-hào
8. 十一月六号 Shíyīyuè liù-hào

3 哪天? Něi-tiān? Which day?

With a partner, take turns asking and saying the dates of the following holidays.

Lì.zi: **A:** St. Patrick's Day是哪天？ St. Patrick's Day shì něi-tiān?
B: St. Patrick's Day是三月十七号。 St. Patrick's Day shì Sānyuè shíqī-hào.

1. Independence Day

2. April Fool's Day

3. Christmas

4. Valentine's Day

5. Halloween

6. Thanksgiving

句型介绍 Jùxíng Jièshào

Language Patterns

The Verb 看 *kàn*

The verb 看 *kàn* means "to look at." However, a better English translation for this usage in the example below might be "it depends on," meaning "we've got to look at (the calculations of the lunar calendar)." Similar to its structure in English, it is followed by a noun, pronoun or clause.

看 *kàn* + **NP**

中国节日得看农历。 Zhōng.guó jié.rì děi kàn nónglì.

你可以点多少吃的东西，得看你有多少钱。

Nǐ kě.yǐ diǎn duō.shǎo chī .de dōng.xī, děi kàn *nǐ* yǒu duō.shǎo qián.

The Question Word 为什么 *wèishén.me* and the Pattern 因为 *yīn.wèi...*, 所以 *suǒ.yǐ...*

The Question Word 为什么 *wèishén.me* means "why," and it is used to inquire about the cause of a consequence. To answer a "why" question, 因为 *yīn.wèi...*, 所以 *suǒ.yǐ...* is used. The cause follows 因为 *yīn.wèi* and the consequence follows 所以 *suǒ.yǐ*. In Chinese, 因为 *yīn.wèi* and 所以 *suǒ.yǐ* are commonly used together.

为什么 *Wèishén.me* + **Sentence**

因为 *Yīn.wèi* + **the cause** , **所以 *suǒ.yǐ*** + **the result**

A: 为什么你不吃这道菜？ Wèishén.me nǐ bù chī zhèi-dào cài?

B: 因为我觉得这道菜太辣了，所以我不吃。

Yīn.wèi wǒ jué.de zhèi-dào cài tài là .le, suǒ.yǐ wǒ bù chī.

A: 为什么你点冰淇淋？ Wèishén.me *nǐ* diǎn bīng.qílín?

B: 因为今天很热，所以我想吃冰的东西。

Yīn.wèi jīn.tiān hěn rè, suǒ.yǐ *wǒ* xiǎng chī bīng .de dōng.xī.

会话 Huìhuà
Dialogue

中国新年 Zhōng.guó Xīnnián *Chinese New Year*

Bai Ping and Dong Jun are riding their bikes home.

董军：	学期快要结束了。	Dǒng Jūn:	Xuéqī kuài yào jiéshù .le.
白苹：	是啊，新年要到了。	Bái Píng:	Shì .a, Xīnnián yào dào .le.
董军：	新年？现在已经是一月二十号了。	Dǒng Jūn:	Xīnnián? Xiànzài yǐ.jīng shì Yīyuè èrshí-hào .le.
白苹：	中国新年通常在一月底到二月初。	Bái Píng:	Zhōng.guó Xīnnián tōngcháng zài Yīyuè dǐ dào Èryuè chū.
董军：	我不懂。中国新年是哪天？	Dǒng Jūn:	Wǒ bù dǒng. Zhōng.guó Xīnnián shì něi-tiān?
白苹：	得看农历。	Bái Píng:	Děi kàn nónglì.
董军：	为什么得看农历？	Dǒng Jūn:	Wèishén.me děi kàn nónglì?
白苹：	因为以前的中国人用农历，所以中国节日得看农历。	Bái Píng:	Yīn.wèi yǐqián .de Zhōng.guórén yòng nónglì, suǒ.yǐ Zhōng.guó jié.rì děi kàn nónglì.
董军：	真有意思。	Dǒng Jūn:	Zhēn yǒu yì.sī.
白苹：	中国新年更有意思，你应该在这儿过年。	Bái Píng:	Zhōng.guó Xīnnián gèng yǒu yì.sī, nǐ yīnggāi zài zhèr guò-nián.

4 对还是错？ Duì hái.shì cuò? *True or false?*

Decide if each statement is true or false. Correct any false statements.

1. 学期已经结束了。 Xuéqī yǐ.jīng jiéshù .le.
2. 中国新年快要到了。 Zhōng.guó Xīnnián kuài yào dào .le.
3. 中国新年通常在一月初。 Zhōng.guó Xīnnián tōngcháng zài Yīyuè chū.

4. 今年的中国新年在一月二十号。 Jīnnián .de Zhōng.guó Xīnnián zài Yīyuè èrshí-hào.

5. 中国节日得看农历。 Zhōng.guó jié.rì děi kàn nónglì.

6. 白苹说(*to say*)中国新年很有意思。 Bái Píng shuō Zhōng.guó Xīnnián *hěn* yǒu yì.sī.

5 懂了吗? Dǒng .le .ma? *Do you understand?*

Answer the following questions in Chinese.

1. 今天是几月几号? Jīn.tiān shì jǐ-yuè jǐ-hào?
2. 学期快要结束了，对不对? Xuéqī kuài yào jiéshù .le, duì .bú .duì?
3. 什么节日快到了? Shén.me jié.rì kuài dào .le?
4. 为什么中国新年得看农历? Wèishén.me Zhōng.guó Xīnnián děi kàn nónglì?
5. 白苹建议(*to suggest*)董军新年的时候可以做什么?
   Bái Píng jiànyì Dǒng Jūn Xīnnián .de .shí.hòu kě.yǐ zuò shén.me?

文化橱窗 Wénhuà Chúchuāng

Culture Window

Chinese New Year

Apart from the Western New Year that is celebrated on January 1st, there is another New Year which is a very important traditional holiday—the Spring Festival, also known as the Lunar New Year—that the Chinese celebrate on the first day of the first month of the Lunar Calendar. In many places with Chinese population, such as Taiwan, Singapore, Korea, Vietnam and Thailand, the Chinese New Year is a national holiday that is celebrated with family and friends.

▲ Spring couplets.

Before the New Year, people prepare for the holiday by cleaning the house and buying New Year goods. They also paste Spring Festival couplets with lucky phrases written on them with Chinese calligraphy on either side of their front doors for good fortune. Sometimes, people paste single character spring posters (such as posters with the words 福 *fú* or 春 *chūn*) upside down on purpose because the word 倒 *dǎo* (upside down) sounds similar to the word 到 *dào* (to come; to arrive). This play on words means that pasting spring posters upside down is to wish for good fortune or spring to come.

The day before New Year's Day is called 除夕 *chúxī*. On New Year's Eve, the whole family gathers around the table and eats dinner together. This dinner is called 年夜饭 *niányèfàn* (New Year's Eve dinner) or 团圆饭 *tuán.yuánfàn* (get-together dinner), and will include dishes that are "lucky," such as fish (a homonym for the word "fish" in Chinese is surplus) or 年年有余 *niánx yǒu yú* (to have surplus every year) and dumplings (to represent riches). However, all kids look forward to the time after dinner, a time when adults will give them 红包 *hóngbāo* (red envelopes). The adults will place some money in red envelopes to give to the children in exchange for some lucky phrases. The elderly are also given red envelopes to wish them good health in the coming year.

▲ Traditional Chinese New Year's Eve dinner.

During the Chinese New Year holidays, people visit their relatives and friends. Normally, people will say something lucky to whomever they meet; the most often used phrase is 恭喜发财 *gōngxǐ fā-cái* (Congratulations and may you be prosperous). Traditionally, New Year's festivities begin on the first day of the first lunar month, and do not end till Lantern Festival on the fifteenth. However, people are much busier nowadays, so people usually return to work after only a few days off. In China, the Chinese New Year holidays usually last only three days—New Year's Eve, New Year's Day and the day after that.

The Lunar Calendar and the Solar Calendar

Apart from the Western calendar that is used throughout the world, the Chinese have their own calendar system called 农历 *nónglì* (the lunar calendar).

The lunar calendar came about because China was originally an agricultural country, so the ancient Chinese observed the heavens and came up with a calendar system that fit agricultural needs of the farmers. In the lunar calendar, a "big month" has 30 days, and a "small month" has 29 days. There are 12 months in a lunar year, with a total of 354 days—11 days shorter than the Western calendar. Therefore, a thirteenth month, or a leap month, is added every two, or sometimes every three years to make up for the additional days.

Although the Chinese now use the Western calendar, the lunar calendar still has its uses. For example, it is used to calculate on which days traditional Chinese holidays (such as the Spring Festival, Mid-Autumn Festival, and Dragon Boat Festival) will fall. This is the reason why traditional Chinese festivals fall on different days of the Western calendar each year.

The Chinese 12-Animal Zodiac

The Western Zodiac has signs that are said to have certain characteristics that people born in that month would have. The Chinese have a similar system called 十二生肖 *Shí'èr Shēngxiāo*. It is a set of twelve animals and each animal corresponds to one lunar year. Every twelve years, the order of animals associated with each year repeats. The twelve animals of the Chinese Zodiac in order are: the rat, ox, tiger, rabbit, dragon, snake, horse, goat, monkey, rooster, dog, and pig.

The legend of the order of the animals comes from a competition. A long time ago, people did not have calendars, so they asked the Emperor of the Heavens for help. The Emperor decided to calculate years using animals. Then, he asked all of the animals to compete in a race across a river. The years would be organized by the order in which the competitors finished. The ox was the best swimmer out of all the animals that came out for the race. The cat and the rat, who were both sneaky, crawled on the ox's back. Half way through the race, the rat pushed the cat off the ox's back and into the river. When the ox was about to reach the finish line, the rat jumped off the ox and climbed onto the riverbank before it, winning the race. The cat, who was sabotaged by the rat, didn't finish the race and naturally developed a grudge. This is why cats nowadays chase rats.

▲ The twelve animals of the Chinese Zodiac.

6 文化动动脑 Wénhuà Dòng.x nǎo / *Culture Check-up*

On a separate sheet of paper, write a short answer in English for each question.

1. What other name does the Chinese New Year have? When is it?
2. What is a spring couplet / poster? What color is it?
3. Why are some spring posters pasted upside down?
4. When is 除夕 *chúxī*? Is there anything special about the dinner on that day? Why can you find fish and dumplings on the 年夜饭 *niányèfàn* dinner table? What special meanings are there for these dishes? What are 红包 *hóngbāo*? Who gets them?
5. If you visit your friend in China during the New Year holidays, what lucky phrase could you say to him / her when you first meet?
6. If you were working in China, how many days would you have off (not including weekends) for the New Year?
7. Chinese traditional festivals are based on which calendar system?
8. Do Chinese people still use the lunar calendar now? When and why?
9. What are the twelve animals of the Chinese Zodiac?
10. What is the animal of this year?

Comparisons

What foods or dishes carry special meanings for Americans?

Language Practice

7 快要还是已经? Kuài yào hái.shì yǐ.jīng? *Soon or already?*

Use 快要 *kuài yào* or 已经 *yǐ.jīng* to complete the phrase based on the picture.

1. 圣诞节___到了。
Shèngdànjié ___ dào .le.

2. 电影___结束了。
Diànyǐng ___ jiéshù .le.

3. 我___回家了。
Wǒ ___ huíjiā .le.

4. 夏天___来了。
Xià.tiān ___ lái .le.

5. 他们___到篮球场了。
Tā.mén ___ dào lánqiúchǎng .le.

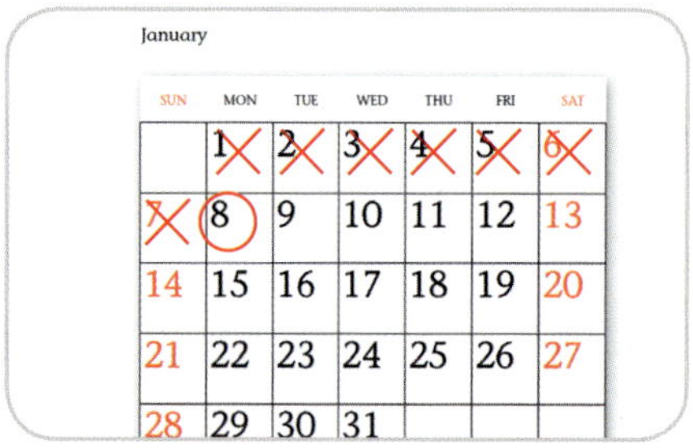

6. 一月九日___到了。
Yīyuè jiǔ-rì ___ dào .le.

8 为什么? Wèishén.me? *Why?*

With a partner, take turns asking and answering the following questions. Answer by using 因为 *yīn.wèi*⋯. Use the cues provided.

Lì.zi: 为什么你点牛肉面? (好吃) Wèishén.me *nǐ* diǎn niúròumiàn? (hǎochī)

A: 为什么你点牛肉面? Wèishén.me *nǐ* diǎn niúròumiàn?

B: 因为牛肉面很好吃。 Yīnwèi niúròumiàn *hěn* hǎochī.

1. 为什么爸爸喜欢打网球? (很有意思) Wèishén.me bà.x xǐ.huān *dǎ*-wǎngqiú? (*hěn* yǒu yì.sī)
2. 为什么你点大杯汽水? (又热又渴) Wèishén.me *nǐ* diǎn dà bēi qìshuǐ? (yòu rè yòu kě)
3. 为什么一共十二块? (面包五块, 果汁七块)
Wèishén.me yígòng shí'èr-kuài? (miànbāo wǔ-kuài, guǒzhī qī-kuài)
4. 为什么你不喜欢数学课? (很难) Wèishén.me nǐ bù xǐ.huān shùxué kè? (hěn nán)
5. 为什么你跟他一起看书? (我没有书) Wèishén.me nǐ gēn tā yìqǐ kàn-shū? (wǒ méi.yǒu shū)

9 因为…，所以… Yīn.wèi…, suǒ.yǐ… Because…, therefore…

With a partner, complete the dialogue by using the pattern 因为 ***yīn.wèi***···，所以 ***suǒ.yǐ***···

Lì.zi: **A:** 你们今天要去海边吗？ Nǐ.mén jīn.tiān yào qù hǎibiān .ma?

B: 我们今天要在家。 Wǒ.mén jīn.tiān yào zài-jiā.

A: 为什么你们今天不去海边？ Wèishén.me nǐ.mén jīn.tiān bú qù hǎibiān?

B: (今天天气不好，又刮风又下雨

Jīn.tiān tiān.qì bù hǎo, yòu guā-fēng yòu xià-yǔ / 我们不去 wǒ.mén bú qù)

因为今天天气不好，又刮风又下雨，所以我们不去。

Yīnwèi jīn.tiān tiān.qì bù hǎo, yòu guā-fēng yòu xià-yǔ, suǒ.yǐ wǒ.mén bú qù.

1. **A:** 你点什么？ *Nǐ* diǎn shén.me?

   B: (色拉和果汁 sèlā hé guǒzhī)

   A: 为什么你不点炸鸡？ Wèishén.me nǐ bù diǎn zhájī?

   B: (炸鸡太油了 zhájī tài yóu .le / 我不喜欢 wǒ bù xǐ.huān)

2. **A:** 这个学期你上什么课？ Zhèi.ge xuéqī nǐ shàng shén.me kè?

   B: (中文、化学和历史 Zhōngwén, huàxué hé lìshǐ)

   A: 为什么你上中文？ Wèishén.me nǐ shàng Zhōngwén?

   B: (中文很有意思 Zhōngwén *hěn* yǒu yì.sī / 我想上 *wǒ* xiǎng shàng)

3. **A:** 你喜欢什么宠物？ *Nǐ* xǐ.huān shén.me chǒng.wù?

   B: (狗 gǒu)

   A: 为什么你喜欢狗？ Wèishén.me *nǐ* xǐ.huān gǒu?

   B: (我觉得狗是最可爱的动物 wǒ jué.de gǒu shì zuì kě'ài .de dòng.wù /
   我很喜欢 *wǒ hěn* xǐ.huān)

4. **A:** 中国新年是几月几日？ Zhōng.guó Xīnnián shì jǐ-yuè jǐ-rì?

   B: (今年的中国新年，二月十三日 jīnnián .de Zhōng.guó Xīnnián, Èryuè shísān-rì)

   A: 为什么中国新年不是一月一日？
   Wèishén.me Zhōng.guó Xīnnián bú shì Yīyuè yī-rì?

   B: (中国新年得看农历 Zhōng.guó Xīnnián děi kàn nónglì /
   中国新年通常在一月底到二月初
   Zhōng.guó Xīnnián tōngcháng zài Yīyuè dǐ dào Èryuè chū)

10 图片会说话 Túpiàn huì Shuō-huà / Pictures Talk

Listen to the recording and choose the picture that best describes each dialogue.

1.

A. 

B. 

2.

A. 

B. 

3.

A. 

B. 

11 个人问题 Gèrén Wèntí / Personal Questions

Use 看 *kàn* (It depends on) to answer the following questions in Chinese.

1. 你每天(*every day*)几点睡觉？ *Nǐ* měitiān *jǐ*-diǎn shuìjiào?
2. 你每天去图书馆吗？ *Nǐ* měitiān qù túshūguǎn .ma?
3. 你今天下午打篮球吗？ Nǐ jīn.tiān xià.wǔ dǎ-lánqiú .ma?
4. 中午的时候，你吃什么？ Zhōng.wǔ .de .shí.hòu, nǐ chī shén.me?
5. 你下个学期上中文课吗？ Nǐ xià.ge xuéqī shàng Zhōngwénkè .ma?
6. 你觉得你的课都很有意思吗？ Nǐ jué.de nǐ.de kè dōu *hěn* yǒu yì.sī .ma?
7. 你每个月都去爷爷奶奶家吗？ *Nǐ* měi.ge yuè dōu qù yé.x nǎi.x jiā .ma?
8. 你这个星期五晚上要看电影吗？

   Nǐ zhèi.ge Xīngqīwǔ wǎn.shàng yào kàn-diànyǐng .ma?

开口说 Kāikǒu Shuō

Communication

12 新年要到了 Xīnnián yào dào .le *The New Year is coming*

Role-play the situation in Chinese with your partner. Talk about how you will spend the Chinese New Year.

- Say what day it is now.
- Tell your friend what activities there are during the Chinese New Year.
- Tell your friend what you plan to do for the coming New Year's celebrations.
- Talk about when the Chinese New Year is.
- Talk about how one finds out the date of the Chinese New Year each year.
- Explain what the lunar calendar is.

13 短信拜年 Duǎnxìn Bài-nián *"Happy New Year" Text Message*

Look at the following text message and then answer the questions.

收件匣 (1/8)

2009/01/28 (五) 09:16

罗意69841172

白华，春到，福到，新年到！新年的第一天，祝你新年快乐！

1. Whose cell phone is this?
2. Who sent the text message?
3. At what time did the recipient receive this message?
4. On what day is New Year's Eve according to this text?
5. What is the cell phone number of the person who sent the text message?

汉字天地 Hànzì Tiāndì

Chinese Characters

火 ■ huǒ ■ fire

The pictograph 火 *huǒ* means "fire." Its earliest form was , meaning "flames." As it evolved, its lines became more linear. Today's character for fire (火) is also a common radical for words related to fire. When 火 *huǒ* is used as a radical, it can be also written as 灬, e.g. 热 *rè* (hot).

Stroke Order

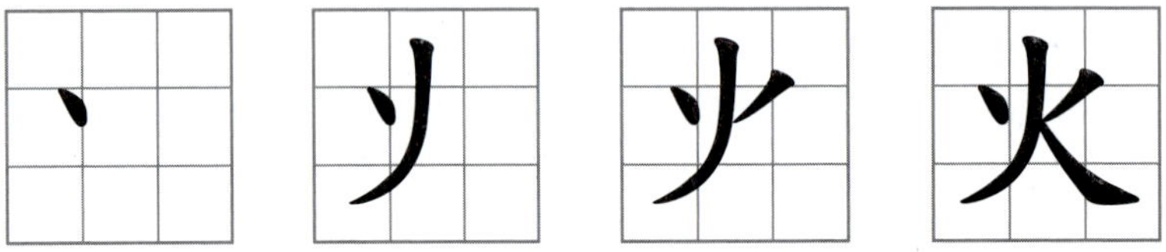

14 词汇延伸 Cíhuì Yánshēn / *Vocabulary Builder*

Below are some characters that can be combined with 火 *huǒ* to create new words. Match the Chinese words on the left with the appropriate English meaning on the right.

柴 chái *n. firewood*	腿 tuǐ *n. leg*	车 chē *n. vehicle*	花 huā *n. flower*	药 yào *n. medicine*

1. 火柴 huǒchái — A. *ham*
2. 火腿 *huǒ*tuǐ — B. *spark*
3. 火车 huǒchē — C. *train*
4. 火花 huǒhuā — D. *match*
5. 火药 huǒyào — E. *gunpowder*

15 汉字侦探 Hànzì Zhēntàn / *Visual Detective*

Can you find 火 in the following pictures?

Lesson D

发音 Fāyīn
Pronunciation

d t n l g k h z c s zh ch sh r + uan uang

词汇 Cíhuì
Vocabulary

中国节日 Zhōng.guó Jié.rì *More Holidays and Festivals*

端午节(端午節)
Duānwǔjié
n. Dragon Boat Festival

龙舟(龍舟)
lóngzhōu
n. dragon boat

中元节(中元節)
Zhōngyuánjié
n. Ghost Festival

冬至(冬至)
Dōngzhì
n. Winter solstice

七夕(七夕)
Qīxī
n. Chinese Valentine's Day

香包(香包)
xiāngbāo
n. scented sachet

粽子(粽子)
zòng.zi
n. zongzi (rice dumplings made and eaten during the Dragon Boat Festival)

Culture Note

Chinese Holidays/Festivals	Chinese Lunar Date
Dragon Boat Festival	May 5th
Chinese Valentine's Day	July 7th
Ghost Festival	July 15th
Winter solstice	December 22nd

A: 你在做什么（你在做什麼）？

Nǐ zài zuò shén.me? *What are you doing?*

B: 我在做香包（我在做香包）。

Wǒ zài zuò xiāngbāo. *I'm making the scented sachet.*

A: 划船很难吧（划船很難吧）？

Huá-chuán hěn nán .ba? *Rowing boats is hard, right?*

B: 不，划船一点儿也不难（不，划船一點兒也不難）！

Bù, huá-chuán yìdiǎnr yě bù nán! *No, rowing boats is not hard at all!*

A: 粽子是什么（粽子是什麼）？

Zòng.zi shì shén.me? *What is zongzi?*

B: 粽子是一种吃的东西。端午节的时候，中国人吃粽子
（粽子是一種吃的東西。端午節的時候，中國人吃粽子）。

Zòng.zi shì yì-zhǒng chī .de dōng.xī. Duānwǔjié .de .shí.hòu, Zhōng.guórén chī zòng.zi.

Zongzi is a kind of food. During the Dragon Boat Festival, Chinese people eat zongzi.

A: 中国人端午节做什么？包粽子吗（中國人端午節做什麼？包粽子嗎）？

Zhōng.guórén Duānwǔjié zuò shén.me? Bāo zòng.zi .ma?

What do Chinese people do during the Dragon Boat Festival? Make zongzi?

B: 除了包粽子以外，中国人也做香包（除了包粽子以外，中國人也做香包）。

Chú.le bāo zòng.zi yǐwài, Zhōng.guórén yě zuò xiāngbāo.

In addition to making zongzi, Chinese people also make scented sachets.

船(船)
chuán
boat

比赛(比賽)
bǐsài
competition; race

Adjectives

好玩儿 (好玩兒)	hǎowánr	*interesting; amusing*

Adverbs

在 (在)	zài	*(indicating an action in progress)*

Idiomatic Expressions

除了…以外… (除了…以外…)	chú.le… yǐwài…	*besides; in addition to; except for*

Measure Words

种 (種)	zhǒng	*kind; sort; type*

Particles

喂 (喂)	wéi	*hello (used to greet people on the phone)*
吧 (吧)	.ba	*(particle of suggestion and supposition)*

Pronouns

大家 (大家)	dàjiā	*all; everybody*

Verbs

包 (包)	bāo	*to wrap*
划 (划)	huá	*to paddle; to row*
带 (帶)	dài	*to take; to bring*

Verb-Objects

划船 (划船)	huá-chuán	*to row a boat*

1 中国节日 Zhōng.guó Jié.rì / *Chinese Festival*

Listen to the recording and select the corresponding photo.

2 我问你答 Wǒ wèn Nǐ dá / *I ask; You answer*

Answer the following questions using the cues provided.

1. 你昨天下午在做什么？ (to study in the library)
   Nǐ zuó.tiān xià.wǔ zài zuò shén.me?

2. 七月初的时候，美国的天气很冷吧？ (not at all)
   Qīyuè chū .de .shíhou, Měi.guó .de tiān.qì *hěn* lěng .ba?

3. 什么时候家人一定(*must*)要一起吃饭？ (New Year's Eve)
   Shén.me shí.hòu jiārén yídìng yào yìqǐ chī-fàn?

4. 端午节的时候，大家做什么？ (to row the dragon boat, to wrap rice dumplings)
   Duānwǔjié .de .shí.hòu, dàjiā zuò shén.me?

5. 除了春节，你还知道什么中国节日(*festival*)？ (Dragon Boat Festival, Mid-Autumn Festival)
   Chú.le Chūnjié, nǐ hái zhī.dào shén.me Zhōng.guó jié.rì?

6. 为什么孩子(*children*)喜欢中国新年？ (to receive red envelopes)
   Wèishén.me hái.zi xǐ.huān Zhōng.guó Xīnnián?

3 个人问题 Gèrén Wèntí / *Personal Questions*

Answer the following questions in Chinese.

1. 你的家人都是美国人吧？ Nǐ.de jiārén dōu.shì Měi.guórén .ba?
2. 你喜欢划船吗？ *Nǐ* xǐ.huān huá-chuán .ma?
3. 你觉得划船很难吗？ Nǐ jué.de huá-chuán hěn nán .ma?
4. 昨天晚上八点，你在念书吗？ Zuó.tiān wǎn.shàng bā-diǎn, nǐ zài niàn-shū .ma?
5. 今天早上六点，你还在睡觉吗？ Jīn.tiān zǎo.shàng liù-diǎn, nǐ hái zài shuìjiào .ma?
6. 除了中文以外，这个学期你还上什么课？ Chú.le Zhōngwén yǐwài, zhèi.ge xuéqī nǐ hái shàng shén.me kè?
7. 中文一点儿也不难，对不对？ Zhōngwén yìdiǎn yě bù nán, duì .bú.duì?

句型介绍 Jùxíng Jièshào

Language Patterns

The Adverb 在 *zài*

Put 在 *zài* before a verb to express that an action is currently under way.

Subject + 在 *zài* + **V-ing**

你等一下，我在打电话。 *Nǐ* děng yí.xià, wǒ zài dǎ-diànhuà.

A: 他在吃什么？ Tā zài chī shén.me?

B: 他在吃三明治。 Tā zài chī-sānmíngzhì.

The Question Particle 吧 *.ba*

The particle 吧 *.ba* is used at the end of a statement for the speaker to suggest or suppose that the statement is true, but wants it to be verified.

Sentence + 吧 *.ba*?

A: 今天的考试不难吧？ Jīn.tiān .de kǎoshì bù nán .ba?

B: 不，我觉得很难。 Bù, wǒ jué.de hěn nán.

A: 这道菜很辣吧？ Zhèi-dào cài hěn là .ba?

B: 嗯，这道菜很辣。 Ēn, zhèi-dào cài hěn là.

Express Intensified Exclusion with 一点儿也/都不 *yìdiǎnr yě/dōu bù*

The word 一点儿 *yìdiǎnr* means "the smallest amount" and it is used to express the least degree of a situation, like "not even a little" or "not at all" in English. To do this, put 一点儿 *yìdiǎnr* followed by 也不 *yě bù* or 都不 *dōu bù* in front of adjectives or verbs. This pattern is only used with negative verbs and adjectives.

Note: The word 也 *yě* can be substituted in this pattern with the word 都 *dōu* with no change in meaning.

Subject + 一点儿 *yìdiǎnr* + 也 *yě* / 都 *dōu* + 不 *bù* + **Adjective / Verb**

中文一点儿也不难。 Zhōngwén yì*diǎnr* yě bù nán.

我一点儿也不喜欢炸鸡。 Wǒ yì*diǎnr* yě bù xǐ.huān zhájī.

The Pattern 除了…以外，也/还… *chú.le... yǐwài, yě / hái...*

The pattern 除了…以外，也/还… *chú.le... yǐwài, yě/hái...* means "besides, in addition to," if a positive statement follows. The subject can be placed at the beginning of 除了…以外 *chú.le... yǐwài* or 还 *hái*.

除了 *chú.le* + **VP_1 / NP_1** + 以外 *yǐwài* , 也 *yě* / 还 *hái* + **VP_2 / NP_2**

Note: If the VP_1 or NP_1 that falls between 除了 *chú.le...*以外 *yǐwài* is short, it is common to drop 以外 *yǐwài*. But if the VP_1 or NP_1 is long, it is good to keep both 除了 *chú.le...* and 以外 *yǐwài*.

A: 你今天上什么课？数学课吗？

Nǐ jīn.tiān shàng shén.me kè? Shùxué kè .ma?

B: 我今天除了上数学课，还上英文课。

Wǒ jīn.tiān chú.le shàng shùxuékè, hái shàng Yīngwénkè.

你想吃什么？牛肉面吗？

Nǐ xiǎng chī shén.me? Niúròumiàn .ma?

我很喜欢运动。打网球以外，我还喜欢游泳。

Wǒ hěn xǐ.huān yùn.dòng. *Dǎ*-wǎngqiú yǐwài, wǒ hái xǐ.huān yóuyǒng.

除了牛肉面，我也想吃饺子。

Chú.le niúròumiàn, *wǒ yě* xiǎng chī-jiǎo.zi.

会话 Huìhuà
Dialogue

端午节 Duānwǔjié *Dragon Boat Festival*

Dong Jun calls Lin Shufang. Lin Shufang is in the kitchen.

董军：	喂，书芳，你在做什么？	Dǒng Jūn:	Wéi, Shūfāng, nǐ zài zuò shén.me?
林书芳：	我在包粽子。	Lín Shūfāng:	Wǒ zài bāo-zòng.zi.
董军：	包粽子？包粽子很难吧？	Dǒng Jūn:	Bāo-zòng.zi? Bāo-zòng.zi hěn nán .ba?
林书芳：	一点儿也不难！包粽子很好玩。	Lín Shūfāng:	Yì*diǎnr* yě bù nán! Bāo-zòng.zi *hěn* hǎowán.
董军：	你为什么要包粽子？	Dǒng Jūn:	Nǐ wèishén.me yào bāo-zòng.zi?
林书芳：	因为下个星期一是端午节，所以大家吃粽子。	Lín Shūfāng:	Yīn.wèi xià.ge Xīngqīyī shì Duānwǔjié, suǒ.yǐ dàjiā chī-zòng.zi.
董军：	端午节的时候，你们还做什么？	Dǒng Jūn:	Duānwǔjié .de shí.hòu, nǐ.mén hái zuò shén.me?
林书芳：	除了吃粽子以外，我们也划龙舟。	Lín Shūfāng:	Chú.le chī-zòng.zi, wǒ.mén yě huá-lóngzhōu.
董军：	划龙舟是什么？	Dǒng Jūn:	Huá-lóngzhōu shì shén.me?
林书芳：	划龙舟是一种划船比赛。下个星期一我带你去看看吧！	Lín Shūfāng:	Huá lóngzhōu shì yì-zhǒng huá-chuán bǐsài. Xià.ge Xīngqīyī wǒ dài nǐ qù kàn.x .ba!
董军：	太好了！我们几点见？	Dǒng Jūn:	Tài hǎo .le! Wǒ.mén *jǐ*-diǎn jiàn?
林书芳：	早上十点半，在我家见。	Lín Shūfāng:	Zǎo.shàng shí-diǎn bàn, zài wǒ jiā jiàn.

4 关键词 Guānjiàncí / Keywords

Complete each statement according to the dialogue.

1. 林书芳在 ___。 Lín Shūfāng zài ___.
2. 董军觉得包粽子 ___。 Dǒng Jūn jué.de bāo-zòng.zi ___.
3. 林书芳说(*to say*)包粽子 ___难。 Lín Shūfāng shuō bāo-zòng.zi ___ nán.
   她觉得包粽子很 ___。 Tā jué.de bāo-zòng.zi hěn ___.
4. 因为 ___要到了，所以林书芳包粽子。 Yīn.wèi ___ yào dào .le, *suǒ*.yǐ Lín Shūfāng bāo-zòng.zi.
5. 端午节的时候，除了吃粽子以外，中国人还 ___。
   Duānwǔjié .de shí.hòu, chú.le chī-zòng.zi yǐwài, Zhōng.guórén hái ___.
6. 划龙舟是一种 ___比赛。 Huá-lóngzhōu shì yì-zhǒng ___ bǐsài.
7. ___星期一是端午节。 ___ Xīngqīyī shì Duānwǔjié.
8. 林书芳要带董军去看 ___。 Lín Shūfāng yào dài Dǒng Jūn qù kàn ___.
9. 他们 ___在林书芳家见。 Tā.mén ___ zài Lín Shūfāng jiā jiàn.

文化橱窗 Wénhuà Chúchuāng
Culture Window

Dragon Boat Festival

The annual Dragon Boat Festival falls on the fifth day of the fifth lunar month, and is one of the three major Chinese festivals, together with the Spring Festival and Mid-Autumn Festival. In 2006, the Chinese government placed the Dragon Boat Festival on their first National Cultural Heritage list, and in 2009 requested that the United Nations include the Dragon Boat Festival on the World Cultural Heritage list, and it was approved.

This festival originated as a way to commemorate the ancient poet, Qu Yuan (340 B.C.-278 B.C.), who was a minister of the Chu State during the Warring States Period. He was very loyal, and was well loved by the emperor. However, this made other people jealous, so they spoke badly of Qu Yuan in front of the emperor. In the end, the emperor exiled Qu Yuan, and in his grief and worry over the state of affairs of his country, he tied rocks to his body and drowned himself in a river on the fifth of May on the lunar calendar. Because the citizens of his country admired Qu Yuan's patriotic spirit, they hurried to the river to look for his body as soon as they heard what had happened. But they couldn't find his body, so to keep the shrimp and fish from destroying his body, they filled bamboo shoots with sticky rice and threw them into the river for shrimp and

▲ Traditional shape of zongzi.

fish to eat while making a lot of noise to scare them away. Henceforth, people ate rice dumplings (粽子 *zòng.zi*) and rowed dragon boats on the lunar fifth of May each year to remember Qu Yuan.

Zongzi are made of sticky rice and other ingredients that are wrapped in bamboo leaves. There are many different kinds of dumplings. For example, some are sweet, and some are salty. People eat them while enjoying the dragon boat races. The Dragon Boat is a boat carved out of wood in the shape of a dragon, and is usually rowed by a crew of 21 people (18 rowers, 1 drummer, 1 helmsman, 1 flag-snatcher). Apart from watching the races by the river, television broadcasts also make it possible for the whole family to watch the races together on TV at home.

There are other Dragon Boat Festival customs apart from eating zongzi and dragon boat competitions, such as hanging Calamus and Artemisia plants on doors to keep the bugs and evil spirits at bay. Traditionally, the Chinese placed antibacterial herbs into cloth sachets, called 香包 *xiāngbāo*, and wore them around their necks to ward off bugs and germs. Because of the advances in medicine since then, people now wear scented sachets for good luck. There is also an "egg standing" activity that takes place during the Dragon Boat Festival. It is believed that people who succeed in making an egg stand on its own on this day will have good luck.

▲ Eggs "stand up" at noon on the day of the Dragon Boat Festival.

5 文化动动脑 Wénhuà Dòng.x nǎo / Culture Check-up

On a separate sheet of paper, write a short answer in English for each question.

1. What are the three major traditional Chinese festivals?
2. When is the Dragon Boat Festival?
3. In which year did the Chinese government place the Dragon Boat Festival on the National Cultural Heritage list?
4. The Dragon Boat Festival is a festival to remember which person, and why?
5. What is *zongzi*?
6. What kind of activity is dragon boat rowing?
7. Why do people eat zongzi and row dragon boats during the Dragon Boat Festival?
8. Why do people hang Calamus and Artemisa plants on doors?
9. What are "scented sachets" used for?
10. What do people believe will happen to people who succeed in standing an egg on its end during the Dragon Boat Festival?

Comparisons

Can you name an American holiday that celebrates or honors a person or people in history? Are there any special traditions or customs that people follow on that holiday?

6 他们在做什么？ Tā.mén zài zuò shén.me? *What are they doing?*

With a partner, take turns asking and answering what the people in the pictures are doing.

Lì.zi: A: 刘明在做什么？ Liú Míng zài zuò shén.me?
B: 他在吃冰淇淋。 Tā zài chī-bīng.qílín.

刘明 Liú Míng

1. 林军 Lín Jūn

3. 妈妈 mā.x

5. 张小姐 Zhāng *xiǎo*.jiě

2. Macy

4. 哥哥 gē.x

6. 王先生 Wáng xiān.shēng

7 句子变化 Jù.zi Biànhuà *Making Suppositions*

Add 吧 *.ba* to the following sentences to turn them into suppositions.

Lì.zi: 学期快要结束了。 Xuéqī kuài yào jiéshù .le.
学期快要结束了吧？ Xuéqī kuài yào jiéshù .le .ba?

1. 你是二年级学生。 Nǐ shì èr niánjí xué.shēng.
2. 她的名字叫董冰冰。 Tā.de míng.zì jiào Dǒng Bīng.x.
3. 董军的爸爸是日本人。 Dǒng Jūn .de bà.x shì Rì.běnrén.
4. 那是你的小狗。 Nà shì nǐ.de *xiǎo*gǒu.
5. 他们家有六口人。 Tā.mén jiā yǒu liù-kǒu rén.
6. 化学课很有意思。 Huàxuékè *hěn* yǒu yì.sī.
7. 我的一共十二元。 Wǒ.de yígòng shí'èr-yuán.
8. 你的不用找钱。 Nǐ.de búyòng zhǎo-qián.

8 一点儿也不！ Yìdiǎnr yě bù! / *Not at all!*

Make sentences using the pattern 一点儿也/都不 *yìdiǎnr yě/dōu bù* and the words provided. Follow the model.

Lì.zi: 中文 / 难 Zhōngwén / nán
中文一点儿也不难。Zhōngwén yì*diǎnr* yě bù nán.

1. 这道菜 / 热 zhè-dào cài / rè
2. 薯条 / 辣 shǔtiáo / là
3. 我 / 渴 wǒ / kě
4. 他的家 / 大 tā.de jiā / dà
5. 你们的狗 / 小 nǐ.mén.de gǒu / xiǎo
6. 上数学课 / 好玩儿 shàng shùxuékè / hǎowánr
7. 越南的冬天 / 冷 Yuènán .de dōng.tiān / lěng
8. 那个服务员 / 客气 nèi.ge fúwùyuán / kè.qì
9. 哥哥 / 饿 gē.x / è
10. 昨天的天气 / 好 zuó.tiān .de tiān.qì / hǎo
11. 这杯果汁 / 甜 zhèi-bēi guǒzhī / tián
12. 那位先生 / 有名 nèi.wèi xiān.shēng / yǒumíng

9 除了… Chú.le… / *In addition to….*

Answer the following questions by using the pattern 除了…以外，还/也… *chú.le… yǐwài, hái/yě…* and the words provided. Follow the model.

Lì.zi: 你想喝水吗？（果汁） *Nǐ* xiǎng hē-shuǐ .ma? (guǒzhǐ)
除了水以外，我还想喝果汁。
Chú.le shuǐ yǐwài, wǒ hái xiǎng hē-guǒzhī.

1. 你要点面吗？（饭） *Nǐ* yào diǎn-miàn .ma? (fàn)
2. 你要不要笔？（三张纸） Nǐ yào .bú.yào bǐ? (sān-zhāng zhǐ)
3. 你家有没有狗？（猫） Nǐ jiā yǒu .méi.yǒu gǒu? (māo)
4. 你想吃汉堡包吗？（炸鸡） *Nǐ* xiǎng chī-hànbǎobāo .ma? (zhájī)
5. 你有哥哥吗？（姐姐和妹妹） *Nǐ* yǒu gē.x .ma? (jiě.x hé mèi.x)
6. 下个星期会下雨吗？（刮风） Xià.ge xīngqī huì xià-yǔ .ma? (guā-fēng)
7. 你喜欢吃巧克力冰淇淋吗？（香草冰淇淋） *Nǐ* xǐ.huān chī-qiǎo.kèlì bīng.qílín .ma? (xiāngcǎo bīng.qílín)
8. 书包里面有化学课本吗？（中文课本） Shūbāo lǐ.miàn yǒu huàxué kèběn .ma? (Zhōngwén kèběn)
9. 这个星期有数学小考吗？（法文大考） Zhèi.ge xīngqī yǒu shùxué *xiǎo*kǎo .ma? (Fǎwén dàkǎo)
10. 你喜欢看日本电影吗？（中国电影） *Nǐ* xǐ.huān kàn Rì.běn diànyǐng .ma? (Zhōng.guó diànyǐng)

开口说 Kāikǒu Shuō

Communication

10 端午节 Duānwǔjié / *Dragon Boat Festival*

Work with a partner to play the roles of two students on a trip to China with their Chinese classes. You have both been learning about the upcoming Dragon Boat Festival and are excited to attend. Take turns asking and answering questions about the Dragon Boat Festival. Follow the cues given below.

- Talk about the Dragon Boat Festival and when it is.
- Talk about which calendar to use to find out the date of the Dragon Boat Festival each year.
- Ask about the activities that take place during the Dragon Boat Festival.
- Explain the reasons for eating zongzi and having dragon boat races.
- Arrange to go to a dragon boat race together.

11 中国节日 Zhōng.guó Jié.rì / *Chinese Festivals*

Conduct a survey of the class. Ask your classmates which of the following festivals they would choose to take part in if they were able to travel to China for only one of them. Poll ten of your classmates.

Lì.zi: A: 你想去哪个中国节日？ *Nǐ* xiǎng qù něi.ge Zhōng.guó jié.rì?

B: 我想去七夕。 *Wǒ* xiǎng qù Qīxī.

春节 Chūnjié

端午节 Duānwǔjié

中元节 Zhōngyuánjié

元宵节 Yuánxiāojié

七夕 Qīxī

中秋节 Zhōngqiūjié

12 龙舟比赛 Lóngzhōu Bǐsài / *Dragon Boat Racing*

Carefully read the flyer promoting a Dragon Boat event and then answer the questions.

1. What sort of race will take place?
2. What is this event in celebration of?
3. What is the date of this event? And what time is it?
4. If you have questions about the event, what number can you call, and whom can you ask for?

汉字天地 Hànzì Tiāndì
Chinese Characters

心 ■ xīn ■ heart; mind

The pictograph 心 *xīn*, was originally in the shape of a heart. In ancient times, Chinese people thought the heart was the organ that we used to think, which is why 心 *xīn* is also the character used for thoughts and emotions. It is also a common radical for words related to the heart or mind. When 心 *xīn* is used as a radical, it can also be written as 忄, e.g. 忆 *yì* (to remember).

Stroke Order

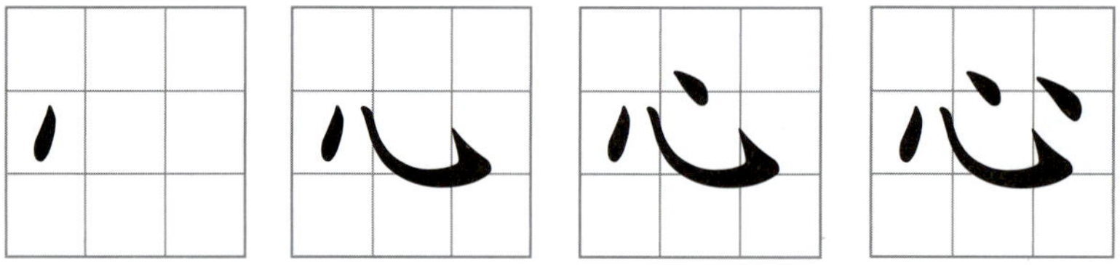

13 词汇延伸 Cíhuì Yánshēn / *Vocabulary Builder*

Below are some characters that can be combined with 心 *xīn* to create new words. Match the Chinese words on the left with the appropriate English meaning on the right.

脏 zàng *n. internal organ*	情 qíng *n. feelings*	意 yì *n. intention*	爱 ài *v. to love*	静 jìng *adj. quiet*

1. 心脏 xīnzàng — A. *mood*
2. 心情 xīnqíng — B. *beloved*
3. 心意 xīnyì — C. *wish*
4. 心爱 xīn'ài — D. *heart*
5. 心静 xīnjìng — E. *calm*

14 汉字侦探 Hànzì Zhēntàn / *Visual Detective*

Can you find 心 in the following pictures?

Unit 6

逛街去 Guàng-jiē .qù

When you have completed this unit, you will be able to...

- identify and discuss appearance, clothing, and shoes
- talk about different kinds of stores
- explain when something happened
- identify and discuss colors
- discuss prices and discounts
- negotiate and bargain
- express choices, preferences, opinions, and advice
- invite others to do something

Lesson A

发音 Fāyīn
Pronunciation

d t n l g k h z
c s zh ch sh r
+ un ong

词汇 Cíhuì
Vocabulary

衣服 Yī.fú *Clothing*

外套（外套）
wàitào
n. jacket

T恤（T恤）
T-xù
n. T-shirt

裤子（褲子）
kù.zi
n. pants

吊带衫（吊帶衫）
diàodàishān
n. spaghetti strap tank

毛衣（毛衣）
máoyī
n. sweater

衬衫（襯衫）
chènshān
n. shirt

连衣裙（連衣裙）
liányīqún
n. dress

西装（西裝）
xīzhuāng
n. suit

大衣（大衣）
dàyī
n. coat

裙子（裙子）
qún.zi
n. skirt

牛仔裤（牛仔褲）
niúzǎikù
n. jeans

背心（背心）
bèixīn
n. vest

商店 Shāngdiàn *Stores*

Language Note

To say the name of a store which sells a certain kind of product, just add 店 *diàn* after the noun to form "Noun + 店 *diàn*." For example, a store selling chocolate is 巧克力店 *qiǎo.kèlì diàn*; a store selling ice cream is 冰淇淋店 *bīng.qílín diàn*.

A: 下课以后，你要去哪里（下課以後，你要去哪裡）？
Xià-kè yǐhòu, nǐ yào qù *nǎ*.lǐ? *Where will you go after class?*

B: 我要去百货商店买几件衣服（我要去百貨商店買幾件衣服）。
Wǒ yào qù bǎihuò shāngdiàn *mǎi* jǐ-jiàn yī.fú. *I'm going to the department store to buy some clothes.*

A: 你要买什么衣服（你要買什麼衣服）？
Nǐ yào mǎi shén.me yī.fú? *What clothes are you going to buy?*

B: 我想买两件衬衫（我想買兩件襯衫）。
Wǒ xiǎng mǎi liǎng-jiàn chènshān. *I want to buy two shirts.*

A: 你自己去书店吗（你自己去書店嗎）？
Nǐ zìjǐ qù shūdiàn .ma? *Are you going to the bookstore by yourself?*

B: 不，我跟国华一起去（不，我跟國華一起去）。
Bù, wǒ gēn Guóhuá yìqǐ qù. *No, I'm going with Guohua.*

A: 星期天我可以去你家玩电子游戏吗(星期天我可以去你家玩電子遊戲嗎)?

Xīngqītiān *wǒ kě*.yǐ qù nǐ jiā wán diànzǐ yóuxì .ma? *Can I go to your house to play video games on Sunday?*

B: 不好意思，这个星期天不行(不好意思，這個星期天不行)。

Bù hǎoyì.sī, zhèi.gè Xīngqītiān bù xíng. *I'm sorry, but I can't this Sunday.*

Reflexive Pronouns			
我 →	我自己(我自己) wǒ zìjǐ, *myself*	我们 →	我们自己(我們自己) wǒ.mén zìjǐ, *ourselves*
你 →	你自己(你自己) nǐ zìjǐ, *yourself*	你们 →	你们自己(你們自己) nǐ.mén zìjǐ, *yourselves*
他 →	他自己(他自己) tā zìjǐ, *himself*	他们 →	他们自己(他們自己) tā.mén zìjǐ, *themselves*
她 →	她自己(她自己) tā zìjǐ, *herself*	她们 →	她们自己(她們自己) tā.mén zìjǐ, *themselves*

Measure Words

件(件)	jiàn	*used for a piece of clothing*
条(條)	tiáo	*used for a pair of pants or a skirt*

Nouns

商店(商店)	shāngdiàn	*store; shop*

Pronouns

自己(自己)	zìjǐ	*oneself*

Time Words

以前(以前)	yǐqián	*before; formerly; previously*
以后(以後)	yǐhòu	*after; afterward*

Verbs

行(行)	xíng	*to be all right*
旅行(旅行)	lǚxíng	*to travel*
买(買)	mǎi	*to buy*

Verb-Objects

下课(下課)	xià-kè	*to finish class*

1 这是什么？ Zhè .shì shén.me? *What is this?*

Listen to the recording and select the letter of the clothing item that you hear.

A.

C.

E.

G.

B.

D.

F.

H.

2 辨认方位 Biànrèn Fāngwèi *Locate Stores*

Say the location of each store according to the map below.

Lì.zi: 宠物店在百货商店右边。 Chǒngwùdiàn zài bǎihuò shāngdiàn yòu.biān.

3 几件衣服? Jǐ-jiàn yī.fú? *How many pieces of clothing?*

Macy is going abroad tomorrow. Look at her luggage and say what clothes she has packed and how many pieces of each item of clothing there are.

4 个人问题 Gèrén Wèntí *Personal Questions*

Answer each question in Chinese.

1. 你今天穿什么衣服? Nǐ jīn.tiān chuān shén.me yī.fú?
2. 上课的时候，你可以穿吊带衫吗? Shàng-kè .de shíhòu, *nǐ kě*yǐ chuān diàodàishān .ma?
3. 你喜欢什么衣服? *Nǐ* xǐ.huān shén.me yī.fú?
4. 你喜欢穿衬衫吗? *Nǐ* xǐ.huān chuān chènshān .ma?
5. 你有几条牛仔裤? *Nǐ yǒu* jǐ-tiáo niúzǎikù?
6. 下课以后，你要去书店吗? Xià-kè yǐhòu, nǐ yào qù shūdiàn .ma?

句型介绍 Jùxíng Jièshào

Language Patterns

The Time Words 以前 yǐqián and 以后 yǐhòu

The verb *以前 yǐqián* means "before," and *以后 yǐhòu* means "after." It is used after a noun phrase, a verb phrase or a clause that refers to a specific action or point in time.

以前 yǐqián and 以后 yǐhòu are Time Words

他以前住在日本。 Tā yǐqián zhù zài Rìběn.

我以后想去中国工作。 *Wǒ* yǐhòu xiǎng qù Zhōng.guó gōngzuò.

Amount of Time + 以前 *yǐqián* / 以后 *yǐhòu* = time ago / after

三年以前 sān nián yǐqián; 两年以后 liǎng nián yǐhòu

Verbal Clause + 以前 *yǐqián* / 以后 *yǐhòu* = Before / After….

上中文课以前，我要读中文。 Shàng Zhōngwén kè yǐqián, wǒ yào dú Zhōngwén.

下课以后，他们要去篮球场。 Xià-kè yǐhòu, tā.mén yào qù lánqiúchǎng.

Comparisons

Is the usage of "before" and "after" in Chinese different than the English?

The Numeral 几 jǐ

The word *几 jǐ* means "several, a few." It is used to indicate an unknown number.

几 *jǐ* + Measure Word + Noun

张小姐想去商店买几件衣服。 Zhāng *xiǎo.jiě* xiǎng qù shāngdiàn *mǎi* jǐ-jiàn yī.fú.

我有几本书可以借给你。 *Wǒ yǒu jǐ*-běn shū *kě*yǐ jiè *gěi* nǐ.

For numbers which are not so precise, the word *几 jǐ* can also be used to refer to the unclear range in the decimal system.

Number (10, 20, 30, …, 90) + 几 *jǐ* + Measure Word + Noun

他有十几件T恤。 Tā yǒu shí jǐ jiàn T-xù.

我的学校有三十几个中国学生。 Wǒ.de xuéxiào yǒu sān.shí jǐ .gè Zhōng.guó xué.shēng.

The Pronoun 自己 zìjǐ

The pronoun 自己 *zìjǐ* means "self." It is combined with a pronoun or a noun to refer "(one)self."

Noun / Pronoun + **自己 *zìjǐ***

昨天我自己去游泳。 Zuó.tiān wǒ zìjǐ qù yóuyǒng.

The personal pronoun (he/she/it) can be omitted if it has already been mentioned.

他不要自己去买衣服。 Tā bú yào zìjǐ qù mǎi yī.fú.

林小姐不喜欢自己旅行。 Lín *xiǎo*.jiě bù xǐ.huān zìjǐ qù lǚxíng.

会话 Huìhuà

Dialogue

下课以后 Xià-kè Yǐhòu *After Class*

In the classroom, Zhang Guohua is talking to Dong Jun.

董军：	下课以后，你要不要打电子游戏？	Dǒng Jūn:	Xià-kè yǐhòu, nǐ yào .bú.yào dǎ diànzǐ yóuxì?
张国华：	不好意思，今天不行。	Zhāng Guóhuá:	Bù hǎoyì.sī, jīn.tiān bù xíng.
董军：	你要做什么？	Dǒng Jūn:	Nǐ yào zuò shén.me?
张国华：	我要去百货商店。	Zhāng Guóhuá:	Wǒ yào qù bǎihuò shāngdiàn.
董军：	百货商店！为什么？	Dǒng Jūn:	Bǎihuò shāngdiàn! Wèishén.me?
张国华：	我要买衣服，下个月我要去日本旅行。	Zhāng Guóhuá:	Wǒ yào mǎi yī.fú, xià.gè yuè wǒ yào qù Rìběn lǚxíng.
董军：	你要买什么衣服？	Dǒng Jūn:	Nǐ yào mǎi shén.me yī.fú?
张国华：	一件外套、几条裤子和几件毛衣。	Zhāng Guóhuá:	Yí-jiàn wàitào, jǐ-tiáo kù.zi hé jǐ-jiàn máoyī.
董军：	你自己去吗？	Dǒng Jūn:	Nǐ zìjǐ qù .ma?
张国华：	不，我跟我妈妈去。	Zhāng Guóhuá:	Bù, wǒ gēn wǒ mā.x qù.

5 要买什么? Yào mǎi shén.me? *What to buy?*

Point to each picture and say in Chinese the clothes that Zhang Guohua wants to buy.

1. 	3. 	5. 
2. 	4. 	6. 

6 选一选 Xuǎn .Yì Xuǎn *Multiple Choice*

Select the correct answer to each question based on the dialogue.

1. 张国华下课以后要做什么? Zhāng Guóhuá xià-kè yǐhòu yào zuò shén.me?
   a. 去董军家 qù Dǒng Jūn jiā　　b. 去图书馆 qù túshūguǎn
   c. 去百货商店 qù bǎihuò shāngdiàn

2. 为什么张国华要去那个地方? Wèishén.me Zhāng Guóhuá yào qù nèi.gè dì.fāng?
   a. 他要念书 tā yào niàn-shū　　b. 他要买衣服 tā yào mǎi yī.fú
   c. 他要玩电子游戏 tā yào wán diànzǐ yóuxì

3. 张国华什么时候要去旅行? Zhāng Guóhuá shén.me shíhòu yào qù lǚxíng?
   a. 下个周末 xià.gè zhōumò　　b. 下个星期五 xià.gè Xīngqīwǔ
   c.下个月 xià.gè yuè

4. 张国华要去哪儿旅行? Zhāng Guóhuá yào qù nǎr lǚxíng?
   a. 日本 Rìběn　　b. 中国 Zhōng.guó
   c. 韩国 Hán.guó

5. 张国华跟谁去买衣服? Zhāng Guóhuá gēn shéi qù mǎi yī.fú?
   a.他自己 tā zìjǐ　　b. 他妈妈 tā mā.x
   c. 董军 Dǒng Jūn

文化橱窗 Wénhuà Chúchuāng

Culture Window

China's Cultural Influences on Japan

▲ Where Japan is to China.

Japan is an archipelago to the northeast of China. Although the two countries are separated by sea, Chinese culture has influenced Japan for a very long time. Japan's first interaction with China was in the second century when Japan sent representatives to render tribute to the Chinese emperor. The interactions between the two countries reached a peak in the Tang Dynasty (618-907 A.D.) when Japan went through the "Taika Reform," during which they incorporated Chinese culture into their own. China's interactions with Japan waned with the demise of the Tang Dynasty. Nowadays, the relationship between the two countries is politically distant, but economically intimate.

During the Taika Reform, Japan sent monks and students to China to learn about Chinese culture, the Chinese political system, Chinese text, Buddhism, art and medicine. During the Reform, the Japanese changed their preexisting aristocratic government to centralize and enhance the power of the imperial court. Nowadays, the Japanese royalty no longer have any actual power, but are still important public figures. Japanese was originally a text-less language. Written Japanese developed gradually from Chinese characters. Even now, many Japanese people enjoy learning how to write Kanji: characters that were adopted from written Chinese and are now used in Japanese text. The Japanese regard the ability to write Kanji as a mark of an educated person. Since 1975, approximately 30,000 people have taken the Japanese Kanji Proficiency Test.

Japan's Kyoto city was modeled after Chinese cities of the Tang Dynasty. At the time, Kyoto was divided into east and west; east was a replica of China's Luoyang, and west was a replica of China's Chang'an. Because western Kyoto is full of swamps, most of Kyoto's urban developments were restricted to the east, which is why some people still call Kyoto "Luoyang."

Japanese Kimonos are also similar to China's Tang-fus or Wu-Fus. Even now, some kimono stores in Japan still have "Wu-fu (吴服)" written on them. Although Japanese kimonos are different from Chinese-style clothing, there are some shared characteristics such as overlapping lapels (right over left) and wide sleeves.

Japan has its famous "three daos" (三道): *chadou* (茶道), *kado* (花道) and *shodo* (书道). *Chadou* and *shodo* were both cultural influences from China. The Japanese *chadou* originated from the Chinese tea culture, which the Japanese have turned into a social ceremony. It is said that "China is the homeland of the *chadou* of Japan." As for calligraphy (*shodo*), this Chinese art form became extremely popular in Japan and is considered by some to be a form of relaxation.

▲ Japanese chadou (dao of tea).

7 文化动动脑 Wénhuà Dòng.x nǎo / *Culture Check-up*

Complete each statement with an appropriate word or expression.

1. Japan's first interaction with China was in the ___ century when Japan sent representatives to render tributes to the Chinese emperor.
2. The interactions between the two countries reached a peak in the ___ (618-907 A.D.)
3. The "___" is to incorporate Chinese culture into Japanese culture.
4. Nowadays, the relationship between the two countries is "___ distant but ___ intimate."
5. Japanese was originally a ___ language.
6. Written Japanese was developed from ___ characters.
7. Japan's ___ city was modeled after Chinese cities of the Tang Dynasty as references.
8. Japan has its famous "three daos" (三道): ___ (茶道), ___ (花道) and ___ (书道).
9. It is said that "China is the homeland of the ___ of Japan."

Language Practice

8 以前还是以后? Yǐqián hái.shì Yǐhòu? / *Before or After?*

Look at the timelines below. Based on the direction of the red arrow, complete the following sentence using 以前 *yǐqián* or 以后 *yǐhòu*. Follow the model.

Lì.zi: 你有几个考试? *Nǐ yǒu* jǐ-.gè kǎoshì?

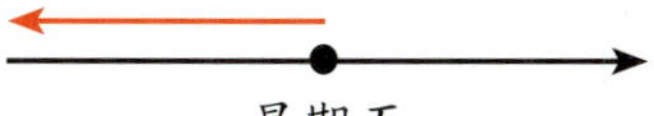

星期五以前，你有几个考试? Xīngqīwǔ yǐqián, *nǐ yǒu* jǐ-.gè kǎoshi?

1.  星期三	3.  下课	5.  吃早餐
她有中文课吗? Tā yǒu Zhōngwén kè .ma?	你要不要打棒球? Nǐ yào .bú.yào dǎ bàngqiú?	他要喝一杯咖啡。 Tā yào hē yì-bēi kāfēi.
2.  十一月	4.  早上九点	6.  中午
我要去美国旅行。 Wǒ yào qù Měi.guó lǚxíng.	我们要去游泳。 Wǒ.mén yào qù yóuyǒng	这儿会下雨。 Zhèr huì xià-yǔ.

9 自己去… Zìjǐ Qù… Go by Oneself

Describe the following pictures using 自己 *zìjǐ*. Follow the model.

Lì.zi: Judy自己看电影。 Judy zìjǐ kàn-diànyǐng.

1. 他 *tā*

3. 姐姐 *jiě.x*

5. 小意 *Xiǎoyì*

2. Lisa

4. 马老师 *Mǎ lǎoshī*

6. 李先生 *Lǐ xiān.shēng*

10 换句话说 Huàn jù huà shuō Paraphrasing

Use 几 *jǐ* to replace the numbers in the sentences below. Follow the model.

Lì.zi: 我的中文课有20~24个人。
Wǒ.de Zhōngwén-kè yǒu èrshí dào èrshísì-.gè rén.

我的中文课有二十几个人。 Wǒ.de Zhōngwén kè yǒu èrshí jǐ .gè rén.

1. 我有12、13枝笔。 *Wǒ* yǒu shí'èr, shísān-zhī bǐ.
2. 他有54、55块。 Tā *yǒu* wǔ.shísì, wǔ.shíwǔ-kuài.
3. 弟弟有35、36件T恤。 Dì.x yǒu sān.shíwǔ, sān.shíliù-jiàn T-xù.
4. 他借给我44、45本中文书。 Tā jiè *gěi* wǒ sì.shísì, sì.shí*wǔ*-běn Zhōngwén-shū.
5. 他们有88、89个中国朋友。 Tā.mén yǒu bā.shíbā, bā.shíjiǔ-.gè Zhōng.guó péng.yǒu.
6. 上个学期我有27、28个考试。 Shàng.gè xuéqī *wǒ* yǒu èr.shíqī, èr.shíbā-.gè kǎoshì.

开口说 Kāikǒu Shuō

Communication

11 想去逛街吗? Xiǎng qù guàng-jiē .ma? *Do you want to go shopping?*

With a partner, play the roles of two people talking about going shopping at a department store.

- A tells B that A wants to go to the department store. B asks why.
- B asks A what A wants to buy.
- B asks A why A wants to buy those things.
- B asks A who A will go to the department store with.

12 他们穿什么? Tā.mén chuān shén.me? *What do they wear?*

With a partner, take turns asking and telling what the following six people are wearing. Follow the model.

Lì.zi: **A:** 他穿什么? Tā chuān shén.me?

B: 他穿T恤和裤子。 Tā chuān T-xù hé kù.zi.

1.

2.

3.

4.

5.

6.

The following is a promotional poster for "NY Fashion" women's clothing store. Read the text, then answer the questions below.

1. What clothing is not sold in NY Fashion?
   a. pants
   b. sweaters
   c. dresses
2. How much is a skirt?
3. Cai Xiaohua bought two dresses and a coat. How much did she spend?
4. Dresses are cheaper if you buy how many at once? How much would you be able to save?

汉字天地 Hànzì Tiāndì

Chinese Characters

衣 ■ yī ■ clothes

The pictograph 衣 *yī* has two parts. The upper part is like the head and shoulders of a person, and the rest resembles an overlapping collar. It is also a common radical for words related to clothes. When 衣 *yī* is used as a radical, it can also be written as 衤, as used in 裙 *qún* and 衫 *shān*.

Stroke Order

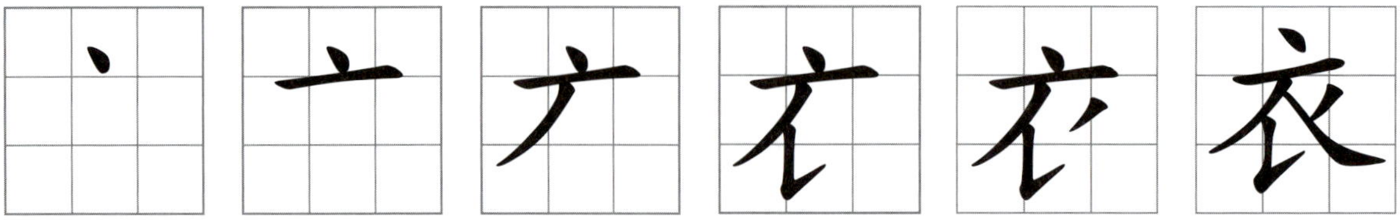

15 词汇延伸 Cíhuì Yánshēn *Vocabulary Builder*

Below are some characters that can be combined with 衣 *yī* to create new words. Match the Chinese words on the left with the appropriate English meaning on the right.

橱 chú	架 jià	毛 máo	内 nèi	睡 shuì
n. cabinet	*n. rack*	*n. wool*	*adj. inside*	*v. to sleep*

1. 衣橱 yīchú
2. 衣架 yījià
3. 毛衣 máoyī
4. 内衣 nèiyī
5. 睡衣 shuìyī

A. *pajamas*
B. *underwear*
C. *sweater*
D. *clothes hanger*
E. *closet*

16 汉字侦探 Hànzì Zhēntàn *Visual Detective*

Can you find 衣 in the following pictures?

Lesson B

发音 Fāyīn
Pronunciation

j q x n l + ü üe

词汇 Cíhuì
Vocabulary

颜色 Yán.sè *Color*

红色 (紅色)
hóng.sè
n. red

蓝色 (藍色)
lán.sè
n. blue

米色 (米色)
mǐ.sè
n. beige

粉红色 (粉紅色)
fěnhóng.sè
n. pink

紫色 (紫色)
zǐ.sè
n. purple

白色 (白色)
bái.sè
n. white

咖啡色 (咖啡色)
kāfēi.sè
n. brown

绿色 (綠色)
lǜ.sè
n. green

灰色 (灰色)
huī.sè
n. gray

橘黄色 (橘黃色)
júhuáng.sè
n. orange

黄色 (黃色)
huáng.sè
n. yellow

黑色 (黑色)
hēi.sè
n. black

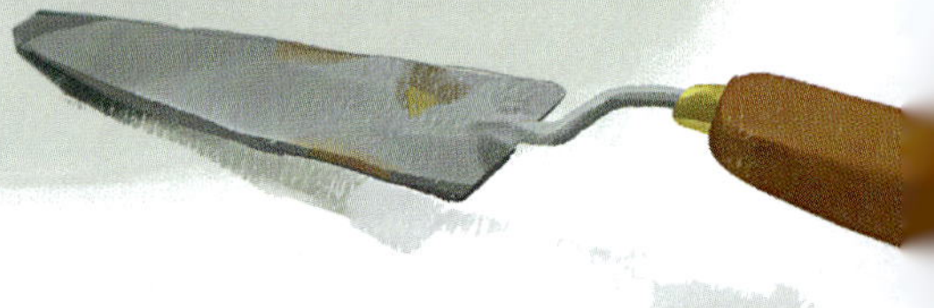

Let's count!

一千 (一千) yì-qiān *one thousand (1,000)*	一万 (一萬) yí-wàn *ten thousand*	十万 (十萬) shí-wàn *one hundred thousand*	百万 (百萬) bǎiwàn *a million*
千万 (千萬) qiānwàn *ten million*	亿 (億) yì *a hundred million*	十亿 (十億) shí-yì *a billion*	

A: 这件大衣多少钱 (這件大衣多少錢)?
Zhèi-jiàn dàyī duō.shǎo qián? *How much is this coat?*

B: 一万三千元 (一萬三千元)。
Yí-wàn sān-qiān yuán. *13 thousand (13,000) yuan.*

A: 中国有多少人 (中國有多少人)?
Zhōng.guó yǒu duō.shǎo rén? *What's the population of China?*

B: 十三亿人 (十三億人)。
Shísān-yì rén. *1.3 billion people.*

A: 这件红色的T恤真漂亮 (這件紅色的T恤真漂亮)。
Zhèi-jiàn hóng.sè .de T-xù zhēn piào.liàng. *This red T-shirt is really pretty.*

B: 这件蓝色的呢 (這件藍色的呢)?
Zhèi-jiàn lán.sè .de .ne? *What about this blue one?*

A: 这件咖啡色的外套多少钱 (這件咖啡色的外套多少錢)?
Zhèi-jiàn kāfēi.sè .de wàitào duō.shǎo qián? *How much is this brown coat?*

B: 两千元 (兩千元)。
Liǎng-qiān yuán. *2,000 yuan.*

A: 牛仔裤有折扣吗 (牛仔褲有折扣嗎)?

Niúzǎikù yǒu zhékòu .ma? *Is there a discount for this pair of jeans?*

B: 有，打八折 (有，打八折)。

Yǒu, dǎ bā-zhé. *Yes, it's 20% off.*

这条裙子打几折
(這條裙子打幾折)?
Zhèi-tiáo qún.zi *dǎ* jǐ-zhé?
How much of a discount does this skirt have?

五折(五折)。
Wǔ-zhé. *50% off.*

Adjectives

长 (長)	cháng	*long*
短 (短)	duǎn	*short*
漂亮 (漂亮)	piào.liàng	*beautiful; pretty*
便宜 (便宜)	pián.yí	*cheap*
好看 (好看)	hǎokàn	*(to look) fine; nice*
贵 (貴)	guì	*expensive*

Nouns

折扣 (折扣)	zhékòu	*discount*

Verbs

知道 (知道)	zhī.dào	*to know*
选 (選)	xuǎn	*to choose; to select*

Verb-Objects

打折 (打折)	dǎ-zhé	*to sell at a discount price*

1 哪个颜色? Něi.gè yán.sè? *Which color?*

With a partner, take turns asking and answering which color each person likes. Follow the model.

Lì.zi: A: 芳芳喜欢哪个颜色? Fāng.fāng xǐ.huān něi.gè yán.sè?

B: 她喜欢白色。Tā xǐ.huān bái.sè.

1. 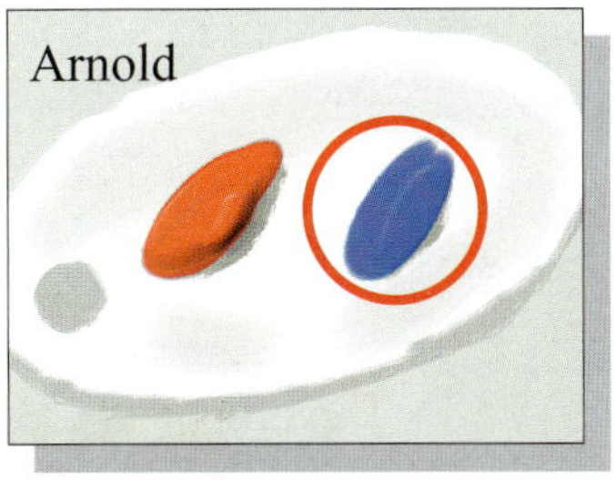

2. 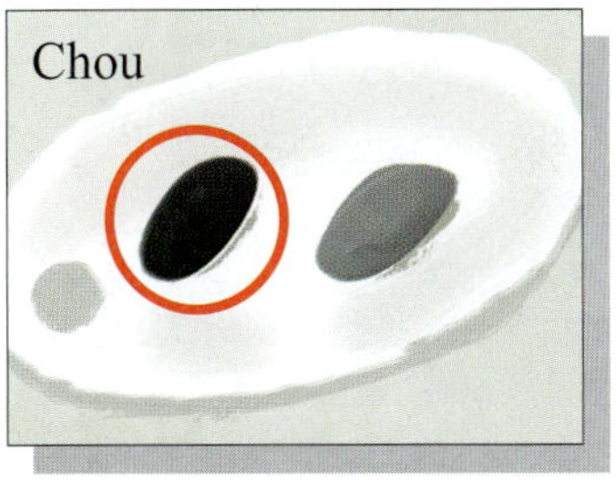

3. 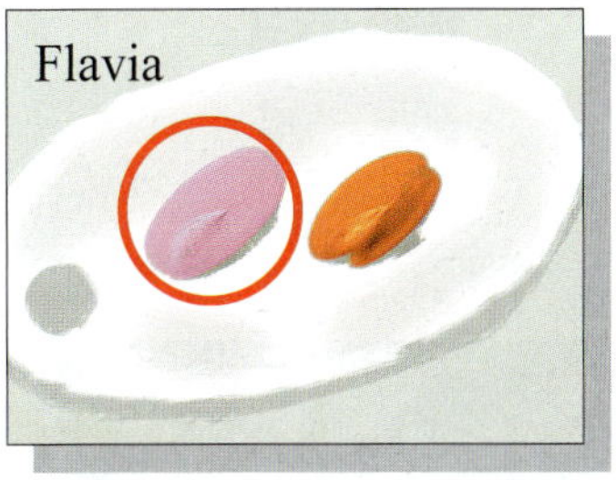

4. 

5. 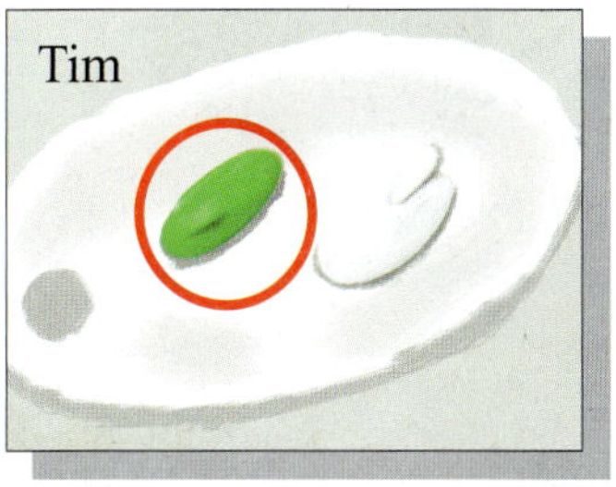

6. 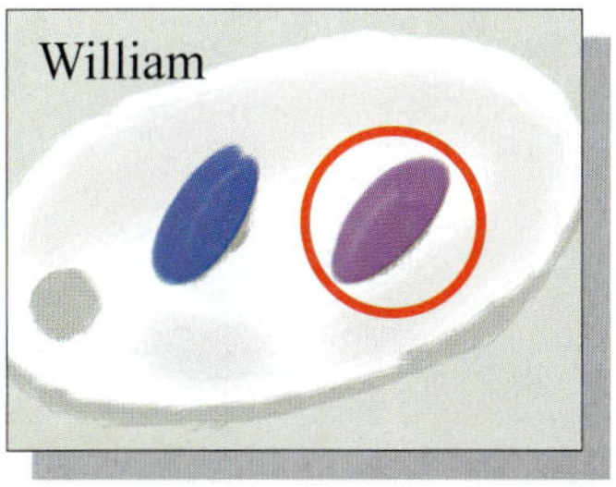

2 这是… Zhè .shì… *This is…*

Look at the pictures and name each object and its color.

Lì.zi: 这是紫色的杯子。Zhè .shì zǐ.sè .de bēi.zi.

1. 

2. 

3. 

4. 

5. 

6. 

3 多少钱? Duō.shǎo qián? *How much?*

Look at the prices below and say how much each item costs.

1. 

3. 

5. 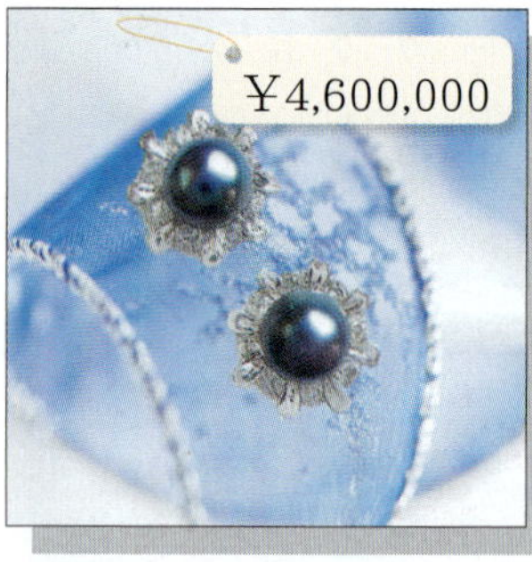

2. 

4. 

6. 

句型介绍 Jùxíng Jièshào

Language Patterns

Omission of Nouns

Either in conversation or in writing, if a certain noun is mentioned again in the dialogue and is clearly known by both listener and speaker, then the noun can be omitted, but 的 *.de* should be kept.

A: 这件蓝色的衬衫真漂亮。 Zhèi-jiàn lán.sè .de chènshān zhēn piào.liàng.
B: 我不喜欢。 Wǒ bù xǐ.huān.
A: 这件灰色的呢? Zhèi-jiàn huī.sè .de .ne?

A: 这是谁的中文课本? Zhè .shì shéi .de Zhōngwén kèběn?
B: 这是我的。 Zhè .shì wǒ .de.

The Phrase 打…折 *dǎ … zhé*

The word 折 *zhé* is short for 折扣 *zhékòu*, which means "discount." 打…折 *dǎ … zhé* means that an item is sold at the certain percentage of the original price. For example, 打九折 *dǎ jiǔ-zhé* means that the item is 10% off, 打八折 *dǎ bā-zhé* means that the item is 20% off, and so forth. To ask how much of a discount something has, use the phrase 打几折 *dǎ jǐ-zhé*.

A: 这本书打几折？ Zhèi-běn shū *dǎ* jǐ-zhé?

B: 打七折。 Dǎ qī-zhé.

A: 这件衣服有折扣吗？ Zhèi-jiàn yī.fú yǒu zhékòu .ma?

B: 有，打四折。 Yǒu, dǎ sì-zhé.

会话 Huìhuà *Dialogue*

跟妈妈逛街 Gēn mā.x guàng-jiē *Shopping with Mom*

Mrs. Zhang and Zhang Guohua are shopping in a department store.

张妈妈：	这条红色的长裤真漂亮。	Zhāng mā.x:	Zhèi-tiáo hóng.sè .de chángkù zhēn piào.liàng.
张国华：	红色的裤子很奇怪。	Zhāng Guóhuá:	Hóng.sè .de kù.zi hěn qíguài.
张妈妈：	这条白色的呢？这件又便宜又好看。	Zhāng mā.x:	Zhèi-tiáo bái.sè .de .ne? Zhèi-jiàn yòu pián.yí yòu hǎokàn.
张国华：	你知道我不喜欢白色。我喜欢黑色。我要自己选。	Zhāng Guóhuá:	Nǐ zhī.dào wǒ bù xǐ.huān bái.sè. *Wǒ* xǐ.huān hēi.sè. Wǒ yào zì*jǐ* xuǎn.

Zhang Guohua is looking through the pants.

张妈妈：	这条黑色的怎么样？	Zhāng Guóhuá:	Zhèi-tiáo hēi.sè .de zěn.meyàng?
张妈妈：	不错。多少钱？	Zhāng mā.x:	Búcuò. Duōshǎo qián?
张国华：	一千两百五十块。	Zhāng Guóhuá:	Yì-qiān *liǎng-bǎi* wǔ.shí-kuài.
张妈妈：	太贵了！没有折扣吗？	Zhāng mā.x:	Tài guì .le! Méi.yǒu zhékòu .ma?
张国华：	有折扣。	Zhāng Guóhuá:	Yǒu zhékòu.
张妈妈：	打几折？	Zhāng mā.x:	*Dǎ* jǐ-zhé?
张国华：	这件打八折。	Zhāng Guóhuá:	Zhèi-jiàn dǎ bā-zhé.

4 什么颜色的裤子? Shén.me yán.sè .de kù.zi? *What color pants?*

Look at the following pictures and say what color pants Mrs. Zhang and Zhang Guohua like.

1. 

2. 

3. 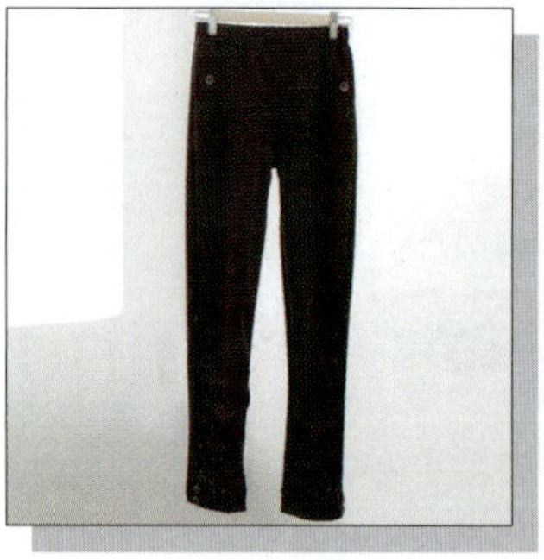

5 对还是错? Duì hái.shì cuò? *True or false?*

Decide if each statement is true or false based on the dialogue. Correct any false statements.

1. 张国华跟爸爸妈妈一起去百货商店。
   Zhāng Guóhuá gēn bà.x mā.x yìqǐ qù bǎihuò shāngdiàn.
2. 张妈妈喜欢粉红色的裤子。
   Zhāng mā.x xǐ.huān fěnhóng.sè .de kù.zi.
3. 张国华喜欢白色的裤子。
   Zhāng Guóhuá xǐ.huān bái.sè .de kù.zi.
4. 张妈妈觉得白色的裤子又便宜又好看。
   Zhāng mā.x jué.de bái.sè .de kù.zi yòu pián.yí yòu hǎokàn.
5. 张国华觉得那条红色的长裤很漂亮。
   Zhāng Guóhuá jué.de nèi-tiáo hóng.sè .de chángkù hěn piào.liàng.
6. 张国华不要妈妈选裤子给他。
   Zhāng Guóhuá bú yào mā.x xuǎn kù.zi gěi tā.
7. 妈妈不喜欢张国华选的裤子。
   Mā.x bù xǐ.huān Zhāng Guóhuá xuǎn .de kù.zi.
8. 张国华选的裤子有折扣。
   Zhāng Guóhuá xuǎn .de kù.zi yǒu zhékòu.
9. 张妈妈觉得一千两百五十块的裤子太贵了。
   Zhāng mā.x jué.de yì-qiān *liǎng-bǎi* wǔshí-kuài .de kù.zi tài guì .le.
10. 打折以后，那条黑色的裤子要一千两百块。
    Dǎ-zhé yǐhòu, nèi-tiáo hēi.sè .de kù.zi yào yì-qiān *liǎng*-bǎi-kuài.

文化橱窗 Wénhuà Chúchuāng

Culture Window

The Meaning of Colors for the Chinese People

The meaning of colors for the Chinese people are mostly influenced by the Wu Xing (五行 *Wǔ Xíng*, Five elements/movements/phases) concepts of metal (金 *jīn*), wood (木 *mù*), water (水 *shuǐ*), fire (火 *huǒ*), earth (土 *tǔ*). Traditionally, the Chinese thought that all things in nature were made up of these five elements, each with its own representative color. This, together with mythical legends and the feudal system, influenced the color preferences of the Chinese people.

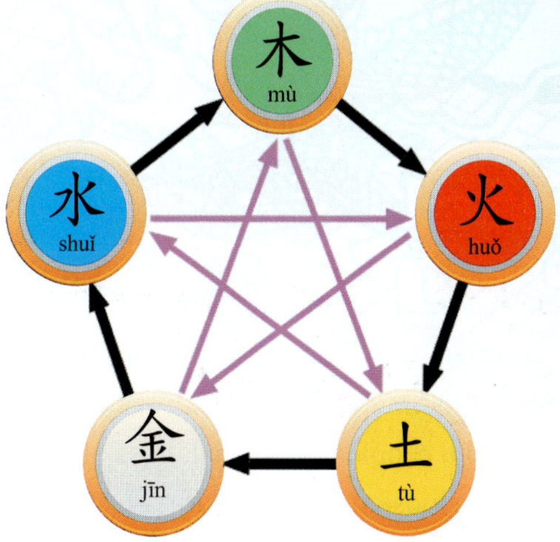

▲ Five elements (Wu Xing).

The color white represents purity in Western countries and Japan, which is why most wedding gowns are white. However, in China, white corresponds to "metal," which represents autumn and mourning. Hence, in countries with historically Chinese roots, white is often used in funerals or to represent surrender.

▲ Bride in red wedding gown.

Green represents "wood" in Wu Xing, and is the color of plants. In Chinese culture, green signifies life and spring.

Red is the color for "fire," and is used in temples to ward off evil and in festivals to represent fortune and happiness. Red is the color that most represents Chinese culture, and is used widely on many occasions such as birthdays, weddings (the color of wedding gowns), and the Chinese New Year (spring couplets and red envelopes, etc.).

In ancient China, black represented the north. Black also represents "water," and means honor and subtlety. For example, rulers of the Qin Dynasty (221-207 B.C.) came from China's northwest, so they especially loved the color black that represented the north and water. They even named black the national color of Qin. In fact, many existing portraits of Qin Shi Huang show him wearing a black robe.

Yellow represents "earth" in Wu Xing. China was an agricultural nation, so ownership of land meant ownership of food. Yellow is also the color of gold, so for the Chinese, yellow came to represent wealth and riches. As Chinese merchants became richer, they started to wear clothes of extravagant yellow silk like the emperor. Thus, a rule was made in the Song Dynasty (10th century, A.D.) that only the emperor could wear bright yellow—an example of the Chinese preference of using colors to implement the rules of feudal society.

Apart from the five colors mentioned above, other colors also have meanings for the Chinese. Purple, for example, is regarded as the color of royalty. Legend has it that purple clouds in the sky are a sign from God that a new ruler has appeared, and the country will be moving into a new dynasty. Hence, purple is a color that is well-loved by rulers of all dynasties, to show that his/her rulership has been blessed by God. Purple is not only loved by the aristocrats, but has also been used to name palaces, such as Qing Dynasty's Purple Forbidden City (紫禁城 *Zǐjìnchéng*).

▲ Yellow, the color for emperors.

Chinese Traditional Dress

Whenever Chinese traditional dress is mentioned, most will think of the cheongsam, changshan or other such clothing. Yet, technically speaking, those are clothing of the Qing Dynasty and thus, clothing of the Manchu people. Traditional dress of the Han Chinese are called Hanfu (or simply referred to as 'silk robes,') and are loose-fitting with large sleeves and belts that open at the collar on the right hand side. Different styles are worn for people of different social status.

Hanfu are linear in design, making them seem like they lack dimension. However, because the cloth used in Hanfu far surpasses the amount necessary to cover up a human body, the excess fabric plus the belt allows for movement and a different sense of beauty when viewed from different angles.

Throughout history, the Chinese have been ruled by different tribes. Using Hanfu as a basic style, each era saw clothing with new elements incorporated into it. In 7th century A.D., the Wu Hu people from the northern border ruled the Tang Dynasty. Compared to the Han Chinese, the Hu were more liberal in their beliefs and loved to ride horses, and so clothing back then had lots of round necks and narrow sleeves; clothes for women were also much more liberal in design.

No matter the origin of clothing, the Chinese place great emphasis on the choice of fabric and fineness of handiwork as well as the aura the clothing would give its wearer.

▶ Qipao (cheongsam for females).

Comparisons

Take 5 minutes to make a list of some traditional or special clothing items worn throughout history in the United States. When time is up, choose one clothing item on your list and compare it with one of the traditional Chinese clothing items mentioned in the reading.

6 文化动动脑 Wénhuà Dòng.x nǎo / *Culture Check-up*

Complete each statement with an appropriate word or expression.

1. The meaning of colors for the Chinese people are mostly influenced by the ___ concepts of metal, wood, water, fire, and earth.
2. In China, white corresponds to "___," which represents autumn and mourning.
3. ___ represents "wood" in Wu Xing, and is the color of plants; it also signifies life and spring in Chinese culture.
4. ___ is the color that most represents Chinese culture.
5. ___ is the color of the Qin Dynasty (221-207 B.C.).
6. For the Chinese, ___ came to represent wealth and riches.
7. ___ is regarded as the color of royalty.
8. Purple is not only loved by the aristocrats, but has also been used to name ___, such as Qing Dynasty's Purple Forbidden City.
9. Whenever Chinese traditional dress is mentioned, most will think of the ___, ___ or other such clothing.
10. Traditional dress of the Han Chinese are called ___ (or simply referred to as 'silk robes.')
11. Compared to the Han Chinese, the Hu were more ___ in their beliefs and the clothing.

Language Practice

7 多少钱? Duō.shǎo qián? / *How much?*

Look at the price tags below and read them aloud in Chinese.

1. 漂亮百货 ¥29
2. 漂亮百货 ¥655
3. 漂亮百货 ¥5,200
4. 漂亮百货 ¥88,888
5. 漂亮百货 ¥74,290
6. 漂亮百货 ¥160,000
7. 漂亮百货 ¥4,200,000
8. 漂亮百货 ¥19,550,000
9. 漂亮百货 ¥12,500,000
10. 漂亮百货 ¥336,000,000

8 打几折? Dǎ jǐ-zhé? How much of a discount?

Below are some discount tags with discounts written on them. Say what each discount would be in Chinese using the 打#折 *dǎ # zhé* phrase.

Lì.zi: 打七折。 Dǎ qī-zhé.

1. 

2. 

3. 

4. 

5. 

6. 

7. 

8. 

9 精打细算 Jīngdǎ Xìsuàn Careful Calculation

Calculate how much each item below will cost after the discount. Then, with a partner, take turns asking and telling the sale price of each item.

Lì.zi: **A:** 这件吊带衫打几折? Zhèi-jiàn diàodàishān *dǎ* jǐ-zhé?

B: 打八折。 Dǎ bā-zhé.

A: 打八折以后,多少钱? Dǎ bā-zhé yǐhòu, duō.shǎo qián?

B: 六十四块。 Liù.shísì-kuài.

1. 

2. 

3. 

4. 

5. 

6. 

7. 

8. 

10 长话短说 Cháng huà Duǎn shuō *Less for More*

Answer each question in a way that only repeats the necessary information. Follow the model.

Lì.zi: 这是中文课的教室吗？(英文课)

Zhè .shì Zhōngwén kè .de jiàoshì .ma? (Yīngwé kè)

不，这是英文课的。

Bù, zhè .shì Yīngwén kè .de.

1. 那是你的电话吗？(Mathew) Nà .shì nǐ .de diànhuà .ma? (Mathew)
2. 你喜欢红色的书包吗？（黑色）*Nǐ* xǐ.huān hóng.sè .de shūbāo .ma? (hēi.sè)
3. 他要大杯的汽水吗？（小杯）Tā yào dà bēi .de qìshuǐ .ma? (xiǎo bēi)
4. 你们想喝冰的饮料吗？（热）Nǐ.mén xiǎng hē bīng .de yǐnliào .ma? (rè)
5. "春节"是日本的节日吗？（中国）Chūnjié shì Rìběn .de jié.rì .ma?(Zhōng.guó)
6. 你买这条绿色的裤子吗？（灰色）*Nǐ* mǎi zhè-tiáo lǜ.sè .de kùzi .ma? (huī.sè)
7. "Bonjour"是德文的 "早上好" 吗？（法文）
   "Bonjour" shì Dewén .de "zǎo.shàng hǎo" .ma? (Fǎwén)
8. Jurassic Park是英国的电影吗？（美国）
   "Jurassic Park" shì Yīng.guó .de diànyǐng .ma? (Měi.guó)

开口说 Kāikǒu Shuō

Communication

11 挑选衣服 Tiāoxuǎn Yī.fú *Picking Out Clothes*

With a partner, play the roles of two friends who are going shopping together.

- A asks B to go to the department store with A to shop for clothes.
- A tells B what sort of clothes A wants to buy.
- A chooses a color and asks B if it looks nice.
- B gives A his/her opinion.
- A tells B why he/she wants to buy this.
- Ask the price of the piece of clothing.
- Ask if there is a discount, and if yes, how much.

12 最受欢迎的颜色 Zuì Shòuhuānyíng .de Yán.sè / *The Most Popular Color*

Survey your classmates on their favorite color. On a separate sheet of paper, draw a table like the one below. In the table, write down six colors in Chinese. Then, ask ten of your classmates for their favorite color.

Lì.zi: **You:** 你最喜欢什么颜色？ Nǐ zuì xǐ.huān shén.me yán.sè?

Lucas: 我最喜欢黑色。 Wǒ zuì xǐ.huān hēi.sè.

You: 你最喜欢什么颜色？ Nǐ zuì xǐ.huān shén.me yán.sè?

Sylvia: 我最喜欢红色。 Wǒ zuì xǐ.huān hóng.sè.

colors / names	黑色 hēi.sè	白色 bái.sè	红色 hóng.sè	黄色 huáng.sè	绿色 lǜ.sè	蓝色 lán.sè
Lucas	✓					
Sylvia			✓			

13 冬季拍卖 Dōngjì Pāimài / *Winter Sale*

Read the following and answer the questions below in Chinese.

1. What is this ad about?
   a. a sale
   b. fashion information
   c. a seasonal tour
2. Is there a sale on the 20th of November?
3. How much of a discount do T-shirts have?
4. T-shirts have the same discount as what other item?
5. What item is 15% off?
6. How much of a discount do dresses have?
7. If your sister buys a shirt originally priced at 300 dollars on November 26, will she get a discount? And if so, how much is the discount price?

汉字天地 Hànzì Tiāndì
Chinese Characters

白 ■ bái ■ white

The ideograph 白 *bái* resembles an acorn, which is creamy white inside.

Stroke Order

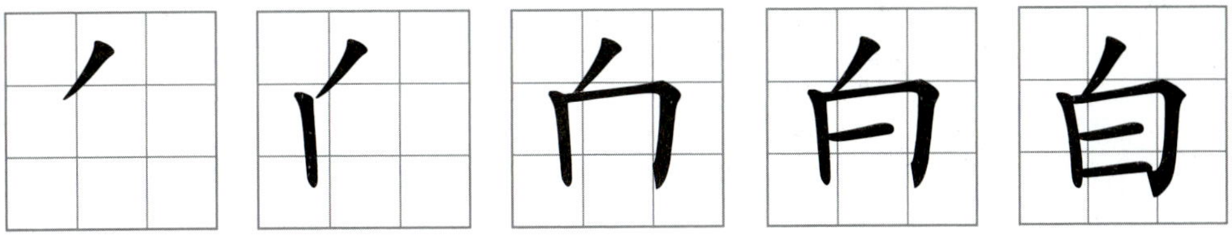

14 词汇延伸 Cíhuì Yánshēn *Vocabulary Builder*

Below are some characters that can be combined with 白 *bái* to create new words. Match the Chinese words on the left with the appropriate English meaning on the right.

宫 gōng *n. palace*	金 jīn *n. gold*	天 tiān *n. sky; day*	板 bǎn *n. board*	明 míng *adj. bright*

1. 白宫 Báigōng — A. *daytime*
2. 白金 báijīn — B. *the White House*
3. 白天 báitiān — C. *to understand*
4. 白板 báibǎn — D. *platinum*
5. 明白 míng.bái — E. *white board*

15 汉字侦探 Hànzì Zhēntàn *Visual Detective*

Can you find 白 in the following pictures?

Lesson C

发音 Fāyīn
Pronunciation

j q x + üan ün

词汇 Cíhuì
Vocabulary

描述衣服 Miáoshù Yī.fú *Describe Clothing*

老 (老)
lǎo
adj. old

年轻 (年輕)
niánqīng
adj. young

新 (新)
xīn
adj. new

旧 (舊)
jiù
adj. used; old

时髦 (時髦)
shímáo
adj. fashionable

过时 (過時)
guòshí
adj. out-of-date

紧 (緊)
jǐn
adj. tight

合身 (合身)
héshēn
adj. good-fitting

松 (鬆)
sōng
adj. loose

这件连衣裙好不好看
(這件連衣裙好不好看)?
Zhèi-jiàn liányīqún hǎo .bù hǎokàn?
Does this dress look nice?

不好看，因为有点儿老
(不好看，因為有點兒老)。
Bù hǎokàn, yīn.wèi *yǒu.diǎnr* lǎo.
No, because it looks a bit "old."

A: 这件毛衣几号 (這件毛衣幾號)?
Zhèi-jiàn máoyī jǐ-hào? *What's the size of this sweater?*

B: 38号 (38號)。 Sān.shíbā-hào. *Size 38.*

A: 我穿什么颜色的裙子比较合适 (我穿什麼顏色的裙子比較合適)?
Wǒ chuān shén.me yánsè .de qún.zi bǐjiào héshì? *What color skirt suits me better?*

B: 白色 (白色)。 Bái.sè. *White.*

A: 你觉得这条裤子好看吗 (你覺得這條褲子好看嗎)?
Nǐ jué.de zhèi-tiáo kù.zi hǎokàn .ma? *Do you think this pair of pants looks good?*

B: 我觉得这条裤子不但好看，而且合身
(我覺得這條褲子不但好看，而且合身)。
Wǒ jué.de zhèi-tiáo kù.zi búdàn hǎokàn, érqiě héshēn. *I not only think that it looks good, but that it also fits very well.*

A: 这件衣服的大小怎么样 (這件衣服的大小怎麼樣)?
Zhèi-jiàn yī.fú .de dàxiǎo zěn.meyàng? *What about the size of this piece of clothing?*

B: 有点儿大，不合身 (有點兒大，不合身)。
Yǒu.diǎnr dà, bù héshēn. *It's a bit big; it doesn't fit well.*

A: 请你帮我买一杯冰咖啡，好吗 (請你幫我買一杯冰咖啡，好嗎)?
Qǐng nǐ bāng *wǒ* mǎi yì-bēi bīng kāfēi, hǎo .ma? *Please buy me a cup of iced coffee, okay?*

B: 好，没问题 (好，沒問題)。 Hǎo, méi wèntí. *Okay, no problem.*

Adjectives

合适 (合適)	héshì	*suitable*
成熟 (成熟)	chéngshú	*mature*

Adverbs

刚 (剛)	gāng	*just; exactly*
有点儿 (有點兒)	*yǒu*.diǎnr	*a bit; somewhat*

Conjunctions

不但 (不但)	búdàn	*not only*
而且 (而且)	érqiě	*but also; and; also; in addition*

Nouns

大小 (大小)	dàxiǎo	*size*
号 (號)	hào	*size; number*

Time Words

下次 (下次)	xià.cì	*next time*

Verbs

穿 (穿)	chuān	*to wear; to put on*

1 品头论足 Pǐn-tóu Lùn-zú / *Fashion Critics*

You will hear four dialogues of friends talking about what they plan to wear to an upcoming event. Select the letter of the picture that corresponds to each dialogue.

Lì.zi:

A.

B.

C.

D.

2 个人问题 Gèrén Wèntí / Personal Questions

Answer each question in Chinese.

1. 你喜欢紧一点的衣服还是松一点的衣服？
   Nǐ xǐ.huān jǐn yìdiǎn hái.shì sōng yìdiǎn .de yī.fú?
2. 你觉得长裙很老吗？ Nǐ jué.de chángqún *hěn* lǎo .ma?
3. 你喜欢穿什么颜色的裤子？ *Nǐ* xǐ.huān chuān shén.me yán.sè .de kù.zi?
4. 你喜欢成熟的衣服吗？ *Nǐ* xǐ.huān chéngshú .de yī.fú .ma?
5. 你有几条牛仔裤？ *Nǐ yǒu* jǐ-tiáo niúzǎikù?
6. 下课以后，你要去书店吗？ Xià-kè yǐhòu, nǐ yào qù shūdiàn .ma?

句型介绍 Jùxíng Jièshào
Language Patterns

To Express Degree Using 有点儿 *yǒu.diǎnr*

The adverb 有点儿 *yǒu.diǎnr* means "a bit, a little." It is followed by adjectives to indicate a small degree of dissatisfaction. It can modify negative adjectives.

Noun + 有点儿 ***yǒu.diǎnr*** + **Adjective**

这条裤子有点儿贵。 Zhèi-tiáo kù.zi *yǒu*.diǎnr guì.
这道菜有点儿辣。 Zhèi-dào cài *yǒu*.diǎnr là.

The Pattern 不但 *búdàn*…, 而且 *érqiě*…

The pattern 不但 *búdàn*…, 而且 *érqiě*… means "not only…, but also…." This pattern is used with verb phrases which are juxtaposed to express two situations of the same importance.

Subject + 不但 ***búdàn*** + **Verb Clause 1** + 而且(也) ***érqiě (yě)*** + **Verb Clause 2**

这件衬衫不但便宜，而且很漂亮。 Zhèi-jiàn chènshān búdàn pián.yí, ér*qiě* hěn piào.liàng.
他不但喜欢看中国电影，也喜欢看法国电影。
Tā búdàn xǐ.huān kàn Zhōng.guó diànyǐng, *yě* xǐ.huān kàn Fǎ.guó diànyǐng.

Asking About Clothing Size with 几号 *jǐ-hào*

To ask about clothing size, use 几号 *jǐ-hào*. 号 *hào* is a measure word, therefore, it is preceded by a number to answer the question "几 *jǐ*" (what number, or how many).

A: 这件衬衫有没有36号的？ Zhè-jiàn chènshān yǒu méi.yǒu sān.shíliù-hào .de?

B: 不好意思，没有。 Bù hǎoyì.sī, méi.yǒu.

The Verb 请 *qǐng*

The verb 请 *qǐng* means "to request; to invite." It can be followed by a person / persons and a verb phrase to mean "to invite somebody to do something."

请 *qǐng* + **somebody** + **Verb Phrase**

下个星期请你带我去看龙舟比赛，好吗?
Xià.ge xīngqī *qǐng* nǐ dài wǒ qù kàn lóngzhōu bǐsài, hǎo .ma?

我想请小华看电影。 *Wǒ xiǎng qǐng* Xiǎohuá kàn-diànyǐng.

To Ask for Agreement with 好吗 *hǎo .ma*

The phrase 好吗 *hǎo .ma* means "okay?" It follows a sentence and is used as a tag question for the purpose of seeking agreement.

Sentence + **好吗 *hǎo ma*** ?

我们下个月一起去日本旅行，好吗？
Wǒ.mén xià.ge yuè yìqǐ qù Rìběn lǚxíng, hǎo .ma?

请借给我一支笔，好吗？ Qǐng jiè *gěi* wǒ yì-zhī bǐ, hǎo .ma?

会话 Huìhuà Dialogue

实话实说 Shíhuà Shíshuō *An Honest Opinion*

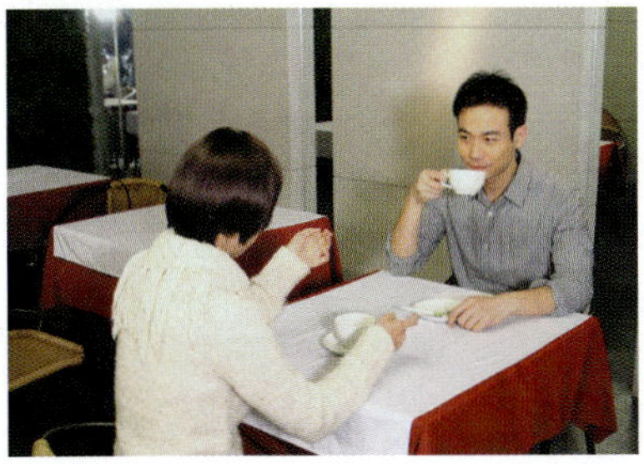

At the cafeteria, Lin Shufang is talking to Zhang Guohua.

林书芳：	这是新衣服吗？	Lín Shūfāng:	Zhè .shì xīn yī.fú .ma?
张国华：	是啊。好不好看？	Zhāng Guóhuá:	Shì .a. Hǎo .bù hǎokàn?
林书芳：	好看，可是有点儿老。	Lín Shūfāng:	Hǎokàn, kě.shì *yǒu.diǎnr* lǎo.
张国华：	老？我觉得这叫"成熟"。	Zhāng Guóhuá:	Lǎo? Wǒ jué.de zhè jiào "chéngshú".
林书芳：	不，这件不但老，而且有点儿小。	Lín Shūfāng:	Bù, zhèi-jiàn búdàn lǎo, érqiě *yǒu.diǎnr* xiǎo.
张国华：	我觉得大小刚好。	Zhāng Guóhuá:	Wǒ jué.de dàxiǎo gāng hǎo.
林书芳：	这件衣服几号？	Lín Shūfāng:	Zhèi-jiàn yī.fú jǐ-hào?
张国华：	42号。	Zhāng Guóhuá:	Sì.shí'èr-hào.
林书芳：	你穿44号比较合适。	Lín Shūfāng:	Nǐ chuān sì.shísì-hào bǐjiào héshì.
张国华：	下次请你跟我去买衣服，好吗？	Zhāng Guóhuá:	Xià.cì *qǐng* nǐ gēn wǒ qù mǎi yī.fú, hǎo .ma?

3 几号？ Jǐ-hào? *What size?*

Answer the following questions based on the dialogue.

1. 张国华的衣服几号？ Zhāng Guóhuá .de yī.fú jǐ-hào?
2. 林书芳觉得张国华的衣服合身吗？ Lín Shūfāng jué.de Zhāng Guóhuá .de yī.fú héshēn .ma?
3. 林书芳觉得张国华穿几号比较合适？ Lín Shūfāng jué.de Zhāng Guóhuá chuān jǐ-hào bǐjiào héshì?

4 选一选 Xuǎn .Yì Xuǎn Choice Questions

Choose the correct answers based on the dialogue.

1. 谁有新衣服? Shéi yǒu xīn yī.fú?
   a. 林书芳 Lín Shūfāng b. 张国华 Zhāng Guóhuá c. 张妈妈 Zhāng mā.x
2. 林书芳觉得新衣服怎么样? Lín Shūfāng jué.de xīn yī.fú zěn.meyàng?
   a. 不好看 bù hǎokàn b. 成熟 chéngshú c. 老 lǎo
3. 张国华觉得新衣服怎么样? Zhāng Guóhuá jué.de xīn yī.fú zěn.meyàng?
   a. 不好看 bù hǎokàn b. 成熟 chéngshú c. 老 lǎo
4. 谁觉得新衣服有点儿小? Shéi jué.de xīn yī.fú *yǒu.diǎnr* xiǎo?
   a. 林书芳 Lín Shūfāng b. 张国华 Zhāng Guóhuá
   c. 林书芳和张国华 Lín Shūfāng hé Zhāng Guóhuá
5. 张国华想请谁跟他去买衣服? Zhāng Guóhuá *xiǎng* qǐng shéi gēn tā qù mǎi yī.fú?
   a. 他妈妈 tā mā.x b. 他爸爸 tā bà.x c. 林书芳 Lín Shūfāng

文化橱窗 Wénhuà Chúchuāng
Culture Window

Chinese and American Sizes

Mainland China, Hong Kong and Taiwan all have their own clothing sizes. Clothing measurements differ from brand to brand, but are usually given in inches or centimeters.

In Mainland China, clothing sizes are often labeled with 号 *hào* or 型 *xíng*. 号 *hào* is used to indicate the height of the intended wearer, and 型 *xíng* is used to label the chest or waistline. The labels are in centimeters, with a 2 cm margin for error. For example, a pair of men's pants with the label 180/100 means that it is suitable for men from 178 cm to 182 cm tall with a waistline of between 98 cm to 102 cm. Clothes in Taiwan are labeled with one of five sizes: 特小号 *tèxiǎohào* (extra small, XS), 小号 *xiǎohào* (small, S), 中号 *zhōnghào* (medium, M), 大号 *dàhào* (large, L), and 特大号 *tèdàhào* (extra large, XL). For each size, there is a number that represents the size of the piece of clothing in inches.

As for footwear, most Asian countries, like Japan, use centimeters for shoe sizes. However, many European or American brands (especially athletic brands) use a separate system.

Asian Fashion Designers

Jason Wu (吴季刚) is a Taiwanese-American fashion designer that rose to fame after Michelle Obama wore his design to the 2009 presidential inauguration ceremony. Wu was born in Taipei, Taiwan, and moved to Canada when he was nine. He learned sculpting when he attended junior high school in Tokyo, and studied at Parsons, The New School for Design in New York. When he was 16 years old, he started to work as a freelancer and designed clothes for dolls for toy companies. In 2008, he received the Fashion Group International's Rising Star Award.

Vera Wang (王薇薇), born on June 27, 1949, is a Chinese American fashion designer based in New York. She is famous for her wedding gown designs, which, unlike the complex and extravagant designs of traditional gowns, are simple, chic and modern. Although her gowns are highly priced, they are very much sought after by Hollywood as they guarantee that the wearer won't be placed on the "worst dressed" list. Vera Wang is also very famous in China. The female actors of many Hong Kong romantic movies and TV shows call Vera Wang in New York to place an order for their wedding gown when they are about to get married.

▲ Vera Wang's wedding dress.

5 文化动动脑 Wénhuà Dòng.x nǎo *Culture Check-up*

Complete each statement with an appropriate word or expression.

1. Clothing measurements differ from brand to brand, but are mostly in ____ or ____.
2. In Mainland China, clothing sizes are often labeled with ____or ____.
3. The labels of clothes in Mainland China are in centimeters, with a ____ margin for error.
4. 号 *hào* is used to indicate the ____ of the intended wearer, and 型 *xíng* is used to label the chest or ____
5. Clothes in Taiwan are labeled with one of five sizes: ____ (extra small), ____ (small), ____ (medium), ____ (large), and ____ (extra large).
6. Most Asian countries, like Japan, use ____ for shoe sizes.
7. Jason Wu (吴季刚) is a Taiwanese-American fashion designer that rose to fame after ____ wore his design to the 2009 presidential inauguration ceremony.
8. Vera Wang (王薇薇), an ____ fashion designer based in New York, who is famous for her ____ designs.

Language Practice

6 有点儿… Yǒu.diǎnr …. A bit….

Use 有点儿 *yǒu.diǎnr* and the adjectives provided to describe the following nouns.

Lì.zi: 那件衣服 / 旧 nèi-jiàn yī.fú / jiù
那件衣服有点儿旧。 Nèi-jiàn yī.fú *yǒu*diǎnr jiù.

1. 红色的裤子 / 奇怪 hóng.sè .de kù.zi / qíguài
2. 这条长裤 / 紧 zhèi-tiáo chángkù / jǐn
3. 这本书 / 贵 zhèi-běn shū / guì
4. 今天天气 / 热 jīntiān tiān.qì / rè
5. 包粽子 / 难 bāo-zòng.zi / nán
6. 这杯果汁 / 甜 zhèi-bēi guǒzhī / tián
7. 吃的东西 / 多 chī .de dōng.xī / duō
8. 这些衬衫 / 过时 zhè.xiē chènshān / guòshí

7 他们穿几号? Tā.mén chuān jǐ-hào? What size do they wear?

With a partner, take turn asking and answering what size each person in the following pictures wears.

1. 李红 Lǐ Hóng / 38号

3. 张书苹 Zhāng Shūpíng / 42号

5. 林军 Lín Jūn / 48号

2. Mike / 46号

4. 哥哥 gē.x / 44号

6. 妹妹 mèi.x / 40号

8 提出请求 Tíchū Qǐngqiú / *Say Your Request*

You would like to ask others to do something by using the pattern 我请… *Wǒ qǐng…*. Follow the model.

Lì.zi: 爸妈 / 带我去中国 bà-mā / dài wǒ qù Zhōng.guó
我请爸妈带我去中国。 *Wǒ* qǐng bà-mā dài wǒ qù Zhōng.guó.

1. 小芳 / 给我三张纸 Xiǎofāng / gěi wǒ sān-zhāng zhǐ
2. 姐姐 / 带我去百货商店 jiě.x / dài wǒ qù bǎihuò shāngdiàn
3. 美美 / 跟我一起打网球 Měi.x / gēn wǒ yìqǐ *dǎ* wǎngqiú
4. 李国 / 跟我一起去买衣服 Lǐ Guó / gēn wǒ yìqǐ qù mǎi yī.fú
5. 董军 / 借给我他的中文书 Dǒng Jūn / jiè *gěi* wǒ tā .de Zhōngwén shū
6. 妈妈 / 买新外套给我 mā.x / mǎi xīn wàitào *gěi* wǒ

9 邀请别人 Yāoqǐng Bié.rén / *Invite Others*

Use the verb 请 *qǐng* to put the following information into sentences to indicate that one wants to invite others to do something. Follow the model.

Lì.zi: 我 / 董军 / 跟我的家人一起过年 wǒ / Dǒng Jūn / gēn wǒ .de jiārén yìqǐ guònián
我请董军跟我的家人一起过年。 *Wǒ qǐng* Dǒng Jūn gēn wǒ .de jiārén yìqǐ guònián.

1. 林文 / 李明 / 去他家玩 Lín Wén / Lǐ Míng / qù tā jiā wán
2. 张华 / 白思 / 去茶店喝茶 Zhāng Huá / Bái Sī / qù chádiàn hē chá
3. 安安 / 我 / 一起玩电子游戏 Ān'ān / wǒ / yìqǐ wán diànzǐ yóuxì
4. 爸爸 / 黄先生 / 去中国餐馆吃饭
bà.x / Huáng xiān.shēng / qù Zhōng.guó cānguǎn chī-fàn
5. 哥哥的墨西哥朋友 / 他 / 去墨西哥玩
gē.x .de Mòxīgē péng.yǒu / tā / qù Mòxīgē wán
6. 姐姐的同学 / 她 / 去他的生日晚会 (*birthday party*)
jiě.x .de tóngxué / tā / qù tā .de shēngrì wǎnhuì

10 征求同意 Zhēngqiú Tóngyì / Seek Agreement

Seek agreement by using 好吗 *hǎo .ma*.

1. 请你打开空调。 *Qǐng nǐ* dǎ-kāi kōngtiáo.
2. 请给我你的照片。 *Qǐng gěi wǒ* nǐ.de zhàopiàn.
3. 明天下午五点见。 Míng.tiān xià.*wǔ wǔ*-diǎn jiàn.
4. 带我去看龙舟比赛。 Dài wǒ qù kàn lóngzhōu bǐsài.
5. 我们不要点辣的菜。 Wǒ.mén bú yào diǎn là .de cài.
6. 我们周末一起去游泳。 Wǒ.mén zhōumò yìqǐ qù yóuyǒng.
7. 我们吃色拉和三明治。 Wǒ.mén chī sèlā hé sānmíngzhì.
8. 请给我你的手机号码。 *Qǐng gěi wǒ* nǐ.de shǒujī hàomǎ.
9. 我买这件黄色的毛衣。 *Wǒ* mǎi zhèi-jiàn huáng.sè .de máoyī.
10. 请借给我一支笔和两张纸。 Qǐng jiè *gěi* wǒ yì-zhī bǐ hé liǎng-zhāng zhǐ.

11 不但…而且… Búdàn ..., érqiě... / Not only..., but also...

Use the provided verb phrases and the pattern 不但…而且(也)… *búdàn ..., érqiě (yě)…* to make sentences. Follow the model.

Lì.zi: 这条裤子 / 贵 / 不好看 zhèi-tiáo kù.zi / guì / bù hǎokàn
这条裤子不但贵，而且不好看。 Zhèi-tiáo kù.zi búdàn guì, érqiě bù hǎokàn.

1. 他 / 修中文课 / 修西班牙文课 tā / xiū Zhōngwén kè / xiū Xībānyáwén kè
2. 他们 / 打篮球 / 踢足球 tā.mén / dǎ-lánqiú/ tī-zúqiú
3. 小芳 / 没有笔 / 没有课本 Xiǎofāng / méi.*yǒu* bǐ / méi.yǒu kèběn
4. 哥哥 / 要吃汉堡 / 要吃炸鸡 gē.x / yào chī hànbǎo / yào chī zhájī
5. 这家餐厅的菜 / 不贵 / 很好吃 zhèi-jiā cāntīng .de cài / bú guì / *hěn* hǎochī
6. 今天 / 会下雨 / 会刮风 jīn.tiān / huì xià-yǔ / huì guā-fēng
7. 端午节 / 吃粽子 / 划龙舟 Duānwǔjié / chī zòng.zi / huá lóngzhōu
8. 这件吊带衫 / 漂亮 / 流行 zhèi-jiàn diàodàishān / piào.liàng / liúxíng
9. 我们家 / 有一只狗和一只猫 / 有三只鸟
   wǒ.mén jiā / yǒu yì-zhī gǒu hé yì-zhī māo / yǒu sān-zhī niǎo
10. 我今天 / 有一个小考 / 有两个大考
    wǒ jīn.tiān / yǒu yí-.ge *xiǎo*kǎo / *yǒu* liǎng-.ge dàkǎo

开口说 Kāikǒu Shuō

Communication

12 讨论衣服 Tǎolùn Yī.fú / *Clothes Talk*

With a partner, play the roles of two friends talking about clothes.

- Tell your partner if you think what he/she is wearing today suits him/her.
- Tell your partner what you think about his/her outfit today.
- Suggest something that you think your partner will look good in.
- Tell your partner what color clothes you think you look good in.
- Tell your partner what color clothes you think he/she will look good in.
- Make plans to go shopping together in the future.

13 衣服标签 Yī.fú Biāoqiān / *Clothing Tags*

Read the following clothing tag and answer the questions below.

合格证

品名：女衬衫
尺寸：42
颜色：黑色
产地：广州
电话：020-86553824
价格：¥150

4927061138

1. What item of clothing is this?
2. What size is this item of clothing?
3. What color is this item of clothing?
4. What number can you call if you wish to get in touch with the manufacturer?
5. How much does this item of clothing cost?

汉字天地 Hànzì Tiāndì

Chinese Characters

小 ■ xiǎo ■ small

The original form of the pictograph 小 *xiǎo* consisted of three short vertical structures which represented tiny grains of sand, symbolizing "small."

Stroke Order

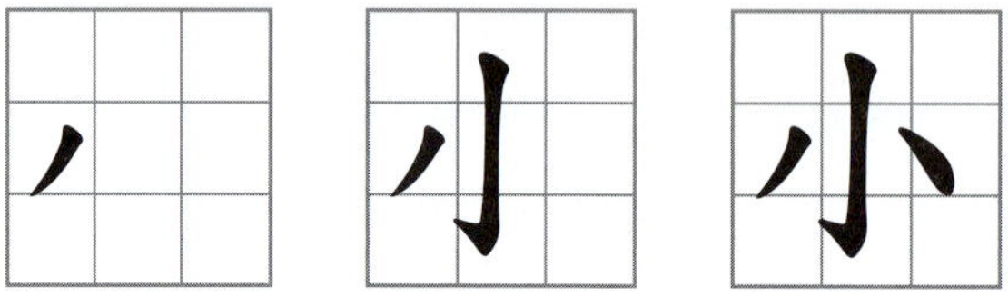

14 词汇延伸 Cíhuì Yánshēn *Vocabulary Builder*

Below are some characters that can be combined with 小 *xiǎo* to create new words. Match the Chinese words on the left with the appropriate English meaning on the right.

刀 dāo	型 xíng	学 xué	心 xīn	腿 tuǐ
n. knife	*n. type*	*n. learning*	*n. heart*	*n. leg*

1. 小刀 xiǎodāo — A. *calf*
2. 小型 xiǎoxíng — B. *careful*
3. 小学 xiǎoxué — C. *small-sized, miniature*
4. 小心 xiǎoxīn — D. *pocket knife*
5. 小腿 *xiǎo*tuǐ — E. *elementary school*

15 汉字侦探 Hànzì Zhēntàn / Visual Detective

Can you find 小 in the following pictures?

Lesson D

发音 Fāyīn
Pronunciation

Group –r Finals

词汇 Cíhuì
Vocabulary

描述外表 Miáoshù Wàibiǎo *Describe Appearance*

美丽 (美麗)
měilì
adj. beautiful; pretty

帅 (帥)
shuài
adj. handsome

丑 (醜)
chǒu
adj. ugly

有型 (有型)
yǒuxíng
adj. stylish

睡衣 (睡衣)
shuìyī
n. pajamas

袜子 (襪子)
wà.zi
n. socks

鞋类 Xiélèi *Shoes*

鞋子 (鞋子)
xié.zi
n. shoes

皮鞋 (皮鞋)
píxié
n. leather shoes

靴子 (靴子)
xuē.zi
n. boots

运动鞋 (運動鞋)
yùndòngxié
n. sneakers

拖鞋 (拖鞋)
tuōxié
n. slippers

夹脚拖鞋 (夾腳拖鞋)
jiā-jiǎo tuōxié
n. flip-flops

A: 你找什么样的衣服 (你找什麼樣的衣服)?

Nǐ zhǎo shén.meyàng .de yī.fú? *What kind of clothes are you looking for?*

B: 我想买黑色的衬衫 (我想買黑色的襯衫)。

Wǒ xiǎng mǎi hēi.sè .de chènshān. *I want to buy a black shirt.*

A: 这条裤子有没有大一点儿的 (這條褲子有沒有大一點兒的)?

Zhèi-tiáo kù.zi yǒu méi.yǒu dà yì.diǎnr .de? *Does this pair of pants come in a larger size?*

B: 有，请等一下 (有，請等一下)。 Yǒu, *qǐng* děng yí.xià. Yes. *Please wait a moment.*

A: 请问您需要帮忙吗 (請問您需要幫忙嗎)?

Qǐngwèn nín xūyào bāng-máng .ma? *Excuse me, do you need any help?*

B: 我想试试这双粉红色的靴子 (我想試試這雙粉紅色的靴子)。

Wǒ xiǎng shì.x zhèi-shuāng fěnhóng.sè .de xuē.zi. *I want to try on this pink pair of boots.*

A: 这双运动鞋现在只要一百块 (這雙運動鞋現在只要一百塊)。

Zhèi-shuāng yùndòngxié xiànzài zhǐ yào yìbǎi-kuài. *This pair of sneakers only cost 100 Yuan now.*

B: 可以便宜一点儿吗 (可以便宜一點兒嗎)?

Kě.yǐ pián.yí yì.diǎnr .ma? *Can they be any cheaper?*

A: 我觉得紫色是最好看的颜色 (我覺得紫色是最好看的顏色)。

Wǒ jué.de zǐ.sè shì zuì hǎokàn .de yán.sè. *I think purple is the prettiest color.*

Adverbs

最 (最)	zuì	*the most*

Complements

一点儿 (一點兒)	yìdiǎnr	*a bit, a little*

Measure Words

样 (樣)	yàng	*kind; type*
套 (套)	tào	*set; suit*

Nouns

价钱 (價錢)	jià.qián	*price*

Verbs

找 (找)	zhǎo	*to look for*
试 (試)	shì	*to try*
要 (要)	yào	*to take*
需要 (需要)	xūyào	*to need*
帮忙 (幫忙)	bāng-máng	*to help*
适合 (適合)	shìhé	*to suit; to fit*

1 穿什么鞋? Chuān shén.me xié? *What shoes are they wearing?*

You will hear a recording about six people and the shoes they are wearing. Match each photo to the correct person.

1. 	4. 
2. 	5. 
3. 	6. 

A. Mandy

B. Jerry

C. 钱先生 Qián xiān.shēng

D. 董华 Dǒng Huá

E. 李小姐 Lǐ *xiǎo*.jiě

F. 黄太太 Huáng tài.x

2 怎么样? Zěn.meyàng? / *What do you think of it?*

Select the letter of the phrase that logically completes each sentence.

1. 这件T恤很…
Zhèi-jiàn T-xù hěn…

4. 这件连衣裙很…
Zhèi-jiàn liányīqún hěn…

2. 这条裤子很…
Zhèi-tiáo kù.zi hěn…

5. 这套衣服很...
Zhèi-tào yī.fú hěn...

3. 这套西装很…
Zhèi-tào xīzhuāng hěn…

A. 美丽 měilì
B. 丑 chǒu
C. 帅 shuài
D. 成熟 chéngshú
E. 有型 yǒuxíng

3 个人问题 Gèrén Wèntí / *Personal Questions*

Answer each question in Chinese.

1. 你有很多鞋子吗？几双？ *Nǐ yǒu* hěn duō shuāng xié.zi .ma? Jǐ-shuāng?
2. 你有皮鞋吗？ *Nǐ* yǒu píxié .ma?
3. 你喜欢穿夹脚拖鞋吗？ *Nǐ* xǐ.huān chuān jiājiǎo tuōxié .ma?
4. 上课的时候，你穿运动鞋还是拖鞋？
Shàng-kè .de shíhòu, nǐ chuān yùndòngxié hái.shì tuōxié?
5. 冬天的时候，你穿袜子睡觉吗？ Dōng.tiān .de shíhòu, nǐ chuān wà.zi shuì-jiào .ma?
6. 你最喜欢什么颜色？ Nǐ zuì xǐ.huān shén.me yán.sè?
7. 你觉得什么口味的冰淇淋最好吃？ Nǐ jué.de shén.me kǒuwèi .de bīng.qílín zuì hǎochī?
8. 你觉得什么样的衣服很丑？ Nǐ jué.de shén.meyàng .de yī.fú *hěn* chǒu?
9. 明天是你朋友的生日晚会，你想穿什么？
Míng.tiān shì nǐ péng.yǒu .de shēngrì wǎnhuì, *nǐ* xiǎng chuān shén.me?

句型介绍 Jùxíng Jièshào

Language Patterns

The Question Pronoun 什么样 *shén.meyàng*

The word 样 *yàng* means "kind, type." The question pronoun 什么样 *shén.meyàng* means "what kind." Unlike the question word 什么 *shén.me* which is used to ask what something is (with a noun as the answer), 什么样 *shén.meyàng* is used to ask for details about the noun.

什么样 *shén.meyàng* + **的 *.de*** + **Object**

A: 那是一件什么样的衣服？ Nà .shì yí-jiàn shén.meyàng .de yī.fú?

B: 那是一件粉红色的短裙。 Nà .shì yí-jiàn fěnhóng.sè .de duǎnqún.

A: 我想买一件毛衣。 *Wǒ xiǎng* mǎi yí-jiàn máoyī.

B: 你想买什么样的(毛衣)？ *Nǐ xiǎng* mǎi shén.meyàng .de (máoyī)?

Language Note

什么 *shén.me* V.S. 什么样 *shén.meyàng*

A: 今天晚上跟李校长吃饭，你要穿什么？
Jīn.tiān wǎn.shàng gēn Lǐ xiàozhǎng chī-fàn, nǐ yào chuān shén.me?
What do you want to wear for the dinner with Principal Li?

B: 我要穿衬衫。 Wǒ yào chuān chènshān. *I want to wear a shirt.*

A: 你要穿什么样的衬衫？ Nǐ yào chuān shén.meyàng .de chènshān? *What kind of shirt do you want to wear?*

B: 我要穿白色的、成熟一点儿的衬衫。 Wǒ yào chuān bái.sè .de, chéngshú yì.diǎnr .de chènshān.
I want to wear a white, mature-looking shirt.

In the first dialogue, Person A asks "what" Person B wants to wear for the dinner, and in the second dialogue Person A asks a follow-up question to ask "what the item of clothing" Person B wants to wear is like.

Moderating Adjectives with 一点儿 *yì.diǎnr*

The word 一点儿 *yì.diǎnr* means "a little." It follows an adjective to imply comparison with something else.

Adjective + **一点儿 *yì.diǎnr***

你们有没有辣一点儿的菜？ Nǐ.mén yǒu méi.yǒu là yì.diǎnr .de cài?

A: 老师，今天的作业可以少一点儿吗？ Lǎoshī, jīn.tiān .de zuòyè *kě.yǐ* shǎo yì.diǎnr .ma?

B: 不行。 Bù xíng.

Language Note

有点儿 *yǒu.diǎnr* V.S. 一点儿 *yì.diǎnr*

Subject + **有点儿 *yǒu.diǎnr*** + **Adjective**

Subject + **Adjective** + **一点儿 *yì.diǎnr***

有点儿 *yǒu.diǎnr* is followed by an adjective and is used to describe the subject and usually connotes some dissatisfaction. 一点儿 *yì.diǎnr* is preceded by an adjective and is used to describe the degree of something in comparison with another.

今天有点儿热。 Jīn.tiān *yǒu*.diǎnr rè. *Today is a bit hot. (Dissatisfaction)*

昨天天气冷，今天热一点儿。 Zuó.tiān tiān qì lěng, jīn.tiān rè yì.diǎnr.

Yesterday the weather was cold. Today it's a bit warmer (hotter). (Comparative)

The Reduplication of Verbs

We reduplicate verbs to express "give something a try" in a casual tone. Reduplication can also indicate a shorter time spent on an action. For example: 想想 *xiǎng.x*; 看看 *kàn.x*.

In the case of a monosyllabic word, 一 *yī* can be inserted between the two iterations of the verb to form "V 一 V." For example: 想一想 *Xiǎng.yì xiǎng*; 看一看 *Kàn.yí kàn*.

In the case of VO constructions, simply reduplicate the verb to make it "V V + O." For example: 念念书 *niàn.x shū*; 吃吃饭 *chī.x fàn*.

Verb + **Verb** + **Object**

我想试试这件短裙。 *Wǒ* xiǎng shì.x zhèi-jiàn duǎnqún.

你看看，这双鞋子好看吗？ Nǐ kàn.x, zhèi-shuāng xié.zi hǎokàn .ma?

The Superlative 最 *zuì*

The adverb 最 *zuì* refers to a superlative, meaning "the most." It is placed before an adjective to express the greatest extent possible.

最 *zuì* + **Adjective**

黄色裙子的价钱最便宜。

Huáng.sè qún.zi .de jià.qián zuì pián.yí.

绿色裙子的价钱最贵。

Lǜ.sè qún.zi .de jià.qián zuì guì.

我觉得巧克力口味的冰淇淋最好吃。

Wǒ jué.de qiǎo.kèlì kǒuwèi .de bīng.qílín zuì hǎochī.

会话 Huìhuà

Dialogue

跟朋友逛街 Gēn Péng.yǒu Guàng-jiē *Shopping with a Friend*

Bai Ping and Lin Shufang are shopping in Wangfujing.

林书芳：	你找什么样的裙子？	Lín Shūfāng:	*Nǐ* zhǎo shén.meyàng .de qún.zi?
白苹：	我要去朋友的生日晚会，所以我想买黑色的短裙。	Bái Píng:	Wǒ yào qù péng.yǒu .de shēngrì wǎnhuì, *suǒ*.yǐ *wǒ xiǎng* mǎi hēi.sè .de duǎn-qún.

A sales clerk approaches.

服务员：	需要帮忙吗？	Fúwùyuán:	Xūyào bāng-máng .ma?
白苹：	你好，这条裙子有没有大一点儿的？	Bái Píng:	*Nǐ* hǎo, zhèi-tiáo qún.zi yǒu méi.yǒu dà yì.diǎnr .de?
服务员：	我看看。你试试38号。	Fúwùyuán:	Wǒ kàn.x. Nǐ shì.x sān.shíbā-hào.

Bai Ping goes to the fitting room to try the skirt on.

白苹：	怎么样？	Bái Píng:	Zěn.meyàng?
林书芳：	我觉得很漂亮，很适合你。	Lín Shūfāng:	Wǒ jué.de hěn piào.liàng, hěn shìhé nǐ.
服务员：	这条裙子现在只要四百块。	Fúwùyuán:	Zhèi-tiáo qún.zi xiànzài zhǐ yào sìbǎi-kuài.
白苹：	可以便宜一点儿吗？	Bái Píng:	*Kě*.yǐ pián.yí yì.diǎnr .ma?
林书芳：	不好意思，这是最便宜的价钱。	Lín Shūfāng:	Bù hǎoyì.sī, zhè .shì zuì pián.yí .de jià.qián.

4 买哪件? Mǎi něi-jiàn? What should she buy?

Based on the dialogue, which of the following skirts should Bai Ping buy?

A.	B.	C.
 size: 36	 size: 38	 size: 38

5 填填看 Tián.x kàn Fill in the blanks

Based on the dialogue, write down the answers to the blanks on a separate sheet of paper.

1. ___ 和白苹一起去买衣服。 ___ hé Bái Píng yìqǐ qù mǎi yī.fú .
2. ___ 想买裙子，因为她要去朋友的 ___ 。
   ___ *xiǎng* mǎi qún.zi, yīn.wèi tā yào qù péng.yǒu .de ___ .
3. 她想买 ___ 色的 ___ 裙子。 Tā *xiǎng* mǎi ___ sè .de ___ qún.zi.
4. 她需要 ___ 一点儿的裙子。 Tā xūyào ___ yì.diǎnr .de qún.zi.
5. 她穿 ___ 号的裙子大小刚好。 Tā chuān ___ hào .de qún.zi dàxiǎo gāng hǎo.
6. 林书芳觉得这条裙子很 ___ 。 Lín Shūfāng jué.de zhèi-tiáo qún.zi hěn ___ .
7. 这条裙子现在 ___ 块。 Zhèi-tiáo qún.zi xiànzài ___ -kuài.
8. 这个价钱是 ___ 的价钱。Zhèi.ge jià.qián shì ___ .de jià.qián.

文化橱窗 Wénhuà Chúchuāng

Culture Window

Wangfujing

Wangfujing (王府井 *Wángfŭjĭng*) is a very famous commercial street located in Beijing's Dongcheng District with the Forbidden City to its west. The street is 1.11 miles long and home to approximately 700 stores. It boasts 700 years of history dating all the way back to the Yuan Dynasty. Wangfujing is one of the few pedestrian areas in China that cars are not allowed to drive through.

The name Wangfujing originated in the Ming Dynasty (14th-17th century A.D.), when many nobles (王爷 *Wángyé*) built their houses (王府 *Wángfŭ*) in the area. The street, which was formerly named after its shape, was thus renamed Wangfu Street (王府街 *Wángfŭ Jiē*). In the Qing Dynasty, the street acquired its present name, Wangfujing, because of a well there that provided water for all the stores.

▲ Wangfujing Street.

▲ Beijing snacks.

At the northern end of the street is Dong'an Market, which is the earliest shopping area in the district. It primarily sells items used for calligraphy, pottery, musical instruments, antique toys, silk textiles, leather goods, furniture, and Chinese-style daily necessities.

The Beijing Department Store Building was once the tallest and newest building on Wangfujing. In front of the building, there is a bronze statue of a famous worker at work, a symbolism of the spirit of service and China's new socialism.

There is a Snack Street in the western section of Wangfujing that provides an assortment of snacks and delicacies. A restaurant famous for its Peking Duck is in one of the alleyways that all tourists to Beijing must visit.

The Story of Silk

There are many stories on how sericulture (silk farming) began in China. One legend is of a beautiful girl from southern China, named Lei Zu, who picked fruit every day for her parents. One day, she discovered many white "fruit" on trees in a certain stretch of woods. Her curiosity led her to discover that fine, delicate threads could be extracted from these inedible white fruits after boiling them in water to weave into light and warm clothing for her parents to wear. News of this traveled to a northern tribe leader, who, attracted by Lei Zu's beauty and lovely nature, proposed to Lei Zu so that she could teach his people the art of silk farming. This northern leader later became the Yellow Emperor, and to thank her, people named Lei Zu the "Silk Goddess."

Silk textiles are woven from the protein fibers extracted from the cocoons of silkworm larvae. It is said that sericulture and silk production originated 3,700 years ago from a Neolithic cultural heritage site near the lower end of the Yellow River in China. Silk textiles are not only warm, they are also soft to the touch and give off a pearlescent shine. Silk has been a favorite of China's aristocracy and merchants for a long time, and there is documented proof that, if well-treated, silk textiles can last as long as a thousand years.

▲ A store of silk cloth.

With the advancement of the ages, silk products no longer hold the same place in world trade. However, China is still trying to improve its silk industry using advanced technology in its silk capitals Suzhou and Hangzhou. Thus, China still remains the country people think of whenever silk is mentioned.

6 文化动动脑 Wénhuà Dòng.x nǎo / Culture Check-up

Complete each statement with an appropriate word or expression.

1. ___ is the street which is 1.11 miles long and home to approximately 700 stores and boasts 700 years of history dating all the way back to the Yuan Dynasty.
2. The name Wangfujing (王府井 *Wángfǔjǐng*) originated in the ___ (14th-17th century A.D.).
3. ___ is the earliest shopping area at the northern end of Wangfu Street.
4. It is said that sericulture and silk production originated 3,700 years ago from a Neolithic cultural heritage site near the lower end of the ___ River in China.
5. Silk textiles are not only warm and absorbent; they are also soft to the touch and give off a ___ shine.
6. ___ has been a favorite of China's aristocracy and merchants for a long time.
7. If well-treated, silk textiles can last as long as a ___ years.
8. Though silk products no longer hold an important place in the Chinese economy, China is still trying to improve its silk industry using advanced technology in its silk capitals ___ and ___.

Comparisons

Now that you have read the legend of how silk farming began in China, think of a Western myth or legend for how something else began.

Language Practice

7 找衣服 Zhǎo Yī.fú / *Looking for Clothes*

With a partner, take turns asking each other what clothes each person below is looking for based on the following pictures. Follow the model.

妈妈 mā.x

Lì.zi: **A:** 妈妈找什么样的衣服? Mā.x zhǎo shén.meyàng .de yī.fú?

B: 她找红色的毛衣。 Tā zhǎo hóng.sè .de máoyī.

1. 爸爸 bà.x 	3. 哥哥 gē.x 	5. 张小姐 Zhāng *xiǎo*.jiě 
2. 妹妹 mèi.x 	4. 王生 Wáng Shēng 	6. 林红 Lín Hóng 

8 重复动词 Chóngfù Dòngcí / *Reduplicate the Verb*

Reduplicate the verbs in the sentences below to soften the tone.

Lì.zi:

我想想这个问题。
Wǒ xiǎng.x zhèi-.ge wèntí.

1. 请你们等。 *Qǐng* nǐ.mén děng.
2. 你听这首(*shǒu, measure words for songs*)歌。 Nǐ tīng zhèi-shǒu gē.
3. 店员请他试40号。 Diànyuán qǐng tā shì sì.shí-hào.
4. 你要不要来我家喝茶。 Nǐ yào .bú.yào lái wǒ jiā hē-chá.

5. 小李星期天想看电影。 *Xiǎo* Lǐ Xīngqītiān xiǎng kàn-diànyǐng.

6. 他们喜欢每天下午打球。 Tā.mén xǐ.huān měi.tiān xià.*wǔ* dǎ-qiú.

7. 下课以后，她要去图书馆看书。 Xià-kè yǐhòu, tā yào qù túshūguǎn kàn-shū.

8. 周末的时候，我喜欢去海边游泳。 Zhōumò .de shí.hòu, *wǒ* xǐ.huān qù hǎibiān yóuyǒng.

9 哪一个? Něi yí-.ge? *Which one?*

Say what each person likes according to the pictures and using the pattern 一点儿 *yì.diǎnr*. Use the sentences provided.

Lì.zi: Melody喜欢…

Melody xǐ.huān…

Melody喜欢成熟一点儿的衣服。

Melody xǐ.huān chéngshú yì.diǎnr .de yī.fú.

1. 老师要喝…
Lǎoshī yào hē…

2. 她们想吃…
Tā.mén xiǎng chī…

3. 弟弟喜欢…
Dì.x xǐ.huān…

4. 妹妹要穿…
Mèi.x yào chuān…

5. 哥哥想买…
Gē.x *xiǎng* mǎi…

6. 考试要到了，所以我要借…
Kǎoshì yào dào .le, *suǒ.yǐ* wǒ yào jiè…

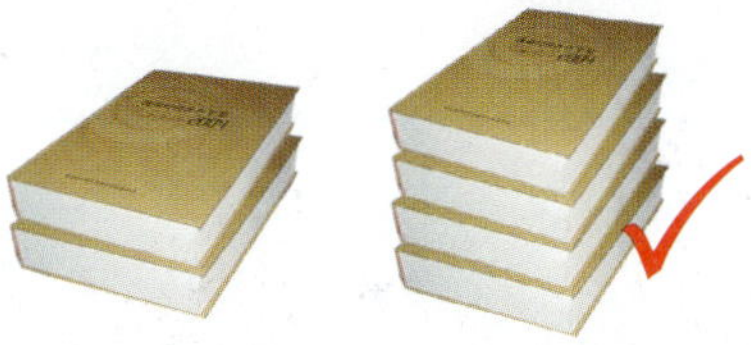

10 最… Zuì… *The most…*

With a partner, take turns asking each other "the most" about each picture below.

Lì.zi: A: 哪条裤子最便宜？ Něi-tiáo kù.zi zuì pián.yí?

B: 黑色的最便宜。哪条裤子最贵？

Hēi.sè .de zuì pián.yí. Něi-tiáo kù.zi zuì guì?

A: 灰色的最贵。 Huī.sè .de zuì guì.

1.

2.

3.

¥7.50 ¥2 ¥8

4.

Joe Maggie Ron

5.

昨天 18°C 今天 20°C 明天 16°C

6.

二月 七月 十二月

开口说 Kāikǒu Shuō
Communication

11 买一件大衣 Mǎi yí-jiàn dàyī / *Buying a coat*

With two other classmates, play the roles of a shop assistant in a clothing store, a person who will go to Canada in December and wants to buy a new coat, and a person who accompanies his/her friend (the shopper) to the store to buy the coat.

- The shop assistant asks the shopper what he/she wants to buy.
- The shopper answers with what he/she is looking for (a coat).
- The shop assistant asks the shopper why he/she wants to buy a coat, and what it is for.
- The shopper picks one and asks the shop assistant if he/she can try it on.
- After trying on the coat, the shopper asks his/her friend for advice and the friend gives his/her opinions.
- The shopper asks the shop assistant if this coat comes in different colors or sizes.
- The shop assistant looks at the shopper and suggests a color and size that would suit him/her.
- The shopper asks the shop assistant the price of the coat.
- The shop assistant tells the shopper how much it is.
- The shopper asks if there is a discount and bargains the price with the shop assistant.

12 传单 Chuándān / *Flyer*

Read the following clothing ad and answer the questions below.

1. What is this ad for?
   a. a new line of clothing
   b. clothing prices
   c. clothing discounts
2. Which season are the products advertised for?
3. What is the style of clothing provided at this store?
4. What are the target buyers of this ad? What kind of clothes might they wear?

汉字天地 Hànzì Tiāndì

Chinese Characters

大 ■ dà ■ big

The pictograph 大 *dà* is shaped like a human with his hands stretching out. In ancient times, people regarded man to be the greatest of all creatures, so a human's image was used to express "big." Therefore, this character looks like a person stretching out his arms and legs to the limit.

Stroke Order

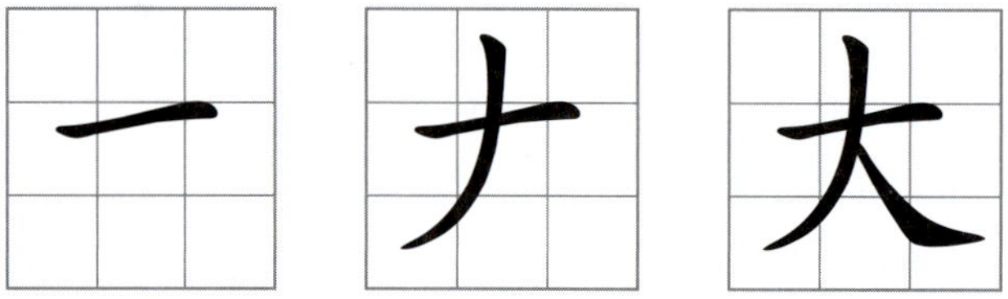

13 词汇延伸 Cíhuì Yánshēn / *Vocabulary Builder*

Below are some characters that can be combined with 大 *dà* to create new words. Match the Chinese words on the left with the appropriate English meaning on the right.

衣 yī *n. clothes*	学 xué *n. learning*	人 rén *n. person*	事 shì *n. thing*	陆 lù *n. land*

1. 大衣 dàyī — A. *university; college*
2. 大学 dàxué — B. *adult*
3. 大人 dàrén — C. *major event*
4. 大事 dàshì — D. *overcoat*
5. 大陆 dàlù — E. *continent*

14 汉字侦探 Hànzì Zhēntàn / Visual Detective

Can you find 大 in the following pictures?

句型介绍 Language Patterns

Unit 1, Lesson A

Unit 1, Lesson B

Unit 1, Lesson C

Unit 1, Lesson D

Unit 2, Lesson A

Unit 2, Lesson B

Unit 2, Lesson C

Unit 2, Lesson D

Unit 3, Lesson A

Unit 3, Lesson B

Unit 3, Lesson C

Unit 3, Lesson D

Unit 4, Lesson A

Unit 4, Lesson B

Unit 4, Lesson C

Unit 4, Lesson D

Unit 5, Lesson A

Unit 5, Lesson B

Unit 5, Lesson C

Unit 5, Lesson D

Unit 6, Lesson A

Unit 6, Lesson B

Unit 6, Lesson C

Unit 6, Lesson D

拼音索引 Pinyin to Chinese and English Vocabulary

Each entry lists the Pinyin, simplified character, traditional character, part of speech, English meaning, unit and lesson.

A

.a	啊	啊	*P.*	a particle with many functions (expressing surprise and at the end of a sentence indicating that strong opinion has been expressed); used at the end of a sentence to convey a feeling of admiration or as a warning	U3B
āi	唉	唉	*Intj.*	oh (a sound of sadness or regret)	U5B
àihào	爱好	愛好	*N.*	pastime	U2D
āiyā	唉呀	唉呀	*Intj.*	oh (to express surprise or unhappiness)	U5A

B

.ba	吧	吧	*P.*	used at the end of a sentence to make a suggestion and supposition	U2D
bā	八	八	*Num.*	eight	U1D
bā.shí	八十	八十	*Num.*	eighty	U1D
bà.x	爸爸	爸爸	*N.*	father	U2A
bǎi	百	百	*Num.*	hundred	U4C
bái.sè	白色	白色	*N.*	white	U6B
báibǎn	白板	白板	*N.*	white board	U3A
bái*bǎn*bǐ	白板笔	白板筆	*N.*	white board marker	U3A
bǎihuò shāngdiàn	百货商店	百貨商店	*N.*	department store	U6A
bǎiwàn	百万	百萬	*Num.*	a million	U6B
bàn	半	半	*Adj.*	half	U3B
bǎncā	板擦	板擦	*N.*	board eraser	U3A
bāng-máng	帮忙	幫忙	*V.*	to help	U6D
bàngqiú	棒球	棒球	*N.*	baseball	U2D
bā-niánjí	八年级	八年級	*N.*	8th grade	U1D
bāo	包	包	*V.*	to wrap	U5D
bāo.zi	包子	包子	*N.*	steamed buns with meat filling	U4C
Bāyuè	八月	八月	*T.W.*	August	U2C
bēi	杯	杯	*M.W.*	measure word for cups	U4B
			N.	cup	U4B
bēibāo	背包	背包	*N.*	backpack	U2B

Běijīng kǎoyā	北京烤鸭	北京烤鴨	*N.*	Beijing roast duck	U4D
bǐ	笔	筆	*N.*	pen	U2B
biānpào	鞭炮	鞭炮	*N.*	firecrackers	U5C
bǐjiào	比较	比較	*Adv.*	fairly; comparatively	U5B
bǐjìběn	笔记本	筆記本	*N.*	notebook	U3B
bīng.qílín	冰淇淋	冰淇淋	*N.*	ice cream	U5B
bīngqiú	冰球	冰球	*N.*	ice hockey	U2D
bīngshā	冰沙	冰沙	*N.*	smoothie	U4B
bǐsài	比赛	比賽	*N.*	competition; race	U5D
bówùguǎn	博物馆	博物館	*N.*	museum	U3D
bú kè.qì	不客气	不客氣	*I.E.*	you're welcome	U3B
bú tài hǎo	不太好	不太好	*Adj.*	not so good	U1B
bù / bú	不	不	*Adv.*	no; not	U1B
búcuò	不错	不錯	*Adj.*	fine	U1B
búdàn	不但	不但	*Conj.*	not only	U6C
búyòng	不用	不用	*C.E.*	no, no need	U4B

C

cài	菜	菜	*N.*	dish	U4D
cānguǎn	餐馆	餐館	*N.*	restaurant	U4D
cāntīng	餐厅	餐廳	*N.*	cafeteria; dining room	U4D
cǎoméi	草莓	草莓	*N.*	strawberry	U5B
CD bōfàngjī	CD播放机	CD播放機	*N.*	CD player	U3A
chá	茶	茶	*N.*	tea	U2B
chádiàn	茶店	茶店	*N.*	tea shop	U6A
cháng	长	長	*Adj.*	long	U6B
chǎng	场	場	*N.*	court	U3D
chàng-gē	唱歌	唱歌	*V.O.*	to sing	U2D
chāopiào	钞票	鈔票	*N.*	paper money	U4C
chéngshú	成熟	成熟	*Adj.*	mature	U6C
chéngzhī	橙汁	橙汁	*N.*	orange juice	U4B
chènshān	衬衫	襯衫	*N.*	shirt	U6A
chǐ	尺	尺	*N.*	ruler	U3B
chī	吃	吃	*V.*	to eat	U4B
chī-fàn	吃饭	吃飯	*V.O.*	to eat a meal	U2D
chōnglàng	冲浪	衝浪	*V.O./N.*	to surf; surfing	U3D
chǒngwù	宠物	寵物	*N.*	pets	U2A
chǒngwùdiàn	宠物店	寵物店	*N.*	pet store	U6A

Chóngyángjié	重阳节	重陽節	*N.*	Double Ninth Festival	U5C
chǒu	丑	醜	*Adj.*	ugly	U6D
chuān	穿	穿	*V.*	to wear; to put on	U6C
chuán	船	船	*N.*	boat	U5D
chúle… yǐwài…	除了…以外…	除了…以外…	*I.E.*	besides; in addition to; except for	U5D
Chūnjié	春节	春節	*N.*	Chinese New Year	U5C
chūnlián	春联	春聯	*N.*	Spring Festival couplets	U5C
chūntiān	春天	春天	*N.*	spring	U5B
Chúxī	除夕	除夕	*N.*	Chinese New Year's Eve	U5C
chūzhōng	初中	初中	*N.*	junior high school	U1D
chūzhōng yì-niánjí	初中一年级	初中一年級	*N.*	7th grade (in China)	U1D
chūzhōng èr-niánjí	初中二年级	初中二年級	*N.*	8th grade (in China)	U1D
chūzhōng sān-niánjí	初中三年级	初中三年級	*N.*	9th grade (in China)	U1D
chūzhōngshēng	初中生	初中生	*N.*	junior high school student	U1D
cuì	脆	脆	*Adj.*	crispy	U4D

D

dǎ	打	打	*V.*	to hit; to play (a ball sport)	U2D
dà	大	大	*Adj.*	big; large	U2A
dà bēi	大杯	大杯	*Adj.*	large (cup)	U4A
dǎ wǎngqiú	打网球	打網球	*V.O.*	to play tennis	U5A
dàchāo	大钞	大鈔	*N.*	large denomination bills	U4C
dài	带	帶	*V.*	to take; to bring	U5D
dàjiā	大家	大家	*Pron.*	everyone; all	U1C
dǎkāi	打开	打開	*V.*	to turn on	U5B
dàkǎo	大考	大考	*N.*	final exam	U3C
dǎléi	打雷	打雷	*V.O.*	to thunder	U5A
dāngrán	当然	當然	*M.A.*	of course	U3B
dào	道	道	*M.W.*	course of a meal	U4D
dào	到	到	*Prep.*	to	U5C
			V.	to arrive; to reach	U5C
dàxiǎo	大小	大小	*N.*	size	U6C
dàyī	大衣	大衣	*N.*	coat	U6A

dǎ-zhé	打折	打折	*V.O.*	to sell at a discount price	U6B
Dé.guó	德国	德國	*N.*	Germany	U1C
Dé.guórén	德国人	德國人	*N.*	German (people)	U1C
děi	得	得	*A.V.*	to need to; to have to	U1B
děng	等	等	*V.*	to wait	U4A
Déyǔ	德语	德語	*N.*	German	U1D
dì.x	弟弟	弟弟	*N.*	younger brother	U2B
diǎn	点	點	*M.W.*	o'clock	U4A
			V.	to order	U3B
diǎncài	点菜	點菜	*V.O.*	to order	U4D
diànnǎo	电脑	電腦	*N.*	computer	U3A
diànshì	电视	電視	*N.*	television	U3D
diànyǐng	电影	電影	*N.*	movie	U2D
diànzǐ yóuxì	电子游戏	電子遊戲	*N.*	video games	U2D
diàodàishān	吊带衫	吊帶杉	*N.*	spaghetti strap tank	U6A
dìlǐ	地理	地理	*N.*	geography	U1D
dìngshūjī	订书机	訂書機	*N.*	stapler	U3B
dìtú	地图	地圖	*N.*	map	U3A
dǒng	懂	懂	*V.*	to understand	U5C
dōngtiān	冬天	冬天	*N.*	winter	U5B
dōng.xī	东西	東西	*N.*	thing(s); stuff	U4B
Dōngzhì	冬至	冬至	*N.*	Winter solstice	U5D
dōu	都	都	*Adv.*	both; all	U1D
dòujiāng	豆浆	豆漿	*N.*	soybean milk	U4C
dù	度	度	*M.W.*	a unit or measurement for temperature	U5B
duǎn	短	短	*Adj.*	short	U6B
duànliàn	锻练	鍛鍊	*V.*	to work out	U3C
Duānwǔjié	端午节	端午節	*N.*	Dragon Boat Festival	U5C
duì	对	對	*Adj.*	correct; right	U1D
duì .bú duì	对不对	對不對	*Ph.*	Is that right?	U1D
duì.le	对了	對了	*I.E.*	by the way	U2D
duìbuqǐ	对不起	對不起	*C.E.*	sorry	U4B
duōyún	多云	多雲	*Adj.*	cloudy	U5A

E

.en	嗯	嗯	*Intj.*	um	U1D
è	饿	餓	*Adj.*	hungry	U5B
èr	二	二	*Num.*	two	U1D
èr.shí	二十	二十	*Num.*	twenty	U1D
érqiě	而且	而且	*Conj.*	but also; and; also; in addition	U6C
Èryuè	二月	二月	*T.W.*	February	U2C

F

Fǎ.guó	法国	法國	*N.*	France	U1C
Fǎ.guórén	法国人	法國人	*N.*	French (people)	U1C
fàn	饭	飯	*N.*	cooked meal	U4D
*Fǎ*yǔ	法语	法語	*N.*	French	U1D
fēn	分	分	*M.W.*	minute; penny	U3B
fèn	份	份	*M.W.*	a share of; a portion of	U4A
*fěn*bǐ	粉笔	粉筆	*N.*	chalk	U3A
fēng	风	風	*N*	wind	U5A
fěnhóng.sè	粉红色	粉紅色	*N.*	pink	U6B
fúwùyuán	服务员	服務員	*N.*	waiter / waitress	U4D

G

.ge	个	個	*M.W.*	a common measure word	U2B
gāng	刚	剛	*Adv.*	just; exactly	U6C
Gǎngbì	港币	港幣	*N.*	Hong Kong dollar	U4C
gāo'ěrfū	高尔夫	高爾夫	*N.*	golf	U3D
gāoxìng	高兴	高興	*Adj.*	happy; glad	U1C
gāozhōng	高中	高中	*N.*	senior high school	U1D
gāozhōng yì-niánjí	高中一年级	高中一年級	*N.*	10th grade (in China)	U1D
gāozhōng èr-niánjí	高中二年级	高中二年級	*N.*	11th grade (in China)	U1D
gāozhōng sān-niánjí	高中三年级	高中三年級	*N.*	12th grade (in China)	U1D
gāozhōngshēng	高中生	高中生	*N.*	senior high school student	U1D
gē.x	哥哥	哥哥	*N.*	older brother	U2B
gěi	给	給	*V.*	to give	U3B
gēn	跟	跟	*Prep.*	with	U3D

gèng	更	更	*Adv.*	more	U5C
gōngbǎo jīdīng	宫保鸡丁	宮保雞丁	*N.*	Kung Pao chicken	U4D
gōngxǐ	恭喜	恭喜	*N.*	congratulations	U5C
gōngyuán	公园	公園	*N.*	park	U3D
gǒu	狗	狗	*N.*	dog	U2A
gòuwù zhōngxīn	购物中心	購物中心	*N.*	mall	U3D
guāfēng	刮风	刮風	*V.O.*	the wind is blowing very hard	U5A
guàn	罐	罐	*N.*	can	U4B
guāngpán	光盘	光盤	*N.*	compact disc (CD)	U3A
guì	贵	貴	*Adj.*	honored; expensive	U1A; U6B
guó	国	國	*N.*	country	U1C
guò	过	過	*V.*	to celebrate; to pass through time	U5C
guójiā	国家	國家	*N.*	country	U1C
guònián	过年	過年	*V.O.*	to celebrate / spend the New Year	U5C
guòshí	过时	過時	*Adj.*	out-of-date	U6C
guǒzhī	果汁	果汁	*N.*	juice	U4A

H

hāi	嗨	嗨	*Intj.*	hi; hello	U1C
hái	还	還	*Adv.*	still; in addition; and also	U3C
hǎi	海	海	*N.*	sea	U3D
hái xíng	还行	還行	*Adj.*	not so bad	U1B
hǎibào	海报	海報	*N.*	poster	U3A
hǎibiān	海边	海邊	*N.*	beach	U3D
háishì	还是	還是	*Conj.*	or	U4A
Hán.guó	韩国	韓國	*N.*	Korea	U1C
Hán.guórén	韩国人	韓國人	*N.*	Korean (people)	U1C
hànbǎobāo	汉堡包	漢堡包	*N.*	hamburger	U4A
Hányuán	韩元	韓元	*N.*	South Korean won	U4C
hào	号	號	*M.W.*	date	U2C
			N.	size; number	U6C
hǎo	好	好	*Adj.*	good	U1A
hǎo .le	好了	好了	*C.E.*	okay	U3C
hǎo jiǔ bú jiàn	好久不见	好久不見	*C.E.*	long time no see	U1B
hǎochī	好吃	好吃	*Adj.*	delicious	U4D

hǎohē	好喝	好喝	*Adj.*	good to drink	U4D
hǎokàn	好看	好看	*Adj.*	(to look) fine; nice	U6B
hàomǎ	号码	號碼	*N.*	number	U2C
hǎowánr	好玩儿	好玩兒	*Adj.*	fun; interesting; amusing	U3C
hē	喝	喝	*V.*	to drink	U4A
hé	和	和	*Conj.*	and	U2B
héchàngtuán	合唱团	合唱團	*N.*	choir	U1D
.hei	嘿	嘿	*Intj.*	hey	U1A
hēi.sè	黑色	黑色	*N.*	black	U6B
hēibǎn	黑板	黑板	*N.*	blackboard	U3A
hěn	很	很	*Adv.*	very	U1B
hěn hǎo	很好	很好	*Adj.*	great	U1B
héshēn	合身	合身	*Adj.*	good-fitting	U6C
héshì	合适	合適	*Adj.*	suitable	U6C
hóng.sè	红色	紅色	*N.*	red	U6B
hóngbāo	红包	紅包	*N.*	red envelopes	U5C
hóngchá	红茶	紅茶	*N.*	black tea	U4B
hóngdòu	红豆	紅豆	*N.*	red bean	U5B
hòu.tiān	后天	後天	*T.W.*	the day after tomorrow	U3C
hú	壶	壺	*N.*	pot	U4B
huá	划	划	*V.*	to paddle; to row	U5D
huábǎn	滑板	滑板	*N.*	skateboarding	U2D
huāchá	花茶	花茶	*N.*	herbal tea	U4B
huá-chuán	划船	划船	*V.O.*	to row a boat	U5D
huà-huà	画画	畫畫	*V.O.*	to paint; to draw	U2D
huài	坏	壞	*Adj.*	broken	U5B
huáng.sè	黄色	黃色	*N.*	yellow	U6B
Huáshì	华氏	華氏	*N.*	Fahrenheit	U5B
huá-xuě	滑雪	滑雪	*V.O.*	to ski	U3D
huàxué	化学	化學	*N.*	chemistry	U1D
huì	会	會	*A.V.*	will	U5A
huī.sè	灰色	灰色	*N.*	grey	U6B
huí-jiā	回家	回家	*V.O.*	to go home	U1B
hún.tún	馄饨	餛飩	*N.*	wontons	U4C
huǒguō	火锅	火鍋	*N.*	hot pot	U4D

J

jǐ	几	幾	*Q.W.*	how many	U2B
jiā	家	家	*N.*	home; family	U2A
jià.qián	价钱	價錢	*N.*	price	U6D
Jiā'nádà	加拿大	加拿大	*N.*	Canada	U1C
Jiā'nádàrén	加拿大人	加拿大人	*N.*	Canadian (people)	U1C
jiā-jiǎo tuōxié	夹脚拖鞋	夾腳拖鞋	*N.*	flip-flops	U6D
jiàn	见	見	*V.*	to see	U1B
	件	件	*M.W.*	measure word for things and matters; used for a piece of clothing	U4C
jiānbǐng	煎饼	煎餅	*N.*	pancake	U4C
jiǎndāo	剪刀	剪刀	*N.*	scissors	U3B
jiǎngtái	讲台	講台	*N.*	podium	U3A
jiànshēnfáng	健身房	健身房	*N.*	fitness center	U3C
jiào	叫	叫	*V.*	to be called	U1A
Jiàoshījié	教师节	教師節	*N.*	Teacher's Day	U5C
jiāoshuǐ	胶水	膠水	*N.*	glue	U3B
jiǎo.zi	饺子	餃子	*N.*	dumplings	U4D
jiārén	家人	家人	*N.*	family members	U2A
jīdàn	鸡蛋	雞蛋	*N.*	eggs	U4C
jiè	借	借	*V.*	to borrow; to lend	U3B
jiě.x	姐姐	姐姐	*N.*	older sister	U2A
jiérì	节日	節日	*N.*	festival	U5C
jiéshù	结束	結束	*V.*	to end	U5C
jǐn	紧	緊	*Adj.*	tight	U6C
jīn.tiān	今天	今天	*T.W.*	today	U3C
jīròu	鸡肉	雞肉	*N.*	chicken	U4D
jíshì hànbǎobāo	吉士汉堡包	吉士漢堡包	*N.*	cheeseburger	U4A
jìsuànjī kēxué	计算机科学	計算機科學	*N.*	computer science	U1D
jiù	旧	舊	*Adj.*	used; old	U6C
jiǔ	九	九	*Num.*	nine	U1D
jiǔ.shí	九十	九十	*Num.*	ninety	U1D
jiǔ-niánjí	九年级	九年級	*N.*	9th grade	U1D
Jiǔyuè	九月	九月	*T.W.*	September	U2C

jué.de	觉得	覺得	*V.*	to feel; think	U3C
júhuáng.sè	橘黄色	橘黃色	*N.*	orange	U6B
jǔzhòng	举重	舉重	*V.O.*	to lift weights	U3D

K

kāfēi	咖啡	咖啡	*N.*	coffee	U4A
kāfēi.sè	咖啡色	咖啡色	*N.*	brown	U6B
kāi diànnǎo	开电脑	開電腦	*V.O.*	to turn on the computer	U3A
kàn	看	看	*V.*	to see; to look at	U2D
kàn-shū	看书	看書	*V.O.*	to read (books)	U2D
kǎoshì	考试	考試	*N.*	test; exam	U3C
kè	课	課	*N.*	class; course	U1C
kě	渴	渴	*Adj.*	thirsty	U5B
kè	刻	刻	*M.W.*	quarter	U3B
kě.shì	可是	可是	*Conj.*	but; however	U2B
kě'ài	可爱	可愛	*Adj.*	cute; adorable	U2A
kèběn	课本	課本	*N.*	textbook	U3A
kělè	可乐	可樂	*N.*	cola	U2B
*kě*yǐ	可以	可以	*A.V.*	can; may	U3B
kōngtiáo	空调	空調	*N.*	air conditioner	U5B
kǒu	口	口	*M.W.*	a measure word for people	U2B
kǒuwèi	口味	口味	*N.*	flavor	U5B
kǔ	苦	苦	*Adj.*	bitter	U4D
kù.zi	裤子	褲子	*N.*	pants	U6A
kuài	块	塊	*M.W.*	dollar (in spoken Chinese)	U4C
	快	快	*Adv.*	soon; before long	U5C
kuàilè	快乐	快樂	*Adj.*	happy; joyful	U3D

L

là	辣	辣	*Adj.*	spicy	U4D
lái	来	來	*V.*	to come	U3C
lán.sè	蓝色	藍色	*N.*	blue	U6B
lánqiú	篮球	籃球	*N.*	basketball	U2D
lánqiúchǎng	篮球场	籃球場	*N.*	basketball court	U3D
lǎo	老	老	*Adj.*	old	U6C
lǎoshī	老师	老師	*N.*	teacher	U1A

le	了	了	*P.*	a particle placed at the end of a sentence to indicate change	U4D
léi	雷	雷	*N.*	thunder	U5A
lěng	冷	冷	*Adj.*	cold	U5B
liáng	凉	涼	*Adj.*	cool	U5B
liǎng	两	兩	*Num.*	two	U2B
liányīqún	连衣裙	連衣裙	*N.*	dress	U6A
líng	零	零	*Num.*	zero	U1D
língqián	零钱	零錢	*N.*	change	U4C
lìshǐ	历史	歷史	*N.*	history	U1D
liù	六	六	*Num.*	six	U1D
liù.shí	六十	六十	*Num.*	sixty	U1D
Liùyuè	六月	六月	*T.W.*	June	U2C
lóngzhōu	龙舟	龍舟	*N.*	dragon boat	U5D
lǜ.sè	绿色	綠色	*N.*	green	U6B
lǜchá	绿茶	綠茶	*N.*	green tea	U4B
lǚxíng	旅行	旅行	*V.*	to travel	U6A

M

.ma	吗	嗎	*Q.W.*	a question particle used at the end of a declarative sentence	U1B
méi.yǒu yì.sī	没有意思	沒有意思	*Adj.*	uninteresting	U3C
mā.x	妈妈	媽媽	*N.*	mother	U2A
mǎi	买	買	*V.*	to buy	U6A
màipiàn	麦片	麥片	*N.*	cereal	U4C
Mǎláixīyà	马来西亚	馬來西亞	*N.*	Malaysia	U1C
Mǎláixīyàrén	马来西亚人	馬來西亞人	*N.*	Malaysian (people)	U1C
mànpǎo	慢跑	慢跑	*N.*	jogging	U3D
			V.	to jog	
mán.tóu	馒头	饅頭	*N.*	steamed bread	U4C
māo	猫	貓	*N.*	cat	U2A
máo	毛	毛	*M.W.*	one tenth of a 元 *yuán*; a dime or 10 pennies	U4C
máoyī	毛衣	毛衣	*N.*	sweater	U6A
mápó dòu.fǔ	麻婆豆腐	麻婆豆腐	*N.*	Mapo Tofu	U4D
mǎshàng	马上	馬上	*Adv.*	at once; right away	U4D

méi wèntí	没问题	沒問題	*C.E.*	no problem	U5B
Měi.guó	美国	美國	*N.*	the United States	U1C
mèi.x	妹妹	妹妹	*N.*	younger sister	U2B
méi.yǒu	没有	沒有	*V.*	to not have (the negation of 有 *yǒu*)	U2B
měilì	美丽	美麗	*Adj.*	beautiful; pretty	U6D
měishù	美术	美術	*N.*	art	U1D
měishùguǎn	美术馆	美術館	*N.*	art museum	U3D
Měiyuán	美元	美元	*N.*	United States dollar	U4C
.mén	们	們	*N.*	a plural suffix for pronouns; sometimes a suffix for nouns	U1A
miàn	面	麵	*N.*	noodles	U4D
miànbāo	面包	麵包	*N.*	bread	U4C
mǐfàn	米饭	米飯	*N.*	cooked rice	U4D
mǐ.sè	米色	米色	*N.*	beige	U6B
míng.tiān	明天	明天	*T.W.*	tomorrow	U2D
míng.zì	名字	名字	*N.*	name	U1A
mǒchá	抹茶	抹茶	*N.*	matcha	U5B
Mòxīgē	墨西哥	墨西哥	*N.*	Mexico	U1C
Mòxīgērén	墨西哥人	墨西哥人	*N.*	Mexican (people)	U1C

N

nà	那	那	*Conj.*	then; in that case	U2D
			Dem.	that	U2A
nǎ	哪	哪	*Q.W.*	which	U1C
nǎi.x	奶奶	奶奶	*N.*	paternal grandmother	U2A
nǎichá	奶茶	奶茶	*N.*	milk tea	U4B
nǎixī	奶昔	奶昔	*N.*	milk shake	U4B
*nǎ*lǐ	哪里	哪裡	*Q.W.*	where	U1C
nán	难	難	*Adj.*	difficult	U3C
nánchī	难吃	難吃	*Adj.*	bad-tasting (for food)	U4D
nánhē	难喝	難喝	*Adj.*	bad-tasting (for drinks)	U4D
nǎr	哪儿	哪兒	*Q.W.*	where	U3A
.ne	呢	呢	*P.*	a final particle used in follow-up questions	U1A
nǐ	你	你	*Pron.*	you	U1A
nǐ.de	你的	你的	*Poss.*	yours	U4C

Nǐ hǎo .ma?	你好吗?	你好嗎?	*C.E.*	How are you?	U1B
nǐ hǎo	你好	你好	*C.E.*	hello	U1A
nǐ.mén	你们	你們	*Pron.*	you (plural)	U1A
niánjí	年级	年級	*M.W.*	grade	U1D
niánqīng	年轻	年輕	*Adj.*	young	U6C
niǎo	鸟	鳥	*N.*	bird	U2A
nǐmen.de	你们的	你们的	*Poss.*	yours	U4C
nín	您	您	*Pron.*	you (polite)	U1A
níngméngshuǐ	柠檬水	檸檬水	*N.*	lemonade	U4B
niúnǎi	牛奶	牛奶	*N.*	milk	U4C
niúròu	牛肉	牛肉	*N.*	beef	U4D
niúzǎikù	牛仔裤	牛仔褲	*N.*	jeans	U6A
nónglì	农历	農曆	*N.*	the lunar calendar	U5C
nuǎnqì	暖气	暖氣	*N.*	heater; heating system	U5B

O

Ōuyuán	欧元	歐元	*N.*	Euro	U4C

P

páiqiú	排球	排球	*N.*	volleyball	U3D
pàng	胖	胖	*Adj.*	fat	U2A
péng.yǒu	朋友	朋友	*N.*	friend	U1C
pián.yí	便宜	便宜	*Adj.*	cheap	U6B
piào.liàng	漂亮	漂亮	*Adj.*	beautiful; pretty	U6B
píng	瓶	瓶	*M.W.*	a measure word for bottles	U4B
			N.	bottle	U4B
píngguǒ	苹果	蘋果	*N.*	apple	U4A
píngguǒzhī	苹果汁	蘋果汁	*N.*	apple juice	U4B
píxié	皮鞋	皮鞋	*N.*	leather shoes	U6D
pútáozhī	葡萄汁	葡萄汁	*N.*	grapefruit juice	U4B

Q

qí	骑	騎	*V.*	to ride	U3D
qī	七	七	*Num.*	seven	U1D
qī.shí	七十	七十	*Num.*	seventy	U1D
qián	钱	錢	*N.*	money	U4C

qián.tiān	前天	前天	*T.W.*	the day before yesterday	U3C
qiānbǐ	铅笔	鉛筆	*N.*	pencil	U3B
qiānbǐhé	铅笔盒	鉛筆盒	*N.*	pencil box	U3B
qiānwàn	千万	千萬	*Num.*	ten million	U6B
qiǎokèlì	巧克力	巧克力	*N.*	chocolate	U5B
qíguài	奇怪	奇怪	*Adj.*	strange	U3A
qǐng	请	請	*V.*	to request ("please")	U3B
qīngdàn	清淡	清淡	*Adj.*	light	U4D
Qīngmíngjié	清明节	清明節	*N.*	Tomb-sweeping Festival	U5C
qíngtiān	晴天	晴天	*N.*	sunny day	U5A
qǐngwèn	请问	請問	*C.E.*	May I ask…?	U4B
qī-niánjí	七年级	七年級	*N.*	7th grade	U1D
qìshuǐ	汽水	汽水	*N.*	soda	U4A
qiú	球	球	*N.*	ball	U2D
qiūtiān	秋天	秋天	*N.*	autumn	U5B
Qīxī	七夕	七夕	*N.*	Chinese Valentine's Day	U5D
Qīyuè	七月	七月	*T.W.*	July	U2C
qù	去	去	*V.*	to go	U1B
qún.zi	裙子	裙子	*N.*	skirt	U6A

R

rè	热	熱	*Adj.*	hot	U5B
rè qiǎokèlì	热巧克力	熱巧克力	*N.*	hot chocolate	U4B
règǒu	热狗	熱狗	*N.*	hotdog	U4A
rén	人	人	*N.*	person; people	U1C
rèn.shì	认识	認識	*V.*	to know (people)	U1C
Rénmínbì	人民币	人民幣	*N.*	Chinese Renminbi	U4C
Rìběn	日本	日本	*N.*	Japan	U1C
Rìyuán	日元	日元	*N.*	Japanese yen	U4C
róngyì	容易	容易	*Adj.*	easy	U3C
ròu	肉	肉	*N.*	meat	U4D

S

sān	三	三	*Num.*	three	U1D
sān.shí	三十	三十	*Num.*	thirty	U1D
sānmíngzhì	三明治	三明治	*N.*	sandwich	U4A

Sānyuè	三月	三月	*T.W.*	March	U2C
sèlā	色拉	色拉	*N.*	salad	U4A
shàng	上	上	*Adj.*	last	U5A
shàng shàng.ge xīngqī	上上个星期	上上個星期	*T.W.*	the week before last	U5A
shāngdiàn	商店	商店	*N.*	store; shop	U6A
shàng.ge xīngqī	上个星期	上個星期	*T.W.*	last week	U5A
shàng-kè	上课	上課	*V.O.*	to go to class	U1B
shàngwǎng	上网	上網	*V.O.*	to surf the Internet	U2D
shāobǐng	烧饼	燒餅	*N.*	sesame seed cake	U4C
shén.me	什么	什麼	*Q.W.*	what	U1A
shēng.rì	生日	生日	*N.*	birthday	U2C
shēng.rì dàngāo	生日蛋糕	生日蛋糕	*N.*	birthday cake	U2C
shēng.rì kǎpiàn	生日卡片	生日卡片	*N.*	birthday card	U2C
shēng.rì kuàilè	生日快乐	生日快樂	*C.E.*	happy birthday	U2C
shēng.rì lǐwù	生日礼物	生日禮物	*N.*	birthday gift	U2C
shēngwù	生物	生物	*N.*	biology	U1D
Shèshì	摄氏	攝氏	*N.*	Celsius	U5B
shí	十	十	*Num.*	ten	U1D
shì	是	是	*V.*	to be	U1A
	事	事	*N.*	matter; affair; thing	U4C
	试	試	*V.*	to try	U6D
shí'èr-niánjí	十二年级	十二年級	*N.*	12th grade	U1D
Shí'èryuè	十二月	十二月	*N.*	December	U2C
shìhé	适合	適合	*V.*	to suit; to fit	U6D
shíhou	时候	時候	*N.*	time; moment	U5B
shímáo	时髦	時髦	*Adj.*	fashionable	U6C
shí-niánjí	十年级	十年級	*N.*	10th grade	U1D
shí-wàn	十万	十萬	*Num.*	one hundred thousand	U6B
shíyī-niánjí	十一年级	十一年級	*N.*	11th grade	U1D
Shíyīyuè	十一月	十一月	*T.W.*	November	U2C
shí-yì	十亿	十億	*Num.*	billion	U6B
Shíyuè	十月	十月	*T.W.*	October	U2C
shǒujīdiàn	手机店	手機店	*N.*	cell phone shop	U6A
shū	书	書	*N.*	book	U2B

shuài	帅	帥	*Adj.*	handsome	U6D
shūbāo	书包	書包	*N.*	schoolbag	U3A
shūdiàn	书店	書店	*N.*	bookstore	U6A
shuǐ	水	水	*N.*	water	U2B
shuì-jiào	睡觉	睡覺	*V.O.*	to sleep	U1B
shuìyī	睡衣	睡衣	*N.*	pajamas	U6D
shuō-huà	说话	說話	*V.O.*	to speak	U2D
shǔtiáo	薯条	薯條	*N.*	French fries	U4A
shùxué	数学	數學	*N.*	math	U1D
sì	四	四	*Num.*	four	U1D
sì jì	四季	四季	*N.*	the four seasons	U5B
sì.shí	四十	四十	*Num.*	forty	U1D
Sìyuè	四月	四月	*T.W.*	April	U2C
sōng	松	鬆	*Adj.*	loose	U6C
suān	酸	酸	*Adj.*	sour	U4D
suānlàtāng	酸辣汤	酸辣湯	*N.*	hot and sour soup	U4D
suì	岁	歲	*M.W.*	year (of age)	U1D
*suǒ*yǐ	所以	所以	*Conj.*	so; therefore	U5C

T

tā	他	他	*Pron.*	he	U1C
tā	她	她	*Pron.*	she	U1C
tā	它	它	*Pron.*	it	U1C
tā.de	他的	他的	*Poss.*	his	U4C
tā.de	她的	她的	*Poss.*	hers	U4C
tā.mén	他们	他們	*Pron.*	they (m.)	U1C
tā.mén	她们	她們	*Pron.*	they (f.)	U1C
tā.mén	它们	它們	*Pron.*	they (neuter)	U1C
tài	太	太	*Adv.*	too	U5B
tài.x	太太	太太	*N.*	Ms.	U1A
Tài.guó	泰国	泰國	*N.*	Thailand	U1C
Tài.guórén	泰国人	泰國人	*N.*	Thai (people)	U1C
táiqiú	台球	台球	*N.*	pool	U3D
tā.mén.de	他们的	他們的	*Poss.*	theirs	U4C
tā.mén.de	她们的	她們的	*Poss.*	theirs	U4C

tāng	汤	湯	*N.*	soup	U4D
táng	堂	堂	*M.W.*	period of class	U3C
tāngmiàn	汤面	湯麵	*N.*	noodle soup	U4D
tào	套	套	*M.W.*	set; suit	U6D
tǎoyàn	讨厌	討厭	*Adj.*	annoying	U5A
tī	踢	踢	*V.*	to kick; to play (soccer)	U2D
tián	甜	甜	*Adj.*	sweet	U4D
tiānqì	天气	天氣	*N*	weather	U5A
tiānzhúshǔ	天竺鼠	天竺鼠	*N.*	guinea pig	U2A
tiáo	条	條	*M.W.*	used for a pair of pants or a skirt	U6A
tiào-wǔ	跳舞	跳舞	*V.O.*	to dance	U2D
tīng-yīnyuè	听音乐	聽音樂	*V.O.*	to listen to music	U2D
tīxù	T恤	T恤	*N.*	T-shirt	U6A
tǐyù	体育	體育	*N.*	physical education	U1D
tóngbǎn	铜板	銅板	*N.*	coin	U4C
tōngcháng	通常	通常	*T.W.*	usually	U5C
tóngxué	同学	同學	*N.*	classmate	U1B
tōngyòng jìshù	通用技术	通用技術	*N.*	general technology	U1D
tóuyǐngjī	投影机	投影機	*N.*	projector	U3A
tù.zi	兔子	兔子	*N.*	rabbit	U2A
tuōxié	拖鞋	拖鞋	*N.*	slippers	U6D
túshūguǎn	图书馆	圖書館	*N.*	library	U3C

W

.wa	哇	哇	*Intj.*	wow	U2C
wà.zi	袜子	襪子	*N.*	socks	U6D
wàigōng	外公	外公	*N.*	maternal grandfather	U2A
wàipó	外婆	外婆	*N.*	maternal grandmother	U2A
wàitào	外套	外套	*N.*	jacket	U6A
wàiyǔ	外语	外語	*N.*	foreign language	U1D
wán	玩	玩	*V.*	to play (sports or recreational activities)	U2D
wǎn.shàng	晚上	晚上	*N.*	night	U1B
wǎn.shàng hǎo	晚上好	晚上好	*C.E.*	good evening	U1B
wǎn'ān	晚安	晚安	*C.E.*	good night	U1B

wǎngqiú	网球	網球	*N.*	tennis	U5A
wéi	喂	喂	*P.*	hello (used to greet people on the phone)	U5D
wèishén.me	为什么	為什麼	*Q.W.*	why	U5C
wèn	问	問	*V.*	to ask	U1C
wénjiànjiā	文件夹	文件夾	*N.*	folder	U3B
wēnnuǎn	温暖	溫暖	*Adj.*	warm	U5B
wénxué	文学	文學	*N.*	literature	U1D
wǒ	我	我	*Pron.*	I	U1A
wǒ.de	我的	我的	*Poss.*	mine	U4C
wǒ.mén	我们	我們	*Pron.*	we	U1C
wǒ.men.de	我们的	我們的	*Poss.*	ours	U4C
wǔ	五	五	*Num.*	five	U1D
wǔ.shí	五十	五十	*Num.*	fifty	U1D
wūguī	乌龟	烏龜	*N.*	turtle	U2B
wùlǐ	物理	物理	*N.*	physics	U1D
wúliáo	无聊	無聊	*Adj.*	boring	U3C
wūlóngchá	乌龙茶	烏龍茶	*N.*	oolong tea	U4B
Wǔyuè	五月	五月	*T.W.*	May	U2C

X

xǐ.huān	喜欢	喜歡	*V.*	to like	U2D
xià	下	下	*Adj.*	next	U5A
xià xià.ge xīngqī	下下个星期	下下個星期	*T.W.*	the week after next	U5A
xià.cì	下次	下次	*T.W.*	next time	U6C
xià.wǔ	下午	下午	*T.W.*	afternoon	U1B
xià.ge xīngqī	下个星期	下個星期	*T.W.*	next week	U5A
xià-kè	下课	下課	*V.O.*	after school	U6A
xián	咸	鹹	*Adj.*	salty	U4D
xiān.shēng	先生	先生	*N.*	Mr.	U1A
xiǎng	想	想	*V.*	to want	U4D
xiāngbāo	香包	香包	*N.*	scented sachet	U5D
xiāngcǎo	香草	香草	*N.*	vanilla	U4B
xiàngpí	橡皮	橡皮	*N.*	eraser	U3B
xiànzài	现在	現在	*T.W.*	now	U3B

xiǎo	小	小	*Adj.*	small	U2A
xiǎo bēi	小杯	小杯	*Adj.*	small (cup)	U4A
*xiǎo*jiě	小姐	小姐	*N.*	Miss	U1A
*xiǎo*kǎo	小考	小考	*N.*	quiz	U3C
xiǎoshì	小事	小事	*I.E.*	a triviality; something petty; It's nothing. (phr.)	U4C
xiàozhǎng	校长	校長	*N.*	principal	U1A
xiàtiān	夏天	夏天	*N.*	summer	U5B
xià*wǔ* hǎo	下午好	下午好	*C.E.*	good afternoon	U1B
xiàxuě	下雪	下雪	*V.O.*	to snow	U5A
xiàyǔ	下雨	下雨	*V.O.*	to rain	U5A
Xībānyá	西班牙	西班牙	*N.*	Spain	U1C
Xībānyárén	西班牙人	西班牙人	*N.*	Spanish (people)	U1C
Xībānyáyǔ	西班牙语	西班牙語	*N.*	Spanish (language)	U1D
xié.zi	鞋子	鞋子	*N.*	shoe(s)	U2B
xiédiàn	鞋店	鞋店	*N.*	shoe shop	U6A
xiě-zì	写字	寫字	*V.O.*	to write	U2D
xiězuò	写作	寫作	*N.*	composition	U1D
xìjù	戏剧	戲劇	*N.*	theater	U1D
xīn	新	新	*Adj.*	new	U6C
xíng	行	行	*V.*	to be all right	U6A
xìng	姓	姓	*V.*	to be surnamed	U1A
Xīngqī'èr	星期二	星期二	*T.W.*	Tuesday	U3C
Xīngqīliù	星期六	星期六	*T.W.*	Saturday	U3C
Xīngqīrì	星期日	星期日	*T.W.*	Sunday	U3C
Xīngqīsān	星期三	星期三	*T.W.*	Wednesday	U3C
Xīngqīsì	星期四	星期四	*T.W.*	Thursday	U3C
Xīngqīwǔ	星期五	星期五	*T.W.*	Friday	U3C
Xīngqīyī	星期一	星期一	*T.W.*	Monday	U3C
Xīnjiāpō	新加坡	新加坡	*N.*	Singapore	U1C
Xīnjiāpōrén	新加坡人	新加坡人	*N.*	Singaporean (people)	U1C
Xīnjiāpōbì	新加坡币	新加坡幣	*N.*	Singapore dollar	U4C
Xīnnián	新年	新年	*N.*	the New Year	U5C
Xīnnián kuàilè	新年快乐	新年快樂	*C.E.*	Happy New Year	U5C
Xīntáibì	新台币	新台幣	*N.*	New Taiwan dollar	U4C

xìnxī jìshù	信息技术	信息技術	*N.*	information technology	U1D
xiū	修	修	*V.*	to take (a class)	U1D
xiūzhèngyì	修正液	修正液	*N.*	correction fluid	U3B
xīzhuāng	西装	西裝	*N.*	suits	U6A
xuǎn	选	選	*V.*	to choose; to select	U6B
xué	学	學	*V.*	to study; to learn	U1D
xuě	雪	雪	*N.*	snow	U5A
xuē.zi	靴子	靴子	*N.*	boots	U6D
xuéqī	学期	學期	*N.*	semester	U5C
xuéxiào kēmù	学校科目	學校科目	*N.*	school subject	U1D
xūyào	需要	需要	*V.*	to need	U6D

Y

yàng	样	樣	*M.W.*	kind; type	U6D
yángròu	羊肉	羊肉	*N.*	lamb	U4D
yángyùpiàn	洋芋片	洋芋片	*N.*	chips	U4A
yào	要	要	*A.V.*	to be going to	U3B
			V.	to want; to need; to take	U3D
yāròu	鸭肉	鴨肉	*N.*	duck (meat)	U4D
yě	也	也	*Adv.*	also; too	U1C
yé.x	爷爷	爺爺	*N.*	paternal grandfather	U2A
yì	亿	億	*Num.*	a hundred million	U6B
yī	一	一	*Num.*	one	U1D
yī.fú	衣服	衣服	*N.*	clothes	U2B
yǐ.zi	椅子	椅子	*N.*	chair	U3A
yībǎi	一百	一百	*Num.*	one hundred	U1D
Yìdàlì	意大利	義大利	*N.*	Italy	U1C
Yìdàlìrén	意大利人	義大利人	*N.*	Italian (people)	U1C
yìdiǎnr	一点儿	一點兒	*C.*	a bit, a little	U6D
			I.E.	a little	U5B
yígòng	一共	一共	*Adv.*	altogether; in all	U4C
yǐhòu	以后	以後	*T.W.*	after; afterward	U6A
yǐjīng	已经	已經	*Adv.*	already	U5C
Yìndù	印度	印度	*N.*	India	U1C
Yìndùrén	印度人	印度人	*N.*	Indian (people)	U1C

Yīng.guó	英国	英國	*N.*	Great Britain	U1C
Yīng.guórén	英国人	英國人	*N.*	British (people)	U1C
Yīngbàng	英镑	英鎊	*N.*	British pound	U4C
yìngbì	硬币	硬幣	*N.*	coin	U4C
yīnggāi	应该	應該	*A.V.*	should	U5C
Yīngyǔ	英语	英語	*N.*	English (language)	U1D
yǐnliào	饮料	飲料	*N.*	beverages; drink	U4A
yīntiān	阴天	陰天	*N.*	cloudy day	U5A
yīnwèi	因为	因為	*Conj.*	because	U5C
yīnyuè	音乐	音樂	*N.*	music	U1D
yìqǐ	一起	一起	*Adv.*	together	U2D
yì-qiān	一千	一千	*Num.*	one thousand	U6B
yǐqián	以前	以前	*T.W.*	before; formerly; previously	U5C
yí-wàn	一万	一萬	*Num.*	ten thousand	U6B
yíxià	一下	一下	*Num. + M.W.*	used after a verb to indicate short duration	U4A
Yīyuè	一月	一月	*T.W.*	January	U2C
yóu	油	油	*Adj.*	greasy	U4D
yǒu	有	有	*V.*	to have	U2B
yòu	又	又	*Adv.*	both… and…	U5B
yǒu tiǎozhànxìng	有挑战性	有挑戰性	*Adj.*	challenging	U3C
yǒu yì.sī	有意思	有意思	*Adj.*	interesting	U3C
yǒu.diǎnr	有点儿	有點兒	*Adv.*	a bit; somewhat	U6C
yǒufēng	有风	有風	*Adj.*	windy	U5A
yǒumíng	有名	有名	*Adj.*	famous	U4D
yóutiáo	油条	油條	*N.*	deep-fried twisted dough sticks	U4C
*yǒu*yǎng yùndòng	有氧运动	有氧運動	*N.*	aerobics	U3D
yóuyǒng	游泳	游泳	*N.*	swimming	U2D
			V.	to swim	
yú	鱼	魚	*N.*	fish	U2A
yǔ	雨	雨	*N*	rain	U5A
Yuánxiāojié	元宵节	元宵節	*N.*	Lantern Festival	U5C
yuánzhūbǐ	圆珠笔	圓珠筆	*N.*	ballpoint pen	U3B
yuè	月	月	*M.W.*	month	U2C

yuèduì	乐队	樂隊	*N.*	band	U1D
Yuènán	越南	越南	*N.*	Vietnam	U1C
Yuènánrén	越南人	越南人	*N.*	Vietnamese (people)	U1C
yújiā	瑜珈	瑜珈	*N.*	yoga	U3D
yún	云	雲	*N.*	cloud	U5A
yùndòngxié	运动鞋	運動鞋	*N.*	sneakers	U6D
yǔtiān	雨天	雨天	*N.*	rainy day	U5A
yǔwén	语文	語文	*N.*	Chinese (for native speakers)	U1D

Z

zài	在	在	*V.*	indicating the position of a person or thing	U3A
zài	在	在	*Adv.*	indicating an action in progress	U5D
zǎo	早	早	*C.E.*	good morning	U1A
zǎo.shàng	早上	早上	*N.*	morning	U1B
zǎo.shàng hǎo	早上好	早上好	*C.E.*	good morning	U1B
zǎocān	早餐	早餐	*N.*	breakfast	U4C
zāogāo	糟糕	糟糕	*Adj.*	awful	U5B
zěn.meyàng	怎么样	怎麼樣	*Q.W.*	how; what about	U5A
zhájī	炸鸡	炸雞	*N.*	fried chicken	U4C
zhāng	张	張	*M.W.*	for a piece of paper	U3B
zhǎo	找	找	*V.*	to look for; to search; to return change after a purchase	U3A
zhàopiàn	照片	照片	*N.*	photo	U2B
zhǎoqián	找钱	找錢	*V.O.*	to give change	U4C
zhè; zhèi	这	這	*Dem.*	this	U1A
zhèi.ge xīngqī	这个星期	這個星期	*T.W.*	this week	U5A
zhékòu	折扣	折扣	*N.*	discount	U6B
zhè.me	这么	這麼	*Adv.*	such; so; like this	U5B
zhēn	真	真	*Adv.*	really	U5A
zhèngzhì	政治	政治	*N.*	political education	U1D
zhī	支	枝	*M.W.*	for stick-like things	U3B
zhǐ	纸	紙	*N.*	paper	U2B
	只	只	*Adv.*	only	U4B
zhī.dào	知道	知道	*V.*	to know	U6B
zhīmá	芝麻	芝麻	*N.*	sesame	U5B

zhōng	中	中	*Adj.*	medium	U4A
zhǒng	种	種	*M.W.*	kind; sort; type	U5D
zhōng bēi	中杯	中杯	*Adj.*	medium (cup)	U4A
Zhōng.guó	中国	中國	*N.*	China	U1C
Zhōng.guórén	中国人	中國人	*N.*	Chinese (people)	U1C
Zhōngqiūjié	中秋节	中秋節	*N.*	Mid-Autumn Festival	U5C
Zhōngwén	中文	中文	*N.*	Chinese (language)	U1A
zhōngwǔ	中午	中午	*N.*	noon	U1B
zhōngxué	中学	中學	*N.*	high school	U1D
zhōngxué.shēng	中学生	中學生	*N.*	high school student	U1D
Zhōngyuánjié	中元节	中元節	*N.*	Ghost Festival	U5D
zhōumò	周末	週末	*N.*	weekend	U3D
zhuō.zi	桌子	桌子	*N.*	table; desk	U3A
zhūròu	猪肉	豬肉	*N.*	pork	U4D
zǐ.sè	紫色	紫色	*N.*	purple	U6B
zijǐ	自己	自己	*Pron.*	oneself	U6A
zìxíngchē	自行车	自行車	*N.*	bicycle	U3D
zǒng	总	總	*Adv.*	always	U5B
zǒngshì	总是	總是	*Adv.*	always	U5B
zòng.zi	粽子	粽子	*N.*	(rice dumplings made and eaten during the Dragon Boat Festival)	U5D
zǒu	走	走	*V.*	to go; to walk	U1B
zuì	最	最	*Adv.*	the most	U6D
zuò	做	做	*V.*	to do; to make	U2D
zuó.tiān	昨天	昨天	*T.W.*	yesterday	U3C
zúqiú	足球	足球	*N.*	soccer	U2D

英文索引 English to Chinese and Pinyin Vocabulary

Each entry lists the English meaning, simplified character, traditional character, Pinyin, part of speech, unit and lesson.

A

a bit, a little	一点儿	一點兒	yìdiǎnr	*C.*	U6D
a little				*I.E.*	U5B
a bit; somewhat	有点儿	有點兒	*yǒu*.diǎnr	*Adv.*	U6C
a common measure word	个	個	.ge	*M.W.*	U2B
aerobics	有氧运动	有氧運動	*yǒu*yǎng yùndòng	*N.*	U3D
after school	下课	下課	xià-kè	*V.O.*	U6A
after; afterward	以后	以後	yǐhòu	*T.W.*	U6A
afternoon	下午	下午	xià.wǔ	*T.W.*	U1B
air conditioner	空调	空調	kōngtiáo	*N.*	U5B
already	已经	已經	yǐjīng	*Adv.*	U5C
all right	行	行	xíng	*V.*	U6A
also; too	也	也	yě	*Adv.*	U1C
altogether; in all	一共	一共	yígòng	*Adv.*	U4C
always	总(是)	總(是)	zǒng(shì)	*Adv.*	U5B
and	和	和	hé	*Conj.*	U2B
annoying	讨厌	討厭	tǎoyàn	*Adj.*	U5A
apple	苹果	蘋果	píngguǒ	*N.*	U4A
apple juice	苹果汁	蘋果汁	píngguǒzhī	*N.*	U4B
April	四月	四月	Sìyuè	*T.W.*	U2C
art	美术	美術	měishù	*N.*	U1D
art museum	美术馆	美術館	měishùguǎn	*N.*	U3D
to arrive; to reach	到	到	dào	*V.*	U5C
to ask	问	問	wèn	*V.*	U1C
at once; right away	马上	馬上	mǎshàng	*Adv.*	U4D
August	八月	八月	Bāyuè	*T.W.*	U2C
autumn	秋天	秋天	qiūtiān	*N.*	U5B
awful	糟糕	糟糕	zāogāo	*Adj.*	U5B

B

backpack	背包	背包	bēibāo	*N.*	U2B

bad-tasting (for food)	难吃	難吃	nánchī	*Adj.*	U4D
bad-tasting (for drinks)	难喝	難喝	nánhē	*Adj.*	U4D
ball	球	球	qiú	*N.*	U2D
ballpoint pen	圆珠笔	圓珠筆	yuánzhūbǐ	*N.*	U3B
band	乐队	樂隊	yuèduì	*N.*	U1D
baseball	棒球	棒球	bàngqiú	*N.*	U2D
basketball	篮球	籃球	lánqiú	*N.*	U2D
basketball court	篮球场	籃球場	lánqiúchǎng	*N.*	U3D
to be	是	是	shì	*V.*	U1A
beach	海边	海邊	hǎibiān	*N.*	U3D
beautiful; pretty	美丽	美麗	měilì	*Adj.*	U6D
beautiful; pretty	漂亮	漂亮	piào.liàng	*Adj.*	U6B
because	因为	因為	yīnwèi	*Conj.*	U5C
beef	牛肉	牛肉	niúròu	*N.*	U4D
before; formerly; previously	以前	以前	yǐqián	*T.W.*	U5C
beige	米色	米色	mǐ.sè	*N.*	U6B
Beijing roast duck	北京烤鸭	北京烤鴨	Běijīng kǎoyā	*N.*	U4D
besides; in addition to; except for	除了…以外…	除了…以外…	chúle… yǐwài…	*I.E.*	U5D
beverages; drink	饮料	飲料	yǐnliào	*N.*	U4A
bicycle	自行车	自行車	zìxíngchē	*N.*	U3D
big; large	大	大	dà	*Adj.*	U2A
billion	十亿	十億	shíyì	*Num.*	U6B
biology	生物	生物	shēngwù	*N.*	U1D
bird	鸟	鳥	niǎo	*N.*	U2A
birthday	生日	生日	shēng.rì	*N.*	U2C
birthday cake	生日蛋糕	生日蛋糕	shēng.rì dàngāo	*N.*	U2C
birthday card	生日卡片	生日卡片	shēng.rì kǎpiàn	*N.*	U2C
birthday gift	生日礼物	生日禮物	shēng.rì lǐwù	*N.*	U2C
bitter	苦	苦	kǔ	*Adj.*	U4D
black	黑色	黑色	hēi.sè	*N.*	U6B
black tea	红茶	紅茶	hóngchá	*N.*	U4B
blackboard	黑板	黑板	hēibǎn	*N.*	U3A
blue	蓝色	藍色	lán.sè	*N.*	U6B
board eraser	板擦	板擦	bǎncā	*N.*	U3A

boat	船	船	chuán	*N.*	U5D
book	书	書	shū	*N.*	U2B
bookstore	书店	書店	shūdiàn	*N.*	U6A
boots	靴子	靴子	xuē.zi	*N.*	U6D
boring	无聊	無聊	wúliáo	*Adj.*	U3C
both; all	都	都	dōu	*Adv.*	U4D
both … and…	又	又	yòu	*Adv.*	U5B
bottle	瓶	瓶	píng	*N.*	U4B
a measure word for bottles				*M.W.*	U2B
bread	面包	麵包	miànbāo	*N.*	U4C
breakfast	早餐	早餐	zǎocān	*N.*	U4C
British (people)	英国人	英國人	Yīng.guórén	*N.*	U1C
British pound	英镑	英鎊	Yīngbàng	*N.*	U4C
broken	坏	壞	huài	*Adj.*	U5B
but also; and; also; in addition	而且	而且	érqiě	*Conj.*	U6C
but; however	可是	可是	kě.shì	*Conj.*	U2B
to borrow; to lend	借	借	jiè	*V.*	U3B
brown	咖啡色	咖啡色	kāfēi.sè	*N.*	U6B
to buy	买	買	mǎi	*V.*	U6A
by the way	对了	對了	duì.le	*I.E.*	U2D

C

cafeteria; dining room	餐厅	餐廳	cāntīng	*N.*	U4D
to be called	叫	叫	jiào	*V.*	U1A
can	罐	罐	guàn	*N.*	U4B
can; may	可以	可以	kěyǐ	*A.V.*	U3B
Canada	加拿大	加拿大	Jiā'nádà	*N.*	U1C
Canadian (people)	加拿大人	加拿大人	Jiā'nádàrén	*N.*	U1C
cat	猫	貓	māo	*N.*	U2A
CD player	CD播放机	CD播放機	CD bōfàngjī	*N.*	U3A
cell phone shop	手机店	手機店	shǒujīdiàn	*N.*	U6A
Celsius	摄氏	攝氏	Shèshì	*N.*	U5B
cereal	麦片	麥片	màipiàn	*N.*	U4C
to celebrate / spend the New Year	过年	過年	guònián	*V.O.*	U5C
to celebrate; to pass through time	过	過	guò	*V.*	U5C

to choose; to select	选	選	xuǎn	*V.*	U6B
chair	椅子	椅子	yǐ.zi	*N.*	U3A
chalk	粉笔	粉筆	fěnbǐ	*N.*	U3A
challenging	有挑战性	有挑戰性	yǒu tiǎozhànxìng	*Adj.*	U3C
change (small change)	零钱	零錢	língqián	*N.*	U4C
cheap	便宜	便宜	pián.yí	*Adj.*	U6B
cheeseburger	吉士汉堡包	吉士漢堡包	jíshì hànbǎobāo	*N.*	U4A
chemistry	化学	化學	huàxué	*N.*	U1D
chicken	鸡肉	雞肉	jīròu	*N.*	U4D
China	中国	中國	Zhōng.guó	*N.*	U1C
Chinese people	中国人	中國人	Zhōng.guórén	*N.*	U1C
Chinese (for native speakers)	语文	語文	yǔwén	*N.*	U1D
Chinese (language)	中文	中文	Zhōngwén	*N.*	U1A
Chinese New Year	春节	春節	Chūnjié	*N.*	U5C
Chinese New Year's Eve	除夕	除夕	Chúxī	*N.*	U5C
Chinese Renminbi	人民币	人民幣	Rénmínbì	*N.*	U4C
Chinese Valentine's Day	七夕	七夕	Qīxī	*N.*	U5D
chips	洋芋片	洋芋片	yángyùpiàn	*N.*	U4A
chocolate	巧克力	巧克力	qiǎokèlì	*N.*	U5B
choir	合唱团	合唱團	héchàngtuán	*N.*	U1D
class; course	课	課	kè	*N.*	U1C
classmate	同学	同學	tóngxué	*N.*	U1B
clothes	衣服	衣服	yī.fú	*N.*	U2B
cloud	云	雲	yún	*N.*	U5A
cloudy	多云	多雲	duōyún	*Adj.*	U5A
cloudy day	阴天	陰天	yīntiān	*N.*	U5A
coat	大衣	大衣	dàyī	*N.*	U6A
coffee	咖啡	咖啡	kāfēi	*N.*	U4A
coin	铜板	銅板	tóngbǎn	*N.*	U4C
coin	硬币	硬幣	yìngbì	*N.*	U4C
cola	可乐	可樂	kělè	*N.*	U2B
cold	冷	冷	lěng	*Adj.*	U5B
to come	来	來	lái	*V.*	U3C
compact disc (CD)	光盘	光盤	guāngpán	*N.*	U3A

competition; race	比赛	比賽	bǐsài	*N.*	U5D
composition	写作	寫作	xiězuò	*N.*	U1D
computer	电脑	電腦	diànnǎo	*N.*	U3A
computer science	计算机科学	計算機科學	jìsuànjī kēxué	*N.*	U1D
congratulations	恭喜	恭喜	gōngxǐ	*N.*	U5C
cooked meal	饭	飯	fàn	*N.*	U4D
cooked rice	米饭	米飯	mǐfàn	*N.*	U4D
cool	凉	涼	liáng	*Adj.*	U5B
correct; right	对	對	duì	*Adj.*	U1D
correction fluid	修正液	修正液	xiūzhèngyè	*N.*	U3B
country	国(家)	國(家)	guó(jiā)	*N.*	U1C
measure word for course of a meal	道	道	dào	*N*	U4D
court	场	場	chǎng	*N.*	U3D
crispy	脆	脆	cuì	*Adj.*	U4D
cute; adorable	可爱	可愛	kě'ài	*Adj.*	U2A

D

date	号	號	hào	*M.W.*	U2C
to dance	跳舞	跳舞	tiào-wǔ	*V.O.*	U2D
the day after tomorrow	后天	後天	hòu.tiān	*T.W.*	U3C
the day before yesterday	前天	前天	qián.tiān	*T.W.*	U3C
December	十二月	十二月	Shí'èryuè	*T.W.*	U2C
deep-fried twisted dough sticks	油条	油條	yóutiáo	*N.*	U4C
delicious	好吃	好吃	hǎochī	*Adj.*	U4D
department store	百货商店	百貨商店	bǎihuò shāngdiàn	*N.*	U6A
difficult	难	難	nán	*Adj.*	U3C
discount	折扣	折扣	zhékòu	*N.*	U6B
dish	菜	菜	cài	*N.*	U4D
dog	狗	狗	gǒu	*N.*	U2A
dollar (in spoken Chinese)	块	塊	kuài	*M.W.*	U4C
Double Ninth Festival	重阳节	重陽節	Chóngyángjié	*N.*	U5C
to do; to make	做	做	zuò	*V.*	U2D
to drink	喝	喝	hē	*V.*	U4A
Dragon Boat Festival	端午节	端午節	Duānwǔjié	*N.*	U5C

dress	连衣裙	連衣裙	liányīqún	*N.*	U6A
duck	鸭肉	鴨肉	yāròu	*N.*	U4D
dumplings	饺子	餃子	jiǎo.zi	*N.*	U4D

E

easy	容易	容易	róngyì	*Adj.*	U3C
to eat	吃	吃	chī	*V.*	U4B
to eat a meal	吃饭	吃飯	chī-fàn	*V.O.*	U2D
eggs	蛋	蛋	dàn	*N.*	U4C
eighty	八十	八十	bā.shí	*Num.*	U1D
eighth grade	八年级	八年級	bā-niánjí	*N.*	U1D
eighth grade (in China)	初中二年级	初中二年級	chūzhōng èr-niánjí	*N.*	U1D
eleventh grade	十一年级	十一年級	shíyī-niánjí	*N.*	U1D
eleventh grade (in China)	高中二年级	高中二年級	gāozhōng èr-niánjí	*N.*	U1D
to end	结束	結束	jiéshù	*V.*	U5C
English (language)	英语	英語	Yīngyǔ	*N.*	U1D
eraser	橡皮	橡皮	xiàngpí	*N.*	U3B
Euro	欧元	歐元	Ōuyuán	*N.*	U4C
everyone; all	大家	大家	dàjiā	*Pron.*	U1C

F

Fahrenheit	华氏	華氏	Huáshì	*N.*	U5B
fairly; comparatively	比较	比較	bǐjiào	*Adv.*	U5B
family members	家人	家人	jiārén	*N.*	U2A
famous	有名	有名	yǒumíng	*Adj.*	U4D
fashionable	时髦	時髦	shímáo	*Adj.*	U6C
fat	胖	胖	pàng	*Adj.*	U2A
father	爸爸	爸爸	bà.x	*N.*	U2A
to feel; think	觉得	覺得	jué.de	*V.*	U3C
February	二月	二月	Èryuè	*T.W.*	U2C
festival	节日	節日	jiérì	*N.*	U5C
five	五	五	wǔ	*Num.*	U1D
fifty	五十	五十	wǔ.shí	*Num.*	U1D
final exam	大考	大考	dàkǎo	*N.*	U3C
fine	不错	不錯	búcuò	*Adj.*	U1B

fine; nice (looking)	好看	好看	hǎokàn	*Adj.*	U6B
firecrackers	鞭炮	鞭炮	biānpào	*N.*	U5C
fish	鱼	魚	yú	*N.*	U2A
fitness center	健身房	健身房	jiànshēnfáng	*N.*	U3C
flavor	口味	口味	kǒuwèi	*N.*	U5B
flip-flops	夹脚拖鞋	夾腳拖鞋	jiā-jiǎo tuōxié	*N.*	U6D
folder	文件夹	文件夾	wénjiànjiā	*N.*	U3B
foreign language	外语	外語	wàiyǔ	*N.*	U1D
four	四	四	sì	*Num.*	U1D
the four seasons	四季	四季	sì-jì	*N.*	U5B
forty	四十	四十	sì.shí	*Num.*	U1D
France	法国	法國	Fǎ.guó	*N.*	U1C
French (people)	法国人	法國人	Fǎ.guórén	*N.*	U1C
French (language)	法语	法語	*Fǎ*yǔ	*N.*	U1D
French fries	薯条	薯條	shǔtiáo	*N.*	U4A
Friday	星期五	星期五	Xīngqīwǔ	*T.W.*	U3C
fried chicken	炸鸡	炸雞	zhájī	*N.*	U4C
friend	朋友	朋友	péng.yǒu	*N.*	U1C
fun; interesting; amusing	好玩儿	好玩兒	hǎowánr	*Adj.*	U3C

G

general technology	通用技术	通用技術	tōngyòng jìshù	*N.*	U1D
geography	地理	地理	dìlǐ	*N.*	U1D
Germany	德国	德國	Dé.guó	*N.*	U1C
German (people)	德国人	德國人	Dé.guórén	*N.*	U1C
German (language)	德语	德語	Déyǔ	*N.*	U1D
Ghost Festival	中元节	中元節	Zhōngyuánjié	*N.*	U5D
to give	给	給	gěi	*V.*	U3B
to give change	找钱	找錢	zhǎoqián	*V.O.*	U4C
glue	胶水	膠水	jiāoshuǐ	*N.*	U3B
to go	去	去	qù	*V.*	U1B
to go home	回家	回家	huí-jiā	*V.O.*	U1B
to go to class	上课	上課	shàng-kè	*V.O.*	U1B
to go; to walk	走	走	zǒu	*V.*	U1B
good afternoon	下午好	下午好	xià.*wǔ* hǎo	*C.E.*	U1B

good evening	晚上好	晚上好	wǎn.shàng hǎo	*C.E.*	U1B
good morning	早	早	zǎo	*C.E.*	U1A
	早上好	早上好	zǎo.shàng hǎo	*C.E.*	U1B
good night	晚安	晚安	wǎn'ān	*C.E.*	U1B
good to drink	好喝	好喝	hǎohē	*Adj.*	U4D
good-fitting	合身	合身	héshēn	*Adj.*	U6C
grade	年级	年級	niánjí	*M.W.*	U1D
grapefruit juice	葡萄汁	葡萄汁	pú.táozhī	*N.*	U4B
greasy	油	油	yóu	*Adj.*	U4D
great	很好	很好	*hěn* hǎo	*Adj.*	U1B
Great Britain	英国	英國	Yīng.guó	*N.*	U1C
green	绿色	綠色	lǜ.sè	*N.*	U6B
green tea	绿茶	綠茶	lǜchá	*N.*	U4B
grey	灰色	灰色	huī.sè	*N.*	U6B
guinea pig	天竺鼠	天竺鼠	tiānzhúshǔ	*N.*	U2A

H

half	半	半	bàn	*Adj.*	U3B
hamburger	汉堡包	漢堡包	hànbǎobāo	*N.*	U4A
handsome	帅	帥	shuài	*Adj.*	U6D
happy birthday	生日快乐	生日快樂	shēng.rì kuàilè	*C.E.*	U2C
Happy New Year	新年快乐	新年快樂	Xīnnián kuàilè	*C.E.*	U5C
happy; glad	高兴	高興	gāoxìng	*Adj.*	U1C
happy; joyful	快乐	快樂	kuàilè	*Adj.*	U3D
to have	有	有	yǒu	*V.*	U2B
to help	帮忙	幫忙	bāng-máng	*V.*	U6D
he	他	他	tā	*Pron.*	U1C
heater; heating system	暖气	暖氣	nuǎnqì	*N.*	U5B
hello	你好	你好	*nǐ* hǎo	*C.E.*	U1A
hello (used to greet people on the phone)	喂	喂	wéi	*Part.*	U5D
herbal tea	花茶	花茶	huāchá	*N.*	U4B
hers	她的	她的	tā.de	*Poss.*	U4C
hey	嘿	嘿	.hei	*Interj.*	U1A
hi; hello	嗨	嗨	hāi	*Interj.*	U1C
to hit; to play (a ball sport)	打	打	dǎ	*V.*	U2D

high school	中学	中學	zhōngxué	*N.*	U1D
high school student	中学生	中學生	zhōngxué.shēng	*N.*	U1D
his	他的	他的	tā.de	*Poss.*	U4C
history	历史	歷史	lìshǐ	*N.*	U1D
home; family	家	家	jiā	*N.*	U2A
Hong Kong dollar	港币	港幣	Gǎngbì	*N.*	U4C
hot	热	熱	rè	*Adj.*	U5B
hot and sour soup	酸辣汤	酸辣湯	suānlàtāng	*N.*	U4D
hot chocolate	热巧克力	熱巧克力	rè qiǎokèlì	*N.*	U4B
hot pot	火锅	火鍋	huǒguō	*N.*	U4D
hotdog	热狗	熱狗	règǒu	*N.*	U4A
How are you?	你好吗	你好嗎	*Nǐ hǎo* .ma?	*C.E.*	U1B
how many	几	幾	jǐ	*Q.W.*	U2B
how; what about	怎么样	怎麼樣	zěmyàng	*Q.W.*	U5A
hundred	百	百	bǎi	*Num.*	U4C
a hundred million	亿	億	yì	*Num.*	U6B
hungry	饿	餓	è	*Adj.*	U5B

I

I	我	我	wǒ	*Pron.*	U1A
ice cream	冰淇淋	冰淇淋	bīng.qílín	*N.*	U5B
ice hockey	冰球	冰球	bīngqiú	*N.*	U2D
India	印度	印度	Yìndù	*N.*	U1C
Indian (people)	印度人	印度人	Yìndùrén	*N.*	U1C
indicating the position of a person or thing	在	在	zài	*V.*	U3A
indicating an action in progress				*Adv.*	U5D
information technology	信息技术	信息技術	xìnxī jìshù	*N.*	U1D
interesting	有意思	有意思	yǒu yì.sī	*Adj.*	U3C
Is that right?	对不对	對不對	duì .bú duì	*Ph.*	U1D
it	它	它	tā	*Pron.*	U1C
Italy	意大利	義大利	Yìdàlì	*N.*	U1C
Italian (people)	意大利人	義大利人	Yìdàlìrén	*N.*	U1C

J

jacket	外套	外套	wàitào	*N.*	U6A
January	一月	一月	Yīyuè	*T.W.*	U2C
Japan	日本	日本	Rìběn	*N.*	U1C
Japanese (people)	日本人	日本人	Rìběnrén	*N.*	U1C
Japanese yen	日元	日元	Rìyuán	*N.*	U4C
jeans	牛仔裤	牛仔褲	niúzǎikù	*N.*	U6A
to jog	慢跑	慢跑	mànpǎo	*V.*	U3D
jogging				*N.*	
juice	果汁	果汁	guǒzhī	*N.*	U4A
June	六月	六月	Liùyuè	*T.W.*	U2C
July	七月	七月	Qīyuè	*T.W.*	U2C
junior high school	初中	初中	chūzhōng	*N.*	U1D
junior high school student	初中生	初中生	chūzhōngshēng	*N.*	U1D
just; exactly	刚	剛	gāng	*Adv.*	U6C

K

kind; sort; type	种	種	zhǒng	*M.W.*	U5D
kind; type	样	樣	yàng	*M.W.*	U6D
to kick; to play (soccer)	踢	踢	tī	*V.*	U2D
to know	知道	知道	zhī.dào	*V.*	U6B
to know (people)	认识	認識	rèn.shì	*V.*	U1C
Korea	韩国	韓國	Hán.guó	*N.*	U1C
Korean (people)	韩国人	韓國人	Hán.guórén	*N.*	U1C
Kung Pao chicken	宫保鸡丁	宮保雞丁	gōngbǎo jīdīng	*N.*	U4D

L

lamb	羊肉	羊肉	yángròu	*N.*	U4D
Lantern Festival	元宵节	元宵節	Yuánxiāojié	*N.*	U5C
large (cup)	大杯	大杯	dà bēi	*Adj.*	U4A
large denomination bills	大钞	大鈔	dàchāo	*N.*	U4C
last	上	上	shàng	*Adj.*	U5A
last week	上个星期	上個星期	shàng.ge xīngqī	*T.W.*	U5A
leather shoes	皮鞋	皮鞋	píxié	*N.*	U6D
lemonade	柠檬水	檸檬水	níngméngshuǐ	*N.*	U4B
library	图书馆	圖書館	túshūguǎn	*N.*	U3C

light (in flavor)	清淡	清淡	qīngdàn	*Adj.*	U4D
to lift weights	举重	舉重	jǔzhòng	*V.O.*	U3D
to like	喜欢	喜歡	xǐ.huān	*V.*	U2D
to listen to music	听音乐	聽音樂	tīng-yīnyuè	*V.O.*	U2D
literature	文学	文學	wénxué	*N.*	U1D
long	长	長	cháng	*Adj.*	U6B
long time no see	好久不见	好久不見	*hǎo* jiǔ bú jiàn	*C.E.*	U1B
loose	松	鬆	sōng	*Adj.*	U6C
to look for; to search; to return change after a purchase	找	找	zhǎo	*V.*	U3A
the lunar calendar	农历	農曆	nónglì	*N.*	U5C

M

Malaysia	马来西亚	馬來西亞	Mǎláixīyà	*N.*	U1C
Malaysian (people)	马来西亚人	馬來西亞人	Mǎláixīyàrén	*N.*	U1C
mall	购物中心	購物中心	gòuwù zhōngxīn	*N.*	U3D
map	地图	地圖	dìtú	*N.*	U3A
Mapo Tofu	麻婆豆腐	麻婆豆腐	mápó dòu.fǔ	*N.*	U4D
March	三月	三月	Sānyuè	*T.W.*	U2C
matcha	抹茶	抹茶	mǒchá	*N.*	U5B
maternal grandfather	外公	外公	wàigōng	*N.*	U2A
maternal grandmother	外婆	外婆	wàipó	*N.*	U2A
math	数学	數學	shùxué	*N.*	U1D
matter; affair; thing	事	事	shì	*N.*	U4C
mature	成熟	成熟	chéngshú	*Adj.*	U6C
May	五月	五月	Wǔyuè	*T.W.*	U2C
may I ask…?	请问	請問	qǐngwèn	*C.E.*	U4B
meat	肉	肉	ròu	*N.*	U4D
a measure word for cup	杯	杯	bēi	*M.W.*	U4B
cup				*N.*	
a measure word for things, matters, or a piece of clothing	件	件	jiàn	*M.W.*	U4C
medium	中	中	zhōng	*Adj.*	U4A

medium (cup)	中杯	中杯	zhōng bēi	*Adj.*	U4A
Mid-Autumn Festival	中秋节	中秋節	Zhōngqiūjié	*N.*	U5C
minute; penny	分	分	fēn	*M.W.*	U3B
milk	牛奶	牛奶	niúnǎi	*N.*	U4C
milk shake	奶昔	奶昔	nǎixī	*N.*	U4B
milk tea	奶茶	奶茶	nǎichá	*N.*	U4B
a million	百万	百萬	bǎiwàn	*Num.*	U6B
mine	我的	我的	wǒ.de	*Poss.*	U4C
Miss	小姐	小姐	*xiǎo*jiě	*N.*	U1A
Monday	星期一	星期一	Xīngqīyī	*T.W.*	U3C
money	钱	錢	qián	*N.*	U4C
month	月	月	yuè	*M.W.*	U2C
more	更	更	gèng	*Adv.*	U5C
morning	早上	早上	zǎo.shàng	*T.W.*	U1B
the most	最	最	zuì	*Adv.*	U6D
mother	妈妈	媽媽	mā.x	*N.*	U2A
movie	电影	電影	diànyǐng	*N.*	U2D
Mr.	先生	先生	xiān.shēng	*N.*	U1A
Ms.	太太	太太	tài.x	*N.*	U1A
museum	博物馆	博物館	bówùguǎn	*N.*	U3D
music	音乐	音樂	yīnyuè	*N.*	U1D
Mexico	墨西哥	墨西哥	Mòxīgē	*N.*	U1C
Mexican (people)	墨西哥人	墨西哥人	Mòxīgērén	*N.*	U1C

N

name	名字	名字	míng.zì	*N.*	U1A
new	新	新	xīn	*Adj.*	U6C
New Taiwan dollar	新台币	新台幣	Xīntáibì	*N.*	U4C
the New Year	新年	新年	Xīnnián	*N.*	U5C
next	下	下	xià	*Adj.*	U5A
next time	下次	下次	xià.cì	*T.W.*	U6C
next week	下个星期	下個星期	xià.ge xīngqī	*T.W.*	U5A
to need	需要	需要	xūyào	*V.*	U6D
to need to; to have to	得	得	děi	*A.V.*	U1B
night	晚上	晚上	wǎn.shàng	*N.*	U1B

nine	九	九	jiǔ	*Num.*	U1D
ninety	九十	九十	jiǔ.shí	*Num.*	U1D
ninth grade	九年级	九年級	jiǔ-niánjí	*N.*	U1D
ninth grade (in China)	初中三年级	初中三年級	chūzhōng sān-niánjí	*N.*	U1D
no, no need	不用	不用	búyòng	*C.E.*	U4B
no problem	没问题	沒問題	méi wèntí	*C.E.*	U5B
no; not	不	不	bù / bú	*Adv.*	U1B
noble; honored; expensive	贵	貴	guì	*Adj.*	U1A
noodle soup	汤面	湯麵	tāngmiàn	*N.*	U4D
noodles	面	麵	miàn	*N.*	U4D
noon	中午	中午	zhōngwǔ	*N.*	U1B
to not have (the negation of 有 *yǒu*)	没有	沒有	méi.yǒu	*V.*	U2B
not only	不但	不但	búdàn	*Conj.*	U6C
not so bad	还行	還行	hái xíng	*Adj.*	U1B
not so good	不太好	不太好	bú tài hǎo	*Adj.*	U1B
notebook	笔记本	筆記本	bǐjìběn	*N.*	U3B
November	十一月	十一月	Shíyīyuè	*T.W.*	U2C
now	现在	現在	xiànzài	*T.W.*	U3B
number	号码	號碼	hàomǎ	*N.*	U2C

O

o'clock	点	點	diǎn	*M.W.*	U3B
October	十月	十月	Shíyuè	*T.W.*	U2C
of course	当然	當然	dāngrán	*M.A.*	U3B
oh (a sound of sadness or regret)	唉	唉	āi	*Intj.*	U5B
oh (to express surprise or unhappiness)	唉呀	唉呀	āiyā	*Intj.*	U5A
okay	好了	好了	hǎo .le	*C.E.*	U3C
old	老	老	lǎo	*Adj.*	U6C
older brother	哥哥	哥哥	gē.x	*N.*	U2B
older sister	姐姐	姐姐	jiě.x	*N.*	U2A
one	一	一	yī	*Num.*	U1D
one hundred	一百	一百	yībǎi	*Num.*	U1D
one hundred thousand	十万	十萬	shí-wàn	*Num.*	U6B
one tenth of a 元 *yuán*; a dime or 10 pennies	毛	毛	máo	*M.W.*	U4C

one thousand	一千	一千	yì-qiān	*Num.*	U6B
oneself	自己	自己	zìjǐ	*Pron.*	U6A
only	只	只	zhǐ	*Adv.*	U4B
oolong tea	乌龙茶	烏龍茶	wūlóngchá	*N.*	U4B
or	还是	還是	háishì	*Conj.*	U4A
orange	橘黄色	橘黃色	júhuáng.sè	*N.*	U6B
orange juice	橙汁	橙汁	chéngzhī	*N.*	U4B
to order	点	點	diǎn	*V.*	U4A
to order	点菜	點菜	diǎn-cài	*V.O.*	U4D
ours	我们的	我們的	wǒ.men.de	*Pron.*	U4C
out-of-date	过时	過時	guòshí	*Adj.*	U6C

P

to paddle; to row	划	划	huá	*V.*	U5D
to paint; to draw	画画	畫畫	huà-huà	*V.O.*	U2D
a measure word for a pair of pants or a skirt	条	條	tiáo	*M.W.*	U6A
a measure word for people	口	口	kǒu	*M.W.*	U2B
pajamas	睡衣	睡衣	shuìyī	*N.*	U6D
pancake	煎饼	煎餅	jiānbǐng	*N.*	U4C
pants	裤子	褲子	kù.zi	*N.*	U6A
paper	纸	紙	zhǐ	*N.*	U2B
paper money	钞票	鈔票	chāopiào	*N.*	U4C
park	公园	公園	gōngyuán	*N.*	U3D
pastime	爱好	愛好	àihào	*N.*	U2D
paternal grandfather	爷爷	爺爺	yé.x	*N.*	U2A
paternal grandmother	奶奶	奶奶	nǎi.x	*N.*	U2A
pen	笔	筆	bǐ	*N.*	U2B
pencil	铅笔	鉛筆	qiānbǐ	*N.*	U3B
pencil box	铅笔盒	鉛筆盒	qiānbǐhé	*N.*	U3B
a measure word for a period of class	堂	堂	táng	*M.W.*	U3C
person; people	人	人	rén	*N.*	U1C
pet store	宠物店	寵物店	chǒngwùdiàn	*N.*	U6A
pets	宠物	寵物	chǒngwù	*N.*	U2A
photo	照片	照片	zhàopiàn	*N.*	U2B
physical education	体育	體育	tǐyù	*N.*	U1D

physics	物理	物理	wùlǐ	*N.*	U1D
a measure word for a piece of paper	张	張	zhāng	*M.W.*	U3B
pink	粉红色	粉紅色	fěnhóng.sè	*N.*	U6B
to play (sports or recreational activities)	玩	玩	wán	*V.*	U2D
to play tennis	打网球	打網球	*dǎ* wǎngqiú	*V.O.*	U5A
podium	讲台	講台	jiǎngtái	*N.*	U3A
political education	政治	政治	zhèngzhì	*N.*	U1D
pool	台球	台球	táiqiú	*N.*	U3D
pork	猪肉	豬肉	zhūròu	*N.*	U4D
poster	海报	海報	hǎibào	*N.*	U3A
pot	壶	壺	hú	*N.*	U4B
price	价钱	價錢	jià.qián	*N.*	U6D
principal	校长	校長	xiàozhǎng	*N.*	U1A
projector	投影机	投影機	tóuyǐngjī	*N.*	U3A
purple	紫色	紫色	zǐ.sè	*N.*	U6B

Q

quarter	刻	刻	kè	*M.W.*	U3B
quiz	小考	小考	*xiǎo*kǎo	*N.*	U3C

R

rabbit	兔子	兔子	tù.zi	*N.*	U2A
rain	雨	雨	yǔ	*N*	U5A
to rain	下雨	下雨	xià-yǔ	*V.O.*	U5A
rainy day	雨天	雨天	yǔtiān	*N.*	U5A
really	真	真	zhēn	*Adv.*	U5A
red	红色	紅色	hóng.sè	*N.*	U6B
red bean	红豆	紅豆	hóngdòu	*N.*	U5B
red envelopes	红包	紅包	hóngbāo	*N.*	U5C
restaurant	餐馆	餐館	cānguǎn	*N.*	U4D
to read (books)	看书	看書	kàn-shū	*V.O.*	U2D
to request ("please")	请	請	qǐng	*V.*	U3B
to ride	骑	騎	qí	*V.*	U3D
rice dumplings made and eaten during the Dragon Boat Festival	粽子	粽子	zòng.zi	*N.*	U5D

to row a boat	划船	划船	huá-chuán	*V.O.*	U5D
ruler	尺	尺	chǐ	*N.*	U3B

S

salad	色拉	色拉	sèlā	*N.*	U4A
salty	咸	鹹	xián	*Adj.*	U4D
sandwich	三明治	三明治	sānmíngzhì	*N.*	U4A
Saturday	星期六	星期六	Xīngqīliù	*T.W.*	U3C
scented sachet	香包	香包	xiāngbāo	*N.*	U5D
school subject	学校科目	學校科目	xuéxiào kēmù	*N.*	U1D
schoolbag	书包	書包	shūbāo	*N.*	U3A
scissors	剪刀	剪刀	jiǎndāo	*N.*	U3B
sea	海	海	hǎi	*N.*	U3D
semester	学期	學期	xuéqī	*N.*	U5C
senior high school	高中	高中	gāozhōng	*N.*	U1D
senior high school student	高中生	高中生	gāozhōngshēng	*N.*	U1D
September	九月	九月	Jiǔyuè	*T.W.*	U2C
sesame	芝麻	芝蔴	zhīmá	*N.*	U5B
sesame seed cake	烧饼	燒餅	shāobǐng	*N.*	U4C
set; suit	套	套	tào	*M.W.*	U6D
seven	七	七	qī	*Num.*	U1D
seventy	七十	七十	qī.shí	*Num.*	U1D
seventh grade	七年级	七年級	qī-niánjí	*N.*	U1D
seventh grade (in China)	初中一年级	初中一年級	chūzhōng yì-niánjí	*N.*	U1D
to see	见	見	jiàn	*V.*	U1B
to see; to look at	看	看	kàn	*V.*	U2D
to sell at a discount price	打折	打折	dǎ-zhé	*V.O.*	U6B
a share of; a portion of	份	份	fèn	*M.W.*	U4A
she	她	她	tā	*Pron.*	U1C
shirt	衬衫	襯衫	chènshān	*N.*	U6A
shoe shop	鞋店	鞋店	xiédiàn	*N.*	U6A
shoe(s)	鞋子	鞋子	xié.zi	*N.*	U2B
short	短	短	duǎn	*Adj.*	U6B
should	应该	應該	yīnggāi	*A.V.*	U5C

Singapore	新加坡	新加坡	Xīnjiāpō	*N.*	U1C
Singapore dollar	新加坡币	新加坡幣	Xīnjiāpōbì	*N.*	U4C
Singaporean (people)	新加坡人	新加坡人	Xīnjiāpōrén	*N.*	U1C
six	六	六	liù	*Num.*	U1D
sixty	六十	六十	liù.shí	*Num.*	U1D
to sing	唱歌	唱歌	chàng-gē	*V.O.*	U2D
size	大小	大小	dàxiǎo	*N.*	U6C
size; number	号	號	hào	*N.*	U6C
skateboarding	滑板	滑板	huábǎn	*N.*	U2D
to ski	滑雪	滑雪	huá-xuě	*V.O.*	U3D
skirt	裙子	裙子	qún.zi	*N.*	U6A
slippers	拖鞋	拖鞋	tuōxié	*N.*	U6D
to sleep	睡觉	睡覺	shuì-jiào	*V.O.*	U1B
small	小	小	xiǎo	*Adj.*	U2A
small (cup)	小杯	小杯	xiǎo bēi	*Adj.*	U4A
smoothie	冰沙	冰沙	bīngshā	*N.*	U4B
sneakers	运动鞋	運動鞋	yùndòngxié	*N.*	U6D
to snow	下雪	下雪	xiàxuě	*V.O.*	U5A
snow	雪	雪	xuě	*N.*	U5A
so; therefore	所以	所以	*suǒ*yǐ	*Conj.*	U5C
soccer	足球	足球	zúqiú	*N.*	U2D
socks	袜子	襪子	wà.zi	*N.*	U6D
soda	汽水	汽水	qìshuǐ	*N.*	U4A
soon; before long	快	快	kuài	*Adv.*	U5C
sorry	对不起	對不起	duì.bùqǐ	*C.E.*	U4B
soup	汤	湯	tāng	*N.*	U4D
sour	酸	酸	suān	*Adj.*	U4D
South Korean won	韩元	韓元	Hányuán	*N.*	U4C
soybean milk	豆浆	豆漿	dòujiāng	*N.*	U4C
spaghetti strap tank	吊带衫	吊帶衫	diàodàishān	*N.*	U6A
Spain	西班牙	西班牙	Xībānyá	*N.*	U1C
Spanish (people)	西班牙人	西班牙人	Xībānyárén	*N.*	U1C
Spanish (language)	西班牙语	西班牙語	Xībānyáyǔ	*N.*	U1D
to speak	说话	說話	shuō-huà	*V.O.*	U2D
spicy	辣	辣	là	*Adj.*	U4D

spring	春天	春天	chūntiān	*N.*	U5B
Spring Festival couplets	春联	春聯	chūnlián	*N.*	U5C
stapler	订书机	訂書機	dìngshūjī	*N.*	U3B
steamed bread	馒头	饅頭	mán.tóu	*N.*	U4C
steamed buns with meat filling	包子	包子	bāo.zi	*N.*	U4C
a measure word for stick-like things	支	枝	zhī	*M.W.*	U3B
still; in addition; and also	还	還	hái	*Adv.*	U3C
store; shop	商店	商店	shāngdiàn	*N.*	U6A
strange	奇怪	奇怪	qíguài	*Adj.*	U3A
strawberry	草莓	草莓	cǎoméi	*N.*	U5B
to study; to learn	学	學	xué	*V.*	U1D
such; so; like this	这么	這麼	zhè.me	*Adv.*	U5B
suitable	合适	合適	héshì	*Adj.*	U6C
suits	西装	西裝	xīzhuāng	*N.*	U6A
summer	夏天	夏天	xiàtiān	*N.*	U5B
Sunday	星期日	星期日	Xīngqīrì	*N.*	U3C
sunny day	晴天	晴天	qíngtiān	*N.*	U5A
to suit; to fit	适合	適合	shìhé	*V.*	U6D
to be surnamed	姓	姓	xìng	*V.*	U1A
to surf the Internet	上网	上網	shàngwǎng	*V.*	U2D
to surf	冲浪	衝浪	chōnglàng	*V.O.*	U3D
surfing				*N.*	U3D
sweater	毛衣	毛衣	máoyī	*N.*	U6A
sweet	甜	甜	tián	*Adj.*	U4D
to swim	游泳	游泳	yóuyǒng	*V.*	U2D
swimming				*N.*	

T

table; desk	桌子	桌子	zhuō.zi	*N.*	U3A
tea	茶	茶	chá	*N.*	U2B
tea shop	茶店	茶店	chádiàn	*N.*	U6A
teacher	老师	老師	lǎoshī	*N.*	U1A
Teacher's Day	教师节	教師節	Jiàoshījié	*N.*	U5C
television	电视	電視	diànshì	*N.*	U3D
ten	十	十	shí	*Num.*	U1D

ten million	千万	千萬	qiānwàn	*Num.*	U6B
ten thousand	一万	一萬	yí-wàn	*Num.*	U6B
tennis	网球	網球	wǎngqiú	*N.*	U5A
tenth grade	十年级	十年級	shí-niánjí	*N.*	U1D
tenth grade (in China)	高中一年级	高中一年級	gāozhōng yì-niánjí	*N.*	U1D
test; exam	考试	考試	kǎoshì	*N.*	U3C
textbook	课本	課本	kèběn	*N.*	U3A
Thailand	泰国	泰國	Tàiguó	*N.*	U1C
Thai (people)	泰国人	泰國人	Tàiguórén	*N.*	U1C
that	那	那	nà	*Dem.*	U2A
the wind is blowing very hard	刮风	刮風	guāfēng	*V.O.*	U5A
theater	戏剧	戲劇	xìjù	*N.*	U1D
theirs (m.)	他们的	他們的	tā.mén.de	*Poss.*	U4C
theirs (f.)	她们的	她們的	tā.mén.de	*Poss.*	U4C
then; in that case	那	那	nà	*Conj.*	U2D
they (f.)	她们	她們	tā.mén	*Pron.*	U1C
they (m.)	他们	他們	tā.mén	*Pron.*	U1C
they (neuter)	它们	它們	tā.mén	*Pron.*	U1C
thing(s); stuff	东西	東西	dōng.xī	*N.*	U4B
thirsty	渴	渴	kě	*Adj.*	U5B
thirty	三十	三十	sān.shí	*Num.*	U1D
this	这	這	zhè; zhèi	*Dem.*	U1A
this week	这个星期	這個星期	zhèi.ge xīngqī	*T.W.*	U5A
three	三	三	sān	*Num.*	U1D
thunder	雷	雷	léi	*N.*	U5A
Thursday	星期四	星期四	Xīngqīsì	*T.W.*	U3C
tight	紧	緊	jǐn	*Adj.*	U6C
time; moment	时候	時候	shí.hòu	*N.*	U5B
to	到	到	dào	*Prep.*	U5C
to take (a class)	修	修	xiū	*V.*	U1D
to take; to bring	带	帶	dài	*V.*	U5D
to thunder	打雷	打雷	dǎléi	*V.O.*	U5A
to travel	旅行	旅行	lǚxíng	*V.*	U6A
to try	试	試	shì	*V.*	U6D

to turn on	打开	打開	dǎkāi	*V.*	U5B
today	今天	今天	jīn.tiān	*T.W.*	U3C
together	一起	一起	yìqǐ	*Adv.*	U2D
Tomb-sweeping Festival	清明节	清明節	Qīngmíngjié	*N.*	U5C
tomorrow	明天	明天	míng.tiān	*T.W.*	U2D
too	太	太	tài	*Adv.*	U5B
a triviality; something petty; It's nothing (phr.).	小事	小事	xiǎoshì	*I.E.*	U4C
T-shirt	T恤	T恤	tīxù	*N.*	U6A
Tuesday	星期二	星期二	Xīngqī'èr	*T.W.*	U3C
to turn on the computer	开电脑	開電腦	kāi diànnǎo	*V.O.*	U3A
turtle	乌龟	烏龜	wūguī	*N.*	U2B
twelfth (in China)	高中三年级	高中三年級	gāozhōng sān-niánjí	*N.*	U1D
twelfth grade	十二年级	十二年級	shí'èr-niánjí	*N.*	U1D
twenty	二十	二十	èr.shí	*Num.*	U1D
two	二	二	èr	*Num.*	U1D
two	两	兩	liǎng	*Num.*	U2B

U

ugly	丑	醜	chǒu	*Adj.*	U6D
um	嗯	嗯	.en	*Interj.*	U1D
uninteresting	没有意思	沒有意思	méi.yǒu yì.sī	*Adj.*	U3C
the United States	美国	美國	Měi.guó	*N.*	U1C
a unit or measurement for temperature	度	度	dù	*M.W.*	U5B
to understand	懂	懂	dǒng	*V.*	U5C
United States dollar	美元	美元	Měiyuán	*N.*	U4C
used after a verb to indicate short duration	一下	一下	yíxià	*Num.+ M.W.*	U4A
used; old	旧	舊	jiù	*Adj.*	U6C
usually	通常	通常	tōngcháng	*T.W.*	U5C

V

vanilla	香草	香草	xiāngcǎo	*N.*	U4B
very	很	很	hěn	*Adv.*	U1B
video games	电子游戏	電子遊戲	diànzǐ yóuxì	*N.*	U2D

Vietnam	越南	越南	Yuènán	*N.*	U1C
Vietnamese (people)	越南人	越南人	Yuènánrén	*N.*	U1C
volleyball	排球	排球	páiqiú	*N.*	U3D

W

waiter / waitress	服务员	服務員	fúwùyuán	*N.*	U4D
warm	温暖	溫暖	wēnnuǎn	*Adj.*	U5B
water	水	水	shuǐ	*N.*	U2B
to wait	等	等	děng	*V.*	U4A
to want	想	想	xiǎng	*V.*	U4D
to want; to need; to take	要	要	yào	*V.*	U3B
to wear; to put on	穿	穿	chuān	*V.*	U6C
we	我们	我們	wǒ.mén	*Pron.*	U1C
weather	天气	天氣	tiān.qì	*N.*	U5A
Wednesday	星期三	星期三	Xīngqīsān	*T.W.*	U3C
the week after next	下下个星期	下下個星期	xià xià.ge xīngqī	*T.W.*	U5A
the week before last	上上个星期	上上個星期	shàng shàng.ge xīngqī	*T.W.*	U5A
weekend	周末	週末	zhōumò	*N.*	U3D
what	什么	什麼	shén.me	*Q.W.*	U1A
where	哪里	哪裡	*nǎ*lǐ	*Q.W.*	U1C
where	哪儿	哪兒	nǎr	*Q.W.*	U3A
which	哪	哪	nǎ	*Q.W.*	U1C
white	白色	白色	bái.sè	*N.*	U6B
white board	白板	白板	báibǎn	*N.*	U3A
white board marker	白板笔	白板筆	bái*bǎn*bǐ	*N.*	U3A
why	为什么	為什麼	wèishén.me	*Q.W.*	U5C
will	会	會	huì	*A.V.*	U5A
wind	风	風	fēng	*N*	U5A
windy	有风	有風	yǒufēng	*Adj.*	U5A
winter	冬天	冬天	dōngtiān	*N.*	U5B
Winter solstice	冬至	冬至	Dōngzhì	*N.*	U5D
with	跟	跟	gēn	*Prep.*	U3D
wontons	馄饨	餛飩	hún.tún	*N.*	U4C
wow	哇	哇	.wa	*Interj.*	U2C

to work out	锻练	鍛鍊	duànliàn	*V.*	U3C
to wrap	包	包	bāo	*V.*	U5D
to write	写字	寫字	xiě-zì	*V.O.*	U2D

Y

year (of age)	岁	歲	suì	*M.W.*	U1D
yellow	黄色	黃色	huáng.sè	*N.*	U6B
yesterday	昨天	昨天	zuó.tiān	*T.W.*	U3C
yoga	瑜珈	瑜珈	yújiā	*N.*	U3D
you	你	你	nǐ	*Pron.*	U1A
you (plural)	你们	你們	nǐ.mén	*Pron.*	U1A
you (polite)	您	您	nín	*Pron.*	U1A
you're welcome	不客气	不客氣	bú kè.qì	*I.E.*	U3B
young	年轻	年輕	niánqīng	*Adj.*	U6C
younger brother	弟弟	弟弟	dì.x	*N.*	U2B
younger sister	妹妹	妹妹	mèi.x	*N.*	U2B
yours	你的	你的	nǐ.de	*Poss.*	U4C
yours	你们的	你們的	nǐ.mén.de	*Poss.*	U4C

Z

zero	零	零	líng	*Num.*	U1D

主题索引 Index of Topics

照片与实物提供者 Photo and Realia Credits

All photos and realia in 真棒! ***Zhēn Bàng!*** Level 1 textbook not supplied by LiveABC Interactive Corporation have been provided by the following:

Akirastock: 362 (top)
Anthony W Seebaran Photography: vii (bottom)
bedo: xii (bottom)
Benedek, Arpad: 318 (right)
Bialy94: 140 (top)
Brey, James: vii (top)
Btrenkel: 59
Craftvision: 134
design56: xi (top)
Donna Coleman Photography: 375 (bottom, 4)
Eurobanks: 420 (bottom)
Fotolinchen: viii (top)
Francesco Ridolfi Photography: 184 (bottom right)
iPandaStudio: 77
Japanthings: 416 (bottom)
L, Aleksandr: 452 (suit)
lypnyk2: 504 (model)
Nicolesy, Inc.: 375 (bottom, 2)
Nirod: vi
Paul Kline Photography: 375 (bottom, 3)
Photo168: 155 (center)
Phototalk: 501
Quavondo: 477
Rafa Irusta Machin: 420 (top left)
Sadeugra: 375 (bottom, 1)
Stratesigns, Inc.: xii (top)
Szefei: 295 (top)
TEDA: 330-331
Terex Foto: 456 (suitcase)
Track5: 264 (bottom)
Urbancow: 402 (top)
Uschools University Images: 21
Videowok: xi (bottom)
Vikram Raghuvanshi Photography: 189 (bottom center)
XGH: viii (bottom)